W9-AHA-375

Essentials of Marketing Research

Fourth Edition

Joseph F. Hair, Jr.
University of South Alabama

Mary Celsi
California State University–Long Beach

David J. Ortinau
University of South Florida

Robert P. Bush
Houston Baptist University

ESSENTIALS OF MARKETING, FOURTH EDITION

Published by McGraw-Hill Education, 2 Penn Plaza, New York, NY 10121. Copyright © 2017 by McGraw-Hill Education. All rights reserved. Printed in the United States of America. Previous editions © 2013, 2010, and 2008. No part of this publication may be reproduced or distributed in any form or by any means, or stored in a database or retrieval system, without the prior written consent of McGraw-Hill Education, including, but not limited to, in any network or other electronic storage or transmission, or broadcast for distance learning.

Some ancillaries, including electronic and print components, may not be available to customers outside the United States.

This book is printed on acid-free paper.

3 4 5 6 7 8 9 QVS 21 20 19 18 17

ISBN 978-0-07-811211-9
MHID 0-07-811211-7

Chief Product Officer, SVP Products & Markets: *G. Scott Virkler*
Vice President, General Manager, Products & Markets: *Michael Ryan*
Managing Director: *Susan Gouijnstook*
Executive Brand Manager: *Meredith Fossel*
Brand Manager: *Laura Hurst Spell*
Director, Product Development: *Meghan Campbell*
Marketing Manager: *Elizabeth Schonagen*
Digital Product Analyst: *Kerry Shanahan*
Director, Content Design & Delivery: *Terri Schiesl*
Program Manager: *Mary Conzachi*
Content Project Manager: *Jeni McAtee*
Buyer: *Sandy Ludovissy*
Cover image: *Mutlu Kurtbas/Getty Images*
Content Licensing Specialist: *Shannon Manderscheid, text*
Cover Image: *Mutlu Kurtbas/Getty Images*
Compositor: *MPS Limited*
Printer: *Quad/Graphics*

All credits appearing on page or at the end of the book are considered to be an extension of the copyright page.

Library of Congress Cataloging-in-Publication Data

Hair, Joseph F., author.
    Essentials of marketing research / Joseph F. Hair, Jr., University of South Alabama, Mary W. Celsi, California State University/Long Beach, David J. Ortinau, University of South Florida, Robert P. Bush, Houston Baptist University.
    Fourth edition. | New York, NY : McGraw-Hill Education, [2017]
    LCCN 2016030404 | ISBN 9780078112119 (alk. paper)
    LCSH: Marketing research.
    LCC HF5415.2 .E894 2017 | DDC 658.8/3—dc23 LC record available at https://lccn.loc.gov/2016030404

The Internet addresses listed in the text were accurate at the time of publication. The inclusion of a website does not indicate an endorsement by the authors or McGraw-Hill Education, and McGraw-Hill Education does not guarantee the accuracy of the information presented at these sites.

mheducation.com/highered

To my wife Dale, our son Joe III, wife Kerrie, and grandsons Joe IV and Declan.

—Joseph F. Hair, Jr., Mobile, Alabama

To my father and mother, William and Carol Finley.

—Mary Wolfinbarger Celsi, Long Beach, CA

To my late mom, Lois and my sister and brothers and their families.

—David J. Ortinau, Tampa, FL

To my late wife Donny Kathleen, and my two boys, Michael and Robert, Jr.

—Robert P. Bush, Sr., Houston, TX

Joseph F. Hair is Professor of Marketing and the Cleverdon Chair of Business at the University of South Alabama, and Director of the DBA degree program in the Mitchell College of Business. He formerly held the Copeland Endowed Chair of Entrepreneurship at Louisiana State University. He has published more than 60 books, including market leaders Multivariate Data Analysis, 7th edition, Prentice Hall, 2010, which has been cited more than 125,000 times; *Marketing Research,* 4th edition, McGraw-Hill/Irwin, 2009; *Principles of Marketing,* 12th edition, Thomson Learning, 2012, used at over 500 universities globally; *A Primer in Partial Least Squared Structural Equation Modeling (PLS-SEM),* 2nd edition, Sage, 2017; and *Essentials of Business Research Methods,* 3rd edition, Taylor & Francis, 2016. In addition to publishing numerous referred manuscripts in academic journals such as *Journal of Marketing Research, Journal of Academy of Marketing Science, Journal of Business/Chicago, Journal of Advertising Research,* and *Journal of Retailing,* he has presented executive education and management training programs for numerous companies, has been retained as consultant and expert witness for a wide variety of firms, and is frequently an invited speaker on research methods and multivariate analysis. He is a Distinguished Fellow of the Academy of Marketing Science, the Society for Marketing Advances (SMA), and has served as president of the Academy of Marketing Sciences, the SMA, the Southern Marketing Association, the Association for Healthcare Research, the Southwestern Marketing Association, and the American Institute for Decision Sciences, Southeast Section. Professor Hair was recognized by the Academy of Marketing Science with its Outstanding Marketing Teaching Excellence Award, and the Louisiana State University Entrepreneurship Institute under his leadership was recognized nationally by *Entrepreneurship Magazine* as one of the top 12 programs in the United States.

Mary W. Celsi is a Professor of Marketing at California State University, Long Beach. She has published research in several top journals, including *Journal of Marketing, Journal of Consumer Research Journal of Retailing, California Management Review,* and *Journal of the Academy of Marketing Science.* She has expertise in qualitative and quantitative research methods. Her publications span a wide range of interests, from internal marketing to digital marketing and consumer culture theory. Her research has been cited more than 5,000 times in scholarly publications.

David J. Ortinau is Professor of Marketing at the University of South Florida (USF). His Ph.D. in Marketing is from Louisiana State University. He began his teaching career at Illinois State University and after completing his degree moved to USF in Tampa. Dr. Ortinau continues to be recognized for both outstanding research and excellence in teaching at the undergradute, graduate, and doctorate levels. His research interests range from research methodologies and scale measurement development, attitude formation, and perceptual differences in retailing and services marketing environments to interactive electronic marketing technologies and their impact on information research problems.

He consults for a variety of corporations and small businesses, with specialties in customer satisfaction, service quality, service value, retail loyalty, and imagery. Dr. Ortinau has presented numerous papers at national and international academic conferences. He continues to make scholarly contributions in such prestigious publications as the *Journal of the Academy of Marketing Science, Journal of Retailing, Journal of Business Research, Journal of Marketing Theory and Practice, Journal of Healthcare Marketing, Journal of Services Marketing, Journal of Marketing Education, and others.* He is a co-author of marketing research textbooks titled *Marketing Research: In a Digital Information Environment,* 4e (2009) as well as guest co-editor of several JBR Special Issues on Retailing. He is an editorial board member for JAMS, JBR, JGSMS, and JMTP as well as an Ad Hoc reviewer for several other journals. He has multiple "Outstanding Editorial Reviewer" Awards from JAMS, JBR, and JMTP, and recently served as the JBR co-associate editor of Marketing and is a member of JMTP Senior Advisory Board. Professor Ortinau remains an active leader in the Marketing Discipline. He has held many leadership positions in the Society for Marketing Advances (SMA), including President; Founder and Chairman of Board of the SMA Foundation; and is a 2001 SMA Fellow. He has been chair of the SMA Doctoral Consortiums in New Orleans, Orlando, and Atlanta. Dr. Ortinau has been an active member of the Academy of Marketing Science (AMS) since the early 1980s, serving AMS in a wide variety of positions such as 2004 AMS Conference Program co-chair, AMS Doctoral Colloquium, Meet the Journal Editorial Reviewers, and special sessions on Research Methods as well as How to Publish Journal Articles. Recently, Dr. Ortinau served as the Program Co-chair of the 2016 AMS World Marketing Congress in Paris, France and became a member of AMS Board of Governors.

Robert P. Bush is a Professor of Marketing, and Associate Dean of the Archie W. Dunham College of Business, Houston Baptist University. He formerly held the Alumni and Friends Endowed Chair in Business at Louisiana State University at Alexandria. Throughout his academic career, he has served as reviewer and special editor for several major Marketing Journals. He has authored, edited, or coauthored six textbooks, published over 25 articles in leading Marketing Journals, and has over 30 publications in national and international proceedings.

Preface

We have prepared this edition with great optimism, but at the same time some degree of trepidation. We live in a global, highly competitive, rapidly changing world that increasingly is influenced by information technology, social media, artificial intelligence, and many other recent developments. The earlier editions of our text *Essentials of Marketing Research* became a premier source for new and essential marketing research knowledge. Many of you, our customers, provided feedback on previous editions of this book as well as our longer text, *Marketing Research*. Some of you like to do applied research projects while others emphasize case studies or exercises at the end of the chapters. Others have requested additional coverage of both qualitative and quantitative methods. Students and professors alike are concerned about the price of textbooks. This fourth edition of *Essentials of Marketing Research* was written to meet the needs of you, our customers. The text is concise, highly readable, and value-priced, yet it delivers the basic knowledge needed for an introductory text. We provide you and your students with an exciting, up-to-date text, and an extensive supplement package. In the following section, we summarize what you will find when you examine, and we hope, adopt, the fourth edition of *Essentials*.

Innovative Features of this Book

First, in the last few years, data collection has migrated quickly to online approaches, and by 2015 reached about 80 percent of all data collection methods. The movement to online methods of data collection has necessitated the addition of considerable new material on this topic. The chapters on sampling, measurement and scaling, questionnaire design, and preparation for data analysis all required new guidelines on how to deal with online related issues. Social media monitoring and marketing research online communities are expanding research methods and are addressed in our chapter on qualitative and observational research.

Second, to enhance student analytical skills we added additional variables to the continuing case on the Santa Fe Grill and Jose's Southwestern Café. Also, there is now a separate data set based on a survey of the employees of the Santa Fe Grill. Findings of the Santa Fe Grill customer and employee data sets are related and can be compared qualitatively to obtain additional insights. The competitor data for the continuing case enables students to make comparisons of customer experiences in each of the two restaurants and to apply their research findings in devising the most effective marketing strategies for the Santa Fe Grill. The exercises for the continuing case demonstrate practical considerations in sampling, qualitative and observational design, questionnaire design, data analysis and interpretation, and report preparation, to mention a few issues. Social media monitoring and marketing research online communities are expanding research methods and are addressed in our chapter on qualitative and observational research.

Third, we have updated the Marketing Research Dashboards in each chapter to include new features that focus on timely, thought-provoking issues in marketing research. Examples of topics covered include ethics, privacy and online data collection, particularly clickstream analysis, the role of Twitter and Linked-In in marketing research, and improving students' critical thinking skills.

Fourth, other texts include little coverage of the task of conducting a literature review to find background information on the research problem. Our text has a chapter that includes substantial material on literature reviews, including guidelines on how to conduct a literature review and the sources to search. Because students rely so heavily on the Internet, the emphasis is on using Google, Yahoo!, Bing, and other search engines to execute the background research. In our effort to make the book more concise, we integrated secondary sources of information with digital media searches. This material is in Chapter 3.

Fifth, our text is the only one that includes a separate chapter on qualitative data analysis. Other texts discuss qualitative data collection, such as focus groups and in-depth interviews, but then say little about what to do with this kind of data. In contrast, we dedicate an entire chapter to the topic that includes interesting new examples and provides an overview of the seminal work in this area by Miles and Huberman, thus enabling professors to provide a more balanced approach in their classes. We also explain important tasks such as coding qualitative data and identifying themes and patterns. An important practical feature in Chapter 9 of the third edition is a sample report on a qualitative research project to help students better understand the differences between quantitative and qualitative reports. We also have an engaging, small-scale qualitative research assignment on product dissatisfaction as a new MRIA at the end of the chapter to help students more fully understand how to analyze qualitative research. We think you and your students will find this assignment to be an engaging introduction to qualitative analysis.

Sixth, as part of the "applied" emphasis of our text, *Essentials* has two pedagogical features that are very helpful to students' practical understanding of the issues. One is the boxed material mentioned above entitled the Marketing Research Dashboard that summarizes an applied research example and poses questions for discussion. Then at the end of every chapter, we feature a Marketing Research in Action (MRIA) exercise that enables students to apply what was covered in the chapter to a real-world situation.

Seventh, as noted above, our text has an excellent continuing case study throughout the book that enables the professor to illustrate applied concepts using a realistic example. Our continuing case study, the Santa Fe Grill Mexican Restaurant, is a fun example students can relate to given the popularity of Mexican restaurant business themes. As mentioned above, for this edition we added an employee data set so students can complete a competitive analysis, including application of importance-performance concepts, and also relate the employee findings to the customer perceptions. Because it is a continuing case, professors do not have to familiarize students with a new case in every chapter, but instead can build on what has been covered earlier. The Santa Fe Grill case is doubly engaging because the story/setting is about two college student entrepreneurs who start their own business, a goal of many students. Finally, when the continuing case is used in later chapters on quantitative data analysis, a data set is provided that can be used with SPSS and SmartPLS to teach data analysis and interpretation skills. Thus, students can truly see how marketing research information can be used to improve decision making.

Eighth, in addition to the Santa Fe Grill case, there are four other data sets in SPSS format. The data sets can be used to assign research projects or as additional exercises throughout the book. These databases cover a wide variety of topics that all students can identify with and offer an excellent approach to enhance teaching of concepts. An overview of these cases is provided below:

Deli Depot is an expanded version of the Deli Depot case included in previous editions. An overview of this case is provided as part of the MRIA (Marketing Research in Action) feature in Chapter 10. The sample size is 200.

Remington's Steak House is introduced as the MRIA in Chapter 11. Remington's Steak House competes with Outback and Longhorn. The focus of the case is analyzing data to identify restaurant images and prepare perceptual maps to facilitate strategy development. The sample size is 200.

QualKote is a business-to-business application of marketing research based on an employee survey. It is introduced as the MRIA in Chapter 12. The case examines the implementation of a quality improvement program and its impact on customer satisfaction. The sample size is 57.

Consumer Electronics is based on the rapid growth of the digital recorder/player market and focuses on the concept of innovators and early adopters. The case overview and variables as well as some data analysis examples are provided in the MRIA for Chapter 13. The sample size is 200.

Ninth, the text's coverage of quantitative data analysis is more extensive and much easier to understand than other books'. Specific step-by-step instructions are included on how to use SPSS and SmartPLS to execute data analysis for many statistical techniques. This enables instructors to spend much less time teaching students how to use the software the first time. It also saves time later by providing a handy reference for students when they forget how to use the software, which they often do. For instructors who want to cover more advanced statistical techniques, our book is the only one that includes this topic. In the fourth edition, we have added additional material on topics such as common methods bias, selecting the appropriate scaling method, and a table providing guidelines to select the appropriate statistical technique. Finally, we include an overview of the increasingly popular variance based approach to structural modeling (PLS-SEM) and much more extensive coverage of how to interpret data analysis findings.

Tenth, as noted earlier, online marketing research techniques are rapidly changing the face of marketing, and the authors have experience with and a strong interest in the issues associated with online data collection. For the most part, other texts' material covering online research is an "add-on" that does not fully integrate online research considerations and their impact. In contrast, our text has extensive new coverage of these issues that is comprehensive and timely because it was written in the last year when many of these trends are now evident and information is available to document them.

Pedagogy

Many marketing research texts are readable. But a more important question is, "Can students comprehend what they are reading?" This book offers a wealth of pedagogical features, all aimed at answering the question positively. Below is a list of the major pedagogical elements available in the fourth edition:

Learning Objectives. Each chapter begins with clear Learning Objectives that students can use to assess their expectations for and understanding of the chapter in view of the nature and importance of the chapter material.

Real-World Chapter Openers. Each chapter opens with an interesting, relevant example of a real-world business situation that illustrates the focus and significance of the chapter material. For example, Chapter 1 illustrates the emerging role of social networking sites such as Twitter in enhancing marketing research activities.

Marketing Research Dashboards. The text includes boxed features in all chapters that act like a dashboard for the student to understand emerging issues in marketing research decision making.

Key Terms and Concepts. These are boldfaced in the text and defined in the page margins. They also are listed at the end of the chapters along with page numbers to make reviewing easier, and they are included in the comprehensive marketing research Glossary at the end of the book.

Ethics. Ethical issues are treated in the first chapter to provide students with a basic understanding of ethical challenges in marketing research. Coverage of increasingly important ethical issues has been updated and expanded from the second edition, and includes online data collection ethical issues.

Chapter Summaries. The detailed chapter Summaries are organized by the Learning Objectives presented at the beginning of the chapters. This approach to organizing summaries helps students remember the key facts, concepts, and issues. The Summaries serve as an excellent study guide to prepare for in-class exercises and for exams.

Questions for Review and Discussion. The Review and Discussion Questions are carefully designed to enhance the self-learning process and to encourage application of the concepts learned in the chapter to real business decision-making situations. There are two or three questions in each chapter directly related to the Internet and designed to provide students with opportunities to enhance their digital data gathering and interpretative skills.

Marketing Research in Action. The short MRIA cases that conclude each of the chapters provide students with additional insights into how key concepts in each chapter can be applied to real-world situations. These cases serve as in-class discussion tools or applied case exercises. Several of them introduce the data sets found on the book's Web site.

Santa Fe Grill. The book's continuing case study on the Santa Fe Grill uses a single research situation to illustrate various aspects of the marketing research process. The Santa Fe Grill continuing case, including competitor Jose's Southwestern Café, is a specially designed business scenario embedded throughout the book for the purpose of questioning and illustrating chapter topics. The case is introduced in Chapter 1, and in each subsequent chapter, it builds on the concepts previously learned. More than 30 class-tested examples are included as well as an SPSS and Excel formatted database covering a customer survey of the two restaurants. In earlier editions, we added customer survey information for competitor Jose's Southwestern Café, as well as employee survey results for the Santa Fe Grill, to further demonstrate and enhance critical thinking and analytical skills.

McGraw-Hill Connect®: connect.mheducation.com

Continually evolving, McGraw-Hill Connect® has been redesigned to provide the only true adaptive learning experience delivered within a simple and easy-to-navigate environment, placing students at the very center.

- Performance Analytics—Now available for both instructors and students, easy-to-decipher data illuminates course performance. Students always know how they are doing in class, while instructors can view student and section performance at-a-glance.
- Mobile—Available on tablets, students can now access assignments, quizzes, and results on-the-go, while instructors can assess student and section performance anytime, anywhere.
- Personalized Learning—Squeezing the most out of study time, the adaptive engine within Connect creates a highly personalized learning path for each student by identifying areas of weakness and providing learning resources to assist in the moment of need.

This seamless integration of reading, practice, and assessment ensures that the focus is on the most important content for that individual.

LearnSmart®

LearnSmart, the most widely used adaptive learning resource, is proven to improve grades. By focusing each student on the most important information they need to learn, LearnSmart personalizes the learning experience so they can study as efficiently as possible.

SmartBook®

SmartBook—an extension of LearnSmart—is an adaptive eBook that helps students focus their study time more effectively. As students read, SmartBook assesses comprehension and dynamically highlights where they need to study more.

Instructor Library

The Connect Instructor Library is your repository for additional resources to improve student engagement in and out of class. You can select and use any asset that enhances your lecture.

Instructor's Resources. Specially prepared Instructor's Manual and Test Bank and PowerPoint slide presentations provide an easy transition for instructors teaching with the book the first time.

Data Sets. Six data sets in SPSS format are available in the Connect Library, which can be used to assign research projects or with exercises throughout the book. (The concepts covered in each of the data sets are summarized earlier in this Preface.)

SmartPLS Student Version. Through an arrangement with SmartPLS (**www.smartple.de**), we provide instructions on how to obtain a free student version of this powerful new software for executing structural modeling, multiple regression, mediation, and many other interesting types of analyses. Specific instructions on how to obtain and use the software are available in the Connect Library.

SPSS Student Version. This powerful software tool enables students to analyze up to 50 variables and 1,500 observations. SPSS data sets are available that can be used in conjunction with data analysis procedures included in the text. Licensing information is available from IBM Analytics for Education: **www.ibm.com/analytics/us/en /industry/education**

Acknowledgments

The authors took the lead in preparing the fourth edition, but many other people must be given credit for their significant contributions in bringing our vision to reality. We thank our colleagues in academia and industry for their helpful insights over many years on numerous research topics: David Andrus, *Kansas State University*; Barry Babin, *Louisiana Tech University*; Joseph K. Ballanger, *Stephen F. Austin State University*; Ali Besharat, *University of South Florida*; Kevin Bittle, *Johnson and Wales University*; Mike Brady, *Florida State University*; John R. Brooks, Jr., *Houston Baptist University*; Mary L. Carsky, *University of Hartford*; Gabriel Perez Cifuentes, *University of the Andes*; Vicki Crittenden, *Boston College*; Diane Edmondson, *Middle Tennessee State University*; Keith Ferguson, *Michigan State University*; Frank Franzak, *Virginia Commonwealth University*; Susan Geringer, *California State University, Fresno*; Anne Gottfried, *University of Southern Mississippi*; Timothy Graeff, *Middle Tennessee State University*; Dana Harrison,

East Tennessee State University; Harry Harmon, *Central Missouri State University*; Lucas Hopkins, *Florida State University*; Gail Hudson, *Arkansas State University*; Beverly Jones, *Kettering University*; Karen Kolzow-Bowman, *Morgan State University*; Michel Laroche, *Concordia University*; Bryan Lukas, *University of Melbourne*; Vaidotas Lukosius, *Tennessee State University*; Lucy Matthews, *Middle Tennessee State University*; Peter McGoldrick, *University of Manchester*; Martin Meyers, *University of Wisconsin, Stevens Point*; Arthur Money, *Henley Management College*; Vanessa Gail Perry, *George Washington University*; Ossi Pesamaa, *Jonkoping University*; Emily J. Plant, *University of Montana*; Michael Polonsky, *Deakin University*; Charlie Ragland, *Indiana University*; Molly Rapert, *University of Arkansas*; Mimi Richard, *University of West Georgia*; John Rigney, *Golden State University*; Jeff Risher, *Kennesaw State University*; Wendy Ritz *Fayetteville State University*; Jean Romeo, *Boston College*; Lawrence E. Ross, *Florida Southern University*; Phillip Samouel, *Kingston University*; Carl Saxby, *University of Southern Indiana*; Donna Smith, *Ryerson University*; Marc Sollosy, *Marshall University*; Bruce Stern, *Portland State University*; Goran Svensson, *University of Oslo*; Armen Taschian, *Kennesaw State University*; Drew Thoeni, *University of North Florida* ; Gail Tom, *California State University, Sacramento*; John Tsalikis, *Florida International University*; Steve Vitucci, *University of Central Texas*; Tuo Wang, *Kent State University*; David Williams, *Dalton State University*;

Our sincere thank goes also to the helpful reviewers who made suggestions and shared their ideas for the fourth edition:

Mary Conran
Fox School of Business at Temple University

Lee Ann Kahlor
University of Texas at Austin

Curt John Dommeyer
California State University at Northridge

Sungho Park
Arizona State University

Finally, we would like to thank our editors and advisors at McGraw-Hill Education. Thanks go to Laura Hurst Spell, sponsoring editor; Elizabeth Schonagen, marketing manager; and Jenilynn McAtee, project manager.

Joseph F. Hair, Jr.
Mary W. Celsi
David J. Ortinau
Robert P. Bush

Brief Contents

Part 1 The Role and Value of Marketing Research Information   **1**

1   Marketing Research for Managerial Decision Making   2
2   The Marketing Research Process and Proposals   24

Part 2 Designing the Marketing Research Project   **47**

3   Secondary Data, Literature Reviews, and Hypotheses   48
4   Exploratory and Observational Research Designs and Data Collection Approaches   74
5   Descriptive and Causal Research Designs   106

Part 3 Gathering and Collecting Accurate Data   **133**

6   Sampling: Theory and Methods   134
7   Measurement and Scaling   158
8   Designing the Questionnaire   190

Part 4 Data Preparation, Analysis, and Reporting the Results   **219**

9   Qualitative Data Analysis   220
10   Preparing Data for Quantitative Analysis   246
11   Basic Data Analysis for Quantitative Research   272
12   Examining Relationships in Quantitative Research   316
13   Communicating Marketing Research Findings   352

Glossary   382
Endnotes   400
Name Index   404
Subject Index   406

Contents

Part 1 The Role and Value of Marketing Research Information   1

1 Marketing Research for Managerial Decision Making   2
Geofencing   3
The Growing Complexity of Marketing Research   4
MARKETING RESEARCH DASHBOARD: CONDUCTING INTERNATIONAL MARKETING RESEARCH   4
The Role and Value of Marketing Research   6
   Marketing Research and Marketing Mix Variables   6
   Marketing Theory   9
MARKETING RESEARCH DASHBOARD: THE PERFECT PRICING EXPERIMENT?   10
The Marketing Research Industry   10
   Types of Marketing Research Firms   10
   Changing Skills for a Changing Industry   11
Ethics in Marketing Research Practices   12
   Ethical Questions in General Business Practices   12
   Conducting Research Not Meeting Professional Standards   13
   Abuse of Respondents   14
   Unethical Activities of the Client/Research User   15
MARKETING RESEARCH DASHBOARD   15
   Unethical Activities by the Respondent   16
   Marketing Research Codes of Ethics   16
CONTINUING CASE STUDY: THE SANTA FE GRILL MEXICAN RESTAURANT   17
Emerging Trends   17
Marketing Research in Action   18
Continuing Case: The Santa Fe Grill   18
Summary   20
Key Terms and Concepts   20
Review Questions   21
Discussion Questions   21
Appendix A   22

2 The Marketing Research Process and Proposals   24
Solving Marketing Problems Using a Systematic Process   25
Value of the Research Process   26
Changing View of the Marketing Research Process   26
Determining the Need for Information Research   27
MARKETING RESEARCH DASHBOARD: DECISION MAKERS AND RESEARCHERS   28
Overview of the Research Process   29
   Transforming Data into Knowledge   30
   Interrelatedness of the Steps and the Research Process   31
Phase I: Determine the Research Problem   31
   Step 1: Identify and Clarify Information Needs   32
   Step 2: Define the Research Questions   34
   Step 3: Specify Research Objectives and Confirm the Information Value   36
Phase II: Select the Research Design   36
   Step 4: Determine the Research Design and Data Sources   36
MARKETING RESEARCH DASHBOARD: MEASURING EFFECTIVENESS OF ONLINE ADVERTISING FORMATS   37
   Step 5: Develop the Sampling Design and Sample Size   38
   Step 6: Examine Measurement Issues and Scales   38
   Step 7: Design and Pretest the Questionnaire   39
Phase III: Execute the Research Design   39
   Step 8: Collect and Prepare Data   39
   Step 9: Analyze Data   39
   Step 10: Interpret Data to Create Knowledge   40
Phase IV: Communicate the Results   40

Step 11: Prepare and Present
  the Final Report   41
Develop a Research Proposal   41
Marketing Research in Action   42
What Does a Research Proposal Look Like?   42
Summary   44
Key Terms and Concepts   45
Review Questions   45
Discussion Questions   46

**Part 2   Designing the Marketing
           Research Project   47**

**3   Secondary Data, Literature Reviews,
     and Hypotheses   48**
Will Brick-and-Mortar Stores
Eventually Turn into Product Showrooms?   49
Value of Secondary Data and
Literature Reviews   50
  Nature, Scope, and Role of
  Secondary Data   50
Conducting a Literature Review   51
  Evaluating Secondary Data Sources   51
  Secondary Data and the Marketing
  Research Process   53
Internal and External Sources
of Secondary Data   54
  Internal Sources of Secondary Data   54
  External Sources of Secondary Data   54
CONTINUING CASE STUDY:
THE SANTA FE GRILL MEXICAN
RESTAURANT USING
SECONDARY DATA   58
MARKETING RESEARCH
DASHBOARD: TRIANGULATING
SECONDARY DATA SOURCES   62
  Synthesizing Secondary Research for the
  Literature Review   62
Developing a Conceptual Model   63
  Variables, Constructs, and
  Relationships   63
  Developing Hypotheses and Drawing
  Conceptual Models   64
CONTINUING CASE STUDY: THE SANTA
FE GRILL MEXICAN RESTAURANT
DEVELOPING RESEARCH QUESTIONS
AND HYPOTHESES   67
Hypothesis Testing   67
Marketing Research in Action   69
The Santa Fe Grill Mexican Restaurant   69

Summary   70
Key Terms and Concepts   71
Review Questions   71
Discussion Questions   71

**4   Exploratory and Observational
     Research Designs and Data
     Collection Approaches   74**
Customer Territoriality in "Third Places"   75
Value of Qualitative Research   76
Overview of Research Designs   77
Overview of Qualitative and Quantitative
Research Methods   77
  Quantitative Research Methods   77
  Qualitative Research Methods   78
Qualitative Data Collection Methods   81
  In-Depth Interviews   81
  Focus Group Interviews   82
  Phase 1: Planning the Focus
  Group Study   85
  Phase 2: Conducting the Focus
  Group Discussions   87
  Phase 3: Analyzing and Reporting
  the Results   89
  Advantages of Focus Group
  Interviews   89
  Purposed Communities/Private
  Community   89
Other Qualitative Data Collection
Methods   91
  Ethnography   91
  Case Study   91
  Projective Techniques   92
CONTINUING CASE:
THE SANTA FE GRILL   92
Observation Methods   93
  Unique Characteristics of Observation
  Methods   94
  Types of Observation Methods   94
  Selecting the Observation Method   96
  Benefits and Limitations of
  Observation Methods   97
  Social Media Monitoring and the
  Listening Platform   97
  Netnography   99
Marketing Research in Action   100
Reaching Hispanics through Qualitative
Research   100
Summary   102
Key Terms and Concepts   103

Review Questions 104
Discussion Questions 104

**5 Descriptive and Causal
Research Designs** **106**
Magnum Hotel's Loyalty Program 107
Value of Descriptive and Causal Survey
Research Designs 108
Descriptive Research Designs
and Surveys 108
Types of Errors in Surveys 109
Sampling Errors 109
Nonsampling Errors 110
Types of Survey Methods 110
Person-Administered Surveys 111
Telephone-Administered Surveys 112
Self-Administered Surveys 115
Selecting the Appropriate Survey Method 118
Situational Characteristics 118
Task Characteristics 119
Respondent Characteristics 120
Causal Research Designs 122
The Nature of Experimentation 123
*Validity Concerns with Experimental
Research* 124
MARKETING RESEARCH DASHBOARD:
RETAILERS USE EXPERIMENTS
TO TEST DISCOUNT STRATEGY 125
*Comparing Laboratory and Field
Experiments* 126
Test Marketing 127
Marketing Research Dashboard 128
Riders Fits New Database into
Brand Launch 128
Summary 130
Key Terms and Concepts 131
Review Questions 131
Discussion Questions 132

**Part 3 Gathering and Collecting
Accurate Data** **133**

**6 Sampling: Theory
and Methods** **134**
Mobile Web Interactions Explode 135
Value of Sampling in Marketing
Research 136
*Sampling as a Part of the
Research Process* 136
The Basics of Sampling Theory 137

Population 137
Sampling Frame 138
*Factors Underlying Sampling
Theory* 138
*Tools Used to Assess the Quality
of Samples* 139
MARKETING RESEARCH IN ACTION
CONTINUING CASE STUDY: THE SANTA
FE GRILL 139
Probability and Nonprobability Sampling 140
Probability Sampling Designs 140
MARKETING RESEARCH DASHBOARD:
SELECTING A SYSTEMATIC RANDOM
SAMPLE FOR THE SANTA FE GRILL 142
MARKETING RESEARCH
DASHBOARD: WHICH IS
BETTER—PROPORTIONATELY OR
DISPROPORTIONATELY STRATIFIED
SAMPLES? 145
Nonprobability Sampling Designs 146
*Determining the Appropriate
Sampling Design* 148
Determining Sample Sizes 148
Probability Sample Sizes 148
CONTINUING CASE STUDY:
THE SANTA FE GRILL 149
Sampling from a Small Population 150
MARKETING RESEARCH
DASHBOARD: USING SPSS
TO SELECT A RANDOM SAMPLE 150
Nonprobability Sample Sizes 151
*Other Sample Size Determination
Approaches* 151
MARKETING RESEARCH DASHBOARD:
SAMPLING AND ONLINE SURVEYS 151
Steps in Developing a Sampling Plan 152
Marketing Research in Action 154
Developing a Sampling Plan for a
New Menu Initiative Survey 154
Summary 155
Key Terms and Concepts 156
Review Questions 156
Discussion Questions 156

7 Measurement and Scaling **158**
Santa Fe Grill Mexican Restaurant:
Predicting Customer Loyalty 159
Value of Measurement in
Information Research 160
Overview of the Measurement Process 160

What Is a Construct?   161
   Construct Development   161
Scale Measurement   163
MARKETING RESEARCH DASHBOARD:
UNDERSTANDING THE DIMENSIONS
OF BANK SERVICE QUALITY   163
   Nominal Scales   164
   Ordinal Scales   164
   Interval Scales   165
   Ratio Scales   166
Evaluating Measurement Scales   167
   Scale Reliability   167
   Validity   168
Developing Scale Measurements   169
   Criteria for Scale Development   169
   Adapting Established Scales   172
Scales to Measure Attitudes and Behaviors   173
   Likert Scale   173
   Semantic Differential Scale   174
   Behavioral Intention Scale   176
Comparative and Noncomparative
Rating Scales   177
Other Scale Measurement Issues   180
   Single-Item and Multiple-Item Scales 180
   Clear Wording   180
Misleading Scaling Formats   181
Marketing Research in Action   184
What Can You Learn from a Customer
Loyalty Index?   184
Summary   186
Key Terms and Concepts   187
Review Questions   187
Discussion Questions   188

8 Designing the Questionnaire   **190**
Can Surveys Be Used to Develop
University Residence Life Plans?   191
Value of Questionnaires in
Marketing Research   192
Pilot Studies and Pretests   192
Questionnaire Design   193
   *Step 1: Confirm Research
   Objectives*   193
   *Step 2: Select Appropriate
   Data Collection Method*   194
   *Step 3: Develop Questions
   and Scaling*   194
MARKETING RESEARCH DASHBOARD:
"FRAMING" YOUR QUESTIONS CAN
INTRODUCE BIAS!   198

   *Step 4: Determine Layout and
   Evaluate Questionnaire*   203
MARKETING RESEARCH DASHBOARD:
SMART QUESTIONNAIRES
ARE REVOLUTIONIZING SURVEYS   204
   *Step 5: Obtain Initial
   Client Approval*   207
   *Step 6: Pretest, Revise, and
   Finalize the Questionnaire*   207
   Step 7: Implement the Survey   207
The Role of a Cover Letter   208
MARKETING RESEARCH DASHBOARD:
COVER LETTER USED WITH THE
AMERICAN BANK SURVEY   209
Other Considerations in Collecting Data   210
   Supervisor Instructions   210
   Interviewer Instructions   211
   Screening Questions   211
   Quotas   211
   Call or Contact Records   211
Marketing Research in Action   212
Designing a Questionnaire to
Survey Santa Fe Grill Customers   212
Summary   217
Key Terms and Concepts   218
Review Questions   218
Discussion Questions   218

**Part 4   Data Preparation, Analysis,
and Reporting the Results   219**

9 Qualitative Data Analysis   **220**
Why Women are "Claiming
the Throttle"   221
Nature of Qualitative Data Analysis   222
Qualitative versus Quantitative Analyses   222
The Process of Analyzing
Qualitative Data   223
   *Managing the Data
   Collection Effort*   223
   Step 1: Data Reduction   223
   Step 2: Data Display   230
   *Step 3: Conclusion Drawing/
   Verification*   231
Writing the Report   235
   Analysis of the Data/Findings   236
   Conclusions and Recommendations 237
CONTINUING CASE: SANTA FE GRILL:
USING QUALITATIVE RESEARCH   238
Marketing Research in Action   239

A Qualitative Approach to Understanding
Product Dissatisfaction 239
Summary 240
Key Terms and Concepts 241
Review Questions 242
Discussion Questions 242
Appendix A 243
Advertising's Second Audience:
Employee Reactions to Organizational
Communications 243

10 Preparing Data for Quantitative
Analysis 246
Scanner Data Improves Understanding
of Purchase Behavior 247
Value of Preparing Data for Analysis 248
Validation 249
Editing and Coding 251
Asking the Proper Questions 251
Accurate Recording of Answers 251
Correct Screening Questions 252
Responses to Open-Ended Questions 255
The Coding Process 256
MARKETING RESEARCH DASHBOARD:
DEALING WITH DATA FROM DATA
WAREHOUSES 258
Data Entry 259
Error Detection 259
Missing Data 259
Organizing Data 261
Data Tabulation 261
One-Way Tabulation 261
Descriptive Statistics 264
Graphical Illustration of Data 264
Marketing Research in Action 267
Deli Depot 267
Summary 270
Key Terms and Concepts 271
Review Questions 271
Discussion Questions 271

11 Basic Data Analysis for Quantitative
Research 272
Data Analysis Facilitates Smarter Decisions 273
Value of Statistical Analysis 274
Measures of Central Tendency 274
MARKETING RESEARCH DASHBOARD:
SPLITTING THE DATABASE INTO SANTA
FE'S AND JOSE'S CUSTOMERS 276
SPSS Applications—Measures of
Central Tendency 276

Measures of Dispersion 277
SPSS Applications—Measures of
Dispersion 278
Preparation of Charts 281
How to Develop Hypotheses 281
MARKETING RESEARCH DASHBOARD:
STEPS IN HYPOTHESIS DEVELOPMENT
AND TESTING 282
Analyzing Relationships of
Sample Data 283
Sample Statistics and Population
Parameters 283
Choosing the Appropriate Statistical
Technique 283
Univariate Statistical Tests 286
SPSS Application—Univariate
Hypothesis Test 287
Bivariate Statistical Tests 287
Cross-Tabulation 288
MARKETING RESEARCH DASHBOARD:
SELECTING THE SANTA FE GRILL
CUSTOMERS FOR ANALYSIS 288
Chi-Square Analysis 290
Calculating the Chi-Square Value 291
SPSS Application—Chi-Square 292
Comparing Means: Independent
Versus Related Samples 293
Using the t-Test to Compare
Two Means 294
SPSS Application—Independent
Samples t-Test 295
SPSS Application—Paired
Samples t-Test 296
Analysis of Variance (ANOVA) 297
SPSS Application—ANOVA 298
n-Way ANOVA 300
SPSS Application—n-Way
ANOVA 301
Perceptual Mapping 304
Perceptual Mapping Applications
in Marketing Research 305
CONTINUING CASE STUDY:
THE SANTA FE GRILL 305
Marketing Research in Action 306
Examining Restaurant Image Positions—
Remington's Steak House 306
Summary 313
Key Terms and Concepts 313
Review Questions 314
Discussion Questions 314

**12 Examining Relationships
in Quantitative Research** 316

Data Mining Helps Rebuild Procter &
Gamble as a Global Powerhouse 317
Examining Relationships
between Variables 318
Covariation and Variable Relationships 319
Correlation Analysis 322
Pearson Correlation Coefficient 323
*SPSS Application—Pearson
Correlation* 323
*Substantive Significance of the
Correlation Coefficient* 325
*Influence of Measurement Scales on
Correlation Analysis* 326
*SPSS Application—Spearman
Rank Order Correlation* 326
What Is Regression Analysis? 327
Fundamentals of Regression Analysis 328
*Developing and Estimating the
Regression Coefficients* 330
*SPSS Application—Bivariate
Regression* 330
Significance 332
Multiple Regression Analysis 333
Statistical Significance 334
Substantive Significance 334
Multiple Regression Assumptions 335
*SPSS Application—Multiple
Regression* 335
What Is Structural Modeling? 339
An Example of Structural Modeling 341
Marketing Research in Action 345
The Role of Employees in Developing a
Customer Satisfaction Program 345
Summary 348
Key Terms and Concepts 349
Review Questions 349
Discussion Questions 349

**13 Communicating Marketing
Research Findings** 352

It Takes More than Numbers to
Communicate 353
Value of Communicating
Research Findings 354
Marketing Research Reports 354
MARKETING RESEARCH DASHBOARD:
CRITICAL THINKING AND MARKETING
RESEARCH 357
Format of the Marketing
Research Report 357
Title Page 358
Table of Contents 358
Executive Summary 358
Introduction 359
Research Methods and Procedures 360
Data Analysis and Findings 361
Conclusions and Recommendations 372
Limitations 374
Appendixes 374
Common Problems in Preparing
the Marketing Research Report 374
The Critical Nature of Presentations 375
*Guidelines for Preparing Oral
Presentations* 375
*Guidelines for Preparing the Visual
Presentation* 376
Marketing Research in Action 377
Who Are the Early Adopters of
Technology? 377
Summary 380
Key Terms and Concepts 381
Review Questions 381
Discussion Questions 381

Glossary 382
Endnotes 400
Name Index 404
Subject Index 406

Part 1

The Role and Value of Marketing Research Information

Marketing Research for Managerial Decision Making

1. Describe the impact marketing research has on marketing decision making.
2. Demonstrate how marketing research fits into the marketing planning process.
3. Provide examples of marketing research studies.
4. Understand the scope and focus of the marketing research industry.
5. Recognize ethical issues associated with marketing research.
6. Discuss new skills and emerging trends in marketing research.

Geofencing

Over the past 15 years, the Internet has sparked a number of significant innovations in marketing research, from online surveys, to mobile surveys, to social media monitoring. The newest Internet technology to influence both marketing and marketing research may be geofencing. Geofencing is a virtual fence that is placed around a geographic location in the real world. Location-enabled smartphone applications can detect entry and exit from these virtual fences. A geofence can be as small as a coffee shop or as wide as a city block. Companies such as Starbucks have used these virtual fences as a way to offer customers in-store benefits such as ease of checkout and local in-store deals.[1] In-store deals can be customized based on the the shopper's previous purchases or other information available in the shopper's profile.

For marketing researchers, geofencing offers a number of possible ways for information to be gleaned from customers. The applications often possess the ability to monitor purchasing behavior as well as the time of day of visits, the number of visits, and the length of visits (often called "loitering time").[2] Perhaps most interesting is the possibility of using geofencing to capture in-the-moment feedback. Early research comparing surveys fielded by geofencing applications to traditional surveys suggests that consumers more accurately report their experiences immediately after they occur.[3] An additional potential benefit for researchers is that online browsing behavior can be matched to data on in-store behavior.

Geofencing should be particularly helpful with collecting data from younger customers who often do not participate in traditional surveys.[4] Of course, consumers must agree to turn on their location-based apps if researchers are to collect data. On the other hand, potential research respondents can easily be offered relevant rewards for participating in research based on geofencing apps. The popularity of retail store apps that include geofencing components along with the value of "in-context" feedback for marketers makes it likely that the use of geofencing to collect marketing research information will grow in the next few years.

▎▎ The Growing Complexity of Marketing Research

Technology and the growth of global business are increasing the complexity of marketing research. Digital technologies bring a great deal of opportunities for marketing research but create challenges as well. Internet-based tools, including web-based surveys, interactive and social networking tools like Facebook and Twitter, and mobile phones are radically remolding data collection. "Big data," a term used to describe the large and complex datasets that information technology enables organizations to gather and store, requires innovative tools to extract insight for businesses and marketers. Some new techniques, such as neuromarketing—which involves scanning the brains of research subjects while showing them ads, for instance—have not yet proven themselves, and may or may not eventually provide useful insights to marketers. Many new data collection tools, including Twitter, clickstream tracking, GPS, and geofencing, pose serious questions in regard to consumer privacy. The current variety of available tools and techniques makes choosing a method for a particular research project increasingly challenging. An additional level of complexity in research design occurs whenever the research effort is global. In our first Marketing Research Dashboard, we address issues in conducting international marketing research. Never before has the research landscape been more complex or more exciting for marketing researchers.

MARKETING RESEARCH DASHBOARD   CONDUCTING INTERNATIONAL MARKETING RESEARCH

Many marketing research firms have a presence in a large number of countries. For example, Gfk Research (www.gfk.com) advertises that it performs marketing research in over 100 countries. Still, performing research in countries around the world poses some challenges. A great deal of marketing theory and practice to date has been developed in the United States. The good news is that many theories and concepts developed to explain consumer behavior are likely to be applicable to other contexts. For example, the idea that consumers may purchase items that reflect their self-concepts and identities likely applies to many countries. Second, marketing research techniques, including sampling, data collection, qualitative and quantitative techniques, and statistical analyses, are tools that are likely to be almost universally applicable.

But there are many challenges. Some marketing researchers study a country's culture and make broad conclusions about the applicability of their findings. However, culture may strongly affect some kinds of purchases and not others. Second, some target segments and subcultures exist across countries, so performing research that focuses on cultural differences at the level of countries may too narrowly define a target market. Last, Yoram Wind and Susan Douglas argue that while consumers in different countries tend to behave somewhat differently, there is often more variance in behavior within a country than between countries. Thus, research making broad conclusions about consumer culture in a particular country may not be useful to a company marketing a specific product to a specific segment. More specific research applicable to the specific marketing opportunity or problem is likely to be necessary.

Research on emerging markets, such as Latin America, Africa, and the Middle East, is important as these marketplaces are growing, but the lack of existing secondary data and market research suppliers in these areas of the world presents challenges for businesses who would like to better understand these marketplaces. Developing research capabilities in these areas is complicated by the fact that identifying representative samples is difficult because existing reliable demographic data in these markets may not be available. Translating survey items into another language may change their meaning even when the precaution of backtranslation is used to identify potential issues. Moreover, establishing conceptual equivalence in surveys may be difficult; for example, the Western notion of "truth" is not applicable in the Confucian philosophy.

Building relationships with marketing research companies in the countries where firms want to collect information is the preferred strategy as firms within countries already have useful knowledge about research challenges and solutions. However, marketing research is not always highly regarded by managers in emerging marketplaces. This may be true for several reasons. Consumer acceptance and participation in surveys may be low. The cost of poor business decisions may be lower and thus the perceived need for research to minimize risk is lessened. And, researchers who engage in both qualitative and quantitative techniques often

(Continued)

have to adjust methodology to more successfully interact with consumers in emerging marketplaces.

Technology presents both opportunities and barriers for international marketing research. 3Com commissioned Harris Interactive to conduct the world's largest interactive Internet-based poll. Fully 1.4 million respondents in 250 countries around the world participated in Project Planet. In many countries, respondents entered their answers in an online survey. In remote areas without telephones and computers, interviewers were sent with portable handheld tablets for data entry. When interviewers returned from the field, the data could be uploaded to the database. In this research effort, 3Com was able to reach even technologically disenfranchised communities. While the results were based on a convenience rather than a representative sample, the effort still represents an important, if imperfect global effort at collecting meaningful cross-cultural information.

What does the future hold? Research firms and companies who can successfully develop methods and concepts that will aid them to better understand and serve marketplaces around the world are likely to be more competitive in a global marketplace. The research firms who are able to provide actionable information will be those who study consumer behavior in context, work with local marketing research firms to develop sound marketing research infrastructure, apply new technologies appropriately to collect valid and reliable data, and develop the analytical sophistication to understand segments within and across country boundaries.

Sources: Yoram Wind and Susan Douglas, "Some Issues in International Consumer Research," *European Journal of Marketing*, 2001, pp. 209–217; C. Samuel Craig and Susan P. Douglas, "Conducting International marketing Research in the 21st Century," 3rd Edition, John Wiley & Sons Ltd, Chichester, West Sussex, England 2005; B. Sebastian Reiche and Anne Wil Harzing, "Key Issues in International Survey Research," *Harzing.com*, June 26, 2007, www .harzing.com/ intresearch_keyissues.htm, accessed August 11, 2011; Fernando Fastoso and Jeryl Whitelock, "Why is so Little Marketing Research on Latin America Published in High Quality Journals and What Can We Do About It?" *International Marketing Research*, 2011, Vol. 28(4), pp. 435–439; Holmes, Paul "3Com's Planet Project: An Interactive Poll of the Human Race," http://www.holmesreport.com /casestudyinfo/581/3Coms-Planet-Project-An-Interactive-Poll-of -the-Human-Race.aspx, May 28, 2011, accessed August 13, 2011.

Despite the explosion of new marketing research tools and concepts, established tools such as hypothesis testing, construct definition, reliability, validity, sampling, and data analysis remain essential to evaluating the uses and value of new data collection approaches. Traditional data collection methods such as focus groups, mystery shopping, and computer-aided telephone interviewing (CATI) are still relevant and widely used tools. Companies increasingly are choosing hybrid research techniques involving multiple research methods to overcome the weaknesses inherent in single methodologies.

Marketing research The function that links an organization to its market through the gathering of information.

The American Marketing Association defines **marketing research** as the function that links an organization to its market through the gathering of information. This information facilitates the identification and definition of market-driven opportunities and problems, as well as the development and evaluation of marketing actions. Finally, it enables the monitoring of marketing performance and improved understanding of marketing as a business process.[5] Organizations use marketing research information to identify new product opportunities, develop advertising strategies, and implement new data-gathering methods to better understand customers.

Marketing research is a systematic process. Tasks in this process include designing methods for collecting information, managing the information collection process, analyzing and interpreting results, and communicating findings to decision makers. This chapter provides an overview of marketing research and its fundamental relationship to marketing. We first explain why firms use marketing research and give some examples of how marketing research can help companies make sound marketing decisions. Next we discuss who should use marketing research, and when.

The chapter provides a general description of the ways companies collect marketing research information. We present an overview of the marketing research industry in order to clarify the relationship between the providers and the users of marketing information. The chapter closes with a description of the role of ethics in marketing research, followed by an appendix on careers in marketing research.

The Role and Value of Marketing Research

Many managers with experience in their industry can make educated guesses based on their experience. But markets and consumer tastes change, sometimes rapidly. No matter how much experience that managers might have with their marketplace, they occasionally find that their educated guesses miss the mark. Behavioral decision theorists such as Dan Ariely, author of *Predictably Irrational*, have documented that even experienced individuals can be very wrong in their decision making even when the decision they are making has important consequences.[6] And many managerial decisions involve new contexts where experience may be absent or even misleading. For example, organizations may be considering new strategies, including marketing to a new segment, using new or evolving media to appeal to their customers, or introducing new products.

Marketing research draws heavily on the social sciences both for methods and theory. Thus, marketing research methods are diverse, spanning a wide variety of qualitative and quantitative techniques and borrowing from disciplines such as psychology, sociology, and anthropology. Marketing research can be thought of as a toolbox full of implements designed for a wide variety of purposes. Tools include surveys, focus groups, experiments, and ethnography, just to name a few. The size of the toolbox has grown in recent years with the advent of "big data," social media, Internet surveys, and mobile phones. And international marketing problems and opportunities have brought complexity to marketing problems and opportunities along with special challenges for marketing researchers who seek to understand these markets. The size and diversity of the toolbox represent exciting opportunities for marketing researchers to grow and develop innovative ways of learning about markets and consumers.

Whether you work for a small, medium, or large business, it is highly likely that sooner or later you or your organization will buy research, commission research, or even engage in do-it-yourself (DIY) research. While some research methods involve techniques that are hard to master in one course, the essential material in a one-semester course can take you a long way toward being a better research client and will enable you to do some projects on your own.

You probably already know that not all research efforts are equally well executed, and poorly conceived efforts result in information that is not useful for decision making. As well, some secondary research may initially appear to be relevant to a decision, but after reviewing the methodology or sample employed by the research firm, you may decide that the research is not useful for your decision problem. Moreover, even well-executed research has some weaknesses and must be critically evaluated. Developing the knowledge and critical stance to evaluate research efforts will help you determine how and when to apply the research that is available to marketing problems at hand.

Marketing research can be applied to a wide variety of problems involving the four Ps: price, place, promotion, and product. Additionally, marketing research is often used to research consumers and potential consumers in vivid detail, including their attitudes, behaviors, media consumption, and lifestyles. Marketers are also interested in consumer subcultures, as products are often used to enact and support subculture participation. Last, marketing academics and consultants often perform theoretical research that helps marketers understand questions applicable to a broad variety of marketing contexts. Below, we explain how marketing research applies to the traditional four Ps; to studying consumers and consumer subcultures; and the role of theoretical research in marketing.

Marketing Research and Marketing Mix Variables

Product Product decisions are varied and include new product development and introduction, branding, and positioning products. New product development often involves a great deal of research identifying possible new product opportunities, designing products that evoke favorable consumer response, and then developing an appropriate marketing mix for new products. *Concept and product testing* or *test marketing* provide information for decisions on product improvements and new-product introductions. Concept testing identifies any weaknesses in a product concept prior to launching a product. Product testing attempts to answer two fundamental questions: "How does a product perform for the customer?" and "How can a product be improved to exceed customer expectations?"

Branding is an important strategic issue both for new and existing products. Some marketing firms such as Namestomers specialize in branding, both identifying possible names and then performing consumer research to choose which name effectively communicates product attributes or image. Even for brands with established identities, research must be undertaken regularly to enable early detection of changes in meaning and attitudes toward a brand.

Perceptual mapping A technique used to picture the relative position of products on two or more product dimensions important to consumer purchase decisions.

Positioning is a process in which a company seeks to understand how present or possible products are perceived by consumers on relevant product attributes. **Perceptual mapping** is a technique that is often used to picture the relative position of products on two or more dimensions important to consumers in making their choice to purchase. To create the map, consumers are asked to indicate how similar or dissimilar a group of relevant brands or products is to each other. The responses are used to construct perceptual maps that transform the positioning data into a picture or graph that shows how brands are viewed relative to one another. Perceptual mapping reflects the criteria customers use to evaluate brands, typically representing major product features important to customers in selecting products or services. See Exhibit 1.1 for an example of a perceptual map of the Fast Food market.

Place/Distribution Distribution decisions in marketing include choosing and evaluating locations, channels, and distribution partners. Retailers, including online retailers, undertake a wide variety of studies, but some needs of retailers are unique. Market research studies peculiar to retailers include trade area analysis, store image studies, in-store traffic patterns,

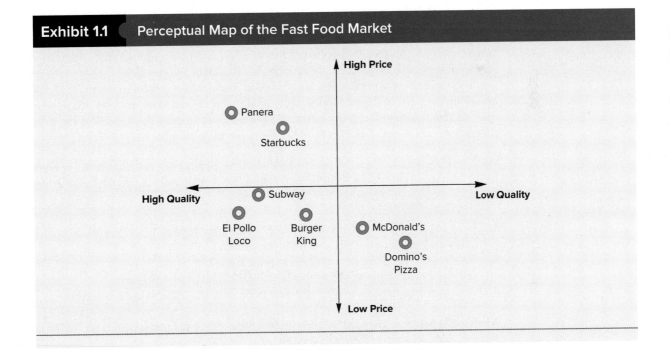

Exhibit 1.1   **Perceptual Map of the Fast Food Market**

Retailing research Research investigations that focus on topics such as trade area analysis, store image/perception, in-store traffic patterns, and location analysis.

and location analysis. Because retailing is a high customer-contact activity, much **retailing research** focuses on database development through optical scanning at the point of purchase. Retailers match data collected at the point of purchase with information on the media customers consume, type of neighborhoods they live in, and the stores they prefer to patronize. This information helps retailers select the kind of merchandise to stock and to understand the factors that influence their customers' purchase decisions.

Online retailers face some unique challenges and data-gathering opportunities. E-tailers can determine when a website is visited, how long the visit lasts, which pages are viewed, and which products are examined and ultimately purchased, and whether or not products are abandoned in online shopping carts. Online retailers who participate in search engine marketing have access to search analytics that help them choose keywords to purchase from search engines. In **behavioral targeting**, e-tailers work with content sites to display ads based on data collected about user behaviors. For example, Weather.com may display ads for a specific pair of shoes that a customer has recently viewed while shopping online at Zappos.com.

Behavioral targeting Displaying ads at one website based on the user's previous surfing behavior.

Shopper marketing Marketing to consumers based on research of the entire process consumers go through when making a purchase.

In recent years, **shopper marketing** has received a lot of attention. The purpose of shopper research is "to help manufacturers and retailers understand the entire process consumers go through in making a purchase, from prestore to in-store to point-of-purchase."[7] Shopper marketing addresses product category management, displays, sales, packaging, promotion, and marketing. Marketing research helps businesses to understand when, where, and how consumers make decisions to purchase products that helps retailers provide the right strategy at the right time to influence consumer choices.

Promotion Promotional decisions are important influences on any company's sales. Billions of dollars are spent yearly on various promotional activities. Given the heavy level of expenditures on promotional activities, it is essential that companies know how to obtain good returns from their promotional budgets. In addition to traditional media, digital media, such as Google, YouTube, and social media such as Facebook, all present special challenges to businesses that require reliable metrics to accurately gauge the return on advertising dollars spent. Market researchers must develop meaningful metrics and then collect the data for those metrics. "Analytics" is the application of statistics to quantify performance. For example, Google analytics reports a number of statistics that measure the performance and value of a marketer's search engine marketing program, for example, clickthroughs and purchases.

The three most common research tasks in integrated marketing communications are advertising effectiveness studies, attitudinal research, and sales tracking. Marketing research that examines the performance of a promotional program must consider the total program as each effort often affects others in the promotional mix.

Price Pricing decisions involve pricing new products, establishing price levels in test marketing, and modifying prices for existing products. Marketing research provides answers to questions such as the following:

1. How large is the demand potential within the target market at various price levels? What are the sales forecasts at various price levels?
2. How sensitive is demand to changes in price levels?
3. Are there identifiable segments that have different price sensitivities?
4. Are there opportunities to offer different price lines for different target markets?

A pricing experiment intended to help Amazon.com choose the optimal price for DVDs is featured in the Marketing Research Dashboard.

Consumers and Markets

Segmentation Studies Creating customer profiles and understanding behavioral characteristics are major focuses of any marketing research project. Determining why consumers behave as they do with respect to products, brands, and media is an important goal of a great deal of marketing research. Marketing decisions involving all four Ps are more successful when target market demographics, attitudes, and lifestyles are clear to decision makers.

Benefit and lifestyle studies
Examine similarities and differences in consumers' needs. Researchers use these studies to identify two or more segments within the market for a particular company's products.

A major component of market segmentation research is **benefit and lifestyle studies** that examine similarities and differences in consumers' needs. Researchers use these studies to identify segments within the market for a particular company's products. The objective is to collect information about customer characteristics, product benefits, and brand preferences. This data, along with information on age, family size, income, and lifestyle, can be compared to purchase patterns of particular products (e.g., cars, food, electronics, financial services) to develop market segmentation profiles. Segmentation studies are also useful for determining how to design communications that will resonate with a target market.

While segmentation studies are useful, more detailed information may sometimes be needed about cultures or subcultures that businesses seek to serve. Marketers may use ethnographic (or netnographic) research to study consumer behavior as activities embedded in a cultural context and laden with identity and other symbolic meanings. Ethnography requires extended observation of consumers in context. Ethnography can highlight problems and opportunities for marketers that are based on consumers' actual behavior. For example, when asked about light in the operating room, surgeons said that they had plenty of light. But when an ethnographer watched operations, he noticed that surgeons often struggled to get enough light as they worked. As a result of this research, a company introduced a throw-away light stick for use during operations.[8] Studying consumer culture and subculture requires immersion by trained, skillful observers. Studying consumers ethnographically broadens businesses' understanding of how consumers view and use products in their day-to-day lives.

Marketing Theory

Some readers see the word *theory* and stop listening and reading. But theory is often quite useful and relevant. Kurt Lewin, a pioneer of social, organizational, and applied psychology famously wrote, "There is nothing so practical as a good theory."[9] The purpose of theory is to generalize relationships between concepts in a way that is applicable to a wide variety of business and often other settings. Thus, marketing theory is important to many businesses. Theory is so important that many major companies are members of Marketing Science Institute (MSI.org), which grants money to academics studying marketing problems that businesses and industry are trying to understand.

Some examples of practical theory most marketing students learn are useful in demonstrating how important theory is to the field of marketing. For example, adoption and diffusion theory (adopted from sociology) has helped marketers understand how new products are adopted and spread through the market and the characteristics of products and adopters that aid or inhibit adoption. Another example of useful theory comes from services marketing research, where marketing researchers have learned that five characteristics—reliability, empathy, responsiveness, assurance, and tangibles—are important to consumers across a wide variety of services contexts. Information overload theory explains why consumers are much more likely to purchase after sampling from a set of 6 versus 24 flavors.[10] In sales research, likability, similarity, and trustworthiness are characteristics that are linked to a salesperson's success. These few examples show how theory can be useful to thinking about business problems and opportunities. In Chapter 3, you will learn about developing conceptual models.

MARKETING RESEARCH DASHBOARD THE PERFECT PRICING EXPERIMENT?

E-tailing presents almost the perfect opportunity for a market research project testing the price elasticity of products. For example, Amazon.com ran a large-scale pricing experiment for several DVDs offered for sale on its website. Customers received random prices (reflecting discounts between 20 and 40 percent) on 68 DVDs when they visited Amazon's site. While the differences were mostly only a few dollars, for a few titles, the price differences were much larger. For example, consumers purchasing *The X-Files: The Complete Second Season* paid prices ranging from $89.99 to $104.99 for a DVD set with a list price of $149.99.

The experimental methodology used by Amazon to determine the optimal price is standard and is widely used both in online and offline settings. Consumers are randomly offered different prices. Then the retailer collects sales data to determine which price performs best. The problem for Amazon was that the giant is both large and online where consumers can easily share information. Consumers got together and learned they paid different prices for the same DVD on the same day. For example, the *E-commerce Times* reported that when they checked the price for the DVD *Mission Impossible* it was $17.99, but several hours later the price was $20.99.

Consumers were outraged and accused Amazon of deceptive pricing policies. As a result, Amazon apologized, admitted they had made a mistake, and agreed to give back the difference between the price paid on any of the affected DVDs and the lowest possible price offered. As a result, Amazon refunded an average of $3.10 to 6,896 customers. Even the best-laid plans for marketing research studies can sometimes create problems.

Sources: Lori Enos, "Amazon Apologizes for Pricing Blunder." *E-commerce Times*, September 28, 2000, www.ecommercetimes .com/story/4411.html; Keith Regan, "Amazon's Friendly Deception," *E-commerce Times*, September 18, 2000, www.eccomercetimes .com/story/4310.html, accessed August 13, 2011; Troy Wolverton, "Amazon Backs Away from Test Prices," September 12, 2000, news. cnet.com/2100-1017-245631.html, accessed August 13, 2011.

The Marketing Research Industry

The marketing research industry has experienced unparalleled growth in recent years. According to an *Advertising Age* study, revenues of U.S. research companies have grown substantially in recent years.[11] The growth in revenues of international research firms has been even more dramatic. Marketing research firms have attributed these revenue increases to postsale customer satisfaction studies (one-third of research company revenues), retail-driven product scanning systems (also one-third of all revenues), database development for long-term brand management, and international research studies.

Types of Marketing Research Firms

Marketing research providers can be classified as either internal or external, custom or standardized, or brokers/facilitators. Internal research providers are typically organizational units that reside within a company. For example, IBM, Procter & Gamble, Kraft Foods, and Kodak all have internal marketing research departments. Kraft Foods and other firms enjoy many benefits by keeping the marketing research function internal. These benefits include research method consistency, shared information across the company, lower research costs, and ability to produce actionable research results.

Other firms choose to use external sources for marketing research. External sources, usually referred to as marketing research suppliers, perform all aspects of the research, including study design, questionnaire production, interviewing, data analysis, and report preparation. These firms operate on a fee basis and commonly submit a research proposal to be used by a client for evaluation and decision purposes. An example of a proposal is provided in the Marketing Research in Action at the end of Chapter 2.

Many companies use external research suppliers because the suppliers can be more objective and less subject to company politics and regulations than internal suppliers.

Also, many external suppliers provide specialized talents that, for the same cost, internal suppliers could not provide. And finally, companies can choose external suppliers on a study-by-study basis and thus gain greater flexibility in scheduling studies as well as match-specific project requirements to the talents of specialized research firms.

Customized research firms Research firms that provide tailored services for clients.

Marketing research firms also provide research that is customized or standardized. **Customized research firms** provide specialized, highly tailored services to the client. Many customized research firms concentrate their activities in one specific area such as brand-name testing, test marketing, or new-product development. For example, Namestormers assists companies in brand-name selection and recognition; Survey Sampling Inc., which recently added mobile sampling to its portfolio, concentrates solely on sample development; and Retail Diagnostics Inc. specializes in collecting research in store environments. In contrast, **standardized research firms** provide more general services. These firms also follow an established, common approach in research design so the results of a study conducted for one client can be compared to norms from studies done for other clients. Examples of these firms are Burke Market Research, which conducts day-after advertising recall; AC Nielsen (separate from Nielsen Media Research), which conducts store audits for a variety of retail firms; and Arbitron Ratings, which provides primary data collection on radio audiences.

Standardized research firms Research firms that provide general results following a standard format so that results of a study conducted for one client can be compared to norms.

Syndicated business services Services provided by standardized research firms that include data made or developed from a common data pool or database.

Many standardized research firms also provide **syndicated business services**, which include the purchase of diary panels, audits, and advertising recall data made or developed from a common data pool or database. A prime example of a syndicated business service is a database established through retail optical scanner methods. This database, available from AC Nielsen, tracks the retail sales of thousands of brand-name products. The data can be customized for a variety of industries (e.g., snack foods, over-the-counter drugs, or cars) to indicate purchase profiles and volume sales in a given industry.

Changing Skills for a Changing Industry

Marketing research employees represent a vast diversity of cultures, abilities, and personalities. As marketing research firms expand their geographic scope to Europe, Asia, and the Pacific Rim, the requirements for successfully executing marketing research projects will change dramatically. Many fundamental skill requirements will remain in place, but new and innovative practices will require a unique skill base that is more comprehensive than ever before. Individuals who are logical and perceptive about human emotions find marketing research to be a rewarding career.

In a survey of 100 marketing research executives, fundamental business skills were rated high for potential employees. Communication skills (verbal and written), interpersonal skills (ability to work with others), and statistical skills were the leading attributes in job aptitude.[12] More specifically, the top five skills executives hope to find in candidates for marketing research positions are (1) the ability to understand and interpret secondary data, (2) presentation skills, (3) foreign-language competency, (4) negotiation skills, and (5) information technology proficiency.[13] In addition to quantitative, teamwork, and communication skills, the Bureau of Labor Statistics emphasizes the importance of being detail oriented, patient, and persistent for market and survey researchers.[14] In the future, analyzing existing databases, multicultural interaction, and negotiation are likely to be important characteristics of marketing researchers. Marketing research jobs are discussed further in the careers appendix at the end of this chapter.

Ethics in Marketing Research Practices

Many opportunities exist for both ethical and unethical behaviors to occur in the research process. The major sources of ethical issues in marketing research are the interactions among the three key groups: (1) the research information providers; (2) the research information users; and (3) the respondents. Research providers face numerous potential ethical challenges and opportunities to go wrong. Some of those involve general business practices, while others involve conducting research that is below professional standards. Clients may behave unethically or deceptively also, as in all business relationships. Respondents may abuse the research relationship or be abused by it. For example, in recent years, Internet marketing research is posing new questions regarding the potential for abuse of respondents with regard to privacy. We address each of these issues below. (See Exhibit 1.2, which lists typical questionable or unethical practices among the key groups.)

Ethical Questions in General Business Practices

Pricing issues, client confidentiality issues, and use of "black-box" methodologies are all potential ethical pitfalls for research providers.

Exhibit 1.2   Ethical Challenges in Marketing Research

Research Provider
General business practices
Padding expenses
Selling unnecessary services
Not maintaining client confidentiality
Selling branded "black box" methodology

Conducting research below professional standards
Research methodology will not answer research question
Doing research to prove predetermined conclusions
Cost-cutting in projects results in inconclusive findings
Interviewer "curbstoning"

Respondent abuse
Not providing promised incentives
Stating that interviews are shorter than they are
Not maintaining respondent confidentiality
Not obtaining respondent agreement before audio or videotaping or otherwise tracking behavior (other than public behavior)

Privacy invasion
Selling under the guise of conducting research (sugging or frugging)
Faking research sponsorship
Respondent deception (without debriefing)
Causing respondent distress

Internet issues
Providing insufficient information to website users about how their clickstream data are tracked and used
Sending unwanted follow-up e-mails to respondents
Deanonymizing data

Client/Research Buyer
Requesting proposals without intent to purchase
Deceptively promising future business
Overstating research findings

Unethical Activity by Respondent
Providing dishonest answers or faking behavior

First, the research firm may engage in unethical pricing. For example, after quoting a fixed overall price for a proposed research project, the researcher may tell the decision maker that variable-cost items such as travel expenses, monetary response incentives, or fees charged for computer time are extra, over, and above the quoted price. Such "soft" costs can be easily used to pad the total project cost. Another unethical practice found all too often in marketing research is the selling of unnecessary or unwarranted research services. While it is perfectly acceptable to sell follow-up research that can aid the decision maker's company, selling nonessential services is unethical.

Research firms are required to maintain client confidentiality. This requirement can be a challenge for firms that specialize in industries (e.g., cars) and regularly collect data about various competitors and the industry in general. Occasionally, a new client may ask for a study very similar to one recently conducted for another client. It may be tempting to simply share the previous results, but those results belong to another client.

Branded "black-box" methodologies Methodologies offered by research firms that are branded and do not provide information about how the methodology works.

A common practice among research firms is selling **branded "black-box" methodologies.** These branded techniques are quite varied and include proprietary scaling, sampling, sample correction, data collection methods, market segmentation, and specialized indexes (e.g., customer satisfaction, loyalty, or quality indexes). Some techniques that are branded do involve sufficient disclosure, so a methodology is not a black box just because it is branded. Methodologies are called black-box methodologies when they are proprietary, and research firms will not fully disclose how the methodology works.

While the desire to maintain a proprietary technique is understandable, without access to the inner workings of the technique, research buyers and others cannot assess its validity. Of course, no one forces clients to choose black-box methodologies. If clients are unable to get sufficient insight into the method's strengths and weaknesses prior to purchase, they can choose other suppliers.

Conducting Research Not Meeting Professional Standards

Research providers may occasionally conduct research that does not meet professional standards. For example, a client may insist that a research firm use a particular methodology even though the research firm feels the methodology will not answer the research question posed by the client. Fearful of losing the business entirely, a firm may go along with their client's wishes. Or a research provider may agree to do a study even though the firm does not have the expertise to conduct the kind of study needed by the client. In this case, the client should be referred to another research provider.

Another unethical situation may arise because of client pressure to perform research to prove a predetermined conclusion. If researchers consciously manipulate the research methodology or reporting to present a biased picture just to please a client, they are engaging in unethical behavior.

One additional pressure that may result in unprofessional research efforts is cost-cutting. A client may not provide a sufficient budget to do a research project that will provide useful information. For example, cost-cuts could result in sample size reductions. As a result, the findings may have large margins of error (e.g., $+/-25$ percent). The provider should advise the client that the results are likely to provide unreliable results before engaging in the research.

Curbstoning Data collection personnel filling out surveys for fake respondents.

Interviewers working for research firms may also engage in unethical behavior. A practice of falsifying data known to many researchers and field interviewers is called curbstoning, or rocking-chair interviewing. **Curbstoning** occurs when the researcher's trained interviewers or observers, rather than conducting interviews or observing respondents' actions as directed in the study, will complete the interviews themselves or make up "observed" respondents' behaviors.

Other data falsification practices include having friends and relatives fill out surveys, not using the designated sample of respondents but rather anyone who is conveniently available to complete the survey, or not following up on the established callback procedures indicated in the research procedure. To minimize the likelihood of data falsification, research companies typically randomly verify 10 to 15 percent of the interviews through callbacks.

Abuse of Respondents

In addition to unethical general business practices and research conducted below professional standards, abuse of respondents can be a problem. There are several potential ways to abuse respondents in marketing research. Research firms may not provide the promised incentive (contest awards, gifts, or money) to respondents for completing interviews or questionnaires. A second way to abuse respondents is to state that interviews are very short when in reality they may last an hour or more. Respondents are also abused if research firms use "fake" sponsors. Clients sometimes fear that identification of the sponsor will affect respondent answers to research questions. While a research firm does not have to reveal its client to respondents, it is nevertheless unethical to create fake sponsors for a study.

Subject debriefing Fully explaining to respondents any deception that was used during research.

Occasionally, it may be necessary to deceive consumers during a study. For example, an experimental study induced consumer variety seeking by having subjects read a "scientific study" claiming that changing hair products frequently improves hair health and cleanliness. At the end of any study involving deception, subjects must be **"debriefed"** and the deception must be explained. Importantly, in no case can respondents be psychologically or physically harmed. An egregious example of doing harm was a study of complaint handling in which a researcher sent letters to restaurant owners stating that he and his wife had been food poisoned at their establishment on their anniversary. Restaurant owners receiving the letters were deceived in a manner that caused them undue concern and anxiety.

Sugging/frugging Claiming that a survey is for research purposes and then asking for a sale or donation.

Researchers typically promise respondents anonymity to encourage cooperation and honesty in their responses. Respondents' confidentiality is breached if their names are shared with the sponsoring company for sales follow-up or if respondents' names and demographic data are given to other companies without their approval. In fact, some "research" is conducted for the purpose of collecting names. This practice, known as **sugging** or **frugging**, is completely unethical and has a negative impact on the entire industry because it leads to consumers turning down legitimate research inquiries because they do not want to be solicited.

Market researchers should not invade customer privacy. While public behavior may be audiotaped or videotaped without prior agreement, behavior in private, including during research interviews, may not be taped without respondents' consent. This issue is even more complicated and controversial in online settings where consumer behavior is digitally tracked (e.g., in clickstream analysis) and conversations about the company and its products are collected and analyzed.

Are the online research methods that track consumers without their consent unethical even when the behavior being tracked is in some sense public and all identifiers are removed from the data stream? What about the use of "cookies," the digital identification files that are placed on individuals' computers by websites and used to collect information about behavior and interests so that advertising and content may be adjusted to consumer needs? While cookies are usually designed to maintain consumer privacy with respect to identity at least, they still nevertheless collect and utilize consumer data. Doubleclick, a business that serves ads to websites all over the Internet, has received a great deal of scrutiny from privacy advocates over the years. Doubleclick uses cookies that collect information from Internet surfers across all the websites it serves and is thus able to assemble a great deal of information about individual (unidentified) consumers.

The Marketing Research Association (MRA) has developed guidelines for Internet marketing research issues. The MRA suggests that websites post a privacy policy to explain how data are used. Similarly, researchers must discontinue follow-up e-mails if requested to by respondents. Recently, researchers have shown that it is possible to "*deanonymize*" information on the Internet by combining different publicly available records available at social networks.[15] The MRA guidelines prohibit market researchers from **deanonymizing data.** MRA guidelines do allow clickstream tracking. But as with other public behavior, online actions may be observed but any identifying information must be removed from the data file. Other digital technologies such as GPS also result in privacy-related issues (see Marketing Research Dashboard on p. 15).

Deanonymizing data
Combining different publicly available information, usually unethically, to determine consumers' identities, especially on the Internet.

Unethical Activities of the Client/Research User

Opportunities for unethical behavior also confront the client or decision maker who requires research data. One such unethical behavior is decision makers requesting detailed research proposals from several competing research providers with no intention of actually selecting a firm to conduct the research. In this case, the "clients" solicit the proposals for the purpose of learning how to conduct the necessary marketing research themselves. They obtain first drafts of questionnaires, suggested sampling frames and sampling procedures, and knowledge on data collection procedures. Then, unethically, they may use the information to either perform the research project themselves or bargain for a better price among interested research companies.

Unfortunately, another common behavior among unethical decision makers at firms requiring marketing research information is promising a prospective research provider a long-term relationship or additional projects in order to obtain a very low price on the initial research project. Then, after the researcher completes the initial project, the client forgets about the long-term promises.

Clients may also be tempted to overstate results of a marketing research project. They may claim, for instance, that consumers prefer the taste of their product when in actual testing, the difference between products was statistically insignificant, even if slightly higher for the sponsoring firm's products.

 MARKETING RESEARCH DASHBOARD

Research and Data Privacy: The Challenge

Are there ethical dimensions to GPS as a research tool? Acme Rent-A-Car of New Haven, Connecticut, placed GPS units on all its rental cars. Thus, the rent-a-car company knows every place a customer goes. Not only do they know where you stop, but how fast you drive on the way there. Acme began sending their customers speeding tickets based on GPS tracking. Eventually a customer sued, alleging that Acme was violating a driver's privacy. Thus far, the courts have ruled in the customer's favor.

Insurance companies also are using GPS technology. What can they find out? They can learn whether you drive at night or on interstate highways, both of which are more dangerous, whether and how often you exceed the speed limit or run stop signs, or whether you stop at a bar on the way home and how long you stay there. Thus, not only can they research driving behavior much better than they could in the past, but are also able to address issues related to pricing. For example, GPS systems used by Progressive Insurance have resulted in drastically reduced rates for some customers and substantially increased rates for others. Drive less, as shown by the GPS, and you pay less. Drive within the speed limit, and you pay less. Just fair isn't it? But some consumer advocates argue that this is a violation of people's right to privacy.

Sources: Annette Cardwell, "Building a Better Speed Trap," *Smartbusiness.com*, December/January 2002, p. 28; Ira Carnahan, "Insurance by the Minute," *Forbes*, December 11, 2000, p. 86; Will Wade, "Insurance Rates Driven by GPS," *Wired*, October 3, 2003.

Unethical Activities by the Respondent

The primary unethical practice of respondents or subjects in any research endeavor is providing dishonest answers or faking behavior. The general expectation in the research environment is that when a subject has freely consented to participate, she or he will provide truthful responses.

Research respondents frequently provide untrue answers when they must answer questions related to their income or to their indulgence in certain sensitive types of behavior such as alcohol consumption or substance abuse.

Consumers may have the prospect of earning money by participating in marketing research surveys and focus groups. To be able to participate in more surveys or groups, would-be respondents may lie to try to match the characteristics that screeners are seeking. For example, potential participants may say they are married when they are not, or may say they own a Toyota, even though they do not. But the reason marketing researchers pay focus group or survey participants is that their research requires them to talk to a specific type of participant. Lying by respondents to make money from participating in marketing research is unethical. Worse than that from the researcher's point of view, it undermines the validity of the research.

Marketing Research Codes of Ethics

Many marketing research companies have established internal company codes of ethics derived from the ethical codes formulated by larger institutions that govern today's marketing research industry. The Code of Ethics for the American Marketing Association applies to all marketing functions, including research, and can be viewed at **www.marketingpower.com**. ESOMAR, the world organization for enabling better research into markets, consumers, and societies, publishes a marketing research code of ethics on their website at **www.esomar.org**. The Marketing Research Society summarizes the central principles in ESOMAR's code as follows:[16]

1. Market researchers will conform to all relevant national and international laws.
2. Market researchers will behave ethically and will not do anything that might damage the reputation of market research.
3. Market researchers will take special care when carrying out research among children and other vulnerable groups of the population.
4. Respondents' cooperation is voluntary and must be based on adequate, and not misleading, information about the general purpose and nature of the project when their agreement to participate is being obtained and all such statements must be honored.
5. The rights of respondents as private individuals will be respected by market researchers, and they will not be harmed or disadvantaged as the result of cooperating in a market research project.
6. Market researchers will never allow personal data they collect in a market research project to be used for any purpose other than market research.
7. Market researchers will ensure that projects and activities are designed, carried out, reported and documented accurately, transparently, objectively, and to appropriate quality.
8. Market researchers will conform to the accepted principles of fair competition.

CONTINUING CASE STUDY: THE SANTA FE GRILL MEXICAN RESTAURANT

To illustrate marketing research principles and concepts in this text, we have prepared a case study that will be used throughout most of the chapters in the book. The case study looks at the Santa Fe Grill Mexican Restaurant, which was started 18 months ago by two former business students at the University of Nebraska, Lincoln. They had been roommates in college and both had an entrepreneurial desire. After graduating, they wanted to start a business instead of working for someone else. The two owners used research to start their business and to make it prosper. The Marketing Research in Action that concludes this chapter provides more details about this continuing case. Exercises relating to the continuing case about the Santa Fe Grill are included in each chapter either in the body of the chapter or in the Marketing Research in Action feature. For example, Chapter 3 has a secondary data assignment. When sampling is discussed in Chapter 6, different sampling approaches are evaluated, and we point out sample size issues for the Santa Fe Grill as well as why the research company recommended exit interviews. Similarly, the questionnaire used to collect primary data for this continuing case is given in Chapter 8 to illustrate measurement and questionnaire design principles. In all the data analysis chapters, we use the continuing case study data to illustrate statistical software and the various statistical techniques for analyzing data. The focus on a single case study of a typical business research problem will enable you to more easily understand the benefits and pitfalls of using research to improve business decision making.

Emerging Trends

The general consensus in the marketing research industry is that five major trends are becoming evident: (1) increased emphasis on secondary data collection methods; (2) movement toward technology-related data management (optical scanning data, database technology, customer relationship management); (3) expanded use of digital technology for information acquisition and retrieval; (4) a broader international client base; and (5) movement beyond data analysis toward a data interpretation/information management environment.

The organization of this book is consistent with these trends. Part 1 (Chapters 1 and 2) explores marketing research information and technology from the client's perspective, including how to evaluate marketing research projects. Part 2 (Chapters 3–5) provides an innovative overview of the emerging role of secondary data, with emphasis on technology-driven approaches for the design and development of research projects. The chapters in Part 2 also discuss traditional marketing research project design issues (survey methods and research designs) as well as collection and interpretation of qualitative data including research techniques emerging in social media environments.

Part 3 of the book (Chapters 6–8) covers sampling, attitude measurement and scaling, and questionnaire design. The impact of growing online data collection on these issues is explained. Part 4 (Chapters 9–13) prepares the reader for management, categorization, and analysis of marketing research data, both qualitative and quantitative. A chapter on analyzing qualitative data explains the basic approach to carrying out this type of analysis. Computer applications of statistical packages give readers a hands-on guide to analyzing quantitative data. Part 4 concludes by showing how to effectively present marketing research findings.

Each chapter in the book concludes with a feature called "Marketing Research in Action." The goal of the examples and illustrations in the Marketing Research in Action feature is to facilitate the student's understanding of chapter topics and especially to provide the reader with a "how-to" approach for marketing research methods.

MARKETING RESEARCH IN ACTION
Continuing Case: The Santa Fe Grill

The Santa Fe Grill Mexican restaurant was started 18 months ago by two former business students at the University of Nebraska, Lincoln. They had been roommates in college and both wanted to become entrepreneurs. After graduating they wanted to start a business instead of working for someone else. The students worked in restaurants while attending college, both as waiters and one as an assistant manager, and believed they had the knowledge and experience necessary to start their own business.

During their senior year, they prepared a business plan in their entrepreneurship class for a new Mexican restaurant concept. They intended to start the restaurant in Lincoln, Nebraska. After a demographic analysis of that market, however, they decided that Lincoln did not match their target demographics as well as they initially thought it would.

After researching the demographic and competitive profile of several markets, they decided Dallas, Texas, would be the best place to start their business. In examining the markets, they were looking for a town that would best fit their target market of singles and families in the age range of 18 to 50. The population of Dallas was almost 5.5 million people, of which about 50 percent were between the ages of 25 and 60. This indicated there were a lot of individuals in their target market in the Dallas area. They also found that about 55 percent of the population earns between $35,000 and $75,000 a year, which indicated the market would have enough income to eat out regularly. Finally, 56 percent of the population was married, and many of them had children at home, which was consistent with their target market. More detailed demographic information for the area is shown below.

The new restaurant concept was based upon the freshest ingredients, complemented by a festive atmosphere, friendly service, and cutting-edge advertising and marketing strategies. The key would be to prepare and serve the freshest "made-from-scratch" Mexican foods possible. Everything would be prepared fresh every single day. In addition to their freshness concept, they wanted to have a fun, festive atmosphere, and fast, friendly service. The atmosphere would be open, brightly lit, and bustling with activity. Their target market would be mostly families with children, between the ages of 18 and 49. Their marketing programs would be memorable, with the advertising designed to provide an appealing, slightly offbeat positioning in the market.

The Santa Fe Grill was not successful as quickly as the owners had anticipated. To improve the restaurant operations, the owners needed to understand what aspects of the restaurant drive customer satisfaction and loyalty, and where they were falling short in serving their customers. So they decided to conduct three surveys. One was designed to obtain information from current customers of the Santa Fe Grill. A second survey would collect information from customers of their primary competitor, Jose's Southwestern Café. The third survey was designed to collect data from the employees who worked for the Santa Fe Grill. They believed the employee survey was important because employee experiences might be affecting how customers evaluated the restaurant.

The Santa Fe Grill was located on an outparcel on the east side near the main entrance of the Cumberland Mall. The mall has 75 or more stores and is considered very successful for the area. A market research company was located in the mall so they decided to use a mall intercept approach to collect customer data. Another Mexican restaurant that had been in business longer and appeared to be more successful was also on an outparcel at the same mall, but its location was on the west side of the mall. The goal was to complete interviews with 250 individuals who had recently eaten at the Santa Fe Grill and 150 diners who had recently eaten at Jose's Southwestern Café. Additionally, employees of the Santa Fe Grill were asked to log on to a website to complete the employee survey.

Over a period of two weeks, a total of 405 customer interviews were completed—152 for Jose's and 253 for the Santa Fe Grill. Of the employee survey, 77 questionnaires were completed. The owners believe the surveys will help them to identify the restaurant's strengths and weaknesses, enable them to compare their restaurant to a nearby competitor, and develop a plan to improve the restaurant's operations.

Selected Demographics for Geographic Area (10-mile radius of Santa Fe Grill)

Households by Type	Number	Percent
Total households	452,000	100
Family households	267,000	59
With children under 18 years	137,000	30
Non-Family households	185,000	41
Householder living alone	148,850	33
Householder 65 years and over	29,570	7
Households with individuals under 18 years	157,850	35
Households with individuals 65 years and over	74,250	16
Average household size	2.6 people	
Average family size	3.4 people	

Gender and Age	Number	Percent
Male	599,000	51
Female	589,000	49
Total	1,188,000	
Under 20 years	98,800	29
20 to 34 years	342,000	29
35 to 44 years	184,000	16
45 to 54 years	132,500	11
55 to 59 years	44,250	4
60 years and over	13,000	11
Median Age (years)	32	
18 years and over	873,000	74

Hands-On Exercise

1. Based on your understanding of Chapter 1, what kind of information about products, services, and customers should the owners of Santa Fe Grill consider collecting?
2. Is a research project actually needed? Is the best approach a survey of customers? Should employees also be surveyed? Why or why not?

■ Summary

Describe the impact marketing research has on marketing decision making.

Marketing research is the set of activities central to all marketing-related decisions regardless of the complexity or focus of the decision. Marketing research is responsible for providing managers with accurate, relevant, and timely information so that they can make marketing decisions with a high degree of confidence. Within the context of strategic planning, marketing research is responsible for the tasks, methods, and procedures a firm will use to implement and direct its strategic plan.

Demonstrate how marketing research fits into the marketing planning process.

The key to successful planning is accurate information—information related to product, promotion, pricing, and distribution. Marketing research also helps organizations better understand consumers and markets. Last, marketing research is used to develop theory that is useful in a broad range of marketing problems.

Provide examples of marketing research studies.

Marketing research studies support decision making for all marketing mix variables as well as providing information about markets and cultures. Examples of research studies include concept and product testing; perceptual mapping; trade area analysis, store image studies, in-store traffic pattern studies, and location analysis; shopper marketing research; advertising effectiveness studies, attitude research and sales tracking; pricing studies for new and existing products; segmentation and consumer culture studies; and marketing theory development.

Understand the scope and focus of the marketing research industry.

Generally, marketing research projects can be conducted either internally by an in-house marketing research staff or externally by independent or facilitating marketing research firms. External research suppliers are normally classified as custom or standardized, or as brokers or facilitators.

Recognize ethical issues associated with marketing research.

Ethical decision making is a challenge in all industries, including marketing research. Ethical issues in marketing research occur for the research information user, the research information provider, and the selected respondents. Specific unethical practices among research providers include unethical general business practices, conducting research below professional standards, respondent abuse, and issues specific to the Internet such as violation of privacy. Unethical behavior by clients includes requesting research proposals with no intent to follow through, promising more business that never materializes to secure low-cost research services, and exaggerating research findings. Respondents can be unethical when they provide dishonest answers or fake behavior.

Discuss new skills and emerging trends in marketing research.

Just as the dynamic business environment causes firms to modify and change practices, so does this changing environment dictate change to the marketing research industry. Specifically, technological and global changes will affect how marketing research will be conducted in the future. Necessary skills required to adapt to these changes include (1) the ability to understand and interpret secondary data, (2) presentation skills, (3) foreign-language competency, (4) negotiation skills, and (5) information technology proficiency.

■ Key Terms and Concepts

Behavioral targeting   8

Benefit and lifestyle studies   9

Branded "black-box" methodologies   13

Curbstoning   13

Customized research firms   11

Deanonymizing data   15

Marketing research   5

Perceptual mapping   7

Retailing research   8

Shopper marketing   8

Standardized research firms   11

Subject debriefing   14

Sugging/frugging   14

Syndicated business services   11

◼️ Review Questions

1. What is the role of marketing research in organizations?
2. What improvements in retailing strategy might be attributed to the results obtained from shopper marketing studies?
3. Discuss the importance of segmentation research. How does it affect the development of market planning for a particular company?
4. What are the advantages and disadvantages for companies maintaining an internal marketing research department? What advantages and disadvantages can be attributed to the hiring of an external marketing research supplier?
5. As the marketing research industry expands, what skills will future executives need to possess? How do these skills differ from those currently needed to function successfully in the marketing research field?
6. Identify the three major groups of people involved in the marketing research process, and then give an example of an unethical behavior sometimes practiced by each group.
7. Sometimes respondents claim they are something they are not (e.g., a Toyota owner or a married person) so they will be selected to participate in a focus group. Sometimes respondents do not accurately reflect their personal income. Is it always unethical for a respondent to lie on a survey? Why or why not?

◼️ Discussion Questions

1. **EXPERIENCE MARKETING RESEARCH.** Go online to one of your favorite search engines (Yahoo!, Google, etc.) and enter the following search term: marketing research. From the results, access a directory of marketing research firms. Select a particular firm and comment on the types of marketing research studies it performs.
2. **EXPERIENCE MARKETING RESEARCH.** Use Google to find a local marketing research firm. E-mail that company and ask to have any job descriptions for positions in that company e-mailed back to you. Once you obtain the descriptions, discuss the particular qualities needed to perform each job.
3. You have been hired by McDonald's to lead a mystery shopper team. The goal of your research is to improve the service quality at the McDonald's restaurant in your area. What attributes of service quality will you attempt to measure? What customer or employee behaviors will you closely monitor?
4. Contact a local business and interview the owner/manager about the types of marketing research performed for that business. Determine whether the business has its own marketing research department or if it hires an outside agency. Also, determine whether the company takes a one-shot approach to particular problems or is systematic over a long period of time.
5. **EXPERIENCE MARKETING RESEARCH.** As the Internet has grown as a medium for conducting various types of marketing research studies, there is growing concern about ethical issues. Identify and discuss three ethical issues pertinent to research conducted using the Internet.

    Now go to the Internet and validate your ethical concerns. Check out ESOMAR's website (ESOMAR.org) and search for ethical issues related to the Internet. What unethical practices are possible in Internet research?

Careers in Marketing Research with a Look at Federal Express

Career opportunities in marketing research vary by industry, company, and size of company. Different positions exist in consumer products companies, industrial goods companies, internal marketing research departments, and professional marketing research firms. Marketing research tasks range from the very simple, such as tabulation of questionnaires, to the very complex, such as sophisticated data analysis. Exhibit A.1 lists some common job titles and the functions as well as compensation ranges for marketing research positions.

Exhibit A.1 Marketing Research Career Outline

Position*	Duties	Compensation Range (Annual, in Thousands)
Director, research and analytical services	Directs and manages business intelligence initiatives, data reports, and/or data modeling efforts.	$63 to $163
Statistician	Acts as expert consultant on application of statistical techniques for specific research problems. Many times responsible for research design and data analysis.	$90 to $110
Research analyst	Plans research project and executes project assignments. Works in preparing questionnaire. Makes analysis, prepares report, schedules project events, and sets budget.	$35 to $81
Senior research manager	Works closely with client to define complex business challenges; oversees one or more research managers.	$85K
Project director	Hires, trains, and supervises field interviewers. Provides work schedules and is responsible for data accuracy.	$60 to $90
Librarian	Builds and maintains a library of primary and secondary data sources to meet the requirements of the research department.	$35 to $56
Administrative coordinator	Handles and processes statistical data. Supervises day-to-day office work.	$35 to $50
Marketing research vice president	Develop and manage clients within an entire geography, sector or industry.	$125+

*Positions are general categories and not all companies employ all of the positions.

Most successful marketing research people are intelligent and creative; they also possess problem-solving, critical-thinking, communication, and negotiation skills. Marketing researchers must be able to function under strict time constraints and feel comfortable working with large volumes of data. Federal Express (FedEx), for example, normally seeks individuals with strong analytical and computer skills to fill its research positions. Candidates should have an undergraduate degree in business, marketing, or information systems. Having an MBA will usually give an applicant a competitive advantage.

As is the case with many companies, the normal entry-level position in the marketing research area at Federal Express is the assistant research analyst. While learning details of the company and the industry, these individuals receive on-the-job training from a research analyst. The normal career path includes advancement to information technician and then research director and/or account executive.

Marketing research at Federal Express is somewhat unusual in that it is housed in the information technology division. This is evidence that, while the research function is integrated throughout the company, it has taken on a high-tech orientation. Marketing research at FedEx operates in three general areas:

1. *Database development and enhancement.* This function is to establish relationships with current FedEx customers and use this information for the planning of new products.
2. *Cycle-time research.* Providing more information for the efficient shipping of packages, tracking of shipments, automatic replenishment of customers' inventories, and enhanced electronic data interchange.
3. *Market intelligence system.* Primarily a logistical database and research effort to provide increased customer service to catalog retailers, direct marketing firms, and electronic commerce organizations.

The entire research function is led by a vice president of research and information technology, to whom four functional units report directly. These four units are responsible for the marketing decision support system operation, sales tracking, new business development, and special project administration.

If you are interested in pursuing a career in marketing research, a good way to start is to visit **www.careers-in-marketing.com/mr.htm**.

Exercise

1. Go to the web home page for Federal Express, and identify the requirements that FedEx is seeking in marketing research personnel. Write a brief description of these requirements, and report your finding to the class.
2. If you were seeking a marketing research position at FedEx, how would you prepare yourself through training and education for such a position? Put together a one-year plan for yourself identifying the college courses, special activities, interests, and related work experience you would engage in to obtain a marketing research position at FedEx.

The Marketing Research Process and Proposals

Chapter 2

1. Describe the major environmental factors influencing marketing research.
2. Discuss the research process and explain the various steps.
3. Distinguish between exploratory, descriptive, and causal research designs.
4. Identify and explain the major components of a research proposal.

Solving Marketing Problems Using a Systematic Process

Bill Shulby is president of Carolina Consulting Company, a marketing strategy consulting firm based in Raleigh-Durham, North Carolina. He recently worked with the owners of a regional telecommunications firm located in Texas on improving service quality processes. Toward the end of their meeting, one of the owners, Dan Carter, asked him about customer satisfaction and perceptions of the company's image as they related to service quality and customer retention. During the discussion, Carter stated that he was not sure how the company's telecommunications services were viewed by current or potential customers. He said, "Just last week, the customer service department received 11 calls from different customers complaining about everything from incorrect bills to taking too long to get DSL installed. Clearly, none of these customers were happy about our service." Then he asked Shulby, "What can I do to find out how satisfied our customers are overall and what can be done to improve our image?"

Shulby explained that conducting a marketing research study would answer Carter's questions. Dan Carter responded that the company had not done research in the past so he did not know what to expect from such a study. Shulby then gave several examples of studies the Carolina Consulting Company had conducted for other clients and explained how the information had been used, making sure not to disclose any confidential information. Carter then asked, "How much would it cost me to do this study and how long would it take to complete?" Shulby then explained he would like to ask a few more questions so he could better understand the issues, and he then would prepare a research proposal summarizing the approach to be used, the deliverables from the study, the cost, and the time frame for completion. The proposal would be ready in about a week, and they would meet to go over it in detail.

Value of the Research Process

Business owners and managers often identify problems they need help to solve. In such situations, additional information typically is needed to make a decision or to solve a problem. One solution is a marketing research study based on a scientific research process. This chapter provides an overview of the research process as well as a preview of some of the core topics in the text.

Changing View of the Marketing Research Process

Organizations, both for-profit and not-for-profit, are increasingly confronted with new and complex challenges and also opportunities that are the result of changing legal, political, cultural, technological, and competitive issues. Perhaps the most influential factor is the Internet. The rapid technological advances and its growing use by people worldwide are making the Internet a driving force in many current and future developments in marketing research. Traditional research philosophies are being challenged as never before. For example, there is a growing emphasis on *secondary data* collection, analysis, and interpretation as a basis of making business decisions. **Secondary data** are information previously collected for some other problem or issue. A by-product of the technology advances is the ongoing collection of data that is placed in a data warehouse and is available as secondary data to help understand business problems and to improve decisions. In contrast, **primary data** are information collected specifically for a current research problem or opportunity.

Secondary data Information previously collected for some other problem or issue.

Primary data Information collected for a current research problem or opportunity.

Many large businesses (e.g., Dell Computers, Bank of America, Marriott Hotels, Coca-Cola, IBM, McDonald's, and Walmart) are linking purchase data collected in-store and online with customer profiles already in company databases, thus enhancing their ability to understand shopping behavior and better meet customer needs. But even medium-sized and small companies are building databases of customer information to serve current customers more effectively and to attract new customers.

Gatekeeper technologies Technologies such as caller ID that are used to prevent intrusive marketing practices such as by telemarketers and illegal scam artists.

Another development is increased use of **gatekeeper technologies** (e.g., caller ID and automated screening and answering devices) as a means of protecting one's privacy against intrusive marketing practices such as by telemarketers and illegal scam artists. Similarly, many Internet users either block the placement of cookies or periodically erase them in order to keep marketers from tracking their behavior. Marketing researchers' ability to collect consumer data using traditional methods such as mail and telephone surveys has been severely limited by the combination of gatekeeper devices and recent federal and state data privacy legislation. For example, marketing researchers must contact almost four times more people today to complete a single interview than was true five years ago. Similarly, online marketers and researchers must provide opt-in/opt-out opportunities when soliciting business or collecting information. Advances in gatekeeper technologies will continue to challenge marketers to be more creative in developing new ways to reach respondents.

A third development affecting marketing decision makers is firms' widespread expansion into global markets. Global expansion introduces marketing decision makers to new sets of cultural issues that force researchers to focus not only on data collection tasks, but also on data interpretation and information management activities. For example, one of the largest full-service global marketing information firms, NFO (National Family Opinion) Worldwide, Inc., located in Greenwich, Connecticut, with subsidiaries in North America, Europe, Australia, Asia, and the Middle East, has adapted many of its measurement and brand tracking services to accommodate specific cultural and language differences encountered in global markets.

Fourth, marketing research is being repositioned in businesses to play a more important role in strategy development. Marketing research is being used increasingly to identify new business opportunities and to develop new product, service, and delivery ideas. Marketing research is also being viewed not only as a mechanism to more efficiently execute CRM (customer relationship management) strategies, but also as a critical component in developing competitive intelligence. For example, Sony uses its PlayStation website (**www.playstation.com**) to collect information about PlayStation gaming users and to build closer relationships. The PlayStation website is designed to create a community of users who can join PlayStation Underground, where they will "feel like they belong to a subculture of intense gamers." To achieve this objective, the website offers online shopping, opportunities to try new games, customer support, and information on news, events, and promotions. Interactive features include online gaming and message boards, as well as other relationship-building aspects.

Collectively, these key influences are forcing managers and researchers to view marketing research as an information management function. The term *information research* reflects the evolving changes occurring in the market research industry affecting organizational decision makers. Indeed, a more appropriate name for the traditional marketing research process is now the information research process. The **information research process** is a systematic approach to collecting, analyzing, interpreting, and transforming data into decision-making information. While many of the specific tasks involved in marketing research remain the same, understanding the process of transforming data into usable information from a broader information processing framework expands the applicability of the research process in solving organizational problems and creating opportunities.

Information research process A systematic approach to collecting, analyzing, interpreting, and transforming data into decision-making information.

◼ Determining the Need for Information Research

Before we introduce and discuss the phases and specific steps of the information research process, it is important that you understand when research is needed and when it is not. More than ever, researchers must interact closely with managers to recognize business problems and opportunities.

Decision makers and researchers frequently are trained differently in their approach to identifying and solving business problems, questions, and opportunities, as illustrated in the accompanying Marketing Research Dashboard. Until decision makers and marketing researchers become closer in their thinking, the initial recognition of the existence of a problem or opportunity should be the primary responsibility of the decision maker, not the researcher. A good rule of thumb is to ask "Can the decision-making problem (or question) be solved based on past experience and managerial judgment?" If the response is "no," research should be considered and perhaps implemented.

Decision makers often initiate the research process because they recognize problem and opportunity situations that require more information before good plans of action can be developed. Once the research process is initiated, in most cases decision makers will need assistance in defining the problem, collecting and analyzing the data, and interpreting the data.

There are several situations in which the decision to undertake a marketing research project may not be necessary.[1] These are listed and discussed in Exhibit 2.1.

The initial responsibility of today's decision makers is to determine if research should be used to collect the needed information. The first question the decision maker must ask is: *Can the problem and/or opportunity be solved using existing information and*

MARKETING RESEARCH DASHBOARD DECISION MAKERS AND RESEARCHERS

Management Decision Makers . . .

Tend to be decision-oriented, intuitive thinkers who want information to confirm their decisions. They want additional information now or "yesterday," as well as results about future market component behavior ("What will sales be next year?"), while maintaining a frugal stance with regard to the cost of additional information. Decision makers tend to be results oriented, do not like surprises, and tend to reject the information when they are surprised. Their dominant concern is market performance ("Aren't we number one yet?"); they want information that allows certainty ("Is it or isn't it?") and advocate being proactive but often allow problems to force them into reactive decision-making modes.

Marketing Researchers . . .

Tend to be scientific, technical, analytical thinkers who love to explore new phenomena; accept prolonged investigations to ensure completeness; focus on information about past behaviors ("Our trend has been . . ."); and are not cost conscious with additional information ("You get what you pay for"). Researchers are results oriented but love surprises; they tend to enjoy abstractions ("Our exponential gain . . ."), the probability of occurrences ("May be," "Tends to suggest that . . ."); and they advocate the proactive need for continuous inquiries into market component changes, but feel most of the time that they are restricted to doing reactive ("quick and dirty") investigations due to management's lack of vision and planning.

managerial judgment? The focus is on deciding what type of information (secondary or primary) is required to answer the research question(s). In most cases, decision makers should undertake the information research process any time they have a question or problem or believe there is an opportunity, but do not have the right information or are unwilling to rely on the information at hand to solve the problem. In reality, conducting secondary and primary research studies costs time, effort, and money. Another key managerial question deals with the availability of existing information. With the assistance of the research expert, decision makers face the next question: *Is adequate information available within the company's internal record systems to address the problem?* If the necessary marketing information is not available in the firm's internal record system, then a customized marketing research project to obtain the information should be considered.

With input from the research expert, decision makers must assess the time constraints associated with the problem/opportunity: *Is there enough time to conduct the necessary research before the final managerial decision must be made?* Decision makers often need

Exhibit 2.1	Situations When Marketing Research Might Not Be Needed

Situation Factors and Comments

Insufficient time frames   When the discovery of a problem situation leaves inadequate time to execute the necessary research activities, a decision maker may have to use informed judgment. Competitive actions/reactions sometimes emerge so fast that marketing research studies are not a feasible option.

Inadequate resources   When there are significant limitations in money, manpower, and/or facilities, then marketing research typically is not feasible.

Costs outweigh the value   When the benefits to be gained by conducting the research are not significantly greater than the costs, then marketing research is not feasible.

information in real time. But in many cases, systematic research that delivers high-quality information can take months. If the decision maker needs the information immediately, there may not be enough time to complete the research process. Sometimes organizations fear that a window of opportunity in a marketplace will close quickly, and they do not have time to wait. Another fundamental question focuses on the availability of marketing resources such as money, staff, skills, and facilities. Many small businesses lack the funds necessary to consider doing formal research.

A cost-benefit assessment should be made of value of the research compared to the cost: *Do the benefits of having the additional information outweigh the costs of gathering the information?* This type of question remains a challenge for today's decision makers. While the cost of doing marketing research varies from project to project, generally the cost can be estimated accurately. On the other hand, determining the true value of the expected information remains difficult.

Some business problems cannot be solved with marketing research. This suggests the question: *Will the research provide useful feedback for decision making?* A good example is in the area of "really new" products. In 1996, Charles Schwab conducted research asking their customers if they would be interested in online trading. The research came back with a resounding "no." At the time, most consumers did not have Internet access and were not able to imagine they would be interested in online trading. Schwab ignored the research and developed their online trading capability. They could have saved time and money by not doing the research at all.

Doing research can tip your hat to competitors: *Will this research give our competitors too much information about our marketing strategy?* For example, when a firm offers a potential new product in a test market, they reveal a great deal to their competitors about the product and the accompanying promotional efforts. Also, some competitors will actively disrupt market testing. Competitors might reduce their prices during the market test to prevent the company from collecting accurate information. This practice is called *jamming*.

Overview of the Research Process

The research process consists of four distinct but related phases: (1) determine the research problem; (2) select the appropriate research design; (3) execute the research design; and (4) communicate the research results (see Exhibit 2.2). The phases of the process must be completed properly to obtain accurate information for decision making. But each phase can be viewed as a separate process that consists of several steps.

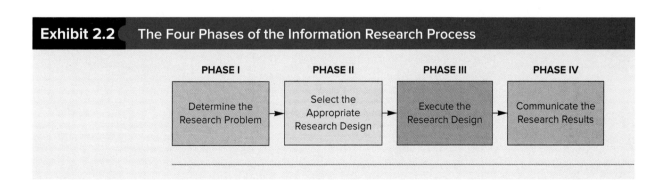

Exhibit 2.2   The Four Phases of the Information Research Process

PHASE I	PHASE II	PHASE III	PHASE IV
Determine the Research Problem	Select the Appropriate Research Design	Execute the Research Design	Communicate the Research Results

Scientific method Research procedures should be logical, objective, systematic, reliable, and valid.

The four phases are guided by the **scientific method.** This means the research procedures should be logical, objective, systematic, reliable, and valid.

Transforming Data into Knowledge

The primary goal of the research process is to provide decision makers with knowledge that will enable them to solve problems or pursue opportunities. Data become **knowledge** when someone, either the researcher or the decision maker, interprets the data and attaches meaning. To illustrate this process, consider the Magnum Hotel. Corporate executives were assessing ways to reduce costs and improve profits. The VP of finance suggested cutting back on the "quality of the towels and bedding" in the rooms. Before making a final decision, the president asked the marketing research department to interview business customers.

Knowledge Information becomes knowledge when someone, either the researcher or the decision maker, interprets the data and attaches meaning.

Exhibit 2.3 summarizes the key results. A total of 880 people were asked to indicate the degree of importance they placed on seven criteria when selecting a hotel. Respondents used a six-point importance scale ranging from "Extremely Important = 6" to "Not At All Important = 1." The average importance of each criterion was calculated for both first-time and repeat customers and statistically significant differences were identified. These results did not confirm, however, whether "quality towels and bedding" should be cut back to reduce operating costs.

When shown the results, the president asked this question: "I see a lot of numbers, but what are they really telling me?" The director of marketing research responded by explaining: "Among our first-time and repeat business customers, the 'quality of the hotel's towels and bedding' is considered one of the three most important selection criteria impacting their choice of a hotel to stay at when an overnight stay is required. In addition, they feel 'cleanliness of the room and offering preferred guest card options' are of comparable importance to the quality of towels and bedding. But first-time customers place significantly higher importance on cleanliness of the room than do repeat customers (5.7 vs. 5.5). Moreover, repeat customers place significantly more importance

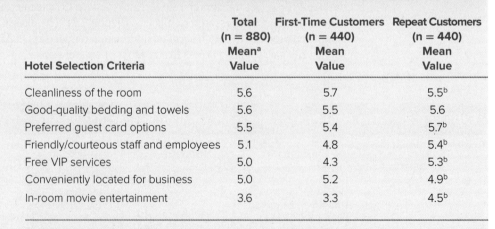

Exhibit 2.3	Summary of Differences in Selected Hotel-Choice Criteria: Comparison of First-Time and Repeat Business Customers		
Hotel Selection Criteria	**Total (n = 880)** Mean[a] Value	**First-Time Customers (n = 440)** Mean Value	**Repeat Customers (n = 440)** Mean Value
Cleanliness of the room	5.6	5.7	5.5[b]
Good-quality bedding and towels	5.6	5.5	5.6
Preferred guest card options	5.5	5.4	5.7[b]
Friendly/courteous staff and employees	5.1	4.8	5.4[b]
Free VIP services	5.0	4.3	5.3[b]
Conveniently located for business	5.0	5.2	4.9[b]
In-room movie entertainment	3.6	3.3	4.5[b]

[a]Importance scale: a six-point scale ranging from 6 (extremely important) to 1 (not at all important).

[b]Mean difference in importance between the two customer groups is significant at $p < 0.05$.

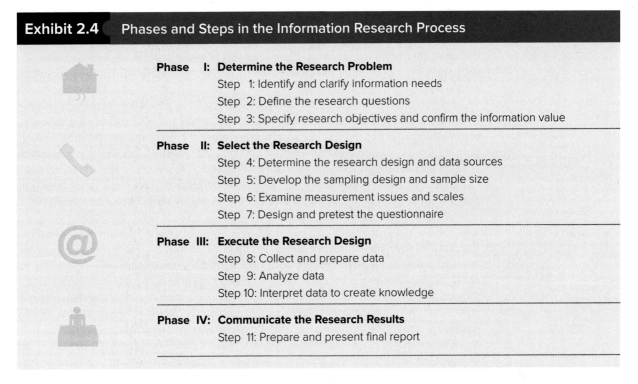

Exhibit 2.4	Phases and Steps in the Information Research Process

Phase   I: Determine the Research Problem
Step   1: Identify and clarify information needs
Step   2: Define the research questions
Step   3: Specify research objectives and confirm the information value

Phase   II: Select the Research Design
Step   4: Determine the research design and data sources
Step   5: Develop the sampling design and sample size
Step   6: Examine measurement issues and scales
Step   7: Design and pretest the questionnaire

Phase   III: Execute the Research Design
Step   8: Collect and prepare data
Step   9: Analyze data
Step 10: Interpret data to create knowledge

Phase   IV: Communicate the Research Results
Step 11: Prepare and present final report

on the availability of our preferred guest card loyalty program than do first-time customers (5.7 vs. 5.4)." Based on these considerations, the executives decided they should not cut back on the quality of towels or bedding as a way to reduce expenses and improve profitability.

Interrelatedness of the Steps and the Research Process

Exhibit 2.4 shows in more detail the steps included in each phase of the research process. Although in many instances researchers follow the four phases in order individual steps may be shifted or omitted. The complexity of the problem, the urgency for solving the problem, the cost of alternative approaches, and the clarification of information needs will directly impact how many of the steps are taken and in what order. For example, secondary data or "off-the-shelf" research studies may be found that could eliminate the need to collect primary data. Similarly, pretesting the questionnaire (step 7) might reveal weaknesses in some of the scales being considered (step 6), resulting in further refinement of the scales or even selection of a new research design (back to step 4).

◼◼ Phase I: Determine the Research Problem

The process of determining the research problem involves three interrelated activities: (1) identify and clarify information needs; (2) define the research questions; and (3) specify research objectives and confirm the information value. These three activities bring researchers and decision makers together based on management's recognition of the need for information to improve decision making.

Step 1: Identify and Clarify Information Needs

Generally, decision makers prepare a statement of what they believe is the problem before the researcher becomes involved. Then researchers assist decision makers to make sure the problem or opportunity has been correctly defined and the information requirements are known.

For researchers to understand the problem, they use a problem definition process. There is no one best process. But any process undertaken should include the following components: researchers and decision makers must (1) agree on the decision maker's purpose for the research, (2) understand the complete problem, (3) identify measurable symptoms and distinguish them from the root problem, (4) select the unit of analysis, and (5) determine the relevant variables. Correctly defining the problem is an important first step in determining if research is necessary. A poorly defined problem can produce research results that are of little value.

Purpose of the Research Request Problem definition begins by determining the research purpose. Decision makers must decide whether the services of a researcher are really needed. The researcher helps decision makers begin to define the problem by asking the decision maker why the research is needed. Through questioning, researchers begin to learn what the decision maker believes the problem is. Having a general idea of why research is needed focuses attention on the circumstances surrounding the problem.

The *iceberg principle* holds that decision makers are aware of only 10 percent of the true problem. Frequently the perceived problem is actually a symptom that is some type of measurable market performance factor, while 90 percent of the problem is not visible to decision makers. For example, the problem may be defined as "loss of market share" when in fact the problem is ineffective advertising or a poorly trained sales force. The real problems are below the waterline of observation. If the submerged portions of the problem are omitted from the problem definition and later from the research design, then decisions based on the research may be incorrect. Referring to the iceberg principle, displayed in Exhibit 2.5, helps researchers distinguish between the symptoms and the causes.

Understand the Complete Problem Situation The decision maker and the researcher must both understand the complete problem. This is easy to say but quite often difficult to accomplish. To gain an understanding, researchers and decision makers should do a situation analysis of the problem. A **situation analysis** gathers and synthesizes background information to familiarize the researcher with the overall complexity of the problem. A situation analysis attempts to identify the events and factors that have led to the situation, as well as any expected future consequences. Awareness of the complete problem situation provides better perspectives on the decision maker's needs, the complexity of the problem, and the factors involved. A situation analysis enhances communication between the researcher and the decision maker. The researcher must understand the client's business, including factors such as the industry, competition, product lines, markets, and in some cases production facilities. To do so, the researcher cannot rely solely on information provided by the client because many decision makers either do not know or will not disclose the information needed. Only when the researcher views the client's business objectively can the true problem be clarified.

Identify and Separate Out Symptoms Once the researcher understands the overall problem situation, he or she must work with the decision maker to separate the possible root problems from the observable and measurable symptoms that may have

Situation analysis Gathers and synthesizes background information to familiarize the researcher with the overall complexity of the problem.

Exhibit 2.5	**The Iceberg Principle**

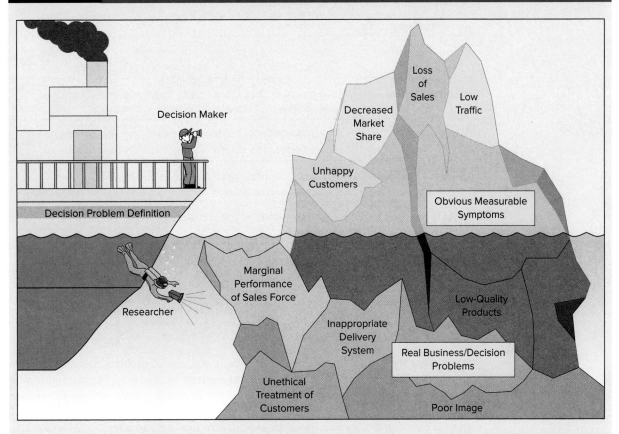

The iceberg principle states that in many business problem situations, the decision maker is aware of only 10 percent of the true problem. Often what is thought to be the problem is nothing more than an observable outcome or symptom (i.e., some type of measurable market performance factor), while 90 percent of the problem is neither visible to nor clearly understood by decision makers. For example, the problem may be defined as "loss of market share" when in fact the problem is ineffective advertising or a poorly trained sales force. The real problems are submerged below the waterline of observation. If the submerged portions of the problem are omitted from the problem definition and later from the research design, then decisions based on the research may be less than optimal.

been initially perceived as being the problem. For example, as we mentioned, many times managers view declining sales or loss of market share as problems. After examining these issues, the researcher may see that they are the result of more specific issues such as poor advertising execution, lack of sales force motivation, or inadequate distribution. The challenge facing the researcher is one of clarifying the real problem by separating out possible causes from symptoms. Is a decline in sales truly the problem or merely a symptom of lack of planning, poor location, or ineffective sales management?

| Exhibit 2.6 | Examples of Variables/Constructs Investigated in Marketing |

Variables/Constructs	Description
Brand Awareness	Percentage of respondents having heard of a designated brand; awareness could be either unaided or aided.
Brand Attitudes	The number of respondents and their intensity of feeling positive or negative toward a specific brand.
Satisfaction	How people evaluate their postpurchase consumption experience with a particular product, service, or company.
Purchase Intention	The number of people planning to buy a specified object (e.g., product or service) within a designated time period.
Importance of Factors	To what extent do specific factors influence a person's purchase choice.
Demographics	The age, gender, occupation, income level, and other characteristics of individuals providing the information.

Determine the Unit of Analysis As a fundamental part of problem definition, the researcher must determine the appropriate **unit of analysis** for the study. The researcher must be able to specify whether data should be collected about individuals, households, organizations, departments, geographical areas, or some combination. The unit of analysis will provide direction in later activities such as scale development and sampling. In an automobile satisfaction study, for example, the researcher must decide whether to collect data from individuals or from a husband and wife representing the household in which the vehicle is driven.

Unit of analysis Specifies whether data should be collected about individuals, households, organizations, departments, geographical areas, or some combination.

Determine the Relevant Variables The researcher and decision maker jointly determine the variables that need to be studied. The types of information needed (facts, predictions, relationships) must be identified. Exhibit 2.6 lists examples of variables that are often investigated in marketing research. Variables are often measured using several related questions on a survey. In some situations, we refer to these variables as *constructs*. We will discuss constructs in Chapters 3 and 7.

Step 2: Define the Research Questions

Next, the researcher must redefine the initial problem as a research question. For the most part, this is the responsibility of the researcher. To provide background information on other firms that may have faced similar problems, the researcher conducts a *review of the literature*. The literature review may uncover relevant theory and variables to include in the research. For example, a literature review of new software adoption research would reveal that two factors—ease of use and functionality—are often included in studies of software adoption because these variables strongly predict adoption and usage. While the literature review ordinarily does not provide data that answer the research question, it can supply valuable perspectives and ideas that may be used in research design and in interpretation of results. *Literature reviews* are described in more detail in Chapter 3.

Breaking down the problem into research questions is one of the most important steps in the marketing research process because how the research problem is defined influences all of the remaining research steps. The researcher's task is to restate the initial variables associated with the problem in the form of key questions: how, what, where, when, or why. For example, management of Lowe's Home Improvement, Inc. was concerned about the overall image of Lowe's retail operations as well as its image among customers within the Atlanta metropolitan market. The initial research question was, "Do our marketing strategies need to be modified to increase satisfaction among our current and future customers?" After Lowe's management met with consultants at Corporate Communications and Marketing, Inc. to clarify the firm's information needs, the consultants translated the initial problem into the specific questions displayed in Exhibit 2.7. With assistance of management, the consultants then identified the attributes in each research question. For example, specific "store/operation aspects" that can affect satisfaction included convenient operating hours, friendly/courteous staff, and wide assortment of products and services.

After redefining the problem into research questions and identifying the information requirements, the researcher must determine the types of data (secondary or primary) that will best answer each research question. Although final decision on types of data is part of step 4 (Determine the Research Design and Data Sources), the researcher begins the process in step 2. The researcher asks the question, "Can the specific research question be addressed with data that already exist or does the question require new data?" To answer this question, researchers consider other issues such as data availability, data quality, and budget and time constraints.

Finally, in step 2 the researcher determines whether the information being requested is necessary. This step must be completed before going on to step 3.

Exhibit 2.7   Initial and Redefined Research Questions for Lowe's Home Improvement, Inc.

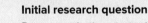

Initial research question

Do our marketing strategies need to be modified to increase satisfaction among our current and future customer segments?

Redefined research questions

- What store/operation aspects do people believe are important in selecting a retail hardware/lumber outlet?
- How do customers evaluate Lowe's retail outlets on store/operation aspects?
- What are the perceived strengths and weaknesses of Lowe's retail operations?
- How do customers and noncustomers compare Lowe's to other retail hardware/lumber outlets within the Atlanta metropolitan area?
- What is the demographic/psychographic profile of the people who patronize Lowe's retail outlets in the Atlanta market?

Step 3: Specify Research Objectives and Confirm the Information Value

The research objectives should be based on the development of research questions in step 2. Formally stated research objectives provide guidelines for determining other steps that must be taken. The assumption is that if the objectives are achieved, the decision maker will have the information needed to answer the research questions.

Before moving to Phase II of the research process, the decision maker and the researcher must evaluate the expected value of the information. This is not an easy task because a number of factors come into play. "Best judgment" answers have to be made to the following types of questions: "Can the information be collected at all?" "Can the information tell the decision maker something not already known?" "Will the information provide significant insights?" and "What benefits will be delivered by this information?" In most cases, research should be conducted only when the expected value of the information to be obtained exceeds the cost of the research.

◼◼ Phase II: Select the Research Design

The main focus of Phase II is to select the most appropriate research design to achieve the research objectives. The steps in this phase are outlined below.

Step 4: Determine the Research Design and Data Sources

The research design serves as an overall plan of the methods used to collect and analyze the data. Determining the most appropriate research design is a function of the research objectives and information requirements. The researcher must consider the types of data, the data collection method (e.g., survey, observation, in-depth interview), sampling method, schedule, and budget. There are three broad categories of research designs: *exploratory, descriptive*, and *causal*. An individual research project may sometimes require a combination of exploratory, descriptive, and/or causal techniques in order to meet research objectives.

Exploratory research has one of two objectives: (1) generating insights that will help define the problem situation confronting the researcher or (2) deepening the understanding of consumer motivations, attitudes, and behavior that are not easy to access using other research methods. Examples of exploratory research methods include literature reviews of already available information, qualitative approaches such as focus groups and in-depth interviews, or pilot studies. Literature reviews will be described in Chapter 3. Exploratory research is discussed in Chapter 4.

Descriptive research involves collecting quantitative data to answer research questions. Descriptive information provides answers to who, what, when, where, and how questions. In marketing, examples of descriptive information include consumer attitudes, intentions, preferences, purchase behaviors, evaluations of current marketing mix strategies, and demographics. In the nearby Marketing Research Dashboard, we highlight Lotame Solutions, Inc., a firm that developed a research methodology called "Time Spent" to measure how many seconds various online advertising formats are visible to individual consumers, which provides information to advertising decision makers.

Descriptive studies may provide information about competitors, target markets, and environmental factors. For example, many chain restaurants conduct annual studies that describe customers' perceptions of their restaurant as well as primary competitors. These studies, referred to as either *image assessment surveys* or *customer satisfaction surveys*,

Exploratory research
Generates insights that will help define the problem situation confronting the researcher or improves the understanding of consumer motivations, attitudes, and behavior that are not easy to access using other research methods.

Descriptive research
Collects quantitative data to answer research questions such as who, what, when, where, and how.

MARKETING RESEARCH DASHBOARD   MEASURING EFFECTIVENESS
OF ONLINE ADVERTISING FORMATS

To help companies make better advertising placement decisions on websites, Lotame Solutions, Inc., developed a technology called Time Spent that measures how much time online ads are visible (completely unobstructed) to individual consumers. The company recently reported a finding that questions conventional wisdom about the effectiveness of three common online ad formats: *the medium rectangle, the leaderboard,* and *the skyscraper.*

Scott Hoffman, CMO of Lotame, says the three advertising formats are often seen as interchangeable in the online marketplace. But the findings indicate they are not equivalent, at least on the basis of amount of time online viewers spend viewing each of the ads. In Lotame's study of nearly 150 million ads, the 300 by 250 pixel format known in the industry as the "medium rectangle" averaged 13 seconds of viewing exposure per user served, as compared to only 5.4 seconds for the long and skinny "leaderboard" format (728 × 90 pixels), and 1.9 seconds for the thin but tall "skyscraper" format (160 × 600 pixels). Even though the findings challenge conventional wisdom, they are not altogether surprising. Leaderboards often appear on the top of pages, so are out of range as soon as a user scrolls down a page. A skyscraper may not fully load before a user scrolls down a page. The medium rectangle is often close to the middle of a web page where the user spends the most time.

Lotame has also conducted research on the effectiveness of online display ads. Their findings indicate a significantly increased likelihood in intent to recommend products among Internet users who have seen an online display ad.

The findings regarding time spent by the Time Spent method (i.e., number of seconds of viewing exposure for the online ad formats) and display ads have implications for both online publishers and online advertisers. The three advertising formats are not equal.

Sources: Adapted from Joe Mandese, "Finding Yields New Angle on Rectangle, Reaps Far More User Time than Leaderboards, Skyscrapers," *Mediapost.com,* April 7, 2009, www.mediapost.com /publications/?fa Articles.showArticle&art_aid 103585&passFuseAction PublicationsSearch.showSearchResults&art_searched Lotame&page _number 0#, accessed December 2011; "Lotame Research Finds 'Rectangle' Online Ads Provide Best Exposure, Beating 'Leaderboards' by Nearly Two and a Half to One," April 7, 2009, www.lotame.com /press/releases/23/, accessed December 2011; and "Display Ads Lift Branding Metrics," www.lotame.com/ 2011/06/display-ads-lift-branding -metrics/, accessed December 2011.

describe how customers rate different restaurants' customer service, convenience of location, food quality, and atmosphere. Some qualitative research is said to be descriptive, in the sense of providing rich or "thick" narrative description of phenomena. However, in the marketing research industry, the term *descriptive research* usually means numeric rather than textual data. Descriptive designs are discussed in Chapter 5.

Causal research Collects data that enables decision makers to determine cause-and-effect relationships between two or more variables.

Causal research collects data that enables decision makers to determine cause-and-effect relationships between two or more variables. Causal research is most appropriate when the research objectives include the need to understand which variables (e.g., advertising, number of salespersons, price) cause a dependent variable (e.g., sales, customer satisfaction) to move.

Understanding cause-effect relationships among market performance factors enables the decision maker to make "If–then" statements about the variables. For example, as a result of using causal research methods, the owner of a men's clothing store in Chicago can predict that, "If I increase my advertising budget by 15 percent, then overall sales volume should increase by 20 percent." Causal research designs provide an opportunity to assess and explain causality among market factors. But they often can be complex, expensive, and time consuming. Causal research designs are discussed in Chapter 5.

Secondary and Primary Data Sources The sources of data needed to address research problems can be classified as either secondary or primary, as we have discussed earlier. The sources used depend on two fundamental issues: (1) whether the data already exist; and (2) if so, the extent to which the researcher or decision maker knows the reason(s) why the existing secondary data were collected. Sources of such secondary data include a company's data warehouse, public libraries and universities, Internet websites, or commercial data purchased from firms specializing in providing secondary information. Chapter 3 covers secondary data and sources.

Primary data are collected directly from firsthand sources to address the current research problem. The nature and collection of primary data are covered in Chapters 4–8.

Step 5: Develop the Sampling Design and Sample Size

When conducting primary research, consideration must be given to the sampling design. If secondary research is conducted, the researcher must still determine that the population represented by the secondary data is relevant to the current research problem. Relevancy of secondary data is covered in Chapter 3.

Target population The population from which the researcher wants to collect data.

Census The researcher attempts to question or observe all the members of a defined target population.

Sample A small number of members of the target population from which the researcher collects data.

If predictions are to be made about market phenomena, the sample must be representative. Typically, marketing decision makers are most interested in identifying and solving problems associated with their target markets. Therefore, researchers need to identify the relevant **target population.** In collecting data, researchers can choose between collecting data from a census or a sample. In a **census,** the researcher attempts to question or observe all the members of a defined target population. For small populations, a census may be the best approach. For example, if your marketing research professor wanted to collect data regarding student reactions to a new lecture she just presented, she would likely survey the entire class, not merely a sample.

A second approach, used when the target population is large, involves selection of a **sample** from the defined target population. Researchers must use a representative sample of the population if they wish to *generalize* the findings. To achieve this objective, researchers develop a sampling plan as part of the overall research design. A sampling plan serves as the blueprint for defining the appropriate target population, identifying the possible respondents, establishing the procedures for selecting the sample, and determining the appropriate sample size. Sampling plans can be classified into two general types: *probability* and *nonprobability*. In probability sampling, each member of the defined target population has a known chance of being selected. For example, if the population of marketing majors at a university is 500, and 100 are going to be sampled, the "known chance" of being selected is one five or 20 percent.

Probability sampling gives the researcher the opportunity to assess sampling error. In contrast, nonprobability sampling plans cannot measure sampling error and thus limit the generalizability of the research findings. Qualitative research designs often use small samples, so sample members are usually hand-selected to ensure a relevant sample. For example, a qualitative study of Californians' perceptions of earthquake risk and preparedness included residents who had been close to sizable earthquakes and those who had not. In addition, researchers attempted to include representatives of major demographic groups in California.

Sample size affects the accuracy and generalizability of research results. Researchers must therefore determine how many people to include or how many objects to investigate. We discuss sampling in more detail in Chapter 6.

Step 6: Examine Measurement Issues and Scales

Step 6 is an important step in the research process for descriptive and causal designs. It involves identifying the concepts to study and measuring the variables related to the research problem. Researchers must be able to answer questions such as: How should a variable such as customer satisfaction or service quality be defined and measured? Should researchers use single- or multi-item measures to quantify variables? In Chapter 7, we discuss measurement and scaling.

Although most of the activities involved in step 6 are related to primary research, understanding these activities is important in secondary research as well. For example, when using data mining with database variables, researchers must understand the measurement approach used in creating the database as well as any measurement biases. Otherwise, secondary data may be misinterpreted.

Step 7: Design and Pretest the Questionnaire

Designing good questionnaires is difficult. Researchers must select the correct type of questions, consider the sequence and format, and pretest the questionnaire. Pretesting obtains information from people representative of those who will be questioned in the actual survey. In a pretest, respondents are asked to complete the questionnaire and comment on issues such as clarity of instructions and questions, sequence of the topics and questions, and anything that is potentially difficult or confusing. Chapter 8 covers questionnaire design.

■ Phase III: Execute the Research Design

The main objectives of the execution phase are to finalize all necessary data collection forms, gather and prepare the data, and analyze and interpret the data to understand the problem or opportunity. As in the first two phases, researchers must be cautious to ensure potential biases or errors are either eliminated or at least minimized.

Step 8: Collect and Prepare Data

There are two approaches to gathering data. One is to have interviewers ask questions about variables and market phenomena or to use self-completion questionnaires. The other is to observe individuals or market phenomena. Self-administered surveys, personal interviews, computer simulations, telephone interviews, and focus groups are just some of the tools researchers use to collect data.

A major advantage of questioning over observation is questioning enables researchers to collect a wider array of data. Questioning approaches can collect information about attitudes, intentions, motivations, and past behavior, which are usually invisible in observational research. In short, questioning approaches can be used to answer not just how a person is behaving, but why.

Once primary data are collected, researchers must perform several activities before data analysis. Researchers usually assign a numerical descriptor (code) to all response categories so that data can be entered into the electronic data file. The data then must be examined for coding, data-entry errors, inconsistencies, availability, and so on. Data preparation is also necessary when information is used from internal data warehouses. Chapter 10 discusses data preparation.

Step 9: Analyze Data

In step 9, the researcher analyzes the data. Analysis procedures vary widely in sophistication and complexity, from simple frequency distributions (percentages) to summary statistics (mean, median, and mode) and multivariate data analysis. In qualitative research studies, textual and/or visual information is examined, categorized, and even sometimes tabulated. Different procedures enable the researcher to statistically test hypotheses for significant differences or correlations among several variables, evaluate data quality, and test models of cause-effect relationships. Chapters 9–12 provide an overview of data analysis approaches.

Step 10: Interpret Data to Create Knowledge

Knowledge is created for decision makers in step 10—interpretation. Knowledge is created through engaged and careful interpretation of results. Interpretation is more than a narrative description of the results. It involves integrating several aspects of the findings into conclusions that can be used to answer the research questions.

◼◼ Phase IV: Communicate the Results

The last phase of the research process is reporting the research findings to management. The overall objective often is to prepare a nontechnical report that is useful to decision makers whether or not they have marketing research backgrounds.

Exhibit 2.8 | General Outline of a Research Proposal

TITLE OF THE RESEARCH PROPOSAL

I. Purpose of the Proposed Research Project

Includes a description of the problem and research objectives.

II. Type of Study

Discusses the type of research design (exploratory, descriptive, or causal), and secondary versus primary data requirements, with justification of choice.

III. Definition of the Target Population and Sample Size

Describes the overall target population to be studied and determination of the appropriate sample size, including a justification of the size.

IV. Sample Design and Data Collection Method

Describes the sampling technique used, the method of collecting data (e.g., observation or survey), incentive plans, and justifications.

V. Specific Research Instruments

Discusses the method used to collect the needed data, including the various types of scales.

VI. Potential Managerial Benefits of the Proposed Study

Discusses the expected values of the information to management and how the initial problem might be solved, including the study's limitations.

VII. Proposed Cost for the Total Project

Itemizes the expected costs for completing the research, including a total cost figure and anticipated time frames.

VIII. Profile of the Research Company Capabilities

Briefly describes the researchers and their qualifications as well as a general overview of the company.

IX. Optional Dummy Tables of the Projected Results

Gives examples of how the data might be presented in the final report.

Step 11: Prepare and Present the Final Report

Step 11 is preparing and presenting the final research report to management. The importance of this step cannot be overstated. There are some sections that should be included in any research report: executive summary, introduction, problem definition and objectives, methodology, results and findings, and limitations of study. In some cases, the researcher not only submits a written report but also makes an oral presentation of the major findings. Chapter 13 describes how to write and present research reports.

◼◗ Develop a Research Proposal

Research proposal A specific document that provides an overview of the proposed research and methodology, and serves as a written contract between the decision maker and the researcher.

By understanding the four phases of the research process, a researcher can develop a **research proposal** that communicates the research framework to the decision maker. A research proposal is a specific document that serves as a written contract between the decision maker and the researcher. It lists the activities that will be undertaken to develop the needed information, the research deliverables, how long it will take, and what it will cost.

The research proposal is not the same as a final research report quite obviously. They are at two different ends of the process, but some of the sections are necessarily similar. There is no best way to write a research proposal. If a client asks for research proposals from two or three different companies for a given research problem, they are likely to be somewhat different in the methodologies and approach suggested for the problem. Exhibit 2.8 shows the sections that should be included in most research proposals. The exhibit presents only a general outline. An actual proposal can be found in the Marketing Research in Action at the end of the chapter.

MARKETING RESEARCH IN ACTION
What Does a Research Proposal Look Like?

Magnum Hotel Preferred Guest Card Research Proposal

The purpose of the proposed research project is to collect attitudinal, behavioral, motivational, and general demographic information to address several key questions posed by management of Benito Advertising and Johnson Properties, Inc., concerning the Magnum Hotel Preferred Guest Card, a recently implemented marketing loyalty program. Key questions are as follows:

1. Is the Preferred Guest Card being used by cardholders?
2. How do cardholders evaluate the privileges associated with the card?
3. What are the perceived benefits and weaknesses of the card, and why?
4. Is the Preferred Guest Card an important factor in selecting a hotel?
5. How often and when do cardholders use their Preferred Guest Card?
6. Of those who have used the card, what privileges have been used and how often?
7. What improvements should be made regarding the card or the extended privileges?
8. How did cardholders obtain the card?
9. Should the Preferred Guest Card membership be complimentary or should cardholders pay an annual fee?
10. If there should be an annual fee, how much should it be? What would a cardholder be willing to pay?
11. What is the demographic profile of the people who have the Magnum Hotel Preferred Guest Card?

To collect data to answer these questions, the research will be a structured, nondisguised design that includes both exploratory and descriptive research. The study will be descriptive because many questions focus on identifying perceived awareness, attitudes, and usage patterns of Magnum Hotel Preferred Guest Card holders as well as demographic profiles. It will be exploratory since it is looking for possible improvements to the card and its privileges, the pricing structure, and the perceived benefits and weaknesses of the current card's features.

The target population consists of adults known to be current cardholders of the Magnum Hotel Preferred Guest Card Program. This population frame is approximately 17,000 individuals across the United States. Statistically a conservative sample size would be 387. But realistically, a sample of approximately 1,500 should be used to enable examination of sample subgroups. The size is based on the likely response rate for the sampling method and questionnaire design, a predetermined sampling error of ± 5 percent and a confidence level of 95 percent, administrative costs and trade-offs, and the desire for a prespecified minimum number of completed surveys.

Probability sampling will be used to draw the sample from the central cardholder database. Using a mail survey, cardholders randomly selected as prospective respondents will be mailed a personalized self-administered questionnaire. Attached to the questionnaire will be a cover letter explaining the study as well as incentives for respondent participation.

Given the nature of the study, the perceived type of cardholder, the trade-offs regarding costs and time considerations, and the use of incentives to encourage respondent participation, a mail survey is more appropriate than other methods.

The questionnaire will be self-administered. That is, respondents will fill out the survey in the privacy of their home and without the presence of an interviewer. All survey questions will be pretested using a convenience sample to assess clarity of instructions, questions, and administrative time dimensions. Response scales for the questions will conform to questionnaire design guidelines and industry judgment.

Given the nature of the proposed project, the findings will enable Magnum Hotel's management to answer questions regarding the Preferred Guest Card as well as other marketing strategy issues. Specifically, the study will help management:

- Better understand the types of people using the Preferred Guest Card and the extent of usage.
- Identify issues that suggest evaluating (and possibly modifying) current marketing strategies or tactics for the card and its privileges.
- Develop insights concerning the promotion and distribution of the card to additional segments.

Additionally, the proposed research project will initiate a customer database and information system so management can better understand customers' hotel service needs and wants. Customer-oriented databases will be useful in developing promotional strategies as well as pricing and service approaches.

Proposed Project Costs

Questionnaire/cover letter design and reproduction costs	$ 3,800
Development, Typing, Pretest, Reproduction (1,500),	
Envelopes (3,000)	
Sample design	2,750
Administration/data collection costs	4,800
Questionnaire packet assembly	
Postage and P.O. Box	
Address labels	
Coding and predata analysis costs	4,000
Coding and setting of final codes	
Data entry	
Computer programming	
Data analysis and interpretation costs	7,500
Written report and presentation costs	4,500
Total maximum proposed project cost*	$27,350

*Costing policy: Some items may cost more or less than what is stated on the proposal. Cost reductions, if any, will be passed on to the client. Additionally, there is a ± 10 percent cost margin for data collection and analysis activities depending on client changes of the original analysis requirements.

Research for this proposed project will be conducted by the Marketing Resource Group (MRG), a full-service marketing research firm located in Tampa, Florida, that has conducted studies for many Fortune 1,000 companies. The principal researcher and project coordinator will be Dr. Alex Smith, senior project director at MRG. Smith holds a PhD in marketing from Louisiana State University, an MBA from Illinois State University, and a

BS from Southern Illinois University. With 25 years of marketing research experience, he has designed and coordinated numerous projects in the consumer packaged-goods products, hotel/resort, retail banking, automobile, and insurance industries. He specializes in projects that focus on customer satisfaction, service/product quality, market segmentation, and general consumer attitudes and behavior patterns as well as interactive electronic marketing technologies. In addition, he has published numerous articles on theoretical and pragmatic research topics.

Hands-On Exercise

1. If this proposal is accepted, will it achieve the objectives of management?
2. Is the target population being interviewed the appropriate one?
3. Are there other questions that should be asked in the project?

Summary

Describe the major environmental factors influencing marketing research.

Several key environmental factors have significant impact on changing the tasks, responsibilities, and efforts associated with marketing research practices. Marketing research has risen from a supporting role within organizations to being integral in strategic planning. The Internet and e-commerce, gatekeeper technologies and data privacy legislation, and new global market structure expansions are all forcing researchers to balance their use of secondary and primary data to assist decision makers in solving decision problems and taking advantage of opportunities. Researchers need to improve their ability to use technology-driven tools and databases. There are also greater needs for faster data acquisition and retrieval, analysis, and interpretation of cross-functional data and information among decision-making teams within global market environments.

Discuss the research process and explain the various steps.

The information research process has four major phases, identified as (1) determine of the research problem; (2) select the appropriate research design; (3) execute the research design; and (4) communicate the results. To achieve the overall objectives of each phase, researchers must be able to successfully execute 11 interrelated task steps: (1) identify and clarify information needs; (2) define the research problem and questions; (3) specify research objectives and confirm the information value; (4) determine the research design and data sources; (5) develop the sampling design and sample size; (6) examine measurement issues and scales; (7) design and pretest questionnaires; (8) collect and prepare data; (9) analyze data; (10) interpret data to create knowledge; and (11) prepare and present the final report.

Distinguish between exploratory, descriptive, and causal research designs.

The main objective of exploratory research designs is to create information that the researcher or decision maker can use to (1) gain a clear understanding of the problem; (2) define or redefine the initial problem, separating the symptoms from the causes; (3) confirm the problem and objectives; or (4) identify the information requirements. Exploratory research designs are often intended to provide preliminary insight for follow-up quantitative research. However, sometimes qualitative exploratory methods are used as standalone techniques because the topic under investigation requires in-depth understanding of a complex web of consumer culture, psychological motivations, and behavior. For some research topics, quantitative research may be too superficial or it may elicit responses from consumers that are rationalizations rather than true reasons for purchase decisions and behavior.

Descriptive research designs produce numeric data to describe existing characteristics (e.g., attitudes, intentions, preferences, purchase behaviors, evaluations of current marketing mix strategies) of a defined target population. The researcher looks for answers to how, who, what, when, and where questions. Information from descriptive designs allows decision makers to draw inferences about their customers, competitors, target markets, environmental factors, or other phenomena.

Finally, causal research designs are most useful when the research objectives include the need to understand why market phenomena happen. The focus of causal research is to collect data that enables the decision maker or researcher to model cause-and-effect relationships between two or more variables.

Identify and explain the major components of a research proposal.

Once the researcher understands the different phases and task steps of the information research process, he or she can develop a research proposal. The proposal serves as a contract between the researcher and decision maker. There are nine sections suggested for inclusion: (1) purpose of the proposed research project; (2) type of study; (3) definition of the target population and sample size; (4) sample design, technique, and data collection method; (5) research instruments; (6) potential managerial benefits of the proposed study; (7) proposed cost structure for the project; (8) profile of the researcher and company; and (9) dummy tables of the projected results.

◼ Key Terms and Concepts

Causal research 37

Census 38

Descriptive research 36

Exploratory research 36

Gatekeeper technologies 26

Information research process 27

Knowledge 30

Primary data 26

Research proposal 41

Sample 38

Scientific method 30

Secondary data 26

Situation analysis 32

Target population 38

Unit of analysis 34

◼ Review Questions

1. Identify the significant changes taking place in today's business environment that are forcing management decision makers to rethink their views of marketing research. Also discuss the potential impact that these changes might have on marketing research activities.

2. In the business world of the 21st century, will it be possible to make critical marketing decisions without marketing research? Why or why not?

3. How are management decision makers and information researchers alike? How are they different? How might the differences be reduced between these two types of professionals?

4. Comment on the following statements:
    a. The primary responsibility for determining whether marketing research activities are necessary is that of the marketing research specialist.
    b. The information research process serves as a blueprint for reducing risks in making marketing decisions.
    c. Selecting the most appropriate research design is the most critical task in the research process.

5. Design a research proposal that can be used to address the following decision problem: "Should the Marriott Hotel in Pittsburgh, Pennsylvania, reduce the quality of its towels and bedding in order to improve the profitability of the hotel's operations?"

Discussion Questions

1. For each of the four phases of the information research process, identify the corresponding steps and develop a set of questions that a researcher should attempt to answer.

2. What are the differences between exploratory, descriptive, and causal research designs? Which design type would be most appropriate to address the following question: "How satisfied or dissatisfied are customers with the automobile repair service offerings of the dealership from which they purchased their new 2013 BMW?"

3. When should a researcher use a probability sampling method rather than a nonprobability method?

4. **EXPERIENCE MARKETING RESEARCH.** Go to the Gallup poll organization's home page at **www .gallup.com**.
   a. Several polls are reported on their home page. After reviewing one of the polls, outline the different phases and task steps of the information research process that might have been used in the Gallup Internet poll.
   b. Is the research reported by the poll exploratory, descriptive, or causal? Explain your choice.

Part 2

Designing
the Marketing
Research Project

Secondary Data, Literature Reviews, and Hypotheses

Chapter 3

Learning Objectives   After reading this chapter, you will be able to:

1. Understand the nature and role of secondary data.
2. Describe how to conduct a literature review.
3. Identify sources of internal and external secondary data.
4. Discuss conceptualization and its role in model development.
5. Understand hypotheses and independent and dependent variables.

Will Brick-and-Mortar Stores Eventually Turn into Product Showrooms?

Research conducted during the recent holiday shopping season provided evidence of an important and growing trend in shopping: using one's mobile phone while shopping in a store as an aid in making purchasing decisions. Pew American and Internet Life conducted a study of 1,000 U.S. adults regarding their mobile phone use while shopping. Over half of consumers (52 percent) reported using their mobile phone to help them make a purchase decision while shopping in a bricks-and-mortar store during the holiday season.

There were three specific ways the mobile phones were used. First, fully 38 percent of respondents reported using the cell phone to call a friend for advice while in a store. Second, 24 percent of respondents used mobile devices to search for online product reviews. Last, one in four shoppers used their mobile phone to compare prices, for example, using Amazon's barcode scan service to search for more competitive prices.

Some categories of consumers were more likely to use the mobile phone to help them while shopping in brick-and-mortar stores. Younger (18–49), non-white, and male consumers were more likely to use their cell phones to search for product information, but the trend is also evident in white and female shopper populations. The research findings show that brick-and-mortar businesses can easily lose business to shoppers looking for better or more competitively priced products. Online retailers have opportunities to increase their sales, especially if they can provide timely information and good prices to shoppers using mobile devices. Another trend relevant to marketers is highlighted by the research as well: while friends and family have always had an important role in recommending products, their availability via mobile devices has enhanced their influence. Businesses and marketers will increasingly have to implement tactics that help them to influence customers in an environment where both personal and online sources are easily available at the point of decision.

Pew Internet and American Life's research on mobile phone use while shopping is available at their website and is published at several other media sites as well. Their study is an example of secondary data, and in this case, the research is available for free. Yet, the information may have relevance to a broad variety of businesses, including offline and online retailers, mobile app developers, and wireless carriers. To use the study effectively, most businesses will have to evaluate how applicable the findings are to their particular industry. For example, to better understand the in-store mobile usage trend, the industries that could benefit might search for other free online sources of similar information, purchase additional secondary research that is more specific to their industry, and if necessary, conduct primary research.[1]

Value of Secondary Data and Literature Reviews

This chapter focuses on the types of secondary data available, how they can be used, the benefits they offer, and the impact of the Internet on the use of secondary data. We also explain how to conduct background research as part of a literature review and how to report information found in completing a literature review. A literature review is an important step in developing an understanding of a research topic and supports the conceptualization and development of hypotheses, the last topic in this chapter.

Nature, Scope, and Role of Secondary Data

One of the essential tasks of marketing research is to obtain information that enables management to make the best possible decisions. Before problems are examined, researchers determine whether useful information already exists, how relevant the information is, and how it can be obtained. Existing sources of information are plentiful and should always be considered first before collecting primary data.

Secondary data Data not gathered for the immediate study at hand but for some other purpose.

The term **secondary data** refers to data gathered for some other purpose than the immediate study. Sometimes it is called "desk research" while primary research is called "field research." There are two types of secondary data: internal and external. **Internal secondary data** are collected by a company for accounting purposes, marketing programs, inventory management, and so forth.

Internal secondary data Data collected by the individual company for accounting purposes or marketing activity reports.

External secondary data are collected by outside organizations such as federal and state governments, trade associations, nonprofit organizations, marketing research services, or academic researchers. Secondary data also are widely available from the Internet and other digital data sources. Examples of these digital information sources include information vendors, federal and government websites, and commercial websites.

External secondary data Data collected by outside agencies such as the federal government, trade associations, or periodicals.

The role of secondary data in marketing research has changed in recent years. Traditionally, secondary data were viewed as having limited value. The job of obtaining secondary data often was outsourced to a corporate librarian, syndicated data collection firm, or junior research analyst. With the increased emphasis on business and competitive intelligence and the ever-increasing availability of information from online sources, secondary data research has gained substantial importance in marketing research.

Secondary research approaches are increasingly used to examine marketing problems because of the relative speed and cost-effectiveness of obtaining the data. The role of the secondary research analyst is being redefined to that of business unit information professional or specialist linked to the information technology area. This individual creates contact and sales databases, prepares competitive trend reports, develops customer retention strategies, and so forth.

◼◼ Conducting a Literature Review

Literature review A comprehensive examination of available information that is related to your research topic.

A **literature review** is a comprehensive examination of available secondary information related to your research topic. Secondary data relevant to your research problem obtained in a literature review should be included in the final report of findings. This section of the report typically is labeled "background research," or "literature review." Secondary research alone may sometimes provide the answer to your research question, and no further research will be required.

But even if analysts plan to conduct primary research, a literature review can be helpful because it provides background and contextual information for the current study; clarifies thinking about the research problem and questions that are the focus of the study; reveals whether information already exists that addresses the issue of interest; helps to define important constructs of interest to the study; and suggests sampling and other methodological approaches that have been successful in researching similar topics.

Reviewing available literature helps researchers stay abreast of the latest thinking related to their topic of interest. In most industries, there are some widely known and cited studies. For example, the Interactive Advertising Bureau (IAB) is an industry organization whose members are a "Who's Who" of online publishers and advertisers. The IAB has conducted a number of high-profile studies that are well known to industry members and available on their website. The studies report what works and doesn't work in online advertising. An analyst conducting research in the area of online advertising who is not familiar with major published studies, such as those conducted by the IAB, would likely have difficulty establishing their expertise with clients, many of whom are aware of these studies.

An important reason for doing a literature review is that it can help clarify and define the research problem and research questions. Suppose an online advertiser wants to study how consumers' engagement with online advertising affects their attitude toward the brand, website visits, and actual purchase behavior. A literature review would uncover other published studies on the topic of consumer advertising engagement, as well as the different ways to define and measure consumer engagement.

A literature review can also suggest research hypotheses to investigate. For example, a literature review may show that frequent Internet shoppers are more likely to be engaged with online advertising; that engagement increases positive attitudes toward the brand; or that younger people are more likely to become engaged with an online ad. The studies you locate may not provide answers to specific research questions. But they will provide some ideas for issues and relationships to investigate.

Importantly, literature reviews can identify scales to measure variables and research methodologies that have been used successfully to study similar topics. For instance, if a researcher wants to measure the usability of a website, a literature review will locate published studies that suggest checklists of important features of usable sites. Reviewing previous studies will save researchers time and effort because new scales will not need to be developed from scratch.

Evaluating Secondary Data Sources

Literature reviews may include a search of popular, scholarly, government, and commercial sources available outside the company. An internal search of available information within the company also should be conducted. With the advent of the Internet, conducting a literature review has become both easier and harder. It is easier in the sense that a wide variety of material may be instantly available. Thus, finding relevant published studies has become easier than ever. But wading through the search results to find the studies that are actually of interest can be overwhelming. It is important, therefore, to narrow your topic so that you can focus your efforts before conducting a search for relevant information.

With the increasing emphasis on secondary data, researchers have developed criteria to evaluate the quality of information obtained from secondary data sources. The criteria used to evaluate secondary data are:

1. *Purpose.* Because most secondary data are collected for purposes other than the one at hand, the data must be carefully evaluated on how it relates to the current research objective. Many times the data collected in a particular study is not consistent with the research objectives at hand. For example, industry research may show that today's consumers are spending less on new cars than they did in the 1980s. But a car company may be more interested in a specific demographic group, for example, high-income women, or the market for a specific type of car, for example, luxury sedans.

2. *Accuracy.* Accuracy is enhanced when data are obtained from the original source of the data. A lot of information in industries may be cited repeatedly without checking the original source.

   In addition to going back to the original source of the data, it is important to evaluate whether or not the data are out of date. For example, a researcher tracking the sales of imported Japanese autos in the U.S. market needs to consider changing attitudes, newly imposed tariffs that may restrict imports, and even fluctuations in the exchange rate.

3. *Consistency.* When evaluating any source of secondary data, a good strategy is to seek out multiple sources of the same data to assure consistency. For example, when evaluating the economic characteristics of a foreign market, a researcher may try to gather the same information from government sources, private business publications (*Fortune, Bloomberg Businessweek*), and specialty import/export trade publications. Researchers should attempt to determine the source(s) of any inconsistencies in the information they gather.

4. *Credibility.* Researchers should always question the credibility of the secondary data source. Technical competence, service quality, reputation, training, and expertise of personnel representing the organization are some of the measures of credibility.

5. *Methodology.* The quality of secondary data is only as good as the methodology employed to gather it. Flaws in methodological procedures can produce results that are invalid, unreliable, or not generalizable beyond the study itself. Therefore, the researcher must evaluate the size and description of the sample, the response rate, the questionnaire, and the data collection method (telephone, mobile device, or personal interview).

6. *Bias.* Researchers must determine the underlying motivation or hidden agenda, if any, of the organization that collected the secondary data. It is not uncommon to find secondary data sources published to advance the interests of commercial, political, or other special interest groups. Researchers must consider whether the organization reporting the data is motivated by a certain purpose. For example, statistics on animal

extinction reported by the National Hardwood Lumber Association or, alternatively, by the People for the Ethical Treatment of Animals (PETA) should be validated before they can be relied on as unbiased sources of information.

Secondary Data and the Marketing Research Process

In many areas of marketing research, secondary research plays a subordinate role to primary research. In product and advertising concept testing, focus groups, and customer satisfaction surveys, only primary research can provide answers to marketing problems. But in some situations, secondary data by itself can address the research problem. If the problem can be solved based on available secondary data alone, then the company can save time, money, and effort.

The amount of secondary information is indeed vast. Secondary data often sought by researchers include demographic characteristics, employment data, economic statistics, competitive and supply assessments, regulations, and international market characteristics. Exhibit 3.1 provides examples of specific variables within these categories.

Exhibit 3.1 **Key Descriptive Variables Sought in Secondary Data Search**

Demographics
Population growth: actual and projected
Population density
In-migration and out-migration patterns
Population trends by age, race, and ethnic background

Employment Characteristics
Labor force growth
Unemployment levels
Percentage of employment by occupation categories
Employment by industry

Economic Data
Personal income levels (per capita and median)
Type of manufacturing/service firms
Total housing starts
Building permits issued
Sales tax rates

Competitive Characteristics
Levels of retail and wholesale sales
Number and types of competing retailers
Availability of financial institutions

Supply Characteristics
Number of distribution facilities
Cost of deliveries
Level of rail, water, air, and road transportation

Regulations
Taxes
Licensing
Wages
Zoning

International Market Characteristics
Transportation and exporting requirements
Trade barriers
Business philosophies
Legal system
Social customs
Political climate
Cultural patterns
Religious and moral backgrounds

Several kinds of secondary sources are available, including internal, popular, academic, and commercial sources. We describe each of these categories of secondary sources.

◼️◀ Internal and External Sources of Secondary Data

Secondary data are available both within the company and from external sources. In this section, we look at the major internal and external sources of secondary data.

Internal Sources of Secondary Data

The logical starting point in searching for secondary data is the company's own internal information. Many organizations fail to realize the wealth of information their own records contain. Additionally, internal data are the most readily available and can be accessed at little or no cost at all. But while this appears to be a good rationale for using internal data, researchers must remember that most of the information comes from past business activities. Nevertheless, internal data sources can be highly effective in helping decision makers plan new-product introductions or new distribution outlets.

Generally, internal secondary data consist of sales, accounting, or cost information. Exhibit 3.2 lists key variables found in each of these internal sources of secondary data.

Other types of internal data that exist among company records can be used to complement the information thus far discussed. Exhibit 3.3 outlines other potential sources of internal secondary data.

A lot of internal company information is available for marketing research activities. If maintained and categorized properly, internal data can be used to analyze product performance, customer satisfaction, distribution effectiveness, and segmentation strategies. These forms of internal data are also useful for planning new-product introductions, product deletions, promotional strategies, competitive intelligence, and customer service tactics.

External Sources of Secondary Data

After searching for internal secondary data, the next logical step for the researcher to focus on is external secondary data. Primary sources of external secondary data include: (1) popular sources; (2) scholarly sources; (3) government sources; (4) North American Industry Classification System (NAICS); and (5) commercial sources.

Popular Sources Many popular sources are available both in the library and on the Internet. Examples of popular sources include *Bloomberg Businessweek, Forbes, Harvard Business Review, Wired,* and so on. Most popular articles are written for newspapers and periodicals by journalists or freelance writers. Popular sources are often more current than scholarly sources and are written using less technical language. However, the findings and ideas expressed in popular sources often involve secondhand reporting of information. Moreover, while scholarly findings are reviewed by peers prior to publication, findings reported in journalistic publications receive much less scrutiny.[2]

Many business students are already familiar with the business articles and resources offered by ABI/Inform or Lexus/Nexus. These databases can be searched

Exhibit 3.2   Common Sources of Internal Secondary Data

1. **Sales invoices**
   a. Customer name
   b. Address
   c. Class of product/service sold
   d. Price by unit
   e. Salesperson
   f. Terms of sales
   g. Shipment point

2. **Accounts receivable reports**
   a. Customer name
   b. Product purchased
   c. Total unit and dollar sales
   d. Customer as percentage of sales
   e. Customer as percentage of regional sales
   f. Profit margin
   g. Credit rating
   h. Items returned
   i. Reason for return

3. **Quarterly sales reports**
   a. Total dollar and unit sales by:
      Customer   Geographic segment
      Customer segment   Sales territory
      Product   Sales rep
      Product segment
   b. Total sales against planned objectives
   c. Total sales against budget
   d. Total sales against prior periods
   e. Actual sales percentage increase/decrease
   f. Contribution trends

4. **Sales activity reports**
   a. Classification of customer accounts
      Mega
      Large
      Medium
      Small
   b. Available dollar sales potential
   c. Current sales penetration
   d. Existing bids/contracts by
      Customer location
      Product

Exhibit 3.3   Additional Sources of Secondary Data

Source	Information
Customer letters	General satisfaction/dissatisfaction data
Customer comment cards	Overall performance data
Mail-order forms	Customer name, address, items purchased, quality, cycle time of order
Credit applications	Detailed biography of customer segments (demographic, socioeconomic, credit usage, credit ratings)
Cash register receipts	Dollar volume, merchandise type, salesperson, vendor, manufacturer
Salesperson expense reports	Sales activities, competitor activities in market
Employee exit interviews	General internal satisfaction/dissatisfaction data, internal company performance data
Warranty cards	Sales volume, names, addresses, zip codes, items purchased, reasons for product return
Past marketing research studies	Data pertaining to the situation in which the marketing research was conducted

through online library gateways at most colleges and universities. The databases cover many publications that are "walled off" and thus not available through major search engines. For example, both *The New York Times* and *The Wall Street Journal* provide excellent business news. However, search engines currently do not access the archives of these and other prominent newspapers. Most libraries pay for access to many newspaper and business publications through arrangements with ABI/Inform and Lexus/Nexus.

A great deal of information is available on the Internet without subscription to library databases. Search engines continually catalog this information and return the most relevant and most popular sites for particular search terms. Google, Yahoo!, and Bing are all good at locating published studies. Before performing an online search, it is useful to brainstorm several relevant keywords to use in search engines. For example, if you are interested in word-of-mouth marketing, several terms might make useful search terms: *buzz marketing, underground marketing,* and *stealth marketing.*

Some popular sources are publications staffed by writers who are marketing practitioners and analysts. For instance, the contributors at **www.Clickz.com** who write articles about a wide variety of online marketing issues are specialists in the areas they cover. Therefore, the opinions and analyses they offer are timely and informed by experience. Nevertheless, their opinions, while reflective of their experience and in-depth knowledge, have not been investigated with the same level of care as those available in scholarly publications.

One more possible source is marketing blogs. Many marketing writers and analysts have their own blogs. These sources must be chosen very carefully because anyone can write and post a blog. Only a blog that is written by a respected expert is worthy of mention in your literature review. Exhibit 3.4 lists some marketing blogs of note. Good blogs that are written by high-profile practitioners and analysts are often provocative and up to date. They often suggest perspectives that are worthy of consideration in the design and execution of your study.

Exhibit 3.4 Marketing Blogs of Note

Hootsuite	e-Consulting.com
Unbounce	Vidyard
OKDork	Seth's Blogs
Buffer	DuctTapeMarketing
Customer.io	Hubspot
MarketingProfs	BrandSavant
Mailchimp	TopRank
Kissmetrics	LinkedInPulse
Drip	Social Media Examiner

Sources: Orinna Weaver, "The Best Blogs of 2015" *Radius.com*, https://radius.com/2015/03/10/the-best-marketing-blogs-of-2015/ (March 10, 2015); Dusti Arab, "Top 16 Marketing Blogs to Follow in 2015", *Instapage, Inc.*, https://instapage.com/landing-pages, January 22, 2016; Jay Baer, "My Top 33 Digital Marketing Blogs," *Convince & Convert*, http://www.convinceandconvert.com/digital-marketing/my-top-33-digital-marketing-blogs/, accessed February 7, 2016.

Blog writers may also provide insightful commentary and critical analysis of published studies and practices that are currently being discussed by experts in the field. However, even blogs written by the most respected analysts express viewpoints that may be speculative and unproven. When writing your literature review, you will want to be clear in noting that these blogs are often more opinion than fact.

All popular sources you find on the web need to be carefully evaluated. Check the "About Us" portion of the website to see who is publishing the articles or studies to see if the source of the material is reputable. Another issue to consider is that marketing studies found on websites sometimes promote the business interest of the publisher. For instance, studies published by the IAB have to be carefully scrutinized for methodological bias because the IAB is a trade organization that represents businesses that will benefit when Internet advertising grows. Ideally, you are looking for the highest quality information by experts in the field. When sources are cited and mentioned more often, studies or blogs are more likely to be credible.[3]

Scholarly Sources Google has a specialized search engine dedicated to scholarly articles called Google Scholar. Using Google's home page search function rather than Google Scholar will identify some scholarly articles, but will include many other kinds of results that make scholarly articles difficult to identify. If you go to Google Scholar, and type "online shopping," for instance, Google Scholar (**www.Scholar.Google.com**) will list published studies that address online shopping. Google Scholar counts how many times a study is referenced by another document on the web and lists that number in the search results; the result says "cited by" and lists the number of citations. The number of citation counts is one measure of the importance of the article to the field.

Some of the studies listed by Google Scholar will be available online from any location. You may have access to others only when you are at school or through a library gateway. Most colleges and universities pay fees for access to scholarly published papers. If you are on campus while you are accessing these sources, many journal publishers read the IP address of the computer you are using, and grant access based on your location. In particular, articles in JSTOR, which hosts many of the top marketing journals, may be accessible through any computer linked to your campus network. However, some journals require you to go through the library gateway to obtain access whether you are on or off campus.

Both popular and scholarly sources can be tracked using web-based bookmarking tools such as Delicious, Google Bookmarks, Xmarks, Bundlr, and Diigo that will help you organize your sources. Using these bookmarking tools, you can keep track of the links for research projects, take notes about each of the sites, and "tag" the links with your choice of search terms to make future retrieval of the source easy. Bookmarking tools also facilitate exchanges with a social network so they can be very helpful in sharing sources with multiple members of the research team.

Government Sources Detail, completeness, and consistency are major reasons for using U.S. government documents. In fact, U.S. Bureau of the Census reports are the statistical foundation for most of the information available on U.S. population and economic activities. You can find census reports and data at census.gov. Exhibit 3.5 lists some of the common sources of secondary data available from the U.S. government.

There are two notes of caution about census data and often other types of secondary data. First, census data are collected only every 10 years with periodic updates, so

---

Exhibit 3.5 Common Government Reports Used as Secondary Data Sources

U.S. Census Data

Census of Agriculture
Census of Construction
Census of Government
Census of Manufacturing
Census of Mineral Industries
Census of Retail Trade
Census of Service Industries
Census of Transportation
Census of Wholesale Trade
Census of Housing
Census of Population

U.S. Census Reports

Economic Indicators
County Business Patterns
American Fact Finder
Foreign Trade

Additional Government Reports

Economic Report of the President
Federal Reserve Bulletin
Statistics of Income
Survey of Current Business
Monthly Labor Review

---

researchers always need to consider the timeliness of census data. Second, census data include only a limited number of topics. As with other secondary data, predefined categories of variables such as age, income, and occupation may not always meet user requirements.

A final source of information available through the U.S. government is the Catalog of Government Publications (**http://catalog.gpo.gov/F**). This catalog indexes major market research reports for a variety of domestic and international industries, markets, and institutions. It also provides an index of publications available to researchers from July 1976 to the current month and year.

CONTINUING CASE STUDY THE SANTA FE GRILL MEXICAN RESTAURANT
USING SECONDARY DATA

The owners of the Santa Fe Grill believe secondary data may be useful in better understanding how to run a restaurant. Based on what you have learned in this chapter about secondary data, that should be true.

1. What kinds of secondary data are likely to be useful?

2. Conduct a search of secondary data sources for material that could be used by the Santa Fe Grill

owners to better understand the problems/opportunities facing them. Use Google, Yahoo!, Twitter, or other search tools to do so.

3. What key words would you use in the search?

4. Summarize what you found in your search.

North American Industry Classification System (NAICS) A system that codes numerical industrial listings designed to promote uniformity in data reporting procedures for the U.S. government.

North American Industry Classification System (NAICS) An initial step in any secondary data search is to use the numeric listings of the **North American Industry Classification System** codes. NAICS codes are designed to promote uniformity in data reporting by federal and state government sources and private business. The federal government assigns every industry an NAICS code. Businesses within each industry report all activities (sales, payrolls, taxation) according to their code. Currently, there are 99 two-digit industry codes representing everything from agricultural production of crops to environmental quality and housing.

Within each two-digit industry classification code is a four-digit industry group code representing specific industry groups. All businesses in the industry represented by a given four-digit code report detailed information about the business to various sources for publication. For example, as shown in Exhibit 3.6, NAICS code 12 is assigned to coal mining and NAICS code 1221 specifies bituminous coal and lignite, surface extraction. It is at the four-digit level where the researcher will concentrate most data searches. NAICS data are now accessible on the Internet at **www.census.gov/eos /www/naics/**.

Commercial Sources—Syndicated Data A major trend in marketing research is toward a greater dependency on syndicated data sources. The rationale for this is that companies can obtain substantial information from a variety of industries at a relatively low cost.

Exhibit 3.6	Sample List of North American Industry Classification System Codes

Numeric Listing

10—Metal Mining
1011 Iron Ores
1021 Copper Ores
1031 Lead & Zinc Ores
1041 Gold Ores
1044 Silver Ores
1061 Ferroalloy Ores except Vanadium
1081 Metal Mining Services
1094 Uranium, Radium & Vanadium Ores
1099 Metal Ores Nec*

12—Coal Mining
1221 Bituminous Coal & Lignite—Surface
1222 Bituminous Coal—Underground
1231 Anthracite Mining
1241 Coal Mining Services

13—Oil & Gas Extraction
1311 Crude Petroleum & Natural Gas
1321 Natural Gas Liquids
1381 Drilling Oil & Gas Wells
1382 Oil & Gas Exploration Services
1389 Oil & Gas Field Services Nec*

14—Nonmetallic Minerals except Fuels
1411 Dimension Stone
1422 Crushed & Broken Limestone
1423 Crushed & Broken Granite
1429 Crushed & Broken Stone Nec*
1442 Construction Sand & Gravel
1446 Industrial Sand

*Not elsewhere classified.

Source: *Ward Business Directory of U.S. Private and Public Companies*, 2007, Gale Cengage Learning.

Syndicated (or commercial) data Data that has been compiled according to some standardized procedure; provides customized data for companies, such as market share, ad effectiveness, and sales tracking.

Syndicated data, or commercial data, are market research data that are collected, packaged, and sold to many different firms. The information is in the form of tabulated reports prepared specifically for a client's research needs, often tailored to specific reporting divisions—examples might include sales of consumer product categories such as coffee, detergents, toilet tissue, carbonated beverages, and so on. Reports also may be organized by geographic region, sales territory, market segment, product class, or brand.

Suppliers traditionally have used two methods of data collection: *consumer panels* and *store audits*. A third method that has increased rapidly in recent years is obtained using *optical-scanner technology*. Scanner data are most often obtained at the point of purchase in supermarkets, drugstores, and other types of retail outlets.

Consumer panels Large samples of households that provide specific, detailed data on purchase behavior for an extended period of time.

Consumer panels consist of large samples of households that have agreed to provide detailed data for an extended period of time. Information provided by these panels typically consists of product purchase information or media habits, often on the consumer package goods industry. But information obtained from optical scanners is increasingly being used as well.

Panels typically are developed by marketing research firms and use a rigorous data collection approach. Respondents are required to record detailed behaviors at the time of occurrence on a highly structured questionnaire. The questionnaire contains a large number of questions related directly to actual product purchases or media exposure. Most often this is an ongoing procedure whereby respondents report data back to the company on a weekly or monthly basis. Panel data are then sold to a variety of clients after being tailored to the client's research needs.

A variety of benefits are associated with panel data. These include (1) lower cost than primary data collection methods; (2) rapid availability and timeliness; (3) accurate reporting of socially sensitive expenditures, for example, beer, liquor, cigarettes, generic brands; and (4) high level of specificity, for instance, actual products purchased or media habits, not merely intentions or propensities to purchase.

There are two types of panel-based data sources: those reflecting actual purchases of products and services and those reflecting media habits. The discussion below provides examples of both types.

A variety of companies offer panel-based purchasing data. NPD Group (**www.npd.com**) provides syndicated research for numerous industry sectors, including automotive, beauty, technology, entertainment, fashion, food, office supplies, software, sports, toys, and wireless. NPD's online consumer panel consists of more than 2 million registered adults and teens who have agreed to participate in their surveys. The consumer panel data can be combined with retail point-of-sale information to offer more complete information about markets.

Two of NPD's most commonly used data sources are the Consumer Report on Eating Share Trends (CREST) and National Eating Trends (NET). CREST tracks consumer purchases of restaurant and prepared meals and snacks in France, Germany, Japan, Spain, the United Kingdom, the United States, and Canada. NET provides continuous tracking of in-home food and beverage consumption patterns in the United States and Canada.

TSN Global offers a myriad of research services, including product tests, concept tests, and attitude, awareness, and brand-usage studies. The research firm has a network of online managed access panels that includes North America, Europe, and Asia Pacific. Consumers can sign up to participate in their online panels at Mysurvey.com. TSN Globals' panels offer not only speed and low cost, but also the ability to efficiently manage international studies.

Mintel has offices in locations around the world, including London, Chicago, Shanghai, Mumbai, Sao Paulo, and Tokyo. The firm tracks consumer spending across 34 countries. Mintel provides syndicated data for specific industries such as beauty, food and drink, and household and personal care. As well, the research firm studies everything about new products, as it collects and categorizes information about 33,000 new products every month by using local shoppers to obtain information directly from the field.[4]

The following list describes additional syndicated data companies and the consumer panels they maintain:

- J. D. Power and Associates maintains a consumer panel of car and light-truck owners to provide data on product quality, satisfaction, and vehicle dependability.
- GfK Roper Consulting offers subscription to their syndicated services. Their reports are available for the United States and Worldwide, providing information about demographics, lifestyles, values, attitudes, and buying behavior. Their panels collectively are representative of 90 percent of the world's GDP.[5]
- Creative and Response Research Services maintains a consumer panel called Youthbeat (www.crresearch.com) that provides monthly tracking of kids', tweens', and teens' opinions of music, media usage, gaming, shopping, cell phones, and awareness of causes. The research provides an "encyclopedic view of youth marketing that covers the world of children from the time they enter grade school through the time they leave high school."[6] Youthbeat also has a panel of parents as well.

Media panels Similar to consumer panels but the information focuses on media usage behavior.

Media panels and consumer panels are similar in procedure, composition, and design. They differ only in that media panels primarily measure media consumption habits as opposed to product or brand consumption. As with consumer panels, numerous media panels exist. The following are examples of the most commonly used syndicated media panels.

Nielsen Media Research is by far the most widely known and accepted source of media panel data. The flagship service of Nielsen is used to measure television audiences, but in recent years, "TV is no longer a distinct medium, but a form of information and entertainment that connects multiple platforms and reaches audiences at every possible touchpoint."[7]

Nielsen collects data on television viewing habits through a device, called a people meter, connected to a television set. The people meter continuously monitors and records when a television set is turned on, what channels are being viewed, how much time is spent on each channel, and who is watching. Nielsen also measures content downloading, listening, and viewing on screens other than the TV. Nielsen's data are used to calculate media efficiency measured as cost per thousand (CPM), that is, how much it costs to reach 1,000 viewers. CPM measures a program's ability to deliver the largest target audience at the lowest cost.

Nielsen Audio conducts ongoing data collection for media, including radio, television, cable, and out of home. They are perhaps best known for radio audience measurement. The research firm uses an electronic measurement device called the Portable People Meter (PPM) to estimate national and local radio audiences. The PPM is a portable, passive electronic measuring system about the size of a cell phone that tracks consumer exposure to media and entertainment. Survey participants carry the PPM throughout the day, and it tracks TV watching and radio listening. The data are used by media planners, advertising agencies, and advertisers.

MARKETING RESEARCH DASHBOARD TRIANGULATING SECONDARY DATA SOURCES

Estimating the market penetration of new technologies—from DVRs to iPhones to Twitter—is important for managers because it impacts business decisions, from promotions to pricing to new-product development. Managers need accurate measurements and data in order to improve their strategic and tactical planning. Getting accurate measurements, however, can be surprisingly difficult.

A case in point is the DVR, a device that uses a hard drive to record television shows. The DVR was introduced to the U.S. marketplace in 2000. A few months after introduction of the DVR, one published estimate concluded that the device had been adopted by 16 percent of all U.S. households. The astonishing growth led some marketers to proclaim the end of traditional advertising because consumers use DVRs to skip ads. Knowledge Metrics/SRI, a business specializing in

household technology, used multiple sources of information to check the estimate. Initially, their own survey research suggested a high adoption rate for the DVR as well. But some fact-checking brought their results into question. The research firm reviewed 10-K filings of the two major DVR firms. Those firms had only shipped a few hundred thousand units, which meant that less than 1 percent of TV households had adopted the DVR at that time.

Based on this information, Knowledge Metrics realized that they needed to improve their survey questions regarding DVR ownership. They learned that consumers experienced confusion when they were asked about the concept of a DVR. Using a revised and improved questionnaire, they learned in a subsequent study that the actual incidence of ownership was less than 0.5 percent of TV households, and not 16 percent.[8]

Store audits Formal examination and verification of how much of a particular product or brand has been sold at the retail level.

Store audits consist of formal examination and verification of how much of a particular product or brand has been sold at the retail level. Based on a collection of participating retailers (typically discount, supermarket, and drugstore retailers), audits are performed on product or brand movement in return for detailed activity reports and cash compensation to the retailer. The audits then operate as a secondary data source. Store audits provide two unique benefits: precision and timeliness. Many of the biases of consumer panels are not found in store audits. By design, store audits measure product and brand movement directly at the point of sale (usually at the retail level).

Key variables measured in a store audit include beginning and ending inventory levels, sales receipts, price levels, price inducements, local advertising, and point-of-purchase (POP) displays. Collectively, these data allow users of store audit services to generate information on the following factors:

- Product/brand sales in relation to competition.
- Effectiveness of shelf space and POP displays.
- Sales at various price points and levels.
- Effectiveness of in-store promotions and point-of-sale coupons.
- Direct sales by store type, product location, territory, and region.

Synthesizing Secondary Research for the Literature Review

Divergent perspectives and findings need to be included in your literature review. It is likely that the findings of some studies will be inconsistent with each other. These differences may include estimates of descriptive data, for example, the percentage of people who buy from catalog marketers, the amount of dollars spent on advertising, or online retail sales numbers. Reports may also disagree as to the nature of theoretical relationships between variables.

Researchers often need to dig into the details of the methodology that is used to define variables and collect data. For example, differences in estimates of online retail spending are caused by several factors. Three major causes of discrepancies in online retail estimates are (1) the inclusion (or not) of travel spending, which is a major category of online spending; (2) methodological differences, for instance, some reports make estimates based on surveying retailers while others survey customers; and (3) there is always some degree of sampling error. It is not enough to say that reports differ in their findings. You want to make intelligent judgments about the sources that may be causing the differences.

◼ Developing a Conceptual Model

In addition to providing background for your research problem, literature reviews can also help conceptualize a model that summarizes the relationships you hope to predict. If you are performing purely exploratory research, you will not need to develop a model before conducting your research. In Chapter 2, we learned that once you have turned your research objectives into research questions, the information needs can be listed and the data collection instrument can be designed. Some of your information needs might involve trying to understand relationships between variables. For example, you might be interested in learning whether or not variables such as respondents' ratings of quality of the product, customer service, and brand image will predict overall satisfaction with the product. If one or more of your research questions require you to investigate relationships between constructs, then you need to *conceptualize* these relationships. The conceptualization process is aided by developing a picture of your model that shows the predicted causal relationship between variables.

Variables, Constructs, and Relationships

Variable An observable item that is used as a measure on a questionnaire.

Construct An unobservable concept that is measured by a group of related variables.

To conceptualize and test a model, you must have three elements: variables, constructs, and relationships. A **variable** is an observable item that is used as a measure on a questionnaire. Variables have concrete properties and are measured directly. Examples of variables include gender, marital status, company name, number of employees, how frequently a particular brand is purchased, and so on. In contrast, a **construct** is an unobservable, abstract concept that is measured indirectly by a group of related variables.

Some examples of commonly measured constructs in marketing include service quality, value, customer satisfaction, and brand attitude. Constructs that represent characteristics of respondents may also be measured, for example, innovativeness, opinion leadership, and deal proneness. In Exhibit 3.7, we show a group of items identified in a literature review that can be used to measure the construct "market maven," defined as an individual who has a lot of information about products and who actively shares that information. Researchers often use the words "variable" and "construct" interchangeably, but constructs are always measured by one or more indicator variables.

Relationships Associations between two or more variables.

Independent variable The variable or construct that predicts or explains the outcome variable of interest.

Relationships are associations between two or more variables. When modeling causal relationships, variables or constructs in relationships can be either independent or dependent variables. An **independent variable** is the variable or construct that predicts or explains the outcome variable of interest. A **dependent variable** is the variable or construct researchers are seeking to explain. For example, if technology optimism and household income predict new technology adoption, then technology optimism and household income are independent variables, and product adoption is the dependent variable.

Dependent variable The variable or construct researchers are seeking to explain.

A literature review will help you identify, define, and measure constructs. Nevertheless, after conducting a literature review and consulting secondary research, an analyst may believe there is not enough information to design a full-scale study. There may be several sources of uncertainty: the definition of important constructs; the identification of variables

Exhibit 3.7 · Measuring the Marketing Maven Construct

1. I like introducing new brands and products to my friends.
2. I like helping people by providing them with information about many kinds of products.
3. People ask me for information about products, places to shop, or sales.
4. If someone asked where to get the best buy on several types of products, I could tell him or her where to shop.
5. My friends think of me as a good source of information when it comes to new products or sales.
6. Think about a person who has information about a variety of products and likes to share this information with others. This person knows about new products, sales, stores, and so on, but does not necessarily feel he or she is an expert on one particular product. How well would you say that this description fits you?

Source: Lawrence F. Feick and Linda L. Price, "The Marketing Maven: A Diffuser of Marketplace Information," *Journal of Marketing* 51 (1987), pp. 83–97.

or items that will measure each construct; and the identification of constructs that may have an important role in affecting an outcome or dependent variable of interest.

For example, an early study of online retailing had as its objective the identification and modeling of constructs that would predict online customer satisfaction and repurchase behavior. A literature review revealed there were existing studies and measures of customer satisfaction and quality in services and in bricks-and-mortar retailing settings. While these published studies are useful in conceptualizing satisfaction with online retailing, researchers decided that the online retailing environment likely had unique aspects that might affect consumer ratings of satisfaction. Thus, researchers used qualitative methods (Chapter 4) and pilot-testing before designing a full-scale study.

Developing Hypotheses and Drawing Conceptual Models

Formulating Hypotheses Hypotheses provide the basis for the relationships between constructs pictured in conceptual models. Many students initially find hypothesis development challenging. However, coming up with hypotheses is often relatively straightforward. There are two types of hypotheses: descriptive and causal. Descriptive hypotheses address possible answers to specific business problems. For example, suppose our research question is, "Why does this retail store attract fewer customers between the ages of 18 and 30 than we anticipated?" **Descriptive hypotheses** are merely answers to this specific applied research problem. Thus, possible hypotheses might be "younger customers believe our prices are too high," "we have not effectively advertised to the younger segment," or "the interior of the store is not attractive to younger consumers." Developing descriptive hypotheses involves three steps:

Descriptive hypotheses
Possible answers to a specific applied research problem.

1. Reviewing the research problem or opportunity (e.g., our research opportunity might be that we are interested in marketing our product to a new segment)
2. Writing down the questions that flow from the research problem or opportunity (e.g., "would a new segment be interested in our product, and if so how could we approach this segment?")

3. Brainstorming possible answers to the research questions (the potential target segment would be interested in this product if we made some modifications to the product and sold the product in outlets where the segment shops)

Causal hypotheses are theoretical statements about relationships between variables. The theoretical statements are based on previous research findings, management experience, or exploratory research. For example, a business might be interested in predicting the factors that lead to increased sales. Independent variables that may lead to sales include advertising spending and price. These two hypotheses can formally be stated as follows:

> Hypothesis 1: Higher spending on advertising leads to higher sales.
> Hypothesis 2: Higher prices lead to lower sales.

Causal hypotheses help businesses understand how they can make changes that, for example, improve awareness of new products, service quality, customer satisfaction, loyalty, and repurchase. For example, if researchers want to predict who will adopt a new technological innovation, there is a great deal of existing research and theory on this topic. The research suggests, for example, that more educated, higher income individuals who are open to learning are more likely to adopt new technologies, while technology discomfort leads to lower likelihood of adoption. The hypotheses could be summarized as follows:

- Individuals with more education are more likely to adopt a new technological innovation.
- Individuals who are more open to learning are more likely to adopt a new technological innovation.
- Individuals who have more income are more likely to adopt a new technological innovation.
- Individuals who have higher technology discomfort are less likely to adopt a new technological innovation.

The first three hypotheses suggest positive relationships. A **positive relationship** between two variables is when the two variables increase or decrease together. But negative relationships can be hypothesized as well. **Negative relationships** suggest that as one variable increases, the other one decreases. For example, the last hypothesis suggests that individuals exhibiting higher technology discomfort are less likely to adopt a new technological innovation.

The literature review, secondary data, and exploratory research may all provide information that is useful in developing both descriptive and causal hypotheses. Experience with a research context can help decision makers and researchers develop hypotheses as well. Both clients and research firms may have a great deal of experience over time with a particular research context that is useful in conceptualizing hypotheses for future studies. For example, restaurant owners know a lot about their customers as do managers of retail clothing stores. They learn this over time by observing customers' behavior and listening to the questions that they ask.

Good hypotheses have several characteristics. First, hypotheses follow from research questions. For example, if a researcher asks, "what leads customers to perceive that a service is high quality," the hypotheses are educated guesses about the answers to that question. For example, we might hypothesize that service provider competence and empathy lead to higher perceptions of service quality. A second important characteristic of a good hypothesis is that it is written clearly and simply. If the hypothesis is a causal hypothesis, it must have both an independent and dependent variable in the statement. In our example about predictors of service quality, empathy

Causal hypotheses Theoretical statements about relationships between variables.

Positive relationship An association between two variables in which they increase or decrease together.

Negative relationship An association between two variables in which one increases while the other decreases.

and competence are independent variables while service quality is the dependent variable. Last, hypotheses must be testable. Constructs that appear in hypotheses must be defined and measured. For example, to test the four hypotheses concerning new technology adoption, researchers would have to define and measure income, education, openness to learning, technology discomfort, and new technology adoption. For example, "openness to learning" can be defined as "open awareness to new experiences," while technology discomfort is "the degree to which a person reports being uneasy with the use and understanding of technology."

To more effectively communicate relationships and variables, researchers follow a process called **conceptualization.** Conceptualization involves (1) identifying the variables for your research; (2) specifying hypotheses and relationships; and (3) preparing a diagram (conceptual model) that visually represents the relationships you will study. The end result of conceptualization is a visual display of the hypothesized relationships using a box and arrows diagram. This diagram is called a *conceptual model.* Preparing a conceptual model early in the research process helps to develop and organize their thinking. As well, conceptual models help the research team to efficiently share and discuss their thoughts about possible causal relationships with the entire research team. The model suggested by the four hypotheses we developed about new technology adoption is shown in Exhibit 3.8. Constructs in all conceptual models are represented in a sequence based on theory, logic, and experience with the business setting. The sequence goes from left to right with the independent (predictive) variables on the left and the dependent (predicted) variables on the right of the diagram. Constructs on the left are thus modeled and preceding and predicting constructs on the right. Single-headed arrows indicate causal relationships between variables.

If a literature review and available secondary data are insufficient to suggest strong candidates for explaining dependent variables of interest, then exploratory research will be necessary (see Chapter 4). Exploratory investigations enable analysts to sit down with respondents and find out what they are thinking and incorporate what they learn into further research.

Conceptualization

Development of a model that shows variables and hypothesized or proposed relationships between variables.

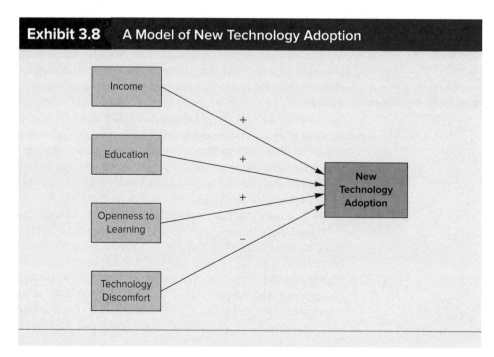

Exhibit 3.8 **A Model of New Technology Adoption**

The owners have concluded that they need to know more about their customers and target market. To obtain a better understanding of each of these issues, they logged on to the Yahoo.com and Google.com search engines. They also spent some time examining trade literature. From this review of the literature, some "Best Practices" guidelines were found on how restaurants should be run. Below is a summary of what was found:

- If you do not have enough customers, first examine the quality of your food, the items on your menu, and the service.

- Examine and compare your lunch and dinner customers and menu for differences.

- Your waitstaff should be consistent with the image of your restaurant. How your employees act and behave is very important. They must be well groomed, knowledgeable, polite, and speak clearly and confidently.

- Menu items should represent a good value for the money.

- Service should be efficient, timely, polished, and cordial.

- The cleanliness and appearance of your restaurant strongly influence the success of your business.

- Follow the marketing premise of "underpromise and overdeliver!"

- Empower your employees to make decisions to keep your customers happy. Train your employees on what to do to resolve customer complaints instead of coming to the manager.

- Create a pleasant dining atmosphere, including furniture and fixtures, decorations, lighting, music, and temperature.

- Learn more about your female customers. For family outings and special occasions, women make the decision on where to dine about 75 percent of the time.

With this information, the owners next need to specify the research questions and hypotheses to be examined.

1. What research questions should be examined?

2. What hypotheses should be tested?

3. Should the literature search be expanded? If yes, how?

The research then takes place in stages. In the first stage, researchers use exploratory research to identify variables, constructs, and relationships that can then be followed up in another study. A conceptual model becomes a theoretical model when the literature review or exploratory research is sufficient to support the model's pictured relationships between variables.

When you prepare your literature review, a section of that review will be dedicated to presenting your model, also called a conceptual framework. This section of your literature review integrates the information previously reviewed, and uses the review to support the development of the relationships pictured in the model. In this section, researchers clearly explain why they expect these relationships to exist, citing theory, business practice, or some other credible source. Based on the framework they have developed, researchers will next design research and collect empirical data that will address the hypotheses sketched in their theoretical model.

Hypothesis Testing

Hypothesis An empirically testable though yet unproven statement developed in order to explain phenomena.

Once researchers have developed hypotheses, they can be tested. As we have already seen, a **hypothesis** suggests relationships between variables. Suppose we hypothesize that men and women drink different amounts of coffee during the day during finals. The independent variable in this case is gender, while the dependent variable is number of cups of coffee. We collect data and find that the average number of cups of coffee consumed by female students per day during finals is 6.1, and the average number of cups of coffee consumed by males is 4.7. Is this finding meaningful? The answer appears to be straightforward (after all, 6.1 is larger than 4.7), but sampling error could have distorted the results enough so that we conclude there are no real differences between men's and women's coffee consumption.

Intuitively, if the difference between two means is large, one would be more confident that there is, in fact, a true difference between the sample means of the two groups. But another important component to consider is the size of the sample used to calculate the means because the size of the sample and the variance in the sample affect sample error. To take sample error into account, we must place an interval around our estimate of the mean. Once we do this, the two means may not be different enough to conclude that men and women consume different amounts of coffee during finals.

Null hypothesis A statistical hypothesis that is tested for possible rejection under the assumption that it is true.

In hypothesis development, the **null hypothesis** states that there is no relationship between the variables. In this case, the null hypothesis would be that there is no difference between male and female coffee consumption. The null hypothesis is the one that is always tested by statisticians and market researchers. Another hypothesis, called the **alternative hypothesis,** states that there is a relationship between two variables. If the null hypothesis is accepted, we conclude that the variables are not related. If the null hypothesis is rejected, we find support for the alternative hypothesis, that the two variables are related.

Alternative hypothesis The hypothesis contrary to the null hypothesis, it usually suggests that two variables are related.

A null hypothesis refers to a population parameter, not a sample statistic. The **parameter** is the actual value of a variable, which can only be known by collecting data from every member of the relevant population (in this case, all male and female college students). The **sample statistic** is an estimate of the population parameter. The data will show that either the two variables are related (reject the null hypothesis) or that once sampling error is considered, there is not a large enough relationship to conclude the variables are related. In the latter case, the researcher would not be able to detect a statistically significant difference between the two groups of coffee drinkers. It is important to note that failure to reject the null hypothesis does not necessarily mean the null hypothesis is true. This is because data from another sample of the same population could produce different results.

Parameter The true value of a variable.

Sample statistic The value of a variable that is estimated from a sample.

In marketing research, the null hypothesis is developed so that its rejection leads to an acceptance of the alternative hypothesis. Usually, the null hypothesis is notated as H0 and the alternative hypothesis is notated as H1. If the null hypothesis (H0) is rejected, then the alternative hypothesis (H1) is accepted. The alternative hypothesis always bears the burden of proof.

MARKETING RESEARCH IN ACTION
The Santa Fe Grill Mexican Restaurant

The owners of the Santa Fe Grill Mexican Restaurant were not happy with the slow growth rate of the restaurant's operations and realized they needed to obtain a better understanding of three important concepts: customer satisfaction, restaurant store image, and customer loyalty. Using, in part, their practical business knowledge and what they learned as business students at the University of Nebraska, Lincoln, they developed several key questions:

1. What makes up customer satisfaction?
2. How are restaurant images created?
3. How is customer loyalty achieved?
4. What are the interrelationships between customer satisfaction, store images, and customer loyalty?

Not really knowing where to begin, they contacted one of their past professors, who taught marketing research at the university, to gain some guidance. Their professor suggested they begin with a literature review of both scholarly and popular press research sources. Using their Internet search skills, they went to Lexus-Nexus, Google, and Google Scholar (**www.Scholar .Google.com**) and found a wealth of past research and popular press articles on customer satisfaction, store image, and customer loyalty.

After reviewing a number of articles, the owners understood that customer satisfaction relates to a restaurant's ability to meet or exceed its customers' dining expectations about a variety of important restaurant attributes such as food quality, acceptable service, competitive prices, restaurant atmosphere, and friendly/courteous staff. Regarding restaurant store image, they learned that image is really an overall impression expressed in either a positive or negative judgment about the restaurant's operations. In addition, customer loyalty reflects customers' willingness to "recommend a restaurant to their friends, family, and/or neighbors," as well as provide positive word of mouth.

Hands-On Exercise

1. Based on your understanding of the material presented in Chapter 3 and the above key research questions, should the owners of the Santa Fe Grill Mexican restaurant go back and restate their questions? If "no," why not? If "yes," why? Suggest how the research questions could be restated.
2. Regarding the owners' desire to understand the interrelationships between customer satisfaction, restaurant store image, and customer loyalty, develop a set of hypotheses that might be used to investigate these interrelationships.

■ Summary

Understand the nature and role of secondary data.

The task of a marketing researcher is to solve the problem in the shortest time, at the least cost, with the highest level of accuracy. Therefore, before any marketing research project is conducted, the researcher must seek out existing information that may facilitate a decision or outcome for a company. Existing data are commonly called secondary data. If secondary data are to be used to assist the decision-making process or problem-solving ability of the manager, they need to be evaluated on six fundamental principles: (1) purpose—how relevant are the data to achieving the specific research objectives at hand?; (2) accuracy of information; (3) consistency—do multiple sources of the data exist?; (4) credibility—how were the data obtained? what is the source of the data?; (5) methodology—will the methods used to collect the data produce accurate and reliable data?; and (6) biases—was the data-reporting procedure tainted by some hidden agenda or underlying motivation to advance some public or private concern?

Describe how to conduct a literature review.

A literature review is a comprehensive examination of available information that is related to your research topic. When conducting a literature review, researchers locate information relevant to the research problems and issues at hand. Literature reviews have the following objectives: provide background information for the current study; clarify thinking about the research problem and questions you are studying; reveal whether information already exists that addresses the issue of interest; help to define important constructs of interest to the study; and suggest sampling and other methodological approaches that have been successful in studying similar topics.

Identify sources of internal and external secondary data.

Internal secondary data are obtained within the company. Company internal accounting and financial information is a major source. These typically consist of sales invoices, accounts receivable reports, and quarterly sales reports. Other forms of internal data include past marketing research studies, customer credit applications, warranty cards, and employee exit interviews.

External secondary data are obtained outside the company. Because of the volume of external data available, researchers need a data search plan to locate and extract the right data. A simple guideline to follow is: define goals the secondary data need to achieve; specify objectives behind the secondary search process; define specific characteristics of data that are to be extracted; document all activities necessary to find, locate, and extract the data sources; focus on reliable sources of data; and tabulate all the data extracted. The most common sources of external secondary data are popular, scholarly, government, and commercial.

Discuss conceptualization and its role in model development.

Literature reviews can also help you conceptualize a model that summarizes the relationships you hope to predict. If you are performing purely exploratory research, you will not need to develop a model before conducting your research. Once you have turned your research objectives into research questions, the information needs can be listed and the data collection instrument can be designed. However, if one or more of your research questions require you to investigate relationships between variables, then you need to conceptualize these relationships. The conceptualization process is aided by developing a picture of your model that shows the predicted causal relationships between variables. To conceptualize and test a model, you must have three elements: variables, constructs, and relationships.

Understand hypotheses and independent and dependent variables.

A variable is an observable item that is used as a measure on a questionnaire. A construct is an unobservable concept that is measured by a group of related variables. Some examples of commonly used constructs in marketing research include service quality, value, customer satisfaction, and brand attitude. Constructs that represent characteristics of respondents may also be measured, for example, innovativeness, opinion leadership, and deal proneness. There are two kinds of hypotheses: descriptive and causal. Descriptive hypotheses are possible answers to specific, applied research problems while causal hypotheses are theoretical statements about relationships between variables. Relationships are associations between two or more variables. The relationships are often illustrated visually by drawing conceptual models. When modeling relationships, variables or constructs depicted in relationships can be either independent or dependent variables. An independent variable is the variable or construct that predicts or explains the outcome variable of interest. A dependent variable is the variable or construct researchers are seeking to explain; that is, the outcome. For example, if technology optimism and household income predict Internet adoption by seniors, then technology optimism and household income are independent variables, and Internet adoption is the dependent variable.

Key Terms and Concepts

Alternative hypothesis   68

Causal hypotheses   65

Conceptualization   66

Construct   63

Consumer panels   60

Dependent variable   63

Descriptive hypothesis   64

External secondary data   50

Hypothesis   67

Independent variable   63

Internal secondary data   50

Literature review   51

Media panels   61

Negative relationship   65

North American Industry Classification System (NAICS)   59

Null hypothesis   68

Parameter   68

Positive relationship   65

Relationships   63

Sample statistic   68

Secondary data   50

Store audits   62

Syndicated (or commercial) data   60

Variable   63

Review Questions

1. What characteristic separates secondary data from primary data? What are three sources of secondary data?
2. Explain why a company should use all potential sources of secondary data before initiating primary data collection procedures.
3. List the six fundamental principles used to assess the validity of secondary data.
4. What are the various reasons to conduct a literature review?
5. What should you look for in assessing whether or not an Internet resource is credible?
6. A researcher develops hypotheses that suggest consumers like ads better when they (1) are truthful; (2) creative; and (3) present relevant information. Picture the conceptual model that would show these relationships. Which variables are the independent and which the dependent variables?
7. What are relationships? What is a positive relationship? What is a negative relationship? Give an example of a positive and a negative relationship.
8. What is the difference between a parameter and a sample statistic?

Discussion Questions

1. It is possible to design a study, collect and analyze data, and write a report without conducting a literature review? What are the dangers and drawbacks of conducting your research without doing a literature review? In your judgment, do the drawbacks outweigh the advantages? Why or why not?
2. **EXPERIENCE MARKETING RESEARCH.** Visit several of the marketing blogs listed in Exhibit 3.4. Do these blogs have any information that might be relevant to practitioners who are conducting research in the topic areas that the blogs address? Why or why not?
3. **EXPERIENCE MARKETING RESEARCH.** Using Google Scholar, identify 10 or so references that are relevant to the topic of service quality. Identify four or five that you think would be helpful to designing a survey to measure the service quality received at a restaurant. List the title of each study, and explain why you think they are relevant to the study you are designing.

4. **EXPERIENCE MARKETING RESEARCH.** Go online and find the home page for your particular state. For example, **www.mississippi.com** would get you to the home page for the State of Mississippi. Once there, seek out the category that gives you information on county and local statistics. Select the county where you reside and obtain the vital demographic and socioeconomic data available. Provide a demographic profile of the residents in your community.

5. **EXPERIENCE MARKETING RESEARCH.** Go to the home page of the U.S. census, **www.census.gov.** Select the category "Economic Indicators" and browse the data provided. What did you learn from browsing this data?

6. You are thinking about opening a new quick service restaurant on your campus after you graduate. What information about your potential consumers would you try to find from secondary research to help you understand your target market?

7. You are planning to open a coffee shop in one of two areas in your local community. Conduct a secondary data search on key variables that would allow you to make a logical decision on which area is best suited for your proposed coffee shop.

8. Based on your experiences in college, draw and label a conceptual model that shows the factors that lead to your satisfaction (or dissatisfaction) with a course.

Exploratory and Observational Research Designs and Data Collection Approaches

1. Identify the major differences between qualitative and quantitative research.
2. Understand in-depth interviewing and focus groups as questioning techniques.
3. Define focus groups and explain how to conduct them.
4. Discuss purposed communities and private communities.
5. Explain other qualitative data collection methods such as ethnography, case studies, netnography, projective techniques, and the ZMET.
6. Discuss observation methods and explain how they are used to collect primary data.
7. Discuss the growing field of social media monitoring.

Customer Territoriality in "Third Places"

Territorial behavior involves personalization or marking of a place or object so as to communicate individual or group ownership. Scholars have long studied and understood territoriality at work and at home. But in recent decades, businesses such as Starbucks and Panera Bread have provided space for customers to social-ize and work, sometimes lingering long past when food and beverages have been consumed. These spaces have been called "third places," a place in addition to work and home where individuals may spend extended time working or studying. An ethnographic study of Starbucks noted territorial behavior at the café, point-ing out that almost all patrons keep to themselves, rarely conversing with other customers that they do not know, creating a "virtual gated community" around themselves when they spend time at Starbucks.

A team of researchers followed up this study by trying to understand territo-rial behaviors in a more detailed fashion. Their multimethod qualitative research used observation (including participant observation), photographs, and in-depth interviews to develop a more complete picture of how and why customers engage in territoriality, and how other customers and employees respond. Observation in context helped the researchers to both learn and document how customers behaved in "third places." The authors observed territorial behaviors for over 100 hours and described them in field notes. With customers' permission, researchers took pictures of territorial behavior.

The researchers then performed 36 in-depth interviews with customers, using some of the pictures they took during the observational phase of their research. The purpose of the in-depth interviews was to glean insights into cus-tomer motivations for territorial behavior. Finally, the researchers used a tech-nique they called "narrative inquiry" to get participants to tell stories about their experiences with territoriality in a way that is less threatening than answering direct questions. Informants were asked to write stories about pictures that showed territorial behaviors such as marking space or territorial intrusion.

The next step was to code and categorize the textual and pictorial data for "themes." The researchers learned that customers often strategically spread items to mark places and claim territory. Purchase or even mere use of an item with the retail establishment's logo is often sufficient to give customers territorial "rights," which discourages other customers to sit, consume, and linger. Some consumers may see the café as an extension of home and thus engage in behavior that strains norms for behavior in public places, for example, washing sand from the beach out of their hair in the bathroom sink or changing their clothes at the café. Employees are often faced with mediating territorial disputes between customers.

There are implications for cafés that are positioned as third places. Territorial behavior can both promote and inhibit the approach behavior of customers. Customers of third space businesses cocreate their experiences, but in doing so, they affect the experiences of other customers. These businesses need to take positions on territorial behaviors, making rules that work for most customers, and designing space to accommodate customers wherever possible. As well, some cafés may want to create a "fourth space" for customer groups looking primarily for a semistructured workplace.

Source: Merlyn A. Griffiths and Mary C. Gilly (2012), "Dibs! Customer Territorial Behaviors," *Journal of Services Research*, 15(2), p. 131–149; Bryant Simon, *Everything but the Coffee* (Berkeley: University of California Press, 2009); Irwin Altman, *The Environment and Social Behavior: Privacy, Personal Space, Territory, Crowding* (Monterey, CA: Wadsworth, 1975).

Value of Qualitative Research

Management quite often is faced with problem situations where important questions cannot be adequately addressed or resolved with secondary information. Meaningful insights can be gained only through the collection of primary data. Recall that primary data are new data gathered specifically for a current research challenge. They are typically collected using a set of systematic procedures in which researchers question or observe individuals and record their findings. The method may involve qualitative or quantitative research or both (we will study the difference in this chapter). As the journey through Phase II of the research process (Select the Appropriate Research Design) continues, attention may move from gathering secondary data to collecting primary data. This chapter begins a series of chapters that discuss research designs used for collecting primary data. As noted in earlier chapters, research objectives and information requirements are the keys to determining the appropriate type of research design for collecting data. For example, qualitative research often is used in exploratory research designs when the research objectives are to gather background information and clarify the research problems and to create hypotheses or establish research priorities. Quantitative research may then be used to follow up and quantify the qualitative findings.

Qualitative research results may be sufficient for decision making in certain situations. For example, if the research is designed to assess customer responses to different advertising approaches while the ads are still in the storyboard phase of development, qualitative research is effective. Qualitative research may also be sufficient when feedback in focus groups or in-depth interviews (IDI) is consistent, such as overwhelmingly favorable (or unfavorable) reactions toward a new product concept.[1] Finally, some topics are more appropriately studied using qualitative research. This is particularly true for complex consumer behaviors that may be affected by factors that are not easily reducible to numbers, such as consumer choices and experiences involving cultural, family, and psychological influences that are difficult to tap using quantitative methods.

Occasionally, qualitative research is conducted as a follow-up to quantitative research. This happens when quantitative findings are contradictory or ambiguous and do not fully answer research questions. This chapter begins with an overview of the three major types of research designs. We then introduce several qualitative research methods used in exploratory research designs. The chapter ends with a discussion of observation, which can be collected and analyzed qualitatively or quantitatively, and how it is used by marketing researchers.

■■ Overview of Research Designs

Recall that the three major types of research designs are exploratory, descriptive, and causal. Each type of design has a different objective. The objective of exploratory research is to discover ideas and insights to better understand the problem. If Apple were to experience an unexpected drop in sales of its iPhone, they might conduct exploratory research with a small sample of current and previous customers, or mine conversations in social media sites and blogs on the Internet to identify some possible explanations. This would help Apple to better define the actual problem.

The objective of descriptive research is to collect information that provides answers to research questions. For example, Coca-Cola would use descriptive research to find out the age and gender of individuals who buy different brands of soft drinks, how frequently they consume them and in which situations, what their favorite brand of soft drink is and reasons why, and so forth. This type of research enables companies to identify trends, to test hypotheses about relationships between variables, and ultimately to identify ways to solve previously identified marketing problems. It also is used to verify the findings of exploratory research studies based on secondary research or focus groups.

The objective of causal research is to test cause-and-effect relationships between specifically defined marketing variables. To do this, the researcher must be able to explicitly define the research question and variables. Examples of causal research projects would be to test the following hypotheses: "Introducing a new energy drink will not reduce the sale of current brands of Coca-Cola soft drinks." "Use of humorous ads for Apple Macs versus PCs will improve the image of Apple products in general." "A 10 percent increase in the price of Nike shoes will have no significant effect on sales."

Depending on the research objective, marketing researchers use all three types of research designs. In this chapter, we focus on exploratory designs. In the following chapters, we discuss descriptive and causal designs in more detail.

■■ Overview of Qualitative and Quantitative Research Methods

There are differences in qualitative and quantitative approaches, but all researchers interpret data and tell stories about the research topics they study.[2] Prior to discussing qualitative techniques used in exploratory research, we give an overview of some of the differences between qualitative and quantitative research methods. The factors listed in Exhibit 4.1 summarize the major differences. Study Exhibit 4.1 carefully.

Quantitative Research Methods

Quantitative research uses formal questions and predetermined response options in questionnaires administered to large numbers of respondents. For example, think of J. D. Power and Associates conducting a nationwide mail survey on customer satisfaction among new car purchasers or American Express doing a nationwide survey on travel behaviors with telephone interviews. With quantitative methods, the research problems

Quantitative research
Research that places heavy emphasis on using formal standard questions and predetermined response options in questionnaires or surveys administered to large numbers of respondents.

Exhibit 4.1	Major Differences between Qualitative and Quantitative Research Methods	
Factor	**Qualitative Methods**	**Quantitative Methods**
Goals/objectives	Discovery/identification of new ideas, thoughts, feelings; preliminary understanding of relationships; understanding of hidden psychological and social processes	Validation of facts, estimates, relationships
Type of research Type of questions Time of execution	Exploratory Open-ended, unstructured, probing Relatively short time frame	Descriptive and causal Mostly structured Typically significantly longer time frame
Representativeness	Small samples, only the sampled individuals	Large samples, with proper sampling can represent population
Type of analysis	Content analysis, interpretative	Statistical, descriptive, causal predictions
Researcher skills	Interpersonal communications, observation, interpretation of text or visual data	Statistical analysis, interpretation of numbers
Generalizability	May be limited	Generally very good, can infer facts and relationships

are specific and well defined, and the decision maker and researcher have agreed on the precise information needs.

Quantitative research methods are most often used with descriptive and causal research designs but are occasionally associated with exploratory designs. For example, a researcher may pilot test items on a questionnaire to see how well they measure a construct before including them in a larger study. Quantitative analysis techniques may be applied to qualitative data (e.g., textual, image, or video). These projects may be exploratory as they seek to detect and measure early problems or successes with products, services, or marketing communication efforts for example.

The main goals of quantitative research are to obtain information to (1) make accurate predictions about relationships between market factors and behaviors, (2) gain meaningful insights into those relationships, (3) validate relationships, and (4) test hypotheses. Quantitative researchers are well trained in construct development, scale measurement, questionnaire design, sampling, and statistical data analysis. Increasingly, marketing researchers are learning to turn qualitative conversational data on the Internet into quantitative analytical measures. We address this special category of quantitative techniques under observation later in this chapter. Finally, quantitative researchers must be able to translate numerical data into meaningful narrative information, ultimately telling a compelling story that is supported by data. Finally, quantitative methods are often statistically projectible to the target population of interest.

Qualitative Research Methods

Qualitative data consists of text, image, audio or video data. The data may be naturally occurring (as on Internet blog and product review sites), or be collected from answers to open-ended questions from researchers. Qualitative data may be analyzed qualitatively or quantitatively, but in this section we focus on qualitative analysis. While qualitative research data collection and analysis can be careful and rigorous, most practitioners regard qualitative research as being less reliable than quantitative research. However, **qualitative research** may probe more deeply. Qualitative researchers seek to understand research participants rather than to fit their answers into predetermined categories with little room for qualifying or explaining their choices. Thus, qualitative research often uncovers unanticipated findings and reactions. Therefore, one common objective of qualitative research is to gain preliminary insights into research problems. These preliminary insights are sometimes followed up with quantitative research to verify the qualitative findings.

A second use of qualitative research is to probe more deeply into areas that quantitative research may be too superficial to access, such as subconscious consumer motivations.[3] Qualitative research enables researchers and clients to get closer to their customers and potential customers than does quantitative research. For example, video and textual verbatims enable participants to speak and be heard in their own words in the researcher's report.

Qualitative researchers usually collect detailed data from relatively small samples by asking questions or observing behavior. Researchers trained in interpersonal communications and interpretive skills use open-ended questions and other materials to facilitate in-depth probing of participants' thoughts. Some qualitative research involves analysis of "found" data, or existing text. For example, qualitative researchers who want to better understand teen consumer culture might analyze a sample of social media entries posted by teens. In most cases, qualitative data is collected in relatively short time periods. Data analysis typically involves content analysis and interpretation. To increase the reliability and trustworthiness of the interpretation, researchers follow consistent approaches that are extensively documented.

The semistructured format of the questions and the small sample sizes limit the researcher's ability to generalize qualitative data to the population. Nevertheless, qualitative data have important uses in identifying and understanding business problems. For example, qualitative data can be invaluable in providing researchers with initial ideas about specific problems or opportunities, theories and relationships, variables, or the design of scale measurements. Finally, qualitative research can be superior for studying topics that involve complex psychological motivations not easily reduced to survey formats and quantitative analyses.

Qualitative research methods have several advantages. Exhibit 4.2 summarizes the major advantages and disadvantages of qualitative research. An advantage of qualitative research, particularly for focus groups and IDIs, is that it can be completed relatively quickly. Due in part to the use of small samples, researchers can complete investigations in a shorter period of time and at a significantly lower cost than is true with quantitative methods. Another advantage is the richness of the data. The unstructured approach of qualitative techniques enables researchers to collect in-depth data about respondents' attitudes, beliefs, emotions, and perceptions, all of which may strongly influence their behaviors as consumers.

The richness of qualitative data can often supplement the facts gathered through other primary data collection techniques. Qualitative techniques enable decision makers to gain firsthand experiences with customers and can provide revealing information that is contextualized. For example, an ethnographic study of Thanksgiving traditions conducted in consumers' homes during their celebrations discovered that the term "homemade" is often applied to dishes that are not made from scratch, but instead use at least some premade, branded ingredients.[4]

Qualitative research The collection of data in the form of text or images using open-ended questions, observation, or "found" data.

Exhibit 4.2	Advantages and Disadvantages of Qualitative Research

Advantages of Qualitative Research	Disadvantages of Qualitative Research
Except for ethnography, data can be collected relatively quickly or may already exist as naturally occurring conversations on the Internet	Lack of generalizability
Richness of the data	Difficulty in estimating the magnitude of phenomena being investigated
Accuracy of recording marketplace behaviors (validity)	Low reliability
Preliminary insights into building models and scale measurements	Difficulty finding well-trained investigators, interviewers, and observers
Insights from qualitative researchers with training in social and behavioral sciences	Reliance on subjective interpretive skills of qualitative researcher

Qualitative research methods often provide preliminary insights useful in developing ideas about how variables are related. Similarly, qualitative research can help define constructs or variables and suggest items that can be used to measure those constructs. For example, before they can successfully measure the perceived quality of online shopping experiences from their customers' perspective, retailers must first ascertain the factors or dimensions that are important to their customers when shopping online. Qualitative data also play an important role in identifying marketing problems and opportunities. The in-depth information enhances the researcher's ability to understand consumer behavior. Finally, many qualitative researchers have backgrounds in the social sciences, such as sociology, anthropology, or psychology, and thus bring knowledge of theories from their discipline to enhance their interpretation of data. For example, a study of grooming behavior of young adults conducted by an anthropologist described grooming behavior as "ritual magic."[5] The legacy of psychology and psychiatry in developing qualitative techniques is seen in the emphasis on subconscious motivations and the use of probing techniques that are designed to uncover motives.[6]

Although qualitative research produces useful information, it has some potential disadvantages, including small sample sizes and the need for well-trained interviewers or observers. The sample size in a qualitative study may be as few as 10 (individual in-depth interviews), and is rarely more than 60 (the number of participants in five six focus groups). Occasionally, companies will undertake large-scale qualitative studies involving thousands of IDIs and hundreds of focus groups, as Forrester Research did to support the development of their e-commerce consulting business,[7] but this is the exception, not the rule. While researchers often handpick respondents to represent their target population, the resulting samples are not representative in the statistical sense. Qualitative researchers emphasize their samples are made up of "relevant" rather than representative consumers. The lack of representativeness of the defined target population may limit the use of qualitative information in selecting and implementing final action strategies.

◼◼ Qualitative Data Collection Methods

A number of approaches can be used to collect qualitative data. Focus groups are the most frequently used qualitative research method (Exhibit 4.3). But the use of projective techniques, ethnography, and similar approaches has been growing in recent years.

In-Depth Interviews

In-depth interview A data-collection method in which a well-trained interviewer asks a participant a set of semistructured questions in a face-to-face setting.

The **in-depth interview,** also referred to as a "depth" or "one-on-one" interview, involves a trained interviewer asking a respondent a set of semistructured, probing questions usually in a face-to-face setting. The typical setting for this type of interview is either the respondent's home or office, or some type of centralized interviewing center convenient for the respondent. Some research firms use hybrid in-depth interviewing techniques combining

Exhibit 4.3	Percent of Research Providers and Clients Already Using Qualitative Data Collection Methods, 2015

Which of these qualitative data methods have you used most this year? (Select up to five.)

Method	Percent
Traditional in-person focus groups	68
Traditional in-person, in-depth interviews (IDIs)	53
Telephone IDIs	31
In-store observation	25
Bulletin Board Studies	21
Online focus groups with Webcams	12
Chat-based online focus groups	16
Online focus groups with webcams	17
Interviews/focus groups using online communities	25
Blog monitoring	8
Mobile (e.g., diaries, images, video)	24
Telephone focus groups	6
Online IDIs with webcams	12
Chat-based IDIs	6
Automate Interviewing	3
Other qualitative method	19

Source: Greenbook Research Industry Trends 2015 Report, www.greenbook.org, accessed March 6, 2016, p. 10.

Internet and phone interviewing. In these cases, the conversation can be extended over several days giving participants more time to consider their answers.[8] Use of the Internet also enables consumers to be exposed to visual and audio stimuli, thus overcoming the major limitation of IDIs over the phone. Two more IDI methods have emerged in recent years: online IDIs using webcams and online text-based chat.

A unique characteristic of in-depth interviewing is that the interviewer uses probing questions to elicit more detailed information on the topic. By turning the respondent's initial response into a question, the interviewer encourages the respondent to further explain the first response, creating natural opportunities for more detailed discussion of the topic. The general rule is that the more a subject talks about a topic, the more likely he or she is to reveal underlying attitudes, motives, emotions, and behaviors.

The major advantages of in-depth interviewing over focus groups include (1) rich detail that can be uncovered when focusing on one participant at a time; (2) lower likelihood of participants responding in a socially desirable manner because there are no other participants to impress; and (3) less cross talk that may inhibit some people from participating in a focus group. In-depth interviewing is a particularly good approach to use with projective techniques, which are discussed later in this chapter.

Skills Required for Conducting In-Depth Interviews For in-depth interviewing to be effective, interviewers must have excellent interpersonal communications and listening skills. Important interpersonal communication skills include the interviewer's ability to ask questions in a direct and clear manner so respondents understand what they are responding to. Listening skills include the ability to accurately hear, record, and interpret the respondent's answers. Most interviewers ask permission from the respondent to record the interview rather than relying solely on handwritten notes.

Without excellent probing skills, interviewers may allow the discussion of a specific topic to end before all the potential information is revealed. Most interviewers have to work at learning to ask good probing questions. For example, IDIs of business students about what they want in their coursework often reveal that "real-world projects" are important learning experiences. But what do they really mean by "real-world projects"? What specifically about these projects makes them good learning experiences? What kinds of projects are more likely to be labeled as "real-world projects"? It takes time and effort to elicit participants' answers, and ending a sequence of questions relatively quickly, as is the tendency in everyday conversation, is not effective in in-depth interviewing.

Interpretive skills refer to the interviewer's ability to accurately understand the respondent's answers. Interpretive skills are important for transforming the data into usable information. Finally, the personality of the interviewer plays a significant role in establishing a "comfort zone" for the respondent during the question/answer process. Interviewers should be easygoing, flexible, trustworthy, and professional. Participants who feel at ease with an interviewer are more likely to reveal their attitudes, feelings, motivations, and behaviors.

Steps in Conducting an In-Depth Interview There are a number of steps to be concerned in planning and conducting an IDI. Exhibit 4.4 highlights those steps. Have a close look at Exhibit 4.4 as we conclude this brief discussion of in-depth interviewing.

Focus Group Interviews

Focus group research A qualitative data collection method in which responses to open-ended questions are collected from a small group of participants who interactively and spontaneously discuss topics of interest to the researcher.

The most widely used qualitative research method in marketing is the focus group, sometimes called the group depth interview. The focus group interview has its roots in the behavioral sciences. **Focus group research** involves bringing a small group of people together for an interactive and spontaneous discussion of a particular topic or concept.

| **Exhibit 4.4** | **Steps in Conducting an In-Depth Interview** |

Steps	Description and Comments
Step #1:	**Understand Initial Questions/Problems** • Define management's problem situation and questions. • Engage in dialogues with decision makers that focus on bringing clarity and understanding of the research problem.
Step #2:	**Create a Set of Research Questions** • Develop a set of research questions (an interview guide) that focuses on the major elements of the questions or problems. • Arrange using a logical flow moving from "general" to "specific" within topic areas.
Step #3:	**Decide on the Best Environment for Conducting the Interview** • Determine best location for the interview based on the characteristics of the participant and select a relaxed, comfortable interview setting. • Setting must facilitate private conversations without outside distractions.
Step #4:	**Select and Screen the Respondents** • Select participants using specific criteria for the situation being studied. • Screen participants to assure they meet a set of specified criteria.
Step #5:	**Respondent Greeted, Given Interviewing Guidelines, and Put at Ease** • Interviewer meets participant and provides the appropriate introductory guidelines for the interviewing process. • Obtain permission to tape and/or videorecord the interview. • Use the first few minutes prior to the start of the questioning process to create a "comfort zone" for the respondent, using warm-up questions. • Begin the interview by asking the first research questions.
Step #6:	**Conduct the In-Depth Interview** • Use probing questions to obtain as many details as possible from the participant on the topic before moving to the next question. • When interview is completed, thank respondents for participating, debrief as necessary, and give incentives.
Step #7:	**Analyze Respondent's Narrative Responses** • Summarize initial thoughts after each interview. In particular, write down categories that may be used later in coding transcripts, a process referred to as memoing. • Follow up on interesting responses that appear in one interview by adding questions to future interviews. • After all data are collected, code each participant's transcripts by classifying responses into categories.
Step #8:	**Write Summary Report of Results** • A summary report is prepared. • The report is similar to writing a report for a focus group.

Focus groups typically consist of 8 to 12 participants who are guided by a professional moderator through a semistructured discussion that most often lasts about two hours. By encouraging group members to talk in detail about a topic, the moderator draws out as many ideas, attitudes, and experiences as possible about the specified issue. The fundamental idea behind the focus group approach is that one person's response will spark comments from other members, thus creating synergy among participants.

In addition to the traditional face-to-face method, focus groups are now conducted online as well. These groups can be either text or video based. Text-based groups are like chat rooms, but with some enhancements. For example, moderators can use video demonstrations, and "push" or "spawn" websites to participants' browsers. Thus, online focus groups are especially appropriate for web-based advertising of products and services because they can be tested in their natural environment.

Online focus groups can be conducted relatively quickly because of the ease of participation and because the focus group transcript is produced automatically during the group. While body language cannot be assessed with text-based online focus groups and asking follow-up questions is somewhat more difficult than it is in 3D or traditional offline focus groups, there are advantages to online focus groups. Software can be used to slow down the responses of more dominant participants, thus giving everyone a chance to participate. Low incidence populations are easier to reach online, more geographically diverse samples can be drawn, response rates can be higher because of increased convenience for participants who can log in from anywhere, and responses often are more candid because there is less social pressure when participants are not face to face.[9] One study that compared offline and online focus groups found that while comments were briefer online, they were more colorful and contained far more humor, a finding that suggests participants are more relaxed in the online setting.[10]

Bulletin board An online research format in which participants agree to post regularly over a period of four to five days.

A variation of online focus groups is the **bulletin board** format. In the bulletin board format, 10–30 participants agree to respond over a period of three to seven days. Participants post to the boards two to three times a day. The moderator posts questions and manages the discussion that unfolds over several days. This format enables people to participate who might otherwise not be able to and is especially useful for specific groups that are difficult to recruit, such as purchasing agents, executives, or medical professionals. In recent years, marketing research companies who offer bulletin boards have added several features, including the ability to post from mobile devices, webcam technology, concept evaluation and image markup tools, and journaling tools. Journaling tools make it possible for participants to respond to questions at any time by text, picture, or video. Journaling makes it possible for participants to provide real-time feedback rather than to rely on their memories after the relevant event occurs.

The primary disadvantage of text-based online focus groups is they lack face-to-face interaction. Thus, some online focus group providers are now offering video formats. One example is QualVu (**www.qualvu.com**), a firm that offers a format called the VideoDiary. The VideoDiary is like a message board where moderators and participants record their questions and answers, which results in an extended visual dialogue. The video answers average 3.5 minutes in length and are described as "rich and candid."[11] Researchers can post text, pictures, or video for participants to view. QualVu also offers speech-to-text transcription, video clip creation, and note-taking. Using tools available from QualVu, researchers can easily create a video clip playlist that can be integrated into a PowerPoint report and delivered in person or online.

Conducting Focus Group Interviews There is no single approach used by all researchers. But focus group interviews can be divided into three phases: planning the study, conducting the focus group discussions, and analyzing and reporting the results (see Exhibit 4.5).

Exhibit 4.5   Three-Phase Process for Developing a Focus Group Interview

Phase 1: Planning the Focus Group Study
- Researcher must understand the purpose of the study, the problem definition, and specific data requirements.
- Key decisions are who the appropriate participants will be, how to select and recruit participants, how many focus groups will be conducted, and where to have the sessions.

Phase 2: Conducting the Focus Group Discussions
- Moderator's guide is developed that outlines the topics and questions to be used.
- Questions are asked, including follow-up probing.
- Moderator ensures all participants contribute.

Phase 3: Analyzing and Reporting the Results
- Researcher debriefs all the key players involved to compare notes.
- Data obtained from the participants are analyzed using content analysis.
- A formal report is prepared and presented.

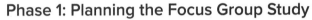

Phase 1: Planning the Focus Group Study

The planning phase is important to the success of focus groups. In this phase, researchers and decision makers must have a clear understanding of the purpose of the study, a definition of the problem, and specific data requirements. The purpose of the focus groups ultimately determines whether face-to-face or online focus groups are the most appropriate. Other important factors in the planning phase relate to decisions about who the participants should be, how to select and recruit respondents, and where to have the focus group sessions.

Focus Group Participants   In deciding who should be included as participants in a focus group, researchers must consider the purpose of the study as well as who can best provide the necessary information. The first step is to consider all types of participants that should be represented in the study. Demographics such as age, sex, and product-related behaviors such as purchase and usage behavior are often considered in the sampling plan. The objective is to choose the type of individuals who will best represent the target population of interest. Depending on the research project the target population might include heavy users, opinion leaders, or consumers currently considering a purchase of the product, for example.

The number of groups conducted usually increases with the number of participant variables (e.g., age and geographic area) of interest. Most research issues can be covered with four to eight groups. Use of more than 10 groups seldom uncovers substantial new information on the same topic. Although some differences in opinion between participants are desirable because they facilitate conversation, participants should be separated into different groups when differences are likely to result in opinions being withheld or modified. For example, including top management with middle management in the same employee focus group can inhibit discussion. Similarly, multiple groups are used to obtain information from different market segments. Depending on the topic being discussed, desirable commonalities among participants may include occupation, education, income, age, or gender.

Selection and Recruitment of Participants Selecting and recruiting appropriate participants are important to the success of any focus group. The general makeup of the target population needs to be represented in the focus groups.

To select participants for a focus group, the researcher must first develop a screening approach that specifies the characteristics respondents must have to qualify for participation. The first questions are designed to eliminate individuals that might provide biased comments in the discussion or report the results to competitors. The next questions ensure that potential respondents meet the demographic criteria and can come at the scheduled time. A final open-ended question is used to evaluate how willing and able the individual might be to talk (or respond online) openly about a particular topic. This question is related to the general topic of the focus groups and gives the potential respondents a chance to demonstrate their communications skills.

Researchers also must choose a method for contacting prospective participants. They can use lists of potential participants either supplied by the company sponsoring the research project or a screening company that specializes in focus group interviewing, or purchased from a list vendor. Other methods include snowball sampling, random telephone screening, and placing ads in newspapers, on bulletin boards, or on the Internet.

Because small samples are inherently unrepresentative, it is usually not possible to recruit a random sample for qualitative methods. Therefore, researchers select sample members purposively or theoretically. **Purposive sampling** involves selecting sample members because they possess particular characteristics. For example, sample members may be chosen because they are typical members of their category, or because they are extreme members (e.g., heavy users or opinion leaders). A **stratified purposive sample** may be chosen so that various target group members (e.g., low-income and high-income consumers) are included or to provide comparisons between groups. **Theoretical sampling** occurs when earlier interviews suggest potentially interesting participants not initially considered in the sampling plan. For example, if discussions with parents reveal that teenagers often have input into household technology purchases, a focus group with teens may be added to the research plan.

Size of the Focus Group Most experts agree that the optimal number of participants in face-to-face focus group interviews is from 10 to 12. Any size smaller than eight participants is not likely to generate synergy between participants. In contrast, having too many participants can easily limit each person's opportunity to contribute insights and observations. Recruiters may qualify more than 12 participants for a focus group because inevitably someone will fail to show. But if more than 12 do show up, some participants are paid and sent home so the group will not be too large.

Focus Group Locations Face-to-face focus groups can be held in the client's conference room, the moderator's home, a meeting room at a church or civic organization, or an office or hotel meeting room, to name a few. While all of these sites are acceptable, in most instances the best location is a professional focus group facility. Such facilities provide specially designed rooms for conducting focus group interviews. Typically, the room has a large table and comfortable chairs for up to 13 people (12 participants and a moderator), a relaxing atmosphere, built-in recording equipment, and a one-way mirror so that researchers and the client can view and hear the discussions without being seen. Also available is digital video cameras that record the participants' nonverbal communication behaviors.

Purposive sampling Selecting sample members to study because they possess attributes important to understanding the research topic.

Stratified purposive sampling Selecting sample members so that groups can be compared.

Theoretical sampling Selecting sample members based on earlier interviews that suggest that particular types of participants will help researchers better understand the research topic.

Phase 2: Conducting the Focus Group Discussions

The success of face-to-face focus group sessions depends heavily on the moderator's communication, interpersonal, probing, observation, and interpretive skills. The **focus group moderator** must be able not only to ask the right questions but also to stimulate and control the direction of the participants' discussions over a variety of predetermined topics. The moderator is responsible for creating positive group dynamics and a comfort zone between himself or herself and each group member as well as among the members themselves.

Focus group moderator
A person who is well trained in the interpersonal communication skills and professional manners required for a focus group.

Moderator's guide   A detailed outline of the topics, questions, and subquestions used by the moderator to lead the focus group session.

Preparing a Moderator's Guide   To ensure that the actual focus group session is productive, a moderator's guide must be prepared. A **moderator's guide** is a detailed outline of the topics and questions that will be used to generate the spontaneous interactive dialogue among group participants. Probes or follow-up questions should appear in the guide to help the moderator elicit more information. Moderator's guides must be developed and used for both face-to-face and online focus group sessions.

Consider asking questions in different ways and at different levels of generality. A common question is to ask what participants think of a specific brand or a product. Asking a focus group to talk about Mercedes-Benz automobiles, for example, will elicit comments about the quality and styling of the vehicle. But a moderator can also ask the question in a more novel way, for instance, "What does the Mercedes-Benz think of you?" This question elicits entirely different information—for example, that the car company thinks participants are the kind of people who are willing to spend a lot of money for the prestige of owning the brand.[12]

Asking key questions in imaginative ways can draw out important information. In a focus group about Oldsmobile, participants were asked, "If the Oldsmobile were an animal, what kind of animal would it be?" Among the answers were "faithful hound," and "dinosaur," which reveals something about the challenges Oldsmobile faces as a brand. Participants were also asked, "What kind of person drives an Oldsmobile?" One participant answered "a middle-aged salesperson," and when asked where the salesman bought his suit, the answer was "Sears." Again, these answers to indirect questions about brand image may sometimes reveal more information than direct questions.

The level of question is also important. For example, asking participants how they feel about transportation, trucks, or luxury cars will all result in different responses than asking more specifically about Mercedes.[13] The level of questions chosen should be dictated by the research problem.

Beginning the Session   When using face-to-face focus groups, after the participants sit down there should be an opportunity (about 10 minutes) for sociable small talk, coupled with refreshments. The purpose of these presession activities is to create a friendly, warm, comfortable environment in which participants feel at ease. The moderator should briefly discuss the ground rules for the session: Participants are told that only one person should speak at a time, everyone's opinion is valued, and that there are no wrong answers. If a one-way mirror or audio/video equipment is being used, the moderator informs participants they are being recorded and that clients are sitting behind the one-way mirror. Sometimes group members are asked to introduce themselves with a few short remarks. This approach breaks the ice, gets each participant to talk, and continues the process of building positive group dynamics and comfort zones. After completing the ground rules and introductions, the moderator asks the first question, which is designed to engage participants in the discussion.

Main Session Using the moderator's guide, the first topic area is introduced to the participants. It should be a topic that is interesting and easy to talk about. As the discussion unfolds, the moderator must use probing questions to obtain as many details as possible. If there is good rapport between group members and the moderator, it should not be necessary to spend a lot of time merely asking selected questions and receiving answers. In a well-run focus group, participants interact and comment on each others' answers.

The most common problem that inexperienced moderators have is insufficient depth of questioning. For example, a moderator of a focus group on videogaming might ask participants, "Why do you enjoy gaming?" A likely answer is "it's fun." If the questioning stops at this point, not much is learned. The moderator must follow up by asking what exactly makes gaming fun. It may take several follow-up questions to all participants to elicit all relevant information.

Moderators may give participants exercises to help stimulate conversation. For example, in a focus group on the topic of online shopping, participants received index cards with instructions to write down their favorite website, along with three reasons the site was their favorite site. The answers on the cards then became the basis for further conversation. Word association can also be used to start conversations about specific topics. For example, participants can be asked to write down all the words that come to mind when a specific company, brand, or product is mentioned. An easel or a whiteboard can be used so that the moderator can write words and comments to facilitate group interaction about the various words that participants wrote down.

Moderators for face-to-face focus groups must have excellent listening skills. Participants are more likely to speak up if they think they are being heard and that their opinion is valued. A moderator can show that she is paying attention by looking at participants while they are talking and nodding at appropriate times, for instance. If a moderator looks away or checks her watch, participants will sense that she is not genuinely interested in what they have to say. Similarly, it is very important to give all participants a chance to talk and to keep one or two participants from dominating the conversation. If someone has been quiet, a moderator should ask that person a question and include them in the conversation. Moderators should generally refrain from interruption and should remain neutral about the topic at hand. Thus, in a discussion about videogames, a moderator should not indicate his opinion of videogaming in general, specific videogames, or anything else that would unduly influence the feedback garnered from the focus group.

Moderators should try to see the topic of discussion from the participants' point of view. When a participant gives feedback that is useful, but which may be uncomfortable for the participant, moderators should support the disclosure by saying something like "thanks so much for bringing that up," or "that's really helpful for us to know." Make room for alternative opinions. A moderator can always ask, "does someone else have a different opinion?" in order to ensure that a specific topic is not being closed too quickly before an important viewpoint is expressed.

Closing the Session After all of the prespecified topics have been covered, participants should be asked a closing question that encourages them to express final ideas or opinions. The moderator may present a final overview of the discussion and then ask the participants, "Have we missed anything?" or "Do you think we've missed anything in the discussion?" Responses to these types of closing questions may reveal some thoughts that were not anticipated. Participants should be thanked for participating and given the promised incentive gift or cash.

Phase 3: Analyzing and Reporting the Results

Debriefing The researchers and the sponsoring client's representatives should conduct debriefing and wrap-up activities as soon as possible after focus group members leave the session. **Debriefing analysis** gives the researcher, client, and moderator a chance to compare notes. Individuals that have heard (or read) the discussion need to know how their impressions compare to those of the moderator. Debriefing is important for both face-to-face and online focus groups.

Content Analysis Qualitative researchers use content analysis to create meaningful findings from focus group discussions. **Content analysis** requires the researcher to systematically review transcripts of individual responses and categorize them into larger thematic categories. Although first "topline" reactions are shared during debriefing, more formal analysis will reveal greater detail and identify themes and relationships that were not remembered and discussed during debriefing. Face-to-face focus groups need to have transcripts converted to electronic format, but online groups are already in electronic format. Software can then be used with the electronic transcripts to identify and summarize overall themes and topics for further discussion. Qualitative data analysis is discussed in more detail in Chapter 9.

Advantages of Focus Group Interviews

There are five major advantages to using focus group interviews. They stimulate new ideas, thoughts, and feelings about a topic; foster understanding of why consumers act or behave in certain market situations; allow client participation; elicit wide-ranging participant responses; and bring together hard-to-reach informants. Because group members interact with each other, the social influence process that affects consumer behavior and attitudes can be observed. For example, a review of Coca-Cola's research concerning New Coke found that the social influence effects apparent in focus groups were more predictive of the failure of New Coke than were individual interviews.[14]

As with any exploratory research design, focus group interviews are not a perfect research method. The major weaknesses of focus groups are inherently similar to all qualitative methods: the findings lack generalizability to the target population, the reliability of the data is limited, and the trustworthiness of the interpretation is based on the care and insightfulness of researchers. Focus groups have an additional drawback: the possibility that group dynamics contaminate results. While the interaction between participants can be a strength of focus group research, groupthink is possible as well. **Groupthink** happens when one or two members of the focus group state an opinion and other members join the bandwagon. Groupthink is most likely when participants do not have a previously well-formed opinion on issues discussed in the group.

Purposed Communities/Private Community

Purposed communities are online social networks that may be specific to marketing research, or they may be broader brand communities, the primary purpose of which is marketing but are also used to provide research insights.[15] For example, MyStarbucksIdea.com is a brand community whose primary focus is producing new ideas, but the site is also used for research.

Private communities are purposed communities, the primary purpose of which is research. Consumers and customers are recruited for the purpose of answering questions and interacting with other participants within the private community. In online

Debriefing analysis An interactive procedure in which the researcher and moderator discuss the subjects' responses to the topics that outlined the focus group session.

Content analysis The systematic procedure of taking individual responses and grouping them into larger theme categories or patterns.

Groupthink A phenomenon in which one or two members of a group state an opinion and other members of the group are unduly influenced.

Purposed communities Online brand communities that can be used for research.

Private communities Purposed communities whose primary purpose is research.

communities, most people participate because they think they can improve products and marketing communication for a brand or product about which they care. For some communities, such as the Harley-Davidson owner community, individuals participate for free and feel honored to do so.[16] Participants are made to feel like part of the inner circle, with intrinsic incentives driving participation.

Participant samples are usually handpicked to be representative of the relevant target market, or they are devoted fans of the brand. Communispace originated private communities and currently operates more than 500 communities for clients such as Proctor & Gamble, Kraft Foods, The Home Depot, BP, Novartis, Verizon, Walmart, and Godiva Chocolates. PepsiCo's director of shopper insights, Bryan Jones, summarizes the benefits of private communities: "Through the evolution of technology, marketers and researchers now have unparalleled access to consumers and the ability to quickly and efficiently communicate with them in real time. Research that cost tens of thousands of dollars and took weeks and months in the past can now be accomplished in days or hours and deliver similar insights for much less money."[17]

Because of the start-up costs involved, most companies outsource community development to a provider, but the site is client branded. Techniques are evolving along with technology. Private community participants are increasingly asked to use mobile phones to provide real-time feedback, as well as posting pictures and video to the community. Private communities may be short or long term, and may involve small or large numbers of participants, from 25 in small groups up to 2,000 for larger groups. There is some controversy about whether private communities should be long term, or whether they are more productive when focused on specific issues for shorter periods of times. One shortcoming of long-term private communities is that members may become more positive about brands and products over time because of their participation in the community and may provide increasingly positive feedback.

EasyJet, a European low-cost airline, has been utilizing a private community that has 2,000 customers for nearly a decade. The community is queried about a variety of issues, including concept screening, product development, and overall customer experience. According to Sophie Dekker, EasyJet's customer research manager, they have been able "to conduct more research, for more areas of the business, in a faster time frame but within the same budgetary constraints."[18] Similarly, Godiva Chocolate used a sample of 400 chocoholics, all women, to help them understand what kinds of products and promotions would help them sell their premium chocolate in a difficult economy. The community helped Godiva to focus on baskets of chocolate priced $25 or less and to develop a heart-shaped lollipop for Valentine's Day that sold for $5.50. Godiva's participants are passionate about chocolate; they often log in to the community every day and participate for monthly gift certificates worth $10.[19]

Private community members may be asked to engage in other research projects such as surveys or in-person ethnography. In-person ethnography asks community members to chronicle an emotion (e.g., what annoys you?), process (e.g., shopping in a grocery store), or ritual (Thanksgiving dinner) using mobile devices. While engagement is much more limited than in traditional ethnography, in-person ethnography does create in-context observations that would be difficult or expensive to record using other research methods.[20]

Short-term private communities may run from two weeks all the way up to three months and typically range from 25 to 300 members. These short-term private communities are less like communities because of their short-term nature, but are often more focused on specific issues. Because these private communities are similar to traditional qualitative focus groups, albeit being more up to date, these short-term communities are increasingly successful at competing with their more traditional counterpart.[21]

◼ Other Qualitative Data Collection Methods

In addition to IDIs, focus groups, and observation, there are several other qualitative data collection methods used by marketing researchers. We provide a brief overview of these methods here.

Ethnography

Ethnography A form of qualitative data collection that records behavior in natural settings to understand how social and cultural influences affect individuals' behaviors and experiences.

Participant observation An ethnographic research technique that involves extended observation of behavior in natural settings in order to fully experience cultural or subcultural contexts.

Most qualitative methods do not allow researchers to actually see consumers in their natural setting. **Ethnography,** however, is a distinct form of qualitative data collection that seeks to understand how social and cultural influences affect people's behavior and experiences. Because of this unique strength, ethnography is increasingly being used to help researchers better understand how cultural trends influence consumer choices. Ethnography records behavior in natural settings, often involves the researcher in extended experience in a cultural or subcultural context, called **participant observation,** produces accounts of behaviors that are credible to the persons who are studied, and involves triangulation among multiple sources of data.[22] An ethnography of skydiving, for example, employed multiple methods, using observation of two skydiving sites over a two-year time period, participant observation of one researcher who made over 700 dives during the research, and IDIs with skydiving participants with varying levels of experience.[23]

There is no one given set of data collection tools used in ethnography. Participant observation is often used because observers can uncover insights by being part of a culture or subculture that informants cannot always articulate in interviews. However, some research questions do not require participant involvement to provide answers to questions. In *nonparticipant observation,* the researcher observes without entering into events. For example, Whirlpool's corporate anthropologist Donna Romero conducted a study for a line of luxury jetted bathtubs. She interviewed 15 families in their homes and videotaped participants as they soaked in bathing suits. Last, Romero asked participants to create a journal of images that included personal and magazine photos. From her research, Romero concluded that bathing is a "transformative experience . . . it's like getting in touch with the divine for 15 minutes."[24]

Because of social media, consumers are used to reporting what they do, when they do it, and why. Thus, mobile ethnography, where consumers provide pictures and videos concerning the research topic in real time, is growing. Consumers can film themselves shopping for particular items, or using products and services, for instance. While not as extensive as traditional ethnography, these methods do provide the ability for researchers to analyze consumers in context.

Case Study

Case study An exploratory research technique that intensively investigates one or several existing situations that are similar to the current problem/opportunity situation.

Case study research focuses on one or a few cases in depth, rather than studying many cases superficially (as does survey research).[25] The case or element studied may be a process (e.g., the organizational purchase decision for large dollar items), a household, an organization, a group, or an industry. It is particularly useful in studying business-to-business purchase decisions because they are made by one or only a few people. Case study research tracks thinking by the same individual, group, or organization using multiple interviews over several weeks and can therefore obtain subconscious thinking and study group interaction over time as problems, projects, and processes are defined and redefined.

Projective Techniques

Projective techniques   An indirect method of questioning that enables a subject to project beliefs and feelings onto a third party, into a task situation, or onto an inanimate object.

Projective techniques use indirect questioning to encourage participants to freely project beliefs and feelings into a situation or stimulus provided by the researcher. Participants are asked to talk about what "other people" would feel, think, or do, interpret or produce pictures, or project themselves into an ambiguous situation. Indirect questioning methods are designed to more nearly reveal a participant's true thoughts than do direct questions, which often prompt people to give rational, conscious, and socially desirable responses.

Projective techniques were developed by clinical psychologists and can be used in conjunction with focus groups or IDIs. These techniques include word association tests, sentence completion tests, picture tests, thematic apperception tests (TAT), cartoon or balloon tests, role-playing activities, and the Zaltman Metaphor Elicitation Technique (ZMET). The stimuli should be ambiguous enough to invite individual participant interpretation, but still specific enough to be associated with the topic of interest.

The major disadvantage of projective techniques is the complexity of interpretation. Highly skilled researchers are required and they can be expensive. There is a degree of subjectivity in all qualitative research analyses, but even more so when projective techniques are used. The background and experiences of the researcher influence the interpretation of data collected by projective techniques.

Word association test   A projective technique in which the subject is presented with a list of words or short phrases, one at a time, and asked to respond with the first thought [word] that comes to mind.

Word Association Tests   In this type of interview, a respondent is read a word or a preselected set of words, one at a time, and asked to respond with the first thing that comes to mind regarding that word. For example, what comes to your mind when you hear the words *mobile phone* or *book*, or brand names such as Target or Nike? Researchers study the responses to **word association tests** to "map" the underlying meaning of the product or brand to consumers.

CONTINUING CASE: THE SANTA FE GRILL

A business consultant with experience in the restaurant industry is hired by the owners of the Santa Fe Grill. After an initial consultation, the business consultant recommends two areas to examine. The first area focuses on the restaurant operations. The proposed variables to be investigated include:

- Prices charged.
- Menu items offered.
- Interior decorations and atmosphere.
- Customer counts at lunch and dinner.
- Average amount spent per customer.

The second area to learn more about are what factors Santa Fe Grill customers consider in selecting a restaurant. Variables to be examined in the project include:

- Food quality.
- Food variety.

- Waitstaff and other restaurant employees.
- Pricing.
- Atmosphere.
- Dining out habits.
- Customer characteristics.

The owners value your opinion of the research project and ask you the following questions:

- Do the two areas of the research project proposed by the consultant include all the areas that need to be researched? If not, which others need to be studied?
- Can these topics be fully understood with qualitative research alone? Is quantitative research needed as well?

Sentence completion test A projective technique where subjects are given a set of incomplete sentences and asked to complete them in their own words.

Sentence Completion Tests In **sentence completion tests**, participants are presented with sentences and asked to complete them in their own words. When successful, sentence completion tests reveal hidden aspects about individuals' thoughts and feelings toward the object(s) studied. From the data collected, researchers interpret the completed sentences to identify meaningful themes or concepts. For example, let's say the local Chili's restaurant in your area wants to find out what modifications to its current image are needed to attract a larger portion of the college student market segment. Researchers could interview college students in the area and ask them to complete the following sentences:

> People who eat at Chili's are ⎯⎯⎯⎯⎯⎯⎯⎯⎯⎯⎯⎯⎯⎯⎯ .
> Chili's reminds me of ⎯⎯⎯⎯⎯⎯⎯⎯⎯⎯⎯⎯⎯⎯⎯⎯⎯ .
> Chili's is the place to be when ⎯⎯⎯⎯⎯⎯⎯⎯⎯⎯⎯⎯⎯ .
> A person who gets a gift certificate for Chili's is ⎯⎯⎯⎯⎯⎯ .
> College students go to Chili's to ⎯⎯⎯⎯⎯⎯⎯⎯⎯⎯⎯⎯ .
> My friends think Chili's is ⎯⎯⎯⎯⎯⎯⎯⎯⎯⎯⎯⎯⎯⎯ .

Zaltman Metaphor Elicitation Technique (ZMET) A visual research technique used in in-depth interviewing that encourages research participants to share emotional and subconscious reactions to a particular topic.

The Zaltman Metaphor Elicitation Technique (ZMET) The **Zaltman Metaphor Elicitation Technique** is the first marketing research tool to be patented in the United States. It is based on the *projective hypothesis,* which holds that a good deal of thought, especially thought with emotional content, is processed in images and metaphors rather than words.[26] In contrast to surveys and focus groups, the most widely used techniques in marketing research, which rely heavily on verbal stimuli, the ZMET uses a visual method. Gerald Zaltman of Olson Zaltman Associates explains that "consumers can't tell you what they think because they just don't know. Their deepest thoughts, the ones that account for their behavior in the marketplace, are unconscious [and] . . . primarily visual."[27]

Several steps are followed in the ZMET. When recruited, participants are told the topic of the study, for example, Coke. Participants are asked to spend a week collecting 10 to 15 pictures or images that describe their reaction to the topic (in this case, Coke) and to bring the pictures to their interview. Each participant is asked to compare and contrast pictures and to explain what else might be in the picture if the frame were to be widened. Then, participants construct a "mini-movie," which strings together the images they have been discussing and describes how they feel about the topic of interest. At the end of the interview, participants create a digital image, which is a summary image of their feelings. When the ZMET was used to study Coke, the company discovered something they already knew— that the drink evokes feelings of invigoration and sociability. But it also found something they did not know—that the drink could bring about feelings of calm and relaxation. This paradoxical view of Coke was highlighted in an ad that showed a Buddhist monk meditating in a crowded soccer field, an image taken from an actual ZMET interview.[28]

◼ Observation Methods

Researchers use observation methods to collect primary data about human behavior and marketing phenomena regardless of the nature of research designs (e.g., exploratory, descriptive, or causal). Observation research can involve collection of either qualitative or quantitative data and may result in qualitative or quantitative summaries and analyses of the collected information. The primary characteristic of observational techniques is that researchers must rely on their observation skills rather than asking participants predetermined questions. That is, with in-person or video observation, the researchers watch and record what people or objects do instead of asking questions. Researchers occasionally combine questioning methods (e.g., IDIs with key informants, surveys, focus groups) with observational research to help them clarify and interpret their findings.

Information about the behavior of people and objects can be observed: physical actions (e.g., consumers' shopping patterns or automobile driving habits), expressive behaviors (e.g., tone of voice and facial expressions), verbal behavior (e.g., phone conversations), temporal behavior patterns (e.g., amount of time spent shopping online or on a particular website), spatial relationships and locations (e.g., number of vehicles that move through a traffic light or movements of people at a theme park), physical objects (e.g., which brand name items are purchased at supermarkets or which make/model SUVs are driven), and so on. This type of data can be used to augment data collected with other research designs by providing direct evidence about individuals' actions.

Observation research Systematic observation and recording of behavioral patterns of objects, people, events, and other phenomena.

Observation research involves systematic observing and recording of behavioral patterns of objects, people, events, and other phenomena. Observation is used to collect data about actual behavior, as opposed to surveys in which respondents may incorrectly report behavior. Observation methods require two elements: a behavior or event that is observable and a system of recording it. Behavior patterns are recorded using trained human observers or devices such as video cameras, cameras, audiotapes, computers, handwritten notes, radio frequency identification (RFID) chips or some other recording mechanism. The main weakness of nonparticipant observation methods is they cannot be used to obtain information on attitudes, preferences, beliefs, emotions, and similar information. A special form of observational research, ethnography, involves extended contact with a natural setting and can even include researcher participation. However, because of the time and expense involved, true ethnographies are rarely undertaken by marketing researchers.

Unique Characteristics of Observation Methods

Observation can be described in terms of four characteristics: (1) directness; (2) awareness; (3) structure; and (4) type of observing mechanism. Exhibit 4.6 is an overview of these characteristics and their impact. Have a close look at Exhibit 4.6.

Types of Observation Methods

The type of observation method refers to how behaviors or events will be observed. Researchers can choose between human observers and technological devices. With human observation, the observer is either a person hired and trained by the researcher or is a member of the research team. To be effective, the observer must have a good understanding of the research objectives and excellent observation and interpretation skills. For example, a marketing research professor could use observation skills to capture not only students' verbal classroom behavior but also nonverbal communication exhibited by students during class (e.g., facial expressions, body postures, movement in chairs, hand gestures). If assiduously practiced by the professor, this enables her or him to determine, in real time, if students are paying attention to what is being discussed, when students become confused about a concept, or if boredom begins to set in.

Technology-mediated observation Data collection using some type of mechanical device to capture human behavior, events, or marketing phenomena.

In many situations, the use of mechanical or electronic devices is more suitable than a person in collecting the data. **Technology-mediated observation** uses a technology to capture human behavior, events, or marketing phenomena. Devices commonly used include video cameras, traffic counters, optical scanners, eye tracking monitors, pupilometers, audio voice pitch analyzers, psychogalvanometers, and software. The devices often reduce the cost and improve the flexibility and accuracy of data collection. For example, when the Department of Transportation conducts traffic-flow studies, air pressure lines are laid

Exhibit 4.6	Unique Characteristics of Observation

Characteristic	Description
Directness	The degree to which the researcher or trained observer actually observes the behavior or event as it occurs. Observation can be either direct or indirect.
Awareness	The degree to which individuals consciously know their behavior is being observed and recorded. Observation can be either disguised or undisguised.
Structure	The degree to which the behavior, activities, or events to be observed are known to the researcher before doing the observations. Observation can be either structured or unstructured.
Observing mechanism	How the behavior, activities, or events are observed and recorded. Alternatives include trained human observers and technological devices.

across the road and connected to a counter box that is activated every time a vehicle's tires roll over the lines. Although the data are limited to the number of vehicles passing by within a specified time span, this method is less costly and more accurate than using human observers to record traffic flows. Other examples of situations where technology-mediated observation would be appropriate include security cameras at ATM locations to detect problems customers might have in operating an ATM, optical scanners and bar-code technology (which relies upon the universal product code or UPC) to count the number and types of products purchased at a retail establishment, turnstile meters to count the number of fans at major sporting or entertainment events, and placing "cookies" on computers to track Internet usage behavior (clickstream analysis).

Advances in technology are making observation techniques more useful and cost effective. For example, AC Nielsen upgraded its U.S. Television Index (NTI) system by integrating its People Meter technology into the NTI system. The People Meter is a technology-based rating system that replaces handwritten diaries with electronic measuring devices. When the TV is turned on, a symbol appears on the screen to remind viewers to indicate who is watching the program using a handheld electronic device similar to a TV remote control. Another device attached to the TV automatically sends prespecified information (e.g., viewer's age, gender, program tuned to, time of program) to Nielsen's computers. Data are used to generate overnight ratings for shows as well as demographic profiles of the audience for various shows.

Scanner technology, a type of electronic observation, is rapidly replacing traditional consumer purchase diary methods. **Scanner-based panels** involve a group of participating households that are assigned a unique bar-coded card that is presented to the clerk at the checkout register. The household's code number is matched with information obtained from scanner transactions during a defined period. Scanner systems enable researchers to observe and develop a purchase behavior database on each household. Researchers also can combine offline tracking information with online-generated information for households, providing more complete customer profiles. Studies that mix online and offline data can show, for

Scanner-based panel A group of participating households that have a unique bar-coded card as an identification characteristic for inclusion in the research study.

instance, if panel members who are exposed to an online ad or website made an offline purchase after their exposure. Scanner data provide week-by-week information on how products are doing in individual stores and track sales against price changes and local ads or promotion activities. They also facilitate longitudinal studies covering longer periods of time.

Scanner technology is also used to observe and collect data from the general population. Market research companies work with drug stores, supermarkets, and other types of retail stores to collect data at check-out counters. The data include products purchased, time of day, day of week, and so forth. Data on advertising campaigns as well as in-store promotions is integrated with the purchase data to determine effectiveness of various marketing strategies.

Perhaps the fastest growing observational research approaches involve the Internet. The Internet, various digital devices, and RFID are enhancing the ability of marketers to electronically track a growing number of behaviors. Online merchants, content sites, and search engines all collect quantitative information about online behavior. These companies maintain databases with customer profiles and can predict probable response rates to ads, the time of day and day of week the ads are likely to be most effective, the various stages of potential buyers in the consideration process for a particular product or service, and the type and level of engagement with a website. Extensive qualitative data from social media is increasingly being harvested on the Internet. The data involves online conversations about products, services, brands, and marketing communications that occur in social media. RFID has expanded the ability to electronically track consumers. PathTracker is a system that consists of RFID tags that are affixed to shopping carts. These signals are picked up every few seconds by antennae around the perimeter of the store. Researchers can match purchase records with path data. One group of researchers used PathTracker data to learn how consumers shop in grocery stores. They found that consumers become more purposeful and less exploratory the more time they spend in the store; are more likely to allow themselves to purchase shop for "vice" products after they've purchased items in "virtue" categories; and other shoppers may discourage consumers from shopping in a specific store zone.[29]

Selecting the Observation Method

The first step in selecting the observation method is to understand the information requirements and consider how the information will be used later. Without this understanding, selecting the observation method is significantly more difficult. First researchers must answer the following questions:

1. What types of behavior are relevant to the research problem?
2. How much detail of the behavior needs to be recorded?
3. What is the most appropriate setting (natural or artificial) to observe the behavior?

Then the various methods of observing behaviors must be evaluated. Issues to be considered include:

1. Is a setting available to observe the behaviors or events?
2. To what extent are the behaviors or events repetitious and frequently exhibited?
3. What degree of directness and structure is needed to observe the behaviors or events?
4. How aware should the subjects be that their behaviors are being observed?
5. Which observation method is most appropriate: in-person or technology-mediated?

The researcher can now determine the proposed method's ability to accurately observe and record the behavior or activity. The costs involved—time, money, and manpower—

Exhibit 4.7	Benefits and Limitations of Observation

Benefits of Observation	Limitations of Observation
Accuracy of recording actual behavior	Difficult to generalize findings
Reduces many types of data collection error	Cannot explain behaviors or events unless combined with another method
Provides detailed behavioral data	Problems in setting up and recording behavior(s) or events

also must be determined and evaluated. Finally, potential ethical issues associated with the proposed observation method must be considered.

Benefits and Limitations of Observation Methods

Observation methods have strengths and weaknesses (see Exhibit 4.7). Among the major benefits is that observation enables collection of actual behavior or activities rather than reported activities. This is especially true in situations where individuals are observed in a natural setting using a disguised technique. In addition, observation methods reduce recall error, response bias, and refusal to participate, as well as interviewer errors. Finally, data can often be collected in less time and at a lower cost than through other types of procedures.

Social Media Monitoring and the Listening Platform

Social media monitoring is observational research based on analyzing conversations in social media, for example, Facebook, Twitter, blogs, and product review sites. The monitoring provides marketing researchers with a rich source of existing, authentic information from the river of news that is being organically shared in social networks online. Blogs, social networking sites, and online communities provide a natural outlet for consumers to share experiences about products, brands, and organizations. The difference between social media monitoring and private communities (covered previously) is that in social media research, the data (text, images, and video) already exists and is not created by interaction with researchers. Thus, one strength of social media monitoring is that researchers can observe people interacting with each other unprompted by the potential bias of interviewers and questions. Another advantage of social media monitoring is individuals who may not fill out surveys or agree to focus groups might nevertheless share their experiences with online social networks.

But social media monitoring has several weaknesses. For example, while the expense is forecasted to decrease, it currently costs thousands of dollars a month just to monitor a few well-chosen keywords.[30] Second, many of the automated techniques for classifying textual data are unproven so the accuracy of the information is unknown. Third, the sample of people interacting about the brand, product, or advertising campaign is a self-selected sample that may not be representative of consumer reactions in the target market. In fact, different social media monitoring tools often produce different results.[31] Last, some social media sites are not publicly available for researchers to mine.

Social media monitoring
Research based on conversations in social media.

For example, most of Facebook is not open to the public. Given all these issues, it is not surprising that analysts suggest viewing results from social monitoring media programs in the context of the organization's larger research program.[32] One industry observer cautions: "Traditional quantitative research has well-established methods of assessing reliability and validity. The methods of assessing the trustworthiness of [traditional] qualitative research are less precise but well established. By contrast, the views about social media research vary widely."[33]

Listening platform/post
An integrated system that monitors and analyzes social media sources to provide insights that will support marketing decision making.

A **listening platform** or **post** is an integrated approach to monitoring and analyzing media sources to provide insights that support marketing decision making. In the past, larger companies often paid for a service that would read and clip articles from newspapers and magazines. Listening platforms are a technologically enhanced version of this older service. Reasons for deploying a listening platform include monitoring online brand image, complaint handling, discovering what customers want, tracking trends, and determining what one's competitors are doing.[34] Listening platforms are in their infancy and are ripe for a large number of research innovations in coming years.[35] Some research firms combine the data mined through their online listening platform with additional online and offline data, for example, sales, awareness, clickstream measures, and inventory movement.

The qualitative data available from social media monitoring can be analyzed qualitatively, quantitatively, or both. Currently, most social media monitoring tools seek to seamlessly mix qualitative and quantitative analyses. The earliest application of quantitative methods is simple counts of mentions of keywords. Another emerging, but controversial, quantitative tool is **sentiment analysis,** also called **opinion mining.** Sentiment analysis relies on the emerging field of natural language processing (NLP) that enables automatic categorization of online comments into positive or negative categories. Initial research applied sentiment analysis tools to product, movie, and restaurant reviews.[36] Quantitative measures of sentiment are still limited as a large amount of data is currently unclassifiable or incorrectly classified with current automation tools. But more advanced sentiment analysis tools are being developed to go beyond grouping by category and enable classification by emotions such as sad, happy, or angry.[37] Thus, in the next few years, sentiment analysis methods are likely to be improved substantially, with their use becoming more pervasive. Common features of social monitoring software include sentiment scoring, identification of influencers who are talking about your brand, and measurement of social media campaigns such as when conversations are happening and the share of conversations that are about your brand.

Sentiment analysis/opinion mining The application of technological tools to identify, extract, and quantify subject information in textual data.

In addition to quantitative metrics, online conversations are typically mined for qualitative insights as well. Online conversations about the topic of interest may be too numerous to efficiently analyze manually. But qualitative researchers can sample comments for intensive analysis. Sampling can be random or can involve oversampling among especially active and connected web posters. In addition to being useful as an independent tool to provide in-depth opinions, qualitative analysis of conversations provides relevant categories of issues and opportunities for automated tools to follow up and quantify.

Social media analytics have some limitations that make it unlikely that the technique will ever fully replace traditional marketing research methods. Many consumers use social media rarely if ever. Moreover, the consumers who engage most heavily in social media conversations about products and brands are more likely to be "eager shoppers."[38] Nevertheless, social media monitoring has already provided researchers with a ready source of existing feedback. As the techniques evolve and improve, they are expected to continue to grow.[39]

Netnography

Netnography A research technique that requires deep engagement with online communities.

Netnography is an observational research technique that requires deep engagement with one or more social media communities. What differentiates netnography from the other social media research techniques is the extensive contact and analysis of online communities and the use of participant observation. These online communities are often organized around interests in industries, products, brands, sports teams, or music groups, and contain fanatic consumers who are lead users or innovators. Rob Kozinets, who developed netnography, used the technique to study an online community of "coffeephiles." Kozinets concluded that devotion to coffee among the members of the community was almost religious: "Coffee is emotional, human, deeply and personally relevant—and not to be commodified . . . or treated as just another product."[40]

In netnography, researchers must (1) gain entrée into the community, (2) gather and analyze data from members of the community, (3) ensure trustworthy interpretation of the data, and (4) provide opportunities for feedback on the research report from members of the community (see Chapter 9 for interpretation and analysis of qualitative data). Before gaining entrée, researchers develop research questions and search to identify online forums that will provide the answers to their research questions. Generally, researchers prefer to collect data from higher traffic forums with larger numbers of discrete message posters and greater between-member interactions.[41]

MARKETING RESEARCH IN ACTION
Reaching Hispanics through Qualitative Research

More than 55.4 million (17.4 percent of the U.S. population) are classified as Hispanic. The Hispanic/Latino population is diverse as it flows from many Spanish-speaking countries around the world characterized by different levels of acculturation. When Hispanics become acculturated, they often strongly identify with both America and their country of origin, an effect that persists across generations. A minority of Hispanics use Spanish as their primary language, with most Hispanics preferring to speak both Spanish and English. Vice president of multicultural business development at Horowitz Associates, Adriana Waterston, emphasizes that approaching the Hispanic segment "has never been exclusively about language as much as cultural relevance."[1] Other researchers have concluded that whatever is the country of origin, themes are relevant in Spanish-speaking communities: family, moral values, religion, music, cooking, dancing, and socializing.

How do these findings influence marketing research? Ricardo Lopez, president of Hispanic Research, Inc., asserts that qualitative research is especially appropriate for the Hispanic marketplace and emphasizes that the population has to be approached differently in order for research to be useful. Quantitative research methods are structured, linear, and dry, suggesting government and academic research rather than connection. In contrast, Latinos prefer qualitative approaches that involve tangents, storytelling, and an expressive process often characterized as lively. This style of interaction is especially noticeable among less-acculturated Latino populations but is evident among acculturated Hispanics as well. Participants in qualitative research projects should be treated like a guest in your home as it is important to form a strong emotional connection to facilitate interaction. Face-to-face focus groups, IDIs, and ethnography are all appropriate for the Latino marketplace. When a relevant population can be recruited that has access to the Internet, IDIs using webcams, bulletin board focus groups, and private communities can also produce high-quality insights into Hispanic populations for clients.

Private communities are increasingly being utilized with Hispanics, including those who prefer to participate in Spanish as well as those who prefer to communicate in English. Communispace has recruited Hispanics of all ages, nationalities, and acculturation levels to participate in Spanish-language brand communities. The facilitators of research among these communities recommend a different approach for engaging these consumers. Facilitators allow members to make the community their space where participants can form close bonds, trading advice and personal stories. Also, participants should be allowed to build personal relationships with each other and the facilitators, replicating the sense of family so important in Hispanic culture. Finally, more facilitation is needed in Hispanic private communities not only because this segment values connectedness, but also because more help is needed for technical issues. If the extra work is invested, the insights generated can be extraordinary.

Traditional marketing research among Hispanics has often focused too heavily on classifying the marketplace in terms of language, acculturation, and generation. Perhaps this is because of overreliance on quantitative research approaches. One strength of qualitative research is the ability to tap deeper contextual, psychological, and cultural issues. As the Latino marketplace continues to grow, marketing researchers will need to adjust their research approach, continually identifying "culturally relevant ways to interact."[2]

Hands-On Exercise

Using the material from the chapter and the earlier information, answer each of the following questions.

1. Should marketing researchers working with Latinos concentrate solely on qualitative research? Explain your answer.
2. Could qualitative research be used to improve quantitative methods such as surveys? Explain your answer.
3. What challenges do researchers face in conducting research with the Latino marketplace online? How can researchers minimize the effects of these difficulties?
4. Think of one or two cultures or subcultures with which you are at least somewhat familiar. Would qualitative research be especially useful for these cultures? Why or why not?

Sources: Sharon R. Ennis, Merarys Rios-Vargas, and Nora G. Albert, "The Hispanic Population: 2010," United States Census Bureau, U.S. Department of Commerce, Economics and Statistics Administration, May 2011; Manila Austin and Josué Jansen, "¿Me Entiende?: Revisiting Acculturation," Communispace.com/UploadedFiles /ResearchInsights/Research_Patterns/MacroTrends_MeEntiendes.pdf, accessed January 16, 2012; Horowitz Associates, "Horowitz Associates Study Reveals That for Many U.S. Latinos Biculturalism Is Key to Self-Identity," July 7, 2011, **www .horowitzassociates.com/press-releases/horowitz-associates-study-reveals-that -for-many-u-s-latinos-biculturalism-is-key-to-self-identity**, accessed January 17, 2012; Ricardo Antonio Lopez, "U.S. Hispanic Market—Qualitative Research Practices and Suggestions," *QRCA Views*, Spring 2008, pp. 44–51; Hispanic Research, Inc., "Online Research," accessed January 16, 2012; Hispanic Research Inc., "Qualitative Research," accessed January 16, 2012; Katrina Lerman, "Spanish-language Facilitators Share Their Best Tips," *MediaPost Blogs*, February 12, 2009, **www.mediapost.com/publications /article/100194/**, accessed January 14, 2012; Thinknow Research, "Communities," Thinknowresearch.com/communities, accessed January 17, 2012.

References

1. Horowitz Associates, "Horowitz Associates Study Reveals that for Many U.S. Latinos Biculturalism Is Key to Self-Identity," July 7, 2011, **www.horowitzassociates.com /press-releases/horowitz-associates-study-reveals-that-for-many-u-s-latinos -biculturalism-is-key-to-self-identity**, accessed January 17, 2012.
2. Manila Austin and Josué Jansen, "¿Me Entiende?: Revisiting Acculturation," Communispace.com/UploadedFiles/ResearchInsights/Research_Patterns /MacroTrends_MeEntiendes.pdf, accessed January 16, 2012, p. 34.

■ Summary

Identify the major differences between qualitative and quantitative research.

In business problem situations where secondary information alone cannot answer management's questions, primary data must be collected and transformed into usable information. Researchers can choose between two general types of data collection methods: qualitative or quantitative. There are many differences between these two approaches with respect to their research objectives and goals, type of research, type of questions, time of execution, generalizability to target populations, type of analysis, and researcher skill requirements.

Qualitative methods may be used to generate exploratory, preliminary insights into decision problems or address complex consumer motivations that may be difficult to study with quantitative research. Qualitative methods are also useful to understand the impact of culture or subculture on consumer decision making and to probe unconscious or hidden motivations that are not easy to access using quantitative research. Qualitative researchers collect detailed amounts of data from relatively small samples by questioning or observing what people do and say. These methods require the use of researchers well trained in interpersonal communication, observation, and interpretation. Data typically are collected using open-ended or semistructured questioning formats that allow for probing attitudes or behavior patterns or observation techniques for current behaviors or events. While qualitative data can be collected quickly (except in ethnography), it requires good interpretative skills to transform data into useful findings. The small nonrandom samples that are typically used make generalization to a larger population of interest questionable.

In contrast, quantitative or survey research methods place heavy emphasis on using formal, structured questioning practices where the response options have been predetermined by the researcher. These questions tend to be administered to large numbers of respondents. Quantitative methods are directly related to descriptive and causal types of research projects where the objectives are either to make more accurate predictions about relationships between market factors and behaviors or to validate the existence of relationships. Quantitative researchers are well trained in scale measurement, questionnaire design, sampling, and statistical data analyses.

Understand in-depth interviewing and focus groups as questioning techniques.

An IDI is a systematic process of asking a subject a set of semistructured, probing questions in a face-to-face setting. Focus groups involve bringing a small group of people together for an interactive and spontaneous discussion of a particular topic or concept. While the success of in-depth interviewing depends heavily on the interpersonal communication and probing skills of the interviewer, success in focus group interviewing relies more on the group dynamics of the members, the willingness of members to engage in an interactive dialogue, and the moderator's abilities to keep the discussion on track.

In-depth interviewing and focus groups are both guided by similar research objectives: (1) to provide data for defining and redefining marketing problem situations; (2) to provide data for better understanding the results from previously completed quantitative survey studies; (3) to reveal and understand consumers' hidden or unconscious needs, wants, attitudes, feelings, behaviors, perceptions, and motives regarding services, products, or practices; (4) to generate new ideas about products, services, or delivery methods; and (5) to discover new constructs and measurement methods.

Define focus groups and explain how to conduct them.

A face-to-face focus group is a small group of people (8–12) brought together for an interactive, spontaneous discussion. Focus groups can also be conducted online. The three phases of a focus group study are planning the study, conducting the actual focus group discussions, and analyzing and reporting the results. In the planning of a focus group, critical decisions have to be made regarding whether to conduct face-to-face or online focus groups, who should participate, how to select and recruit the appropriate participants, what size the group should be, what incentives to offer to encourage and reinforce participants' willingness and commitment to participate, and where the group sessions should be held.

Discuss purposed communities and private communities.

Purposed communities are online social networks that may be specific to marketing research, or they may be broader brand communities whose primary purpose is marketing but are also used to provide research insights. Private communities are purposed communities whose primary purpose is research. Consumers and customers are recruited for the purpose of answering questions and interacting with other participants within the private community. Participant samples are usually handpicked to be representative of the relevant target market, or they are devoted fans of the brand. Private communities may be short or long term, and may involve small or large numbers of participants, from 25 in small groups up to 2,000 for larger groups.

Discuss other qualitative data collection methods such as ethnography, case studies, projective techniques, and the ZMET.

There are several useful qualitative data collection methods other than IDIs and focus groups. These methods include ethnography and case studies, which both involve extended contact with research settings. Researchers may also use projective techniques such as word association tests, sentence completion tests, and the ZMET, which use indirect techniques to access consumers' feelings, emotions, and unconscious motivations. These techniques are less frequently used than are focus groups but are considered useful approaches for understanding more emotional and less rational motivations.

Discuss observation methods and explain how they are used to collect primary data.

Observation methods can be used by researchers in all types of research designs (exploratory, descriptive, causal). The major benefits of observation are the accuracy of collecting data on actual behavior, reduction of confounding factors such as interviewer or respondent biases, and the amount of detailed behavioral data that can be recorded. The unique characteristics that underline observation data collection methods are their (1) directness, (2) subject's awareness, (3) structure, and (4) observing mechanism. The unique limitations of observation methods are lack of generalizability of the data, inability to explain current behaviors or events, and the complexity of observing the behavior.

Discuss the growing field of social media monitoring.

Social media monitoring is research based on analyzing conversations in social media, for example, Facebook, Twitter, blogs, and product review sites. The monitoring provides marketing researchers with a rich source of existing, authentic information and organic conversations in social networks online. The data from these conversations may be analyzed qualitatively and quantitatively. One strength of social media monitoring is that researchers can observe people interacting with each other unprompted by the potential bias of interviewers and questions. Another advantage of social media monitoring is individuals who may not fill out surveys or agree to focus groups might nevertheless share their experiences with online social networks. Weaknesses include expense, accuracy of automatic categorization, and the non-representativeness of online posts. However, expenses are forecasted to fall, while the accuracy and depth of categorization tools is expected to increase over time.

◼️◗ Key Terms and Concepts

Bulletin board 84

Case study 91

Content analysis 89

Debriefing analysis 89

Ethnography 91

Focus group moderator 87

Focus group research 82

Groupthink 89

In-depth interview 81

Listening platform/post 98

Moderator's guide 87

Netnography 99

Observation research 94

Participant observation 91

Private communities 89

Projective techniques 92

Purposed communities 89

Purposive sampling 86

Qualitative research 79

Quantitative research 77

Scanner-based panel 95

Sentence completion test 93

Sentiment analysis/opinion mining 98

Social media monitoring 97

Stratified purposive sampling 86

Technology-mediated observation 94

Theoretical sampling 86

Word association test 92

Zaltman Metaphor Elicitation Technique (ZMET) 93

Review Questions

1. What are the major differences between quantitative and qualitative research methods? What skills must a researcher have to develop and implement each type of design?

2. Compare and contrast the unique characteristics, main research objectives, and advantages/disadvantages of the in-depth and focus group interviewing techniques.

3. Explain the pros and cons of using qualitative research in each of the following situations:

   a. Adding carbonation to Gatorade and selling it as a true soft drink.

   b. Finding new consumption usages for Arm & Hammer baking soda.

   c. Inducing customers who have stopped shopping at Sears to return to Sears.

   d. Advising a travel agency that wants to enter the cruise ship vacation market.

4. What are the characteristics of a good focus group moderator? What is the purpose of a moderator's guide?

5. Why is it important to have 8 to 12 participants in a focus group? What difficulties might exist in meeting that objective?

6. Why are the screening activities so important in the selection of focus group participants? Develop a screening form that would allow you to select participants for a focus group on the benefits and costs of leasing new automobiles.

7. What are the advantages and disadvantages of online focus group interviews compared to face-to-face group interviews?

8. What are the advantages and disadvantages of ethnography as compared to other qualitative techniques?

9. Develop a word association test that will provide some insight to the following information research question: What are college students' perceptions of their university's student union?

Discussion Questions

1. What type of exploratory research design (observation, projective technique, in-depth interview, focus group, case study, ethnography, netnography, ZMET) would you suggest for each of the following situations and why?

   a. A jewelry retailer wants to better understand why men buy jewelry for women and how they select what they buy.

   b. An owner of a McDonald's restaurant is planning to build a playland and wants to know which play equipment is most interesting to children.

   c. Victoria's Secret wants to better understand women's body images.

   d. The senior design engineer for the Ford Motor Company wishes to identify meaningful design changes to be integrated into the 2018 Ford Taurus.

   e. Apple wants to better understand how teenagers discover and choose popular music to download.

   f. Nike wants to better understand the concepts of customization and personalization to support the online product customization services provided by NikeID.

2. Develop a moderator's guide that could be used in a focus group interview to investigate the following question: What does "cool" mean to teens and how do teens decide what products are "cool"?

3. Apple hires you to study Apple's brand image with college students on your campus. Draft a list of 10 questions you would ask in a focus group. Make sure you think of alternative ways to ask questions instead of simply asking direct questions.

4. Thinking about how most participants are recruited for focus groups, identify and discuss three ethical issues the researcher and decision maker must consider when using a focus group research design to collect primary data and information.

5. Conduct an in-depth interview and write a brief summary report that would allow you to address the following decision question: What do students want from their educations?

6. Outback Steak, Inc., is concerned about the shifting attitudes and feelings of the public toward the consumption of red meat. Chris Sullivan, CEO and cofounder of Outback Steak, Inc., thinks that the "red meat" issues are not that important because his restaurants also serve fish and chicken entrées. Select any two "projective interviewing" techniques that you think would be appropriate in collecting data for the above situation. First, defend your choice of each of your selected projective interviewing techniques. Second, describe in detail how each of your two chosen techniques would be applied to Sullivan's research problem at hand.

7. **EXPERIENCE MARKETING RESEARCH.** Visit QualVu.com and locate information about their video diary technique (a video is located and other information can be found on the site). Is this technique superior to text-based online focus groups? Why or why not? How does the online diary compare to face-to-face focus groups?

8. **EXPERIENCE MARKETING RESEARCH.** Visit Context Research Group at **www.contextresearch .com**. Review one of the studies they have online. Could the research topic be addressed with surveys or focus groups? What insights, if any, do you think the researchers gained because they used ethnography rather than surveys or focus groups?

9. **EXPERIENCE MARKETING RESEARCH.** Visit Trackur.com (**www.trackur.com**) and read about the services Trackur offers. Some analysts have referred to the practice of mining social media as being similar to conducting a focus group. Is mining media similar to conducting a focus group? Why or why not?

10. Visit Communispace at Communispace.com. Read their information about what they do and some of the news or case histories at their site. After reviewing the website, evaluate whether and to what extent private communities might replace focus groups.

Descriptive and Causal Research Designs

Chapter 5

1. Explain the purpose and advantages of survey research designs.
2. Describe the types of survey methods.
3. Discuss the factors influencing the choice of survey methods.
4. Explain experiments and the types of variables used in causal designs.
5. Define test marketing and evaluate its usefulness in marketing research.

Magnum Hotel's Loyalty Program

Magnum Hotel's management team recently implemented a new loyalty program designed to attract and retain customers traveling on business. The central feature was a VIP hotel loyalty program for business travel customers offering privileges to members not available to other hotel patrons. The program was similar to the airline industry's "frequent flier" programs. To become a member of the preferred guest program, a business traveler had to complete an application using a dedicated link on the hotel's website. There was no cost to join and no annual fee to members. But benefits increased as members stayed at the hotels more often. Magnum Hotel's database records for the program indicated the initial costs associated with the program were approximately $55,000 and annual operating costs were about $85,000. At the end of the program's third year, there were 17,000 members.

At a recent management team meeting, the CEO asked the following questions concerning the loyalty program: "Is the loyalty program working?" "Does it give us a competitive advantage?" "Has the program increased the hotel's market share of business travelers?" "Is the company making money from the program?" "Is the program helping to create loyalty among our business customers?" Surprised by this line of questions, the corporate VP of marketing replied by saying those were great questions but he had no answers at that time. After having his assistants examine corporate records, the marketing VP realized all he had was a current membership listing and the total program costs to date of about $310,000. Information had not been collected on the attitudes and behaviors of program members, and his best estimate of revenue benefits was about $85,000 a year.

The VP then contacted Alex Smith, senior project director at Marketing Resource Group (MRG). After a meeting they identified two major problems:

1. Magnum Hotel needed information to determine whether or not the company should continue the loyalty program.
2. Attitudinal, behavioral, motivational, and demographic information was needed to design promotional strategies to attract new members, retain current members, and increase the frequency of members staying at Magnum Hotel properties.

Before undertaking a survey, they decided to conduct qualitative exploratory research using in-depth interviews with the General Managers of several Magnum Hotel properties and focus group sessions with loyalty program members. This additional information was used to develop the following research questions:

- What are the usage patterns among Magnum Hotel Preferred Guest loyalty program members?
- What is business travelers' awareness of the loyalty program?
- How important is the loyalty program as a factor in selecting a hotel for business purposes?
- Which features of the loyalty program are most valued? Which are least valued?
- Should Magnum Hotel charge an annual fee for membership in the loyalty program?
- What are the differences between heavy users, moderate users, light users, and nonusers of the loyalty program?

Can qualitative research adequately answer these questions, or is quantitative research needed?

Value of Descriptive and Causal Survey Research Designs

Some research problems require primary data that can be gathered only by obtaining information from a large number of respondents considered to be representative of the target population. Chapter 4 covered qualitative methods that are based on smaller samples. This chapter discusses quantitative methods of collecting primary data generally involving much larger samples, including survey designs used in descriptive and causal research.

We begin this chapter by discussing the relationship between descriptive research designs and survey methods. We then provide an overview of the main objectives of survey research methods. The next section examines the various types of survey methods and the factors influencing survey method selection. The remainder of the chapter reviews causal research designs, including experiments and test marketing.

Descriptive Research Designs and Surveys

We begin with an explanation of the relationships among descriptive research designs, quantitative research, and survey methods. Selection of a descriptive research design is based on three factors: (1) the nature of the initial problem or opportunity; (2) the research questions; and (3) the research objectives. When the research problem/opportunity is either to describe characteristics of existing market situations or to evaluate current marketing mix strategies, then a descriptive research design is the appropriate choice. If research questions include issues such as who, what, where, when, and how for target populations or marketing strategies, then a descriptive research design also is most appropriate. Finally, if the task is to identify relationships between variables or determine whether differences exist between groups, then descriptive research designs are generally best.

Exhibit 5.1	Advantages and Disadvantages of Quantitative Survey Research Designs

Advantages of Survey Methods
- Can accommodate large sample sizes so that results can be generalized to the target population
- Produce precise enough estimates to identify even small differences
- Easy to administer and record answers to structured questions
- Facilitate advanced statistical analysis
- Concepts and relationships not directly measurable can be studied

Disadvantages of Survey Methods
- Questions that accurately measure respondent attitudes and behavior can be challenging to develop
- In-depth data difficult to obtain
- Low response rates can be a problem

Survey research methods
Research procedures for collecting large amounts of data using question-and-answer formats.

Two general approaches are used to collect data for descriptive research: asking questions and observation. Descriptive designs frequently use data collection methods that involve asking respondents structured questions about what they think, feel, and do. Thus, descriptive research designs often result in the use of **survey research methods** to collect quantitative data from large groups of people through the question/answer process. But with the emergence of scanner data and tracking of digital media behavior, observation is being used more often in descriptive designs.

The term "descriptive" is sometimes used to describe qualitative research, but the meaning is different than when the word is used to describe quantitative research. Qualitative research is descriptive in the sense that it often results in vivid and detailed textual descriptions of consumers, consumption contexts, and culture. Quantitative studies are descriptive in the sense that they use numbers and statistics to summarize demographics, attitudes, and behaviors.

Survey research methods are a mainstay of quantitative marketing research and are most often associated with descriptive and causal research designs. The main goal of quantitative survey research methods is to provide facts and estimates from a large, representative sample of respondents. The advantages and disadvantages of quantitative survey research designs are summarized in Exhibit 5.1.

Types of Errors in Surveys

Errors can reduce the accuracy and quality of data collected by researchers. Survey research errors can be classified as being either *sampling* or *nonsampling* errors.

Sampling Errors

Any survey research design that involves collecting data from a sample will have some error. Sampling error is the difference between the findings based on the sample and the true values for a population. Sampling error is caused by the method of sampling used and the size of the sample. It can be reduced by increasing sample size and using the appropriate sampling method. We learn more about sampling error in Chapter 6.

Nonsampling Errors

Errors that occur in survey research design not related to sampling are called nonsampling errors. Most types of nonsampling errors are from four major sources: respondent error, measurement/questionnaire design errors, incorrect problem definition, and project administration errors. We discuss respondent errors here and the other types of errors in later chapters.

Nonsampling errors have several characteristics. First, they tend to create "systematic variation" or bias in the data. Second, nonsampling errors are controllable. They are the result of some human mishap in either design or survey execution. Third, unlike random sampling error that can be statistically measured, nonsampling errors cannot be directly measured. Finally, one nonsampling error can create other nonsampling errors. That is, one type of error, such as a poorly worded question, causes respondent mistakes. Thus, nonsampling errors reduce the quality of the data being collected and the information being provided to the decision maker.

Respondent errors Consist of both nonresponse error and response error.

Nonresponse error A systematic bias that occurs when the final sample differs from the planned sample.

Respondent Errors   This type of error occurs when respondents either cannot be reached, are unwilling to participate, or intentionally or unintentionally respond to questions in ways that do not reflect their true answers. **Respondent errors** can be divided into nonresponse error and response error.

Nonresponse error is a systematic bias that occurs when the final sample differs from the planned sample. Nonresponse error occurs when a sufficient number of the preselected prospective respondents in the sample refuse to participate or cannot be reached. Nonresponse is caused by many factors. Some people do not trust the research sponsor or have little commitment about responding,[1] while others resent what is perceived as an invasion of their privacy. The differences between people who do respond and those who do not can be striking. For example, some research has shown that for mail surveys, respondents tend to be more educated than nonrespondents and have higher scores on related variables such as income. In addition, women are more likely than men to respond.[2] Methods for improving response rates include multiple callbacks (or online contacts), follow-up mailings, incentives, enhancing the credibility of the research sponsor, indicating the length of time required to complete online or other types of questionnaires, and shorter questionnaires.[3]

Response error When respondents have impaired memory or do not respond accurately.

When researchers ask questions, respondents search their memory, retrieve thoughts, and provide them as responses. Sometimes respondents give the correct answer, but other times they give what they believe is the socially desirable response—whatever makes them look more favorable—or they may simply guess. Respondents may forget when reporting their past behavior, so human memory is also a source of response errors. When respondents have impaired memory or do not respond accurately, this is termed **response error** or faulty recall. Memory is subject to selective perception (noticing and remembering what we want to) and time compression (remembering events as being more recent than they actually were). Respondents sometimes use averaging to overcome memory retrieval problems, for example, telling the interviewer what is typically eaten for dinner on Sunday, rather than what was actually consumed on the previous Sunday.

◼ Types of Survey Methods

Improvements in information technology and telecommunications have created new survey approaches. Nevertheless, survey methods can be classified as person-administered, self-administered, or telephone-administered. Exhibit 5.2 provides an overview of the major types of survey methods.

Exhibit 5.2	Major Types of Survey Research Methods

Type of Survey Research	Description
Person-Administered	
In-home interview	An interview takes place in the respondent's home or, in special situations, within the respondent's work environment (in-office).
Mall-intercept Interview	Shopping patrons are stopped and asked for feedback during their visit to a shopping mall.
Telephone-Administered	
Traditional telephone interview	An interview takes place over the telephone. Interviews may be conducted from a central telephone location or the interviewer's home.
Computer-assisted telephone interview (CATI)	A computer is used to assist in a telephone interview.
Wireless phone surveys	Wireless phones are used to collect data. The surveys may be text-based or web-based.
Self-Administered	
Mail survey	Questionnaires are distributed to and returned from respondents via the postal service or overnight delivery.
Online surveys	The Internet is used to ask questions and record responses from respondents.
Mail panel survey	Surveys are mailed to a representative sample of individuals who have agreed in advance to participate.
Drop-off survey	Questionnaires are left with the respondent to be completed at a later time. The surveys may be picked up by the researcher or returned via mail.

Person-Administered Surveys

Person-administered survey methods have a trained interviewer that asks questions and records the subject's answers. Exhibit 5.3 highlights some of the advantages and disadvantages associated with person-administered surveys.

In-Home Interviews An **in-home interview** is a face-to-face structured question-and-answer exchange conducted in the respondent's home. Interviews are also occasionally conducted in office environments. This method has several advantages. The interviewer can explain confusing or complex questions, and use visual aids. Respondents can try new products or watch potential ad campaigns and evaluate them. In addition, respondents are in a comfortable, familiar environment thus increasing the likelihood of respondents' willingness to answer the survey's questions.

In-home interviewing may be completed through door-to-door canvassing of geographic areas. This canvassing process is one of the disadvantages of in-home interviewing. Interviewers who are not well supervised may skip homes they find threatening or even fabricate interviews. In-home and in-office interviews are expensive and time consuming.

Person-administered surveys Data collection techniques that require the presence of a trained human interviewer who asks questions and records the subject's answers.

In-home interview A structured question-and-answer exchange conducted in the respondent's home.

Exhibit 5.3   Advantages and Disadvantages of Person-Administered Surveys

Advantages

Adaptability	Trained interviewers can quickly adapt to respondents' differences.
Rapport	Not all people are willing to talk with strangers when asked to answer a few questions. Interviewers can help establish a "comfort zone" during the questioning process and make the process of taking a survey more interesting to respondents.
Feedback	During the questioning process, interviewers can answer respondents' questions and increase the respondents' understanding of instructions and questions and capture additional verbal and nonverbal information.
Quality of responses	Interviewers can help ensure respondents are screened to represent the target population. Respondents are more truthful in their responses when answering questions in a face-to-face situation as long as questions are not likely to result in social desirability biases.

Disadvantages

Possible recording error	Interviewers may incorrectly record responses to questions.
Interviewer-respondent interaction error	Respondents may interpret the interviewer's body language, facial expression, or tone of voice as a clue to how to respond to a question.
High expense	Overall cost of data collection using an interviewer is higher than other data collection methods.

Mall-Intercept Interviews The expense and difficulties of in-home interviews have forced many researchers to conduct surveys in a central location, frequently within regional shopping centers. A **mall-intercept interview** is a face-to-face personal interview that takes place in a shopping mall. Mall shoppers are stopped and asked to complete a survey. The survey may take place in a common area of the mall or in the researcher's on-site offices.

Mall-intercept interviews share the advantages of in-home and in-office interviews, but the environment is not as familiar to the respondent. But mall-intercepts are less expensive and more convenient for the researcher. A researcher spends little time or effort in securing a person's agreement to participate in the interview because both are already at a common location.

The disadvantages of mall-intercept interviews are similar to those of in-home or in-office interviews except that interviewer's travel time is reduced. Moreover, mall patrons are not likely to be representative of the target population, even if they are screened. Typically, mall-intercept interviews must use some type of nonprobability sampling, which adversely affects the ability to generalize survey results.

Mall-intercept interview
A face-to-face personal interview that takes place in a shopping mall.

Telephone-Administered Surveys

Telephone interviews are another source of market information. Compared to face-to-face interviews, telephone interviews are less expensive, faster, and more suitable for gathering data from large numbers of respondents. Interviewers working from their homes or from central locations use telephones to ask questions and record responses.

Telephone interviews
Question-and-answer exchanges that are conducted via telephone technology.

Telephone survey methods have a number of advantages over face-to-face survey methods. One advantage is that interviewers can be closely supervised if they work out of a central location. Supervisors can record calls and review them later, and they can listen in on calls. Reviewing or listening to interviewers ensures quality control and can identify training needs.

Although there is the added cost of the telephone call, they are still less expensive than face-to-face interviews. Telephone interviews facilitate interviews with respondents across a wide geographic area, and data can be collected relatively quickly. Another advantage of telephone surveys is that they enable interviewers to call back respondents who did not answer the telephone or who found it inconvenient to grant interviews when first called. Using the telephone at a time convenient to the respondent facilitates collection of information from many individuals who would be almost impossible to interview personally. A last advantage is that random digit dialing can be used to select a random sample.

The telephone method also has several drawbacks. One disadvantage is that pictures or other nonaudio stimuli cannot be presented over the telephone. Recently some research firms overcame this disadvantage by using the Internet to show visual stimuli during telephone interviewing. A second disadvantage is that some questions become more complex when administered over the telephone. For example, imagine a respondent trying to rank eight to ten products over the telephone, a task that is much less difficult in a mail survey. Third, telephone surveys tend to be shorter than personal interviews because some respondents hang up when a telephone interview becomes too lengthy. Telephone surveys also are limited, at least in practice, by national borders; the telephone is seldom used in international research. Finally, many people are unwilling to participate in telephone surveys so refusal rates are high and have increased substantially in recent years.

Many people are annoyed by telephone research because it interrupts their privacy, their dinner, or their relaxation time. Moreover, the increased use of telemarketing and the illegal and unethical act of "sugging," or selling under the guise of research, has contributed to a poor perception of telephone interviewing among the public.

Computer-Assisted Telephone Interviews (CATI)   Most research firms have computerized the central location telephone interviewing process. With faster, more powerful computers and affordable software, even very small research firms can use computer-assisted telephone interviewing (CATI) systems. Interviewers are equipped with a hands-free headset and seated in front of a keyboard, touch-screen computer terminal, or personal computer.

Computer-assisted telephone interview (CATI) Integrated telephone and computer system in which the interviewer reads the questions from a computer screen and enters respondents' answers directly into the computer program.

Most **computer-assisted telephone interview** systems have one question per screen. The interviewer reads each question and records the respondent's answer. The program automatically skips questions that are not relevant to a particular respondent. CATI systems overcome most of the problems associated with manual systems of callbacks, complex quota samples, skip logic, rotations, and randomization.

Although the major advantage of CATI is lower cost per interview, there are other advantages as well. Sometimes people need to stop in the middle of an interview but are willing to finish at another time. Computer technology can send inbound calls to a particular interviewer who "owns" the interview and who can complete the interview at a later time. Not only is there greater efficiency per call, there also can be cost savings.

CATI eliminates the need for separate editing and data entry tasks associated with manual systems. The possibility for coding or data entry errors is eliminated with CATI because it is impossible to accidentally record an improper response from outside the set of prelisted responses established for a given question.

Results can be tabulated in real time at any point in the study. Quick preliminary results can be beneficial in determining when certain questions can be eliminated because enough information has been obtained or when some additional questions are needed because of unexpected patterns uncovered in the earlier part of the interviewing process. Use of CATI systems continues to grow because decision makers have embraced the cost savings, quality control, and time-saving aspects of these systems.

Wireless phone survey
Method of conducting a marketing survey in which the data are collected using wireless phones.

Wireless Phone Surveys   In a **wireless phone survey,** data are collected from wireless phone users. Wireless phone surveys are growing in use due to the high percentage of wireless phone usage, the availability of wireless phone applications (apps), and the rapid decline in landline phone penetration. Many research firms are expanding usage of wireless phone surveys as a result of two advantages over Internet and landline phone surveys: immediacy and portability. Wireless phone surveys provide immediacy in the sense that consumers can fill out surveys close to the moments of shopping, decision making, and consuming. For example, wireless phone surveys have been used to (1) capture impulse purchases as they are made and consumed, (2) collect data about side effects in real time from patients who are participating in pharmacological testing, and (3) survey wireless customers. A company named Kinesis Survey Research offers researchers the option of attaching a miniature bar code reader to a mobile phone that will discretely collect and store bar codes of purchased items. Finally, wireless phone panels may be especially appropriate for surveying teens, early adopters, and impulse buyers.[4]

Researchers primarily survey in either text-based or web-based formats. In short messaging (text messaging) format, the respondent can access the survey and display it as text messages on a wireless phone screen. The texting format is used for simple polling and very short surveys. In Europe, mobile phone penetration rates are very high and text message usage is higher than in the United States, so it is often preferred to wireless web surveys.[5]

In the United States, wireless web surveys are used more often than text message surveys. As compared to text messaging, the web facilitates a continuous session, with no time delay between questions and receipt of responses. Wireless web surveys tend to be cheaper for both the recipient and administrator of the survey. Wireless web surveys also permit some functionality associated with CATI and Internet surveys to be used, including conditional branching and display of images. When CATI abilities are added to wireless web surveys, the result is called CAMI, or computer-aided mobile interviewing.[6] Mobile surveys can be combined with pictures, audio clips, and videos taken by respondents. The images can be collected and linked to survey responses.

Marketing researchers usually do not call wireless phone users to solicit participation as often as they do over landlines. One reason is that Federal Communications Commission (FCC) regulations prevent the use of autodialing. Thus, when potential respondents are called, each one must be dialed by hand. Second, wireless phone respondents may incur a cost when taking a survey. Third, wireless phone respondents could be anywhere when they are called, meaning they are likely to be distracted by other activities, and may disconnect in the middle of the call. Safety is a potential issue since the respondents could be driving when they get the call from researchers.[7] Typically, respondents are recruited using a solicitation method other than the mobile phone, such as landlines, the Internet, mall-intercept, or in-store. Wireless panels are created from participants who have "opted in" or agreed to participate in advance.

We have already mentioned that immediacy is an advantage of wireless web surveys. A second advantage of wireless surveys is their ability to reach mobile phone-only households, which are increasing. For example, a recent study indicated nearly one out of every six homes in the United States (15.8 percent) had only wireless telephones by the end of 2007, up from 6.1 percent in 2004. Moreover, in states such as New York and New Jersey, landlines have plummeted 50 percent or more since 2000.[8] Thus, one motivation for the market research industry to use wireless phone surveys is their need to obtain representative samples.[9] Wireless-only households are skewed by gender, race, income, and age. Therefore, utilizing wireless phone surveys along with other methods enables research firms to reach consumers they otherwise could not include in their surveys.

Several challenges are facing the use of wireless phone surveys. Because of limited screen space, wireless phone surveys are not suitable for research that involves long and/or complex questions and responses. Second, even though mobile phones have some capacity to handle graphics, that capacity is somewhat limited. Third, wireless panels currently provide relatively small sample sizes. In spite of these challenges, this method of surveying is expected to increase over the next decade.

Self-Administered Surveys

Self-administered survey
A data collection technique in which the respondent reads the survey questions and records his or her own answers without the presence of a trained interviewer.

A **self-administered survey** is a data collection technique in which the respondent reads survey questions and records his or her own responses without the presence of a trained interviewer. The advantages and disadvantages of self-administered surveys are shown in Exhibit 5.4. We discuss four types of self-administered surveys: mail surveys, mail panels, drop-off, and Internet.

Exhibit 5.4	Advantages and Disadvantages of Self-Administered Surveys	
Advantages		
Low cost per survey	With no need for an interviewer or computerized assistance device, self-administered surveys are by far the least costly method of data acquisition.	
Respondent control	Respondents are in total control of how fast, when, and where the survey is completed, thus the respondent creates his/her own comfort zone.	
No interviewer-respondent bias	There is no chance of introducing interviewer bias or interpretive error based on the interviewer's body language, facial expression, or tone of voice.	
Anonymity in responses	Respondents are more comfortable in providing honest and insightful responses because their true identity is not revealed.	
Disadvantages		
Limited flexibility	The type of data collected is limited to the specific questions initially put on the survey. It is impossible to obtain additional in-depth data because of the lack of probing and observation capabilities.	
High nonresponse rates	Most respondents will not complete and return the survey.	
Potential response errors	The respondent may not fully understand a survey question and provide incorrect responses or mistakenly skip sections of the survey. Respondents may unconsciously commit errors while believing they are responding accurately.	
Slow data acquisition	The time required to obtain the data and enter it into a computer file for analysis can be significantly longer than other data collection methods.	
Lack of monitoring capability	Not having an interviewer present can increase misunderstanding of questions and instructions.	

Mail surveys Surveys sent to respondents using the postal service.

Mail Surveys **Mail surveys** typically are sent to respondents using the postal service. An alternative, for example, in business-to-business surveys where sample sizes are much smaller, is to send questionnaires out by overnight delivery. But overnight delivery is much more expensive.

This type of survey is inexpensive to implement. There are no interviewer-related costs such as compensation, training, travel, or search costs. The costs include postage, printing, and the cost of the incentive. Another advantage is that mail surveys can reach even hard-to-interview people.

One major drawback is lower response rates than with face-to-face or telephone interviews, which create nonresponse bias. Another problem is that of misunderstood or skipped questions. People who simply do not understand a question may record a response the researcher did not intend or expect. Finally, mail surveys are slow since there can be a significant time lag between when the survey is mailed and when it is returned.

Mail panel survey A questionnaire sent to a group of individuals who have agreed in advance to participate.

Mail Panel Surveys To overcome some of the drawbacks of mail surveys, a researcher may choose a mail panel survey method. A **mail panel survey** is a questionnaire sent to a group of individuals who have agreed to participate in advance. The panel can be tested prior to the survey so the researcher knows the panel is representative. This prior agreement usually results in high response rates. In addition, mail panel surveys can be used for longitudinal research. That is, the same people can be questioned several times over an extended period. This enables the researcher to observe changes in panel members' responses over time.

The major drawback to mail panels is that members are often not representative of the target population at large. For example, individuals who agree to be on a panel may have a special interest in the topic or may simply have a lot of time available.

Drop-off survey A self-administered questionnaire that a representative of the researcher hand-delivers to selected respondents; the completed surveys are returned by mail or picked up by the representative.

Drop-Off Surveys A popular combination technique is termed the **drop-off survey.** In this method, a representative of the researcher hand-delivers survey forms to respondents. Completed surveys are returned by mail or picked up by the representative. The advantages of drop-off surveys include the availability of a person who can answer general questions, screen potential respondents, and create interest in completing the questionnaire. The disadvantage of drop-offs is they are more expensive than mail surveys.

Online surveys Survey data collected using the Internet.

Online Survey Methods The most frequently used survey method today in marketing research is **online surveys,** which collect data using the Internet (see Exhibit 5.5). Why has the use of online surveys grown so rapidly in a relatively short time? There are several reasons. An important advantage for online surveys is they are less expensive per respondent than other survey methods. There is no cost of copying surveys or buying postage, and no interviewer cost. Surveys are self-administered, and no coding is necessary. Thus, the results are ready for statistical analysis almost immediately.

The ability of Internet surveys to collect data from hard-to-reach samples is another important reason for the growth of online surveys. Some market research firms maintain large panels of respondents that can be used to identify specific targets, for example, allergy sufferers, or doctors. One of the largest online panels, Harris Interactive, has a worldwide panel that numbers in the millions. Their specialty panels include executives, teens, and gays, lesbians, and transgender individuals. Access to hard-to-reach samples is also possible through community, blog, or social networking sites dedicated to specific demographic or interest groups, such as seniors, fans of *The Simpsons*, coffee lovers, or Texas Instrument calculator enthusiasts, just to name a few.[10]

Other advantages of online surveys include the improved functional capabilities of website technologies over pen and pencil surveys. One functional improvement is the

Exhibit 5.5	Usage of Types of Survey Methods

Method	Percent
Online surveys	88
CATI (Computer-assisted telephone interviewing)	39
Face-to-face/Intercepts	32
CAPI (Computer-assisted personal interviewing)	24
Social media monitoring	33
Mobile phone surveys	44
Mail	11
Other	11

Note: Percentages represent frequency of usage of methods.

Source: *Greenbook Research Industry Trends 2015 Report*, pp. 11–21, www.greenbook.org, accessed March 2016.

ability to randomize the order of questions within a group, so that the effects of question order on responses are removed. Another important improvement over other types of surveys is that missing data can be eliminated. Whenever respondents skip questions, they are prompted to answer them before they can move to the next screen. Third, marketing research firms are now learning how to use the improved graphic and animation capabilities of the web. Scaling methods that previously were difficult to use are much easier in an online format. For example, Qualtrics has a slider scale that facilitates the use of graphic rating scales, which are superior to traditional Likert scales, and ranking questions can be completed by respondents by clicking and dragging the items into the appropriate order. Words that might describe the respondent's personality, a brand, a product, or a retailer can be animated to move from left to right, with the respondent clicking on the appropriate words. Pictures and videos can be used, so that full color 3D pictures and videos of store interiors, products, ads, or movie reviews can be shown in the context of online surveys. Graphic improvements to survey design can make tasks more realistic and more engaging for respondents although online survey designers must carefully test the graphics to ensure they do not bias responses or add unnecessary complexity.

In addition to using online panels created by marketing research firms, companies may survey their own customers using their existing e-mail lists to send out invitations to participate in surveys. Small businesses can use online survey creation software, offered by businesses like **www.qualtrics.com**, **www.surveygizmo.com**, **www.Zoomerang.com** and **www.Surveymonkey.com**, to design an online survey and collect data relatively easily and inexpensively. Qualtrics is used by many universities and companies globally. Survey Gizmo is used by companies such as Walgreens, Skype, and ING to collect data from customers and employees. Both companies provide extensive support documentation for developing online surveys. Many online retailers use research contests to gather information as well as increase customer engagement with their company. For instance, graphic designers post pictures of possible T-shirts at **www.Threadless.com**. Designs that garner the most votes are printed and offered for sale on the site.

While the benefits of online surveys include low cost per completed interview, quick data collection, and the ability to use visual stimuli, Internet samples are rarely representative and nonresponse bias can be high. About 70 percent of individuals in the

Propensity scoring Used
to adjust survey results to
be more like those a rep-
resentative sample would
have produced.

United States have home access to the Internet, which limits the ability to generalize to the general population. **Propensity scoring** can be used to adjust the results to look more like those a representative sample would have produced, but the accuracy of this procedure must be evaluated. With propensity scoring, the responses of underrepresented sample members are weighted more heavily to adjust for sampling inadequacies. For example, if respondents who are 65 or older are only half as likely to be in an Internet sample as their actual incidence in the population, each senior would be counted twice in the sample. The primary disadvantage with propensity scoring is that respondents who are demographically similar may be otherwise different.

Selecting the Appropriate Survey Method

Researchers must consider situational, task, and respondent factors when choosing a survey method. The following sections describe situational, task, and respondent characteristics in more detail.

Situational Characteristics

In an ideal situation, researchers could focus solely on the collection of accurate data. We live in an imperfect world, however, and researchers must cope with the competing objectives of budget, time, and data quality. In choosing a survey research method, the goal is to produce usable data in as short a time as possible at the lowest cost. But there are trade-offs. It is easy to generate large amounts of data in a short time if quality is ignored. But excellent data quality often can be achieved only through expensive and time-consuming methods. In selecting the survey method, the researcher commonly considers a number of situational characteristics in combination.

Budget The budget includes all the resources available to the researcher. While budgets are commonly thought of in terms of dollar amount, other resources such as staff size can also constrain research efforts. Budget determinations are frequently much more arbitrary than researchers would prefer. However, it is rare when the budget is the sole determinant of the survey method. Much more commonly, the budget is considered along with data quality and time in selecting a survey method.

Completion Time Frame Long time frames give researchers the luxury of selecting the method that will produce the highest quality data. In many situations, however, the affordable time frame is much shorter than desired, forcing the researcher to choose a method that may not be ideal. Some surveys, such as direct mail or personal interviews, require relatively long time frames. Other methods, such as Internet surveys, telephone surveys, or mall intercepts, can be done more quickly.

Quality Requirements Data quality is a complex issue that encompasses issues of scale measurement, questionnaire design, sample design, and data analysis. A brief overview of three key issues will help explain the impact of data quality on the selection of survey methods.

Completeness of Data Completeness refers to the depth and breadth of the data. Having complete data allows the researcher to paint a total picture, fully describing the information from each respondent. Incomplete data will lack some amount of detail, resulting in a picture that is somewhat vague or unclear. Personal interviews and Internet surveys tend to be complete, while mail surveys may not be. In some cases, the depth of information needed to make an informed decision will dictate that a personal survey is the appropriate method.

Data Generalizability Data that are **generalizable** accurately represent the population being studied and can be accurately projected to the target population. Data collected from mail surveys are frequently less generalizable than those collected from phone interviews or personal interviews due to low response rates. Small sample size will limit the generalizability of data collected using any technique. Generalizability often is a problem with online surveys as well.

Data Precision Precision refers to the degree of accuracy of a response in relation to some other possible answer. For example, if an automobile manufacturer needs to know the type of colors that will be popular for their new models, respondents can indicate that they prefer bright colors for their new automobiles. In contrast, if "red" and "blue" are the two most preferred colors, the automobile manufacturer needs to know exactly that. Moreover, if "red" is preferred over "blue" by twice as many respondents, then the degree of exactness (precision) is two-to-one. This indicates that a more precise measure of the respondents' preference for "red" over "blue" is needed, even though both colors are popular with respondents. Mail and Internet surveys can frequently deliver precise results, but might not always produce the most generalizable results, most often because of the difficulty of obtaining a representative sample. Telephone surveys may be generalizable but might lack precision due to short questions and brief interview times.

Generalizable Projectable to the population represented by the sample in a study.

Task Characteristics

Researchers ask respondents to engage in tasks that take time and effort. Task characteristics include: (1) task difficulty; (2) required stimuli; (3) amount of information asked from respondents; and (4) sensitivity of the research topic.

Difficulty of the Task Answering some kinds of survey questions can be somewhat difficult for respondents. For example, product or brand preference testing may involve comparing and rating many similar products and therefore can be laborious for the respondents. In general, more complex survey environments require more highly trained individuals to conduct the interviews. Regardless of the difficulty of the survey task, the researcher should try to make it as easy as possible for respondents to answer the questions.

Stimuli Needed to Elicit the Response Frequently, researchers need to expose respondents to some type of stimulus in order to elicit a response. Common examples of stimuli are products (as in taste tests) and promotional visuals (as in advertising research). An interviewer is often needed in situations where respondents must touch or taste something. The Internet and personal surveys can be used whenever visual stimuli are required in the research.

The actual form of the personal interview may vary. It is not always necessary to design a one-on-one interview. For example, people may come in groups to a central location for taste testing, or people in mall-intercepts can be shown video to obtain their opinions on advertising.

Amount of Information Needed from the Respondent Generally speaking, if a large amount of detailed information is required from respondents, the need for personal interaction with a trained interviewer increases. As with any survey method, however, collecting more data lowers response rates and increases respondent fatigue. The survey researcher's goal is to achieve the best match between the survey method and the amount of information needed.

Research Topic Sensitivity In some cases, the research problem requires researchers to ask socially or personally sensitive questions. **Topic sensitivity** is the degree to which a specific survey question leads the respondent to give a socially acceptable response. When asked about a sensitive issue, some respondents will feel they should give a socially acceptable response even if they actually feel or behave otherwise. Phone and face-to-face interaction increases the tendency to report socially desirable attitudes and behavior. Less desirable behaviors such as cigarette smoking are likely to be underreported during personal interviews while desirable behaviors such as recycling are likely to be overreported. Even behaviors that are seemingly benign may be under- or overreported based on the social desirability of the behavior. For example, Quaker Oats conducted a study using both an online and mall-intercept survey. They found that the online sample reported significantly more daily snacking behavior. Quaker Oats concluded that the online respondents were more honest.[11] In addition, some respondents simply refuse to answer questions they consider too personal or sensitive. Others may even terminate the interview.

> **Topic sensitivity** The degree to which a survey question leads the respondent to give a socially acceptable response.

Respondent Characteristics

Since most marketing research projects target prespecified groups of people, the third major factor in selecting the appropriate survey method is the respondents' characteristics. The extent to which members of the target group of respondents share common characteristics influences the survey method selected.

Diversity Diversity of respondents refers to the degree to which respondents share characteristics. The more diverse the respondents the fewer similarities they share. The less diverse the respondents the more similarities they share. For example, if the defined target population is specified as people who have access to the Internet, then diversity is low and an Internet survey can be an effective and cost-efficient method. However, if the defined target population does not have convenient access to the Internet, Internet surveys will fail.

There are cases where the researcher may assume a particular personal characteristic or behavior is shared by many people in the defined target population, when in fact very few share that characteristic. For example, the rates of unlisted telephone numbers vary significantly by geographic area. In some areas (e.g., small rural towns in Illinois), the rate of unlisted numbers is very low (<10%), while in others (e.g., large cities like New York or Los Angeles), the rate is very high (>50%).

> **Incidence rate** The percentage of the general population that is the subject of the market research.

Incidence Rate The **incidence rate** is the percentage of the general population that is the focus of the research. Sometimes researchers are interested in a segment of the general population that is relatively large and the incidence rate is high. For example, the incidence rate of auto drivers is very high in the general population. In contrast, if the defined target group is small in relation to the total general population, then the incidence rate is low. The incidence rate of airplane pilots in the general population is much lower than that of car drivers. Normally, the incidence rate is expressed as a percentage. Thus, an incidence rate of 5 percent means that 5 out of 100 members of the general population have the qualifying characteristics sought in a given study.

Complicating the incidence factor is the persistent problem of contacting prospective respondents. For example, researchers may have taken great care in generating a list of prospective respondents for a telephone survey, but may then discover that a significant number of them have moved, changed their telephone number, or simply been disconnected (with no further information), resulting in the incidence rate being lower than initially anticipated. When incidence rates are very low, researchers will spend considerably more time and money in locating and gaining the cooperation of enough respondents. In low-incidence situations, personal interview surveys would be used very sparingly because it costs too much to find that rare individual who qualifies. Here a direct mail survey may be the best choice. In other cases, telephone surveys can be very effective as a method of screening. Individuals who pass the telephone screen, for example, could receive a mail survey. In doing survey research, researchers have the goal of reducing search time and costs of qualifying prospective respondents while increasing the amount of actual, usable data.

Respondent Participation   Respondent participation involves three components: the respondent's ability to participate, the respondent's willingness to participate, and the respondent's knowledge. **Ability to participate** refers to the ability of both interviewers and respondents to get together in a question-and-answer interchange. The ability of respondents to share thoughts with interviewers is an important selection consideration. It is frustrating to researchers to find qualified respondents willing to respond but for some reason unable to participate in the study. For example, personal interviews require uninterrupted time. Finding an hour to interview busy executives can present real problems for both researchers and executives. Similarly, while they might like to participate in a mall-intercept survey, some shoppers may be in a hurry to pick up children from day care or school. An optometrist may have only five minutes until the next patient. The list of distractions is endless. A method such as a mail survey, in which the time needed to complete the questions does not need to be continuous, may be an attractive alternative in such cases. As the above examples illustrate, the inability-to-participate problem is very common. To get around it, most telephone surveys, for example, allow for respondents to be called back at a more convenient time. This illustrates the general rule that marketing researchers make every possible effort to respect respondents' time constraints.

A second component of survey participation is prospective respondents' **willingness to participate** or their inclination to share their thoughts. Some people will respond simply because they have some interest in the subject. Others will not respond because they are not interested, wish to preserve their privacy, are too busy or otherwise occupied, or find the topic objectionable for some reason. Nevertheless, a self-selection process is in effect. The type of survey method influences the self-selection process. For example, people find it much easier to ignore a mail survey or hang up on a telephone call than to refuse a person in a mall-intercept or personal in-home interview.

Knowledge level is the degree to which the selected respondents feel they have the knowledge or experience to answer questions about the survey topic. Respondents' knowledge levels play a critical role in whether or not they agree to participate, and directly impacts the quality of data collected. For example, a large manufacturer of computer software wanted to identify the key factors small wholesalers use to decide what electronic inventory tracking system (EITS) they would need for improving their just-in-time delivery services to retailers. The manufacturer decided to conduct a telephone survey among a selected group of 100 small wholesalers who do not currently use any type of EITS. In the process of trying to set up the initial interviews, the interviewers noticed that about 80 percent or the responses were "not interested." In probing that response, they discovered that most of the respondents felt they were not familiar enough with the details of EITS to be able to discuss the survey issues. The more detailed the information needed, the higher respondents' knowledge level must be to get them to participate in the survey.

Marketing researchers have developed "best practices" to increase participation levels. One strategy is offering some type of incentive. Incentives can include both monetary "gifts" and

Ability to participate The ability of both the interviewer and the respondent to get together in a question-and-answer interchange.

Willingness to participate The respondent's inclination or disposition to share his or her thoughts.

Knowledge level Degree to which the selected respondents feel they have knowledge of or experience with the survey's topics.

nonmonetary items such as a pen, a coupon to be redeemed for a product or service, or entry into a drawing. Another strategy is to personally deliver questionnaires to potential respondents. In survey designs involving group situations, researchers can use social influence to increase participation, for example, mentioning that neighbors or colleagues have already participated. But incentive strategies should not be promoted as "rewards" for respondent participation because this often is the wrong motivator for people deciding to participate in surveys.

In summary, researchers try to get as much participation as possible to avoid problems associated with nonresponse bias.

◼️ Causal Research Designs

Causal research Studies that enable researchers to assess "cause-effect" relationships between two or more variables.

Independent variables Variables whose values are directly manipulated by the researcher.

Dependent variables Measures of effects or outcomes that occur as a result of changes in levels of the independent or causing variable(s).

Experiment An empirical investigation that tests for hypothesized relationships between dependent variables and manipulated independent variables.

Causal research designs differ from exploratory or descriptive research designs in several ways. First, the primary focus of causal research is to obtain data that enables researchers to assess "cause-effect" relationships between two or more variables. In contrast, data from exploratory and survey research designs enables researchers to assess noncausal relationships between variables. The concept of *causality* between several **independent variables** (X) and one **dependent variable** (Y) in research designs specifies relationships that are investigated in causal research studies and stated as "If X, then Y."

Three fundamental conditions must exist in order to accurately conclude that a cause-effect relationship exists between variables. Researchers must establish that there is temporal order between the independent X and the dependent Y variables such that variable X (or a change in X) must occur prior to observing or measuring variable Y (or a change in Y). Second, researchers must establish that collected data confirm there is some type of meaningful association between variable X and variable Y. Finally, researchers must account for (or control for) all other possible variables other than X that might cause a change in variable Y.

Another difference between causal and descriptive research is that causal research requires researchers to collect data using experimental designs. An **experiment** involves carefully designed data collection procedures in which researchers manipulate a proposed causal independent variable and observe (measure) the proposed effect on a dependent variable, while controlling all other influencing variables. Exploratory and survey research designs typically lack the "control" mechanism of causal designs. Typically, researchers use either a controlled laboratory environment where the study is conducted in an artificial setting where the effect of all, or nearly all, uncontrollable variables is minimized. In a field environment, researchers use a natural setting similar to the context of the study in which one or more of the independent variables are manipulated under conditions controlled as carefully as the situation will permit. Finally, while exploratory and descriptive designs almost always involve data collection using surveys, experimental designs collect data using both surveys and observation. In fact, in recent years, one of the most often executed experimental designs is online research that observes online activity to determine which marketing mix variables are likely to influence website traffic patterns and ultimately purchases.

A third difference is the framing of research questions for causal designs. In exploratory and survey research designs, initial research questions are typically framed broadly and hypotheses focus on the magnitude and/or direction of the association, and not on causality. To illustrate noncausal hypotheses, consider the example of a corporate merchandise VP of Macy's department stores who is concerned about the decreased revenues generated by current marketing tactics. Several questions needing answers are framed as: "Should Macy's current marketing tactics (store, product, service, etc.) be modified to increase revenues and market share?" "Do merchandise quality, prices, and service quality significantly impact customer satisfaction, in-store traffic patterns, and store loyalty?" and "Should Macy's expand its marketing efforts to include a mobile commerce option?" While these questions suggest examining associations (or broad relationships) between the specified variables, none of the questions focus on determining the causality of relationships. Consequently, researchers would use exploratory or descriptive survey research designs.

In contrast, questions examining causal relationships between variables are framed with the focus being on the specific impact (or influence) one variable causes on another variable. To illustrate, Macy's VP of merchandise might ask the following types of questions: "Will exchanging customer service policy A (e.g., merchandise returns) with customer service policy B lead to a significant increase in store loyalty among current customers?" "Can the profitability of the casual women's clothing line be improved by increasing prices by 18 percent?" "Will decreasing the current number of brands of shoes from eight to four significantly lower the sales in the shoe department?" and "Will offering storewide sales of 'buy one get a second one for half price' versus a '20 percent discount' lead to a marked increase in store traffic patterns?" Accurate answers to these questions can be obtained only through some type of controlled causal research design.

The Nature of Experimentation

Exploratory and descriptive research designs are useful for many types of studies. But they do not verify causal links between marketing variables. In contrast, experiments are causal research designs and can explain cause-and-effect relationships between variables/ constructs and determine why events occur.

Variable A concept or construct that can vary or have more than one value.

Marketing research often involves measurement of variables. Recall that a **variable** is an observable, measurable element, such as a characteristic of a product or service or an attitude or behavior. In marketing, variables include demographics such as age, gender and income, attitudes such as brand loyalty and customer satisfaction, outcomes such as sales and profits, and behaviors such as media consumption, website traffic, purchase, and product usage.

When conducting an experiment, researchers attempt to identify the relationships between variables of interest. Let's consider, for example, the following research question: "How long does it take a customer to receive an order from the drive-through at a Wendy's fast-food restaurant?" The time it takes to receive a food order is a variable that can be measured quantitatively. That is, the different values of the order time variable are determined by some method of measurement. But how long it takes a particular customer to receive a food order is complicated by a number of other variables. For instance, what if there were ten cars waiting in line, or it was 12:00 noon, or it was raining? Other factors such as the number of drive-up windows, the training level of order takers, and the number of customers waiting also are variables. Consequently, all of these variables can have an effect on the order time variable.

Other variables include the make of the car the person is driving, the number of brothers or sisters they have, and the quantity of food ordered. The first two variables are unlikely to have an effect on order time. But there is likely to be a relationship between the quantity of items in the order and waiting time. If it is true that the quantity of food ordered increases customer wait time at a drive-through, the researcher can conclude that there is a relationship between food quantity ordered and waiting time. In causal research designs involving experiments, the focus is on determining if there is systematic change in one variable as another variable changes.

Experimental research is primarily a hypothesis-testing method that examines hypotheses about relationships between independent and dependent variables. Researchers develop hypotheses and then design an experiment to test them. To do so, researchers must identify the independent variables that might bring about changes in one or more dependent variables. Experiments and other causal designs are most appropriate when the researcher wants to find out why certain events occur, and why they happen under certain

Exhibit 5.6 Types of Variables Used in Experimental Research Designs

Type of Variable	Comments
Independent variable	Also called a *cause, predictor*, or *treatment* variable (X). Represents an attribute (or element) of an object, idea, or event whose values are directly manipulated by the researcher. The independent variable is hypothesized to be the causal factor in a functional relationship with a dependent variable.
Dependent variable	Also called an *effect, outcome*, or *criterion* variable (Y). Represents an observable attribute or element that is the outcome of specified tests that is derived from manipulating the independent variable(s).
Control variables	Variables the researcher control so they do not affect the functional relationship between the independent and dependent variables included in the experiment.
Extraneous variables	Uncontrollable variables that should average out over a series of experiments. If not accounted for, they can have a confounding impact on the dependent variable measures that could weaken or invalidate the results of an experiment.

conditions and not others. Experiments provide stronger evidence of causal relationships than exploratory or descriptive designs because of the control made possible by causal research designs.

Experiments enable marketing researchers to control the research situation so that causal relationships among the variables can be examined. In a typical experiment, the independent variable is manipulated (changed) and its effect on another variable (dependent variable) is measured and evaluated. Researchers attempt to measure or control the influence of any variables other than the independent variable that could affect the dependent variable; these are **control variables.** If a research team wants to test the impact of package design on sales, they will need to control for other factors that can affect sales, including price and level of advertising, for example. Any variables that might affect the outcome of the experiment and that are not measured or controlled are called **extraneous variables.** Extraneous variables include the respondent's mood or feelings, the temperature of the room in which the experiment is taking place, or even the general weather conditions at the time of the experiment. After the experiment, the researcher measures the dependent variable to see if it has changed. If it has, the researcher concludes that the change in the dependent variable is caused by the independent variable. The material in Exhibit 5.6 explains these concepts in more detail.

Control variables Variables that the researcher does not allow to vary freely or systematically with independent variables; control variables should not change as the independent variable is manipulated.

Extraneous variables Any variables that experimental researchers do not measure or control that may affect the dependent variable.

Validity Concerns with Experimental Research

In any type of research design, but particularly in causal designs, researchers must understand *validity* and take steps to ensure they have achieved it. There often are numerous uncontrollable variables that impact research findings, and this is particularly true with findings obtained using experimental design approaches. Uncontrollable variables can make it difficult to determine whether the results of the experiment are valid. That is, was

MARKETING RESEARCH DASHBOARD   RETAILERS USE EXPERIMENTS TO TEST DISCOUNT STRATEGY

Walk into any large retail store and you will find price promotions being offered on big national brands. These discounts are primarily funded by manufacturers and may not be profitable for many retailers. While lower prices can increase sales of national brands, they may also hurt sales of private label store brands that earn higher margins. One retailer decided to conduct experiments to determine how it could protect its market share on private label store brands by promoting these brands at the same time national brands were on sale.

Six experimental conditions were designed using one control and five discount levels ranging from 0 to 35 percent for private label store brands. The retailer divided its stores into six groups and the treatments were randomized across the groups. Each store had a mixture of the experimental conditions distributed across different products being studied. Examples of experimental

conditions were Store A, in which private label store brands for men's shirts were discounted 20 percent, and private label store brands of men's socks were full price. Similarly, in Store B, Men's socks were discounted and men's shirts were not. The experimental designs enabled the retailer to control for variations in sales that might occur because the store groups were not identical.

The test revealed that matching the national brand promotions with small discounts on private label store brands generated 10 percent more profit than by not promoting the private label store brands. The retailer now automatically discounts private label store brands when national brands are being promoted.

What major benefits can retailers learn by conducting such experiments? Do you feel these experiments would produce similar results for brick and mortar stores as well as on line stores? Explain and justify your answers.

Validity The extent to which the conclusions drawn from an experiment are true.

the change in the dependent variable caused by the independent variable or something else? **Validity** is the extent to which the conclusions drawn from a particular research design, such as an experiment, are true. The issue of validity, particularly external validity, becomes more important in developing experimental research designs due to controlled environments, variable manipulation, and measurement considerations.

Internal validity The extent to which the research design accurately identifies causal relationships.

Internal Validity **Internal validity** refers to the extent to which the research design accurately identifies causal relationships. In other words, internal validity exists when the researcher can rule out competing explanations for the conclusions about the hypothesized relationship. The following example illustrates the importance of ruling out competing hypotheses and thus establishing internal validity. A bakery in White Water, Wisconsin, wanted to know whether or not putting additional frosting on its cakes would cause customers to like the cakes better. Researchers used an experiment to test the hypothesis that customers prefer additional frosting on their cakes. However, when the amount of frosting was increased, it also made the cakes more moist. Customers reacted favorably to this change. But was the favorable reaction caused by the moistness of the cakes or by the additional frosting? In this case, moistness is an extraneous variable.

External validity The extent to which a causal relationship found in a study can be expected to be true for the entire target population.

External Validity **External validity** means the results of the experiment can be generalized to the target population. For example, imagine that a food company wants to find out if its new dessert would appeal to a market segment between the ages of 18 and 35. It would be too costly to ask every 18- to 35-year-old in the United States to taste the product. But using experimental design methods, the company can randomly select individuals in the target population (ages 18–35) and assign them to different treatment groups, varying one component of the dessert for each group. Respondents in each treatment group would then taste the new dessert. If 60 percent of the respondents indicated they would purchase the product, and if in fact 60 percent of the targeted population did purchase the new product when it was marketed, then the results of the study would be considered externally valid. Random selection of

| Exhibit 5.7 | Types of Experimental Research Designs in Marketing Research |

Pre-experimental Designs

One-shot study	A single group of test subjects is exposed to the independent variable treatment X, and then a single measure on the dependent variable is obtained (Y).
One-group, pretest-posttest	First a pretreatment measure of the dependent variable is obtained (Y), then the test subjects are exposed to the independent treatment X, and then a posttreatment measure of the dependent variable is obtained (Y).
Static group comparison	There are two groups of test subjects: one group is the experimental group (EG), which is exposed to the independent treatment. The second group is the control group (CG) and is not given the treatment. The dependent variable is measured in both groups after the treatment.

True Experimental Designs

Pretest-posttest, control group	Test subjects are randomly assigned to either the experimental or control group, and each group receives a pretreatment measure of the dependent measure. Then the independent treatment is exposed to the experimental group, after which a posttreatment measure of the dependent variable is obtained.
Posttest-only, control group	Test subjects are randomly assigned to either the experimental or control group. The experimental group is then exposed to the independent treatment, after which a posttreatment measure of the dependent variable is obtained.
Solomon Four Group	This method combines the "pretest-posttest, control group" and "posttest-only, control group" designs and provides both direct and reactive effects of testing. It is not often used in marketing research because of complexity and lengthy time requirements.

Quasi-experimental Designs

| Nonequivalent control group | This design is a combination of the "static group comparison" and the "one-group, pretest-posttest" pre-experimental designs. |
| Field experiment | This is a causal design that manipulates the independent variables in order to measure the dependent variable in the natural setting of the event or test. |

subjects and random assignment to treatment conditions are usually necessary for external validity, but they are not necessarily sufficient to confirm that the findings can be generalized. Examples of experimental designs used in marketing research are illustrated in Exhibit 5.7.

Comparing Laboratory and Field Experiments

Laboratory (lab) experiments
Causal research designs that are conducted in an artificial setting.

Marketing researchers use two types of experiments: (1) laboratory and (2) field. **Laboratory (lab) experiments** are conducted in an artificial setting. If a researcher recruits participants for an experiment where several different kinds of ads are shown and asks them to come to a research facility to view and evaluate the TV ads, this would be a laboratory experiment. The setting is different than would be natural for viewing TV ads, which would be in the home, and is therefore considered artificial. Laboratory experiments enable the researcher to control the setting and therefore achieve high internal validity. But the trade-off is that laboratory experiments lack external validity.

Field experiments Causal research designs that manipulate the independent variables in order to measure the dependent variable in a natural setting.

Field experiments are performed in natural or "real" settings. Field experiments are often conducted in retail environments such as malls or supermarkets. These settings provide a high level of realism. But high levels of realism mean the independent and extraneous variables are difficult to control. Problems with control occur in several ways. For example, conducting a field experiment of a new product in a supermarket requires the retailer's permission to put the product in the store. Given the large number of new-product introductions each year, retailers are becoming more hesitant about adding new products. Even if the retailer cooperates, proper display and retailer support are needed to conduct the experiment.

Besides realism and control, there are at least three other issues to consider when deciding whether to use a field experiment: (1) time frames; (2) costs; and (3) competitive reactions. Field experiments take longer to complete than laboratory experiments. The planning stage—which can include determining which test market cities to use and which retailers to approach with product experiments, securing advertising time, and coordinating the distribution of the experimental product—adds to the length of time needed to conduct field experiments. Field experiments are more expensive to conduct than laboratory experiments because of the high number of independent variables that must be manipulated. For example, the cost of an advertising campaign alone can increase the cost of the experiment. Other items adding to the cost of field experiments are coupons, product packaging development, trade promotions, and product sampling. Because field experiments are conducted in a natural setting, competitors can learn about the new product almost as soon as it is introduced and respond by using heavy promotional activity to invalidate the results of the experiment or by rushing similar products to market. If secrecy is desired, then laboratory experiments are generally more effective.

Test Marketing

Test marketing Using controlled field experiments to gain information on specified market performance indicators.

The most common type of field experiment, test marketing, is a special type of experimental design used to assess customer attitudes toward new product ideas, service delivery alternatives, or marketing communication strategies. **Test marketing** is the use of experiments to obtain information on market performance indicators. For example, marketing mix variables (product, price, place, and promotion) are manipulated and changes in dependent variables such as sales volume or website traffic are measured.

Test marketing, often referred to as a controlled field experiment, has three broad applications in marketing research. First, test marketing has long been used to pilot test new product introductions or product modifications. This approach tests a product on a small-scale basis with realistic market conditions to determine if the product is likely to be successful in a national launch. Second, test marketing is used to explore different options of marketing mix elements. Different marketing plans, using different variations of marketing mix elements are tested and evaluated relative to the likely success of a particular product. Third, product weaknesses or strengths, or inconsistencies in the marketing strategies are frequently examined in test marketing. In sum, the main objectives of test marketing are to predict sales, identify possible customer reactions, and anticipate adverse consequences of marketing programs. Test marketing measures the sales potential of a product or service and evaluates variables in the marketing mix.

The cost of conducting test marketing experiments can be high. But with the failure rate of new consumer products and services estimated to be between 80 and 90 percent, many companies believe the expense of conducting test marketing can help them avoid the more expensive mistake of an unsuccessful product or service rollout. Read the Marketing Research Dashboard to see how the Lee Apparel Company used test marketing procedures to build a unique customer database to successfully launch a new brand of female jeans.

MARKETING RESEARCH DASHBOARD
Riders Fits New Database into Brand Launch

The Lee Apparel Company used market test data from a field experiment to build a customer database and help successfully launch a new brand of jeans. A few years ago, the company decided to market a new apparel line of jeans under the name Riders. The management team seized the opportunity to begin building a customer database. Unlike the typical process of building a customer database around promotions, merchandising, and advertising efforts that directly benefit retailers, their goal was to use marketing dollars to build both the brand and the database. The initial launch of the Riders apparel line went well with rollouts in the company's Midwest and Northeast regional markets. The initial positioning strategy called for the products to be priced slightly higher than competitive brands and marketed at mass-channel retailers like Ames, Bradlee's, Caldor, Target, and Venture. During the first year, the communication program emphasized the line's "comfortable fit," and within two years, the rollouts went national, using major retail channels like Walmart.

Initially, Riders used a spring promotion called "Easy Money" to generate product trial and to gather name, address, and demographic information about the line's first customers. These data were collected using a rebate card and certificate from the retailer. Upon completing and mailing the rebate card to Riders, the customer was rewarded with a check in the mail. This initial market test provided valuable data on each customer, such as the exact type of product purchased, how much was spent, whom they bought for, where they heard of the Riders brand, and their lifestyle interests. As part of the test market, Riders supported the effort with point-of-purchase (POP) displays and promotions in Sunday newspaper circulars. In addition, the management team funded the promotion and handled all development, redemption, and fulfillment in-house. Results of the first test market were as follows: A total of $1.5 million in certificates were distributed yielding a 2.1 percent response, or just over 31,000 customer names. About 20 percent of the buyers bought more than one item.

Another part of the test market design was the follow-up phone survey among new customers three months after the initial promotion. Of the customers surveyed, 62 percent had purchased Riders products. The survey provided detailed information to salespeople and consumers. Riders then repeated the test market design, adding a postcard mailing to existing database names. The promotional effort netted over 40,000 new customer names and information for the database. It also proved the responsiveness of database customers—33.8 percent of the database customers who received the postcard promotion came into the store to make a purchase, compared to a 2.8 percent response to the POP and circular ads.

To build a successful customer database from test market designs, the critical first step is figuring out the most efficient way to gather the names. The second step is deciding how you want to use the information with customers, prospects, and retailers. Finally, you begin the process of testing and evaluating the relationships, and applying what you have learned to build customer loyalty.

Focus on Retail Partnerships

The main goal of the test marketing was to create valuable information that could be used to build relationships with Riders consumers and those retail accounts Riders depended on for distribution. The growing philosophy within the Riders brand management team was "The more we know about our customers, the better the decisions we'll be able to make in dealing both with them and with our retailers." Moreover, the detailed information such as hard dollar results of each promotion as well as the demographic profiles is shared with retailers, as is the research showing the consumer behavior benefits. For example, a tracking study found that purchase intent of database customers was twice that of nondatabase customers in a given trade area. Unaided brand awareness likewise was high (100 percent, compared to 16 percent of the general population), and awareness of Riders advertising was 53 percent compared to 27 percent.

The Riders team believed so strongly in tying database information with promotional efforts that they insisted a database component be part of any chain-specific promotions. Management hoped to convince the retailers to build their own database capabilities to share their information. For example, retail account information can identify more product and promotion opportunities. Riders believed the real payoff comes when both manufacturer and retailer use data, from either source, to do a better job of attracting and keeping the key assets for both channel members—the customer. Riders must continue convincing retailers that putting Riders merchandise on their shelves is bringing people into their stores. From test marketing to creating complete customer databases, the Riders team has begun to put a major part of its marketing investment into image-building advertising strategies focused on print and television media.

For instance, they say, "The more we know about our customers and their preferences, the better we'll be able to hone our advertising messages and media buys, pinpoint what kind of promotions work best, and understand what new products we ought to be developing. As competitive pressures continue to mount, Riders expects detailed customer information to become more valuable in helping define the brand position clearly. Defining ourselves and what's different about Riders products is going to be an increasingly important element in drawing customers who have a great many choices to stores where Riders products are on the shelves. Although it initially began with test markets guiding the development of a complete customer database program, it's now the databases that are guiding the inclusion of key elements in our test market research. Riders' ultimate goal is creating a tool that is going to make its products more attractive to retailers and to consumers."

Hands-On Exercise

Using your knowledge from reading about market tests, answer the following questions:

1. What was Lee Apparel Company's overall goal for conducting such an extensive test market of its new line of jeans under the brand name "Riders"? In your opinion did the company achieve its goal? Why or why not?
2. Identify and explain the strengths and weaknesses associated with the test market process used by the Lee Apparel Company.
3. In your opinion, should the company give consideration to the development and implementation of Internet-based test marketing strategies? Why or why not?

◼◼ Summary

Explain the purpose and advantages of survey research designs.

The main advantages of using descriptive survey research designs to collect primary data from respondents are large sample sizes are possible, generalizability of results, ability to distinguish small differences between diverse sampled groups, ease of administering, and the ability to identify and measure factors that are not directly measurable (such as customer satisfaction). In contrast, disadvantages of descriptive survey research designs include the difficulty of developing accurate survey instruments, inaccuracy in construct definition and scale measurement, and limits to the depth of the data that can be collected.

Describe the types of survey methods.

Survey methods are generally divided into three generic types. One is the person-administered survey, in which there is significant face-to-face interaction between the interviewer and the respondent. The second is the telephone-administered survey. In these surveys, the telephone is used to conduct the question-and-answer exchanges. Computers are used in many ways in telephone interviews, especially in data recording and telephone-number selection. The third type is the self-administered survey. In these surveys, there is little, if any, actual face-to-face contact between the researcher and prospective respondent. The respondent reads the questions and records his or her answers. Online surveys are the most frequent method of data collection, with almost 60 percent of all data collection being completed with online surveys.

Discuss the factors influencing the choice of survey methods.

There are three major factors affecting the choice of survey method: (1) situational characteristics; (2) task characteristics; and (3) respondent characteristics. With situational factors, consideration must be given to elements such as available resources, completion time frame, and data quality requirements. Also, the researcher must consider the overall task requirements and ask questions such as "How difficult are the tasks?" "What stimuli (e.g., ads or products) will be needed to evoke responses?" "How much information is needed from the respondent?" and "To what extent do the questions deal with sensitive topics?" Finally, researchers must consider the diversity of the prospective respondents, their likely incidence rate, and the degree of survey participation. Maximizing the quantity and quality of data collected while minimizing the cost and time of the survey generally requires the researcher to make trade-offs.

Explain experiments and the types of variables used in causal designs.

Experiments enable marketing researchers to control the research situation so that causal relationships among the variables can be examined. In a typical experiment, the independent variable is manipulated (changed) and its effect on another variable (dependent variable) is measured and evaluated. During the experiment, the researcher attempts to eliminate or control all other variables that might impact the relationship being measured. After the manipulation, the researcher measures the dependent variable to see if it has changed. If it has, the researcher concludes that the change in the dependent variable is caused by the manipulation of the independent variable.

To conduct causal research, the researcher must understand the four types of variables in experimental designs (independent, dependent, extraneous, control) as well as the key role of random selection and assignment of test subjects to experimental conditions. Theory is important in experimental design because researchers must conceptualize as clearly as possible the roles of the four types of variables. The most important goal of any experiment is to determine which relationships exist among different variables (independent, dependent). Functional (cause-effect) relationships require careful measurement of change in one variable as another variable changes.

Define test marketing and evaluate its usefulness in marketing research.

Test markets are a specific type of field experiment commonly conducted in natural field settings. Data gathered from test markets provide both researchers and practitioners with invaluable information concerning customers' attitudes, preferences, purchasing habits/patterns, and demographic profiles. This information can be useful in predicting new product or service acceptance levels and advertising and image effectiveness, as well as in evaluating current marketing mix strategies.

Key Terms and Concepts

Ability to participate 121
Causal research 122
Computer-Assisted Telephone Interview (CATI) 113
Control variables 124
Dependent variables 122
Drop-off survey 116
Experiment 122
External validity 125
Extraneous variables 124
Field experiments 127
Generalizable 119
Incidence rate 120
Independent variables 122
In-home interview 111
Internal validity 125
Knowledge level 121
Laboratory (lab) experiments 126
Mall-intercept interview 112

Mail panel survey 116
Mail surveys 116
Nonresponse error 110
Online surveys 116
Person-administered survey 111
Propensity scoring 118
Respondent errors 110
Response error 110
Self-administered survey 115
Survey research methods 109
Telephone interviews 112
Test marketing 127
Topic sensitivity 120
Validity 125
Variable 123
Willingness to participate 121
Wireless phone survey 114

Review Questions

1. Identify and discuss the advantages and disadvantages of using quantitative survey research methods to collect primary data in marketing research.
2. What are the three factors that affect choice of appropriate survey method? How do these factors differ in person-administered surveys as opposed to self-administered surveys?
3. Explain why survey designs that include a trained interviewer are more appropriate than computer-assisted survey designs in situations where the task difficulty and stimuli requirements are extensive.
4. Explain the major differences between in-home interviews and mall-intercept interviews. Make sure you include their advantages and disadvantages.
5. How might measurement and design errors affect respondent errors?
6. Develop three recommendations to help researchers increase the response rates in direct mail and telephone-administered surveys.
7. What is "nonresponse"? Identify four types of nonresponse found in surveys.
8. What are the advantages and disadvantages associated with online surveys?
9. How might a faulty problem definition error affect the implementation of a mail survey?
10. Explain the difference between internal validity and external validity.
11. What are the advantages and disadvantages of field experiments?

Discussion Questions

1. Develop a list of the factors used to select from person-administered, telephone-administered, self-administered, and computer-assisted survey designs. Then discuss the appropriateness of those selection factors across each type of survey design.
2. What impact, if any, will advances in technology have on survey research practices? Support your thoughts.
3. **EXPERIENCE MARKETING RESEARCH.** Go to the Gallup Poll site (**www.gallup.com**) and locate information about the Gallup World Poll. After reviewing the material, make a list of the challenges in conducting polls that represent 7 billion citizens across the world.
4. **EXPERIENCE MARKETING RESEARCH.** Go to Kinesis Research (**www.kinesissurvey.com**) and find and view the short wireless survey demonstration video. What are the advantages and disadvantages of wireless surveys?
5. Comment on the ethics of the following situations:
   a. A researcher plans to use invisible ink to code his direct mail questionnaires to identify those respondents who return the questionnaire.
   b. A telephone interviewer calls at 10:00 p.m. on a Sunday and asks to conduct an interview.
   c. A manufacturer purchases 100,000 e-mail addresses from a national e-mail distribution house and plans to e-mail out a short sales promotion under the heading of "We Want to Know Your Opinions."
6. The store manager of a local independent grocery store thought customers might stay in the store longer if slow, easy-to-listen-to music were played over the store's intercom system. After some thought, the manager considered whether he should hire a marketing researcher to design an experiment to test the influence of music tempo on shoppers' behaviors. Answer the following questions:
   a. How would you operationalize the independent variable?
   b. What dependent variables do you think might be important in this experiment?
   c. Develop a hypothesis for each of your dependent variables.

Part 3

Gathering and Collecting Accurate Data

Sampling: Theory and Methods

Chapter 6

1. Explain the role of sampling in the research process.

2. Distinguish between probability and nonprobability sampling.

3. Understand factors to consider when determining sample size.

4. Understand the steps in developing a sampling plan.

Mobile Web Interactions Explode

Mobile devices are taking over the wired world, and web interactions with mobile phones are exploding. More than Almost 90% of adults are internet users and more than 70% are smartphone users. Almost 40% of smartphone owners use messaging apps such as iMessage, WhatsApp or Kik, more than 20% use apps that automatically delete sent messages, such as Snapchat. Smartphone users are accessing all kinds of content from news and information, to social networking sites and blogs, stock reports and entertainment, and are making payments of services like ApplePay. News and information (such as maps and directions) are still the most popular content in the mobile world, with literally millions of daily users. And not only are more people accessing the web while on the go, they're doing so with mobile applications for smartphones like Apple's iPhone, Samsung, and more recently phones manufactured in China. Research studies indicate almost 90% of marketers use or plan to use search engine marketing, yet less than one-half of retail marketers and consumer-product/goods marketers expect to use mobile search in their marketing mixes. Media companies are most receptive, with about 80 percent planning to use mobile search in their promotion mixes. Forrester Research studies indicate that 80 percent of marketers use or plan to use search engine marketing (SEM), yet less than a third of retail marketers and one-half of consumer-product/goods marketers expect to use mobile search in their marketing mixes. Media companies are most receptive, with about 70 percent planning to use mobile search in their promotion mixes.

While Americans are embracing the mobile web as smartphone capabilities increase, most people are still not willing to give up their nice big desktop monitors and laptops for the mobile web only. But as the mobile web becomes more important (and secure), regular and mobile Internet access will begin to merge. Two reasons consumers resist mobile search activities are (1) searching on a 2-inch mobile screen is not yet a good user experience and (2) consumers mistakenly believe a mobile search should be the same as an Internet search. The findings of one study by UpSnap, a search firm that offers free weather, sports scores, and subscription content, indicate that users must remember that mobile search is not the Internet on a phone and mobile search needs to be considered as one alternative to finding a specific, quick hit.

From a marketing research perspective, there are two key questions to be asked about mobile interaction usage studies. First, *What respondents should be included in a study about consumer acceptance of mobile search?* And second, *How many respondents should be included in each study?* These might be difficult questions to answer for companies that do not have good customer demographics, attitudes, and behavior databases. But specialty research firms like Survey Sampling International (SSI) can help. SSI (**www.ssisamples.com**) has the technology and skills to generate samples that target consumers and/or businesses based on lifestyles, topics of interest, and demographics such as age, presence of children, occupation, marital status, education level, and income. The firm is well respected for its Internet, RDD, telephone, B2B, and mail sampling designs. As you read this chapter, you will learn the importance of knowing which groups to sample, how many elements to sample, and the different methods available to researchers for selecting high-quality, reliable samples.[1]

■■ Value of Sampling in Marketing Research

Sampling is a concept we practice in our everyday activities. Consider, for example, going on a job interview. Making a good first impression in a job interview is important because based on the initial exposure (i.e., sample), people often make judgments about the type of person we are. Similarly, people sit in front of their TV with a remote control in their hand and rapidly flip through a number of different channels, stopping a few seconds to take a sample of the program on each channel until they find a program worth watching. Next time you have a free moment, go to a bookstore like Barnes and Noble and observe sampling at its best. People at a bookstore generally pick up a book or magazine, look at its cover, and read a few pages to get a feel for the author's writing style and content before deciding whether to buy the book. When people go automobile shopping, they want to test-drive a particular car for a few miles to see how the car feels and performs before deciding whether to buy it. One commonality in all these situations is that a decision is based on the assumption that the smaller portion, or sample, is representative of the larger population. From a general perspective, **sampling** involves selecting a relatively small number of elements from a larger defined group of elements and expecting that the information gathered from the small group will enable accurate judgments about the larger group.

Sampling Selection of a small number of elements from a larger defined target group of elements and expecting that the information gathered from the small group will allow judgments to be made about the larger group.

Census A research study that includes data about every member of the defined target population.

Sampling as a Part of the Research Process

Sampling is often used when it is impossible or unreasonable to conduct a census. With a **census**, primary data is collected from every member of the target population. The best example of a census is the U.S. Census, which takes place every ten years.

It is easy to see that sampling is less time-consuming and less costly than conducting a census. For example, American Airlines may want to find out what business travelers like and dislike about flying with them. Gathering data from 2,000 American business travelers would be much less expensive and time-consuming than surveying several million travelers. No matter what type of research design is used to collect data, decision makers are concerned about the time and cost required, and shorter projects are more likely to fit the decision maker's time frames.

Samples also play an important indirect role in designing questionnaires. Depending on the research problem and the target population, sampling decisions influence the type of research design, the survey instrument, and the actual questionnaire. For example, by having a general idea of the target population and the key characteristics that will be used to draw the sample of respondents, researchers can customize the questionnaire to ensure that it is of interest to respondents and provides high-quality data.

◼ The Basics of Sampling Theory

Population

Population The identifiable set of elements of interest to the researcher and pertinent to the information problem.

A **population** is an identifiable group of elements (e.g., people, products, organizations) of interest to the researcher and pertinent to the information problem. For example, Mazda Motor Corporation could hire J. D. Power and Associates to measure customer satisfaction among automobile owners. The population of interest could be all people who own automobiles. It is unlikely, however, that J. D. Power and Associates could draw a sample that would be truly representative of such a broad, heterogeneous population—any data collected would probably not be applicable to customer satisfaction with Mazda. This lack of specificity unfortunately is common in marketing research. Most businesses that collect data are not really concerned with total populations, but with a prescribed segment. In this chapter, we use a modified definition of population: *defined target population*. A **defined target population** consists of the complete group of elements (people or objects) that are identified for investigation based on the objectives of the research project. A precise definition of the target population is essential and is usually done in terms of elements, sampling units, and time frames. **Sampling units** are target population elements actually available to be used during the sampling process. Exhibit 6.1 clarifies several sampling theory terms.

Defined target population The complete set of elements identified for investigation.

Sampling units The target population elements available for selection during the sampling process.

| **Exhibit 6.1** | **Examples of Elements, Sampling Units, and Time Frames** |

Mazda Automobiles

Elements	Adult purchasers of automobiles
Sampling unit	New Mazda automobile purchasers
Time frame	January 1, 2012 to September 30, 2013

Nail Polish

Elements	Females between the ages of 18 and 34 who purchased at least one brand of nail polish during the past 30 days
Sampling units	U.S. cities with populations between 100,000 and 1 million people
Time frame	June 1 to June 15, 2013

Retail Banking Services

Elements	Households with checking accounts
Sampling units	Households located within a 10-mile radius of Bank of America's central location in Charlotte, North Carolina
Time frame	January 1 to April 30, 2013

Sampling Frame

Sampling frame The list of all eligible sampling units.

After defining the target population, the researcher develops a list of all eligible sampling units, referred to as a **sampling frame**. Some common sources of sampling frames are lists of registered voters and customer lists from magazine publishers or credit card companies. There also are specialized commercial companies (for instance, Survey Sampling, Inc., American Business Lists, Inc., and Scientific Telephone Samples) that sell databases containing names, addresses, and telephone numbers of potential population elements. Although the costs of obtaining sampling lists will vary, a list typically can be purchased for between $150 and $300 per 1,000 names.[2]

Regardless of the source, it is often difficult and expensive to obtain accurate, representative, and current sampling frames. It is doubtful, for example, that a list of individuals who have eaten a taco from Taco Bell in a particular city in the past six months will be readily available. In this instance, a researcher would have to use an alternative method such as random-digit dialing (if conducting telephone interviews) or a mall-intercept interview to generate a sample of prospective respondents.

Factors Underlying Sampling Theory

To understand sampling theory, you must know sampling-related concepts. Sampling concepts and approaches are often discussed as if the researcher already knows the key population parameters prior to conducting the research project. However, because most business environments are complex and rapidly changing, researchers often do not know these parameters prior to conducting research. For example, retailers that have added online shopping alternatives for consumers are working to identify and describe the people who are making their retail purchases over the Internet rather than at traditional "brick-and-mortar" stores. Experts estimate that the world's online population exceeds 570 million people,[3] but the actual number of online retail shoppers is more difficult to estimate. One of the major goals of researching small, yet representative, samples of members of a defined target population is that the results of the research will help to predict or estimate what the true population parameters are within a certain degree of confidence.

If business decision makers had complete knowledge about their defined target populations, they would have perfect information about the realities of those populations, thus eliminating the need to conduct primary research. Better than 95 percent of today's marketing problems exist primarily because decision makers lack information about their problem situations and who their customers are, as well as customers' attitudes, preferences, and marketplace behaviors.

Central limit theorem (CLT) The sampling distribution derived from a simple random sample will be approximately normally distributed.

Central Limit Theorem The **central limit theorem (CLT)** describes the theoretical characteristics of a sample population. The CLT is the theoretical backbone of survey research and is important in understanding the concepts of sampling error, statistical significance, and sample sizes. In brief, the theorem states that for almost all defined target populations, the sampling distribution of the mean $\bar{x}$ or the percentage value $(\bar{p})$ derived from a simple random sample will be approximately normally distributed, provided the sample size is sufficiently large (i.e., when n is > or = 30). Moreover, the mean $\bar{x}$ of the random sample with an estimated sampling error $(S_{\bar{x}})$ fluctuates around the true population mean (μ) with a standard error of $\sigma/\sqrt{n}$ and an approximately normal sampling distribution, regardless of the shape of the probability frequency distribution of the overall target population. In other words, there is a high probability that the mean of any sample $\bar{x}$ taken from the target population will be a close approximation of the true target population mean (μ), as one increases the size of the sample (n).

With an understanding of the basics of the CLT, the researcher can do the following:

1. Draw representative samples from any target population.
2. Obtain sample statistics from a random sample that serve as accurate estimates of the target population's parameters.
3. Draw one random sample, instead of many, reducing the costs of data collection.
4. More accurately assess the reliability and validity of constructs and scale measurements.
5. Statistically analyze data and transform it into meaningful information about the target population.

Tools Used to Assess the Quality of Samples

There are numerous opportunities to make mistakes that result in some type of bias in any research study. This bias can be classified as either sampling error or nonsampling error. Random sampling errors could be detected by observing the difference between the sample results and the results of a census conducted using identical procedures. Two difficulties associated with detecting sampling error are (1) a census is very seldom conducted in survey research and (2) sampling error can be determined only after the sample is drawn and data collection is completed.

Sampling error Any type of bias that is attributable to mistakes in either drawing a sample or determining the sample size.

Sampling error is any bias that results from mistakes in either the selection process for prospective sampling units or in determining the sample size. Moreover, random sampling error tends to occur because of chance variations in the selection of sampling units. Even if the sampling units are properly selected, those units still might not be a perfect representation of the defined target population, but they generally are reliable estimates. When there is a discrepancy between the statistic estimated from the sample and the actual value from the population, a sampling error has occurred. Sampling error can be reduced by increasing the size of the sample. In fact, doubling the size of the sample can reduce the sampling error, but increasing the sample size primarily to reduce the standard error may not be worth the cost.

Nonsampling error A bias that occurs in a research study regardless of whether a sample or census is used.

Nonsampling error occurs regardless of whether a sample or a census is used. These errors can occur at any stage of the research process. For example, the target population may be inaccurately defined causing population frame error; inappropriate question/scale measurements can result in measurement error; a questionnaire may be poorly designed

MARKETING RESEARCH IN ACTION CONTINUING CASE STUDY   THE SANTA FE GRILL

The business consultant has recommended a survey of Santa Fe Grill customers. To interview the customers, the consultant has suggested several approaches for collecting the data. One is to ask customers to complete the questionnaires at their table either before or after they get their food. Another is to stop them on the way out of the restaurant and ask them to complete a questionnaire. A third option is to give the questionnaire to them and ask that they complete it at home and mail it back, and a fourth option is to intercept them in the mall. A fifth option is to load software on the computer, write a program to randomly select customers, and when they pay their bill, give them instructions on how to go to a website and

complete the survey. The last option, however, is most expensive because setting up the Internet survey is more expensive than handing paper surveys to customers in the restaurant.

The consultant has been brainstorming with other restaurant industry experts on how to best collect the data. He has not yet decided which options to suggest to the owners.

1. Which of the data collection options is best? Why?
2. Should data be collected from customers of competitive restaurants? If yes, what are some possible ways to collect data from their customers?

causing response error; or there may be other errors in gathering and recording data or when raw data are coded and entered for analysis. In general, the more extensive a study, the greater the potential for nonsampling errors. Unlike sampling error, there are no statistical procedures to assess the impact of nonsampling errors on the quality of the data collected. Yet, most researchers realize that all forms of nonsampling errors reduce the overall quality of the data regardless of the data collection method. Nonsampling errors usually are related to the accuracy of the data, whereas sampling errors relate to the representativeness of the sample to the defined target population.

◼◼ Probability and Nonprobability Sampling

There are two basic sampling designs: (1) probability and (2) nonprobability. Exhibit 6.2 lists the different types of both sampling methods.

Probability sampling Each sampling unit in the defined target population has a known probability of being selected for the sample.

In **probability sampling**, each sampling unit in the defined target population has a known probability of being selected for the sample. The actual probability of selection for each sampling unit may or may not be equal depending on the type of probability sampling design used. Specific rules for selecting members from the population for inclusion in the sample are determined at the beginning of a study to ensure (1) unbiased selection of the sampling units and (2) proper sample representation of the defined target population. Probability sampling enables the researcher to judge the reliability and validity of data collected by calculating the probability that the sample findings are different from the defined target population. The observed difference can be partially attributed to the existence of sampling error. The results obtained by using probability sampling designs can be generalized to the target population within a specified margin of error.

Nonprobability sampling Sampling designs in which the probability of selection of each sampling unit is not known. The selection of sampling units is based on the judgment of the researcher and may or may not be representative of the target population.

In **nonprobability sampling**, the probability of selecting each sampling unit is not known. Therefore, sampling error is not known. Selection of sampling units is based on intuitive judgment or researcher knowledge. The degree to which the sample is representative of the defined target population depends on the sampling approach and how well the researcher executes the selection activities.

Probability Sampling Designs

Simple random sampling A probability sampling procedure in which every sampling unit has a known and equal chance of being selected.

Simple Random Sampling **Simple random sampling** is a probability sampling procedure. With this approach, every sampling unit has a known and equal chance of being selected. For example, an instructor could draw a sample of ten students from among 30 students in a marketing research class. The instructor could write each student's name on a separate, identical piece of paper and place all of the names in a hat. Each student

---

Exhibit 6.2 Types of Probability and Nonprobability Sampling Methods

Probability Sampling Methods	Nonprobability Sampling Methods
Simple random sampling	Convenience sampling
Systematic random sampling	Judgment sampling
Stratified random sampling	Quota sampling
Cluster sampling	Snowball sampling

would have an equal, known probability of selection. Many software programs including SPSS have an option to select a random sample.

Advantages and Disadvantages Simple random sampling has several advantages. The technique is easily understood and the survey's results can be generalized to the defined target population with a prespecified margin of error. Another advantage is that simple random samples produce unbiased estimates of the population's characteristics. This method guarantees that every sampling unit has a known and equal chance of being selected, no matter the actual size of the sample, resulting in a valid representation of the defined target population. The primary disadvantage of simple random sampling is the difficulty of obtaining a complete and accurate listing of the target population elements. Simple random sampling requires that all sampling units be identified. For this reason, simple random sampling works best for small populations where accurate lists are available.

Systematic Random Sampling **Systematic random sampling** is similar to simple random sampling but requires that the defined target population be ordered in some way, usually in the form of a customer list, taxpayer roll, or membership roster. In research practices, systematic random sampling has become a popular method of drawing samples. Compared to simple random sampling, systematic random sampling is less costly because it can be done relatively quickly. When executed properly, systematic random sampling creates a sample of objects or prospective respondents that is very similar in quality to a sample drawn using simple random sampling.

To use systematic random sampling, the researcher must be able to secure a complete listing of the potential sampling units that make up the defined target population. But unlike simple random sampling, there is no need give the sampling units any special code prior to drawing the sample. Instead, sampling units are selected according to their position using a skip interval. The skip interval is determined by dividing the number of potential sampling units in the defined target population by the number of units desired in the sample. The required skip interval is calculated using the following formula:

$$\text{Skip interval} = \frac{\text{Defined target population list size}}{\text{Desired sample size}}$$

For instance, if a researcher wants a sample of 100 to be drawn from a population of 1,000, the skip interval would be 10 (1,000/100). Once the skip interval is determined, the researcher would then randomly select a starting point and take every 10th unit until he or she had proceeded through the entire target population list. Exhibit 6.3 displays the steps that a researcher would take in drawing a systematic random sample.

Advantages and Disadvantages Systematic sampling is frequently used because it is a relatively easy way to draw a sample while ensuring randomness. The availability of lists and the shorter time required to draw a sample versus simple random sampling makes systematic sampling an attractive, economical method for researchers. The greatest weakness of systematic random sampling is the possibility of hidden patterns in the list of names that create bias. Hidden patterns represent populations that researchers may be interested in studying, but often are hard to reach or "hidden". Such populations may be hidden because they exhibit some type of social stigma (certain medical conditions), illicit or illegal behaviors (drug usage), or are atypical or socially marginalized (homeless). Another difficulty is the number of sampling units in the target population must be known. When the size of the target population is large or unknown, identifying the number of units is difficult, and estimates may not be accurate.

Systematic random sampling Similar to simple random sampling but the defined target population is ordered in some way, usually in the form of a customer list, taxpayer roll, or membership roster, and selected systematically.

Exhibit 6.3 Steps in Drawing a Systematic Random Sample

Step 1 → **Obtain a List of Potential Sampling Units That Contains an Acceptable Frame of the Target Population Elements.**
Example: Current list of students (names, addresses, telephone numbers) enrolled at your university or college from the registrar's office.

Step 2 → **Determine the Total Number of Sampling Units Making Up the List of the Defined Target Population's Elements and the Desired Sample Size.**
Example: 30,000 current student names on the list. Desired sample size is 1,200 students, for a confidence level of 95%, P value equal to 50%, and tolerance sampling error of ± 2.83 percentage points.

Step 3 → **Compute the Needed Skip Interval by Dividing the Number of Potential Sampling Units on the List by the Desired Sample Size.**
Example: 30,000 current student names on the list, desired sample of 1,200, so the skip interval would be every 25th name.

Step 4 → **Using a Random Number-Generation System, Randomly Determine a Starting Point to Sample the List of Names.**
Examples: Select: Random number for starting page of the multiple-page listing (e.g., 8th page).
Select: Random number for name position on that starting page (e.g., Carol V. Clark).

Step 5 → **With Carol V. Clark as the First Sample Unit, Apply the Skip Interval to Determine the Remaining Names That Should Be Included in the Sample of 1,200.**
Examples: Clark, Carol V. (Skip 25 names).
Cobert, James W. (Skip 25 names).
Damon, Victoria J. (Skip 25 names; repeat process until all 1,200 names are drawn).

Note: The researcher must visualize the population list as being continuous or "circular"; that is, the drawing process must continue past those names that represent the Z's and include names representing the A's and B's so that the 1,200th name drawn will basically be the 25th name prior to the first drawn name (i.e., Carol V. Clark).

MARKETING RESEARCH DASHBOARD SELECTING A SYSTEMATIC RANDOM SAMPLE FOR THE SANTA FE GRILL

Over the past three years, the owners of the Santa Fe Grill have compiled a listing of 1,030 customers arranged in alphabetical order. A systematic sample of 100 customers' opinions is the research objective. Having decided on a sample size of 100 to be selected from the sampling frame of 1,030 customers, the owner calculates the size of the interval between successive elements of the sample by computing 1,030/100. The size of the interval is determined by dividing the target population (sampling frame) size by the desired sample size (1,030/100 = 10.3). In situations such as this, where the result is a decimal instead of a round number, you round to the nearest integer. Thus, we have effectively partitioned the sampling frame into 100 intervals of size 10. From the numbers in the interval of 1 to 10, we then must randomly select a number to identify the first element for the systematic sample. If, for example, that number is 4, then we begin with the 4th element in the sampling frame and every 10th element thereafter is chosen. The initial starting point is the 4th element and the remaining elements selected for the sample are the 14th, 24th, 34th, and so on until the final element chosen is the 1,024th. This will result in a sample of 103 customers to be interviewed in the survey.

Stratified random sampling
Separation of the target
population into different
groups, called strata, and
the selection of samples
from each stratum.

Stratified Random Sampling **Stratified random sampling** involves the separation of
the target population into different groups, called strata, and the selection of samples from
each stratum. Stratified random sampling is similar to segmentation of the defined target
population into smaller, more homogeneous sets of elements.

To ensure that the sample maintains the required precision, representative samples
must be drawn from each of the smaller population groups (stratum). Drawing a stratified
random sample involves three basic steps:

1. Dividing the target population into homogeneous subgroups or strata.
2. Drawing random samples from each stratum.
3. Combining the samples from each stratum into a single sample of the target population.

As an example, if researchers are interested in the market potential for home security systems in a specific geographic area, they may wish to divide the homeowners into several
different strata. The subdivisions could be based on such factors as assessed value of the
homes, household income, population density, or location (e.g., sections designated as
high- and low-crime areas).

**Proportionately stratified
sampling**   A stratified
sampling method in which
each stratum is dependent
on its size relative to the
population.

Two common methods are used to derive samples from the strata: proportionate and
disproportionate. In **proportionately stratified sampling**, the sample size from each stratum is dependent on that stratum's size relative to the defined target population. Therefore, the larger strata are sampled more heavily because they make up a larger percentage
of the target population. In **disproportionately stratified sampling**, the sample size
selected from each stratum is independent of that stratum's proportion of the total defined
target population. This approach is used when stratification of the target population produces sample sizes for subgroups that differ from their relative importance to the study.

**Disproportionately strati-
fied sampling**   A stratified
sampling method in which
the size of each stratum is
independent of its relative
size in the population.

For example, stratification of manufacturers based on number of employees will usually
result in a large segment of manufacturers with fewer than ten employees and a very small
proportion with, say, 500 or more employees. The economic importance of those firms
with 500 or more employees would dictate taking a larger sample from this stratum and
a smaller sample from the subgroup with fewer than ten employees than indicated by the
proportionality method.

An alternative type of disproportionate stratified method is **optimal allocation
sampling**. In this method, consideration is given to the relative size of the stratum
as well as the variability within the stratum to determine the necessary sample size
of each stratum. The basic logic underlying optimal allocation is that the greater the
homogeneity of the prospective sampling units within a particular stratum, all else
being equal, the fewer the units that would have to be selected to accurately estimate
the true population parameter (u or P) for that subgroup. In contrast, more units would
be selected for any stratum that has considerable variance among its sampling units or
that is heterogeneous.

In some situations, **multisource sampling** is being used when no single source can
generate a large or low incidence sample. While researchers have shied away from using
multiple sources, mainly because sampling theory dictates the use of a defined single population, changing respondent behaviors (e.g., less frequent use of e-mail and more frequent
use of social media) are supporting multisource sampling. For example, if the manufacturer
of golfing equipment used a stratified random sample of country club members as the sampling frame, the likelihood of visitors or invited guests to the country club would be hidden
from the researcher. Excluding these two groups could omit valuable data that would be
available in a multisource approach. Exhibit 6.4 displays the steps that a researcher would
take in drawing a stratified random sample.

Exhibit 6.4 Steps in Drawing a Stratified Random Sample

Step 1 → **Obtain a List of Potential Sampling Units That Contains an Acceptable Frame of the Defined Target Population Elements.**
Example: List of known performance arts patrons (names, addresses, telephone numbers) living in a three-county area from the current database of the Asolo Performing Arts Centre. Total number of known patrons on the current database is 10,500.

Step 2 → **Using Some Type of Secondary Information or Past Experience with the Defined Target Population, Select a Stratification Factor for Which the Population's Distribution Is Skewed (Not Bell-Shaped) and Can Be Used to Determine That the Total Defined Target Population Consists of Separate Subpopulations of Elements.**
Example: Using attendance records and county location, identify strata by county and number of events attended per season (i.e., regular, occasional, or rare). Total: 10,500 patrons with 5,900 "regular" (56.2%); 3,055 "occasional" (29.1%); and 1,545 "rare" (14.7%) patrons.

Step 3 → **Using the Selected Stratification Factor (or Some Other Surrogate Variable), Segment the Defined Target Population into Strata Consistent with Each of the Identified Separate Subpopulations. That is, use the stratification factor to regroup the prospective sampling units into their mutually exclusive subgroups. Then determine both the actual number of sampling units and their percentage equivalents for each stratum.**
Example: County A: 5,000 patrons with 2,500 "regular" (50%); 1,875 "occasional" (37.5%); and 625 "rare" (12.5%) patrons.
County B: 3,000 patrons with 1,800 "regular" (60%); 580 "occasional" (19.3%); and 620 "rare" (20.7%) patrons.
County C: 2,500 patrons with 1,600 "regular" (64%); 600 "occasional" (24%); and 300 "rare" (12%) patrons.

Step 4 → **Determine Whether There Is a Need to Apply a Disproportionate or Optimal Allocation Method to the Stratification Process; Otherwise, Use the Proportionate Method and Then Estimate the Desired Sample Sizes.**
Example: Compare individual county strata percentage values to overall target population strata values. Let's assume a proportionate method and a confidence level of 95% and a tolerance for sampling error of ±2.5 percentage points. Estimate the sample size for total target population with no strata needed and assuming $P = 50\%$. The desired sample size would equal 1,537 people. Then proportion that size by the total patron percentage values for each of the three counties determined in step 2 (e.g., County A = 5,000/10,500 [47.6%]; County B = 3,000/10,500 [28.6%]; County C = 2,500/10,500 [23.8%]). New sample sizes for each county would be: County A = 732; County B = 439; County C = 366. Now for each county sample size, proportion the sample sizes by the respective within-county estimates for "regular," "occasional," and "rare" strata percentages determined in step 3.

Step 5 → **Select a Probability Sample from Each Stratum, Using either the SRS or SYMRS Procedure.**
Example: Use the procedures discussed earlier for drawing SRS or SYMRS samples.

Advantages and Disadvantages Dividing the target population into homogeneous strata has several advantages, including (1) the assurance of representativeness in the sample; (2) the opportunity to study each stratum and make comparisons between strata; and (3) the ability to make estimates for the target population with the expectation of greater precision and less error. The primary difficulty encountered with stratified sampling is determining the basis for stratifying. Stratification is based on the target population's characteristics of interest. Secondary information relevant to the required stratification factors might not be readily available, therefore forcing the researcher to use less desirable criteria as the factors for stratifying the target population. Usually, the larger the number of relevant strata, the more precise the results. Inclusion of irrelevant strata, however, will waste time and money without providing meaningful results.

Cluster sampling A probability sampling method in which the sampling units are divided into mutually exclusive and collectively exhaustive subpopulations, called clusters.

Cluster Sampling **Cluster sampling** is similar to stratified random sampling, but is different in that the sampling units are divided into mutually exclusive and collectively exhaustive subpopulations called clusters. Each cluster is assumed to be representative of the heterogeneity of the target population. Examples of possible divisions for cluster sampling include customers who patronize a store on a given day, the audience for a movie shown at a particular time (e.g., the matinee), or the invoices processed during a specific week. Once the cluster has been identified, the prospective sampling units are selected for the sample by either using a simple random sampling method or canvassing all the elements (a census) within the defined cluster.

Area sampling A form of cluster sampling in which the clusters are formed by geographic designations.

A popular form of cluster sampling is **area sampling**. In area sampling, the clusters are formed by geographic designations. Examples include metropolitan statistical areas (MSAs), cities, subdivisions, and blocks. Any geographical unit with identifiable boundaries can be used. When using area sampling, the researcher has two additional options: the

MARKETING RESEARCH DASHBOARD   WHICH IS BETTER—PROPORTIONATELY OR DISPROPORTIONATELY STRATIFIED SAMPLES?

The owners of the Santa Fe Grill have a list of 3,000 potential customers broken down by age. Using a statistical formula, they have decided that a proportionately stratified sample of 200 customers will produce information that is sufficiently accurate for decision making. The number of elements to be chosen from each stratum using a proportionate sample based on age is shown in the fourth column of the table. But if they believe the sample size in each stratum should be relative to its economic importance,

and the 18 to 49 age group are the most frequent diners and spend the most when dining out, then the number of selected elements would be disproportionate to stratum size as illustrated in the fifth column. The numbers in the disproportionate column would be determined based on the judgment of each stratum's economic importance.

Should proportionate or disproportionate sampling be used? That is, should the decision be based on economic importance, or some other criteria?

			Number of Elements Selected for the Sample	
(1) Age Group	(2) Number of Elements in Stratum	(3) % of Elements in Stratum	(4) Proportionate Sample Size	(5) Disproportionate Sample Size
18–25	600	20	40 = 20%	50 = 25%
26–34	900	30	60 = 30%	50 = 25%
35–49	270	9	18 = 9%	50 = 25%
50–59	1,020	34	68 = 34%	30 = 15%
60 and Older	210	7	14 = 7%	20 = 10%
Total	3,000	100	200	200

one-step approach or the two-step approach. When deciding on a one-step approach, the researcher must have enough prior information about the various geographic clusters to believe that all the geographic clusters are basically identical with regard to the specific factors that were used to initially identify the clusters. By assuming that all the clusters are identical, the researcher can focus his or her attention on surveying the sampling units within one designated cluster and then generalize the results to the population. The probability aspect of this particular sampling method is executed by randomly selecting one geographic cluster and sampling all units in that cluster.

Advantages and Disadvantages Cluster sampling is widely used because of its cost-effectiveness and ease of implementation. In many cases, the only representative sampling frame available to researchers is one based on clusters (e.g., states, counties, MSAs, census tracts). These lists of geographic regions, telephone exchanges, or blocks of residential dwellings usually can be easily compiled, thus avoiding the need of compiling lists of all the individual sampling units making up the target population.

Cluster sampling methods have several disadvantages. A primary disadvantage of cluster sampling is that the clusters often are homogeneous. The more homogeneous the cluster, the less precise the sample estimates. Ideally, the people in a cluster should be as heterogeneous as those in the population.

Another concern with cluster sampling is the appropriateness of the designated cluster factor used to identify the sampling units within clusters. While the defined target population remains constant, the subdivision of sampling units can be modified depending on the selection of the factor used to identify the clusters. As a result, caution must be used in selecting the factor to determine clusters in area sampling situations.

Nonprobability Sampling Designs

Convenience sampling
A nonprobability sampling method in which samples are drawn at the convenience of the researcher.

Convenience Sampling **Convenience sampling** is a method in which samples are drawn based on convenience. For example, interviewing individuals at shopping malls or other high-traffic areas is a common method of generating a convenience sample. The assumption is that the individuals interviewed at the shopping mall are similar to the overall defined target population with regard to the characteristic being studied. In reality, it is difficult to accurately assess the representativeness of the sample. Given self-selection and the voluntary nature of participating in the data collection, researchers should consider the impact of nonresponse error when using sampling based on convenience only.

Advantages and Disadvantages Convenience sampling enables a large number of respondents to be interviewed in a relatively short time. For this reason, it is commonly used in the early stages of research, including construct and scale measurement development as well as pretesting of questionnaires. But using convenience samples to develop constructs and scales can be risky. For example, assume a researcher is developing a measure of service quality and in the preliminary stages uses a convenience sample of 300 undergraduate business students. While college students are consumers of services, serious questions should be raised about whether they are truly representative of the general population. By developing constructs and scales using a convenience sample of college students, the constructs might be unreliable if used to study a broader target population. Another major disadvantage of convenience samples is that the data are not generalizable to the defined target population. The representativeness of the sample cannot be measured because sampling error estimates cannot be calculated.

Judgment sampling A nonprobability sampling method in which participants are selected according to an experienced individual's belief that they will meet the requirements of the study.

Judgment Sampling In **judgment sampling**, sometimes referred to as *purposive sampling*, respondents are selected because the researcher believes they meet the requirements of the study. For example, sales representatives may be interviewed rather than customers to determine whether customers' wants and needs are changing or to assess the firm's product or service performance. Similarly, consumer packaged goods companies such as Procter & Gamble may select a sample of key accounts to obtain information about consumption patterns and changes in demand for selected products, for example, Crest toothpaste or Cheer laundry detergent. The assumption is that the opinions of a group of experts are representative of the target population.

Advantages and Disadvantages If the judgment of the researcher is correct, the sample generated by judgment sampling will be better than one generated by convenience sampling. As with all nonprobability sampling procedures, however, you cannot measure the representativeness of the sample. Thus, data collected from judgment sampling should be interpreted cautiously.

Quota sampling A nonprobability sampling method in which participants are selected according to prespecified quotas regarding demographics, attitudes, behaviors, or some other criteria.

Quota Sampling **Quota sampling** involves the selection of prospective participants according to prespecified quotas for either demographic characteristics (e.g., age, race, gender, income), specific attitudes (e.g., satisfied/dissatisfied, liking/disliking, great/marginal/no quality), or specific behaviors (e.g., regular/occasional/rare customer, product user/nonuser). The purpose of quota sampling is to assure that prespecified subgroups of the population are represented.

Advantages and Disadvantages The major advantage of quota sampling is that the sample generated contains specific subgroups in the proportions desired by researchers. Use of quotas ensures that the appropriate subgroups are identified and included in the survey. Also, quota sampling reduces selection bias by field workers. An inherent limitation of quota sampling is that the success of the study is dependent on subjective decisions made by researchers. Since it is a nonprobability sampling method, the representativeness of the sample cannot be measured. Therefore, generalizing the results beyond the sampled respondents is questionable.

Snowball sampling A nonprobability sampling method, also called referral sampling, in which a set of respondents is chosen, and they help the researcher identify additional people to be included in the study.

Snowball Sampling **Snowball sampling** involves identifying a set of respondents who can help the researcher identify additional people to include in the study. This method of sampling is also called *referral sampling* because one respondent refers other potential respondents. Snowball sampling typically is used in situations where (1) the defined target population is small and unique and (2) compiling a complete list of sampling units is very difficult. Consider, for example, researching the attitudes and behaviors of people who volunteer their time to charitable organizations like the Children's Wish Foundation. While traditional sampling methods require an extensive search effort both in time and cost to find a sufficient number of prospective respondents, the snowball method yields better results at a much lower cost. Here the researcher interviews a qualified respondent, then solicits his or her help to identify other people with similar characteristics. While membership in these types of social circles might not be publicly known, intracircle knowledge is very accurate. The underlying logic of this method is that rare groups of people tend to form their own unique social circles.

Advantages and Disadvantages Snowball sampling is a reasonable method of identifying respondents who are members of small, hard-to-reach, uniquely defined target populations. As a nonprobability sampling method, it is most useful in qualitative research. But snowball sampling allows bias to enter the study. If there are significant differences between people who are known in certain social circles and those who are not, there may be problems with this sampling technique. Like all other nonprobability sampling approaches, the ability to generalize the results to members of the target population is limited.

| Exhibit 6.5 | Factors to Consider in Selecting the Sampling Design |

Selection Factors	Questions
Research objectives	Do the research objectives call for the use of qualitative or quantitative research designs?
Degree of accuracy	Does the research call for making predictions or inferences about the defined target population, or only preliminary insights?
Resources	Are there tight budget constraints with respect to both dollars and human resources that can be allocated to the research project?
Time frame	How quickly does the research project have to be completed?
Knowledge of the target population	Are there complete lists of the defined target population elements? How easy or difficult is it to generate the required sampling frame of prospective respondents?
Scope of the research	Is the research going be international, national, regional, or local?
Statistical analysis needs	To what extent are accurate statistical projections and/or testing of hypothesized differences in the data required?

Determining the Appropriate Sampling Design

Determining the best sampling design involves consideration of several factors. In Exhibit 6.5 we provide an overview of the major factors that should be considered. Take a close look at Exhibit 6.5 and review your understanding of these factors.

Determining Sample Sizes

Determining the sample size is not an easy task. The researcher must consider how precise the estimates must be and how much time and money are available to collect the required data, since data collection is generally one of the most expensive components of a study. Sample size determination differs between probability and nonprobability designs.

Probability Sample Sizes

Three factors play an important role in determining sample sizes with probability designs:

1. *The population variance, which is a measure of the dispersion of the population, and its square root, referred to as the population standard deviation.* The greater the variability in the data being estimated, the larger the sample size needed.
2. *The level of confidence desired in the estimate.* Confidence is the certainty that the true value of what we are estimating falls within the precision range we have selected. For example, marketing researchers typically select a 90 or 95 percent confidence level for their projects. The higher the level of confidence desired is the larger the sample size needed.
3. *The degree of precision desired in estimating the population characteristic.* **Precision** is the acceptable amount of error in the sample estimate. For example, if we want to estimate the likelihood of returning in the future to the Santa Fe Grill (based on a

Precision The acceptable amount of error in the sample estimate.

CONTINUING CASE STUDY   THE SANTA FE GRILL

The business consultant has recommended a survey of customers. The restaurant is open seven days a week for lunch and dinner. The consultant is considering both probability and nonprobability sampling methods as ways to collect customer data.

1. Which of the sampling options is best for the survey of the Santa Fe Grill customers? Why?

2. What are some possible sampling methods with which to collect data from customers of competitive restaurants?

7-point scale), is it acceptable to be within ±1 scale point? The more precise the required sample results, that is, the smaller the desired error, the larger the sample size.

For a particular sample size, there is a trade-off between degree of confidence and degree of precision, and the desire for confidence and precision must be balanced. These two considerations must be agreed upon by the client and the marketing researcher based on the research situation.

Formulas based on statistical theory can be used to compute the sample size. For pragmatic reasons, such as budget and time constraints, alternative "ad hoc" methods often are used. Examples of these are sample sizes based on rules of thumb, previous similar studies, one's own experience, or simply what is affordable. Irrespective of how the sample size is determined, it is essential that it should be of a sufficient size and quality to yield results that are seen to be credible in terms of their accuracy and consistency.

When formulas are used to determine sample size, there are separate approaches for determining sample size based on a predicted population mean and a population proportion. The formulas are used to estimate the sample size for a simple random sample. When the situation involves estimating a population mean, the formula for calculating the sample size is

$$n = \left(Z_{B,CL}^2\right)\left(\frac{\sigma^2}{e^2}\right)$$

where

$Z_{B,CL}$ = The standardized z-value associated with the level of confidence
σ_μ = Estimate of the population standard deviation (σ) based on some type of prior information
e = Acceptable tolerance level of error (stated in percentage points)

In situations where estimates of a population proportion are of concern, the standardized formula for calculating the needed sample size would be

$$n = \left(Z_{B,CL}^2\right)\left(\frac{[P \times Q]}{e^2}\right)$$

where

$Z_{B,CL}$ = The standardized z-value associated with the level of confidence
P = Estimate of expected population proportion having a desired characteristic based on intuition or prior information
Q = −[1 − P], or the estimate of expected population proportion not holding the characteristic of interest
e = Acceptable tolerance level of error (stated in percentage points)

When the defined target population size in a consumer study is 500 elements or less, the researcher should consider taking a census of the population rather than a sample. The logic behind this is based on the theoretical notion that at least 384 sampling units need to be included in most studies to have a ±5 percent confidence level and a sampling error of ±5 percentage points.

Sample sizes in business-to-business studies present a different problem than in consumer studies where the population almost always is very large. With business-to-business studies, the population frequently is only 200 to 300 individuals. What then is an acceptable sample size? In such cases, an attempt is made to contact and complete a survey from all individuals in the population. An acceptable sample size may be as small as 30 percent or so but the final decision would be made after examining the profile of the respondents. For example, you could look at position titles to see if you have a good cross-section of respondents from all relevant categories. You likely will also determine what proportion of the firm's annual business is represented in the sample to avoid having only smaller firms or accounts that do not provide a representative picture of the firm's customers. Whatever approach you use, in the final analysis you must have a good understanding of who has responded so you can accurately interpret the study's findings.

Sampling from a Small Population

In the previously described formulas, the size of the population has no impact on the determination of the sample size. This is always true for "large" populations. When working with small populations, however, use of the earlier formulas may lead to an unnecessarily large sample size. If, for example, the sample size is larger than 5 percent of the population then the calculated sample size should be multiplied by the following correction factor:

$$N/(N + n - 1)$$

where

N = Population size

n = Calculated sample size determined by the original formula

Thus, the adjusted sample size is

Sample size = (Specified degree of confidence × Variability/Desired precision)^2
× $N/(N + n - 1)$

 MARKETING RESEARCH DASHBOARD   USING SPSS TO SELECT A RANDOM SAMPLE

Our sampling objective is to draw a random sample of 100 customers of the two Mexican restaurants that were interviewed in the survey. Each of the 405 interviews represents a sampling unit. The sampling frame is the list of 405 customers of the Santa Fe Grill and Jose's Southwestern Café that were interviewed in the survey. The SPSS click-through sequence to select the random sample is DATA → SELECT CASES → RANDOM SAMPLE OF CASES → SAMPLE → EXACTLY → "100" CASES → FROM THE FIRST "405" CASES → CONTINUE → OK. In the preceding sequence you must click on each of the options and place "100" in the cases box and "405" in the blank from the first cases box. The interviews (cases) not included in the random sample are indicated by the slash (/) through the case ID number on the left side of your computer screen.

Any data analysis done with the random sample will be based only on the random sample of 100 persons interviewed. For example, the table below shows the number and percentage of individuals in the sample that drove various distances to eat at the two restaurants. Data in the frequency column indicates the sample included 27 individuals who drove less than 1 mile, 37 who drove 1 to 5 miles, and 37 who drove more than 5 miles, for a total of 100 customers. This table is an example of what you get when you use the SPSS software.

X30—Distance Driven	Frequency	Percent	Cumulative Percent
Less than 1 mile	27	27	27
1–5 miles	37	37	64
More than 5 miles	36	36	100
Total	100	100	

Nonprobability Sample Sizes

Sample size formulas cannot be used for nonprobability samples. Determining the sample size for nonprobability samples is usually a subjective, intuitive judgment made by the researcher based on either past studies, industry standards, or the amount of resources available. Regardless of the method, the sampling results cannot be used to make statistical inferences about the true population parameters. Researchers can compare specific characteristics of the sample, such as age, income, and education, and note that the sample is similar to the population. But the best that can be offered is a description of the sample findings.

Other Sample Size Determination Approaches

Sample sizes are often determined using less formal approaches. For example, the budget is almost always a consideration, and the sample size then will be determined by what the client can afford. A related approach is basing sample size on similar previous studies that are considered comparable and judged as having produced reliable and valid findings. Consideration also is often given to the number of subgroups that will be examined and the minimum sample size per subgroup needed to draw conclusions about each subgroup. Some researchers suggest the minimum subgroup sample size should be 100 while many believe subgroup sample sizes as small as 50 are sufficient. If the minimum subgroup sample size is 50 and there are five subgroups, then the total sample size would be 250. Finally, sometimes the sample size is determined by the number of questions on a questionnaire. For example, typical rules of thumb are five respondents for each question asked. Thus, if there are 25 questions then the recommended sample size would be 125. Decisions on which of these approaches, or combinations or approaches, to use require the judgment of both research experts and managers to select the best alternative.

 MARKETING RESEARCH DASHBOARD SAMPLING AND ONLINE SURVEYS

Online data collection is increasing rapidly and now represents almost 60 percent of data collection in the United States. Below are some of the problems associated with sampling using online data collection methods:

1. The sampling population is difficult to define and to reach. E-mail participation solicitation can potentially contact a broad geographic cross-section of participants, but who actually responds? For example, younger demographic groups are less likely to use e-mail and can more easily be contacted via texting. Similarly, e-mail solicitations may not reach potential respondents because they are considered junk mail, or there may be browser or other compatibility issues.

2. Random samples are difficult and perhaps impossible to select. Lists generally are either unavailable or unreliable.

3. Some recent research suggests that samples drawn from opt-in online panels produce survey data that is less accurate, even after weighting for underrepresented groups. Moreover, the reduced accuracy of survey data from nonprobability web panels likely offsets their lower cost and ability to survey subpopulations with the precision needed for complex research studies. One study suggests that online samples should not be "volunteers" recruited online, but should be solicited using probability methods tied to landline and mobile telephone contacts.[4]

4. If random samples cannot be used, then it clearly is highly questionable to generalize findings.

These problems should not always stop researchers from using online data collection. Instead, they represent issues that need to be carefully evaluated before data collection begins.

Steps in Developing a Sampling Plan

After understanding the key components of sampling theory, the methods of determining sample sizes, and the various designs available, the researcher is ready to use them to develop a **sampling plan.** A sampling plan is the blueprint to ensure the data collected are representative of the population. A good sampling plan includes the following steps: (1) define the target population; (2) select the data collection method; (3) identify the sampling frames needed; (4) select the appropriate sampling method; (5) determine necessary sample sizes and overall contact rates; (6) create an operating plan for selecting sampling units; and (7) execute the operational plan.

Sampling plan The blueprint or framework needed to ensure that the data collected are representative of the defined target population.

Step 1: Define the Target Population In any sampling plan, the first task of the researcher is to determine the group of people or objects that should be investigated. With the problem and research objectives as guidelines, the characteristics of the target population should be identified. An understanding of the target population helps the researcher to successfully draw a representative sample.

Step 2: Select the Data Collection Method Using the problem definition, the data requirements, and the research objectives, the researcher chooses a method for collecting the data from the population. Choices include some type of interviewing approach (e.g., personal or telephone), a self-administered survey, or perhaps observation. The method of data collection guides the researcher in selecting the sampling frame(s).

Step 3: Identify the Sampling Frame(s) Needed A list of eligible sampling units must be obtained. The list includes information about prospective sampling units (individuals or objects) so the researcher can contact them. An incomplete sampling frame decreases the likelihood of drawing a representative sample. Sampling lists can be created from a number of different sources (e.g., customer lists from a company's internal database, random-digit dialing, an organization's membership roster, or purchased from a sampling vendor).

Step 4: Select the Appropriate Sampling Method The researcher chooses between probability and nonprobability methods. If the findings will be generalized, a probability sampling method will provide more accurate information than will nonprobability sampling methods. As noted previously, in determining the sampling method, the researcher must consider seven factors: (1) research objectives; (2) desired accuracy; (3) availability of resources; (4) time frame; (5) knowledge of the target population; (6) scope of the research; and (7) statistical analysis needs.

Step 5: Determine Necessary Sample Sizes and Overall Contact Rates In this step of a sampling plan, the researcher decides how precise the sample estimates must be and how much time and money are available to collect the data. To determine the appropriate sample size, decisions have to be made concerning (1) the variability of the population characteristic under investigation, (2) the level of confidence desired in the estimates, and (3) the precision required. The researcher also must decide how many completed surveys are needed for data analysis.

At this point the researcher must consider what impact having fewer surveys than initially desired would have on the accuracy of the sample statistics. An important question is "How many prospective sampling units will have to be contacted to ensure the estimated sample size is obtained, and at what additional costs?"

Step 6: Create an Operating Plan for Selecting Sampling Units   The researcher must decide how to contact the prospective respondents in the sample. Instructions should be written so that interviewers know what to do and how to handle problems contacting prospective respondents. For example, if the study data will be collected using mall-intercept interviews, then interviewers must be given instructions on how to select respondents and conduct the interviews.

Step 7: Execute the Operational Plan   This step is similar to collecting the data from respondents. The important consideration in this step is to maintain consistency and control.

MARKETING RESEARCH IN ACTION
Developing a Sampling Plan for a New Menu Initiative Survey

Owners of the Santa Fe Grill realize that in order to remain competitive in the restaurant industry, new menu items need to be introduced periodically to provide variety for current customers and to attract new customers. Recognizing this, the owners of the Santa Fe Grill believe three issues need to be addressed using marketing research. The first is should the menu be changed to include items beyond the traditional southwestern cuisine? For example, should they add items that would be considered standard American, Italian, or European cuisine? Second, regardless of the cuisine to be explored, how many new items (e.g., appetizers, entrées, or desserts) should be included on the survey? And third, what type of sampling plan should be developed for selecting respondents, and who should those respondents be? Should they be current customers, new customers, and/or old customers?

Hands-On Exercise

Understanding the importance of sampling and the impact it will have on the validity and accuracy of the research results, the owners have asked the local university if a marketing research class could assist them in this project. Specifically, the owners have posed the following questions that need to be addressed:

1. How many questions should the survey contain to adequately address all possible new menu items, including the notion of assessing the desirability of new cuisines? In short, how can it be determined that all necessary items will be included on the survey without the risk of ignoring menu items that may be desirable to potential customers?
2. How should the potential respondents be selected for the survey? Should customers be interviewed while they are dining? Should customers be asked to participate in the survey upon exiting the restaurant? Or should a mail or telephone approach be used to collect information from customers/noncustomers?

Based on the above questions, your task is to develop a procedure to address the following issues:

1. How many new menu items can be examined on the survey? Remember, all potential menu possibilities should be assessed but you must have a manageable number of questions so the survey can be performed in a timely and reasonable manner. Specifically, from a list of all possible menu items that can be included on the survey, what is the optimal number of menu items that should be used? Is there a sampling procedure one can use to determine the maximum number of menu items to place on the survey?
2. Determine the appropriate sample design. Develop a sample design proposal for the Santa Fe Grill that addresses the following: Should a probability or nonprobability sample be used? Given your answer, what type of sampling design should be employed (simple random, stratified, convenience, etc.)? Given the sample design suggested, how will potential respondents be selected for the study? Finally, determine the necessary sample size and suggest a plan for selecting the sampling units.

◼ Summary

Explain the role of sampling in the research process.

Sampling uses a portion of the population to make estimates about the entire population. The fundamentals of sampling are used in many of our everyday activities. For instance, we sample before selecting a TV program to watch, test-drive a car before deciding whether to purchase it, and take a bite of food to determine if our food is too hot or if it needs additional seasoning. The term target population is used to identify the complete group of elements (e.g., people or objects) that are identified for investigation. The researcher selects sampling units from the target population and uses the results obtained from the sample to make conclusions about the target population. The sample must be representative of the target population if it is to provide accurate estimates of population parameters.

Sampling is frequently used in marketing research projects instead of a census because sampling can significantly reduce the amount of time and money required in data collection.

Distinguish between probability and nonprobability sampling.

In probability sampling, each sampling unit in the defined target population has a known probability of being selected for the sample. The actual probability of selection for each sampling unit may or may not be equal depending on the type of probability sampling design used. In nonprobability sampling, the probability of selection of each sampling unit is not known. The selection of sampling units is based on some type of intuitive judgment or knowledge of the researcher.

Probability sampling enables the researcher to judge the reliability and validity of data collected by calculating the probability the findings based on the sample will differ from the defined target population. This observed difference can be partially attributed to the existence of sampling error. Each probability sampling method, simple random, systematic random, stratified, and cluster, has its own inherent advantages and disadvantages.

In nonprobability sampling, the probability of selection of each sampling unit is not known. Therefore, potential sampling error cannot be accurately known either. Although there may be a temptation to generalize nonprobability sample results to the defined target population, for the most part the results are limited to the people who provided the data in the survey. Each nonprobability sampling method—convenience, judgment, quota, and snowball—has its own inherent advantages and disadvantages.

Understand factors to consider when determining sample size.

Researchers consider several factors when determining the appropriate sample size. The amount of time and money available often affect this decision. In general, the larger the sample, the greater the amount of resources required to collect data. Three factors that are of primary importance in the determination of sample size are (1) the variability of the population characteristics under consideration, (2) the level of confidence desired in the estimate, and (3) the degree of precision desired in estimating the population characteristic. The greater the variability of the characteristic under investigation, the higher the level of confidence required. Similarly, the more precise the required sample results, the larger the necessary sample size.

Statistical formulas are used to determine the required sample size in probability sampling. Sample sizes for nonprobability sampling designs are determined using subjective methods such as industry standards, past studies, or the intuitive judgments of the researcher. The size of the defined target population does not affect the size of the required sample unless the population is large relative to the sample size.

Understand the steps in developing a sampling plan.

A sampling plan is the blueprint or framework needed to ensure that the data collected are representative of the defined target population. A good sampling plan will include, at least, the following steps: (1) define the target population; (2) select the data collection method; (3) identify the sampling frames needed; (4) select the appropriate sampling method; (5) determine necessary sample sizes and overall contact rates; (6) create an operating plan for selecting sampling units; and (7) execute the operational plan.

Key Terms and Concepts

Area sampling 145

Census 136

Central limit theorem (CLT) 138

Cluster sampling 145

Convenience sampling 145

Defined target population 137

Disproportionately stratified sampling 143

Judgment sampling 147

Nonprobability sampling 140

Nonsampling error 139

Population 137

Precision 148

Probability sampling 140

Proportionately stratified sampling 143

Quota sampling 147

Sampling 136

Sampling error 139

Sampling frame 138

Sampling plan 152

Sampling units 137

Simple random sampling 140

Snowball sampling 147

Stratified random sampling 143

Systematic random sampling 141

Review Questions

1. Why do many research studies place heavy emphasis on correctly defining a target population rather than a total population?
2. Explain the relationship between sample sizes and sampling error. How does sampling error occur in survey research?
3. The vice president of operations at Busch Gardens knows that 70 percent of the patrons like roller-coaster rides. He wishes to have an acceptable margin of error of no more than ±2 percent and wants to be 95 percent confident about the attitudes toward the "Gwazi" roller coaster. What sample size would be required for a personal interview study among on-site patrons?

Discussion Questions

1. Summarize why a current telephone directory is not a good source from which to develop a sampling frame for most research studies.
2. **EXPERIENCE MARKETING RESEARCH:** Go to **www.surveysampling.com** and select from the menu "the frame." Once there, select "archive" and go to a particular year (e.g., 2012) and review the articles available on the topic of sampling. Select two articles and write a brief summary on how sampling affects the ability to conduct accurate market research.

Measurement and Scaling

Chapter 7

1. Understand the role of measurement in marketing research.
2. Explain the four basic levels of scales.
3. Describe scale development and its importance in gathering primary data.
4. Discuss comparative and noncomparative scales.

Santa Fe Grill Mexican Restaurant: Predicting Customer Loyalty

About 18 months after opening their first restaurant near Cumberland Mall in Dallas, Texas, the owners of the Santa Fe Grill Mexican Restaurant concluded that although there was another Mexican theme competitor located nearby (Jose's Southwestern Café), there were many more casual dining competitors within a 3-mile radius. These other competitors included several well-established national chain restaurants, including Chili's, Applebee's, T.G.I. Friday's, and Ruby Tuesday, which also offered some Mexican food items. Concerned with growing a stronger customer base in a very competitive restaurant environment, the owners had initially just focused on the image of offering the best, freshest "made-from-scratch" Mexican foods possible in hopes of creating satisfaction among their customers. Results of several satisfaction surveys of current customers indicated many customers had a satisfying dining experience, but intentions to revisit the restaurant on a regular basis were low. After reading a popular press article on customer loyalty, the owners wanted to better understand the factors that lead to customer loyalty. That is, what would motivate customers to return to their restaurant more often?

To gain a better understanding of customer loyalty, the Santa Fe Grill owners contacted Burke's (**www.burke.com**) Customer Satisfaction Division. They evaluated several alternatives including measuring customer loyalty, intention to recommend and return to the restaurant, and sales. Burke representatives indicated that customer loyalty directly influences the accuracy of sales potential estimates, traffic density is a better indicator of sales than demographics, and customers often prefer locations where several casual dining establishments are clustered together so more choices are available. At the end of the meeting, the owners realized that customer loyalty is a complex behavior to predict.

Several insights about the importance of construct and measurement developments can be gained from the Santa Fe Grill experience. First, not knowing the critical elements that influence customers' restaurant loyalty can lead to intuitive guesswork and unreliable sales predictions. Second, developing loyal customers requires identifying and precisely defining constructs that predict loyalty (i.e., customer attitudes, emotions, behavioral factors). When you finish this chapter, read the Marketing Research in Action at the end of the chapter to see how Burke Inc. defines and measures customer loyalty.

Value of Measurement in Information Research

Measurement is an integral part of the modern world, yet the beginnings of measurement lie in the distant past. Before a farmer could sell his corn, potatoes, or apples, both he and the buyer had to decide on a common unit of measurement. Over time this particular measurement became known as a bushel or four pecks or, more precisely, 2,150.42 cubic inches. In the early days, measurement was achieved simply by using a basket or container of standard size that everyone agreed was a bushel.

From such simple everyday devices as the standard bushel basket, we have progressed in the physical sciences to an extent that we are now able to measure the rotation of a distant star, the altitude of a satellite in microinches, or time in picoseconds (1 trillionth of a second). Today, precise physical measurement is critical to airline pilots flying through dense fog or to physicians controlling a surgical laser.

In most marketing situations, however, the measurements are applied to things that are much more abstract than altitude or time. For example, most decision makers would agree that it is important to have information about whether or not a firm's customers are going to like a new product or service prior to introducing it. In many cases, such information makes the difference between business success and failure. Yet, unlike time or altitude, people's preferences can be very difficult to measure accurately. The Coca-Cola Company introduced New Coke after incompletely conceptualizing and measuring consumers' preferences, and consequently suffered substantial losses.

Because accurate measurement is essential to effective decision making, this chapter provides a basic understanding of the importance of measuring customers' attitudes and behaviors and other marketplace phenomena. We describe the measurement process and the decision rules for developing scale measurements. The focus is on measurement issues, construct development, and scale measurements. The chapter also discusses popular scales that measure attitudes and behavior.

Overview of the Measurement Process

Measurement An integrative process of determining the intensity (or amount) of information about constructs, concepts, or objects.

Measurement is the process of developing methods to systematically characterize or quantify information about persons, events, ideas, or objects of interest. As part of the measurement process, researchers assign either numbers or labels to phenomena they measure. For example, when gathering data about consumers who shop for automobiles online, a researcher may collect information about their attitudes, perceptions, past online purchase behaviors, and demographic characteristics. Then, numbers are used to represent how individuals responded to questions in each of these areas.

The *measurement process* consists of two tasks: (1) construct selection/development and (2) scale measurement. To collect accurate data, researchers must understand what they are attempting to measure before choosing the appropriate scale measurements. The goal of the construct development process is to precisely identify and define what is to be measured. In turn, the scale measurement process determines how to precisely measure each construct. For example, a 10-point scale results in a more precise measure than a 2-point scale. We begin with construct development and then move to scale measurement.

What Is a Construct?

A construct is an abstract idea or concept formed in a person's mind. This idea is a combination of a number of similar characteristics of the construct. The characteristics are the variables that collectively define the concept and make measurement of the concept possible. For example, the variables listed below were used to measure the concept of "customer interaction."[1]

- This customer was easy to talk with.
- This customer genuinely enjoyed my helping her/him.
- This customer likes to talk to people.
- This customer was interested in socializing.
- This customer was friendly.
- This customer tried to establish a personal relationship.
- This customer seemed interested in me, not only as a salesperson, but also as a person.

By using Agree-Disagree scales to obtain scores on each of the individual variables, you can measure the overall concept of customer interaction. The individual scores are then combined into a single score, according to a predefined set of rules. The resultant score is often referred to as a scale, an index, or a summated rating. In the above example of customer interaction, the individual variables (items) are scored using a 5-point scale, with 1 = Strongly Disagree and 5 = Strongly Agree.

Suppose the research objective is to identify the characteristics (variables) associated with a restaurant satisfaction construct. The researcher is likely to review the literature on satisfaction, conduct both formal and informal interviews, and then draw on his or her own experiences to identify variables like quality of food, quality of service, and value for money as important components of a restaurant satisfaction construct. Logical combination of these characteristics then provides a theoretical framework that represents the satisfaction construct and enables the researcher to conduct an empirical investigation of the concept of restaurant satisfaction.

Construct Development

Construct A hypothetical variable made up of a set of component responses or behaviors that are thought to be related.

Marketing constructs must be clearly defined. Recall that a **construct** is an unobservable concept that is measured indirectly by a group of related variables. Thus, constructs are made up of a combination of several related indicator variables that together define the concept being measured. Each individual indicator has a scale measurement. The construct being studied is indirectly measured by obtaining scale measurements on each of the indicators and adding them together to get an overall score for the construct. For example, customer satisfaction is a construct while an individual's positive (or negative) feeling about a specific aspect of their shopping experience, such as attitude toward the store's employees, is an indicator variable.

Construct development
An integrative process in which researchers determine what specific data should be collected for solving the defined research problem.

Construct development begins with an accurate definition of the purpose of the study and the research problem. Without a clear initial understanding of the research problem, the researcher is likely to collect irrelevant or inaccurate data, thereby wasting a great deal of time, effort, and money. **Construct development** is the process in which researchers identify characteristics that define the concept being studied by the researcher. Once the characteristics are identified, the researcher must then develop a method of indirectly measuring the concept.

Exhibit 7.1 — **Examples of Concrete Features and Abstract Constructs of Objects**

Objects

Consumer
Concrete properties: age, sex, marital status, income, brand last purchased, dollar amount of purchase, types of products purchased, color of eyes and hair

Abstract properties: attitudes toward a product, brand loyalty, high-involvement purchases, emotions (love, fear, anxiety), intelligence, personality

Organization
Concrete properties: name of company, number of employees, number of locations, total assets, Fortune 500 rating, computer capacity, types and numbers of products and service offerings

Abstract properties: competence of employees, quality control, channel power, competitive advantages, company image, consumer-oriented practices

Marketing Constructs

Brand loyalty
Concrete properties: the number of times a particular brand is purchased, the frequency of purchases of a particular brand, amount spent

Abstract properties: like/dislike of a particular brand, the degree of satisfaction with the brand, overall attitude toward the brand

Customer satisfaction
Concrete properties: identifiable attributes that make up a product, service, or experience

Abstract properties: liking/disliking of the individual attributes making up the product, positive feelings toward the product

Service quality
Concrete properties: identifiable attributes of a service encounter, for example amount of interaction, personal communications, service provider's knowledge

Abstract properties: expectations held about each identifiable attribute, evaluative judgment of performance

Advertising recall
Concrete properties: factual properties of the ad (e.g., message, symbols, movement, models, text), aided and unaided recall of ad properties

Abstract properties: favorable/unfavorable judgments, attitude toward the ad

At the heart of construct development is the need to determine exactly what is to be measured. Objects that are relevant to the research problem are identified first. Then the objective and subjective properties of each object are specified. When data are needed only about a concrete issue, the research focus is limited to measuring the object's objective properties. But when data are needed to understand an object's subjective (abstract) properties, the researcher must identify measurable subcomponents that can be used as indicators of the object's subjective properties. Exhibit 7.1 shows examples of objects and their concrete and abstract properties. A rule of thumb is that if an object's features can be directly measured using physical characteristics, then that feature is a concrete variable and not an abstract construct. Abstract constructs are not physical characteristics and are measured indirectly. The Marketing Research Dashboard demonstrates the importance of using the appropriate set of respondents in developing constructs.

Scale Measurement

Scale measurement The process of assigning descriptors to represent the range of possible responses to a question about a particular object or construct.

Scale points Designated degrees of intensity assigned to the responses in a given questioning or observation method.

The quality of responses associated with any question or observation technique depends directly on the scale measurements used by the researcher. **Scale measurement** involves assigning a set of scale descriptors to represent the range of possible responses to a question about a particular object or construct. The *scale descriptors* are a combination of labels, such as "Strongly Agree" or "Strongly Disagree" and numbers, such as 1 to 7, which are assigned using a set of rules.

Scale measurement assigns degrees of intensity to the responses. The degrees of intensity are commonly referred to as **scale points.** For example, a retailer might want to know how important a preselected set of store or service features is to consumers in deciding where to shop. The level of importance attached to each store or service feature would be determined by the researcher's assignment of a range of intensity descriptors (scale points) to represent the possible degrees of importance associated with each feature. If labels are

MARKETING RESEARCH DASHBOARD UNDERSTANDING THE DIMENSIONS OF BANK SERVICE QUALITY

Hibernia National Bank needs to identify the areas customers might use in judging banking service quality. As a result of a limited budget and based on the desire to work with a local university marketing professor, several focus groups were conducted among undergraduate students in a basic marketing course and graduate students in a marketing management course. The objective was to identify the service activities and offerings that might represent service quality. The researcher's rationale for using these groups was that the students had experience in conducting bank transactions, were consumers, and it was convenient to obtain their participation. Results of the focus groups revealed that students used four dimensions to judge a bank's service quality: (1) interpersonal skills of bank staff; (2) reliability of bank statements; (3) convenience of ATMs; and (4) user-friendly Internet access to banking functions.

A month later, the researcher conducted focus groups among current customers of one of the large banks in the same market area as the university. Results suggested these customers used six dimensions in judging a bank's service quality. The dimensions were: (1) listening skills of bank personnel; (2) understanding banking needs; (3) empathy; (4) responses to customers' questions or problems; (5) technological competence in handling bank transactions; and (6) interpersonal skills of contact personnel.

The researcher was unsure whether customers perceive bank service quality as having four or six components, and whether a combined set of dimensions should be used. Which of the two sets of focus groups should be used to better understand the construct of bank service quality? What would you do to better understand the bank service quality construct? How would you define banking service quality?

used as scale points to respond to a question, they might include the following: definitely important, moderately important, slightly important, and not at all important. If numbers are used as scale points, then a 10 could mean very important and a 1 could mean not important at all.

All scale measurements can be classified as one of four basic scale levels: (1) nominal; (2) ordinal; (3) interval; and (4) ratio. We discuss each of the scale levels next.

Nominal Scales

Nominal scale The type of scale in which the questions require respondents to provide only some type of descriptor as the raw response.

A **nominal scale** is the most basic and least powerful scale design. With nominal scales, the questions require respondents only to provide some type of descriptor as the response. Responses do not contain a level of intensity. Thus, a ranking of the set of responses is not possible. Nominal scales allow the researcher only to categorize the responses into mutually exclusive subsets that do not have distances between them. Thus, the only possible mathematical calculation is to count the number of responses in each category and to report the mode. Some examples of nominal scales are given in Exhibit 7.2.

Ordinal Scales

Ordinal scale A scale that allows a respondent to express relative magnitude between the answers to a question.

Ordinal scales are more powerful than nominal scales. This type of scale enables respondents to express relative magnitude between the answers to a question and responses can be rank-ordered in a hierarchical pattern. Thus, relationships between responses can be determined such as "greater than/less than," "higher than/lower than," "more often/less often," "more important/less important," or "more favorable/less favorable." The mathematical calculations that can be applied with ordinal scales include mode, median, frequency distributions, and ranges. Ordinal scales cannot be used to determine the absolute difference between rankings. For example, respondents can indicate they prefer Coke over Pepsi, but

---

Exhibit 7.2 **Examples of Nominal Scales**

Example 1:
Please indicate your marital status.

____ Married   ____ Single   ____ Separated   ____ Divorced   ____ Widowed

Example 2:
Do you like or dislike chocolate ice cream?

____ Like   ____ Dislike

Example 3:
Which of the following supermarkets have you shopped at in the past 30 days? Please check all that apply.

____ Albertson's   ____ Winn-Dixie   ____ Publix   ____ Safeway   ____ Walmart

Example 4:
Please indicate your gender.

____ Female   ____ Male   ____ Transgender

Exhibit 7.3 Examples of Ordinal Scales

Example 1:

We would like to know your preferences for actually using different banking methods. Among the methods listed below, please indicate your top three preferences using a "1" to represent your first choice, a "2" for your second preference, and a "3" for your third choice of methods. Please write the numbers on the lines next to your selected methods. Do not assign the same number to two methods.

_____ Inside the bank   _____ Bank by mail

_____ Drive-in (Drive-up) windows   _____ Bank by telephone

_____ ATM   _____ Internet banking

_____ Debit card

Example 2:

Which one statement best describes your opinion of the quality of an Intel PC processor? (Please check just one statement.)

_____ Higher than AMD's PC processor

_____ About the same as AMD's PC processor

_____ Lower than AMD's PC processor

Example 3:

For each pair of retail discount stores, circle the one store at which you would be more likely to shop.

_____ Costco or Target

_____ Target or Walmart

_____ Walmart or Costco

researchers cannot determine how much more the respondents prefer Coke. Exhibit 7.3 provides several examples of ordinal scales.

Interval Scales

Interval scale A scale that demonstrates absolute differences between each scale point.

Interval scales can measure absolute differences between scale points. That is, the intervals between the scale numbers tell us how far apart the measured objects are on a particular attribute. For example, the satisfaction level of customers with the Santa Fe Grill and Jose Southwestern Café was measured using a 7-point interval scale, with the end points 1 = Strongly Disagree and 7 = Strongly Agree. This approach enables us to compare the relative level of satisfaction of the customers with the two restaurants. Thus, with an interval scale we could say that customers of the Santa Fe Grill are more satisfied than customers of Jose's Southwestern Café.

In addition to the mode and median, the mean and standard deviation of the respondents' answers can be calculated for interval scales. This means that researchers can report findings not only about hierarchical differences (better than or worse than) but

Exhibit 7.4	Examples of Interval Scales

Example 1:

How likely are you to recommend the Santa Fe Grill to a friend?	Definitely Will Not Recommend						Definitely Will Recommend
	1	2	3	4	5	6	7

Example 2:

Using a scale of 0–10, with "10" being Highly Satisfied and "0" being Not Satisfied At All, how satisfied are you with the banking services you currently receive from (read name of primary bank)?
Answer: _____

Example 3:

Please indicate how frequently you use different banking methods. For each of the banking methods listed below, circle the number that best describes the frequency you typically use each method.

Banking Methods	Never Use								Use Very Often		
Inside the bank	0	1	2	3	4	5	6	7	8	9	10
Drive-up window	0	1	2	3	4	5	6	7	8	9	10
24-hour ATM	0	1	2	3	4	5	6	7	8	9	10
Debit card	0	1	2	3	4	5	6	7	8	9	10
Bank by mail	0	1	2	3	4	5	6	7	8	9	10
Bank by phone	0	1	2	3	4	5	6	7	8	9	10
Bank by Internet	0	1	2	3	4	5	6	7	8	9	10

also the absolute differences between the data. Exhibit 7.4 gives several examples of interval scales.

Ratio Scales

Ratio scale A scale that allows the researcher not only to identify the absolute differences between each scale point but also to make comparisons between the responses.

Ratio scales are the highest level scale because they enable the researcher not only to identify the absolute differences between each scale point but also to make absolute comparisons between the responses. For example, in collecting data about how many cars are owned by households in Atlanta, Georgia, a researcher knows that the difference between driving one car and driving three cars is always going to be two. Furthermore, when comparing a one-car family to a three-car family, the researcher can assume that the three-car family will have significantly higher total car insurance and maintenance costs than the one-car family.

Ratio scales are designed to enable a "true natural zero" or "true state of nothing" response to be a valid response to a question. Generally, ratio scales ask respondents to provide a specific numerical value as their response, regardless of whether or not a set of scale points is used. In addition to the mode, median, mean, and standard deviation, one can make comparisons between levels. Thus, if you are measuring weight, a familiar ratio scale, one can then say a person weighing 200 pounds is twice as heavy as one weighing only 100 pounds. Exhibit 7.5 shows examples of ratio scales.

Exhibit 7.5	Examples of Ratio Scales

Example 1:

Please circle the number of children under 18 years of age currently living in your household.

0   1   2   3   4   5   6   7   If more than 7, please specify: _____

Example 2:

In the past seven days, how many times did you go shopping at a retail shopping mall?

_____ # of times

Example 3:

In years, what is your current age?

_____ # of years old

Evaluating Measurement Scales

All measurement scales should be evaluated for reliability and validity. The following paragraphs explain how this is done.

Scale Reliability

Scale reliability refers to the extent to which a scale can reproduce the same or similar measurement results in repeated trials. Thus, reliability is a measure of consistency in measurement. Random error produces inconsistency in scale measurements that leads to lower scale reliability. But researchers can improve reliability by carefully designing scaled questions. Two of the techniques that help researchers assess the reliability of scales are test-retest and equivalent form.

First, the *test-retest* technique involves repeating the scale measurement with either the same sample of respondents at two different times or two different samples of respondents from the same defined target population under as nearly the same conditions as possible. The idea behind this approach is that if random variations are present, they will be revealed by variations in the scores between the two sampled measurements. If there are very few differences between the first and second administrations of the scale, the measuring scale is viewed as being stable and therefore reliable. For example, assume that determining the teaching effectiveness associated with your marketing research course involved the use of a 28-question scale designed to measure the degree to which respondents agree or disagree with each question (statement). To gather the data on teaching effectiveness, your professor administers this scale to the class after the sixth week of the semester and again after the 12th week. Using a mean analysis procedure on the questions for each measurement period, the professor then runs correlation analysis on those mean values. If the correlation is high between the mean value measurements from the two assessment periods, the professor concludes that the reliability of the 28-question scale is high.

There are several potential problems with the test-retest approach. First, some of the students who completed the scale the first time might be absent for the second administration of the scale. Second, students might become sensitive to the scale measurement and therefore alter their responses in the second measurement. Third, environmental or personal factors may change between the two administrations, thus causing changes in student responses in the second measurement.

Some researchers believe the problems associated with test-retest reliability technique can be avoided by using the *equivalent form* technique. In this technique, researchers create two similar yet different (e.g., equivalent) scale measurements for the given construct (e.g., teaching effectiveness) and administer both forms to either the same sample of respondents or to two samples of respondents from the same defined target population. In the marketing research course "teaching effectiveness" example, the professor would construct two 28-question scales whose main difference would lie in the wording of the item statements, not the Agree/Disagree scaling points. Although the specific wording of the statements would be changed, their meaning is assumed to remain constant. After administering each of the scale measurements, the professor calculates the mean values for each question and then runs correlation analysis. Equivalent form reliability is assessed by measuring the correlations between the scores on the two scale measurements. High correlation values are interpreted as meaning high-scale measurement reliability.

There are two potential drawbacks with the equivalent form reliability technique. First, even if equivalent versions of the scale can be developed, it might not be worth the time, effort, and expense of determining that two similar yet different scales can be used to measure the same construct. Second, it is difficult and perhaps impossible to create two totally equivalent scales. Thus, questions may be raised as to which scale is the most appropriate to use in measuring teaching effectiveness.

The previous approaches to examining reliability are often difficult to complete in a timely and accurate manner. As a result, marketing researchers most often use internal consistency reliability. *Internal consistency* is the degree to which the individual questions of a construct are correlated. That is, the set of questions that make up the scale must be internally consistent.

Two popular techniques are used to assess internal consistency: (1) split-half tests and (2) coefficient alpha (also referred to as Cronbach's alpha). In a *split-half test,* the scale questions are divided into two halves (odd versus even, or randomly) and the resulting halves' scores are correlated against one another. High correlations between the halves indicate good (or acceptable) internal consistency. A *coefficient alpha* calculates the average of all possible split-half measures that result from different ways of dividing the scale questions. The coefficient value can range from 0 to 1, and, in most cases, a value of less than 0.7 would typically indicate marginal to low (unsatisfactory) internal consistency. In contrast, when reliability coefficient is too high (0.95 or greater), it suggests that the items making up the scale are too consistent with one another (i.e., measuring the same thing) and consideration should be given to eliminating some of the redundant items from the scale.

Researchers need to remember that just because their scale measurement designs are reliable, the data collected are not necessarily valid. Separate validity assessments must be made on the constructs being measured.

Validity

Since reliable scales are not necessarily valid, researchers also need to be concerned about validity. *Scale validity* assesses whether a scale measures what it is supposed to measure. Thus, validity is a measure of accuracy in measurement. For example, if you want to know a family's disposable income, this is different from total household income. You may start with questions about total family income to arrive at disposable income, but total family income by itself is not a valid indicator of disposable income. A construct with perfect validity contains no measurement error. An easy measure of validity would be to compare observed measurements with the true measurement. The problem is that we very seldom know the true measure.

Validation, in general, involves determining the suitability of the questions (statements) chosen to represent the construct. One approach to assess scale validity involves examining face validity. *Face validity* is based on the researcher's intuitive evaluation of whether the statements look like they measure what they are supposed to measure. Establishing the face validity of a scale involves a systematic but subjective assessment of a scale's ability to measure what it is supposed to measure. Thus, researchers use their expert judgment to determine face validity.

A similar measure of validity is *content validity,* which is a measure of the extent to which a construct represents all the relevant dimensions. Content validity requires more rigorous statistical assessment than face validity, which only requires intuitive judgments. To illustrate content validity, let's consider the construct of job satisfaction. A scale designed to measure the construct job satisfaction should include questions on compensation, working conditions, communication, relationships with coworkers, supervisory style, empowerment, opportunities for advancement, and so on. If any one of these major areas does not have questions to measure it then the scale would not have content validity.

Content validity is assessed before data are collected in an effort to ensure the construct (scale) includes items to represent all relevant areas. It is generally carried out in the process of developing or revising scales. In contrast, face validity is a post hoc claim about existing scales that the items represent the construct being measured. Several other types of validity typically are examined after data are collected, particularly when multi-item scales are being used. For example, *convergent validity* is evaluated with multi-item scales and represents a situation in which the multiple items measuring the same construct share a high proportion of variance, typically more than 50 percent. Similarly, *discriminant validity* is the extent to which a single construct differs from other constructs and represents a unique construct. Two approaches typically are used to obtain data to assess validity. If sufficient resources are available, a pilot study is conducted with 100 to 200 respondents believed to be representative of the defined target population. When fewer resources are available, researchers assess only content validity using a panel of experts.

◼︎ Developing Scale Measurements

Designing measurement scales requires (1) understanding the research problem, (2) establishing detailed data requirements, (3) identifying and developing constructs, and (4) selecting the appropriate measurement scale. Thus, after the problem and data requirements are understood, the researcher must develop constructs and then select the appropriate scale format (nominal, ordinal, interval, or ratio). If the problem requires interval data, but the researcher asks the questions using a nominal scale, the wrong level of data will be collected and the findings may not be useful in understanding and explaining the research problem.

Criteria for Scale Development

Questions must be phrased carefully to produce accurate data. To do so, the researcher must develop appropriate scale descriptors to be used as the scale points.

Understanding of the Questions   The researcher must consider the intellectual capacity and language ability of individuals who will be asked to respond to the scales. Researchers should not automatically assume that respondents understand the questions and response choices. Appropriate language must be used in both the questions and the answers.

Simplicity in word choice and straightforward, simple sentence construction improve understanding. All scaled questions should be pretested to evaluate their level of understanding. Respondents with a high school education or comparable can easily understand and respond to 7-point scales, and in most instances 10-point and 100-point scales.

Discriminatory power

The scale's ability to discriminate between the categorical scale responses (points).

Discriminatory Power of Scale Descriptors   The **discriminatory power** of scale descriptors is the scale's ability to differentiate between the scale responses. Researchers must decide how many scale points are necessary to represent the relative magnitudes of a response scale. The more scale points, the greater the discriminatory power of the scale.

There is no absolute rule about the number of scale points that should be used in creating a scale. For some respondents, scales should not be more than 5 points because it may be difficult to make a choice when there are more than five levels. This is particularly true for respondents with lower education levels and less experience in responding to scales. The more scale points researchers use, the greater the variability in the data—an important consideration in statistical analysis of data. Indeed, as noted earlier with more educated respondents, 10 and even 100-point scales work quite well. Previously published scales based on 5 points should almost always be extended to more scale points to increase the accuracy of respondent answers.

Balanced versus Unbalanced Scales   Researchers must consider whether to use a balanced or unbalanced scale. A *balanced scale* has an equal number of positive (favorable) and negative (unfavorable) response alternatives. An example of a balanced scale is,

> Based on your experiences with your new vehicle since owning and driving it, to what extent are you presently satisfied or dissatisfied with the overall performance of the vehicle? Please check only one response.
> _____ Completely satisfied (no dissatisfaction)
> _____ Generally satisfied
> _____ Slightly satisfied (some satisfaction)
> _____ Slightly dissatisfied (some dissatisfaction)
> _____ Generally dissatisfied
> _____ Completely dissatisfied (no satisfaction)

An *unbalanced scale* has a larger number of response options on one side, either positive or negative. For most research situations, a balanced scale is recommended because unbalanced scales often introduce bias. One exception is when the attitudes of respondents are likely to be predominantly one-sided, either positive or negative. When this situation is expected, researchers typically use an unbalanced scale. One example is when respondents are asked to rate the importance of evaluative criteria in choosing to do business with a particular company, they often rate all criteria listed as very important. An example of an unbalanced scale is,

> Based on your experiences with your new vehicle since owning and driving it, to what extent are you presently satisfied with the overall performance of the vehicle? Please check only one response.
> _____ Completely satisfied
> _____ Definitely satisfied
> _____ Generally satisfied
> _____ Slightly satisfied
> _____ Dissatisfied

Forced or Nonforced Choice Scales A scale that does not have a neutral descriptor to divide the positive and negative answers is referred to as a *forced-choice scale*. It is forced because the respondent can only select either a positive or a negative answer, and not a neutral one. In contrast, a scale that includes a center neutral response is referred to as a *nonforced* or *free-choice scale*. Exhibit 7.6 presents several different examples of both "even-point, forced-choice" and "odd-point, nonforced" scales.

Some researchers believe scales should be designed as "odd-point, nonforced" scales[2] since not all respondents will have enough knowledge or experience with the topic to be able to accurately assess their thoughts or feelings. If respondents are forced to choose, the scale may produce lower-quality data. With nonforced choice scales, however, the so-called neutral scale point provides respondents an easy way to express their feelings.

Many researchers believe that there is no such thing as a neutral attitude or feeling, that these mental aspects almost always have some degree of a positive or negative orientation

Exhibit 7.6   Examples of Forced-Choice and Nonforced Scale Descriptors

Even-Point, Forced-Choice Rating Scale Descriptors

Purchase Intention (Not Buy–Buy)

___ Definitely will not buy ___ Probably will not buy ___ Probably will buy ___ Definitely will buy

Personal Beliefs/Opinions (Agreement–Disagreement)

Definitely Disagree	Somewhat Disagree	Somewhat Agree	Definitely Agree
____	____	____	____

Cost (Inexpensive–Expensive)

Extremely Inexpensive	Definitely Inexpensive	Somewhat Inexpensive	Somewhat Expensive	Definitely Expensive	Extremely Expensive
____	____	____	____	____	____

Odd-Point, Nonforced Choice Rating Scale Descriptors

Purchase Intentions (Not Buy–Buy)

Definitely Will Not Buy	Probably Will Not Buy	Neither Will nor Will Not Buy	Probably Will Buy	Definitely Will Buy
____	____	____	____	____

Personal Beliefs/Opinions (Disagreement–Agreement)

Definitely Disagree	Somewhat Disagree	Neither Disagree nor Agree	Somewhat Agree	Definitely Agree
____	____	____	____	____

Cost (Inexpensive–Expensive)

Definitely Inexpensive	Somewhat Inexpensive	Neither Expensive nor Inexpensive	Somewhat Expensive	Definitely Expensive
____	____	____	____	____

attached to them. A person either has an attitude or does not have an attitude about a given object. Likewise, a person will either have a feeling or not have a feeling. An alternative approach to handling situations in which respondents may feel uncomfortable about expressing their thoughts or feelings because they have no knowledge of or experience with it would be to incorporate a "Not Applicable" response choice.

Negatively Worded Statements   Scale development guidelines traditionally suggested that negatively worded statements should be included to verify that respondents are reading the questions. In more than 40 years of developing scaled questions, the authors have found that negatively worded statements almost always create problems for respondents in data collection. Moreover, based on pilot studies negatively worded statements have been removed from questionnaires more than 90 percent of the time. As a result, inclusion of negatively worded statements should be minimized and even then approached with caution.

Desired Measures of Central Tendency and Dispersion   The type of statistical analyses that can be performed on data depends on the level of the data collected, whether nominal, ordinal, interval, or ratio. In Chapters 11 and 12, we show how the level of data collected influences the type of analysis. Here we focus on how the scale's level affects the choice of how we measure central tendency and dispersion. *Measures of central tendency* locate the center of a distribution of responses and are basic summary statistics. The mean, median, and mode measure central tendency using different criteria. The mean is the arithmetic average of all the data responses. The median is the sample statistic that divides the data so that half the data are above the statistic value and half are below. The mode is the value most frequently given among all of the responses.

Measures of dispersion describe how the data are dispersed around a central value. These statistics enable the researcher to report the variability of responses on a particular scale. Measures of dispersion include the frequency distribution, the range, and the estimated standard deviation. A *frequency distribution* is a summary of how many times each possible response to a scale question/setup was recorded by the total group of respondents. This distribution can be easily converted into percentages or histograms. The *range* represents the distance between the largest and smallest response. The standard deviation is the statistical value that specifies the degree of variation in the responses. These measures are explained in more detail in Chapter 11.

Given the important role these statistics play in data analysis, an understanding of how different levels of scales influence the use of a particular statistic is critical in scale design. Exhibit 7.7 displays these relationships. Nominal scales can only be analyzed using frequency distributions and the mode. Ordinal scales can be analyzed using medians and ranges as well as modes and frequency distributions. For interval or ratio scales, the most appropriate statistics to use are means and standard deviations. In addition, interval and ratio data can be analyzed using modes, medians, frequency distributions, and ranges.

Adapting Established Scales

There are literally hundreds of previously published scales in marketing. The most relevant sources of these scales are: William Bearden, Richard Netemeyer and Kelly Haws, *Handbook of Marketing Scales,* 3rd ed. (Thousand Oaks, CA: Sage Publications, 2011); Gordon Bruner, *Marketing Scales Handbook*, 3rd ed. (Chicago, IL: American Marketing Association, 2006), and the online Measures Toolchest by the Academy of Management, available at: **http:// measures.kammeyer-uf.com/wiki/Main_Page**. Some of the scales described in these sources can be used in their published form to collect data. But most scales need to be adapted to meet current psychometric standards. For example, many scales include double-

Exhibit 7.7	Relationships between Scale Levels and Measures of Central Tendency and Dispersion			

| | **Basic Levels of Scales** | | | |
Measurements	**Nominal**	**Ordinal**	**Interval**	**Ratio**
Central Tendency				
Mode	**Appropriate**	Appropriate	Appropriate	Appropriate
Median	Inappropriate	**More Appropriate**	Appropriate	Appropriate
Mean	Inappropriate	Inappropriate	**Most Appropriate**	**Most Appropriate**
Dispersion				
Frequency distribution	**Appropriate**	Appropriate	Appropriate	Appropriate
Range	Inappropriate	**More Appropriate**	Appropriate	Appropriate
Estimated standard deviation	Inappropriate	Inappropriate	**Most Appropriate**	**Most Appropriate**

barreled questions (discussed in Chapter 8). In such cases, these questions need to be adapted by converting a single question into two separate questions. In addition, most of the scales were developed prior to online data collection approaches and used 5-point Likert scales. As noted earlier, more scale points create greater variability in responses, which is desirable in statistical analysis. Therefore, previously developed scales should in almost all instances be adapted by converting the 5-point scales to 7-, 10-, or even 100-point scales. Moreover, in many instances, the Likert scale format should be converted to a graphic ratings scale (described in next section), which provides more accurate responses to scaled questions.

Scales to Measure Attitudes and Behaviors

Now that we have presented the basics of construct development as well as the rules for developing scale measurements, we are ready to discuss attitudinal and behavioral scales frequently used by marketing researchers.

Scales are the "rulers" that measure customer attitudes, behaviors, and intentions. Well-designed scales result in better measurement of marketplace phenomena, and thus provide more accurate information to marketing decision makers. Several types of scales have proven useful in many different situations. This section discusses three scale formats: *Likert scales, semantic differential scales,* and *behavioral intention scales.* Exhibit 7.8 shows the general steps in the construct development/scale measurement process. These steps are followed in developing mostly all types of scales, including the three discussed here.

Likert scale An ordinal scale format that asks respondents to indicate the extent to which they agree or disagree with a series of mental belief or behavioral belief statements about a given object.

Likert Scale

A **Likert scale** asks respondents to indicate the extent to which they either agree or disagree with a series of statements about a subject. Usually the scale format is balanced between agreement and disagreement scale descriptors. Named after its original developer, Rensis Likert, this scale initially had five scale descriptors: "strongly agree," "agree," "neither agree nor disagree," "disagree," "strongly disagree." The Likert scale is often

---

Exhibit 7.8 — Construct/Scale Development Process

Steps	Activities
1. Identify and define construct	Determine construct dimensions/factors
2. Create initial pool of attribute statements	Conduct qualitative research, collect secondary data, identify theory
3. Assess and select reduced set of items/statements	Use qualitative judgment and item analysis
4. Design scales and pretest	Collect data from pretest
5. Complete statistical analysis	Evaluate reliability and validity
6. Refine and purify scales	Eliminate poorly designed statements
7. Complete final scale evaluation	Most often qualitative judgment, but may involve further reliability and validity tests

---

Exhibit 7.9 — Example of a Likert Scale

For each listed statement below, please check the one response that best expresses the extent to which you agree or disagree with that statement.

Statements	Definitely Disagree	Somewhat Disagree	Slightly Disagree	Slightly Agree	Somewhat Agree	Definitely Agree
I buy *many* things with a credit card.	____	____	____	____	____	____
I wish we had *a lot more* money.	____	____	____	____	____	____
My friends *often* come to me for advice.	____	____	____	____	____	____
I am *never* influenced by advertisements.	____	____	____	____	____	____

---

expanded beyond the original 5-point format to a 7-point scale, and most researchers treat the scale format as an interval scale. Likert scales are best for research designs that use self-administered surveys, personal interviews, or online surveys. Exhibit 7.9 provides an example of a 6-point Likert scale in a self-administered survey.

While widely used, there can be difficulties in interpreting the results produced by a Likert scale. Consider the last statement in Exhibit 7.9 (I am *never* influenced by advertisements). The key words in this statement are *never influenced.* If respondents check "Definitely Disagree," the response does not necessarily mean that respondents are very much influenced by advertisements.

Semantic Differential Scale

Semantic differential scale
A unique bipolar ordinal scale format that captures a person's attitudes or feelings about a given object.

Another rating scale used quite often in marketing research is the **semantic differential scale.** This scale is unique in its use of bipolar adjectives (good/bad, like/dislike, competitive/noncompetitive, helpful/unhelpful, high quality/low quality, dependable/undependable) as the endpoints of a continuum. Only the endpoints of the scale are labeled. Usually there will be one object and a related set of attributes, each with its own set of bipolar adjectives. In most cases, semantic differential scales use either 5 or 7 scale points.

Means for each attribute can be calculated and mapped on a diagram with the various attributes listed, creating a "perceptual image profile" of the object. Semantic differential scales can be used to develop and compare profiles of different companies, brands, or products. Respondents can also be asked to indicate how an ideal product would rate, and then researchers can compare ideal and actual products.

To illustrate semantic differential scales, assume the researcher wants to assess the credibility of Tiger Woods as a spokesperson in advertisements for the Nike brand of personal grooming products. A credibility construct consisting of three dimensions is used: (1) expertise; (2) trustworthiness; and (3) attractiveness. Each dimension is measured using five bipolar scales (see measures of two dimensions in Exhibit 7.10).

Non-bipolar Descriptors A problem encountered in designing semantic differential scales is the inappropriate narrative expressions of the scale descriptors. In a well-designed semantic differential scale, the individual scales should be truly bipolar. Sometimes researchers use a negative pole descriptor that is not truly an opposite of the positive descriptor. This creates a scale that is difficult for the respondent to interpret correctly. Consider, for example, the "expert/not an expert" scale in the "expertise" dimension. While the scale is dichotomous, the words *not an expert* do not allow the respondent to interpret any of the other scale points as being relative magnitudes of that phrase. Other than that one endpoint which is described as "not an expert," all the other scale points would have to represent some intensity of "expertise," thus creating a skewed scale toward the positive pole.

Researchers must be careful when selecting bipolar descriptors to make sure the words or phrases are truly extreme bipolar in nature and allow for creating symmetrical scales.

Exhibit 7.10	Example of a Semantic Differential Scale Format for Tiger Woods as a Credibility Spokesperson[3]

We would like to know your opinions about the expertise, trustworthiness, and attractiveness you believe Tiger Woods brings to Nike advertisements. Each dimension below has five factors that may or may not represent your opinions. For each listed item, please check the space that best expresses your opinion about that item.

Expertise:

Knowledgeable	—	—	—	—	—	—	—	Unknowledgeable
Expert	—	—	—	—	—	—	—	Not an expert
Skilled	—	—	—	—	—	—	—	Unskilled
Qualified	—	—	—	—	—	—	—	Unqualified
Experienced	—	—	—	—	—	—	—	Inexperienced

Trustworthiness:

Reliable	—	—	—	—	—	—	—	Unreliable
Sincere	—	—	—	—	—	—	—	Insincere
Trustworthy	—	—	—	—	—	—	—	Untrustworthy
Dependable	—	—	—	—	—	—	—	Undependable
Honest	—	—	—	—	—	—	—	Dishonest

Exhibit 7.11 Example of a Semantic Differential Scale for Midas Auto Systems

From your personal experiences with Midas Auto Systems' service representatives, please rate the performance of Midas on the basis of the following listed features. Each feature has its own scale ranging from "one" (1) to "six" (6). Please circle the response number that best describes how Midas has performed on that feature. For any feature(s) that you feel is (are) not relevant to your evaluation, please circle the (NA)—Not applicable—response code.

Cost of repair/maintenance work	(NA)	Extremely high	6	5	4	3	2	1	Very low, almost free
Appearance of facilities	(NA)	Very professional	6	5	4	3	2	1	Very unprofessional
Customer satisfaction	(NA)	Totally dissatisfied	6	5	4	3	2	1	Truly satisfied
Promptness in delivering service	(NA)	Unacceptably slow	6	5	4	3	2	1	Impressively quick
Quality of service offerings	(NA)	Truly terrible	6	5	4	3	2	1	Truly exceptional
Understands customer's needs	(NA)	Really understands	6	5	4	3	2	1	Doesn't have a clue
Credibility of Midas	(NA)	Extremely credible	6	5	4	3	2	1	Extremely unreliable
Midas's keeping of promises	(NA)	Very trustworthy	6	5	4	3	2	1	Very deceitful
Midas services assortment	(NA)	Truly full service	6	5	4	3	2	1	Only basic services
Prices/rates/charges of services	(NA)	Much too high	6	5	4	3	2	1	Great rates
Service personnel's competence	(NA)	Very competent	6	5	4	3	2	1	Totally incompetent
Employee's personal social skills	(NA)	Very rude	6	5	4	3	2	1	Very friendly
Midas's operating hours	(NA)	Extremely flexible	6	5	4	3	2	1	Extremely limited
Convenience of Midas's locations	(NA)	Very easy to get to	6	5	4	3	2	1	Too difficult to get to

For example, the researcher could use descriptors such as "complete expert" and "complete novice" to correct the scale descriptor problem described in the previous paragraph.

Exhibit 7.11 shows a semantic differential scale used by Midas Auto Systems to collect attitudinal data on performance. The same scale can be used to collect data on several competing automobile service providers, and each of the semantic differential profiles can be displayed together.

Behavioral Intention Scale

Behavioral intention scale
A special type of rating scale designed to capture the likelihood that people will demonstrate some type of predictable behavior intent toward purchasing an object or service in a future time frame.

One of the most widely used scale formats in marketing research is the **behavioral intention scale.** The objective of this type of scale is to assess the likelihood that people will behave in some way regarding a product or service. For example, market researchers may measure purchase intent, attendance intent, shopping intent, or usage intent. In general, behavioral intention scales have been found to be reasonably good predictors of consumers' choices of frequently purchased and durable consumer products.[4]

Behavioral intention scales are easy to construct. Consumers are asked to make a subjective judgment of their likelihood of buying a product or service, or taking a specified action. An example of scale descriptors used with a behavioral intention scale is "definitely will," "probably will," "not sure," "probably will not," and "definitely will not." When designing a behavioral intention scale, a specific time frame should be included in the instructions to the respondent. Without an expressed time frame, it is likely respondents will bias their response toward the "definitely would" or "probably would" scale categories.

Behavioral intentions are often a key variable of interest in marketing research studies. To make scale points more specific, researchers can use descriptors that indicate the

| Exhibit 7.12 | Retail Store: Shopping Intention Scale for Casual Clothes |

When shopping for casual wear for yourself or someone else, how likely are you to shop at each of the following types of retail stores? **(Please check one response for each store type.)**

Type of Retail Store	Definitely Would Shop At (90–100% chance)	Probably Would Shop At (50–89% chance)	Probably Would Not Shop At (10–49% chance)	Definitely Would Not Shop At (less than 10% chance)
Department stores (e.g., Macy's, Dillard's)	❏	❏	❏	❏
Discount department stores (e.g., Walmart, Costco, Target)	❏	❏	❏	❏
Clothing specialty shops (e.g., Wolf Brothers, Surrey's George Ltd.)	❏	❏	❏	❏
Casual wear specialty stores (e.g., The Gap, Banana Republic, Aca Joe's)	❏	❏	❏	❏

percentage chance they will buy a product, or engage in a behavior of interest. The following set of scale points could be used: "definitely will (90–100 percent chance)"; "probably will (50–89 percent chance)"; "probably will not (10–49 percent chance)"; and "definitely will not (less than 10 percent chance)." Exhibit 7.12 shows what a shopping intention scale might look like.

No matter what kind of scale is used to capture people's attitudes and behaviors, there often is no one best or guaranteed approach. While there are established scale measures for obtaining the components that make up respondents' attitudes and behavioral intentions, the data provided from these scale measurements should not be interpreted as being completely predictive of behavior. Unfortunately, knowledge of an individual's attitudes may not predict actual behavior. Intentions are better than attitudes at predicting behavior, but the strongest predictor of future behavior is past behavior.

■ Comparative and Noncomparative Rating Scales

Noncomparative rating scale A scale format that requires a judgment without reference to another object, person, or concept.

Comparative rating scales A scale format that requires a judgment comparing one object, person, or concept against another on the scale.

A **noncomparative rating scale** is used when the objective is to have a respondent express his or her attitudes, behavior, or intentions about a specific object (e.g., person or phenomenon) or its attributes without making reference to another object or its attributes. In contrast, a **comparative rating scale** is used when the objective is to have a respondent express his or her attitudes, feelings, or behaviors about an object or its attributes on the basis of some other object or its attributes. Exhibit 7.13 gives several examples of graphic rating scale formats, which are among the most widely used noncomparative scales.

Graphic rating scales use a scaling descriptor format that presents a respondent with a continuous line as the set of possible responses to a question. For example, the first graphic rating scale displayed in Exhibit 7.13 is used in situations where the researcher wants to collect "usage behavior" data about an object. Let's say Yahoo! wants to determine how

| Exhibit 7.13 | Examples of Graphic Rating Scales |

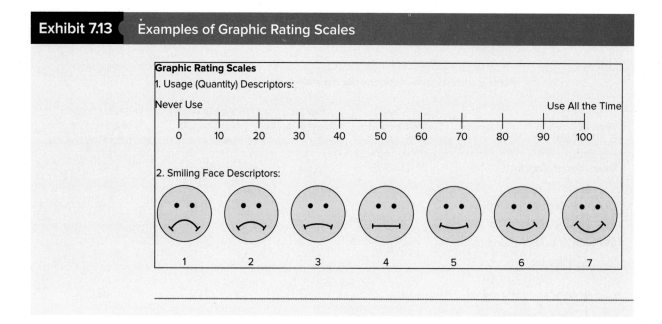

Graphic rating scales A scale measure that uses a scale point format that presents the respondent with some type of graphic continuum as the set of possible raw responses to a given question.

satisfied Internet users are with its search engine without making reference to any other available search engine alternative such as Google. In using this type of scale, the respondents would simply place an "X" along the graphic line, which is labeled with extreme narrative descriptors, in this case "Not at all Satisfied" and "Very Satisfied," together with numeric descriptors, 0 and 100. The remainder of the line is sectioned into equal-appearing numeric intervals.

Another popular type of graphic rating scale descriptor design utilizes smiling faces. The smiling faces are arranged in order and depict a continuous range from "very happy" to "very sad" without providing narrative descriptors of the two extreme positions. This visual graphic rating design can be used to collect a variety of attitudinal and emotional data. It is most popular in collecting data from children. Graphic rating scales can be constructed easily and are simple to use.

Turning now to comparative rating scales, Exhibit 7.14 illustrates rank-order and constant-sums scale formats. A common characteristic of comparative scales is that they can be used to identify and directly compare similarities and differences between products or services, brands, or product attributes.

Rank-order scales These allow respondents to compare their own responses by indicating their first, second, third, and fourth preferences, and so forth.

Rank-order scales use a format that enables respondents to compare objects by indicating their order of preference or choice from first to last. Rank-order scales are easy to use as long as respondents are not asked to rank too many items. Use of rank-order scales in traditional or computer-assisted telephone interviews may be difficult, but it is possible as long as the number of items being compared is kept to four or five. When respondents are asked to rank objects or attributes of objects, problems can occur if the respondent's preferred objects or attributes are not listed. Another limitation is that only ordinal data can be obtained using rank-order scales.

Constant-sum scales Require the respondent to allocate a given number of points, usually 100, among each separate attribute or feature relative to all the other listed ones.

Constant-sum scales ask respondents to allocate a given number of points. The points are often allocated based on the importance of product features to respondents. Respondents are asked to determine the value of each separate feature relative to all the other listed features. The resulting values indicate the relative magnitude of importance each feature has to the respondent. This scaling format usually requires that the individual

Exhibit 7.14   Examples of Comparative Rating Scales

Rank-Order Scale

Thinking about the different types of music, please rank your top three preferences of types of music you enjoy listening to by writing in your first choice, second choice, and third choice on the lines provided below.

First Preference: _____

Second Preference: _____

Third Preference: _____

Constant-Sum Scale

Below is a list of seven banking features Allocate 100 points among the features. Your allocation should represent the importance each feature has to you in selecting your bank. The more points you assign to a feature, the more importance that feature has in your selection process. If the feature is "not at all important" in your process, you should not assign it any points. When you have finished, double-check to make sure your total adds to 100.

Banking Features	Number of Points
Convenience/location	____
Banking hours	____
Good service charges	____
The interest rates on loans	____
The bank's reputation	____
The interest rates on savings	____
Bank's promotional advertising	____
	100 points

Paired-Comparison Scales

Below are several pairs of traits associated with salespeople's on-the-job activities. For each pair, please circle either the "a" or "b" next to the trait you believe is more important for a salesperson to be successful in their job.

a. trust	b. competence
a. communication skills	b. trust
a. trust	b. personal social skills
a. communication skills	b. competence
a. competence	b. personal social skills
a. personal social skills	b. communication skills

Note: Researchers randomly list the order of these paired comparisons to avoid possible order bias.

values must add up to 100. Consider, for example, the constant-sum scale displayed in Exhibit 7.14. Bank of America could use this type of scale to identify which banking attributes are more important to customers in influencing their decision of where to bank. More than five to seven attributes should not be used to allocate points because of the difficulty in adding to reach 100 points.

◼️ Other Scale Measurement Issues

Attention to scale measurement issues will increase the usefulness of research results. Several additional design issues related to scale measurement are reviewed below.

Single-Item and Multiple-Item Scales

Single-item scale A scale format that collects data about only one attribute of an object or construct.

A **single-item scale** involves collecting data about only one attribute of the object or construct being investigated. One example of a single-item scale would be age. The respondent is asked a single question about his or her age and supplies only one possible response to the question. In contrast, many marketing research projects that involve collecting attitudinal, emotional, and behavioral data use some type of multiple-item scale. A **multiple-item scale** is one that includes several statements relating to the object or construct being examined. Each statement has a rating scale attached to it, and the researcher often will sum the ratings on the individual statements to obtain a summated or overall rating for the object or construct.

Multiple-item scale A scale format that simultaneously collects data on several attributes of an object or construct.

The decision to use a single-item versus a multiple-item scale is made when the construct is being developed. Two factors play a significant role in the process: (1) the number of dimensions of the construct and (2) the reliability and validity. First, the researcher must assess the various factors or dimensions that make up the construct under investigation. For example, studies of service quality often measure five dimensions: (1) empathy; (2) reliability; (3) responsiveness; (4) assurance; and (5) tangibles. If a construct has several different, unique dimensions, the researcher must measure each of those subcomponents. Second, researchers must consider reliability and validity. In general, multiple-item scales are more reliable and more valid. Thus, multiple-item scales generally are preferred over single item scales. Researchers are reminded that internal consistency reliability values for single-item or two-item scales cannot be accurately determined and should not be reported as representing the scale's internal consistency. Furthermore, when determining the internal consistency reliability of a multi-item scale, any negatively worded items (questions) must be reverse coded prior to calculating the reliability of the construct.

Clear Wording

When phrasing the question setup element of the scale, use clear wording and avoid ambiguity. Also avoid using "leading" words or phrases in any scale measurement's question. Regardless of the data collection method (personal, telephone, computer-assisted interviews, or online surveys), all necessary instructions for both respondent and interviewer are part of the scale measurement's setup. All instructions should be kept simple and clear. When determining the appropriate set of scale point descriptors, make sure the descriptors are relevant to the type of data being sought. Scale descriptors should have adequate discriminatory power, be mutually exclusive, and make sense to the respondent. Use only scale descriptors and formats that have been pretested and evaluated for scale reliability and validity. Exhibit 7.15 provides a summary checklist for evaluating the appropriateness of scale designs. The guidelines are also useful in developing and evaluating questions to be used on questionnaires, which are covered in Chapter 8.

Exhibit 7.15   Guidelines for Evaluating the Adequacy of Scale and Question Designs

1. Scale questions/setups should be *simple* and *straightforward*.

2. Scale questions/setups should be *expressed clearly*.

3. Scale questions/setups should avoid *qualifying phrases* or *extraneous references*, unless they are being used to screen out specific types of respondents.

4. The scale's question/setup, attribute statements, and data response categories should use singular (or one-dimensional) phrasing, except when there is a need for a *multiple-response scale question/setup*.

5. Response categories (scale points) should be *mutually exclusive*.

6. Scale questions/setups and response categories should be *meaningful to the respondent*.

7. Scale questions/scale measurement formats should avoid *arrangement* of response categories that *might bias* the respondent's answer.

8. Scale questions/setups should avoid *undue stress* on particular words.

9. Scale questions/setups should avoid *double negatives*.

10. Scale questions/scale measurements should avoid *technical* or *sophisticated language*.

11. Scale questions/setup should be phrased in a *realistic setting*.

12. Scale questions/setups and scale measurements should be *logical*.

13. Scale questions/setups and scale measurements should not have *double-barreled items*.

Misleading Scaling Formats

A **double-barreled question** includes two or more different attributes or issues in the same question, but responses allow respondent to comment on only a single issue. The following examples illustrate some of the pitfalls to avoid when designing questions and scale measurements. Possible corrective solutions are also included.

Example:

How happy or unhappy are you with your current phone company's rates and customer service? (Please check only one response)

Very Unhappy	Unhappy	Somewhat Unhappy	Somewhat Happy	Happy	Very Happy	Not Sure
[ ]	[ ]	[ ]	[ ]	[ ]	[ ]	[ ]

Possible Solution:

In your questionnaire, include more than a single question—one for each attribute, or topic. How happy or unhappy are you with your current phone company's rates? (Please check only one response)

Very Unhappy	Unhappy	Somewhat Unhappy	Somewhat Happy	Happy	Very Happy	Not Sure
[ ]	[ ]	[ ]	[ ]	[ ]	[ ]	[ ]

How happy or unhappy are you with your current phone company's customer service? (Please check only one response)

Very Unhappy	Unhappy	Somewhat Unhappy	Somewhat Happy	Happy	Very Happy	Not Sure
[ ]	[ ]	[ ]	[ ]	[ ]	[ ]	[ ]

A **leading question** introduces bias and often influences the way a respondent answers a question. The question below likely influences some respondents to check the Agree option because it indicates what "Experts" think.

Example:

Retail experts believe that all consumers should comparison shop. Do you agree?

[ ] Agree   [ ] Neutral   [ ] Disagree

Possible Solution:

To what extent do you agree or disagree that all consumers should comparison shop.

Definitely Disagree	Disagree	Somewhat Disagree	Neither/Nor	Somewhat Agree	Agree	Definitely Agree
[ ]	[ ]	[ ]	[ ]	[ ]	[ ]	[ ]

A **loaded question** is a situation where the question/setup suggests a socially desirable answer or involves an emotionally charged issue.

Example:

Should Americans buy imported automobiles that take away American jobs?

[ ] Definitely Should Not [ ] Should Not [ ] Should [ ] Definitely Should [ ] Not Sure

Possible Solution:

Please circle the number that best expresses your feelings of what Americans should do when shopping for a car.

Avoid Imports   1   2   3   4   5   6   7   Buy Imports

Ambiguous questions involve a situation in which possible responses can be interpreted a number of different ways. When this is present, it typically creates confusion among respondents about how to respond. The below example is confusing because the terms, such as occasionally or sometimes, are not defined, and could easily differ for different respondents.

Example:

In the past month, how often did you shop in department stores? (Please check only one response category.)

[ ] Never   [ ] Occasionally   [ ] Sometimes   [ ] Often   [ ] Regularly   [ ] Do Not Know

Possible Solution:

In the past month, how often did you shop in department stores? (Please check only one response category.)

[ ] Never   [ ] 1–2 Times   [ ] 3–5 Times   [ ] 6–10 Times   [ ] More Than 10 Times

Complex questions are situations in which the question is worded in a way the respondent is not sure how they are supposed to respond. In the example below, it is unclear what is meant by the word "adequate."

Example:

Do you think that soft drink distribution is adequate? (Please check one response.)

Definitely Disagree	Disagree	Somewhat Disagree	Neither/Nor	Somewhat Agree	Agree	Definitely Agree
[ ]	[ ]	[ ]	[ ]	[ ]	[ ]	[ ]

Possible Solution:

To what extent do you agree or disagree that soft drinks are easy to find whenever you want to buy one?

Definitely Disagree	Disagree	Somewhat Disagree	Neither/Nor	Somewhat Agree	Agree	Definitely Agree
[ ]	[ ]	[ ]	[ ]	[ ]	[ ]	[ ]

A **double negative question** involves a situation where the question/setup contains two negative thoughts in the same question. Double negative expressions in a question create cognitive confusion and respondents find it difficult to understand the question and therefore respond correctly.

Example:

To what extent do you agree that you are not incompetent when part of a multidisciplinary team?

Definitely Disagree	Disagree	Somewhat Disagree	Neutral	Somewhat Agree	Agree	Definitely Agree
[ ]	[ ]	[ ]	[ ]	[ ]	[ ]	[ ]

Possible Solution:

To what extent do you agree or disagree that you are competent when part of a multidisciplinary team?

Definitely Disagree	Disagree	Somewhat Disagree	Neutral	Somewhat Agree	Agree	Definitely Agree
[ ]	[ ]	[ ]	[ ]	[ ]	[ ]	[ ]

Scale responses should be **mutually exclusive** and not overlap. Using response choices that overlap with other response choices creates confusion in the respondent's choice. In the below example, the same numbers (ages) are shown in more than a single category.

Example:

Please check the one category that best represents your current age.

[ ] 0–10 years [ ] 10–20 years [ ] 20–30 years [ ] 30–40 years [ ] 40–50 years [ ] 50 or more years

Possible Solution:

Please check the category that best represents your current age.

[ ] under 10 years [ ] 10–20 years [ ] 21–30 years [ ] 31–40 years [ ] 41–50 years [ ] over 50 years

MARKETING RESEARCH IN ACTION
What Can You Learn from a Customer Loyalty Index?

The idea that loyal customers are especially valuable is not new. Loyal customers repeatedly purchase products or services. They recommend a company to others. And they stick with a business over time. Loyal customers are worth the special effort it may take to keep them. But how can you provide that special treatment if you don't know your customers and how their loyalty is won and lost?

To better understand the concept of customer loyalty, we can first define what customer loyalty is not. Customer loyalty is not customer satisfaction. Satisfaction is a necessary component of loyal or secure customers. However, just because customers are satisfied with your company does not mean they will continue to do business with you in the future.

Customer loyalty is not a response to trial offers or incentives. Customers who respond to a special offer or incentive may be just as quick to respond to your competitors' incentives.

Customer loyalty is not high market share. Many businesses mistakenly look at their sales numbers and market share and think, "We wouldn't be enjoying high levels of market share if our customers didn't love us." However, this may not be true. Many other factors can drive up market share, including poor performance by competitors or pricing issues.

Customer loyalty is not repeat buying or habitual buying. Many repeat customers may be choosing your products or services because of convenience or habit. However, if they learn about a competitive product that they think may be less expensive or of better quality, they may quickly switch to that product.

So what does customer loyalty mean? Customer loyalty is a composite of a number of qualities. It is driven by customer satisfaction, yet it also involves a commitment on the part of the customer to make a sustained investment in an ongoing relationship with a brand or company. Finally, customer loyalty is reflected by a combination of attitudes and behaviors. These attitudes include,

- The intention to buy again and/or buy additional products or services from the same company.
- A willingness to recommend the company to others.
- A commitment to the company demonstrated by a resistance to switching to a competitor.

Customer behaviors that reflect loyalty include,

- Repeat purchasing of products or services.
- Purchasing more and different products or services from the same company.
- Recommending the company to others.

Burke, Inc. (burke.com) developed a Secure Customer Index® (SCI®) using the combined scores on three components of customer loyalty (Exhibit 7.16).[5] They ask, for example, "Overall, how satisfied were you with your visit to this restaurant?" To examine their likelihood to recommend, "How likely would you be to recommend this restaurant to a friend or associate?" And finally, to examine likelihood of repeat purchases, they ask, "How likely are you to choose to visit this restaurant again?"

| **Exhibit 7.16** | The Secure Customer Index® (i.e., Customer Loyalty Index) |

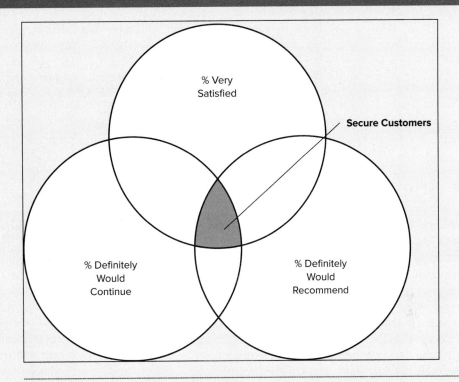

Source: From Burke, Inc. and Amanda Prus and D. Randall Brandt, "Understanding Your Customers – What You Can Learn from a Customer Loyalty Index," *Marketing Tools* (July/August 1995), pp. 10–14.

With these three components and the appropriate scales for each, "secure customers" are defined as those giving the most positive responses across all three components. All other customers would be considered vulnerable or at risk of defecting to a competitor.

Companies are increasingly able to link customer satisfaction and customer loyalty to bottom-line benefits. By examining customer behaviors over time and comparing them to SCI® scores, a strong connection can be shown between secure customers and repeat purchasing of products or services. In comparing cases across customer and industry types, Burke, Inc. has found other illustrations that show a connection between the index scores and financial or market performance.

Using a customer loyalty index helps companies better understand their customers. By listening to customers, implementing change, and continuously monitoring the results, companies can focus their improvement efforts with the goal of winning and keeping customers.

Hands-On Exercise

Using the material from the chapter and the preceding information, answer each of the following questions:

1. In your judgment, what level of scale design would be the most appropriate in creating the necessary scale measurements for collecting primary data on each construct?
2. For each construct, design an example of the actual scale measurement that could be used by Burke, Inc. to collect the data.

3. What are several weaknesses associated with how Burke, Inc. measured its Secure Customer Index® (SCI®)? Make sure you clearly identify each weakness and explain why you feel it is a weakness.
4. If you were the lead researcher, what types of scale measurement would you have used to collect the needed data for calculating SCI®? Why? Write some scale measurements you would use.
5. Do you agree or disagree with the Burke, Inc. interpretation of the value they provide their clients using the Customer Loyalty Index? Support your response.

Source: **www.burke.com**. Reprinted by permission

Summary

Understand the role of measurement in marketing research.

Measurement is the process of developing methods to systematically characterize or quantify information about persons, events, ideas, or objects of interest. As part of the measurement process, researchers assign either numbers or labels to phenomena they measure. The measurement process consists of two tasks: construct selection/development and scale measurement. A construct is an unobservable concept that is measured indirectly by a group of related variables. Thus, constructs are made up of a combination of several related indicator variables that together define the concept being measured. Construct development is the process in which researchers identify characteristics that define the concept being studied by the researcher.

When developing constructs, researchers must consider the abstractness of the construct and its dimensionality, as well as reliability and validity. Once the characteristics are identified, the researcher must then develop a method of indirectly measuring the concept. Scale measurement is the process of assigning a set of descriptors to represent the range of possible responses a person may give in answering a question about a particular object or construct.

Explain the four basic levels of scales.

The four basic levels of scales are nominal, ordinal, interval, and ratio. Nominal scales are the most basic and provide the least amount of data. They assign labels to objects and respondents but do not show relative magnitudes between them. Nominal scales ask respondents about their religious affiliation, gender, type of dwelling, occupation, last brand

of cereal purchased, and so on. To analyze nominal data researchers use modes and frequency distributions. Ordinal scales require respondents to express relative magnitude about a topic. Ordinal scales enable researchers to create a hierarchical pattern among the responses (or scale points) that indicate "greater than/less than" relationships. Data derived from ordinal scale measurements include medians and ranges as well as modes and frequency distributions. An example of an ordinal scale would be "complete knowledge," "good knowledge," "basic knowledge," "little knowledge," and "no knowledge." Ordinal scales determine relative position, but they cannot determine how much more or how much less since they do not measure absolute differences. Interval scales enable researchers to show absolute differences between scale points. With interval data, means and standard deviations can be calculated, as well as the mode, median, frequency distribution and range. Ratio scales enable researchers to identify absolute differences between each scale point and to make absolute comparisons between the respondents' responses. Ratio questions are designed to allow "true natural zero" or "true state of nothing" responses. Ratio scales also can develop means, standard deviations and other measures of central tendency and variation.

Describe scale development and its importance in gathering primary data.

There are three important components to scale measurement: (1) question/setup; (2) dimensions of the object, construct, or behavior; and (3) the scale point descriptors. Some of the criteria for scale development are the intelligibility of the questions, the appropriateness of the primary descriptors, and the discriminatory power of the scale descriptors. Likert scales use agree/disagree scale descriptors to obtain a person's attitude toward a given object or behavior. Semantic differential scale formats are used to obtain perceptual image profiles of an object or behavior. This scale format is unique in that it uses a set of bipolar scales to measure several different attributes of a given object or behavior. Behavioral intention scales measure the likelihood that people will purchase an object or service, or visit a store. Scale point descriptors such as "definitely would," "probably would," "probably would not," and "definitely would not" are often used with intentions scales.

Discuss comparative and noncomparative scales.

Comparative scales require the respondent to make a direct comparison between two products or services, whereas noncomparative scales rate products or services independently. Data from comparative scales is interpreted in relative terms. Both types of scales are generally considered interval or ratio and more advanced statistical procedures can be used with them. One benefit of comparative scales is they enable researchers to identify small differences between attributes, constructs, or objects. In addition, comparative scales require fewer theoretical assumptions and are easier for respondents to understand and respond to than are many noncomparative scales.

Key Terms and Concepts

Behavioral intention scale 176

Comparative rating scale 177

Constant-sum scales 178

Construct 161

Construct development 162

Discriminatory power 170

Graphic rating scales 178

Interval scale 165

Likert scale 173

Measurement 160

Multiple-item scale 180

Nominal scale 164

Noncomparative rating scale 177

Ordinal scale 164

Rank-order scales 178

Ratio scale 166

Scale measurement 163

Scale points 163

Semantic differential scale 174

Single-item scale 180

Review Questions

1. What is measurement?
2. Among the four basic levels of scales, which one provides the researcher with the most information?
3. Explain the main differences between interval and ratio scale measurements.
4. What are the major differences between ordinal and interval scales? In your response include an example of each type of scale.
5. Explain the major differences between "rating" and "ranking" scales. Which is a better scale measurement technique for collecting attitudinal data on sales force performance of people who sell commercial laser printers? Why?
6. What are the benefits and limitations of comparative scale measurements? Design a ranking order scale that will enable you to determine brand preference between Bud Light, Miller Lite, Coors Light, and Old Milwaukee Light beers.

◼️ Discussion Questions

1. Develop a semantic differential scale that can identify the perceptual profile differences between Outback Steakhouse and Longhorn Steakhouse restaurants.

2. Design a behavioral intention scale that can answer the following research question: To what extent are college students likely to purchase a new automobile within six months after graduating? Discuss the potential shortcomings of your scale design.

3. For each of the scales shown below (A, B, and C), answer the following questions:
   a. What type of data is being collected?
   b. What level of scale measurement is being used?
   c. What is the most appropriate measure of central tendency?
   d. What is the most appropriate measure of dispersion?
   e. What weakness, if any, exists with the scale?

A. How do you pay for your travel expenses?

_____ Cash	_____ Company charge
_____ Check	_____ Personal charge
_____ Credit card	_____ Other _____

B. How often do you travel for business or pleasure purposes?

For Business	**For Pleasure**
_____ 0–1 times per month	_____ 0–1 times per year
_____ 2–3 times per month	_____ 2–3 times per year
_____ 4–5 times per month	_____ 4–5 times per year
_____ 6 or more times per year	_____ 6 or more times per month

C. Check the one category that best approximates your total family annual income, before taxes. (Check only one category.)

_____ Under $10,000	_____ $30,001–$40,000	_____ $60,001–$70,000
_____ $10,000–$20,000	_____ $40,001–$50,000	_____ $70,001–$100,000
_____ $20,001–$30,000	_____ $50,001–$60,000	_____ Over $100,000

4. For each of the listed concepts or objects, design a scale measurement that would enable you to collect data on that concept or object.
   a. An excellent long-distance runner
   b. A person's favorite Mexican restaurant
   c. Size of the listening audience for a popular country and western radio station
   d. Consumers' attitudes toward the Colorado Rockies professional baseball team
   e. The satisfaction a person has toward his or her automobile
   f. Purchase intentions for a new tennis racket

5. Identify and discuss the key issues a researcher should consider when choosing a scale for capturing consumers' expressions of satisfaction.

6. AT&T is interested in capturing the judgments people make of its new wireless cell phone services. Determine and justify what service attributes should be used to capture the _performance_ of its wireless cell phone service. Design two scale measurements that would allow AT&T to accurately collect the data.

7. The local Ford dealership is interested in collecting data to answer the following research question: How likely are young adults to purchase a new automobile within a year after graduating from college? Design a nominal, ordinal, interval, and ratio scale measurement that will enable the dealership to collect the required data. In your opinion, which one of your designs would be most useful to the dealership and why?

Designing the Questionnaire

1. Describe the steps in questionnaire design.
2. Discuss the questionnaire development process.
3. Summarize the characteristics of good questionnaires.
4. Understand the role of cover letters.
5. Explain the importance of other documents used with questionnaires.

Can Surveys Be Used to Develop University Residence Life Plans?

University administrators implemented a "Residence Life" program to identify factors likely to enrich the academic and social experiences of on-campus students. The main goals were to ensure the university offered high-quality on-campus living experiences with facilities and programs for attracting new students to the university, increasing on-campus housing occupancy rates, and improving retention levels of students, thus increasing the likelihood that students would renew their on-campus housing contracts for multiple years. MPC Consulting Group, Inc., a national firm specializing in on-campus housing programs, was retained to oversee the project. The firm had an excellent reputation but seldom conducted primary marketing research.

After clarifying the objectives of the project, MPC determined that a self-administered survey instrument would be used to obtain students' information, attitudes, and feelings regarding on-campus living experiences. The survey would be administered using the university's newly acquired "Blackboard" electronic learning management system. The rationale for using this method was that all 43,000 students had access and it would save time and costs. MPC's consulting team brainstormed a list of 59 questions to be asked of both on-campus and off-campus students currently enrolled at the university. The questionnaire began by asking about personal demographic characteristics followed by some questions concerning students' current housing situations and an evaluation of those conditions. Next, questions were asked about the importance of a list of preselected housing characteristics, then questions about students' intentions of living on-campus versus off-campus and reasons for those intentions. After asking about marital status and children, questions were asked on the desirability of types of housing structures and amenities. The survey ended with personal thoughts about the need for child care services.

When placed on "Blackboard" for access, the questionnaire took 24 screens with six different "screener" questions requiring respondents to skip back and forth between computer screens depending on how they responded to the screening questions. After being in the field three weeks, only 17 students had responded, and eight of those surveys were incomplete. University officials were disappointed in the response rate and asked MPC three simple but critical questions: (1) "Why such a low response rate?" (2) "Was the survey a good or bad instrument for capturing the needed information?" and (3) "What was the value of the data for addressing the given goals?"

Based on your knowledge and understanding of research practices to this point, answer the three questions. What are the potential problems (weaknesses) created by MPC's process described earlier?

Value of Questionnaires in Marketing Research

This chapter focuses on the importance of questionnaire design and the process that should be undertaken in the development of data collection instruments. Understanding questionnaire design will require integration of many of the concepts discussed in earlier chapters.

Most surveys are designed to be descriptive or predictive. Descriptive research designs use questionnaires to collect data that can be turned into knowledge about a person, object, or issue. For example, the U.S. Census Bureau uses descriptive survey questionnaires to collect attributes and behavioral data that can be translated into facts about the U.S. population (e.g., income levels, marital status, age, occupation, family size, usage rates, consumption quantities). In contrast, predictive survey questionnaires require the researcher to collect a wider range of data that can be used in predicting changes in attitudes and behaviors as well as in testing hypotheses.

You may never actually design a questionnaire. But you likely will be in the position of determining whether a survey is good or bad. Thus, you should know the activities and principles involved in designing survey questionnaires. A **questionnaire** is a document consisting of a set of questions and scales designed to gather primary data. Good questionnaires enable researchers to collect reliable and valid information. Advances in communication systems, the Internet, and software have influenced how questions are asked and recorded. Yet the principles followed in designing questionnaires remain essentially unchanged. Whether developing a survey to use online or offline, the steps researchers follow in designing questionnaires are similar.

Questionnaire A formal framework consisting of a set of questions and scales designed to generate primary raw data.

Pilot Studies and Pretests

Prior to discussing the development and execution of questionnaires (or surveys) used in marketing research practices, it is useful to understand the distinctions and similarities of a pilot study (also referred to as pilot test) and a pretest. Depending on the reference source, some scholars, books, journal articles, and conference proceedings use these two terms "pilot study" and "pretest" interchangeably referring to the same meaning, that is, a smaller scale study before the actual study. Several characteristics make a pilot study different beginning with its focus. A **pilot study** is a small-scale version of the intended main research study, including all the subcomponents that make up the main study, including the data collection and analysis from about 50 to 100 respondents that have representation of the main study's defined target population. A pilot study normally serves a guide for conducting a larger main study. In some situations, a pilot study is employed for examining specific subcomponents of the overall research plan to see if the selected procedures work as expected or if refinements are needed prior to conducting the main study. For example, a pilot study among 50 to 100 representative respondents is used to obtain data for refining scale measurements and gain preliminary insights about construct reliability and validity assessments, finetuning research objectives and questions as well as data collection procedures, reducing the risk that the main study will be fatally flawed. While pilot studies can be included in any form of research (i.e., exploratory, descriptive, or causal research designs), they are most often associated with empirical descriptive or predictive quantitative research studies. In contrast, a **pretest** is a descriptive research activity representing a small-scale investigation of 5 to 30 subjects that are representative of the main study's defined target population but focus on a specific sub-component of the main study. The results of a pretest are only preliminary and intended only to assist researchers in designing or executing a particular subcomponent of a larger study (or experiment). While researchers do conduct pretests in the development of a pilot study, pre-tests are more associated with exploratory and causal experimental research designs. As we begin discussions of the development and execution of questionnaires in marketing research, more insights concerning how and when researchers use pretests will be acknowledged.

Questionnaire Design

Researchers follow a systematic approach to designing questionnaires. Exhibit 8.1 lists the steps followed in developing survey questionnaires. Discussion of the steps is based on a study conducted for American Bank in Baton Rouge, the capital city of Louisiana. The bank would like to expand regionally. To improve decision making, information is needed on banking habits and patterns, satisfaction and commitment, as well as demographic and lifestyle characteristics of current and potential customers.

Step 1: Confirm Research Objectives

In the initial phase of the development process, the research objectives are agreed upon by the researcher and bank management. The research objectives are listed below:

1. To collect data on selected demographic characteristics that can be used to create a profile of current American Bank customers as well as potential future customers.
2. To collect data on selected lifestyle dimensions that can be used to better understand current American Bank customers and their banking habits and those of potential customers.

Exhibit 8.1 Steps in Questionnaire Design

Step 1: Confirm research objectives

Step 2: Select appropriate data collection method

Step 3: Develop questions and scaling

Step 4: Determine layout and evaluate questionnaire

Step 5: Obtain initial client approval

Step 6: Pretest, revise, and finalize questionnaire

Step 7: Implement the survey

3. To identify preferred banking services, as well as attitudes and feelings toward those services.
4. To identify demographic and lifestyle characteristics of market segments as well as satisfaction with and commitment to current primary banking relationships.

Step 2: Select Appropriate Data Collection Method

To select the data collection method, the researcher first must determine the data requirements to achieve each of the objectives as well as the type of respondent demographic information desired. In doing so, the researcher should follow a general-to-specific order. The data requirements and flow for the American Bank study are described below:

Section I: Banking Services

1. The bank most often patronized by customers; that is, the primary banking relationship.
2. Bank characteristics perceived as important in selecting a bank (convenience and location, banking hours, good service charges, interest rates on savings accounts, knowing an employee of the bank, bank's reputation, bank's promotional advertisements, interest rates on loans, and Internet banking services).
3. Personal savings accounts held by household members at various types of financial institutions.
4. Preferences for and usage of selected banking methods (inside the bank, drive-up window, 24-hour ATM, electronic banking, bank by mail, bank by phone).

Section II: Lifestyle Dimensions
This section includes belief statements to classify bank customer's lifestyles in terms of segments such as financial optimist, financially dissatisfied, information exchanger, credit or debit card user, family oriented, price conscious, and so forth.

Section III: Banking Relationships
This section includes questions to examine satisfaction and commitment to current primary banking relationship.

Section IV: Demographic Characteristics
This section includes characteristics such as gender, length of time in area and at current residence, employment status, marital status, spouse or partner's current employment status, number of dependent children, education, age, occupation, income, and zip code.

The researcher considered several approaches to data collection, including random telephone calls and online surveys. On the basis of the research objectives, information requirements, and the desire for a random sample of current bank customers, bank management and the researcher decided that an initial phone contact followed by a direct mail survey would be the best method of collecting data for current customers along with a telephone survey for potential customers.

Step 3: Develop Questions and Scaling

Questionnaire design is systematic and includes a series of logical activities. Researchers select the appropriate scales and design the questionnaire format to meet the data requirements. The researcher decides on question format (unstructured or structured), wording of questions, scales, and instructions for responding to questions and scales, and type of data required (nominal, ordinal, interval, or ratio). In making these decisions, researchers must consider how the data are to be collected. For example, appropriate questions and scaling often differ between online, mail, and telephone surveys. Constructs and scaling were discussed in a previous chapter. We discuss the other topics in the following sections:

Unstructured questions
Open-ended questions formatted to allow respondents to reply in their own words.

Question Format **Unstructured questions** are open-ended questions that enable respondents to reply in their own words. There is no predetermined list of responses available to aid or limit respondents' answers. Open-ended questions are more difficult to code for analysis. Perhaps more importantly, these questions require more thinking and effort on the part of respondents. As a result, with quantitative surveys there are generally only a few open-ended questions. Unless the question is likely to be interesting to respondents, open-ended questions are often skipped.

Structured questions
Closed-ended questions that require the respondent to choose from a predetermined set of responses or scale points.

Structured questions are closed-ended questions that require the respondent to choose from a predetermined set of responses or scale points. Structured formats reduce the amount of thinking and effort required by respondents, and the response process is faster. In quantitative surveys, structured questions are used much more often than unstructured ones. They are easier for respondents to fill out and easier for researchers to code. Examples of structured questions are shown in Exhibit 8.2.

Wording Researchers must carefully consider the words used in creating questions and scales. Ambiguous words and phrases as well as vocabulary that is difficult to understand must be avoided. For example, asking a question such as "How frequently do you eat Domino's Pizza?" and using a 7-point "Very Frequently" to "Very Infrequently" scale would likely result in inaccurate answers. What is very frequent for one person is likely to be different for another person. Similarly, words easily understood by the researcher may not be familiar to respondents. For example, questionnaires often ask for the respondent's ethnic origin and list one alternative as Caucasian. But many individuals do not know that Caucasian means white. Researchers must select words carefully to make sure respondents are familiar with them, and when unsure, questionable words should be examined in a pretest.

Words and phrases can influence a respondent's answer to a given question. For example, small changes in wording can produce quite different answers to questions. The following illustrates this point:

1. Do you think anything *could* be done to make it more convenient for students to register for classes at your university or college?
2. Do you think anything *should* be done to make it more convenient for students to register for classes at your university or college?
3. Do you think anything *will* be done to make it more convenient for students to register for classes at your university or college?

Sensitive questions
Include income, sexual beliefs or behaviors, medical conditions, financial difficulties, alcohol consumption, and so forth that respondents are likely to respond to incorrectly.

Some question topics are considered sensitive and must be structured carefully to increase response rates. Examples of **sensitive questions** include income, sexual beliefs or behaviors, medical conditions, financial difficulties, alcohol consumption, and so forth. These types of behaviors are often engaged in but may be considered socially unacceptable. As an example, consider the question below:

Have you ever consumed five or more drinks in one sitting? For the purposes of this study, a drink is defined as a bottle of beer, a glass of wine, a wine cooler, a shot glass of liquor, a mixed drink, or a similar drink containing alcohol.

_____ Yes _____ No

Exhibit 8.2	Examples of Structured Questions

Personal Interview

HAND RESPONDENTS THE CARD. Please look at this card and tell me the letters that indicate what toppings, if any, you typically add to a pizza other than cheese when ordering a pizza for yourself from Pizza Hut. Interviewer: Record all mentioned toppings by circling the letters below, and make sure you probe for any other toppings.

[a] anchovies   [b] bacon   [c] barbecue beef
[d] black olives   [e] extra cheese   [f] green olives
[g] green peppers   [h] ground beef   [i] ham
[j] hot peppers   [k] mushrooms   [l] onions
[m] pepperoni   [n] sausage   [o] some other topping: _____

Telephone Interview (Traditional or Computer-Assisted)

I'm going to read you a list of pizza toppings. As I read each one, please tell me whether or not that topping is one that you usually add to a pizza when ordering a pizza for yourself from Pizza Hut. Interviewer: Read each topping category slowly and record all mentioned toppings by circling their corresponding letter below, and make sure you probe for any other toppings.

[a] anchovies   [b] bacon   [c] barbecue beef
[d] black olives   [e] extra cheese   [f] green olives
[g] green peppers   [h] ground beef   [i] ham
[j] hot peppers   [k] mushrooms   [l] onions
[m] pepperoni   [n] sausage   [o] some other topping: _____

Self-Administered Survey (Online or Offline)

Among the pizza toppings listed below, what toppings, if any, do you usually add to a pizza other than cheese when ordering a pizza for yourself from Pizza Hut? Check as many boxes as apply.

❑ anchovies   ❑ bacon   ❑ barbecue beef
❑ black olives   ❑ extra cheese   ❑ green olives
❑ green peppers   ❑ ground beef   ❑ ham
❑ hot peppers   ❑ mushrooms   ❑ onions
❑ pepperoni   ❑ sausage   ❑ some other topping: _____

Researchers are likely to get a high response rate to this question. But how accurate will the answers be? How is "one sitting" defined? Moreover, the size of a drink in ounces is unclear. An even worse approach to asking this question, however, would be to frame it as shown below.

"Binge drinking" has been defined as consuming five or more drinks in one sitting. Have you ever consumed alcohol in a manner that meets this definition? _____ Yes _____ No

The earlier definition of binge drinking was developed by the Harvard School of Public Health, but leading this question with the definition will result in very few people answering yes—in spite of the fact that many individuals who watch sports programs or other activities have actually consumed five drinks.

Guidelines for asking sensitive questions start with not asking them unless they are required to achieve your research objectives. If they are necessary, assure respondents that their answers will be kept completely confidential. Another guideline is to indicate the behavior is not unusual. For example, if asking about financial problems, before asking your questions say something like "Many individuals have financial problems" so respondents do not feel as though they are the only ones with such problems. Another approach is to phrase questions so they are referring to other people to obtain general as opposed to specific answers. For example, "Do you think most college students take drugs? Explain your answer." Responses about the behavior of others are often a reflection of the respondent's behavior.

Questions and Scaling   Questions and scale format directly impact survey designs. To collect accurate data, researchers must devise good questions and select the correct type of scale. Several types of scales were discussed in the previous chapter. Whenever possible, metric scales should be used. Also, researchers must be careful to maintain consistency in scales and coding to minimize confusion among respondents in answering questions.

Once a particular question or scale is selected, the researcher must ensure it is introduced properly and easy to respond to accurately. **Bad questions** prevent or distort communications between the researcher and the respondent. If the respondent cannot answer a question in a meaningful way, it is a bad question. Some examples of bad questions are those that are the following:

> **Bad questions** Any questions that prevent or distort the fundamental communication between the researcher and the respondents.

1. *Unanswerable* either because the respondent does not have access to the information needed or because none of the answer choices apply to the respondent. Examples would be: "What was your parents' yearly after-tax income last year?" or "How much did you spend on food last month?" In general, respondents do not know the answer to this type of question but will still attempt to answer it. They give an "informed guess" based on what they think about is right. Some researchers believe that providing response alternatives is a solution, but that introduces bias, too. When ranges are given, respondents tend to select an average amount based on the range given, and if the range is $200 to $500 then the amount selected will be lower than if the range is $400 to $600. An open-ended question to these types of situations often is the best alternative.

2. *Leading (or loaded)* in that the respondent is directed to a response that would not ordinarily be given if all possible response categories or concepts were provided, or if all the facts were provided for the situation, An example of this would be: "We care about the customer service you receive from our business. How would you rate the quality of service you received?" Another example would be asking a question by first saying, "Most Americans are against raising taxes. Are you in favor of raising taxes?"

3. *Double-barreled* in that they ask the respondent to address more than one issue at a time. An example would be: "Do you drink Pepsi with breakfast, lunch, and dinner?" or "Do you agree or disagree that Home Depot employees are friendly and helpful?"

When designing specific questions and scales, researchers should act as if they are two different people: one thinking like a technical, systematic researcher and the other like a respondent. The questions and scales must be presented in a logical order. After selecting a title for the questionnaire, the researcher includes a brief introductory section and any general instructions prior to asking the first question. Questions should be asked in a natural general-to-specific order to reduce the potential for sequence bias. Also, any sensitive or more difficult questions should be placed later in the questionnaire after the respondent becomes engaged in the process of answering questions.

Skip questions Used if the next question (or set of questions) should be responded to only by respondents who meet a previous condition.

Some questionnaires have skip or branching questions. **Skip questions** can appear anywhere within the questionnaire and are used if the next question (or set of questions) should be responded to only by respondents who meet a previous condition. A simple expression of a skip command might be: "If you answered 'yes' to question 5, skip to question 9." Skip questions help ensure that only specifically qualified respondents answer certain items. When skip questions are used, the instructions must be clearly communicated to respondents or interviewers. If the survey is online, then skip questions are easy to use and handled automatically.

Respondents should be made aware of the time it will take to complete the questionnaire and of their progress in completing it. This begins in the introductory section when the respondent is told how long it will take to complete the questionnaire, but it continues throughout the questionnaire. For online surveys this is easy and most surveys have an icon or some other indicator of the number of questions remaining or progress toward completion. Another approach is at the beginning of the demographic section to use a statement similar to the following: "The survey is almost completed. There are only a few more questions." This is a "transition phrase" that serves two purposes. First, it communicates to the respondents that a change in their thinking process is about to take place. They can clear their minds before thinking about their personal data. Second, it indicates that the task of completing the survey is almost over. The questionnaire used in the banking survey is shown in Exhibit 8.3.

Prior to developing the layout for the survey questionnaire, the researcher should assess the reliability and validity of the scales, such as the statements in Section II: General Opinions shown in Exhibit 8.3. To ensure high quality data, including reliable and valid measures, researchers need to use both qualitative and quantitative procedures to assess validity. In the development stage of understanding what particular aspects make up a construct, such as "brand image", a researcher can use a number of qualitative data collection procedures. For example, a small group of industry brand experts might be asked to review the researcher's list of topics and constructs using a non-structured expert interview procedure, or focus group interviews could be used to obtain the opinions of representative customers about the questions, topics and scaling. The main objective of using qualitative procedures at this point is to establish that the constructs have face validity. Once the

MARKETING RESEARCH DASHBOARD   "FRAMING" YOUR QUESTIONS CAN INTRODUCE BIAS!

On a Saturday morning one spring day, one of the authors was out working in the yard. A group of young folks got out of a van and began knocking on doors to solicit participation in a survey on exercise-related topics. They were students from a local college doing a class project for a local health club. The students were pleasant and polite in soliciting participation, and upon agreement from participants they began asking the questions on the survey. About halfway through the survey, one of the interviewers asked the following:

"When people were asked this question in the past, 90 percent said 'Yes.' Do you think belonging to a health club motivates people to exercise? Yes or no?"

The author refused to answer the question and proceeded to inform the student interviewers that the question had not asked if he believed belonging to a health club motivates people to exercise. In essence they had asked: "How willing are you to give a response that differs from 90 percent of others who have responded to this question in the past?" The students were shocked, but courteous. The author then informed them if they would like to learn how to design valid questionnaires, they should take his research methods course at the local state university.

Exhibit 8.3 Consumer Banking Opinion Survey

Thank you for participating in this study. Your participation will help us determine what people think about the products and services offered by banks. The results will provide insights on how to better serve the banking customers. Your attitudes and opinions are important to this study. All of your answers will be kept strictly confidential.

DIRECTIONS: PLEASE READ EACH QUESTION CAREFULLY. ANSWER THE QUESTION BY FILLING IN THE APPROPRIATE BOX(ES) THAT REPRESENT YOUR RESPONSES.

SECTION I: GENERAL BANKING HABITS

1. Which one of the following banks is the one you use most often in conducting banking or financial transactions? Please check only one box.
   - ❑ American Bank
   - ❑ Capital Bank
   - ❑ Hibernia National Bank
   - ❑ Baton Rouge Bank
   - ❑ City National Bank
   - ❑ Louisiana National Bank
   - ❑ Some other bank; please specify: _____

2. How important were each of the following factors to you in selecting the bank mentioned in Q.1 above?

   Please check only one response for each factor.

Factor	Extremely Important	Important	Somewhat Important	Not at All Important
Convenient locations	❑	❑	❑	❑
Banking hours	❑	❑	❑	❑
Reasonable service charges	❑	❑	❑	❑
Interest rates on savings	❑	❑	❑	❑
Personally knew someone at the bank	❑	❑	❑	❑
Bank's reputation	❑	❑	❑	❑
Bank's promotional advertising	❑	❑	❑	❑
Interest rate on loans	❑	❑	❑	❑
Internet banking services	❑	❑	❑	❑

   If there was some other reason (factor) you considered important in selecting your bank mentioned in Q.1, please specify: _____

3. At which of the following financial institutions do you or some member of your immediate household have a personal savings account? Please check as many or as few as necessary.

Financial Institution	Both You and Some Other Member	Some Other Member	Yourself
A credit union	❑	❑	❑
American Bank	❑	❑	❑
Baton Rouge Bank	❑	❑	❑
City National Bank	❑	❑	❑
Hibernia National Bank	❑	❑	❑
Louisiana National Bank	❑	❑	❑
Another institution (Please specify): _____			

(continued)

Exhibit 8.3 Consumer Banking Opinion Survey, *continued*

4. We would like to know your feelings about each of the following banking methods. For each banking method listed, please check the response that best describes your preference for using that method. Please check only one response for each banking method.

Banking Methods	Definitely Like Using	Somewhat Like Using	Somewhat Dislike Using	Definitely Dislike Using
Inside the bank	❏	❏	❏	❏
Drive-in (Drive-up)	❏	❏	❏	❏
24-hour machine	❏	❏	❏	❏
Bank by phone	❏	❏	❏	❏
Bank by mail	❏	❏	❏	❏
Online banking	❏	❏	❏	❏

5. Now we would like to know to what extent you actually use each of the following banking methods. Please check only one response for each banking method.

Banking Methods	Usually	Occasionally	Rarely	Never
Inside the bank	❏	❏	❏	❏
Drive-in (Drive-up)	❏	❏	❏	❏
24-hour machine	❏	❏	❏	❏
Bank by phone	❏	❏	❏	❏
Bank by mail	❏	❏	❏	❏
Online banking	❏	❏	❏	❏

SECTION II: GENERAL OPINIONS

A list of general statements is included in this section. There are no right or wrong answers to the statements. We are just interested in your opinions.

6. Next to each statement, please fill in the one response that best expresses the extent to which you agree or disagree with the statement. Remember, there are no right or wrong answers—we just want your opinions.

Statements	Definitely Agree	Somewhat Agree	Neither Agree or Disagree	Somewhat Disagree	Definitely Disagree
I often seek out the advice of my friends regarding a lot of different things.	❏	❏	❏	❏	❏
I buy many things with credit cards.	❏	❏	❏	❏	❏
I wish we had a lot more money.	❏	❏	❏	❏	❏
Security is most important to me.	❏	❏	❏	❏	❏
I am definitely influenced by advertising.	❏	❏	❏	❏	❏
I like to pay cash for everything I buy.	❏	❏	❏	❏	❏

Exhibit 8.3   *continued*

Statements	Definitely Agree	Somewhat Agree	Neither Agree or Disagree	Somewhat Disagree	Definitely Disagree
My neighbors or friends often come to me for advice on many different matters.	❑	❑	❑	❑	❑
It is good to have charge accounts.	❑	❑	❑	❑	❑
I will probably have more money to spend next year than I have now.	❑	❑	❑	❑	❑
A person can save a lot of money by shopping around for bargains.	❑	❑	❑	❑	❑
For most products or services, I try the ones that are most popular.	❑	❑	❑	❑	❑
Unexpected situations often catch me without enough money in my pocket.	❑	❑	❑	❑	❑
Five years from now, my income will probably be much higher than it is now.	❑	❑	❑	❑	❑

SECTION III: BANKING RELATIONSHIPS

Please indicate your view on each of the following questions. Check the box that most closely represents your feelings.

	Not Very Satisfied				Highly Satisfied
7. How satisfied are you with the bank you do most of your business with? (i.e., your primary banking relationship)	❑	❑	❑	❑	❑

	Not Very Likely				Highly Likely
8. How likely are you to continue doing business with your current primary bank?	❑	❑	❑	❑	❑
9. How likely are you to recommend your primary bank to a friend?	❑	❑	❑	❑	❑

SECTION IV: CLASSIFICATION DATA

The next few questions ask for your demographic information. We ask these questions so we can properly generalize survey results to the greater population. Your answers help us to ensure that we have sufficient diversity among our respondents.

10. What is your sex?   ❑ Female   ❑ Male

(continued)

Exhibit 8.3 Consumer Banking Opinion Survey, *continued*

11. Approximately how long have you lived at your current address?
   - ❑ Less than 1 year
   - ❑ 4–6 years
   - ❑ 11–20 years
   - ❑ 1–3 years
   - ❑ 7–10 years
   - ❑ Over 20 years

12. What is your current employment status?
   - ❑ Employed full-time
   - ❑ Employed part-time
   - ❑ Not currently employed
   - ❑ Retired

13. What is your current marital status?
   - ❑ Married
   - ❑ Single (never married)
   - ❑ Single (widowed, divorced, or separated)

14. **IF MARRIED,** please indicate your spouse's current employment status.
   - ❑ Employed full-time
   - ❑ Employed part-time
   - ❑ Not currently employed
   - ❑ Retired

15. **IF YOU HAVE CHILDREN,** please indicate the number of children under 18 years of age in your household.

   0 ❑ 1 ❑ 2 ❑ 3 ❑ 4 ❑ 5 ❑ 6 ❑ 7 ❑ 8 ❑   More than 8; please specify: _____

16. Which one of the following categories best represents your last completed year in school?
   - ❑ Postgraduate studies or advanced degree
   - ❑ Completed high school
   - ❑ Graduate studies or degree
   - ❑ Some high school
   - ❑ Completed college (4-year degree)
   - ❑ Completed grammar school
   - ❑ Some college or technical school
   - ❑ Some grammar school

17. What is your current age?
   - ❑ Under 18
   - ❑ 26–35
   - ❑ 46–55
   - ❑ 66–70
   - ❑ 18–25
   - ❑ 36–45
   - ❑ 56–65
   - ❑ Over 70

18. Which one of the following categories best describes the type of work you do?
   - ❑ Government (Federal, State, City)
   - ❑ Legal
   - ❑ Financial
   - ❑ Insurance
   - ❑ Petrochemical
   - ❑ Manufacturing
   - ❑ Transportation
   - ❑ Consulting
   - ❑ Educational
   - ❑ Medical
   - ❑ Retailing
   - ❑ Wholesaling
   - ❑ Some other area, please specify: _____

19. In which of the following categories does your total annual family income, before taxes, fall?
   - ❑ Under $10,000
   - ❑ $30,001–$50,000
   - ❑ $10,000–$15,000
   - ❑ $50,001–$75,000
   - ❑ $15,001–$20,000
   - ❑ $75,001–$100,000
   - ❑ $20,001–$30,000
   - ❑ Over $100,000

20. What is the five-digit zip code of your residence address? ❑ ❑ ❑ ❑ ❑

THANK YOU VERY MUCH FOR PARTICIPATION IN THIS STUDY!
YOUR TIME AND OPINIONS ARE APPRECIATED.

researcher develops the measures for the constructs, quantitative data collection procedures in the form of a pretest or pilot study are needed to quantitatively assess the construct's reliability and validity. Once this is completed, the focus is on preparing instructions and making required revisions. Methods for assessing reliability and validity were discussed in Chapter 7.

Step 4: Determine Layout and Evaluate Questionnaire

In good questionnaire design, questions flow from general to more specific information, and end with demographic data. Questionnaires begin with an **introductory section** that gives the respondent an overview of the research. The section begins with a statement to establish the legitimacy of the questionnaire. For example, the research company would be identified and the respondent would be assured their responses will be anonymous. Next, there typically are screening questions. **Screening questions** (also referred to as *screeners* or *filter questions*) are used on most questionnaires. Their purpose is to identify qualified prospective respondents and prevent unqualified respondents from being included in the study. It is difficult to use screening questions in many self-administered questionnaires, except for computer-assisted surveys. Screening questions are completed before the beginning of the main portion of the questionnaire that includes the research questions. The introductory section also includes general instructions for filling out the survey.

The second section of the questionnaire focuses on the research questions. This is called the **research questions section,** and based on the research objectives the sequence is arranged from general questions to more specific questions. If the study has multiple research objectives then questions designed to obtain information on each of the objectives also should be sequenced from general to specific. One exception to this would be when two sections of a questionnaire have related questions. In such a situation the researcher would typically separate the two sections (by inserting a nonrelated set of questions) to minimize the likelihood that answers to one set of questions might influence the answers given in a second set of questions. Finally, any difficult or sensitive questions should be placed toward the end of each section.

The last section includes demographic questions for the respondents. Demographic questions are placed at the end of a questionnaire because they often ask personal information and many people are reluctant to provide this information to strangers. Until the "comfort zone" is established between the interviewer and respondent, asking personal questions could easily bring the interviewing process to a halt. The questionnaire ends with a thank-you statement.

Questionnaires should be designed to eliminate or at least minimize response order bias. **Response order bias** occurs when the order of the questions, or of the closed-end responses to a particular question, influences the answer given. Answers that appear at the beginning or the end of a list tend to be selected most often. With numeric alternatives (prices or quantities) respondents tend to select central values. With online surveys this is not a problem because the order of presentation can be randomized. It also is less of a problem with mail surveys because the respondent can see all the possible responses. Another way to reduce order bias with mail or self-administered surveys is to prepare several different forms of the questionnaire using a different order and average the responses. Phone surveys often present the most opportunities for response order bias to emerge.

Some researchers have recently expressed concerns that questionnaire design might result in common methods variance (CMV) being embedded in respondent data collected from surveys. **Common methods variance** is biased variance that results from the measurement method used in a questionnaire instead of the scales used to obtain the data. CMV is present in survey responses when the answers given by respondents to the independent

Introductory section Gives the respondent an overview of the research.

Screening questions (also referred to as screeners or filter questions) Used in most questionnaires, their purpose is to identify qualified prospective respondents and prevent unqualified respondents from being included in the study.

Research questions section The second section of the questionnaire that focuses on the research questions.

Response order bias Occurs when the order of the questions, or of the closed-end responses to a particular question, influences the answer given.

Common methods variance (CMV) A biased variance that results from the measurement method used in a questionnaire.

and dependent variable questions are falsely correlated. The bias introduced by CMV is most likely to occur when the same respondent answers at the same time both independent and dependent variable questions that are perceptual in nature, and the respondent recognizes a relationship between the two types of variables. An example of a situation in which CMV might occur is when a respondent is asked to evaluate "How they liked the food" or "How they liked the restaurant atmosphere" (independent variables and perceptions questions) in the initial section of a restaurant questionnaire. Then, in a later section of the same questionnaire, the same respondent is asked "How satisfied were you with your dining experience at the Santa Fe Grill?" (dependent variable and a perceptions question).

Many researchers believe the prevalence of CMV in surveys is exaggerated. More recently, research investigating the extent to which CMV bias is caused by using only one type of scale measure in capturing a respondent's responses found no empirical evidence of problematic bias due to CMV. The research indicates that CMV resulting from these types of variables (e.g., attitudes, emotions, and behaviors) investigated in most marketing studies would not exist until over half of the variance in data is common across all variables. Thus, a sufficient level of CMV to cause concern exceeds even high estimates of how much CMV may exist across studies.[1]

If a researcher is concerned about the possible presence of CMV, one approach to reduce the likelihood of CMV being present in data is to collect independent and dependent variable data at different points in time, or from different sources (e.g., investigate the relationship between the workplace environment and performance by obtaining perceptions of the work environment from employees and performance evaluations from supervisors). Unfortunately, this is often not possible in marketing studies. Other approaches to reduce the possible presence of CMV include using more than one type of scale in the questionnaire (e.g., use both semantic differential and graphic-ratings formats) or using scales with a different number of scale points. For example, a questionnaire could be designed so that 10-point scales are used to answer the independent variable questions and 100-point scales are used to answer the dependent variable questions.

An easy to use test for determining the influence of CMV bias is the so-called Harmon One Factor test.[2] This procedure applies exploratory factor analysis as a diagnostic tool for

MARKETING RESEARCH DASHBOARD   SMART QUESTIONNAIRES ARE REVOLUTIONIZING SURVEYS

"Smart" questionnaires are the state-of-the-art in marketing research surveys. The questionnaires are structured using mathematical logic that enables the computer to customize them for each respondent as the interview progresses. Through the use of interactive software, the computer constantly evaluates new information and personalizes survey questions. Based on responses, more specific questions are posed to probe and clarify an individual respondent's reasons behind his or her initial responses. Thus, with smart questionnaire surveys, different respondents taking the same questionnaire answer different sets of questions, each custom-designed to provide the most relevant data.

For global corporations with diverse product lines, computerized questionnaires can provide information related to each product line. Before computerized questionnaires, corporations had to rely on survey data that used scripted questions that often did not provide relevant data. With smart questionnaires, however, the information obtained is relevant to the specific needs of the organization.

Important advantages of smart questionnaires over traditional structured surveys include increased ease of participation, decreased time requirements, and fewer resources needed to conduct surveys, thereby reducing the overall cost of survey administration. For many companies, smart questionnaires increasingly are the logical choice for data collection.

investigating CMV effects. If the first factor from the analysis accounts for less than 40% of all variance, there would be no concern about CMV bias, and a factor that accounts for as much as 50% is not likely to indicate a CMV problem.

Questionnaire formatting and layout should make it easy for respondents to read and follow instructions. If the researcher fails to consider questionnaire layout, the quality of the data can be substantially reduced. The value of a well-constructed questionnaire is difficult to estimate. The main function of a questionnaire is to obtain people's true thoughts and feelings about issues or objects. Data collected using questionnaires should improve understanding of the problem or opportunity that motivated the research. In contrast, bad questionnaires can be costly in terms of time, effort, and money without yielding good results.

After preparing the questionnaire but before submitting it to the client for approval, the researcher should review the document carefully. The focus is on determining whether each question is necessary and if the overall length is acceptable. Also, the researcher checks to make sure that the survey meets the research objectives, that the scale format and instructions work well, and that the questions move from general to specific. If the survey is online, it should be viewed on the screen as the respondent will see it. If the survey is mail or drop-off, it should be physically inspected. All forms of self-administered questionnaires should look professional and be visually appealing. A summary of the major considerations in questionnaire design is given in Exhibit 8.4.

Online Survey Considerations The design of online surveys requires additional planning. A primary metric for traditional data collection methods is response rate. To determine response rates, the researcher must know the number of attempts to contact respondents and complete a questionnaire. With mail or phone surveys, this task is relatively easy. With online surveys, researchers must work with the online data collection field service to plan how respondents will be solicited. If the data collection service sends out a "blanket" invitation to complete a survey, there is no way to measure response rates. Even if the invitation to complete a survey is sent to an organized panel of respondents,

---

Exhibit 8.4   **Considerations in Questionnaire Design**

1. Confirm the research objectives before starting to design the questionnaire.
2. Determine data requirements to complete each research objective.
3. The introduction section should include a general description of the study.
4. Instructions should be clearly expressed.
5. Questions and scale measurements should follow a logical order, that is, one that appears logical to the respondent rather than to the researcher or practitioner.
6. Begin an interview or questionnaire with simple questions that are easy to answer, and then gradually lead up to the more difficult questions. Use a general-to-specific questions and topic sequence.
7. Ask personal questions at the end of the interview or survey.
8. Place questions that involve personal opinions, attitudes, and beliefs toward the end of the interview or survey, but before demographics.
9. Avoid asking questions using a different measurement format in the same section of the questionnaire.
10. End the interview or survey with a thank-you statement.

calculating response rates can be a problem. This is because panels may involve millions of individuals with broad criteria describing them. As a result, a survey targeted to males between the ages of 18 and 35 may be sent to a group with much broader demographic characteristics. Another issue is recruiting of participants. If individuals are invited to participate and they decline, should they be included in the response rate metric? Or should the response rate metric be based on just those individuals who say they qualify and agree to respond, whether or not they actually respond? To overcome these problems, researchers must work closely with data collection vendors to identify, target, and request participation from specific groups so accurate response rates can be calculated. Moreover, a clear understanding of how individuals are recruited for online surveys is necessary before data collection begins.

A related problem in calculating the response rate metric online is the possibility of recruitment of participants outside the official online data collection vendor. For example, it is not uncommon for an individual included in the official invitation to participate to recruit online friends and suggest that they participate. Recruited friends then go to the data collection website and respond because they are interested in the survey topic. Effective control mechanisms, such as a unique identifier that must be entered before taking the survey, must be put in place ahead of time to prevent this type of unsolicited response.

Another problem with online surveys is the length of time it takes some respondents to complete the survey. It is not uncommon for some respondents to zip through in less than five minutes a survey that should take 15 minutes to complete. On the other hand, it also is not uncommon for individuals to take an hour or two to complete the same 15-minute survey. To deal with this issue with online data collection vendors, first make sure "time for completion" is a metric that is measured. If you do not collect this information, there is no way to deal with this problem. When data collection is complete and you are reviewing this metric, we suggest researchers follow the approach often used to deal with outliers in calculating the mean. That is, apply the "trimmed mean" approach in which the 5 percent tails on either end (very short and very long response times) are removed from the sample. This will remove the extreme outlying observations and reduce the likelihood of biased responses being included in the data analysis.

Research firms are just beginning to analyze online questionnaire design issues. Three specific issues that have been addressed to date are (1) the effect of response box size on length of answer in open-ended questions, (2) use of radio buttons versus pull-down menus for responses, and (3) appropriate use of visuals. With regard to response box size, respondents will write more when boxes are bigger. Some research firms cope with this by offering respondents the choice between small, medium, and large boxes so that the box size does not affect their response. In regard to the second issue, use of pull-down menus, if a response is immediately visible at the top of the pull-down menu, it will be selected more often than if it is simply one of the responses on the list. Thus, if a pull-down menu is used, the top option should be "select one." Generally, radio buttons should be used as much as possible. Third, the use of visuals can affect respondents. For example, two versions of a question about attending a baseball game featured either a full baseball stadium or a small stadium with little attendance. Respondents were more likely to say they attended more sporting events in the previous year when the question was accompanied by a visual of a full baseball stadium as compared to a small, sparsely attended stadium.[3]

Online formats facilitate the use of improved rating and ranking scales, as well as extensive graphics and animation. For example, Qualtrics enables researchers to obtain responses using their slider scale—a graphic ratings scale that improves response accuracy. For example, the slider scale is a true metric measure of responses and facilitates the use of

10-point and 100-point scales. Programming surveys in the online environment offers the opportunity to use graphics and scales in new ways, some of which are helpful and some of which are not. As with traditional data collection methods and questionnaire design, the best guideline is the KISS test—Keep It Simple and Short! Complex formats or designs can produce biased findings and should be avoided.

Step 5: Obtain Initial Client Approval

Copies of the questionnaire should be given to all parties involved in the project. This is the client's opportunity to provide suggestions of topics overlooked or to ask any questions. Researchers must obtain final approval of the questionnaire prior to pretesting. If changes are necessary, this is where they should occur. Changes at a later point will be more expensive and may not be possible.

Step 6: Pretest, Revise, and Finalize the Questionnaire

The final version of the questionnaire is evaluated using a pretest. In the **pretest,** the survey questionnaire is given to a small, representative group of respondents that are asked to fill out the survey and provide feedback to researchers. The number of respondents is most often between 10 and 20 individuals. In a pretest, respondents are asked to pay attention to words, phrases, instructions, and question sequence. They are asked to point out anything that is difficult to follow or understand. Returned questionnaires are checked for signs of boredom or tiring on the part of the respondent. These signs include skipped questions or circling the same answer for all questions within a group. The pretest helps the researcher determine how much time respondents will need to complete the survey, whether to add or revise instructions, and what to say in the cover letter.

Complex questionnaires involving scale development or revision often execute a pilot study. The terms "pilot study" and "pretest" are sometimes used interchangeably but actually are different. A **pilot study** is a small-scale version of the intended main research study, including the data collection and analysis and typically involving 100 to 200 respondents that are similar to the study's defined target population. In some situations, a pilot study is conducted to examine specific subcomponents of the overall research plan, such as the experimental design manipulations, to see if the proposed procedures work as expected or if refinements are needed. For example, a pilot study with 100 representative respondents could be used to collect data to assess the reliability and validity of scaled questions. While pilot studies can be included in any form of research (i.e., exploratory, descriptive, or causal research designs), they are most often associated with quantitative descriptive or predictive research studies. If problems or concerns arise in the pretest or pilot study, modifications must be made and approved by the client prior to moving to the next step.

Step 7: Implement the Survey

The focus here is on the process followed to collect the data using the agreed-upon questionnaire. The process varies depending on whether the survey is self-administered or interviewer-completed. For example, self-completed questionnaires must be distributed to respondents and methods used to increase response rates. Similarly, with Internet surveys, the format, sequence, skip patterns, and instructions after the questionnaire is uploaded to the web must be thoroughly checked. Thus, implementation involves following up to ensure all previous decisions are properly implemented.

■■ The Role of a Cover Letter

Cover letter A separate written communication to a prospective respondent designed to enhance that person's willingness to complete and return the survey in a timely manner.

A **cover letter** is used with a self-administered questionnaire. The primary role of the cover letter is to obtain the respondent's cooperation and willingness to participate in the research project. With personal or telephone interviews, interviewers use a verbal statement that includes many of the points covered by a mailed or drop-off cover letter. Similarly, for online surveys, there is a written introduction designed to motivate respondents to participate and to explain the nature of the survey. Self-administered surveys often have low response rates (25 percent or less). Good cover letters increase response rates. Exhibit 8.5 provides guidelines for developing cover letters. While the exact wording of a cover letter will vary from researcher to researcher and from situation to situation, a good cover letter should incorporate as many of these guidelines as possible. To illustrate how a researcher might incorporate these guidelines, see the MARKETING RESEARCH DASHBOARD: Cover Letter used with the American Bank Survey shown in Exhibit 8.3. The bold number inserts in the cover letter refer to the guidelines listed in Exhibit 8.5.

Exhibit 8.5	**Guidelines for Developing Cover Letters**
Factors	**Description**
1. Personalization	Cover letters should be addressed to the prospective respondent. The research firm's professional letterhead stationery should be used.
2. Identification of the organization	Clear identification of the name of the research firm conducting the survey or interview. A disguised approach is most often used but an undisguised approach that reveals the actual client (or sponsor) of the study may be used.
3. Clear statement of the study's purpose and importance	Describe the general topic of the research and emphasize its importance to the prospective respondent.
4. Anonymity and confidentiality	Give assurances that the prospective respondent's name will not be revealed. Explain how the respondent was chosen, and stress that his or her input is important to the study's success.
5. General time frame of doing the study	Communicate the overall time frame of the survey or study.
6. Reinforce the importance of respondent's participation	Communicate the importance of the prospective respondent's participation.
7. Acknowledge reasons for nonparticipation in survey or interview	Point out "lack of leisure time," "surveys classified as junk mail," and "forgetting about survey" reasons for not participating, and defuse them.
8. Time requirements and incentive	Communicate the approximate time required to complete the survey. Discuss incentive, if any.
9. Completion date and where and how to return the survey	Communicate to the prospective respondent all instructions for returning the completed questionnaire.
10. Advance thank-you statement for willingness to participate	Thank the prospective respondent for his or her cooperation.

MARKETING RESEARCH DASHBOARD   COVER LETTER USED WITH THE
AMERICAN BANK SURVEY

MARKETING **R**ESOURCES **G**ROUP
2305 Windsor Oaks Drive, Suite 1105
Baton Rouge, Louisiana 70814

March 10, 2018

Ms. Caroline V. Livingstone **[1]**
873 Patterson Drive
Baton Rouge LA 70801

Dear Ms. Livingstone:

[2] The Marketing Resources Group in Baton Rouge is conducting an interesting study on people's banking habits and services **[5]** this month and would like to include your opinions.

[3] Consumer-banking practices are rapidly changing. With many new electronic bank services, online technologies, the growth of credit unions and savings and loans, and the increased complexity of people's financial needs and wants, financial institutions are indeed changing. These changes are having important effects on you and your family. We would like to gain insights into these changes and their impact from the consumer's perspective by better understanding your opinions about different banking services, habits, and patterns.

[4] Your name was one of only 600 names randomly selected from a representative list of people currently living in Baton Rouge. **[6]** Because the success of the survey depends upon the cooperation of all the selected people, we would especially appreciate your willingness to help us in this study.

[4] The information obtained from the survey will in no way reflect the identities of the people participating. Your cooperation, attitudes, and opinions are very important to the success of the study and will be kept strictly confidential, and only used when grouped with those of the other people taking part in the study.

[7] We realize that people in the community receive many things through the mail that we classify as "junk mail" and often are not important to respond to, but please do not consider the attached survey as being "junk mail." **[6]** Your opinions, attitudes, and viewpoints toward each question are very important to us.

[7] To most of us in the community, our leisure time is scarce and important, and we do not like to spend it filling out a questionnaire for some unknown organization's survey. Please remember that you are among a few people asked to participate in this study and **[6]** your opinions are very important to the success of the study. **[8]** We have designed the questionnaire to include all the directions and instructions necessary to complete the survey without the assistance of an interviewer. The survey will take only about 15 minutes of your time. Please take your time in responding to each question. **[6]** Your honest responses are what we are looking for in the study.

[8] To show our appreciation for your taking the time to participate in this important study, you will be entered into a drawing to receive one of ten Apple iPads for those who donate some of your leisure time to complete this survey. The drawing procedure is designed so that everyone who completes and returns the questionnaire will have an equal opportunity to receive one of the iPads.

[7] Past research suggests that many questionnaires received through the mail, if not completed and returned within the first 36 hours, are misplaced or forgotten about. Upon receiving this survey, please take the time to complete it. **[6]** Your opinions are very important to us.

[9] Please use the enclosed stamped and addressed envelope to return your completed survey and enter you into the drawing for a new iPad. To help us complete the study in a timely fashion, we need your cooperation in returning the survey by **no later than Friday, March 24, 2018.**

Again, we are not trying to sell you something. If you have any doubts, concerns, or questions about this survey, please give me a call at (504) 974-6236.

[10] Thank you in advance. We deeply appreciate your cooperation in taking part in our study.

Sincerely,

Thomas L. Kirk
MRG Project Director

■■ Other Considerations in Collecting Data

When data are collected, supervisor and interviewer instructions often must be developed as well as screening questions and call records. These mechanisms ensure the data collection process is successful. Some of these are needed for interviews and others for self-administered questionnaires. In this section, we summarize each of these mechanisms.

Supervisor Instructions

Supervisor instruction form A form that serves as a blueprint for training people on how to execute the interviewing process in a standardized fashion; it outlines the process by which to conduct a study that uses personal and telephone interviewers.

Many researchers collect data using interviews conducted by field interviewing companies. A **supervisor instruction form** serves as a blueprint for training people to complete the interviewing process in a consistent fashion. The instructions outline the process for conducting the study and are important to any research project that uses personal or telephone interviews. They include detailed information on the nature of the study, start and completion dates, sampling instructions, number of interviewers required, equipment and facility requirements, reporting forms, quotas, and validation procedures. Exhibit 8.6 displays a sample page from a set of supervisor instructions for a restaurant study.

Exhibit 8.6	Supervisor Instructions for a Restaurant Study Using Personal Interviews
Purpose	To determine students' dining-out patterns and attitudes toward selected restaurants located within 1 mile of campus.
Number of interviewers	A total of 90 trained student interviewers (30 interviewers per class, three different classes).
Location of Interviews	Interviews will be conducted over a two-week period beginning March 10 and ending March 24, 2013. They will be conducted between the hours of 8:00 a.m and 9:00 p.m., Monday through Friday. The locations of the interviews will be outside the campus buildings housing the four colleges one making up the university plus the library and student union. There will be three shifts of interviewers, 30 interviewers per shift, working the time frames of 8:00 a.m. to 12:00 noon or 12:01 p.m. to 5:00 p.m. or 5:01 p.m. to 9:00 p.m.
Quota	Each interviewer will conduct and complete 30 interviews, with a maximum of five completed interviews for each of the following named restaurants: Mellow Mushroom, Pizza Hut, Domino's Pizza, Chili's, Outback Steakhouse, and any five "local restaurants." All completed interviews should come from their assigned location and time period.
	For each shift of 30 interviewers, there will be a minimum of 150 completed interviews for each of the five named restaurants in the study and maximum of 150 completed interviews representing the set of "local restaurants."
Project materials	For this study, you are supplied with the following materials: 2,701 personal questionnaires, 91 interviewer instruction-screening-quota forms, 91 sets of "rating cards," with each set consisting of six different rating cards, 91 "verification of interview" forms, and 1 interviewer scheduling form.
Preparation	Using your set of materials, review all material for complete understanding. Set a two-hour time frame for training your 90 student interviewers on how they should select a prospective respondent, screen for eligibility, and conduct the interviews. Make sure each interviewer understands the embedded "interviewer's instructions" in the actual questions making up the survey. In addition, assign each interviewer to a specified location and time frame for conducting the interviews. Make sure all locations and time frames are properly covered. Prepare a backup plan for anticipated problems.

Interviewer Instructions

Interviewer instructions
Used to train interviewers
how to select prospective
respondents, screen them
for eligibility, and conduct
the actual interview.

Interviewer instructions are used for training interviewers to correctly select a prospective respondent for inclusion in the study, screen prospective respondents for eligibility, and to properly conduct the actual interview. The instructions include detailed information about the nature of the study, start and completion dates, sampling instructions, screening procedures, quotas, number of interviews required, guidelines for asking questions, use of rating cards, recording responses, reporting forms, and verification form procedures.

Screening Questions

Screening questions ensure the respondents included in a study are representative of the defined target population. Screening questions are used to confirm the eligibility of a prospective respondent for inclusion in the survey and to ensure that certain types of respondents are not included in the study. This occurs most frequently when a person's direct occupation or a family member's occupation in a particular industry eliminates the person from inclusion in the study. For example, a study of the perceived quality of automobiles manufactured by Ford Motor Company would exclude people who work for Ford Motor Company or an automobile dealership that sells Ford vehicles. Individuals who work for marketing research firms or advertising agencies also are routinely excluded from participation in studies.

Quotas

Quotas A tracking system
that collects data from
respondents and helps
ensure that subgroups are
represented in the sample
as specified.

Quotas are used to ensure that data are collected from the correct respondents. When a particular quota for a subgroup of respondents is filled, questionnaires for that subgroup are no longer completed. If interviewers are used, they record quota information and tabulate it to know when interviews for targeted groups have been completed. If the survey is online, then the computer keeps track of questionnaires completed to ensure quotas for targeted groups are met. In the retail banking example, each interviewer completed 30 interviews, with five each from customers of six different banks: Bank of America, SunTrust Bank, Citicorp, Chase, First Union, and "Other Banks." Once the quota was reached for a particular bank, such as Chase, any prospective respondent who indicated that Chase was his or her primary bank would be excluded from participating in the survey.

Call or Contact Records

Call records A recording
document that gathers
basic summary informa-
tion about an interviewer's
performance efficiency
(e.g., number of contact
attempts, number of com-
pleted interviews, length of
time of interview).

Call records, also referred to as either reporting or tracking approaches, are used to estimate the efficiency of interviewing. These records typically collect information on the number of attempts to contact potential respondents made by each interviewer and the results of those attempts. Call and contact records are often used in data collection methods that require the use of an interviewer, but also can be used with online surveys. Information gathered from contact records includes number of calls or contacts made per hour, number of contacts per completed interview, length of time of the interview, completions by quota categories, number of terminated interviews, reasons for termination, and number of contact attempts.

Your understanding of the activities needed to develop a survey instrument completes the third phase of the research process, gathering and collecting accurate data, and prepares you to move into the last phase: data preparation and analysis. Chapter 9 covers coding, editing, and preparing data for analysis.

MARKETING RESEARCH IN ACTION
Designing a Questionnaire to Survey Santa Fe Grill Customers

This illustration extends the chapter discussion on questionnaire design. Read through this example and, using the actual Screening Questions (Exhibit 8.7) and Questionnaire (Exhibit 8.8), answer the questions at the end.

In early 2013, two recent college business graduates (one majored in Finance and the other in Management) came together with a new restaurant concept for a southwestern casual dining experience that focused on a Mexican theme with a variety of fresh food items and a friendly family-oriented atmosphere. After several months of planning and creating detailed business and marketing plans, the two entrepreneurs were able to get the necessary capital to build and open their restaurant, calling it the Santa Fe Grill Mexican Restaurant.

After the initial six months of success, they noticed that revenues, traffic flow, and sales were declining and realized that they knew only the basics about their customers. Neither of the owners had taken any marketing courses beyond basic marketing in college, so they turned to a friend who advised them to hire a marketing research firm to collect some primary data about people's dining-out habits and patterns. A marketing research firm was located in their mall so they contracted with them to design a self-administered survey to collect the needed data. The following six research objectives were used to guide the design of their survey instrument shown in Exhibit 8.8.

1. To identify the factors people consider important in making casual dining restaurant choice decisions.
2. To determine the characteristics customers use to describe the Santa Fe Grill and its competitor, Jose's Southwestern Café.
3. To develop a psychographic/demographic profile of the restaurant customers.
4. To determine the patronage and positive word-of-mouth advertising patterns of the restaurant customers.
5. To assess the customer's willingness to return to the restaurant in the future.
6. To assess the degree to which customers are satisfied with their Mexican restaurant experiences.

Exhibit 8.7 Screening and Rapport Questions for the Mexican Restaurant Study

Hello. My name is _____ and I work for DSS Research. We are talking with individuals today (tonight) about dining-out habits.

1. "Do you regularly eat out at casual dining restaurants?" __ Yes __ No
2. "Have you eaten at more than one Mexican restaurant in the last six months?" __ Yes __ No
3. "Is your gross annual household income $20,000 or more?" __ Yes __ No
4. At which of the following Mexican restaurants have you eaten most recently?
   a. First response is Santa Fe Grill—Yes, continue.
   b. First response is Jose's Southwestern Café—Yes, continue.
   c. First response is Other Restaurant—thank them and terminate interview.

If respondent answers "yes" to first three questions, and also indicates either the Santa Fe Grill or Jose's Southwestern Café, then say:

We would like you to answer a few questions about yourself and your experiences eating at the __???__ restaurant. The questions will take only a few minutes and it will be very helpful in better serving our customers.

Exhibit 8.8 The Mexican Restaurant Dining-Out Survey

Please read all questions carefully. If you do not understand a question, ask the interviewer to help you. In the first section, a number of statements are given about interests and opinions. Using a scale from 1 to 7, with 7 being "Strongly Agree" and 1 being "Strongly Disagree," please indicate the extent to which you agree or disagree a particular statement describes you. Circle only one number for each statement.

Section 1: Lifestyle Questions

1. I often try new and different things. Strongly Disagree ... Strongly Agree   1 2 3 4 5 6 7
2. I like parties with music and lots of talk. Strongly Disagree ... Strongly Agree   1 2 3 4 5 6 7
3. People come to me more often than I go to them for information about products. Strongly Disagree ... Strongly Agree   1 2 3 4 5 6 7
4. I try to avoid fried foods. Strongly Disagree ... Strongly Agree   1 2 3 4 5 6 7
5. I like to go out and socialize with people. Strongly Disagree ... Strongly Agree   1 2 3 4 5 6 7
6. Friends and neighbors often come to me for advice about products and brands. Strongly Disagree ... Strongly Agree   1 2 3 4 5 6 7

(continued)

Exhibit 8.8   The Mexican Restaurant Dining-Out Survey, *continued*

7. I am self-confident about myself and my future.

Strongly Disagree   Strongly Agree

1   2   3   4   5   6   7

8. I usually eat balanced, nutritious meals.

Strongly Disagree   Strongly Agree

1   2   3   4   5   6   7

9. When I see a new product in stores, I often buy it.

Strongly Disagree   Strongly Agree

1   2   3   4   5   6   7

10. I am careful about what I eat.

Strongly Disagree   Strongly Agree

1   2   3   4   5   6   7

11. I often try new brands before my friends and neighbors do.

Strongly Disagree   Strongly Agree

1   2   3   4   5   6   7

Section 2: Perceptions Measures

Listed below is a set of characteristics that could be used to describe the Mexican restaurant at which you ate most recently. Using a scale from 1 to 7, with 7 being "Strongly Agree" and 1 being "Strongly Disagree," to what extent do you agree or disagree the _____ restaurant:

12. has friendly employees.

Strongly Disagree   Strongly Agree

1   2   3   4   5   6   7

13. is a fun place to eat.

Strongly Disagree   Strongly Agree

1   2   3   4   5   6   7

14. has large size portions.

Strongly Disagree   Strongly Agree

1   2   3   4   5   6   7

15. has fresh food.

Strongly Disagree   Strongly Agree

1   2   3   4   5   6   7

16. has reasonable prices.

Strongly Disagree   Strongly Agree

1   2   3   4   5   6   7

17. has an attractive interior.

Strongly Disagree   Strongly Agree

1   2   3   4   5   6   7

Exhibit 8.8 *continued*

18. has excellent food taste.

Strongly Disagree   Strongly Agree

1   2   3   4   5   6   7

19. has knowledgeable employees.

Strongly Disagree   Strongly Agree

1   2   3   4   5   6   7

20. serves food at the proper temperature.

Strongly Disagree   Strongly Agree

1   2   3   4   5   6   7

21. has quick service.

Strongly Disagree   Strongly Agree

1   2   3   4   5   6   7

Section 3: Relationship Measures

Please indicate your view on each of the following questions:

22. How satisfied are you with _____?

Not Satisfied At All   Very Satisfied

1   2   3   4   5   6   7

23. How likely are you to return to _____ in the future?

Definitely Will Not Return   Definitely Will Return

1   2   3   4   5   6   7

24. How likely are you to recommend _____ to a friend?

Definitely Will Not Recommend   Definitely Will Recommend

1   2   3   4   5   6   7

25. How often do you eat at _____?

1 = Very Infrequently
2 = Somewhat Infrequently
3 = Occasionally
4 = Somewhat Frequently
5 = Very Frequently

Section 4: Selection Factors

Listed below are some reasons many people use in selecting a restaurant where they want to dine. Think about your visits to casual dining restaurants in the last three months and please rank each attribute from 1 to 4, with 1 being the most important reason for selecting the restaurant and 4 being the least important reason. There can be no ties so make sure you rank each attribute with a different number.

Attribute	Ranking
26. Prices	
27. Food Quality	
28. Atmosphere	
29. Service	

(continued)

Exhibit 8.8   The Mexican Restaurant Dining-Out Survey, *continued*

Section 5: Classification Questions

Please circle the number that classifies you best.

30. How far did you drive to get to the restaurant?

1	Less than 1 mile
2	1–5 miles
3	More than 5 miles

31. Do your recall seeing any advertisements in the last 60 days for _____?

0	No
1	Yes

32. What is your gender?

0	Male
1	Female

33. How many children under the age of 18 are living in your home?

1	None
2	1–2
3	More than 2 children at home

34. What is your age in years?

1	18–25
2	26–34
3	35–49
4	50–59
5	60 and older

35. What is your annual total household income?   Please specify _____

Thank you very much for your help. Please give your questionnaire back to the interviewer.

Interviewer: Check answers to questions 22, 23, and 24. If respondent answers 1, 2, or 3, ask the following questions:

You indicated you are not too satisfied with the Santa Fe Grill. Could you please tell me why?

Record answer here: _____

_____

You indicated you are not likely to return to the Santa Fe Grill. Could you please tell me why?

Record answer here: _____

_____

You indicated you are not likely to recommend the Santa Fe Grill. Could you please tell me why?

Record answer here: _____

_____

Could I please have your name and phone number for verification purposes?

_____   _____

Name   Phone #

I hereby attest that this is a true and honest interview and complete to the best of my knowledge. I guarantee that all information relating to this interview shall be kept strictly confidential.

_____   _____

Interviewer's Signature   Date and Time completed

Hands-On Exercise

1. Based on the research objectives, does the self-administered questionnaire, in its current form, correctly illustrate sound questionnaire design principles? Please explain why or why not.
2. Overall, is the current survey design able to capture the required data needed to address all the stated research objectives? Why or why not? If changes are needed, how would you change the survey's design?
3. Evaluate the "screener" used to qualify the respondents. Are there any changes needed? Why or why not?
4. Redesign questions #26 to 29 on the survey using a rating scale that will enable you to obtain the "degree of importance" a customer might attach to each of the four listed attributes in selecting a restaurant to dine at.

Summary

Describe the steps in questionnaire design.

Researchers follow a systematic approach to designing questionnaires. The steps include: confirm research objectives, select appropriate data collection method, develop questions and scaling, determine layout and evaluate questionnaire, obtain initial client approval, pretest, revise and finalize questionnaire, and implement the survey.

Discuss the questionnaire development process.

A number of design considerations and rules of logic apply to the questionnaire development process. The process requires knowledge of sampling plans, construct development, scale measurement, and types of data. A questionnaire is a set of questions/scales designed to collect data and generate information to help decision makers solve business problems. Good questionnaires enable researchers to gain a true report of the respondent's attitudes, preferences, beliefs, feelings, behavioral intentions, and actions. Through carefully worded questions and clear instructions, a researcher has the ability to focus a respondent's thoughts and ensure answers that faithfully represent respondents' attitudes, beliefs, intentions, and knowledge. By understanding good communication principles, researchers can avoid bad questions that might result in unrealistic information requests, unanswerable questions, or leading questions that prohibit or distort the respondent's answers.

Summarize the characteristics of good questionnaires.

Survey information requirements play a critical role in the development of questionnaires. For each objective, the researcher must choose types of scale formats (nominal, ordinal, interval, or ratio); question formats (open-ended and closed-ended); and the appropriate scaling. Researchers must be aware of the impact that different data collection methods (personal, telephone, self-administered, computer-assisted) have on the wording of both questions and response choices. With good questionnaires, the questions are simple, clear, logical, and meaningful to the respondent, and move from general to specific topics.

Understand the role of cover letters.

The primary role of a cover letter should be to obtain the respondent's cooperation and willingness to participate in the project. Ten factors should be examined in developing cover letters. Observing these guidelines will increase response rates.

Explain the importance of other documents used with questionnaires.

When data are collected using interviews, supervisor and interviewer instructions must be developed as well as screening forms and call record sheets. These documents ensure the data collection process is successful. Supervisor instructions serve as a blueprint for training people to complete the interviewing process in a consistent fashion. The instructions outline the process for conducting the study and are important to any research project that uses personal or telephone interviews. Interviewer instructions are used to train interviewers to correctly select a prospective respondent for inclusion in the study, screen prospective respondents for eligibility, and how to properly conduct the actual interview. Screening forms are a set of preliminary questions used to confirm the eligibility of a prospective respondent for inclusion in the survey. Quota sheets are tracking forms that enable the interviewer to collect data from the right type of respondents. All of these documents help improve data collection and accuracy.

◖▶ Key Terms and Concepts

Bad questions   197

Call records   211

Common methods variance (CMV)   203

Cover letter   208

Interviewer instructions   211

Introductory section   203

Questionnaire   192

Quotas   211

Research questions section   203

Response order bias   203

Screening questions   203

Sensitive questions   195

Skip questions   198

Structured questions   195

Supervisor instruction form   210

Unstructured questions   195

◖▶ Review Questions

1. Discuss the advantages and disadvantages of using unstructured (open-ended) and structured (closed-ended) questions in developing an online, self-administered survey instrument.
2. Explain the role of a questionnaire in the research process. What should be the role of the client during the questionnaire development process?
3. What are the guidelines for deciding the format and layout of a questionnaire?
4. What makes a question bad? Develop three examples of bad questions. Rewrite your examples so they could be judged as good questions.
5. Discuss the value of a good questionnaire design.
6. Discuss the main benefits of including a brief introductory section in questionnaires.
7. Unless needed for screening purposes, why shouldn't demographic questions be asked up front in questionnaires?

◖▶ Discussion Questions

1. Assume you are doing exploratory research to find out students' opinions about the purchase of a new digital music player. What information would you need to collect? What types of questions would you use? Suggest six to eight questions you would ask and indicate in what sequence you would ask them. Pretest the questions on a sample of students from your class.
2. Assume you are conducting a study to determine the importance of brand names and features of mobile phone handsets. What types of questions would you use—open-ended, closed-ended, scaled?—and why? Suggest six to eight questions you would ask and in what sequence you would ask them. Pretest the questions on a sample of students from your class.
3. Discuss the guidelines for developing cover letters. What are some of the advantages of developing good cover letters? What are some of the costs of a bad cover letter?
4. Using the questions asked in evaluating any questionnaire design (see Exhibit 8.4), evaluate the Santa Fe Grill restaurant questionnaire. Write a one-page assessment.
5. What are the critical issues involved in pretesting a questionnaire?

Part 4

Data Preparation, Analysis, and Reporting the Results

Qualitative Data Analysis

Chapter 9

1. Contrast qualitative and quantitative data analyses.
2. Explain the steps in qualitative data analysis.
3. Describe the processes of categorizing and coding data and developing theory.

4. Clarify how credibility is established in qualitative data analysis.
5. Discuss the steps involved in writing a qualitative research report.

Why Women are "Claiming the Throttle"

Why are women increasingly choosing to ride motorcycles? Motorcycle riding has been described as a hypermasculine "outlaw" subculture. Thus, women who choose to ride motorcycles are resisting or expanding existing cultural ideas of women's roles. Currently, about 5 percent of motorcycle riders are women, with estimates as high as 17 percent of riders from Generation X.

In an ethnographic research project, a team of researchers that included one woman and two men studied female motorcycle riders. Data collection included participant observation by the female member of the research team and observation of motorcycle-riding events. In-depth interviews of 18 women were also conducted, including riders of different ages and experience levels. During the in-depth interviews, researchers toured the homes and garages of participants. In addition to videotaping the interviews, researchers wrote field notes detailing what they saw and added these notes to the data set.

The researchers found that initiation and socialization into the "boys' club" of motorcycle riding occur in different ways. Some women had been "rebels" or "bad girls" when they were teenagers, riding on the backs of motorcycles even though their parents had forbidden them to do so. Other girls grew up with motorcycles of their own, often dirt bikes. Competition on bikes had been their way into the "boy's club." Within couples, women either started riding or encouraged their spouse to ride so that they could ride together, side by side. A last route for socialization into riding was seeing other women ride. These women riders experienced riding among other women as a sisterhood and actively encouraged other women to ride.

Freedom and empowerment were the overarching themes emerging from analysis of the qualitative data. Like men, women ride for the sense of freedom—the freedom to slow down and to enjoy, and the freedom to accept physical risk. Women also experience freedom in a unique way as riding broadens their definitions and experiences of femininity. Most women riders are attracted at least to some degree to the hypermasculinity of biking cultures, which they associate with empowerment and fulfillment. Perhaps most impressively, women riders reported carrying over the sense of empowerment gained from riding to other areas of their lives.[1]

◼◼ Nature of Qualitative Data Analysis

In this chapter, you will learn the processes used by researchers to interpret qualitative data and form insights about their meaning. We often think of data analysis as involving numbers. But the data qualitative researchers analyze consists of text (and sometimes images) rather than numbers. Some researchers criticize qualitative research as "soft," lacking rigor, and being inferior. But measurement and statistical analysis do not ensure that research is useful or accurate. What increases the likelihood of good research is a deliberate, thoughtful, knowledgeable approach whether qualitative or quantitative research methods are used. While the reliability and validity of quantitative analysis can be evaluated numerically, the trustworthiness of qualitative analysis depends fundamentally on the rigor of the process used for collecting and analyzing the data.

As we explained in Chapter 4, when magnitude of response and statistical projectability are important, quantitative research should be used to verify and extend qualitative findings. But when the purpose of a research project is to better understand psychoanalytical or cultural phenomena, quantitative research may not offer a great deal of insight or depth. For these topics, qualitative research and analysis often is superior to quantitative research in providing useful knowledge for decision makers.

This chapter details a process that can be followed to ensure qualitative data analyses are careful and rigorous. In this chapter, we first compare qualitative and quantitative analyses. Next we describe the steps involved in qualitative data analysis. We explain categorization, coding, and assessing trustworthiness or credibility. The chapter concludes by providing guidelines on writing a qualitative research report.

◼◼ Qualitative versus Quantitative Analyses

All marketing researchers construct stories that are based on the data they have collected. The goal of these stories, whether they are based on qualitative or quantitative data, is to provide actionable answers to research questions. Yet, there are many differences between the processes of analyzing and interpreting qualitative and quantitative data. The most apparent difference stems from the nature of the data itself. Qualitative data is textual (and occasionally visual), rather than numerical. While the goal of quantitative analysis is quantifying the magnitude of variables and relationships, or explaining causal relationships, *understanding* is the goal of qualitative analysis. A second contrast between the two kinds of analysis is that qualitative analyses tend to be ongoing and iterative. This means the data is analyzed as it is collected, which may affect further data collection efforts in terms of who is sampled and what questions are asked. Another difference between the methods is that quantitative analyses are guided entirely by the researchers, while good qualitative researchers employ *member checking*. **Member checking** involves asking key informants to read the researchers' report to verify that the story they are telling about the focal problem or situation is accurate.

Member checking Asking key informants to read the researcher's report to verify that the analysis is accurate.

Qualitative data analysis is largely inductive. The categories, themes, and patterns analysts describe in their reports emerge from the data, rather than being defined prior to data collection, as in quantitative analyses. Because an inductive process is used, the theory that emerges is often called *grounded theory*.[2] The categories and corresponding codes for categories are developed as researchers work through the texts and images and find what is there. Of course, rarely is the development of categories and theory completely inductive. Researchers bring with them knowledge, theory, and training that suggests categories, themes, and theories that might exist in the data they have collected.

There is no one process for analyzing qualitative data, although the three-step process described in this chapter has been useful to the thinking of many qualitative researchers. Some researchers prefer a more impressionistic approach to qualitative analysis and do not go through transcripts and other documents with the degree of care that we suggest here. Nevertheless, "careful and deliberate analysis remains crucial to sound qualitative research."[3]

Qualitative researchers differ in their beliefs about the use of quantifying their data. Some feel that quantification is completely useless and likely misleading. But others find that quantification can be useful in both counting responses and in model development. We discuss tabulation (counting) later in this chapter.

Qualitative researchers use different techniques for data collection. These differences affect the kinds of analyses that can be performed with the data. Analysts use the collected and transcribed textual data to develop themes, categories, and relationships between variables. Categories are usually developed as the transcripts (and images) are reviewed by researchers. Codes are attached to the categories, which are then used to mark the portions of text (or images) where the category is mentioned.

In this chapter, we review the process of analyzing qualitative data. We explain the process of data reduction, data display, and conclusion making/verification. We also explain how qualitative researchers develop analyses that are credible, which means the analyses are authentic and believable. Finally, we explain how to write a qualitative research report.

The Process of Analyzing Qualitative Data

After data is collected, researchers engage in a three-step process of analysis: data reduction, data display, and conclusion drawing/verification.[4] The three steps and relationships between the steps and data collection efforts are pictured in Exhibit 9.1.

Managing the Data Collection Effort

Whether the collection method is focus groups or in-depth interviews, the data will be transcribed for further analysis. Data from online focus groups, private communities, and social media sites is collected in one database to facilitate analysis. Occasionally, participants are asked to write stories or respond to open-ended questions, and their written responses become the data set. The project in the Marketing Research in Action at the end of this chapter makes use of this technique.

Qualitative researchers often enter their interim thoughts in the database. Field notes, which are observations written down during the data collection effort, also become part of the data set. Finally, key participants may be asked to evaluate researchers' initial research draft. Their feedback becomes part of the official data set as well.

Step 1: Data Reduction

The amount of data collected in a qualitative study can be extensive. Researchers must make decisions about how to categorize and represent the data. This results in

Exhibit 9.1	Components of Data Analysis: An Interactive Model

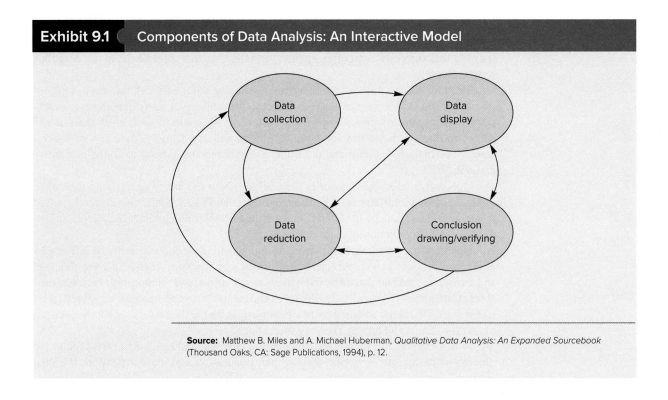

Source: Matthew B. Miles and A. Michael Huberman, *Qualitative Data Analysis: An Expanded Sourcebook* (Thousand Oaks, CA: Sage Publications, 1994), p. 12.

Data reduction The categorization and coding of data that is part of the theory development process in qualitative data analysis.

data reduction. The most systematic method of analysis is to read through transcripts and develop categories to represent the data. When similar topics are encountered, they are coded similarly. Researchers may simply write codes in the margins of their transcripts. But increasingly, software such as QSR NVIVO and Atlas/ti is used to track the passages that are coded. Computer coding enables researchers to view all similarly coded passages at the same time, which facilitates comparison and deeper coding. Computer coding also makes it easier to study relationships in the data. Data reduction consists of several interrelated processes: categorization and coding; theory development; and iteration and negative case analysis.

Data Reduction: Categorization and Coding The first step in data reduction is **categorization.** Researchers categorize sections of the transcript and label the categories with names and sometimes code numbers. There may be some categories that are determined before the study because of existing researcher knowledge and experience. However, most often the codes are developed inductively as researchers read through transcripts and discover new themes of interest and code new instances of categories that have already been discovered. The sections that are coded can be one word long or several pages. The same sections of data can be categorized in multiple ways. If a passage refers to several different themes that have been identified by researchers, the passage will be coded for all the different relevant themes. Some portions of the transcripts will not contain information that is relevant to the analysis and will not be coded at all.[5] A **code sheet** is a piece of paper with all the codes (see Exhibit 9.2 for an example from a senior Internet adoption study). The coded data may be entered into a computer, but the first round of coding usually occurs in the margins (Exhibit 9.3). The **codes** can be words or numbers that refer to categories on the coding sheet. In the example in Exhibit 9.3,

Categorization Placing portions of transcripts into similar groups based on their content.

Code sheet A document that lists the different themes or categories for a particular study.

Codes Labels or numbers that are used to track categories in a qualitative study.

Exhibit 9.2   Senior Adoption of the Internet Study Initial Code Sheet

I. Antecedents
  A. Observability
     1. Seeing others use the Internet
     2. Having an "a-ha" experience
     3. Marketing influences
  B. Trialability
     1. Family
     2. Community centers
     3. Friends
     4. Work
  C. Complexity
     1. Physical challenges
     2. Learning challenges
     3. Initial fear
  D. Relative advantage
     1. Cultural currency
     2. Ability to engage in hobbies
     3. Finding information
     4. Communication
     5. Creativity
  E. Compatibility
     1. Openness to experience/life involvement
     2. Technology optimism
     3. Self-efficacy/proactive coping
     4. Financial resources
     5. Time in retirement
     6. Previous experience w/computing

II. Processes
  A. Attend formal classes
  B. Consult published sources
  C. Mentors
  D. Bricolage (learning by doing)
  E. Ancillary systems (e.g., handwritten notes)
  F. Flow
  G. Multitasking

III. Uses
  A. Communication (e-mail, jokes, support groups)
  B. Gather info
     1. health
     2. hobbies
     3. places
     4. news
     5. financial
     6. product
     7. travel
  C. Banking
  D. Shop selectively
  E. Later life uses (Keeper of the meaning, generativity, integrity)
  F. Intended uses
  G. Acting as an intermediary/proxy
  H. Entertainment
  I. Word processing, etc.
  J. Creativity

IV. Outcomes
  1. Connectedness
     a. Companionship
     b. Social support
     c. Linkages to places visited, lived
  2. Self-efficacy/independence
  3. Cultural currency
     a. Computer skills
     b. Increased knowledge
  4. Excitement
  5. Evangelism
  6. Fun
  7. Self-extension

V. Coping Strategies
  A. Security–personal info
  B. Protecting privacy
  C. Flow/limiting flow
  D. Ease
  E. Satisficing

Codes for Senior Characteristics

B = Broadband	S = Self-adopted
M = Modem	O = Other adopted
OO = Old old 75+	SA = Self-assisted
Y = Young old 65–74	

Exhibit 9.3   Coding Transcripts in the Margins

Moderator: What's a typical session like? You sit down at the computer and . . .

III I

III2 D
III2 C

Nisreen: I sit down at the computer and then I go into my e-mails. I check my emails and I make the replies. Then I want to find out about certain things, then I find out about those things and then I go to World News. Then I go to the different countries I'm interested in, then I go to the newspapers. I get the news about Pakistan right now. I go into Asia and then I go into Pakistan and then I get the news right there before I think my relatives know in Pakistan. I know the news before that. So isn't it wonderful? IV D

Moderator: Yes. It really is. It's amazing.

IV A I

Nisreen: My cousin in Australia . . . before he thought he was leaving Australia from Sydney and I knew all about it, it's faster than telegram. It's so wonderful. I almost feel like I'm sitting on a magic carpet and I press
IV D   a button and boom, I'm there.   IV C

IV F   **Moderator: That's interesting. Just reading the paper makes you feel like you are there.**

III 2D

III 2C
Nisreen: And then I want to read the viewpoint of different newspapers, so I go into different countries like India, Bangladesh or Pakistan, or the Middle East. In the Middle East, I used to be a voluntary assistant of the, *Perspective*, which is the only women's magazine in the Middle East. At that time, Jordan
IV A   was a very peaceful place. The rest of the world was up in arms and that kind of thing. So you see, I feel like I'm in touch with the whole world. It's such a wonderful feeling at my age to be in touch with the world. I
IV C2   wish more and more . . . because I think in the near future, that would be the order of the day.

numbers are used as codes to help organize themes and subthemes in the study. The numbers written in the margin correspond to themes and categories in the coding sheet developed by the researchers.

An example of the process of data coding comes from an online shopping study based on data collected from both online and offline focus groups. One theme that emerged from the data was the importance of freedom and control as desirable outcomes when shopping online.[6] The following are some examples of passages that were coded as representing the freedom and control theme:

- "You're not as committed [online]. You haven't driven over there and parked and walked around so you have a little more flexibility and can get around a lot faster."
- ". . . when I go to a store and a salesperson's helping me for a long time and it's not really what I wanted . . . I'll oblige them, they spent all this time with me . . . but . . . online, I know I will get to the point and be ready to order, but I know I don't have to, I can come back anytime I want to."
- "You can sit on your arse and eat while you shop. You kin even shop nekked!"
- "For me, online browsing is similar [to offline browsing], but I have more of a sense of freedom. I'll browse stores I might not go into offline . . . Victoria's Secret comes to mind . . . also I'll go into swank stores that I might feel intimidated in going into offline . . . when you're a 51-year-old chubby gramma, online Victoria's Secret just feels a bit more comfortable."

Categories may be modified and combined as data analysis continues. The researcher's understanding evolves during the data analysis phase and often results in revisiting, recoding, and recategorizing data.

Comparison The process of developing and refining theory and constructs by analyzing the differences and similarities in passages, themes, or types of participants.

Data Reduction: Comparison Comparison of differences and similarities is a fundamental process in qualitative data analysis. There is an analogy to experimental design, in which various conditions or manipulations (for instance, price levels, advertising appeals) are compared to each other or to a control group. Comparison first occurs as researchers identify categories. Each potential new instance of a category or theme is compared to already coded instances to determine if the new instance belongs in the existing category. When all transcripts have been coded and important categories and themes identified, instances within a category will be scrutinized so that the theme can be defined and explained in more detail. For example, in a study of employee reactions to their own employers' advertising, the category "effectiveness of advertising with consumers" was a recurring theme. Because of the importance of advertising effectiveness in determining employees' reactions to the ad, employees' views of what made ads effective were compared and contrasted. Employees most often associated the following qualities with effective organizational ads to consumers: (1) likely to result in short-term sales; (2) appealing to the target audience; (3) attention grabbing; (4) easily understandable; and (5) authentically portraying the organization and its products.[7]

Comparison processes are also used to better understand the differences and similarities between two constructs of interest. In the study of online shopping, two types of shopping motivations emerged from analyses of transcripts: goal-oriented behavior (shopping to buy or find information about specific products) and experiential behavior (shopping to shop). Comparison of shopper motivations, descriptions, and desired outcomes from each type of behavior reveals that consumers' online shopping behavior is different depending on whether or not the shopping trip is goal-oriented or experiential.[8]

Comparisons can also be made between different kinds of informants. In a study of high-risk leisure behavior, skydivers with different levels of experience were interviewed. As a result of comparing more and less experienced skydivers, the researchers were able to show that motivations changed and evolved, for example, from thrill, to pleasure, to flow, as skydivers continued their participation in the sport.[9] Similarly, in a study of postsocialist Eastern European women who were newly exposed to cosmetics and cosmetics brands, researchers compared women who embraced cosmetics to those who were either ambivalent about cosmetics or who rejected them entirely.[10]

Integration The process of moving from the identification of themes and categories to the development of theory.

Recursive A relationship in which a variable can both cause and be caused by the same variable.

Selective coding Building a storyline around one core category or theme; the other categories will be related to or subsumed to this central overarching category.

Data Reduction: Theory Building Integration is the process through which researchers build theory that is grounded, or based on the data collected. The idea is to move from the identification of themes and categories to the development of theory.

In qualitative research, relationships may or may not be conceptualized and pictured in a way that looks like the traditional causal model employed by quantitative researchers. For instance, relationships may be portrayed as circular or **recursive.** In recursive relationships, variables may both cause and be caused by the same variable. A good example is the relationship between job satisfaction and financial compensation. Job satisfaction tends to increase performance and thus compensation earned on the job, which in turn increases job satisfaction.

Qualitative researchers may look for one core category or theme to build their storyline around, a process referred to as **selective coding.** All other categories will be related to or subsumed to this central category or theme. Selective coding is evident in the following studies that all have an overarching viewpoint or frame:

- A study of personal websites finds that posting a website is an imaginary digital extension of self.
- A study of an online Newton (a discontinued Apple PDA) user group finds several elements of religious devotion in the community.
- A study of Hispanic consumer behavior in the United States uses the metaphor of boundary crossing to explore Hispanic purchase and consumption.[11]

Given its role as an integrating concept, it is not surprising that selective coding generally occurs in the later stages of data analysis. Once the overarching theme is developed, researchers review all their codes and cases to better understand how they relate to the larger category, or central storyline, that has emerged from their data.

Iteration Working through the data several times in order to modify early ideas.

Data Reduction: Iteration and Negative Case Analysis **Iteration** means working through the data in a way that permits early ideas and analyses to be modified by choosing cases and issues in the data that will permit deeper analyses. The iterative process may uncover issues that the already collected data do not address. In this case, the researcher will collect data from more informants, or may choose specific types of informants that he or she believes will answer questions that have arisen during the iterative process. The iterative procedure may also take place after an original attempt at integration. Each of the interviews (or texts or images) may be reviewed to see whether it supports the larger theory that has been developed. This iterative process can result in revising and deepening constructs as well as the larger theory based on relationships between constructs.

Memoing Writing down thoughts as soon as possible after each interview, focus group, or site visit.

An important element of iterative analysis is note taking or **memoing.** Researchers should write down their thoughts and reactions as soon after each interview, focus group, or site visit that time will allow. Researchers may want to write down not only what participants say they feel, but also whether or not what they say is credible.

Negative case analysis Deliberately looking for cases and instances that contradict the ideas and theories that researchers have been developing.

Perhaps most important, during the iterative process researchers use **negative case analysis,** which means that they deliberately look for cases and instances that contradict the ideas and theories that they have been developing. Negative case analysis helps to establish boundaries and conditions for the theory that is being developed by the qualitative researcher. The general stance of qualitative researchers should be skepticism toward the ideas and theory they have created based on the data they have collected.[12] Otherwise they are likely to look for evidence that confirms their preexisting biases and early analysis. Doing so may result in important alternative conceptualizations that are legitimately present in the data being completely overlooked.

Iterative and negative case analyses begin in the data reduction stage. But they continue through the data display and conclusion drawing/verification stages. As analysis continues in the project, data displays are altered. Late in the life of the project, iterative analysis and negative case analysis provide verification for and qualification of the themes and theories developed during the data reduction phase of research.

Data Reduction: The Role of Tabulation The use of tabulation in qualitative analyses is controversial. Some analysts feel that any kind of tabulation will be misleading. After all, the data collected are not like survey data where all questions are asked of all respondents in exactly the same way. Each focus group or in-depth interview asks somewhat different questions in somewhat different ways. Moreover, frequency of mention is not always a good measure of research importance. A unique answer from a lone wolf in an interview

		Documents
Themes	**Passages**	**(Participants)**
Communication—uses	149	27
Self-directed values and behavior	107	23
Shopping/conducting biz—uses	66	24
Gather information—uses	65	25
Classes to learn the Internet	64	22
Future intended uses	63	20
Mentors/teachers helping to learn	55	20
Difficulty in learning	50	20
Self-efficacy/proactive coping—outcome	46	16
Later life cycle uses (e.g., genealogy)	45	19
Entertainment—uses	43	24
Excitement about the Internet	40	14
Adopting to facilitate hobbies	40	15
Technology optimism	40	18
Proactive coping	38	19
Health information on Internet—uses	34	19
Bricolage (Tinkering to learn the Internet)	34	20

Exhibit 9.4 Tabulation of Most Frequently Appearing Categories in the Senior Adoption of the Internet Study

may be worthy of attention because it is consistent with other interpretation and analysis, or because it suggests a boundary condition for the theory and findings.[13]

Exhibit 9.4 shows a tabulation from the study of senior adoption of the Internet. The most frequently coded response was "communication," followed by "self-directed values/ behavior." While this result may seem meaningful, a better measure of the importance of communications to seniors over the Internet is likely to be found using surveys. But the result does provide some guidance. All 27 participants in the study mentioned the use of the Internet for communication, so researchers are likely to investigate this theme in their analysis even if the tabulations are not included in the final report. Note that qualitative researchers virtually never report percentages. For example, they seldom would report four out of ten that are positive about a product concept as 40 percent. Using percentages would inaccurately imply that the results are statistically projectable to a larger population of consumers.

Tabulation can also keep researchers honest. For example, researchers involved in the senior Internet adoption study were initially impressed by informants who made the decision to adopt the Internet quickly and dramatically when someone showed them an Internet function that supported a preexisting interest or hobby (coded as "a-ha"). But the code only appeared three times across the 27 participants in the study. While researchers

Exhibit 9.5	Relationships between Categories: Co-Mentions of Selected Constructs in the Senior Adoption of the Internet Study

	Curiosity	Technology Optimism	Proactive Coping Skills	Cultural Currency
Curiosity	**107***			
Technology optimism	16	**40**		
Proactive coping skills	19	10	**38**	
Cultural currency	12	8	7	**26**

*Diagonal contains total number of mentions of each concept.

may judge the theme worthy of mention in their report, they are unlikely to argue that "a-ha" moments are central in the senior adoption decision process. Counting responses can help keep researchers honest in the sense that it provides a counterweight to biases they may bring to the analysis.[14]

Another way to use tabulation is to look at co-occurrences of themes in the study. Exhibit 9.5 shows the number of times selected concepts were mentioned together in the same coded passage. In the exhibit, the categories or themes most often mentioned together with curiosity were technology optimism, proactive coping skills ("I can figure it out even if it makes me feel stupid sometimes"), and cultural currency (adopting to keep up with the times). The co-mentions with curiosity suggest that qualitative analysts would consider the idea that curious people are more likely to be technology optimists, to be interested in keeping up with the times, and to have strong proactive coping skills. But interpreting these numbers too literally is risky. Further iterative analysis is required to develop these conceptual ideas and to support (or refute) their credibility. Whenever the magnitude of a finding is important to decision makers, well-designed quantitative studies are likely to provide better measures than are qualitative studies.

Some researchers suggest a middle ground for reporting tabulations of qualitative data. They suggest using "fuzzy numerical qualifiers" such as "often," "typically," or "few" in their reports.[15] Marketing researchers usually include a section in their reports about limitations of their research. A caution about the inappropriateness of estimating magnitudes based on qualitative research typically is included in the limitations section of the report. Therefore, when reading qualitative findings, readers would be cautioned that any numerical findings presented should not be read too literally.

Step 2: Data Display

Qualitative researchers typically use visual displays to summarize data. Data displays are important because they help reduce and summarize the extensive textual data collected in the study in a way that conveys major ideas in a compact fashion. There is no one way to display and present data in qualitative analysis. Any perusal of qualitative reports will find a wide variety of formats, each developed in response to the combination of research problem, methodology (ethnography, case study, focus group, or in-depth interview, for instance), and focus of analysis. Coming up with ideas for useful data displays is a creative task that can be both fun and satisfying. Some data displays provide interim analysis and thus may not be included in the final report. In any case, the displays will probably change over the course of analysis as researchers interpret and re-read their data and modify and qualify their initial impressions. The displays also evolve as researchers seek to better display their findings.

Displays may be tables or figures. Tables have rows or row by column formats that cross themes and/or informants. Figures may include flow diagrams, traditional box and arrow causal diagrams (often associated with quantitative research), diagrams that display circular or recursive relationships, trees that display consumers' taxonomies of products, brands, or other concepts, consensus maps, which picture the collective connections that informants make between concepts or ideas, and checklists that show all informants and then indicate whether or not each informant possesses a particular attitude, value, behavior, ideology, or role, for instance. While displays of qualitative findings are quite diverse, some common types of displays include the following:

- A table that explains central themes in the study. For example, a study of technology products uncovered eight themes that represent the paradoxes or issues in technology adoption and use (see Exhibit 9.6).
- A diagram that suggests relationships between variables. An example of a diagram that pictures relationships between themes comes from the earlier mentioned study of skydiving (see Exhibit 9.7). The diagram pictures how three sets of motivations evolve over time as skydivers become more experienced. The arrows are double-sided because movement to a higher level is not complete, since skydivers revisit and experience the lower level motivations.
- A matrix including quotes for various themes from representative informants. An example of this is a table from the previously mentioned study of involvement with cosmetics and brand attitudes in post-socialist Europe, which shows attitudes of women who are ambivalent about cosmetics (see Exhibit 9.8). Other tables included in the study contain parallel verbatims for women who have embraced cosmetics and women who have rejected cosmetics.

Step 3: Conclusion Drawing/Verification

The iterative process and negative case analysis continues through the verification phase of the project. The process includes checking for common biases that may affect researcher conclusions. A list of the most common biases to watch out for is shown in Exhibit 9.9. In addition to actively considering the possibility of bias in the analysis, researchers also must establish credibility for their findings. We explain credibility next.

Verification/Conclusion Drawing: Credibility in Qualitative Research   Quantitative researchers establish credibility in data analysis by demonstrating that their results are reliable (measurement and findings are stable, repeatable, and generalizable) and valid (the research measures what it was intended to measure). In contrast, the credibility of qualitative data analysis is based on the rigor of "the actual strategies used for collecting, coding, analyzing, and presenting data when generating theory."[16] The essential question in developing credibility in qualitative research is "How can (a

Exhibit 9.6	Eight Central Paradoxes of Technological Products

Paradox	Description
Control/chaos	Technology can facilitate regulation or order, and technology can lead to upheaval or disorder
Freedom/enslavement	Technology can facilitate independence or fewer restrictions, and technology can lead to dependence or more restrictions
New/obsolete	New technologies provide the user with the most recently developed benefits of scientific knowledge, and new technologies are already or soon to be outmoded as they reach the marketplace
Competence/incompetence	Technology can facilitate feelings of intelligence or efficacy, and technology can lead to feelings of ignorance or ineptitude
Efficiency/inefficiency	Technology can facilitate less effort or time spent in certain activities, and technology can lead to more effort or time in certain activities
Fulfills/creates needs	Technology can facilitate the fulfillment of needs or desires, and technology can lead to the development or awareness of needs or desires previously unrealized
Assimilation/isolation	Technology can facilitate human togetherness, and technology can lead to human separation
Engaging/disengaging	Technology can facilitate involvement, flow, or activity, and technology can lead to disconnection, disruption, or passivity

Source: David Glen Mick and Susan Fournier, "Paradoxes of Technology: Consumer Cognizance, Emotions and Coping Strategies," *Journal of Consumer Research* 25 (September 1998), p. 126. © 1998 by JOURNAL OF CONSUMER RESEARCH, Inc.

Emic validity An attribute of qualitative research that affirms that key members within a culture or subculture agree with the findings of a research report.

Cross-researcher reliability The degree of similarity in the coding of the same data by different researchers.

researcher) persuade his or her audiences that the research findings of an inquiry are worth paying attention to?"[17]

The terms *validity* and *reliability* have to be redefined in qualitative research. For example, in qualitative research the term **emic validity** means that the analysis presented in the report resonates with people inside the studied culture or subculture, a form of validity established by member checking. Similarly, **cross-researcher reliability** means the text and images are coded similarly among multiple researchers. However, many qualitative researchers prefer terms such as *quality, rigor, dependability, transferability,* and *trustworthiness* to the traditionally quantitative terms *validity* and *reliability*. Moreover, some qualitative researchers completely reject any notions of validity and reliability, believing there is no single "correct" interpretation of qualitative data.[18] In this

Exhibit 9.7	Evolution of Motives for High-Risk Consumption in Relation to Risk Acculturation and Experience

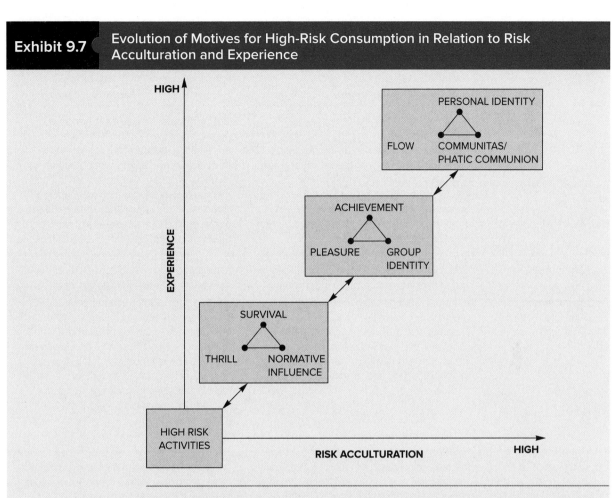

Source: Richard L. Celsi, Randy L. Rose, and Tom W. Leigh, "An Exploration of High Risk Leisure Consumption through Skydiving," *Journal of Consumer Research* 20 (June 1993), p. 14. Copyright 1993 by the University of Chicago Press.

Credibility The degree of rigor, believability, and trustworthiness established by qualitative research.

Triangulation Addressing the analysis from multiple perspectives, including using multiple methods of data collection and analysis, multiple data sets, multiple researchers, multiple time periods, and different kinds of relevant research informants.

chapter, we use the term **credibility** to describe the rigor and believability established in qualitative analysis.

Triangulation is the technique most often associated with credibility in qualitative research.[19] Triangulation requires that research inquiry be addressed from multiple perspectives. Several kinds of triangulation are possible:

- Multiple methods of data collection and analysis.
- Multiple data sets.
- Multiple researchers analyzing the data, especially if they come from different backgrounds or research perspectives.
- Data collection in multiple time periods.
- Providing selective breadth in informants so that different kinds of relevant groups that may have different and relevant perspectives are included in the research.

Credibility is also increased when key informants and other practicing qualitative researchers are asked to review the analyses. As mentioned, soliciting feedback from key

Exhibit 9.8	Postsocialist Eastern European Women's Product Involvement and Brand Commitment: Informants Who Were Ambivalent about Cosmetics	
	Alexandra	**Laura**
Cosmetics use and involvement	3.1: Normally I wash my hair twice a week. But . . . I knew we would meet, so I washed it yesterday. It depends on my mood. I use corrector and cream powder in winter when I am not so brown, but in the summer. . . . It is disgusting. If I go to a movie I don't. So, I always say, "Okay, you have to have a nice look, but you don't have to prepare for the next beauty contest every morning."	3.8: Only if something bad happened, a disaster, and then I wouldn't think about appearance. Mascara, this is something that I always use, and powder everyday for my face. I like it. . . . Mascara, I can put that on myself. But I can't put on makeup. I can give advice, but I don't know how to do it for myself. Maybe I am too stressed, I won't get the effect that I want. I feel better without makeup.
Consumer as interpreter	3.2: When I'll be the grandparent then it will be okay for the parent, because I've changed my way of thinking. I will give it to my children.	3.9: I buy things that I don't really need. I know that I don't need it, but it, and then I am sorry. . . . Those things can wait.
Cultural ideologies and intermediaries	3.3: I mean during the socialist communist regime there wasn't a choice. People weren't conscious about cosmetics. The only thing that was important was to have a workplace and to meet the requirement of the socialist men and women.	3.10: Romanian women are more attractive than five years ago because they have the chance to find out new things from TV and magazines—how to put on makeup and how to dress. For instance, my mother doesn't take care of herself. . . . You know we didn't learn how to use cosmetics from her. We watched TV, read books. My mother didn't tell me anything.
Local context and social networks	3.4: There is *Cosmopolitan* in Hungarian, but it is not as good as in English. It is thinner, and there are only advertisements in it and about sex and that is all. I am lucky because we have an English teacher at the university, and they subscribe to this magazine, and I can read it. And there are fashion models, as well and cooking advice and so on. So, it is much nicer.	3.11: They judge you according to appearance. Even in the job, women discuss . . . and then you also have to buy it, because you want to be at the same level. I saw this, and after they buy the products, they show off. Look what I have. Those who cannot buy suffer, even if they don't admit it. It is painful. . . . After the Revolution, I guess this is when it started—with jeans.
Ideological positions	3.5: We have to forget about communism, and we have to change our way of thinking, but it is very, very hard to change the thinking of the whole country.	3.12: If you look good, you get a good guy, a good job, even though you are not very smart. But many have problems because of this . . . it is risky to look good. Everyone wants to look better than the other. They think that if you are dressed according to the latest fashion, everyone will think that you have money and have a good life.
Involvement with branded products	3.6: If I have money I get cosmetics at a pharmacy, If I don't have much money I go to a drugstore. Usually (pharmacists) have creams that they do themselves. They are good ones because they know what to put in them, but they don't have names. And they are cheaper. . . . The name isn't	3.13: I saw many women that want to use branded products, not because they know it is good, but because they saw a commercial, or they want to show off. They don't think it is possible that the products don't fit you. Branded products might not fit you. At some point, we had Pantene shampoos. All the

(continued)

	Alexandra	Laura
Brand commitment and brand experimentation	important to me, what is important is quality. If I find an unknown product, but it is good for me, I buy it. . . . And I don't trust these (products) . . . it would be cheaper to buy them, but I haven't heard about them. I don't trust them. 3.7: This is my favorite. I just found it. . . . It is brand new. I tried Wash & Go. It was advertised very frequently, and everybody ran to the shops and bought it. But I said, "OK, it's very popular, but it is not good for me (it tangled my hair)."	commercial breaks had ads with Pantene. I didn't want to buy. I got it as a gift and used it, and I wasn't happy with it. I didn't like. It might be a good brand, but it didn't fit me, so brand is not enough. 3.14: I prefer L'Oreal, and Avon and Oriflame have good body lotion. I still like to try other things. I like to try only things that I have heard of.

Exhibit 9.8 Postsocialist Eastern European Women's Product Involvement and Brand Commitment: Informants Who Were Ambivalent about Cosmetics, *continued*

Source: Robin A. Coulter, Linda L. Price, and Lawrence Feick, "Rethinking the Origins of Involvement and Brand Commitment: Insights from Postsocialist Europe," *Journal of Consumer Research* 30 (September 2003), p. 159. © 2003 by JOURNAL OF CONSUMER RESEARCH, Inc.

Exhibit 9.9 Threats to Drawing Credible Conclusions in Qualitative Analysis

- Salience of first impressions or of observations of highly concrete or dramatic incidents.
- Selectivity which leads to overconfidence in some data, especially when trying to confirm a key finding.
- Co-occurrences taken as correlations or even as causal relationships.
- Extrapolating the rate of instances in the population from those observed.
- Not taking account of the fact that information from some sources may be unreliable.

Source: Adapted from Matthew B. Miles and A. Michael Huberman, *Handbook of Qualitative Research, An Expanded Sourcebook* (Thousand Oaks, CA: Sage Publications, 1994), p. 438.

Peer review A process in which external qualitative methodology or topic area specialists are asked to review the research analysis.

informants or member checking strengthens the credibility of qualitative analysis. Seeking feedback from external expert reviewers, called **peer review,** also strengthens credibility. Key informants and external qualitative methodology and topic area experts often question the analyses, push researchers to better clarify their thinking, and occasionally change key interpretations in the research. When member checking and peer review are utilized in a qualitative design, it is reported in the methodological section of the report.

Writing the Report

Researchers should keep in mind that research reports are likely to be read by people in the company who are not familiar with the study. Moreover, the study may be reviewed years later by individuals who were not working at the company at the time the research was conducted. Therefore, the research objectives and procedures should be well explained both to current and future decision makers. Qualitative research reports typically contain three sections:[20]

1. Introduction
   a. Research objectives
   b. Research questions
   c. Description of research methods
2. Analysis of the data/findings
   a. Literature review and relevant secondary data
   b. Data displays
   c. Interpretation and summary of the findings
3. Conclusions and recommendations

The introductory portion of the report should present the research problem, objectives of the research, and the methodology used. As do quantitative researchers, qualitative researchers report the procedures they used to collect and analyze data. The methodology section of a qualitative report usually contains:

- Topics covered in questioning and other materials used in questioning informants.
- If observational methods are used, the locations, dates, times, and context of observation.
- Number of researchers involved and their level of involvement in the study. Any diversity in background or training of researchers may be highlighted as positive for the study because multiple viewpoints have been brought to the analysis.
- Procedure for choosing informants.
- Number of informants and informant characteristics, such as age, gender, location, and level of experience with the product or service. This information is often summarized in a table.
- The number of focus groups, interviews, or transcripts.
- The total number of pages of the transcripts, number of pictures, videos, number, and page length of researcher memos.
- Any procedures used to ensure that the data collection and analysis were systematic. For example, coding, iterative analysis of transcripts, member checking, peer reviews, and so forth.
- Procedures used for negative case analyses and how the interpretation was modified.
- Limitations of qualitative methodology in general, and any limitations that are specific to the particular qualitative method used.

Two examples of explaining the general limitations of qualitative methodology in a report are:

> "The reader is cautioned that the findings reported here are qualitative, not quantitative in nature. The study was designed to explore *how* respondents feel and behave rather than to determine *how many* think or act in specific ways."
> "Respondents constitute a small nonrandom sample of relevant consumers and are therefore not statistically representative of the universe from which they have been drawn."[21]

Analysis of the Data/Findings

The sequence of reported findings should be written in a way that is logical and persuasive. Secondary data may be brought into the analysis to help contextualize the findings. For instance, in the senior adoption of the Internet study, the demographics of senior adopters were included in the report to contextualize the qualitative findings. Also, general topics precede more specific topics. For example, a discussion of findings related to seniors' general attitudes toward and adoption of technology will precede the discussion of senior Internet adoption.

Verbatims Quotes from research participants that are used in research reports.

Data displays that summarize, clarify, or provide evidence for assertions should be included with the report. **Verbatims,** or quotes from research participants, are often used in the textual report as well as in data displays. When they are well chosen, verbatims are a particularly powerful way to underscore important points because they express consumer viewpoints in their own voice. Video verbatims can be used in live presentations. Of course, the power of verbatims is a double-edged sword. Colorfully stated, interesting verbatims do not always make points that are well-grounded in the body of data collected. Researchers need to take care that they do not select, analyze, and present verbatims that are memorable rather than revealing of patterns in their data.

Conclusions and Recommendations

Researchers should provide information that is relevant to the research problem articulated by the client. As two qualitative researchers stated, "A psychoanalytically rich interpretation of personal hygiene and deodorant products is ultimately of little value to the client if it cannot be linked to a set of actionable marketing implications—for example, a positioning which directly reflects consumer motivations or a new product directed at needs not currently addressed."[22] As with quantitative research, knowledge of both the market and the client's business is useful in translating research findings into managerial implications.

When the magnitude of consumer response is important to the client, researchers are likely to report what they have found, and suggest follow-up research. Even so, qualitative research should be reported in a way that reflects an appropriate level of confidence in the findings. Exhibit 9.10 lists three examples of forceful, but realistic recommendations based on qualitative research.

A sample qualitative report appears in Appendix 9A. The sample is a summary of a longer report. A longer report should explain each theme in more detail and include participant verbatims.

| **Exhibit 9.10** | **Making Recommendations Based on Qualitative Research When Magnitude Matters** |

- "The qualitative findings give reason for optimism about market interest in the new product concept . . . We therefore recommend that the concept be further developed and formal executions be tested."
- "While actual market demand may not necessarily meet the test of profitability, the data reported here suggest that there is widespread interest in the new device."
- "The results of this study suggest that ad version #3 is most promising because it elicited more enthusiastic responses and because it appears to describe situations under which consumers actually expect to use the product."

Source: Alfred E. Goldman and Susan Schwartz McDonald, *The Group Depth Interview* (Englewood Cliffs, N J: Prentice Hall, 1987), p. 176.

CONTINUING CASE SANTA FE GRILL: USING QUALITATIVE RESEARCH

The business consultant hired by the owners of the Santa Fe Grill has recommended a quantitative survey of lunch and dinner customers. He has not recommended any qualitative research. The owners are not experts in research methods, but they do know the difference between qualitative and quantitative research. They are wondering if some kind of qualitative research approach would be better to understand the challenges facing them. Or perhaps both qualitative and quantitative research should be undertaken?

1. Could observation be used to collect qualitative information?

2. If yes, when and how could observation be used?

3. Are there topics that could be explored better using focus groups?

4. If yes, suggest topics to be used in the focus group studies.

MARKETING RESEARCH IN ACTION

A Qualitative Approach to Understanding Product Dissatisfaction

Product dissatisfaction has important negative consequences for businesses. In this assignment, you will be investigating the nature of product dissatisfaction qualitatively. Your instructor will form groups of three or four. In your group, you will be conducting a small-scale qualitative project about the nature of product dissatisfaction. There are seven project-related assignments that will help step you through the process of qualitative analysis. As you work your way through the assignments, you will be analyzing textual data. Your instructor may ask you to present your findings after each step, or when you have completed all seven steps.

Project Assignment 1 Write a two-page summary about an unsatisfactory purchase experience you have made recently. In your narrative essay, you should include (1) the product or service, (2) your expectations when you bought the product or service, (3) any interactions with salespeople or customer service people before, during, or after the purchase, (4) the feelings and emotions that accompanied your dissatisfaction, and (5) the outcomes of your dissatisfaction. You should include any other details you remember as well.

The narrative should be posted to the class discussion group, or alternately, each student should bring five copies to class. In class, your instructor will help your group to solicit 10 different product or service dissatisfaction summaries from students outside their group to form the textual data set you will be analyzing in subsequent steps.

Project Assignment 2 With your group members, collectively go through three of the product dissatisfaction narratives, writing codes in the margins of the narratives to represent categories or themes. As you go, write codes directly on the narratives and create a separate code sheet. You will likely need to create new codes as you go through the narrative, but the number of new codes needed will be smaller the more narratives that are coded. Look at the sample code sheet in Exhibit 9.2 and a coded section of a transcript in Exhibit 9.3. The exhibit uses numbers, but it is probably easier for you to simply label your data with the name of the category. For example, you may write "emotion: disappointment" in the margin any time you encounter an instance of disappointment. *Hint:* In coding, relevant categories for this project may include (1) factors that lead to dissatisfaction (e.g., poor product quality), (2) emotions and thoughts related to dissatisfaction (e.g., disappointment and frustration), and (3) outcomes of dissatisfaction (e.g., returning the product, telling others). Your categories may need to be broken down into subcategories. For example, there may be several outcomes of dissatisfaction, each one of which is a subcategory of the more general category "outcomes."

You are likely to uncover categories and codes other than those suggested here as you go through the transcripts. Please work from the data as much as possible to develop your categories. We have suggested categories only to get you started.

When your group has coded three narratives together, the remaining seven can be divided among individuals in the group to be coded. Some codes may still have to be added to the code sheet as individual group members code. Any new codes should be added to the master code sheet that group members are utilizing. The result should be ten coded narratives and one master code sheet.

Project Assignment 3 Your group has now read and coded all ten narratives, so you are familiar with your data set. With your group members, make a list of how the cases are similar. Then make a list of how the cases are dissimilar. Do your lists suggest any issues for further qualitative research to investigate? If yes, please make a list of the issues. What have you learned from the process of comparison that helps you better understand product dissatisfaction? Is the product dissatisfaction experience similar across the narratives, or are there differences?

Project Assignment 4 Create a data display or two that usefully summarizes your findings. Exhibits 9.6 through 9.8 show sample displays. *Hint:* It is likely easiest in this case to create a list of your themes along with representative verbatims and/or a conceptual diagram showing variables leading to product dissatisfaction and the outcomes (thoughts, emotions, and behaviors) that result from dissatisfaction. The result will be data display(s) that will be used as part of your presentation of the results.

Project Assignment 5 Perhaps the most difficult task for new researchers is to come up with an overarching concept that integrates your categories. Re-read the section on integration on pp. 227 and 228 in your text. As a group, come up with one idea or concept that integrates all your themes into one overarching theme.

Project Assignment 6 If your group were to further refine your analysis, which of the techniques that help ensure credibility would you use? Write down your choices and briefly explain why they would improve the credibility of the analysis.

Project Assignment 7 Based on your group's analysis in project assignments #1 to #6, make a presentation to the class that includes slides that address methodology, findings (including some relevant verbatims and your data display(s)), research limitations, and conclusions and recommendations. Your findings should develop a theory of product dissatisfaction based on your data set and should be informed by the analyses you have done across steps #1 to #6. Your group's recommendations should flow from your analyses and be useful to businesses in both reducing product dissatisfaction and managing product dissatisfaction after it occurs.

Turn in a copy of your presentation along with the coded narratives, and your master code sheet.

◧ Summary

Contrast qualitative and quantitative data analyses.
There are many differences between qualitative and quantitative data analyses. The data that are analyzed in qualitative research include text and images, rather than numbers. In quantitative research, the goal is to quantify the magnitude of variables and relationships, or explain causal relationships. In qualitative analysis, the goal of research is deeper understanding. A second difference is that qualitative analysis is iterative, with researchers revisiting data and clarifying their thinking during each iteration. Third, quantitative analysis is driven entirely by researchers, while good qualitative research employs member checking, or

asking key informants to verify the accuracy of research reports. Last, qualitative data analysis is inductive, which means that the theory grows out of the research process rather than preceding it, as it does in quantitative analysis.

Explain the steps in qualitative data analysis.

After data collection, there are three steps in analyzing qualitative data. Researchers move back and forth between these steps iteratively rather than going through them one step at a time. The steps are data reduction, constructing data displays, and drawing/verifying conclusions. Data reduction consists of several interrelated processes: categorization and coding, theory development and iteration, and negative case analysis. Categorization is the process of coding and labeling sections of the transcripts or images into themes. Then the categories can be integrated into a theory through iterative analysis of the data. Data displays are the second step. Data displays picture findings in tables or figures so that the data can be more easily digested and communicated. After a rigorous iterative process, researchers can draw conclusions and verify their findings. During the verification/conclusion drawing stage, researchers work to establish the credibility of their data analysis.

Describe the processes of categorizing and coding data and developing theory.

During the categorization phase, researchers develop categories based both on preexisting theory and the categories that emerge from the data. They code the data in margins and develop a code sheet that shows the various labels that they are developing. The codes are revised and revisited as the theory develops. Comparison of differences and similarities between instances of a category, between related categories, and between different participants is particularly useful in better defining constructs and refining theory.

Integration is the process of moving from identification of themes and categories to the investigation of relationships between categories. In selective coding, researchers develop an overarching theme or category around which to build their storyline.

Clarify how credibility is established in qualitative data analysis.

Credibility in data analysis is established through (1) careful, iterative analysis in categorization and theory development, (2) the use of negative case analysis, and (3) triangulation. In negative case analysis, researchers systematically search the data for information that does not conform to their theory. This helps to establish the credibility of their analysis and to identify boundary conditions for their theory. Triangulation is especially important in developing credibility for qualitative data analyses. There are several forms of triangulation, including using multiple methods of data collection and analysis; multiple data sets; multiple researchers; data collection in multiple time periods; and informants with different perspectives and experiences. Credibility is also enhanced with member checking, which is soliciting feedback about the accuracy of the analysis from key informants. In peer review, qualitative methodology experts are asked to critique the qualitative report.

Discuss the steps involved in writing a qualitative research report.

A qualitative report has three sections: (1) introduction; (2) analysis of the data/findings; and (3) conclusions and recommendations. In the introductory portion of the report, the objectives of the research and methodology are explained. In the data analysis section, the reported findings are written in a way that is logical and persuasive. Data displays and verbatims may be used to enhance the communication of the findings. The Conclusion includes the marketing implications section. In this part of the report, researchers provide information that is relevant to the research problem articulated by the client.

▶ Key Terms and Concepts

Categorization 224

Codes 224

Code sheet 224

Comparison 227

Credibility 233

Cross-researcher reliability 232

Data reduction 224

Emic validity 232

Integration 227

Iteration 228

Member checking 222

Memoing 228

Negative case analysis 228

Peer review 235

Recursive 227

Selective coding 227

Triangulation 233

Verbatims 237

Review Questions

1. How are quantitative and qualitative data analyses different?
2. Describe the three steps in qualitative data analysis and explain how and why these steps are iterative.
3. What are the interrelated steps in data reduction?
4. How do you build theory in qualitative analysis?
5. What is negative case analysis and why is it important to the credibility of qualitative analysis?
6. Give some specific examples data displays and explain of how they may be used in qualitative data analysis.
7. What are some of threats to drawing credible conclusions in qualitative data analysis?
8. What is triangulation and what is its role in qualitative analysis?
9. What are the various ways that credibility can be established in qualitative analysis?

Discussion Questions

1. Compare and contrast reliability and validity in quantitative analysis with the concept of credibility used in qualitative analysis. Do you believe the concepts are really similar? Why or why not?
2. Let's say your college has as a goal increasing participation in student activities on campus. To help this effort, you are doing an ethnographic study to better understand why students do or do not participate in student activities. How would you plan for triangulation in this study?
3. **EXPERIENCE MARKETING RESEARCH.** Ask permission from three people to analyze the content of their Facebook or similar site (of course, you should promise them anonymity). If the sites are extensive, you may need a plan to sample a portion of the website (at least five to ten representative pages). As you go through the sites, develop a coding sheet. What did you learn about social networking sites from your coding? What content categories are the most frequently occurring? What do you conclude based on the fact that these categories are the most frequently occurring at these three websites? Are there any implications of your findings for advertisers that are considering advertising on social networking sites?
4. An anthropology professor over the age of 50 took a year of leave, and spent the year undercover as a student at her college. She did not take classes in her own department, but instead signed up, attended classes, took exams, and wrote papers just like any other freshmen. She lived in the dorm for part of the year. At the end of a year, she wrote a book entitled *My Freshman Year,*[23] which details her findings. In reporting the research methodology of her study, what methodological strengths and weaknesses should the anthropology professor address?
5. Conduct three or four in-depth interviews with college students who are not business majors. You will be conducting an investigation of the associations that college students make with the word *marketing.* You can ask students to bring five to ten images of any type (pictures, cutouts from magazines) that most essentially picture what they think marketing is all about. You may also conduct a word association exercise with the students. During the interview, you may want to tell informants that you are an alien from another planet and have never heard of marketing. Based on your interviews, develop a diagram that shows the concepts that students relate to marketing. Draw a circle around the most frequently occurring connections in your diagram. What did you learn about how college students view marketing?

SAMPLE QUALITATIVE RESEARCH REPORT

■ Advertising's Second Audience: Employee Reactions to Organizational Communications

Advertising consists of specialized statements that are, first and foremost, attempts by the organization to create situations in which consumers and others will be motivated to engage in actions that are favorable to the organization. Nevertheless, employees are a potentially important "second audience." Advertising can be a tool for communicating with, motivating, and educating employees.

In this study, we examine the effects, both positive and negative, of advertising on organizational employees. We also suggest ways in which advertising managers can include this internal audience in their decision making.

Methodology

A qualitative research design was used because research to date is not sufficiently rich to model the possible effects. Thus, the study was designed not to test specific hypotheses, but instead to uncover all the possible effects of outcomes of organizational advertising on employees. Four companies were recruited from the Marketing Science Institute (MSI) roster of member companies to participate in the research.

We conducted interviews and focus groups with employees, marketing and advertising managers, and human relations managers at four different companies. Two data collection methods were used at each participating company. First, in-depth interviews were conducted with advertising decision makers and advertising agency contacts (n = 19). All individual interviews were audiotaped and transcribed for analysis. The second source of data was focus groups with employees. Four to five focus groups were recruited from a variety of employee categories within the organization. A total of 151 individuals participated in the focus group data collection.

How Do Employees Evaluate Advertising?

We found that employees evaluate not only the accuracy of organizational advertising; they judge its effectiveness and appropriateness as well. Employees want their organization to do well, and they see effective advertising as an important component in this success. Employees view themselves, and are viewed by friends and family, as organizational representatives. As such, they are frequently called upon to "explain" their company's actions, including advertising. Thus, they also want ads to appropriately reflect their values and their image of the company.

Several factors were found to affect the intensity of employee reactions to organizational advertising. The foremost is whether a given employee is in a customer contact position, and thus is more likely to feel the effects of customer comments and requests. But regardless of whether employees are in contact with customers, organizational communication with regard to an advertising campaign—its strategy, goals, purposes—can strongly affect employee reception of that campaign. Importantly, employees who more strongly identified with, and expressed more loyalty to, their organization were more psychically invested in their organization's advertising.

Gaps between Decision Makers and Employees

The study also identified four potential gaps between decision maker and employee perceptions of organizational advertising:

1. Knowledge gap: Decision makers have a greater degree of knowledge about the field of advertising in general and about company strategy in particular; employees have greater knowledge of concrete functions and performances of employees.
2. Employee role gap: Decision makers lack knowledge about how employees view their own roles and their roles as organizational representatives in their personal networks.
3. Priority gap: Decision makers' priorities are to make persuasive, effective ads; employees believe that ads should reflect their vision of the company and their values.
4. Evaluation criteria gap: Decision makers evaluate advertising based on particular goals and objectives; employees evaluate ads by comparing them to past organizational ads and to competitors' ads.

Exhibit 9.11 Advertising Perceptions of Decision Makers and Employees

Gap	Source	Solution
Knowledge gap	Employees don't understand strategy.	Explain company strategy in internal communications.
	Decision makers don't know about the portrayed employee function.	Pretest any ads featuring employees or their function with employees.
	Employees lack knowledge of advertising as a body of knowledge.	Communicate with employees concerning the benefits of the particular approach taken in current advertising.
Employee role gap	Decision makers don't understand employees' self-role.	If employees are featured, match with employee group self-role should be attempted. Don't overlook support personnel.
	Decision makers don't understand that others view employees as company representatives.	"Sell" advertising and new products to employees.
Priority gap	Decision makers need to make effective, creative ads.	Explain how minor inaccuracies were tolerated for impact; employees understand need for impact.
	Employees want ads to reflect their vision of the company and their values.	Research employees' vision and values; communicate that they have been heard.
Evaluation criteria gap	Decision makers evaluate ads relative to achievement of objectives.	Communicate to employees how ads are helping the company meet objectives.
	Employees evaluate ads by comparing them to past ads and competitors' ads.	Knowing how employees "frame" their judgments, position organization's ads within the frame.

Source: From Mary C. Gilly and Mary Wolfinbarger (1996), "Advertising's Second Audience: Employee Reactions to Organizational Communications," Working Paper Series, *Report Summary #96-116*, Marketing Science Institute.

Strategies for closing these gaps include the following:

- Explaining advertising strategies and outcomes to employees in internal communications and premieres (at a minimum, advertising should be premiered with customer contact personnel).
- Pretesting advertisements featuring employees or their functions with the employees themselves.
- Understanding employees' vision and values regarding the organization.
- In communicating with employees, positioning advertising with respect to employees' frame of reference.

The gaps and strategies for closing them are summarized in Exhibit 9.11.

Conclusion

This study strongly indicates that advertising decision makers may underestimate the importance of the employee audience for ads. Given that employees will be influenced by ads, it is important for companies to make every effort to ensure that this influence is positive or, at least, to avoid the possible negative influence of ads. Decision makers must recognize that employees enjoy an "insider" role and want to be informed in advance of marketing communications.

If messages and themes can be identified to have positive effects on employees as well as on customers, such messages may be incorporated into advertising campaigns that contribute to employee commitment to the organization. Employee commitment in turn will increase the quality of the organization's products and services.

Source: Report adapted from Mary C. Gilly and Mary Wolfinbarger, "Advertising's Second Audience: Employee Reactions to Organizational Communications," Working Paper Series, Report Summary #96-116, Marketing Science Institute, 1996.

Preparing Data for Quantitative Analysis

1. Describe the process for data preparation and analysis.
2. Discuss validation, editing, and coding of survey data.
3. Explain data entry procedures and how to detect errors.
4. Describe data tabulation and analysis approaches.

Scanner Data Improves Understanding of Purchase Behavior

When you purchase something in a drugstore, supermarket, or almost any retail store, the item you purchase is scanned into a computer. The bar code enables each store to know exactly what products are selling, when, and at what price. Store managers also can keep accurate control of inventory so they can easily order more products when they run low. Walmart is among the leaders in the use of scanner data. Walmart does not own most of the products on its shelves. Instead, the product manufacturers arrange to put them on Walmart shelves but still own the products. With its scanning system, Walmart always knows what is on their shelves, where in the store it is placed, what products are selling, and which ones need to be reordered. Scanner data has enabled Walmart and other retailers to build and manage larger inventories than would have been possible a few years ago.

Scanner equipment can also be used with bar-coded customer cards so customers can be associated with their purchases and the data stored in a central database. The process takes a second or two per transaction, and requires only that the customers produce the card at purchase time. Scanner technology is widely used in the marketing research industry. Questionnaires can be prepared using word processing software and printed on a laser printer. Respondents can complete the questionnaire with any type of writing instrument. With the appropriate software and scanning device, the researcher can scan the completed questionnaires and the data are checked for errors, categorized, and stored in a matter of seconds. Retailers often collect 400 to 500 completed surveys in a week or so. Thus, scanner technology offers many benefits for data collection at a very reasonable cost.[1]

Value of Preparing Data for Analysis

Data collected using traditional methods (i.e., personal interviews, telephone interviews, CATI, direct mail, and drop-off) must be converted to an electronic format for data analysis. Data from Internet or web-based surveys, handheld PCs, scanner databases, and company data warehouses are already in electronic format, but also require preparation. For example, data may be obtained in Excel format and must be converted to SPSS format. Or data collected using open-ended questions will have to be coded for analysis. Converting information from surveys or other data sources so it can be used in statistical analysis is referred to as *data preparation*.

The data preparation process typically follows a four-step approach, beginning with *data validation*, then *editing* and *coding*, followed by *data entry* and *data tabulation*. Data preparation is essential in converting raw data into usable coded data for data analysis. But data preparation also plays an important role in assessing and controlling *data integrity* and ensuring *data quality* by detecting potential response and nonresponse biases created by interviewer errors and/or respondent errors, as well as possible coding and data entry errors. Data preparation also is important in dealing with inconsistent data from different sources or in converting data in multiple formats to a single format that can be analyzed with statistical software.

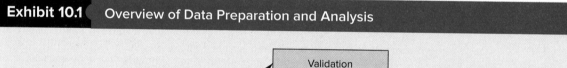

Exhibit 10.1 Overview of Data Preparation and Analysis

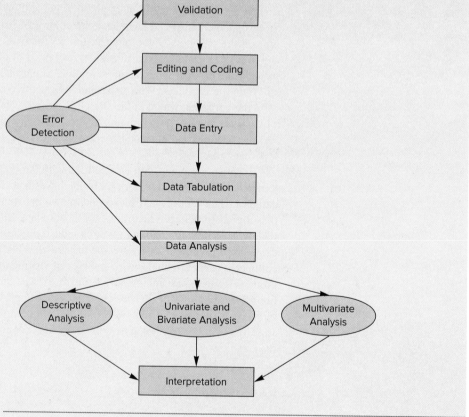

With traditional data collection methods, the data preparation process starts after the interviews, questionnaires, or observation forms have been completed and returned to the field supervisor or researcher. But new technology associated with online surveys and data collection methods involving handheld terminals or scanners enables researchers to complete some data preparation tasks in real time and also eliminate data collection errors. In fact, technology advances are reducing and sometimes eliminating the need to manually code, verify, and enter data when creating electronic files.

The stages of data preparation and analysis are shown in Exhibit 10.1. Some data collection methods require activities in all stages while other methods involve only limited data preparation. For example, online surveys are already in electronic format and do not require data entry, unless some questions are open-ended. This chapter discusses the data preparation process and Chapters 11 and 12 provide an overview of data analysis for quantitative research.

◾ Validation

The purpose of validation is to determine if surveys, interviews, and observations were conducted correctly and free of bias, and if data from other sources is accurate and consistent. Data collection often is not easy to monitor closely. To facilitate accurate data collection in surveys, each respondent's name, address, zip code, phone number, e-mail address, or similar information may be recorded. Similarly, to validate data from other sources, for example, an internal company data warehouse, information must be recorded on when and where the data were obtained, any manipulations that were conducted, and so forth. While information on respondents or sources and nature of internal data may not be used for analysis, it does enable the validation process to be completed.

Data validation The process of determining, to the extent possible, whether a survey's interviews or observations were conducted correctly and are free of fraud or bias.

The initial concern of researchers with surveys is to determine whether questionnaires or observation methods are completed and valid. The purpose of **data validation** is to determine if surveys, interviews, and observations were conducted correctly and free of errors. When data collection involves trained interviewers obtaining data from respondents, the emphasis in validation most often is on interviewer errors, or failure to follow instructions. If data collection involves online surveys, validation often involves checking to see if instructions were correctly followed. For example, if quotas such as 70 percent male respondents, or 80 percent in a specific age range, or only U.S. citizens were specified, then these guidelines must be checked to ensure they were met. Similarly, if observation involves online studies, researchers must verify that specified websites or Internet locations were visited, or whether other execution criteria were followed consistently. Online surveys also should incorporate approaches to verify that the recruited individuals actually completed the survey. As with traditional survey methods, this typically involves requesting specific types of information or including similar questions to assess consistency in responding. Thus, the main goal of validation is to detect, control, and eliminate fraud, misrepresentation, failure to follow predetermined instructions, inconsistent or inaccurate data, and so forth.

Curbstoning Cheating or falsification in the data collection process.

In marketing research, interviewers submitting false data for surveys are referred to as **curbstoning.** As the name implies, *curbstoning* is when interviewers find an out-of-the-way location, such as a curbstone, and fill out the survey themselves rather than follow procedures with an actual respondent. Because of the potential for such falsification, data validation is an important step when the data acquisition process involves interviewers.

To minimize fraudulent responses, marketing researchers target between 10 percent and 30 percent of completed interviews for "callbacks." Specifically for telephone, mail, and personal interviews, a certain percentage of respondents from the completed interviews are recontacted by the research firm to make sure the interview was conducted correctly. Often through telephone recontact, respondents will be asked several short questions as a way of validating the returned interview. Generally, the process of validation covers five areas:

1. *Fraud.* Was the person actually interviewed, or was the interview falsified? Did the interviewer contact the respondent simply to get a name and address, and then proceed to fabricate responses? Did the interviewer use a friend to obtain the necessary information?

2. *Screening.* Data collection often must be conducted only with qualified respondents. To ensure accuracy of the data collected, respondents are screened according to some preselected criteria, such as household income level, recent purchase of a specific product or brand, brand or service awareness, gender, or age. For example, the data collection instructions may specify that only female heads of households with an annual household income of $25,000 or more, who are familiar with and have recently visited a Mexican-themed restaurant, be interviewed. In this case, a validation callback could verify each of these factors if an interviewer was involved.

    When online data collection is used, screening control methods must be included in the design, and this is often difficult to do. For example, online surveys may specify screening criteria but it is up to the respondent to provide accurate information. How can you prevent a child from completing a survey targeted for their parents if all they have to do is provide information that meets the requested profile? Follow-up e-mails are possible but not as effective as follow-up phone calls. One approach is to include multiple similar questions so the consistency of responses can be assessed.

3. *Procedure.* In many marketing research projects, data must be collected according to a specific procedure. For example, customer exit interviews typically must occur in a designated place as the respondent leaves a certain retail establishment. In this particular example, a validation callback may be necessary to ensure that the interview took place at the proper setting, not some social gathering area like a party or a park. For online surveys, procedure checking involves verifying that screening instructions, skip patterns, recruitment, quotas, and so forth were adhered to in data collection.

4. *Completeness.* In order to speed through the data collection process, an interviewer may ask the respondent only a few of the questions. In such cases, the interviewer asks the respondent a few questions from the beginning of the questionnaire and then skips to the end, omitting questions from other sections. The interviewer may then make up answers to the remaining questions. To determine if the interview is valid, the researcher could recontact a sample of respondents and ask about questions from different parts of the questionnaire. This is not a problem with online surveys that have controls to prevent respondents from skipping questions. But these controls likely cause some respondents to stop completing the survey before finishing, particularly if the questions are unclear, difficult, or uninteresting.

    Another problem could arise if the data collection process incorporates "skip" questions to direct interviewers (or respondents) to different parts of the questionnaire. If the interviewer (or respondent on a self-administered survey) fails to follow instructions for those skip questions, the respondent is asked the wrong questions. With some data collection approaches the research supervisor can recontact respondents and verify their response to skip questions. Skip questions are not a problem with online surveys since the computer controls the sequence of answering questions. But researchers should go online before a survey begins and complete the questionnaire themselves to ensure skip patterns are executed like they are supposed to be.

5. *Courtesy*. Respondents should be treated with courtesy and respect during the interviewing process. Situations can occur, however, where the interviewer may inject a tone of negativity into the interviewing process. To ensure a positive image, respondent callbacks are common to determine whether the interviewer was courteous. Other aspects of the interviewer that are checked during callbacks include appearance, communication and interpersonal skills.

◼◖ Editing and Coding

Editing The process where the raw data are checked for mistakes made by either the interviewer or the respondent.

Following validation, the data must be edited for mistakes. **Editing** is the process of checking the data for mistakes made by the interviewer, the respondent, or in the process of transferring information from scanner databases or other sources to the company data warehouse. By reviewing completed interviews from primary research, the researcher can check several areas of concern: (1) asking the proper questions, (2) accurate recording of answers, (3) correct screening of respondents, and (4) complete and accurate recording of open-ended questions. All of the above steps are necessary for traditional data collection methods. Online surveys must verify respondent screening (at minimum to ensure that specified instructions were adhered to in programming the survey) and open-ended questions must be checked and coded if they are used. When information is obtained from internal data warehouses, it must be checked for availability, consistency, correct format, and so on.

Asking the Proper Questions

One aspect of the editing process especially important to interviewing methods is to make certain the proper questions were asked of the respondent. As part of the editing process, the researcher will check to make sure all respondents were asked the proper questions. In cases where they were not, respondents are recontacted to obtain a response to omitted questions. This task is not necessary with online surveys if they were designed and set up correctly.

Accurate Recording of Answers

Completed questionnaires sometimes have missing information. The interviewer may have accidentally skipped a question or not recorded it in the proper location. With a careful check of all questionnaires, these problems can be identified. In such cases, if it is possible, respondents are recontacted and the omitted responses recorded. This task is not necessary with online surveys if they were designed to prevent respondents from skipping questions.

Sometimes a respondent will accidentally not complete one or more questions for various reasons (carelessness, in a hurry to complete the survey, not understanding how to answer the question, etc.), resulting an incomplete response. For example, the questionnaire has a two-part question where answering the second part is based on the respondent's answer to the first part, and the respondent may answer only one part of the question. In this example, the following two-part question creates the need for the in-house editing supervisor to adjust or correct the respondent's answer for completeness.

Does your family use more than one brand of toothpaste?
[ ] Yes   [ ] No
If yes, how many brands?   _3_

If the respondent initially did not check either "yes" nor "no," but indicated "3" brands, the supervisor should check "yes" to the first part of the question, unless there is other information to indicate that would be wrong to assume. This situation should not arise with online questionnaires because the software is designed to prevent it.

Correct Screening Questions

Recall from the continuing case description in Chapter 1 that a survey of Santa Fe Grill employees also was completed. The first two questions on the Santa Fe Grill employee questionnaire shown in Exhibit 10.2 are actually screening questions that determine whether the respondent is eligible to complete the survey. During the editing phase, the researcher makes certain only qualified respondents were included in a survey. It is also critical in the editing process to establish that the questions were asked and (for self-administered surveys) answered in the proper sequence. If the proper sequence is not followed in self-completion surveys, the respondent must be recontacted to verify the accuracy of the recorded data.

Exhibit 10.2	**The Santa Fe Grill Employee Questionnaire**

This is a survey to be completed by employees of the Santa Fe Grill.

- Are you currently an employee of the Santa Fe Grill? Yes _____ (continue) No _____ (terminate)

- How long have you been an employee of the Santa Fe Grill?

  0 = Three months or less (terminate)
  1 = More than three months but less than one year
  2 = One year to three years
  3 = More than three years

If respondents answer "yes" to the first question, and indicate that they have worked at the Santa Fe Grill for more than three months then they are permitted to continue answering the questions on the survey.

The Santa Fe Grill would like to better understand how its employees feel about the work environment so improvements can be made as needed. Please log on to this URL http://santafe.qualtrics.com?SE/?SID=SV_10QkhmnGMiTCJ5C to complete the survey.

The survey will take only about 10 minutes to complete, and it will be very helpful to management in ensuring the work environment meets both employee and company needs. There are no right or wrong answers. We are simply interested in your opinions, whatever they may be. All of your answers will be kept strictly confidential.

WORK ENVIRONMENT SURVEY

Section 1: How You Feel About Your Work Environment

The statements lead in below may or may not describe your work environment at the Santa Fe Grill. Using a scale from 1 to 7, with 7 being "Strongly Agree" and 1 being "Strongly Disagree," to what extent do you agree or disagree that each statement describes your work environment at the Santa Fe Grill:

1. My job teaches me valuable new skills.

Strongly Disagree						Strongly Agree
1	2	3	4	5	6	7

2. I enjoy my work at the Santa Fe Grill.

Strongly Disagree						Strongly Agree
1	2	3	4	5	6	7

Exhibit 10.2   *continued*

3. Supervisors at Santa Fe Grill give praise and recognition for doing good work.

Strongly Disagree ... Strongly Agree

1   2   3   4   5   6   7

4. My team at the Santa Fe Grill has the training and skills needed to do a good job meeting customers' needs.

Strongly Disagree ... Strongly Agree

1   2   3   4   5   6   7

5. I am paid fairly at the Santa Fe Grill compared to other jobs.

Strongly Disagree ... Strongly Agree

1   2   3   4   5   6   7

6. Supervisors at the Santa Fe Grill recognize each worker's potential.

Strongly Disagree ... Strongly Agree

1   2   3   4   5   6   7

7. In general I like working at the Santa Fe Grill.

Strongly Disagree ... Strongly Agree

1   2   3   4   5   6   7

8. My pay is reasonable for the effort I put into my work.

Strongly Disagree ... Strongly Agree

1   2   3   4   5   6   7

9. My work team functions well together.

Strongly Disagree ... Strongly Agree

1   2   3   4   5   6   7

10. Supervisors at the Santa Fe Grill are knowledgeable and helpful.

Strongly Disagree ... Strongly Agree

1   2   3   4   5   6   7

11. My team members cooperate to get the work done right.

Strongly Disagree ... Strongly Agree

1   2   3   4   5   6   7

12. My overall level of pay is reasonable.

Strongly Disagree ... Strongly Agree

1   2   3   4   5   6   7

Section 2: Your Feelings About Working at the Santa Fe Grill

Please answer using the scale provided.

13. For me, the Santa Fe Grill is the best possible of all organizations to work for.

Strongly Disagree ... Strongly Agree

1   2   3   4   5   6   7

continued

Exhibit 10.2	The Santa Fe Grill Questionnaire, *continued*

14. I feel a strong sense of "belonging" to the Santa Fe Grill.

Strongly Disagree   Strongly Agree

     1   2   3   4   5   6   7

15. I tell my friends the Santa Fe Grill is a great place to work.

Strongly Disagree   Strongly Agree

     1   2   3   4   5   6   7

16. I feel like "part of the family" at the Santa Fe Grill.

Strongly Disagree   Strongly Agree

     -1   2   3   4   5   6   7

17. Select a number between 0 and 100 that represents how likely you are to look for another job in the next year.

0 = Not At All Likely   100 = Very Likely

18. Select a number between 0 and 100 that represents how often you think about quitting your job at the Santa Fe Grill.

0 = Not Very Often   100 = All the Time

Section 3: Classification Questions

Please indicate the number that classifies you best.

19. Are you a part-time or full-time worker? 0 = Full Time
                                                      1 = Part Time

20. What is your gender?
                                               0 = Male
                                               1 = Female

21. What is your age in years? _____

22. How long have you been an employee of the Santa Fe Grill?

Note: Data from the screening question for employees working at the restaurant more than three months was recorded here.   1 = More than three months but less than one year
                                                     2 = One year to three years
                                                     3 = More than three years

Thank you very much for your help.

_____

Note: Santa Fe Grill management evaluated the performance of all employees. These scores were added to the employee survey data file.

23. Performance: Employees were rated on a 100-point scale with 0 = very low performer and 100 = very high performer.

Increasingly surveys are completed online. When online surveys are used, respondents are automatically asked the screening questions and are not allowed to continue if the questions are not correctly answered.

Responses to Open-Ended Questions

Responses to open-ended questions often provide very meaningful data. Open-ended questions may provide greater insight into the research questions than forced-choice questions. A major part of editing the answers to open-ended questions is interpretation. Exhibit 10.3 shows some typical responses to an open-ended question and thus points to problems associated with interpreting these questions. For example, one response to the question "Why are you coming to the Santa Fe Grill more often?" is simply "They have good service." This answer by itself is not sufficient to determine what the respondent means by "good service." The interviewer needed to probe for a more specific response. For example, are the employees friendly, helpful, courteous? Do they appear neat and clean? Do they smile when taking an order? Probes such as these would enable the researcher to better interpret the "good service" answer. In cases such as these, the individual doing the editing must use judgment in classifying responses. At some point the responses must be placed in standard categories. Answers that are incomplete are considered useless.

Coding is necessary in online surveys if they have open-ended questions. As with traditional data collection methods, the responses must be reviewed, themes and common words and patterns must be identified, and then codes must be assigned to facilitate quantitative data analysis. See the next section and Chapter 9 for additional comments on coding qualitative data.

Exhibit 10.3	**Responses to Open-Ended Questions**

Why are you eating at the Santa Fe Grill more often?

- They have good service.
- Found out how good the food is.
- I enjoy the food.
- We just moved here and where we lived there were no good Mexican restaurants.
- That part of town is building up so fast.
- They have a couple of offers in the newspaper.
- It is right beside where my husband works.
- Tastes better—grilled.
- They started giving better value packages.
- We really like their chicken sandwiches, so we go more often now.
- The good food.
- Only because they only put one in within the last year.
- Just opened lately.
- It is located right by Walmart.
- Just moved into this area and they have good food.
- There is one in the area where I work.

The Coding Process

Coding Grouping and assigning values to various responses from the survey instrument.

Coding involves grouping and assigning values to responses to the survey questions. It is the assignment of numerical values to each individual response for each question on the survey. Typically, the codes are numerical—a number from 0 to 9—because numbers are quick and easy to input, and computers work better with numbers than alphanumerical values. Like editing, coding can be tedious if certain issues are not addressed prior to collecting the data. A well-planned and constructed questionnaire can reduce the amount of time spent on coding and increase the accuracy of the process if it is incorporated into the design of the questionnaire. The restaurant questionnaire shown in Exhibit 10.2 has built-in coded responses for all questions except the open-ended ones asked by the interviewer at the end of the survey. In the "Lifestyle Questions," for example, a respondent has the option of responding from 1 to 7, based on his or her level of agreement or disagreement with a particular statement. Thus, if the respondent circled "5" as his or her choice, then the value of 5 would become the coded value for a particular question.

In contrast, open-ended questions pose unique problems to the coding process. An exact list of potential responses cannot be prepared ahead of time for open-ended questions. Thus, a coding process must be prepared after data is collected. But the value of the information obtained from open-ended questions often outweighs the problems of coding the responses.

In conducting quantitative research, the format for a question/scale sometimes needs to allow the respondent to provide more than one response using a structured closed-end question. The uniqueness of a multiple response question is that the researcher uses a specific type of instruction (e.g., check as many topics as apply) to communicate clearly to the respondent the appropriateness of selecting more than one listed response. To illustrate coding for this type of structured question format, refer back to the Pizza Hut example for a self-administered survey in Exhibit 8.2. With an online survey, the researcher asks respondents the question "Among the pizza toppings listed below, what toppings, if any, do you usually add to a pizza other than cheese when ordering a pizza for yourself from Pizza Hut? (Check as many boxes as apply)," followed by a list of 14 different topping choices, such as vegetables and types of meats, as well as a write-in option for "some other topping _____." From a coding perspective, a researcher can use either a multiple-dichotomy or a multiple-response coding method. With the multiple dichotomy method, each prelisted topping is treated as a separate variable to which respondents provide a YES answer by checking the corresponding box (or an implied NO answer by leaving the corresponding box unchecked). The researcher would then assign a specific numerical code (e.g., 1) for each topping's checked box and another specific numerical code (e.g., 0) for each topping left blank.

When the questionnaire involves a structured open-ended question as part of a survey, the coding task for multiple responses becomes more time consuming. In these situations, a multiple-response method similar to coding the responses for a content analysis is used. The objective of the coding process is to reduce the large number of individual responses to a smaller set of general, yet mutually exclusive categories of answers that can be assigned numerical codes. Therefore, instead of creating a separate variable for each answer, a smaller set of more general categorical type variables is created so that it includes all of the responses in some combination. A multistep process is followed in which the first step is to identify a portion of the initial written answers that have something in common. The questions with a common theme are then combined to form mutually exclusive general categorical variables. This process can be carried out by the researcher, other experts, or trained coders. Finally, specific numerical codes are assigned to each of the new general categorical variables.

Although a categorization coding scheme should be tailored to meet the specific needs of the study, there is a general rule of thumb to keep in mind: if the categorical data is coded in a way that retains the detail of the initial responses, those codes can always be further combined into broader categories. If the respondents' actual answers are initially coded into broad categories, however, the researcher can never analyze them in more detail. If multiple coders or experts are used to code the responses, cross-researcher reliability (referred to as intercoder reliability) can be calculated. To facilitate this type of coding process, several software programs are available (e.g., the Ethnograph, HyperQual, QUALOG, and Atlas.ti).

Researchers typically use a four-step process to develop codes for responses. The procedure is similar for all types of data collection and begins by generating a list of as many potential responses as possible. Responses are then assigned values within a range determined by the actual number of separate responses identified. When reviewing responses to the open-ended questions, the researcher attaches a value from the developed response list. If responses do not appear on the list, the researcher adds a new response and corresponding value to the list or places the response into one of the existing categories.

Consolidation of responses is the second phase of the four-step process. Exhibit 10.4 illustrates several actual responses to the question "Why are you dining less frequently at the _____ restaurant?" Four of these—related to not liking the food—can be consolidated into a single response category because they all have the same shared meaning. Developing consolidated categories is a subjective decision that should be made only by an experienced research analyst with input from the project's sponsor.

The third step of the process is to assign a numerical value as a code. While at first this may appear to be a simple task, the structure of the questionnaire and the number of

Exhibit 10.4	**Illustration of Response Consolidation for Open-Ended Questions**

Why are you dining less frequently at the _____ restaurant?

Respondent # 2113
- I am a state employee. I look for bargains. Need more specials.
- Family doesn't like it.
- My husband didn't like the way the burgers tasted.

Respondent # 2114
- I do not like the food.
- The order is never right.
- Health reasons.

Respondent # 2115
- They never get my order right.
- I got tired of the hamburgers. I don't like the spices.
- Prices are too high.
- They should give more with their combos than they do. More fries.
- Because they always got our orders wrong and they are rude.
- I work longer hours, and don't think about food.

Respondent # 2116
- Cannot eat the food.
- We started eating at _____.
- The location of my work moved so I am not near a _____.

responses per question need to be considered. For example, if a question has more than ten responses, then double-digit codes need to be used, such as 01, 02, . . . 11. Another good practice is to assign higher value codes to positive responses than to negative responses. For instance, "no" responses are coded 0 and "yes" responses coded 1; "dislike" responses are coded as 1 and "like" responses coded as 5. Coding makes subsequent analysis easier. For example, the researcher will find it easier to interpret means or averages if higher values occur as the average moves from "dislike" to "like."

If correlation or regression is used in data analysis, then for categorical data there is another consideration. The researcher may wish to create "dummy" variables in which the coding is "0" and "1." To learn more about dummy coding, go to our website at **connect.mheducation.com**.

Assigning a coded value to missing data is very important. For example, if a respondent completes a questionnaire except for the very last question and a recontact is not possible, how do you code the response to the unanswered question? A good practice in this situation is to first consider how the response is going to be used in the analysis phase. In certain types of analysis, if the response is left blank and has no numerical value, the entire questionnaire (not just the individual question) will be deleted. The best way to handle the coding of omitted responses is first to check on how your data analysis software treats missing data. This should be the guide for determining whether omissions are coded or left blank. We discuss missing data more in a later section.

The fourth step in the coding process is to assign a coded value to each response. This is probably the most tedious process because it is done manually. Unless an optical scanning approach is used to enter the data, this task is almost always necessary to avoid problems in the data entry phase.

 MARKETING RESEARCH DASHBOARD   DEALING WITH DATA FROM DATA WAREHOUSES

Researchers increasingly must analyze and make recommendations on data from data warehouses. This trend has both advantages and disadvantages. The advantages are related mostly to the fact that data from data warehouses are secondary data and therefore are quicker and easier to obtain, as well as less expensive. But there are numerous disadvantages that must be dealt with before the data can be analyzed and used. Below is a list of typical problems managers face in using data from data warehouses.

- Outdated data, for example, too old to be relevant.
- Incomplete data, for example, data available from one time period but not another.
- Data that supposedly are available but cannot be found. In large companies this is often due to having several data warehouses in different locations maintained by different divisions of the company.
- Supposedly same data from various internal sources are different, for example, information on sales by territory is different from two different sources such as internal sales records versus scanner data, which generally does not represent all distribution outlets.

Managers must decide which source to rely on in a particular situation, or how to combine the data from two sources.

- Data that are in an unusable or incompatible format, or cannot be understood.
- Disorganized data not in a central location.
- Software to access data is not working at all, or not working as it should.
- Too much data.

How are the above problems resolved? Sometimes they cannot be resolved, at least in a timely manner, that is, in time to be used to make decisions. The best approach to avoid or minimize these problems is to establish a good working relationship between the marketing and information technology departments. This means marketing managers must start early to communicate their expectations of what data are needed, how often, in what format, and so on. Then on an ongoing basis they must continue to work closely together to anticipate and deal with data management and utilization issues as they arise.

Each questionnaire is assigned a numerical value. The numerical value typically is a three-digit code if there are fewer than 1,000 questionnaires to code, and a four-digit code if there are 1,000 or more. For example, if 452 completed questionnaires were returned, the first would be coded 001, the second 002, and so on, finishing with 452.

◖ Data Entry

Data entry Those tasks involved with the direct input of the coded data into some specified software package that ultimately allows the research analyst to manipulate and transform the raw data into useful information.

Data entry follows validation, editing, and coding. **Data entry** is the procedure used to enter the data into a computer file for subsequent data analysis. Data entry is the direct input of the coded data into a file that enables the research analyst to manipulate and transform the data into useful information. This step is not necessary when online data collection is used.

There are several ways of entering coded data into an electronic file. With CATI and Internet surveys, the data are entered simultaneously with data collection and a separate step is not required. However, other types of data collection require the data to be entered manually, which typically is done using a personal computer.

Scanning technology also can be used to enter data. This approach enables the computer to read alphabetic, numeric, and special character codes through a scanning device. Respondents use a number two pencil to fill in responses, which are then scanned directly into a computer file.

Online surveys are becoming increasingly popular for completing marketing research studies. Indeed, online surveys now represent almost 60 percent of all data collection approaches. They not only are often faster to complete but also eliminate entirely the data entry process.

Error Detection

Error detection identifies errors from data entry or other sources. The first step in error detection is to determine whether the software used for data entry and tabulation performs "error edit routines" that identify the wrong type of data. For example, say that for a particular field on a given data record, only the codes of 1 or 2 should appear. An error edit routine can display an error message on the data output if any number other than 1 or 2 has been entered. Such routines can be quite thorough. A coded value can be rejected if it is too large or too small for a particular scaled item on the questionnaire. In some instances, a separate error edit routine can be established for every item on the questionnaire. With online surveys, controls are built in ahead of time to prevent respondents from keying in incorrect responses.

Another approach to error detection is for the researcher to review a printed representation of the entered data. Exhibit 10.5, for example, shows the coded values for observations 377 to 405 in the restaurant database. In this example, the top row indicates the variable names assigned to each data field (i.e., "id" is the label for the questionnaire number, "X_s1" represents the first screening question, X_1 is the first question on the survey after the four screening questions, etc.). The numbers in the columns are the coded values that were entered. While the process is somewhat tedious, the analyst can view the actual entered data for accuracy and can tell where any errors occurred. Another approach is to run a tabulation (frequency count) of all survey questions so responses can be examined for completeness and accuracy.

Missing Data

Missing data are often a problem in data analysis. Missing data are defined as a situation in which respondents do not provide an answer to a question. Sometimes respondents

Exhibit 10.5   SPSS Data View of Coded Values for Santa Fe Grill Customer Observations

	id	x_s1	x_s2	x_s3	X_s4	x1	x2	x3	x4	x5	x6
385	385	1	1	1	0	7	5	4	4	5	4
386	386	1	1	1	0	7	6	7	4	3	7
387	387	1	1	1	1	7	4	7	3	2	6
388	388	1	1	1	1	3	4	6	3	4	6
389	389	1	1	1	0	7	7	6	2	7	6
390	390	1	1	1	0	7	5	5	2	5	5
391	391	1	1	1	1	7	3	4	6	5	4
392	392	1	1	1	0	7	6	5	3	5	5
393	393	1	1	1	0	7	5	6	2	5	5
394	394	1	1	1	1	7	4	7	5	4	6
395	395	1	1	1	1	7	4	6	6	4	5
396	396	1	1	1	1	3	4	4	5	4	4
397	397	1	1	1	0	7	5	6	2	6	6
398	398	1	1	1	1	7	3	4	6	5	4
399	399	1	1	1	1	3	3	3	5	3	3
400	400	1	1	1	0	7	5	5	4	6	5
401	401	1	1	1	1	3	4	6	3	4	6
402	402	1	1	1	1	7	4	7	3	2	6
403	403	1	1	1	1	3	4	7	3	4	7
404	404	1	1	1	1	4	4	3	5	4	3
405	405	1	1	1	1	4	3	3	6	3	3
406											
407											

*Customer Database_Santa Fe Grill_Essn 3e_N=405_11-20-2011.sav [DataSet2] - IBM SPSS Statistics Data Editor

File Edit View Data Transform Analyze Graphs Utilities Add-ons Window Help

Visible: 40 of 40 Variables

Data View   Variable View

IBM SPSS Statistics Processor is ready

2:01 PM
12/17/2011

purposely do not answer a question creating a missing data situation. This most often arises when questions of a sensitive nature are asked, such as asking for a respondent's age or income. It also may occur because a respondent simply does not see a question, or is in a hurry to complete the survey and simply skips a question. Missing data are most often a problem with self-completion surveys. With online surveys respondents can be required to answer all questions, but this may cause some respondents to simply stop answering questions and terminate the survey. In general, with online surveys it is recommended to require answers on all questions since the problem of respondents quitting a survey is not as substantial as is the problem of missing data.

If missing data are encountered, there are several ways to deal with it. One approach is to replace the missing value with a value from a similar respondent. For example, if the demographics of the respondent are male, aged 35 to 49, with some college education, then the appropriate approach is to find one or more other respondents with similar characteristics and use their responses as a guide to determine a replacement value for the missing data. Another approach, if there are other similar questions to the one with missing data, is to use the answers to the other similar questions as a guide in determining the replacement value. A third approach is to use the mean of a subsample of the respondents with similar characteristics that answered the question to determine a replacement value. A final alternative is to use the mean of the entire sample that answered the question as a replacement value, but this is not recommended because it reduces the overall variance in the question.

Organizing Data

Several useful data organizing functions are available in SPSS. One function under the Data pull-down menu is Sort Cases. This can be used to sort your data cases (observations) in either ascending or descending order. Another is the Split File function, which can be used, for example, to split the Santa Fe Grill and Jose's Southwestern Café customer respondents into two groups so they can be compared. A third useful function is the Select Cases option, which can be used to select only males, or only customers over age 35, and so on. This option can also be used to select a random subsample of your total sample. The specific steps to execute these and other functions are explained in the SPSS instructions available from the book's website.

■ Data Tabulation

Tabulation The simple process of counting the number of observations (cases) that are classified into certain categories.

One-way tabulation Categorization of single variables existing in a study.

Cross-tabulation Simultaneously treating two or more variables in the study; categorizing the number of respondents who have answered two or more questions consecutively.

Tabulation, sometimes referred to as a frequency count, is counting the number of responses in categories. Two common forms of tabulation are used in marketing research projects: one-way tabulation and cross-tabulations. A **one-way tabulation** shows responses for a single variable. In most cases, a one-way tabulation shows the number of respondents (frequency count) who gave each possible answer to each question on the questionnaire. The number of one-way tabulations is determined by the number of variables measured in the study.

Cross-tabulation simultaneously compares two or more variables in the study. Cross-tabulations categorize the number of responses to two or more questions, thus showing the relationship between those two variables. For example, a cross-tabulation could show the number of male and female respondents who spent more than $7.00 eating at McDonald's versus those who spent less. Cross-tabulation is most often used with nominal or ordinal scaled data.

One-way and cross-tabulation are considered descriptive statistics. The overview of these two types of tabulations in this chapter provides a foundation for other types of descriptive statistics discussed in the next chapter. We show you how to use software to develop all types of descriptive statistics in the next chapter.

One-Way Tabulation

One-way tabulations serve several purposes. First, they can be used to determine the amount of nonresponse to individual questions. Based on the coding scheme used for missing data, one-way tabulations identify the number of respondents who did not answer various questions on the questionnaire. Second, one-way tabulations can be used to locate mistakes in data entry.

If a specific range of codes has been established for a given response to a question, say 1 through 5, a one-way tabulation can illustrate if an inaccurate code was entered, say, a 7 or 8. It does this by providing a list of all responses to the particular question. In addition, means, standard deviations, and related descriptive statistics often are determined from a one-way tabulation. Finally, one-way tabulations are also used to communicate the results of the research project. One-way tabulations can profile sample respondents, identify characteristics that distinguish between groups (e.g., heavy users vs. light users), and show the percentage of respondents who respond differently to different situations. For instance, a one-way tabulation might show the percentage of people who purchase fast food from drive-through windows versus those who use dine-in facilities.

The most basic way to illustrate a one-way tabulation is to construct a one-way frequency table. A one-way frequency table shows the number of respondents who answered each possible response to a question given the available alternatives. An example of a one-way frequency table is shown in Exhibit 10.6, which shows which Mexican restaurants the respondents dined at in the last 30 days. The information indicates that 99 individuals (20.1 percent) ate at Superior Grill in the last 30 days, 74 (15.0 percent) ate at Mamacita's, 110 (22.3 percent) ate at Ninfa's, and so on. Typically, a computer printout will be prepared with one-way frequency tables for each question on the survey. In addition to listing the number of responses, one-way frequency tables also identify missing data and show valid percentages and summary statistics. In reviewing the output, look for the following:

1. *Indications of missing data.* One-way frequency tables show the number of missing responses for each question. As shown in Exhibit 10.7, a total of 13 respondents,

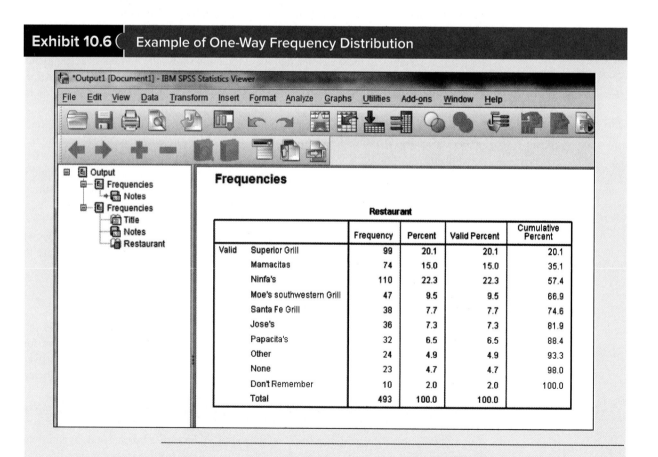

Exhibit 10.6 **Example of One-Way Frequency Distribution**

Frequencies

Restaurant

		Frequency	Percent	Valid Percent	Cumulative Percent
Valid	Superior Grill	99	20.1	20.1	20.1
	Mamacitas	74	15.0	15.0	35.1
	Ninfa's	110	22.3	22.3	57.4
	Moe's southwestern Grill	47	9.5	9.5	66.9
	Santa Fe Grill	38	7.7	7.7	74.6
	Jose's	36	7.3	7.3	81.9
	Papacita's	32	6.5	6.5	88.4
	Other	24	4.9	4.9	93.3
	None	23	4.7	4.7	98.0
	Don't Remember	10	2.0	2.0	100.0
	Total	493	100.0	100.0	

or 3 percent of the sample, did not respond to how frequently they patronized the two restaurants. It is important to recognize the actual number of missing responses when estimating percentages from a one-way frequency table. In order to establish valid percentages, missing responses must be removed from the calculation.

2. *Determining valid percentages.* To determine valid percentages one must remove incomplete surveys or particular questions. For example, the one-way frequency table in Exhibit 10.7 actually constructs valid percentages (the third column). While the total number of responses for this particular question was 427, only 414 are used to develop the valid percentage of response across categories because the 13 missing responses were removed from the calculations.

3. *Summary statistics.* Finally, one-way frequency tables illustrate a variety of summary statistics. In Exhibit 10.7 the summary statistics for question X_{25} are the

Exhibit 10.7   One-Way Frequency Table Illustrating Missing Data

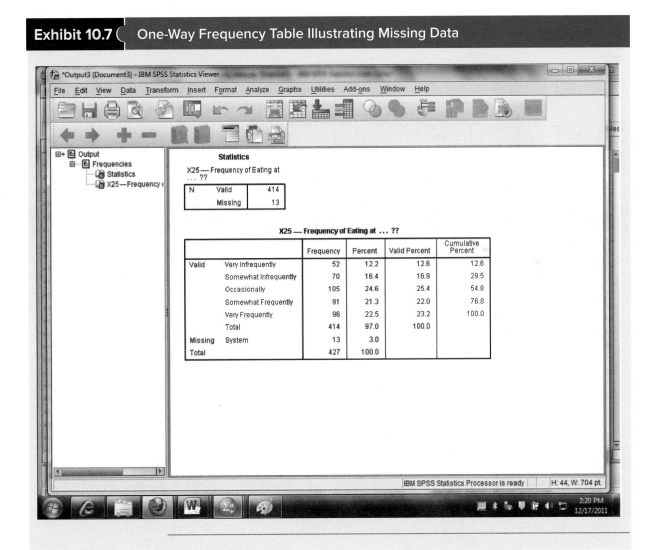

mean, median, mode, and standard deviation. These statistics help the researcher better understand the average responses. For example, the mean of 3.26 indicates that many respondents are occasional patrons of the two restaurants. Note that variable X_{25} ranges from one to five, with larger numbers indicating higher dining frequency.

Descriptive Statistics

Descriptive statistics are used to summarize and describe the data obtained from a sample of respondents. Two types of measures are often used to describe data. One of those is measures of central tendency and the other is measures of dispersion. Both are described in detail in the next chapter. Understanding the six basic descriptive statistics (e.g., mean, median, mode, frequency distribution, range, and standard deviation) is essential to properly applying data editing and coding, error detection (data cleaning), handling missing data, and tabulation. For now we refer you to Exhibit 10.8, which provides an overview of the major types of descriptive statistics used by marketing researchers.

Graphical Illustration of Data

The next logical step following development of frequency tables is to translate them into graphical illustrations. Graphical illustrations can be very powerful for communicating key research results generated from preliminary data analysis. We discuss graphical illustration of data using bar charts, pie charts, and similar techniques in Chapter 13.

Exhibit 10.8   Overview of Descriptive Statistics

To clarify descriptive statistics, we use a simple data set to illustrate each of the major ones. Assume that data have been collected from ten students about satisfaction with their Apple iPOD. Satisfaction is measured on a 7-point scale with the end points labeled "Highly Satisfied = 7" and "Not Satisfied at All = 1". The results of this survey are shown below by respondent.

Respondent	Satisfaction Rating
1	7
2	5
3	6
4	4
5	6
6	5
7	7
8	5
9	4
10	5

Exhibit 10.8 *continued*

Descriptive Statistics

Frequency = the number of times a number (response) is in the data set.

To compute it, count how many times the number is in the data set. For example, the number 7 is in the data set twice.

Frequency distribution = a summary of how many times each possible response to a question appears in the data set.

To develop a frequency distribution, count how many times each number appears in the data set and make a table that shows the results. For example, create a chart like the one shown below:

Satisfaction Rating	Count
7	2
6	2
5	4
4	2
3	0
2	0
1	0
Total	10

Percentage distribution = the result of converting a frequency distribution into percentages.

To develop a percentage distribution, divide each frequency count for each rating by the total count.

Satisfaction Rating	Count	Percentage
7	2	20
6	2	20
5	4	40
4	2	20
3	0	0
2	0	0
1	0	0
Total	10	100%

Cumulative percentage distribution = each individual percentage added to the previous to get a total.

To develop a cumulative percentage distribution, arrange the percentages in descending order and sum the percentages one at a time and show the result.

Satisfaction Rating	Count	Percentage	Cumulative Percentage	
7	2	20	20	
6	2	20	40	
5	4	40	80	← median
4	2	20	100%	
3	0	0		
2	0	0		
1	0	0		
Total	10	100%		

continued

Exhibit 10.8	Overview of Descriptive Statistics, *continued*

Mean = the arithmetic average of all the raw responses.

To calculate the mean, add up all the values of a distribution of responses and divide the total by the number of valid responses.

The mean is: $(7 + 5 + 6 + 4 + 6 + 5 + 7 + 5 + 4 + 5) = 54/10 = 5.4$

Median = the descriptive statistic that splits the data into a hierarchical pattern where half the data are above the median value and half are below.

To determine the median, look at the cumulative percentage distribution and find either where the cumulative percentage is equal to 50 percent or where it includes 50 percent. The median is marked in the table above.

Mode = the most frequently occurring response to a given set of questions.

To determine the mode, find the number which has the largest frequency (count). In the responses above, the number 5 has the largest count and is the mode.

Range = a statistic that represents the spread of the data and is the distance between the largest and the smallest values of a frequency distribution.

To calculate the range, subtract the lowest rating point from the highest rating point and the difference is the range. For the above data, the maximum number is 7 and the minimum number is 4 so the range is $7 - 4 = 3$.

Standard deviation = the measure of the average dispersion of the values in a set of responses about their mean. It provides an indication of how similar or dissimilar the numbers are in the set of responses.

To calculate the standard deviation, subtract the mean from the square of each number and sum them. Then divide that sum by the total number of responses minus one, and then take the square root of the result.

MARKETING RESEARCH IN ACTION
Deli Depot

In this chapter, we have shown you simple approaches to examine data. In later chapters, we show you more advanced statistical techniques to analyze data. The most important consideration in deciding how to analyze data is to enable businesses to use data to make better decisions. To help students more easily understand the best ways to examine data, we have prepared several databases that can be applied to various research problems. This case is about Deli Depot, a sandwich restaurant. The database is available at **connect .mheducation.com**.

Deli Depot sells cold and hot sandwiches, soup and chili, yogurt, and pies and cookies. The restaurant is positioned in the fast-food market to compete directly with Subway and similar sandwich restaurants. Its competitive advantages include special sauces on sandwiches, supplementary menu items like soup and pies, and quick delivery within specified zones. As part of their marketing research class, students conducted a survey for the owner of a local restaurant near their campus.

The students obtained permission to conduct interviews with customers inside the restaurant. Information was collected for 17 questions. Customers were first asked their perceptions of the restaurant on six factors (variables X_1–X_6) and then asked to rank the same six factors in terms of their importance in selecting a restaurant where they wanted to eat (variables X_{12}–X_{17}). Finally, respondents were asked how satisfied they were with the restaurant, how likely they were to recommend it to a friend, how often they eat there, and how far they drove to eat a meal at Deli Depot. Interviewers recorded the sex of the respondents without asking it. The variables, sample questions, and their coding are shown below.

Performance Perceptions Variables

The performance perceptions were measured as follows.

Listed below is a set of characteristics that could be used to describe Deli Depot. Using a scale from 1 to 10, with 10 being "Strongly Agree" and 1 being "Strongly Disagree," to what extent do you agree or disagree that Deli Depot has:

X_1–Friendly Employees
X_2–Competitive Prices
X_3–Competent Employees
X_4–Excellent Food Quality
X_5–Wide Variety of Food
X_6–Fast Service

If a respondent chose a 10 on the Friendly Employees category, this would indicate strong agreement that Deli Depot has friendly employees. On the other hand, if a respondent chose a 1 for Fast Service, this would indicate strong disagreement and the perception that Deli Depot offers relatively slower service.

Classification Variables

Data for the classification variables were asked at the end of the survey, but in the database they are recorded as variables X_7–X_{11}. Responses were coded as follows:

X_7–Gender (1 = Male; 0 = Female)

X_8–Recommend to Friend (7 = Definitely Recommend; 1 = Definitely Not Recommend)

X_9–Satisfaction Level (7 = Highly Satisfied; 1 = Not Very Satisfied)

X_{10}–Usage Level (1 = Heavy User—eats at Deli Depot two or more times each week; 0 = Light User—eats at Deli Depot fewer than two times a week)

X_{11}–Market Area (1 = Came from within 1 mile; 2 = Came from 1–3 miles; 3 = Came from more than 3 miles)

Selection Factor Rankings

Data for the selection factors were collected as follows:

Listed below is a set of attributes (reasons) many people use when selecting a fast-food restaurant. Regarding your visits to fast-food restaurants in the last 30 days, please rank each attribute from 1 to 6, with 6 being the most important reason for selecting the fast-food restaurant and 1 being the least important reason. There can be no ties, so make sure you rank each attribute with a different number.

X_{12}–Friendly Employees
X_{13}–Competitive Prices
X_{14}–Competent Employees
X_{15}–Excellent Food Quality
X_{16}–Wide Variety of Food
X_{17}–Fast Service

The questionnaire for the Deli Depot survey is shown in Exhibit 10.9.

Hands-On Exercise

1. Should the Deli Depot questionnaire have screening questions?
2. Run a frequency count on variable X_3–Competent Employees. Do the customers perceive employees to be competent?
3. Consider the guidelines on questionnaire design you learned in Chapter 8. How would you improve the Deli Depot questionnaire?

Exhibit 10.9 Deli Depot Questionnaire

Screening and Rapport Questions

Hello. My name is ——— and I work for Decision Analyst, a market research firm in Dallas, Texas. We are talking to people today/tonight about eating out habits.

1. "How often do you eat out?"   __ Often   __ Occasionally   __ Seldom

2. "Did you just eat at Deli Depot?"   __ Yes   __ No

3. "Have you completed a restaurant
   questionnaire on Deli Depot before?"   __ Yes   __ No

If respondent answers "Often or Occasionally" to the 1st question, "Yes" to the 2nd question, and "No" to the 3rd question, then say:

We would like you to answer a few questions about your experience today/tonight at Deli Depot, and we hope you will be willing to give us your opinions. The survey will only take a few minutes and it will be very helpful to management in better serving its customers. We will pay you $5.00 for completing the questionnaire.

If the person says yes, give them a clipboard with the questionnaire on it, briefly explain the questionnaire, and show them where to complete the survey.

DINING OUT SURVEY

Please read all questions carefully. If you do not understand a question, ask the interviewer to help you.

Section 1: Perceptions Measures

Listed below is a set of characteristics that could be used to describe Deli Depot. Using a scale from 1 to 10, with 10 being "Strongly Agree" and 1 being "Strongly Disagree," to what extent do you agree or disagree that Deli Depot has: Circle the correct response.

		Strongly Disagree									Strongly Agree
1.	Friendly Employees	1	2	3	4	5	6	7	8	9	10
2.	Competitive Prices	1	2	3	4	5	6	7	8	9	10
3.	Competent Employees	1	2	3	4	5	6	7	8	9	10
4.	Excellent Food Quality	1	2	3	4	5	6	7	8	9	10
5.	Wide Variety of Food	1	2	3	4	5	6	7	8	9	10
6.	Fast Service	1	2	3	4	5	6	7	8	9	10

Section 2: Classification Variables

Circle the response that describes you.

7. Your Gender   1   Male
                          0   Female

continued

Exhibit 10.9   Deli Depot Questionnaire, *continued*

8. How likely are you to recommend Deli Depot to a friend?

Definitely Not Recommend   Definitely Recommend
1 2 3 4 5 6 7

9. How satisfied are you with Deli Depot?

Not Very Satisfied   Highly Satisfied
1 2 3 4 5 6 7

10. How often do you patronize Deli Depot?

1 = eat at Deli Depot 2 or more times each week.
0 = eat at Deli Depot fewer than 2 times each week.

11. How far did you drive to get to Deli Depot?

1 = came from within one mile.
2 = 1–3 miles.
3 = came from more than 3 miles.

Section 3: Selection Factors

Listed below is a set of attributes (reasons) many people use when selecting a fast-food restaurant. Regarding your visits to fast-food restaurants in the last 30 days, please rank each attribute from 1 to 6, with 6 being the most important reason for selecting the restaurant and 1 being the least important reason. There can be no ties so make sure you rank each attribute with a different number.

Attribute	Ranking
12. Friendly Employees	
13. Competitive Prices	
14. Competent Employees	
15. Excellent Food Quality	
16. Wide Variety of Food	
17. Fast Service	

Thank you very much for your help. Please give your questionnaire to the interviewer and you will be given your $5.00.

Summary

Describe the process for data preparation and analysis.

The value of marketing research is its ability to provide accurate decision-making information to the user. To accomplish this, the data must be converted into usable information or knowledge. After collecting data through the appropriate method, the task becomes one of ensuring the data provide meaning and value. Data preparation is the first part of the process of transforming data into useful knowledge. This process involves several steps: (1) data validation; (2) editing and coding; (3) data entry; (4) error detection; and (5) data tabulation. Data analysis follows data preparation and facilitates proper interpretation of the findings.

Discuss validation, editing, and coding of survey data.

Data validation attempts to determine whether surveys, interviews, or observations were conducted correctly and are free from fraud. In recontacting selected respondents, the researcher asks whether the interview (1) was falsified; (2) was conducted with a qualified respondent; (3) took place in the proper procedural setting; (4) was completed correctly and accurately; and (5) was accomplished in a courteous manner. The editing process involves scanning of interviews or questionnaire responses to determine whether the proper questions were asked, the answers were recorded according to the instructions given, and the screening questions were executed properly, as well as whether open-ended questions were recorded accurately. Once edited, the questionnaires are coded by assigning numerical values to all responses. Coding is the process of providing numeric labels to the data so they can be entered into a computer for subsequent statistical analysis.

Explain data entry procedures and how to detect errors.

There are several methods for entering coded data into a computer. First is the PC keyboard. Data also can be entered through terminals having touch-screen capabilities, or through the use of a handheld electronic pointer or light pen. Finally, data can be entered through a scanner using optical character recognition. Data entry errors can be detected through the use of error edit routines in the data entry software. Another approach is to visually scan the actual data after it has been entered.

Describe data tabulation and analysis approaches.

Two common forms of data tabulation are used in marketing research. A one-way tabulation indicates the number of respondents who gave each possible answer to each question on a questionnaire. Cross-tabulation provides categorization of respondents by treating two or more variables simultaneously. Categorization is based on the number of respondents who have responded to two or more consecutive questions.

◗ Key Terms and Concepts

Coding   256

Cross-tabulation   261

Curbstoning   249

Data entry   259

Data validation   249

Editing   251

One-way tabulation   261

Tabulation   261

◗ Review Questions

1. Briefly describe the process of data validation. Specifically discuss the issues of fraud, screening, procedure, completeness, and courtesy.
2. What are the differences between data validation, data editing, and data coding?
3. Explain the differences between developing codes for open-ended questions and for closed-ended questions.
4. Briefly describe the process of data entry. What changes in technology have simplified this procedure?
5. What is the purpose of a simple one-way tabulation? How does this relate to a one-way frequency table?

◗ Discussion Questions

1. Explain the importance of following the sequence for data preparation and analysis described in Exhibit 10.1.
2. Identify four problems a researcher might find while screening questionnaires and preparing data for analysis.
3. How can data tabulation help researchers better understand and report findings?
4. **SPSS Exercise**. Using SPSS and the Santa Fe Grill employee database, develop frequencies, means, modes, and medians for all the relevant variables on the questionnaire.

Basic Data Analysis for Quantitative Research

Chapter 11

1. Explain measures of central tendency and dispersion.
2. Describe how to test hypotheses using univariate and bivariate statistics.
3. Apply and interpret analysis of variance (ANOVA).
4. Utilize perceptual mapping to present research findings.

Data Analysis Facilitates Smarter Decisions

In his book *Thriving on Chaos,* Tom Peters says, "We are drowning in information and starved for knowledge." Indeed, the amount of information available for business decision making has grown tremendously over the last decade. But until recently, much of that information just disappeared. It was either not used or discarded because collecting, storing, extracting, and interpreting it were too expensive. Now, decreases in the cost of data collection and storage, development of faster data processors and user-friendly client–server interfaces, and improvements in data analysis and interpretation made possible through data mining enable businesses to convert what had been a "waste by-product" into a new resource to improve business and marketing decisions. The data may come from secondary sources or surveys of customers, or be internally generated by enterprise or CRM software, such as SAP. To convert this information into knowledge so it can be useful for decision making, the data must be organized, categorized, analyzed, and shared among company employees.

Data analysis facilitates the discovery of interesting patterns in databases that are difficult to identify and have potential for improving decision making and creating knowledge. Data analysis methods are widely used today for commercial purposes. Fair Isaac & Co. (**www.fairisaac.com**) is an $800 million business built around the commercial use of multivariate statistical techniques. The firm developed a complex analytical model that can accurately predict who will pay bills on time, who will pay late, who will not pay at all, who will file for bankruptcy, and so on. Its models are useful for both the consumer and business-to-business markets. Similarly, the IRS uses data analysis to identify which returns to audit. State Farm uses multivariate statistics to decide who to sell insurance to, and Progressive Insurance combines multivariate methods with global positioning technology to identify where and how fast you drive so that they can raise your auto insurance premiums if you drive in a hazardous manner.

To make accurate business decisions in today's increasingly complex environment, intricate relationships with many intervening variables must be examined. Sophisticated statistical methods, such as data mining, are powerful analytical techniques used by marketing researchers to examine and better understand these relationships.

Value of Statistical Analysis

Once data have been collected and prepared for analysis, several statistical procedures can help to better understand the responses. It can be difficult to understand the entire set of responses because there are too many numbers to look at. For example, Nokia analyzed 6 billion pieces of data in designing its N-Series wireless phone. This amount of data could only be analyzed and understood with multivariate analysis. Consequently, almost all data needs summary statistics to describe the information it contains. Basic statistics and descriptive analysis achieve this purpose.

We describe some of the statistics common to almost all research projects in this chapter. First we explain measures of central tendency and dispersion. Next, we discuss the Chi-square statistic to examine cross tabulations, and then the t statistic for testing differences in means. Finally, the chapter closes with an introduction to analysis of variance, a powerful technique for detecting differences between three or more sample means.

Measures of Central Tendency

Frequency distributions can be useful for examining the different values for a variable. Frequency distribution tables are easy to read and provide a great deal of basic information. There are times, however, when the amount of detail is too great. In such situations, the researcher needs a way to summarize and condense all the information in order to get at the underlying meaning. Researchers use descriptive statistics to accomplish this task. The mean, median, and mode are measures of central tendency. These measures locate the center of the distribution. For this reason, the mean, median, and mode are sometimes also called measures of location.

We use variable X_{25}–Frequency of Eating from the restaurant database to illustrate the measures of central tendency (Exhibit 11.1). Note that for this example we look first at the frequency distribution, which is the lower table. It is based on the 427 respondents who participated in the survey, including 13 responses that included some missing data on this question. Respondents used a 5-point scale, with 1 = Very Infrequently, 2 = Somewhat Infrequently, 3 = Occasionally, 4 = Somewhat Frequently, and 5 = Very Frequently. The numbers in the Percent column are calculated using the total sample size of 427, while the numbers in the Valid % and Cumulative % columns are calculated using the total sample size minus the number of missing responses to this question ($427 - 13 = 414$).

Mean The arithmetic average of the sample; all values of a distribution of responses are summed and divided by the number of valid responses.

Mean The **mean** is the average value within the distribution and is the most commonly used measure of central tendency. The mean tells us, for example, the average number of cups of coffee the typical student drinks during finals to stay awake. The mean can be calculated when the data scale is either interval or ratio. Generally, the data will show some degree of central tendency, with most of the responses distributed close to the mean.

The mean is a very robust measure of central tendency. It is fairly insensitive to data values being added or deleted. The mean can be subject to distortion, however, if extreme values are included in the distribution. For example, suppose you ask four students how many cups of coffee they drink in a single day. Respondent answers are as follows: Respondent A = 1 cup; Respondent B = 10 cups; Respondent C = 5 cups; and Respondent D = 6 cups. Let's also assume that we know that respondents A and B are males and respondents B and C are females and we want to compare consumption of coffee between males and females. Looking at the males first (Respondents A and B), we calculate the mean number of cups to be 5.5 ($1 + 10 = 11/2 = 5.5$). Similarly, looking

Exhibit 11.1   Measures of Central Tendency

Frequencies

Statistics

X25—Frequency of Eating at ... ??

Jose's Southwestern Cafe	N	Valid	156
		Missing	8
	Mean		3.77
	Median		4.00
	Mode		3
Santa Fe Grill	N	Valid	258
		Missing	5
	Mean		2.96
	Median		3.00
	Mode		2

at the females next (Respondents C and D), we calculate the mean number of cups to be 5.5 (5 + 6 = 11/2 = 5.5). If we look only at the mean number of cups of coffee consumed by males and females, we would conclude there are no differences in the two groups. If we consider the underlying distribution, however, we must conclude there are some differences and the mean in fact distorts our understanding of coffee consumption patterns of males and females.

Median The **median** is the middle value of the distribution when the distribution is ordered in either an ascending or a descending sequence. For example, if you interviewed a sample of students to determine their coffee-drinking patterns during finals, you might find that the median number of cups of coffee consumed is 4. The number of cups of coffee consumed above and below this number would be the same (the median number is the exact middle of the distribution). If the number of data observations is even, the median is generally considered to be the average of the two middle values. If there is an odd number of observations, the median is the middle value. The median is especially useful as a measure of central tendency for ordinal data and for data that are skewed to either the right or left. For example, income data are skewed to the right because there is no upper limit on income.

Median The middle value of a rank-ordered distribution; exactly half of the responses are above and half are below the median value.

Mode The **mode** is the value that appears in the distribution most often. For example, the average number of cups of coffee students drink per day during finals may be 5 (the mean), while the number of cups of coffee that most students drink is only 3 (the mode). The mode is the value that represents the highest peak in the distribution's graph. The mode is especially useful as a measure for data that have been somehow grouped into categories.

Mode The most common value in the set of responses to a question; that is, the response most often given to a question.

To split the sample into the Santa Fe Grill responses and those from Jose's Southwestern Café, the click-through sequence is DATA → SPLIT FILE. First click on the Data pull-down menu and scroll down and highlight and click on Split File. You now see the Split File dialog box where the default is Analyze all cases. Click on the Compare groups option, highlight the variable you want to split the groups with (e.g., screening variable X_s4) and click on the arrow box to move it into the Groups Based on: window. Next click on OK and you will be analyzing the Santa Fe Grill customers and Jose's customers separately. Thus, your output will have the results for the two competitors separately. Remember too that all data analysis following this change will split the file. To analyze the total sample you must follow the same sequence and click again on Analyze all cases.

The mode for the Jose's Southwestern Café data distribution in Exhibit 11.1 is "Occasionally" because when you look in the Frequency column you will see the largest number of responses is 62 for the "Occasionally" label, which was coded as a 3.

Each measure of central tendency describes a distribution in its own manner, and each measure has its own strengths and weaknesses. For nominal data, the mode is the best measure. For ordinal data, the median is generally best. For interval or ratio data, the mean is appropriate, except when there are extreme values within the interval or ratio data, which are referred to as *outliers*. In this case, the median and the mode are likely to provide more information about the central tendency of the distribution.

SPSS Applications—Measures of Central Tendency

You can use the Santa Fe Grill database with the SPSS software to calculate measures of central tendency. After splitting the file into the two restaurant samples, the SPSS click-through sequence is ANALYZE → DESCRIPTIVE STATISTICS → FREQUENCIES. Let's use X_{25}–Frequency of Eating as a variable to examine. Click on X_{25} to highlight it and then on the arrow box for the Variables window to use in your analysis. Next, open the Statistics box and click on Mean, Median, and Mode, and then Continue and OK. The dialog boxes for this sequence are shown in Exhibit 11.2.

Let's look at the output for the measures of central tendency shown in Exhibit 11.1. In the Statistics table we see the mean for Jose's Southwestern Café is 3.77, the median is 4.00, the mode is 3, and there are eight observations with missing data. Recall that this variable is measured on a 5-point scale, with lower numbers indicating lower frequency of eating and larger numbers indicating higher frequency. The three measures of central tendency can all be different within the same distribution, as described previously in the coffee-drinking example. But it also is possible that all three measures can be the same. In our example, the mean, median, and mode are all different.

Interpretation of Results The mean frequency of dining at Jose's is 3.77 and at the Santa Fe Grill the mean frequency is 2.96. Similarly, the median for Jose's is 4.0 and the mode is 3 while the median for the Santa Fe Grill is 3.0 and the mode 2. All three measures of central tendency indicate, therefore, that the customers of Jose's dine there more frequently. This identifies an area of improvement for the Santa Fe Grill. The owners need to determine why their customers eat there less often (or why Jose's customers eat in that restaurant more frequently) and develop a plan to overcome this weakness.

| Exhibit 11.2 | Dialog Boxes for Calculating the Mean, Median, and Mode |

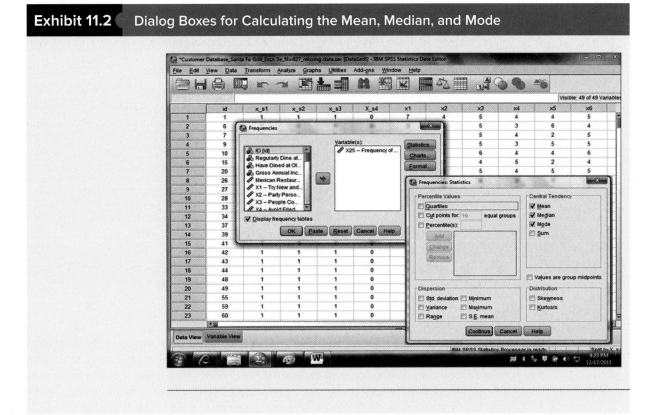

Measures of Dispersion

Measures of central tendency often do not tell the whole story about a distribution of responses. For example, if data have been collected about consumers' attitudes toward a new brand of a product, you could calculate the mean, median, and mode of the distribution of answers. However, you might also want to know if most of the respondents had similar opinions. One way to answer this question is to examine the measures of dispersion associated with the distribution of responses to your questions. Measures of dispersion describe how close to the mean or other measure of central tendency the rest of the values in the distribution fall. Two measures of dispersion that describe the variability in a distribution of numbers are the range and the standard deviation.

Range The distance between the smallest and largest values in a set of responses.

Range The **range** defines the spread of the data. It is the distance between the smallest and largest values of the variable. Another way to think about it is that the range identifies the endpoints of the distribution of values. For variable X_{25}–Frequency of Eating, the range is the difference between the response category Very Frequently (largest value coded 5) and response category Very Infrequently (smallest value coded 1). Thus, the range is 4. In this example, there were only five response categories. But some questions have a much wider range. For example, if we asked how often in a month respondents record TV shows on their DVR, or how much they would pay for a new Smartphone, the range likely would be much larger. In these examples, the respondents, not the researchers, are defining the range by their answers. For this reason, the range is more often used to describe the variability of open-ended questions such as our examples. Recall that for variable X_{25}–Frequency of Eating, the range is calculated as the distance between the largest and smallest values in the set of responses and equals 4 ($5 - 1 = 4$).

Standard deviation The average distance of the distribution values from the mean.

Standard Deviation The **standard deviation** describes the average distance of the distribution values from the mean. The difference between a particular response and the distribution mean is called a deviation. Since the mean of a distribution is a measure of central tendency, there should be about as many values above the mean as there are below it (particularly if the distribution is symmetrical). Consequently, if we subtracted each value in a distribution from the mean and added them up, the result would be close to zero (the positive and negative results would cancel each other out).

The solution to this difficulty is to square the individual deviations before we add them up (squaring a negative number produces a positive result). To calculate the estimated standard deviation, we use the formula below.

$$\text{Standard deviation (s)} = \sqrt{\frac{\sum_{i=1}^{n}(X_i - \overline{X})^2}{n - 1}}$$

Once the sum of the squared deviations is determined, it is divided by the number of respondents minus 1. The number 1 is subtracted from the number of respondents to help produce an unbiased estimate of the standard deviation. The result of dividing the sum of the squared deviations is the average squared deviation. To convert the result to the same units of measure as the mean, we take the square root of the answer. This produces the estimated standard deviation of the distribution. Sometimes the average squared deviation is also used as a measure of dispersion for a distribution. The average squared deviation, called the **variance**, is used in a number of statistical processes.

Variance The average squared deviation about the mean of a distribution of values.

Since the estimated standard deviation is the square root of the average squared deviations, it represents the average distance of the values in a distribution from the mean. If the estimated standard deviation is large, the responses in a distribution of numbers do not fall very close to the mean of the distribution. If the estimated standard deviation is small, you know that the distribution values are close to the mean.

Another way to think about the estimated standard deviation is that its size tells you something about the level of agreement among the respondents when they answered a particular question. For example, in the restaurant database, respondents were asked to rate their satisfaction (X_{22}) with the two restaurants. We will use the SPSS program later to examine the standard deviations for this question.

Together with the measures of central tendency, these descriptive statistics can reveal a lot about the distribution of a set of numbers representing the answers to an item on a questionnaire. Often, however, marketing researchers are interested in more detailed questions that involve more than one variable at a time. The next section, on hypothesis testing, provides some ways to analyze those types of questions.

SPSS Applications—Measures of Dispersion

We will use the restaurant database with the SPSS software to calculate measures of dispersion, just as we did with the measures of central tendency. Note that to calculate the measures of dispersion we will be using the database with a sample size of 405, so we have eliminated all respondents with missing data. Also, before running this analysis make sure your database is split between the two restaurants. The SPSS click-through sequence is ANALYZE → DESCRIPTIVE STATISTICS → FREQUENCIES. Let's use X_{22}–Satisfaction as a variable to examine. Click on X_{22} to highlight it and then on the arrow box to move X_{22} to the Variables window. Next open the Statistics box, go to the Dispersion box in the lowerleft-hand corner, and click on Standard deviation, Range, Minimum and Maximum, and then Continue.

Interpretation of Results Exhibit 11.3 shows the output for the measures of dispersion for variable X_{22}–Satisfaction. First, the highest response on the 7-point scale is 7 (maximum) for both restaurants, and the lowest response for the two restaurants is 3 (minimum). The range for both restaurants is 4 (7 – 3 = 4), while the standard deviation for Jose's is 1.141 and for Santa Fe 1.002. The mean for Jose's is 5.31 and for Santa Fe Grill 4.54. A standard deviation of 1.002 on a 7-point scale for the Santa Fe Grill indicates the responses to this question are dispersed relatively closely around the mean of 4.54. The results again suggest an area of improvement since the reported satisfaction of Santa Fe Grill customers is lower (4.54) than for Jose's Southwestern Café (5.31). At this point we have not examined whether the mean satisfaction levels of the two restaurants are statistically different, however, so that is a question that needs to be examined.

Exhibit 11.3 Measures of Dispersion

Statistics

X22—Satisfaction

Jose's Southwestern Cafe	N	Valid	152
		Missing	0
	Std. Deviation		1.141
	Range		4
	Minimum		3
	Maximum		7
Santa Fe Grill	N	Valid	253
		Missing	0
	Std. Deviation		1.002
	Range		4
	Minimum		3
	Maximum		7

Exhibit 11.4 Frequency Count of X_{25}–Frequency of Eating at Santa Fe Grill

X25—Frequency of Eating at … ??		Frequency	Percent	Valid Percent	Cumulative Percent
Valid	Very Infrequently	49	19.4	19.4	19.4
	Somewhat Infrequently	62	24.5	24.5	43.9
	Occasionally	43	17.0	17.0	60.9
	Somewhat Frequently	59	23.3	23.3	84.2
	Very Frequently	40	15.8	15.8	100.0
	Total	253	100.0	100.0	

Exhibit 11.5 Bar Chart for Frequency of Eating at Santa Fe Grill

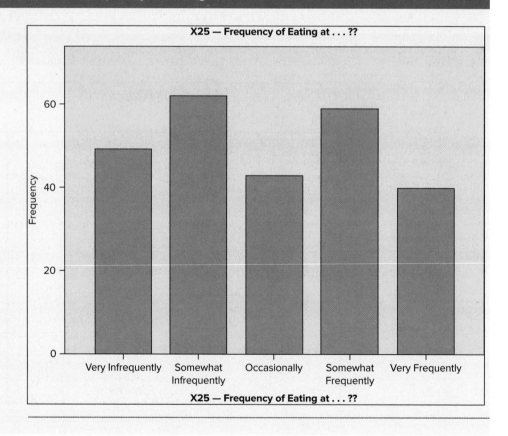

Preparation of Charts

Many types of charts and graphics can be prepared easily using the SPSS software. Charts and other visual communication approaches should be used whenever practical. They help information users to quickly grasp the essence of the results developed in data analysis, and also can be an effective visual aid to enhance the communication process and add clarity and impact to research reports and presentations.

In this section, we show how to prepare bar charts. We use variable X_{25}–Frequency of Eating from the restaurant database to develop the frequency tabulation in Exhibit 11.4. Note that we have 253 responses so this is the data only for the customers of the Santa Fe Grill. The table shows how frequently the customers eat at the Santa Fe Grill using a 5-point scale, with 1 = Very Infrequently, 2 = Somewhat Infrequently, 3 = Occasionally, 4 = Somewhat Frequently, and 5 = Very Frequently. The most frequent response is 2 (Somewhat Infrequently) with 62 of the 253 respondents indicating that alternative.

A *bar chart* shows tabulated data in the form of bars that may be horizontally or vertically oriented. Bar charts are excellent tools to depict both absolute and relative magnitudes, differences, and change. Exhibit 11.5 is an example of a vertical bar chart based on the data from Exhibit 11.4. For example, the frequency for the value label of Very Infrequently = 1 (N = 49) is the first vertical bar on the left side of the chart, and the next bar is Somewhat Infrequently = 2 (N = 62). The remaining bars are developed in the same way.

Marketing researchers need to exercise caution when using charts and figures to explain data. It is possible to misinterpret information in a chart and lead marketing research information users to inappropriate conclusions. In Chapter 13, on marketing research reports, we explain charts and graphics in much more detail.

■ How to Develop Hypotheses

Measures of central tendency and dispersion are useful tools for marketing researchers. But researchers often have preliminary ideas regarding data relationships based on the research objectives. These ideas are derived from previous research, theory, and/or the current business situation, and typically are called hypotheses. Recall that a hypothesis is an unproven supposition or proposition that tentatively explains certain facts or phenomena. A hypothesis also may be thought of as an assumption about the nature of a particular situation. Statistical techniques enable us to determine whether the proposed hypotheses can be confirmed by the empirical evidence. An example of a hypothesis would be "The average number of Cokes consumed by an individual on a hot day will be greater than on a cooler day."

Hypotheses are developed prior to data collection, generally as a part of the research plan. One example of testing a hypothesis is to examine a theory that men eat more hamburgers than women at a McDonald's restaurant in a typical week. To test this hypothesis, the number of hamburgers eaten by men and women could be calculated by observing purchasing behavior in a typical week. To do so, we would compare the number of hamburgers eaten by the male and female customers and determine if there are differences. For example, let's say the average number of McDonald's hamburgers eaten by women per week is 1.2, and the average number of McDonald's hamburgers eaten by men is 2.7. We could conclude that there is a difference in the number of hamburgers eaten by men and women and that our theory is confirmed. This finding could be very useful to a marketing researcher working for McDonald's, or perhaps a competitor.

When we test hypotheses that compare two or more groups, if the groups are different subsets of the same sample then the two groups must be considered related samples for conducting statistical tests. In contrast, if we assume the groups are from separate populations then the different groups are considered independent samples. In both situations, the researcher is interested in determining if the two groups are different but different statistical tests are appropriate for each situation. We examine this in more detail in a later section.

Many theories could be used to develop hypotheses for the restaurant databases. For example, the owners have a theory that the recession has resulted in customers eating at the Santa Fe Grill less often. To test that hypothesis we first calculate that of the 253 Santa Fe Grill customers surveyed, 10 percent said they visited the restaurant at least two times per month. But in a similar survey conducted last year, 15 percent said they visited the restaurant at least two times per month. In this example, the samples are independent. One question is whether or not the difference in the percentages confirms the hypothesis that frequency of eating at the Santa Fe Grill is down. If it is down, as the data suggest, this is useful information in developing a marketing plan for the Santa Fe Grill. In other words, "Has the percentage of persons eating at the Santa Fe Grill two times per month actually decreased from 15 percent last year to 10 percent this year?" or is this finding a result of sampling error?

There is a difference in the percentages that visit the Santa Fe Grill at least two times per month. We noted, however, that sampling error could distort the results enough so there may not be any statistical differences between this year's and last year's percentages. If the difference between the percentages is quite large, the researcher would be more confident that there is in fact a true difference between the groups. Some uncertainty would still exist, however, as to whether the observed difference is meaningful. In this instance we have intuitively considered the amount of difference between the means. But we have not considered the size of the sample used to calculate the means or the sample standard deviations.

The null hypothesis is no difference in the group means. It is based on the notion that any change from the past is due entirely to random error. In this case, the null hypothesis would be no difference between the 15 percent visiting the restaurant an average of two times

MARKETING RESEARCH DASHBOARD STEPS IN HYPOTHESIS DEVELOPMENT AND TESTING

To be consistent with the scientific method, marketing researchers need a systematic approach to develop hypotheses. Below is a recommended set of steps.

1. Review the research objectives and background information obtained from the literature review.

2. Develop the null and alternative hypotheses based on research objectives and other information.

3. Make an informed judgment about the sampling distribution of the population and then select the appropriate statistical test based on data distribution, number of variables, and type of scale measurement.

4. Select the desired level of statistical significance (p = .05, for example).

5. Collect the sample data, apply the statistical method selected, and determine if the differences are statistically significant and meaningful.

6. Accept or reject the null hypothesis. That is, determine whether the deviation of the sample value from the expected value occurred by chance alone or represents a true difference.

a month last year and the 10 percent found this year. Statisticians and marketing researchers typically test the *null hypothesis*. Another hypothesis, called the *alternative hypothesis,* states the opposite of the null hypothesis. The alternative hypothesis is that there is a difference between the group means. If the null hypothesis is accepted, we do not have change in the status quo. But if the null hypothesis is rejected and the alternative hypothesis accepted, the conclusion is there has been a change in behavior, attitudes, or some similar measure.

◼️ Analyzing Relationships of Sample Data

Marketing researchers often wish to test hypotheses about proposed relationships in the sample data. In this section, we discuss several methods used to test hypotheses. We first introduce Chi-square analysis, a statistic used with nominal and ordinal data. We then discuss the *t* distribution and describe its function for testing hypotheses using interval and ordinal data. Before discussing these methods of testing hypotheses, we review some basic statistical terminology and suggest ways to select the appropriate statistical technique.

Sample Statistics and Population Parameters

The purpose of inferential statistics is to make a determination about a population on the basis of a sample from that population. As we explained in Chapter 6, a sample is a subset of the population. For example, if we wanted to determine the average number of cups of coffee consumed per day by students during finals at your university, we would not interview all the students. This would be costly, take a long time, and could be impossible since we might not be able to find them all or some would decline to partici-pate. Instead, if there are 16,000 students at your university, we may decide that a sample of 200 females and 200 males is sufficiently large to provide accurate information about the coffee-drinking habits of all 16,000 students.

You may recall that sample statistics are measures obtained directly from the sample or calculated from the data in the sample. A population parameter is a variable or some sort of measured characteristic of the entire population. Sample statistics are useful in making inferences regarding the population's parameters. Generally, the actual population parameters are unknown since the cost to perform a true census of almost any population is prohibitive.

A frequency distribution displaying the data obtained from the sample is commonly used to summarize the results of the data collection process. When a frequency distribution displays a variable in terms of percentages, then this distribution represents proportions within a population. For example, a frequency distribution showing that 40 percent of the people patronize Burger King indicates the percentage of the population that meets the cri-terion (eating at Burger King). The proportion may be expressed as a percentage, a decimal value, or a fraction.

Choosing the Appropriate Statistical Technique

After the researcher has developed the hypotheses and selected an acceptable level of risk (statistical significance), the next step is to test the hypotheses. To do so, the researcher must select the appropriate statistical technique to test the hypotheses. A number of sta-tistical techniques can be used to test hypotheses. Several considerations influencing the choice of a particular technique are (1) the number of variables, (2) the scale of measure-ment, and (3) parametric versus nonparametric statistics.

Number of Variables The number of variables examined together is a major consideration in the selection of the appropriate statistical technique. Univariate statistics uses only one variable at a time to generalize about a population from a sample. For example, if the researcher wants to examine the average number of cups of Starbucks coffee college students drink during finals, only a single variable is used and univariate statistics is appropriate. If the researcher is interested in the relationship between the average number of cups of Starbucks coffee college students drink during finals and the number of hours spent studying for finals, two variables are involved and a bivariate statistical technique is required. Often researchers will need to examine many variables at the same time to represent the real world and fully explain relationships in the data. In such cases, multivariate statistical techniques are required. We examine univariate and bivariate statistics in this chapter and more advanced statistical techniques in later chapters.

Scale of Measurement We discussed measurement and scaling in Chapter 7. We use that information here to show which statistical techniques are used with a particular type of scale. Exhibit 11.6 provides an overview of the types of scales used in different situations. Suppose the researcher has a nominal scale like Starbucks brand coffee drinkers versus Maxwell House coffee drinkers. The mode would be the only appropriate measure of central tendency. A Chi-square test could be used to test whether the observed number of Starbucks brand coffee drinkers is what one would expect it to be. For example, if a sample survey showed that 34 percent of college students at your university drink Starbucks coffee and you expected it to be 40 percent based on a national survey, you could use Chi-square to determine whether the differences were statistically significant.

With ordinal data you can use only the median, percentile, and Chi-square. For example, if we have ranking data for two factors that are thought to be important in the selection of a coffee brand, we would use the median, percentile, and Chi-square. If the two ranking factors are coffee taste and brand name, we could use the Chi-square statistic to determine whether Starbucks coffee drinkers and Maxwell House drinkers ranked these factors differently. Finally, if we have the actual count of the number of cups of coffee the typical Starbucks consumer drank during finals versus the Maxwell House consumer, we have ratio data and could calculate the standard deviation and determine if there are differences in the mean number of cups consumed using the *t*-test or ANOVA.

Parametric Versus Nonparametric Statistics There are two major types of statistics. They are referred to as *parametric* and *nonparametric*. The major difference between these two types of statistics lies in the underlying assumptions about the data. When the data are measured using

Exhibit 11.6 Type of Scale and Appropriate Statistic

Type of Scale	Measure of Central Tendency	Measure of Dispersion	Statistic
Nominal	Mode	None	Chi-square (nonparametric)
Ordinal	Median	Percentile	Chi-square (nonparametric)
Interval or ratio	Mean	Standard deviation	*t*-test, ANOVA (parametric)

an interval or ratio scale and the sample size is large, parametric statistics are appropriate. It is also assumed the sample data are collected from populations with normal (bell-shaped) distributions. In contrast, when a normal distribution cannot be assumed, the researcher must use nonparametric statistics. Moreover, when data are measured using an ordinal or nominal scale it is generally not appropriate to assume that the distribution is normal and, therefore, nonparametric or distribution-free statistics should be used. In this chapter, we discuss the nonparametric statistic Chi-square and the parametric statistics *t*-test and ANOVA. Exhibit 11.6 shows a chart that provides further guidelines on selecting the appropriate statistic.

After considering the measurement scales and data distributions, there are three approaches for analyzing sample data that are based on the number of variables. We can use univariate, bivariate, or multivariate statistics. Univariate means we statistically analyze only one variable at a time. Bivariate analyzes two variables. Multivariate examines many variables simultaneously.

Exhibit 11.7 provides guidelines on selecting the appropriate statistical test to assess univariate and bivariate relationships. The combination of data types presented by the IV and DV (i.e., nominal, ordinal, interval, or ratio), and the nature of the relationship examined (hypothesis), determines the correct statistical test. For example, if the IV is gender (nominal data) and the DV is age (ratio data), and your objective is examining differences in the groups, then that combination calls for the *t*-test. But if the IV is gender (nominal data) and the DV is age (ratio/metric data), and your objective is examining association between the groups, that combination calls for the Spearman correlation. Thus, it is the combination of the type of data and the objective of the analysis (differences or association) that determines the correct statistical test.

Exhibit 11.7	Univariate and Bivariate Relationships: Selecting the Appropriate Test

Two or More Variables		Relationship	
Independent Variable (IV)	**Dependent Variable (DV)**	**Examined (hypothesis)**	**Statistical Test**
Nominal	Nominal	Differences	X^2 Crosstabs test (NP)
Ordinal	Ordinal	Association	Spearman correlation (NP)
Metric	Ordinal	Association	Spearman correlation (NP)
Ordinal	Metric	Association	Spearman correlation (NP)
Metric	Metric	Association	Pearson correlation (P)
Two groups	Ordinal	Differences	Median test (NP)
Three or more groups	Ordinal	Differences	Kruskal-Wallis one way analysis of variance (NP)
Two groups	Metric	Differences	*t*-test (independent samples) (P)
Three or more groups	Metric	Differences	One way analysis of variance (P)

Single Variable			
Nominal			X^2 Goodness-of-fit test (NP)

Note: (NP) = Nonparametric test and (P) = Parametric test

Univariate Statistical Tests

Testing hypotheses using statistical tests involves much more than the tabulations included in a frequency distribution or the calculation of measures of central tendency or dispersion. Researchers not only describe data using means or percentages. They also provide tests of the likelihood that the sample numbers are correct or incorrect estimates of the population characteristics. The simplest types of tests are univariate tests of significance. Univariate tests of significance are used to test hypotheses when the researcher wishes to test a proposition about a sample characteristic against a known or given standard. The following are some examples of propositions:

- The new product or service will be preferred by 80 percent of our current customers.
- The average monthly electric bill in Miami, Florida, exceeds $250.00.
- The market share for Community Coffee in south Louisiana is at least 70 percent.
- More than 50 percent of current Diet Coke customers will prefer the new Diet Coke that includes a lime taste.

We can translate these propositions into a null hypotheses and test them. Remember, hypotheses are developed based on theory, previous relevant experiences, and current market conditions. In the following paragraphs, we provide an example from the Santa Fe Grill database of a univariate hypothesis test.

The process of testing hypotheses regarding population characteristics based on sample data often begins by calculating frequency distributions and averages, and then moves on to further analysis that actually tests the hypotheses. When the hypothesis testing involves examining one variable at a time, it is referred to as a univariate statistical test. When the hypothesis testing involves two variables, it is called a bivariate statistical test. We first discuss univariate statistical tests.

Suppose the Santa Fe Grill owners based on observation of competitors believe their menu prices are reasonable and want to test the hypothesis of whether customers think their menu prices are reasonable. Respondents have answered a pricing question using a 7-point scale where 1 = "Strongly Disagree" and 7 = "Strongly Agree." The scale is assumed to be an interval scale, and previous research using this measure has shown the responses to be approximately normally distributed.

Researchers must perform a couple of tasks before attempting to answer the question posed above. First, the null and alternative hypotheses must be developed. Then the level of significance for rejecting the null hypothesis and accepting the alternative hypothesis must be selected. At that point, the researchers can conduct the statistical test and determine the answer to the research question.

In this example, the owners believe that customers will perceive the prices of food at the Santa Fe Grill to be about average. If the owners are correct, the mean response to this question will be around 4 (halfway between 1 and 7 on the response scale). The null hypothesis is that the mean of the X_{16}–Reasonable Prices will not be significantly different from 4. Recall the null hypothesis asserts the status quo: Any difference from what is thought to be true is due to random sampling. The alternative hypothesis is that the mean of the answers to X_{16}–Reasonable Prices will not be 4. If the alternative hypothesis is true, then there is in fact a true difference between the sample mean we find and the mean the owners are expected to find (4).

Assume also the owners want to be 95 percent certain the mean is not 4. Therefore, the significance level will be set at .05. Using this significance level means that if the survey of Santa Fe Grill customers is conducted many times, the probability of incorrectly rejecting the null hypothesis when it is true would happen less than five times out of 100 (.05).

SPSS Application—Univariate Hypothesis Test

Using the SPSS software, you can test the responses in the Santa Fe Grill database to find the answer to the research question posed earlier. First you must select only the Santa Fe Grill customers that took the survey—see nearby Marketing Research Dashboard for instructions. The click-through sequence is, ANALYZE → COMPARE MEANS → ONE-SAMPLE T-TEST. When you get to the dialog box, click on X_{16}–Reasonable Prices to highlight it. Then click on the arrow to move X_{16} into the Test Variables box. In the window labeled Test Value, enter the number 4. This is the number you want to compare the respondents' answers against. Click on the Options box and enter 95 in the confidence interval box. This is the same as setting the significance level at 0.05. Then, click on the Continue button and OK to execute the program.

The SPSS output is shown in Exhibit 11.8. The top table is labeled One-Sample Statistics and shows the mean, standard deviation, and standard error for X_{16}– Reasonable Prices (a mean of 4.47 and standard deviation of 1.384). The One-Sample Test table below shows the results of the t-test for the null hypothesis that the average response to X_{16} is 4 (Test Value $= 4$). The t-test statistic is 5.404, and the significance level is .000. This means that the null hypothesis can be rejected and the alternative hypothesis accepted with a high level of confidence from a statistical perspective.

Interpretation of Results   From a practical standpoint, in terms of the Santa Fe Grill, the results of the univariate hypothesis test indicate respondents perceived that menu prices are slightly above the midpoint of the scale. The mean of 4.47 is somewhat higher than the midpoint of 4 on the 7-point scale (7 = Strongly Agree prices are reasonable). Thus, the Santa Fe Grill owners can conclude that their prices are not perceived as unreasonable. But on the other hand, there is a lot of room to improve between the mean of 4.47 on the 7-point scale and the highest value of 7. This is definitely an area the owners need to examine and develop a plan to improve.

Bivariate Statistical Tests

In many instances marketing researchers test hypotheses that compare the characteristics of two groups or two variables. For example, the marketing researcher may be interested in

Exhibit 11.8   Univariate Hypothesis Test Using X_{16}–Reasonable Prices

T-Test

One-Sample Statistics

	N	Mean	Std. Deviation	Std. Error Mean
X16—Reasonable Prices	253	4.47	1.384	.087

One-Sample Test

	Test Value = 4					
					95% Confidence Interval of the Difference	
	t	df	Sig. (2-tailed)	Mean Difference	Lower	Upper
X16—Reasonable Prices	5.404	252	.000	.470	.30	.64

determining whether there is a difference in the importance of a GPS (global positioning system) between older and younger new car purchasers. In this situation, bivariate (two variable) analysis is appropriate.

In the following section, we first explain the concept of cross tabulation, which examines two variables. We then describe three types of bivariate hypothesis tests: Chi-square, which is used with nominal data, and the *t*-test (to compare two means) and analysis of variance (compares three or more means), both of which are used with either interval or ratio data.

Cross-Tabulation

In Chapter 10, we introduced one-way frequency tables to report the findings for a single variable. The next logical step in data analysis is to perform cross-tabulation using two variables. *Cross-tabulation* is useful for examining relationships and reporting the findings for two variables. The purpose of cross tabulation is to determine if differences exist between subgroups of the total sample. In fact, cross tabulation is the primary form of data analysis in some marketing research projects. To use cross tabulation you must understand how to develop a cross tabulation table and how to interpret the outcome.

Cross-tabulation is one of the simplest methods for describing sets of relationships. A cross-tabulation is a frequency distribution of responses on two or more sets of variables. To conduct cross tabulation, the responses for each of the groups are tabulated and compared. Chi-square (X^2) analysis enables us to test whether there are any statistical differences between the responses for the groups. Below are examples of questions that could be answered using cross-tabulations and testing with Chi-square analysis:

- Do restaurant selection factor rankings (most important, second most important, third in importance, etc.) differ between customers and noncustomers?
- Does frequency of dining (very frequent, somewhat frequent, occasional) differ between the Santa Fe Grill and Jose's Southwestern Café?
- Is Internet usage (heavy, moderate, low) related to educational levels (elementary, middle, high school, some college, college degree, post-graduate work)?
- Is brand awareness (unaware, aware) related to the geographic area in which individuals live (North America, Europe, Asia, Africa, etc.)?

Researchers can use the Chi-square test to determine whether responses observed in a survey follow the expected pattern. For example, Exhibit 11.9 shows a cross-tabulation between gender and respondents' recall of restaurant ads. The cross-tabulation shows

MARKETING RESEARCH DASHBOARD SELECTING THE SANTA FE GRILL CUSTOMERS FOR ANALYSIS

To select the Santa Fe Grill responses (253) from the total sample of 405 responses, the click-through sequence is DATA → SELECT CASES. First click on the Data pull-down menu and scroll down and highlight and click on Select Cases. You now see the Select Cases dialog box where the default is All cases. Click on the If condition is satisfied option, and then on the If tab. Next highlight the screening variable X_s4 and click on the arrow box to move it

into the window. Then click on the equal sign (=) and 1 for the Santa Fe Grill customers. Now click Continue and then OK and you will be analyzing only the Santa Fe Grill customers. Thus, your output will have the results for only one restaurant. Remember too that all data analysis following this change will analyze only the Santa Fe customers. To analyze the total sample you must follow the same sequence and click again on All cases.

Exhibit 11.9   Example of a Cross-Tabulation: Gender by Ad Recall

Cross-tabs

X31—Ad Recall * X32—Gender Cross-tabulation

			X32—Gender		Total
			Male	Female	
X31—Ad Recall	Do Not Recall Ads	Count	188	82	270
		Expected Count	176.0	94.0	270.0
		% within X31—Ad Recall	69.6%	30.4%	100.0%
		% within X32—Gender	71.2%	58.2%	66.7%
		% of Total	46.4%	20.2%	66.7%
	Recall Ads	Count	76	59	135
		Expected Count	88.0	47.0	135.0
		% within X31—Ad Recall	56.3%	43.7%	100.0%
		% within X32—Gender	28.8%	41.8%	33.3%
		% of Total	18.8%	14.6%	33.3%
Total		Count	264	141	405
		Expected Count	264.0	141.0	405.0
		% within X31—Ad Recall	65.2%	34.8%	100.0%
		% within X32—Gender	100.0%	100.0%	100.0%
		% of Total	65.2%	34.8%	100.0%

frequencies and percentages, with percentages existing for both rows and columns. To obtain these results, the SPSS sequence is Analyze–Descriptive Statistics–Crosstabs. When you see the Crosstabs dialog box, move X_{31} into the Rows window and X_{32} into the Columns window. Then click on the Statistics tab and check Chi-square and Continue. Next click on the Cells tab and check Observed and Expected under the Counts box and then Row, Column, and Total under the Percentages box, and Continue, and then OK.

Interpretation of Results One way to interpret the numbers in Exhibit 11.9, for example, would be to look at those individuals who do not recall advertising. Overall only 33.3 percent of the sample recall any advertisements. But of all the males interviewed just 28.8 percent (76/264 = 28.8 percent) recall ads, while 41.8 percent of the females interviewed recall ads. Thus, our preliminary interpretation suggests that males are less likely to recall restaurant advertisements than females. But be careful not to be confused by the results for individuals who recall ads. Those results show that of the 135 people who recall ads, 56.3 percent are males and 43.7 percent are females, which you may think conflicts with the previous conclusion that females recall ads at a higher rate than males. The higher percentage of males in the recall ads group is due to the fact that more males than females were interviewed in this study.

The next step to better understand this situation would be to look at this same cross tabulation but divide the analysis into Santa Fe Grill customers and Jose's customers. This would enable the Santa Fe Grill owners to compare the recall of their advertisements compared to that for Jose's.

Several other issues must be considered in developing and interpreting cross tabulation tables. Looking at Exhibit 11.9, note that percentages were calculated for each cell of the cross tabulation table. The top number within each cell represents the absolute frequency (count) of responses for each variable or question (e.g., 188 male respondents do not recall ads). Below the absolute frequency is the Expected Count and then the row percentage per cell. For example, the 188 male respondents who do not recall ads represent 69.6 percent of the total in the "Do Not Recall" category (188/270 = 69.6 percent). The cell also shows the total percentage of respondents within cells based on the total sample. So, for example, with a total sample of 405, 46.4 percent of the sample are males who do not recall ads, and 18.8 percent are males that do recall ads. This suggests that in general males are not recalling advertisements as frequently as females, but neither has a high recall of restaurant ads. This is definitely an area the Santa Fe Grill owners need to understand better.

When constructing a cross-tabulation table, the researcher selects the variables to use when examining relationships. Selection of variables should be based on the objectives of the research project and the hypotheses being tested. But in all cases remember that Chi-square is the statistic to analyze nominal (count) or ordinal (ranking) scaled data. Paired variable relationships (e.g., gender of respondent and ad recall) are selected on the basis of whether the variables answer the research questions in the research project and are either nominal or ordinal data.

Demographic variables or lifestyle/psychographic characteristics are typically the starting point in developing cross tabulations. These variables are usually the columns of the cross tabulation table, and the rows are variables like purchase intention, usage, or actual sales data. Cross-tabulation tables show percentage calculations based on column variable totals. Thus, the researcher can make comparisons of behaviors and intentions for different categories of predictor variables such as income, sex, and marital status.

Cross-tabulation provides the research analyst with a powerful tool to summarize survey data. It is easy to understand and interpret and can provide a description of both total and subgroup data. Yet the simplicity of this technique can create problems. It is easy to produce an endless variety of cross tabulation tables. In developing these tables, the analyst must always keep in mind both the project objectives and specific research questions of the study.

Chi-Square Analysis

Marketing researchers often analyze survey data using one-way frequency counts and cross-tabulations. One purpose of cross tabulations is to study relationships among variables. The research question is "Do the numbers of responses that fall into different categories differ from what is expected if there is no relationship between the variables?" The null hypothesis is always that the two variables are not related. Thus, the null hypothesis in our example would be that the percentage of men and women customers who recall Santa Fe Grill ads is the same. The alternative hypothesis is that the two variables are related, or that men and women differ in their recall of Santa Fe Grill ads. This hypothesis can be answered using Chi-square analysis. Below are some other examples of research questions that could be examined using Chi-square statistical tests:

- Is usage of the Internet (low, moderate, and high) related to the gender of the respondent?
- Does frequency of dining (infrequent, moderately frequent, and very frequent) differ between males and females?
- Do part-time and full-time workers differ in terms of how often they are absent from work (seldom, occasionally, frequently)?
- Do college students and high-school students differ in their preference for Coke versus Pepsi?

Chi-square (X^2) analysis
Assesses how closely the observed frequencies fit the pattern of the expected frequencies and is referred to as a "goodness-of-fit" test.

Chi-square (X^2) analysis enables researchers to test for statistical significance between the frequency distributions of two (or more) nominally scaled variables in a cross-tabulation table to determine if there is any association between the variables. Categorical data from questions about sex, education, or other nominal variables can be tested with this statistic. Chi-square analysis compares the observed frequencies (counts) of the responses with the expected frequencies. The Chi-square statistic tests whether or not the observed data are distributed the way we would expect them to be, given the assumption that the variables are not related. The expected cell count is a theoretical value, while the observed cell count is the actual cell count based on your study. For example, to test whether women recall Santa Fe Grill ads better than men, we would compare the observed recall frequency for each sex with the frequency we would expect to find if there is no difference between women's and men's ad recall. The Chi-square statistic answers questions about relationships between nominally scaled data that cannot be analyzed with other types of statistical analysis, such as ANOVA or t-tests.

Calculating the Chi-Square Value

To help you better understand the Chi square statistic, we will show you how to calculate it. The formula is shown below:

$$\text{Chi-square formula } x^2 = \sum_{i-1}^{n} \frac{(\text{Observed}_i - \text{Expected}_i)^2}{\text{Expected}_i}.$$

where

$$\text{Observed}_i = \text{observed frequency in cell } i$$
$$\text{Expected}_i = \text{expected frequency in cell } i$$
$$n = \text{number of cells}$$

When you apply the above formula to the restaurant data shown in Exhibit 11.9, you get the following calculation of Chi-square value:

$$\frac{(188-176)^2}{176} + \frac{(82-94)^2}{94} + \frac{(76-88)^2}{88} + \frac{(59-47)^2}{47} = \text{Chi-square value} = 7.05 \, (P = 0.011; \text{two-tailed})$$

As the above equation indicates, we subtract the expected frequency from the observed frequency and then square it to eliminate any negative values before we use the results in further calculations. After squaring, we divide the resulting value by the expected frequency to take into consideration cell size differences. Then each of these calculations, which we performed for each cell of the table, is summed over all cells to arrive at the final Chi-square value. The Chi-square value tells you how far the observed frequencies are from the expected frequencies. Conceptually, the larger the Chi-square is, the more likely it is that the two variables are related. This is because Chi-square is larger whenever the number actually observed in a cell is more different than what we expected to find, given the assumption that the two variables are not related. The computed Chi-square statistic is compared to a table of Chi-square values to determine if the differences are statistically significant. If the calculated Chi-square is larger than the Chi-square reported in standard statistical tables, then the two variables are related for a given level of significance, typically .05.

Some marketing researchers call Chi-square a "goodness of fit" test. That is, the test evaluates how closely the actual frequencies "fit" the expected frequencies. When the differences between observed and expected frequencies are large, you have a poor fit and you reject your null hypothesis. When the differences are small, you have a good fit and you would accept the null hypothesis that there is no relationship between the two variables.

One word of caution is necessary in using Chi-square. The Chi-square results will be distorted if more than 20 percent of the cells have an expected count of less than 5, or if any cell has an expected count of less than 1. In such cases, you should not use this test. SPSS will tell you if these conditions have been violated. One solution to small counts in individual cells is to collapse them into fewer cells to get larger counts.

SPSS Application—Chi-Square

Based on their conversations with customers, the owners of the Santa Fe Grill believe that female customers drive to the restaurant from farther away than do male customers. The Chi-square statistic can be used to determine if this is true. The null hypothesis is that the same proportion of male and female customers make up each of the response categories for X_{30}–Distance Driven. The alternative hypothesis is that these proportions differ by gender.

To conduct this analysis, first use the Data pull-down menu and go to Select Cases, as shown in the accompanying Marketing Research Dashboard. Select only the Santa Fe Grill customers to analyze. Next, the click-through sequence is ANALYZE → DESCRIPTIVE STATISTICS → CROSSTABS. Click on X_{30}–Distance Driven for the Row variable and on X_{32}–Gender for the Column variable. Click on the Statistics button and the Chi-square box, and then Continue. Next click on the Cells button and on Expected frequencies (Observed frequencies is usually already checked), and then on Row, Column, and Total Percentages. Now click Continue and OK to execute the program.

The SPSS results are shown in Exhibit 11.10. The top table shows the actual number of responses (count) for males and females for each of the categories of X_{30}–Distance Driven. Also in this table you will see the expected frequencies, or the number that we expect to find in the cell if the null hypothesis of no difference is true. For example, 74 males drove a distance of less than 1 mile (59.8 were "expected" in this cell) while 12 females drove from this same distance (we expected to find 26.2).

The expected frequencies (count) are calculated on the basis of the proportion of the sample represented by a particular group. For example, the total sample of Santa Fe Grill customers is 253 and 176 are males and 77 are females. This means 69.6 percent of the sample is male and 30.4 percent is female. When we look in the Total column for the distance driven category labeled "Less than 1 mile" we see that there are a total of 86 male and female respondents. To calculate the expected frequencies, you multiply the proportion a particular group represents times the total number in that group. For example, with males you calculate 69.6 percent of 86 and the expected frequency is 59.8. Similarly, females are 30.4 percent of the sample so the expected number of females = 26.2 (30.4×86). The other expected frequencies are calculated in the same way.

Look again at the observed frequencies, but this time at those who drove More than 5 Miles. Note that a lower number of male customers of Santa Fe Grill than expected drive farther to get to the restaurant. That is, we would expect 63.3 males to drive to the Santa Fe Grill from more than 5 miles, but actually only 57 men drove from this far away. In contrast, there are more female customers than expected who drive from more than five miles away (expected = 27.7 and actual 34).

Interpretation of Results Information in the Chi-Square tests table shows the results for this test. The Pearson Chi-Square value is 16.945 and it is significant at the .000 level.

Exhibit 11.10	Crosstab Chi-Square Example of Santa Fe Grill Customers

x30—Distance Driven to Restaurant * X32—Gender Cross-tabulation

			X32—Gender Male	X32—Gender Female	Total
x30—Distance Driven to Restaurant	Less than 1 mile	Count	74	12	86
		Expected Count	59.8	26.2	86.0
		% within x30—Distance Driven to Restaurant	86.0%	14.0%	100.0%
		% within X32—Gender	42.0%	15.6%	34.0%
		% of Total	29.2%	4.7%	34.0%
	1–5 miles	Count	45	31	76
		Expected Count	52.9	23.1	76.0
		% within x30—Distance Driven to Restaurant	59.2%	40.8%	100.0%
		% within X32—Gender	25.6%	40.3%	30.0%
		% of Total	17.8%	12.3%	30.0%
	More than 5 miles	Count	57	34	91
		Expected Count	63.3	27.7	91.0
		% within x30—Distance Driven to Restaurant	62.6%	37.4%	100.0%
		% within X32—Gender	32.4%	44.2%	36.0%
		% of Total	22.5%	13.4%	36.0%
Total		Count	176	77	253
		Expected Count	176.0	77.0	253.0
		% within x30—Distance Driven to Restaurant	69.6%	30.4%	100.0%
		% within X32—Gender	100.0%	100.0%	100.0%
		% of Total	69.6%	30.4%	100.0%

Chi-Square Tests

	Value	df	Asymp. Sig. (2-sided)
Pearson Chi-Square	16.945[a]	2	.000
Likelihood Ratio	18.390	2	.000
Linear-by-Linear Association	11.153	1	.001
N of Valid Cases	253		

a. 0 cells (.0%) have expected count less than 5. The minimum expected count is 23.13.

Since this level of significance is much lower than our standard criterion of .05, we can reject the null hypothesis of no difference with a high degree of confidence. The interpretation of this finding suggests that there is a high probability that female customers drive from farther away to get to the Santa Fe Grill. There also is a tendency for males to drive shorter distances to get to the restaurant.

Comparing Means: Independent Versus Related Samples

In addition to examining frequencies, marketing researchers often want to compare the means of two groups. In fact, one of the most frequently examined questions in marketing research is whether the means of two groups of respondents on some attitude or behavior are significantly different. For example, in a sample survey we might examine any of the following questions:

- Do the coffee consumption patterns (measured using the mean number of cups consumed daily) of males and females differ?
- Does the number of hours an individual spends on the Internet each week differ by income level? By gender? By education?
- Do younger workers exhibit higher job satisfaction than do older workers?
- Do Fortune 500 firms have a more favorable image than do smaller, family-owned firms?

The above research questions typically are based upon theory or practical experience suggesting one or more hypotheses to be tested. Thus, when we examine questions like the above, we first consider the theory and then develop the null and alternative hypotheses. Then we select the significance level for testing the null hypothesis. Finally, we select the appropriate statistical test and apply it to our sample data.

There are two types of situations when researchers compare means. The first is when the means are from independent samples, and the second is when the samples are related. An example of an **independent samples** comparison would be the results of interviews with male and female coffee drinkers. The researcher may want to compare the average number of cups of coffee consumed per day by male students with the average number of cups of coffee consumed by female students. An example of the second situation, **related samples**, is when the researcher compares the average number of cups of coffee consumed per day by male students with the average number of soft drinks consumed per day by the same sample of male students.

In a related sample situation, the marketing researcher must take special care in analyzing the information. Although the questions are independent, the respondents are the same. This is called a *paired sample*. When testing for differences in related samples, the researcher must use what is called a paired samples *t*-test. The formula to compute the *t* value for paired samples is not presented here. Students are referred to more advanced texts for the actual calculation of the *t* value for related samples. The SPSS package contains options for both the related-samples and the independent samples situations.

Independent samples Two or more groups of responses that are tested as though they may come from different populations.

Related samples Two or more groups of responses that originated from the sample population.

Using the *t*-Test to Compare Two Means

Just as with the univariate *t*-test, the bivariate *t*-test requires interval or ratio data. Also, the *t*-test is especially useful when the sample size is small ($n < 30$) and when the population standard deviation is unknown. Unlike the univariate test, however, we assume that the samples are drawn from populations with normal distributions and that the variances of the populations are equal.

The ***t*-test** for differences between group means can be conceptualized as the difference between the means divided by the variability of the means. The *t* value is a ratio of the difference between the two sample means and the standard error. The *t*-test provides a mathematical way of determining if the difference between the two sample means occurred by chance. The formula for calculating the *t* value is

t-Test A hypothesis test that utilizes the *t* distribution; used when the sample size is smaller than 30 and the standard deviation is unknown.

$$Z = \frac{\bar{X}_1 - \bar{X}_2}{S\bar{X}_1 - \bar{X}_2}$$

where

$$\overline{X}_1 = \text{mean of sample 1}$$
$$\overline{X}_2 = \text{mean of sample 2}$$
$$S\overline{X}_1 - \overline{X}_2 = \text{standard error of the difference between the two means}$$

SPSS Application—Independent Samples t-Test

To illustrate the use of a t-test for the difference between two group means, we turn to the restaurant database. Based on their experiences observing customers in the restaurant, the Santa Fe Grill owners believe there are differences in the levels of satisfaction between male and female customers. To test this hypothesis we can use the SPSS "Compare Means" program. To execute this analysis, first use the Data pull-down menu and go to Select Cases, as shown in the Marketing Research Dashboard. Select only the Santa Fe Grill customers to analyze.

The SPSS click-through sequence is Analyze → Compare Means → Independent-Samples T-Test. When you get to this dialog box click variable X_{22}–Satisfaction into the Test Variables box and variable X_{32}–Gender into the Grouping Variable Box. For variable X_{32} you must define the range in the Define Groups box. Enter a 0 for Group 1 and a 1 for Group 2 (males were coded 0 in the database and females were coded 1) and then click Continue. For the Options we will use the defaults, so just click OK to execute the program.

Interpretation of Results In Exhibit 11.11 the top table shows the Group Statistics. Note that 176 male customers and 77 female customers are in the Santa Fe restaurant data set. Also, the mean satisfaction level for males is a bit higher at 4.70, compared with 4.18 for the female customers. The standard deviation for females is somewhat smaller (0.823) than for the males (1.034).

To find out if the two means are significantly different, we look at the information in the Independent Samples Test table. The statistical significance of the difference in two means is calculated differently if the variances of the two means are equal versus unequal. The Levene's test for equality of variances is reported on the left side of the table. In this case the test shows the two variances are not equal (Sig. value of .000 indicated the variances are significantly different). When this value is < .05 you would use the "Equal variances not assumed" test. In the column labeled "Sig. (2-tailed)," you will note that the two means are significantly

---

Exhibit 11.11 Comparing Two Means with the Independent Samples t-Test

(Processing...)

Group Statistics

	X32—Gender	N	Mean	Std. Deviation	Std. Error Mean
X22—Satisfaction	Male	176	4.70	1.034	.078
	Female	77	4.18	.823	.094

Independent Samples Test

		Levene's Test for Equality of Variances		t-test for Equality of Means					95% Confidence Interval of the Difference	
		F	Sig.	t	df	Sig. (2-tailed)	Mean Difference	Std. Error Difference	Lower	Upper
X22—Satisfaction	Equal variances assumed	19.800	.000	3.882	251	.000	.517	.133	.255	.779
	Equal variances not assumed			4.241	179.954	.000	.517	.122	.276	.758

different (< .000), whether we assume equal or unequal variances. Thus, there is no support for the null hypothesis that the two means are equal, and we conclude that male customers are significantly more satisfied than female customers with the Santa Fe Grill. There is other information in this table, but we do not need to concern ourselves with it at this time.

SPSS Application—Paired Samples *t*-Test

Sometimes marketing researchers want to test for differences in two means for variables in the same sample. For example, the owners of the Santa Fe Grill noticed that the taste of their food is rated 4.78 while the food temperature is rated only 4.38. Since the two food variables are likely to be related, they want to know if the ratings for taste really are significantly higher (more favorable) than for temperature. To examine this, we use the paired samples test for the difference in two means. This test examines whether two means from two different questions using the same scaling and answered by the same respondents are significantly different. The null hypothesis is that the mean ratings for the two food variables (X_{18} and X_{20}) are equal.

To test this hypothesis we use the SPSS paired-samples *t*-test and data only for the Santa Fe Grill customers. The click-through sequence is Analyze → Compare Means → Paired-Samples T-Test. When you get to this dialog box, highlight first X_{18}–Food Taste and click the arrow button, and then highlight X_{20}–Food Temperature and click on the arrow button to move them into the Paired Variables box. For the "Options" we will use the defaults, so just click OK to execute the program.

Interpretation of Results In Exhibit 11.12 the top table shows the Paired Samples Statistics. The mean for food taste is 4.78 and for food temperature is 4.38. The *t* value for this comparison is 8.421 (see Paired Samples Test table) and it is significant at the 0.000 level. Thus, we can reject the null hypothesis that the two means are equal. Moreover, we can conclude that Santa Fe Grill customers have somewhat more favorable perceptions of food taste than food temperature.

Exhibit 11.12 **Paired Samples *t*-Test**

T-Test

Paired Samples Statistics

		Mean	N	Std. Deviation	Std. Error Mean
Pair 1	X18—Excellent Food Taste	4.78	253	.881	.055
	X20—Proper Food Temperature	4.38	253	1.065	.067

Paired Samples Test

		Paired Differences							
					95% Confidence Interval of the Difference				
		Mean	Std. Deviation	Std. Error Mean	Lower	Upper	t	df	Sig. (2-tailed)
Pair 1	X18—Excellent Food Taste - X20—Proper Food Temperature	.395	.747	.047	.303	.488	8.421	252	.000

Analysis of Variance (ANOVA)

Analysis of variance (ANOVA) A statistical technique that determines whether three or more means are statistically different from one another.

Researchers use **analysis of variance (ANOVA)** to determine the statistical difference between three or more means. For example, if a researcher finds that the average number of cups of coffee consumed per day by freshmen during finals is 3.7, while the average number of cups of coffee consumed per day by seniors and graduate students is 4.3 cups and 5.1 cups, respectively, are these observed differences statistically significant?

In this section, we show how one-way ANOVA is used to examine group means. The term *one-way* is used because the comparison involves only one independent variable. In a later section, we show how researchers also can use ANOVA to examine the effects of several independent variables simultaneously. This enables analysts to estimate both the individual and combined effects of several independent variables on the dependent variable.

An example of a one-way ANOVA problem may be to compare light, medium, and heavy drinkers of Starbucks coffee on their attitude toward a particular Starbucks advertising campaign. In this instance, there is one independent variable—consumption of Starbucks coffee—but it is divided into three different levels. Our earlier *t* statistics won't work here because we are comparing the means of more than two groups.

ANOVA requires that the dependent variable, in this case the attitude toward the Starbucks advertising campaign, be metric. That is, the dependent variable must be either interval or ratio scaled. A second data requirement is that the independent variable, in this case the coffee consumption variable, be categorical (nonmetric).

The null hypothesis for ANOVA always states that there is no difference between the dependent variable groups—in this situation, the ad campaign attitudes of the groups of Starbucks coffee drinkers. Thus, the null hypothesis would be

$$\mu1 = \mu2 = \mu3$$

ANOVA examines the variance within a set of data. Recall from the earlier discussion of measures of dispersion that the variance of a variable is equal to the average squared deviation from the mean of the variable. The logic of ANOVA is that if we calculate the variance between the groups and compare it to the variance within the groups, we can make a determination as to whether the group means (attitudes toward the advertising campaign) are significantly different.[1] When within-group variance is high, it swamps any between group differences we see unless those differences are large.

F-test The test used to statistically evaluate the differences between the group means in ANOVA.

Determining Statistical Significance in ANOVA Researchers use the **F-test** with ANOVA to evaluate the differences between group means for statistical significance. For example, suppose the heavy users of Starbucks coffee rate the advertising campaign 4.4 on a 5-point scale, with 5 = Very favorable. The medium users of Starbucks coffee rate the campaign 3.9, and the light users of Starbucks coffee rate the campaign 2.5. The F-test in ANOVA will tell us if these observed differences are statistically significant.

The *total variance* in a set of responses to a question is made up of between-group and within-group variance. The *between-group variance* measures how much the sample means of the groups differ from one another. In contrast, the *within-group variance* measures how much the responses within each group differ from one another. The F distribution is the ratio of these two components of total variance and can be calculated as follows:

$$\text{F ratio} = \frac{\text{Variance between groups}}{\text{Variance within groups}}$$

The larger the difference in the variance between groups, the larger the F ratio. Since the total variance in a data set is divisible into between- and within-group components, if there is more variance explained or accounted for by considering differences between groups than there is within groups, then the independent variable probably has a significant impact on the dependent variable. Larger F ratios imply significant differences between the groups. Thus, the larger the F ratio, the more *likely* it is that the null hypothesis will be rejected.

SPSS Application—ANOVA

The owners of the Santa Fe Grill would like to know if there is a difference in the likelihood of returning to the restaurant based on how far customers have driven to get to the restaurant. They believe it is important to know the answer not only for their customers but for customers of Jose's as well. They therefore ask the researcher to test the hypothesis that there are no differences in likelihood of returning (X_{23}) and distance driven to get to the restaurants (X_{30}). To do so, the researcher analyzed all 405 responses for the survey.

To test this hypothesis we use the SPSS compare means test. The click-through sequence is Analyze → Compare Means → One-Way ANOVA. When you get to the One-Way ANOVA dialog box, highlight X_{23}–Likely to Return and move it into the Dependent List window. Next highlight X_{30}–Distance Driven and then click on the arrow button to move it into the Factor window. Now click on the Options tab and then on Descriptive. Click Continue and OK to execute the program.

Interpretation of ANOVA Results The results are shown in Exhibit 11.13. First, the numbers in the N column indicate that 116 individuals drive less than 1 mile, 129 drive 1 to 5 miles, and 160 drive more than 5 miles. Thus, a larger number of people are driving from farther away to get to the restaurants. The question is, however, is distance driven related to likelihood of returning? Looking at the numbers in the Mean column, we see that the likelihood of returning is lower as individuals drive farther. That is, the numbers in the Mean

Exhibit 11.13 Example of One-Way ANOVA

Oneway

Descriptives

X23 – Likely to Return

	N	Mean	Std. Deviation	Std. Error	95% Confidence Interval for Mean		Minimum	Maximum
					Lower Bound	Upper Bound		
Less than 1 mile	116	4.91	.734	.068	4.77	5.04	3	6
1–5 miles	129	4.63	1.146	.101	4.43	4.83	3	7
More than 5 miles	160	4.01	1.133	.090	3.84	4.19	2	7
Total	405	4.46	1.104	.055	4.36	4.57	2	7

ANOVA

X23 – Likely to Return

	Sum of Squares	df	Mean Square	F	Sig.
Between Groups	58.659	2	29.330	27.163	.000
Within Groups	434.071	402	1.080		
Total	492.731	404			

column indicate that individuals driving less than 1 mile report a likelihood of returning of 4.91. Recall that this question uses a 7-point scale with 7 = Highly Likely and 1 = Highly Unlikely. Individuals that drive 1 to 5 miles indicate their likelihood of returning is 4.63 and those who drive more than 5 miles are even less likely to return—mean of 4.01. Thus, the likelihood of returning means become smaller as the distance driven increases.

The question remains, however, are these means significantly different? The ANOVA table at the bottom of Exhibit 11.13 provides this answer. The Sig. column has the number .000 in it. The correct interpretation of this number is if this survey were repeated 1,000 times, the result would always be statistically significant. Another way of saying this is there are no chances in 1,000 that we could be wrong if we said that the hypothesis of no differences is rejected and concluded that in fact there truly are differences in the means of likelihood of returning based on distance driven.

Statistical Significance and Individual Group Differences A weakness of ANOVA, however, is that the test enables the researcher to determine only that statistical differences exist between at least one pair of the group means. The technique cannot identify which pairs of means are significantly different from each other. In our example of Starbucks coffee drinkers' attitudes toward the advertising campaign, we can conclude that differences in attitudes toward the advertising campaign exist among light, medium, and heavy coffee drinkers, but we would not be able to determine if the differences are between light and medium, or between light and heavy, or between medium and heavy, and so on. We are able to say only that there are significant differences somewhere among the groups. Thus, the marketing researcher still must determine where the mean differences lie.

The difficulty of the Starbucks example above is also true of the restaurant ANOVA results for the restaurant survey. That is, we can conclude that there are differences between the three groups based on distance driven. But we do not know if the differences are between the drive less than 1 mile group and the 1 to 5 miles group, or the 1 to 5 miles group and the more than 5 miles group, and so on. To answer this question, we must apply follow-up "post-hoc" tests. These tests will identify the pairs of groups that have significantly different mean responses.

Many **follow-up tests** are available in statistical software packages such as SPSS and SAS. All of the methods involve multiple comparisons, or simultaneous assessment of confidence interval estimates of differences between the means. That is, all means are compared two at a time. The differences between the methods are based on their ability to control the error rate. We shall briefly describe one follow-up test, the Scheffé procedure. Relative to other follow-up tests, the *Scheffé procedure* is a more conservative method for detection of significant differences between group means.

The Scheffé follow-up test establishes simultaneous confidence intervals around all groups' responses and imposes an error rate at a specified α level. The test identifies differences between all pairs of means at high and low confidence interval ranges. If the difference between each pair of means falls outside the range of the confidence interval, then the null hypothesis is rejected and we conclude that the pairs of means are statistically different. The Scheffé test will show whether one, two, or all three pairs of means in our restaurant example are different. The Scheffé test is equivalent to simultaneous two-tailed hypothesis tests. Because the technique holds the experimental error rate to α (typically .05), the confidence intervals tend to be wider than in the other methods, but the researcher has more assurance that true mean differences exist. Recall that the Scheffé test is conservative so you may wish to look at one of the other tests available in your statistical software.

To run the Scheffé post-hoc test, we use the SPSS compare means test. The click-through sequence is Analyze → Compare Means → One-Way ANOVA. When you get to the One-Way ANOVA dialog box, highlight X_{23}–Likely to Return and move it into the Dependent

Follow-up tests A test that flags the means that are statistically different from each other; follow-up tests are performed after an ANOVA determines there are differences between means.

Exhibit 11.14	Results for Post-hoc ANOVA Tests

Multiple Comparisons

X23—Likely to Return
Scheffé

(I) x30—Distance Driven to Restaurant	(J) x30—Distance Driven to Restaurant	Mean Difference (I-J)	Std. Error	Sig.	95% Confidence Interval	
					Lower Bound	Upper Bound
Less than 1 mile	1–5 miles	.277	.133	.115	-.05	.60
	More than 5 miles	.893*	.127	.000	.58	1.20
1–5 miles	Less than 1 mile	-.277	.133	.115	-.60	.05
	More than 5 miles	.615*	.123	.000	.31	.92
More than 5 miles	Less than 1 mile	-.893*	.127	.000	-1.20	-.58
	1–5 miles	-.615*	.123	.000	-.92	-.31

*.The mean difference is significant at the 0.05 level.

List window. Next highlight X_{30}–Distance Driven and then click on the arrow button to move it into the Factor window. Now click on the Options tab and then on Descriptive. Next click on the Post Hoc tab and then on Scheffé. Then click Continue and OK to get the post-hoc test results.

Interpretation of Results Results for the Scheffé test for the restaurant example are shown in Exhibit 11.14. Recall from Exhibit 11.13 that the means for the three groups indicated less likelihood to return to the restaurants as the customers drove from farther away. The research question is, "Do statistically significant differences exist between all the distance driven customer groups, or only some?" Looking at the information in the Sig. column we see that differences between some of the group means are statistically significant (.000) while others are not (.115). Specifically, the means of the less than 1 mile and 1–5 mile groups are not statistically different. In contrast, the means of the less than 1 mile and more than 5 miles groups are statistically different and so also are the means of the 1 to 5 miles group and the more than five miles group. As a general conclusion, we can state that distance from the restaurant does influence likelihood of returning, but the influence is not significant until a customer drives from farther than 5 miles away. Thus, marketing efforts based on distance from the restaurant can be similar for individuals within a 5-mile radius of the restaurant, the typical primary target area for a restaurant. But for individuals driving farther than 5 miles, some kind of incentive should be considered to increase their likelihood of returning.

n-Way ANOVA

n-Way ANOVA This is a type of ANOVA that can analyze several independent variables at the same time.

Discussion of ANOVA to this point has been devoted to one-way ANOVA in which there is only one independent variable. In the Starbucks example, the usage category (consumption of Starbucks coffee) was the independent variable. Similarly, for the restaurant example, distance driven (three separate groups) was the independent variable. Marketing researchers may, however, be interested in analyzing several independent variables simultaneously. In such cases an **n-way ANOVA** would be used.

Interaction effect Multiple independent variables in an ANOVA can act together to affect dependent variable group means.

Researchers often are interested in the region of the country where a product is sold as well as consumption patterns. Using multiple independent factors creates the possibility of an **interaction effect.** That is, the multiple independent variables can act together to affect dependent variable group means. For example, heavy consumers of Starbucks coffee in the Northeast may have different attitudes about advertising campaigns than heavy consumers of Starbucks coffee in the West, and there may be still further differences between the various coffee-consumption-level groups, as described earlier.

Another situation that may require n-way ANOVA is the use of experimental designs (causal research), where the researcher uses different levels of a stimulus (e.g., different prices or ads) and then measures responses to those stimuli. For example, a marketer may be interested in finding out whether consumers prefer a humorous ad to a serious one and whether that preference varies across gender. Each type of ad could be shown to different groups of customers (both male and female). Then, questions about their preferences for the ad and the product it advertises could be asked. The primary difference between the groups would be the difference in ad execution (humorous or nonhumorous) and customer gender. An n-way ANOVA could be used to find out whether the ad execution differences helped cause differences in ad and product preferences, as well as what effects might be attributable to customer gender.

From a conceptual standpoint, n-way ANOVA is similar to one-way ANOVA, but the mathematics is more complex. However, statistical packages such as SPSS will conveniently perform n-way ANOVA.

SPSS Application—n-Way ANOVA

To help you understand how ANOVA is used to answer research questions, we refer to the restaurant database to answer a typical question. The owners want to know first whether customers who come to the restaurant from greater distances differ from customers who live nearby in their willingness to recommend the restaurant to a friend. Second, they also want to know whether that difference in willingness to recommend, if any, is influenced by the gender of the customers. The database variables are X_{24}–Likely to Recommend, measured on a 7-point scale, with 1 = "Definitely Will Not Recommend" and 7 = "Definitely Recommend"; X_{30}–Distance Driven, where 1 = "Less than 1 mile," 2 = "1–3 miles," and 3 = "More than 3 miles"; and X_{32}–Gender, where 0 = male and 1 = female.

On the basis of informal comments from customers, the owners believe customers who come from more than 5 miles will be more likely to recommend the restaurant. Moreover, they hypothesize male customers will be more likely to recommend the restaurant than females. The null hypotheses are that there will be no difference between the mean ratings for X_{24}–Likely to Recommend for customers who traveled different distances to come to the restaurant (X_{30}), and there also will be no difference between females and males (X_{32}).

The purpose of the ANOVA analysis is to see if the differences that do exist are statistically significant and meaningful. To statistically assess the differences, ANOVA uses the F-ratio. The bigger the F-ratio, the bigger the difference among the means of the various groups with respect to their likelihood of recommending the restaurant.

SPSS can help you conduct the statistical analysis to test the null hypotheses. The best way to analyze the restaurant survey data to answer the owner's questions is to use a factorial model. A factorial model is a type of ANOVA in which the individual effects of each independent variable on the dependent variable are considered separately, and then the combined effects (an interaction) of the independent variables on the dependent variable are analyzed.

To examine this hypothesis we will use only the Santa Fe Grill customer survey data. To separate out the Santa Fe sample, first use the Data pull-down menu and go to Select

Cases, as shown in the Research Dashboard. Select only the Santa Fe Grill customers to analyze. After selecting the Santa Fe sample, the click-through sequence is ANALYZE → GENERAL LINEAR MODEL → UNIVARIATE. Highlight the dependent variable X_{24}–Likely to Recommend by clicking on it and move it to the Dependent Variable box. Next, highlight X_{30}–Distance Driven and X_{32}–Gender, and move them to the Fixed Factors box. Now click on the Options box on the right side of the SPSS screen and look in the Estimated Marginal Means box and highlight (OVERALL) as well as X_{30}, X_{32}, and $X_{30} * X_{32}$ and move them all into the Display Means for box. Next place a check on "Compare main effects" and Descriptive Statistics. Then click Continue and finally click OK.

Interpretation of Results The SPSS output for ANOVA is shown in Exhibit 11.15. The Tests of Between-Subjects Effects table shows that the F-ratio for X_{30}–Distance Driven is 48.927, which is statistically significant at the .000 level. This means that customers who come from different distances to eat at the restaurant vary in their likelihood of recommending the restaurant. The F-ratio for X_{32}–Gender is 13.046, which also is statistically significant at the .000 level. This means the gender of customers influences their likelihood of recommending the restaurant.

Exhibit 11.15   **n-Way ANOVA Results—Santa Fe Grill**

Between-Subjects Factors

		Value Label	N
x30—Distance Driven to Restaurant	1	Less than 1 mile	86
	2	1–5 miles	76
	3	More than 5 miles	91
X32—Gender	0	Male	176
	1	Female	77

Tests of Between-Subjects Effects

Dependent Variable: X24—Likely to Recommend

Source	Type III Sum of Squares	df	Mean Square	F	Sig.
Corrected model	99.421*	5	19.884	37.034	.000
Intercept	2258.291	1	2258.291	4206.033	.000
x30	52.540	2	26.270	48.927	.000
x32	7.005	1	7.005	13.046	.000
x30 * x32	2.590	2	1.295	2.412	.092
Error	132.618	247	.537		
Total	3534.000	253			
Corrected total	232.040	252			

*R Squared = .428 (Adjusted R Squared = .417)

Exhibit 11.16	n-Way ANOVA Means Result

Descriptive Statistics

Dependent Variable:X24—Likely to Recommend

x30—Distance Driven...	X32—Gender	Mean	Std. Deviation	N
Less than 1 mile	Male	4.39	.569	74
	Female	3.67	.888	12
	Total	4.29	.666	86
1–5 miles	Male	3.78	.850	45
	Female	3.68	1.077	31
	Total	3.74	.943	76
More than 5 miles	Male	3.00	.463	57
	Female	2.65	.812	34
	Total	2.87	.636	91
Total	Male	3.78	.861	176
	Female	3.22	1.059	77
	Total	3.61	.960	253

Pairwise Comparisons

Dependent Variable:X24—Likely to Recommend

(I) x30—Distance Driven to Restaurant	(J) x30—Distance Driven to Restaurant	Mean Difference (I-J)	Std. Error	Sig.†	95% Confidence Interval for Difference†	
					Lower Bound	Upper Bound
Less than 1 mile	1–5 miles	.302*	.143	.035	.021	.582
	More than 5 miles	1.206*	.139	.000	.932	1.479
1–5 miles	Less than 1 mile	-.302*	.143	.035	-.582	-.021
	More than 5 miles	.904*	.117	.000	.674	1.134
More than 5 miles	Less than 1 mile	-1.206*	.139	.000	-1.479	-.932
	1–5 miles	-.904*	.117	.000	-1.134	-.674

Based on estimated marginal means

*. The mean difference is significant at the .05 level.
†. Adjustment for multiple comparisons: Least Significant Difference (equivalent to no adjustments).

n-Way ANOVA Means We now know that both X_{30}–Distance Driven and X_{32}–Gender influence likelihood of recommending the Santa Fe Grill. But we do not know how. To answer this question we must look at the means for these two variables, which are shown in Exhibit 11.16.

Interpretation of Results Look at the numbers in the Descriptive Statistics table of Exhibit 11.16. The means (see Total rows) show that the average likelihood of recommending the Santa Fe Grill to a friend increases as the distance driven by the respondent decreases. In short, customers who come from within 1 mile of the Santa Fe Grill show an average likelihood to recommend of 4.29, compared with a 3.74 and 2.87 average likelihood for customers who come from 1–5 and more than 5 miles away, respectively.

The Santa Fe Grill owners were also interested in whether there is a difference in the likelihood of males versus females recommending the Santa Fe Grill. The F-ratio for gender is again large (13.046; see Exhibit 11.15) and statistically significant (.000). Looking at the means of the customer groups based on gender (see Exhibit 11.16), we see that indeed males are more likely to recommend the Santa Fe Grill as compared to females. The null hypothesis of no differences based on gender is rejected. Moreover, we conclude there is a difference in the average likelihood of male and female customers to recommend the Santa Fe Grill, with males being significantly more likely than females to recommend the restaurant.

The interaction between distance traveled and gender has an F-ratio of .456, with a probability level of .634, meaning that the difference in the likelihood of recommendation when both independent variables are considered together is not statistically significant. This means there is no interaction between distance driven, gender, and likelihood of recommending the Santa Fe Grill.

Perceptual Mapping

Perceptual mapping A process that is used to develop maps showing the perceptions of respondents. The maps are visual representations of respondents' perceptions of a company, product, service, brand, or any other object in two dimensions.

Perceptual mapping is a process that is used to develop maps that show the perceptions of respondents. The maps are visual representations of respondents' perceptions of a company, product, service, brand, or any other object in two dimensions. A perceptual map typically has a vertical and a horizontal axis that are labeled with descriptive adjectives. Possible adjectives for our restaurant example might be food temperature and/or freshness, speed of service, good value for the money, and so on.

Several different approaches can be used to develop perceptual maps. These include rankings, medians and mean ratings. To illustrate perceptual mapping, data from an example involving ratings of fast-food restaurants are shown in Exhibit 11.17. Researchers gave customers a set of six fast-food restaurants and asked them to express how they perceive each restaurant. The perceptions of the respondents are then plotted on a two-dimensional map using two of the adjectives, freshness of food and food temperature. Inspection of the map, shown in Exhibit 11.18, illustrates that customers perceive Wendy's and Back Yard Burgers as quite similar to each other, as are McDonald's and Burger King. Customers perceive Arby's and Hardee's as somewhat similar, but do not view these restaurants as favorably as the others. However, Back Yard Burgers and McDonald's were perceived as very dissimilar. To better understand how to develop perceptual maps, read the Marketing Research in Action on Remington's Steak House at the end of this chapter.

Exhibit 11.17	Ratings of Six Fast-Food Restaurants

	Food Freshness	Food Temperature
McDonald's	1.8	3.7
Burger King	2.0	3.5
Wendy's	4.0	4.5
Back Yard Burger	4.5	4.8
Arby's	4.0	2.5
Hardee's	3.5	1.8

Key: Food temperature, 1 = Warm, 5 = Hot, Food freshness, 1 = Low, 5 = High.

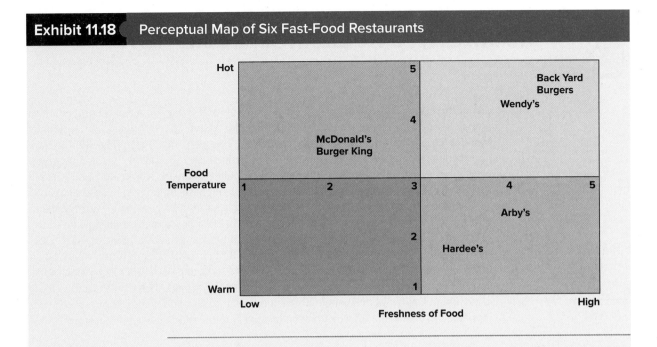

Exhibit 11.18 Perceptual Map of Six Fast-Food Restaurants

Perceptual Mapping Applications in Marketing Research

While our fast-food example illustrates how perceptual mapping groups pairs of restaurants together based on perceived ratings, perceptual mapping has many other important applications in marketing research. Other applications include

- *New-product development.* Perceptual mapping can identify gaps in perceptions and thereby help to position new products.
- *Image measurement.* Perceptual mapping can be used to identify the image of the company to help to position one company relative to the competition.
- *Advertising.* Perceptual mapping can assess advertising effectiveness in positioning the brand.
- *Distribution.* Perceptual mapping could be used to assess similarities of brands and channel outlets.

 CONTINUING CASE STUDY THE SANTA FE GRILL

With the survey completed, edited, and entered into a digital file, researchers will now make decisions regarding the best way to analyze the data to understand the interviewed individuals. Then, researchers and decision makers will determine how the information can be used to improve the restaurant's operations. The data analysis should be connected directly to the research objectives. The researcher and the owners have been brainstorming about how to best analyze the data to better understand the situation.

1. Draw several conceptual models to represent relationships that could be tested with the survey. Be sure to include comparisons of the Santa Fe Grill and Jose's Southwestern Café.

2. Which statistical techniques would be appropriate to test the proposed relationships?

3. Give examples of relationships that could be tested with Chi-square. . . . with ANOVA.

MARKETING RESEARCH IN ACTION
Examining Restaurant Image Positions—Remington's Steak House

About three years ago, John Smith opened Remington's Steak House, a retail theme restaurant located in a large midwestern city. Smith's vision was to position his restaurant as a unique, theme-oriented specialty restaurant. The plan was for the restaurant to have an excellent reputation for offering a wide assortment of high-quality yet competitively priced entrees, excellent service, and knowledgeable employees who understand customers' needs. The overriding goal was to place heavy emphasis on satisfying customers.

Smith used this vision to guide the development and implementation of his restaurant's positioning and marketing strategies. Although Smith knew how to deliver dining experience, he did not know much about developing, implementing, and assessing marketing strategies.

Recently, Smith began asking himself some fundamental questions about his restaurant's operations and the future of his business. Smith expressed these questions to an account representative at a local marketing research firm and, as a result, decided to do some research to better understand his customers' attitudes and feelings. More specifically, he wanted to gain some information and insights into the following set of questions:

1. What are the major factors customers use when selecting a restaurant, and what is the relative importance of each of these factors?
2. What image do customers have of Remington's and its two major competitors?
3. Is Remington's providing quality and satisfaction to its customers?
4. Do any of Remington's current marketing strategies need to be changed, and if so in what ways?

To address Smith's questions, the account representative recommended completing an image survey using an Internet panel approach. Initial contact was made with potential respondents using a random digit dialing telephone survey to screen for individuals who were patrons of Remington's as well as customers of competitors' restaurants (including their main competitors, Outback Steak House and Longhorn Steak House) within the market area. Respondents must also have a minimum annual household income of $20,000, and be familiar enough with one of the three restaurant competitors to accurately rate them. If an individual was qualified for the study based on the screening questions, they were directed to a website where they completed the survey.

Because this was the first time Smith had conducted any marketing research, the consultant suggested an exploratory approach and recommended a small sample size of 200. She said that if the results of the initial 200 surveys were helpful, the sample size could be increased so that the findings would be more precise. The questionnaire included questions about the importance of various reasons in choosing a restaurant, perceptions of the images of the three restaurant competitors on the same factors, and selected classification information on the respondents. When the researcher reached the quota of 200 usable completed questionnaires, the sample included 86 respondents who were most familiar with Outback, 65 who were most familiar with Longhorn, and 49 who were most familiar with Remington's. This last criterion was used to determine which of Remington's restaurant competitors a respondent evaluated. A database for the questions in this case is available in SPSS format at **connect.mheducation.com.** The name of the database is Remingtons MRIA_essn.sav. A copy of the questionnaire is in Exhibit 11.19.

Exhibit 11.19	The Remington's Steak House Questionnaire

Screening and Rapport Questions

Hello. My name is _____ and I work for DSS Research. We are talking to individuals today/ tonight about dining out habits.

1. "Do you regularly dine at casual dining restaurants?"   _____ Yes _____ No
2. "Have you eaten at other casual restaurants in the last six months?" _____ Yes _____ No
3. "Is your gross annual household income $20,000 or more?"   _____ Yes _____ No
4. There are three casual steakhouse restaurants in you neighborhood—Outback, Longhorn, and Remington's. Which of these restaurants are you most familiar with?
   a. Outback _____
   b. Longhorn _____
   c. Remington's _____
   d. None _____

If respondent answers "Yes" to the first three questions, and is familiar with one of the three restaurants, then say:

We would like you to answer a few questions about your recent dining experiences at Outback/ Longhorn/Remington's restaurant. The survey will only take a few minutes and it will be very helpful in better serving restaurant customers in this area.

If the person says yes, give them instructions on how to access the website and complete the survey.

DINING OUT SURVEY

Please read all questions carefully. In the first section a number of reasons are listed that people use in selecting a particular restaurant to dine at. Using a scale from 1 to 7, with 7 being "Very Important" and 1 being "Not Important at All," please indicate the extent to which a particular selection reason is important or unimportant. Circle only one number for each selection reason.

Section 1: Importance Ratings

How important is/are _____ in selecting a particular restaurant to dine at?

	Not Important At All					Very Important
1. Large portions	1	2	3	4	5	6 7
2. Competent employees	1	2	3	4	5	6 7
3. Food quality	1	2	3	4	5	6 7
4. Speed of service	1	2	3	4	5	6 7
5. Atmosphere	1	2	3	4	5	6 7
6. Reasonable prices	1	2	3	4	5	6 7

(continued)

Exhibit 11.19   *continued*

Section 2: Perceptions Measures

Listed below is a set of characteristics that could be used to describe [Outback/Longhorn/Remington's]. Using a scale from 1 to 7, with 7 being "Strongly Agree" and 1 being "Strongly Disagree," to what extent do you agree or disagree that [Remington's—Outback—Longhorn's]: (a particular restaurant's name appeared on the screen based on the familiarity question in the telephone screener)

7. has large portions

Strongly Disagree   Strongly Agree
1   2   3   4   5   6   7

8. has competent employees

Strongly Disagree   Strongly Agree
1   2   3   4   5   6   7

9. has excellent food quality

Strongly Disagree   Strongly Agree
1   2   3   4   5   6   7

10. has quick service

Strongly Disagree   Strongly Agree
1   2   3   4   5   6   7

11. has a good atmosphere

Strongly Disagree   Strongly Agree
1   2   3   4   5   6   7

12. reasonable prices

Strongly Disagree   Strongly Agree
1   2   3   4   5   6   7

Section 3: Relationship Measures

Please indicate your view on each of the following questions:

13. How satisfied are you with _____ ?

Not Satisfied At All   Very Satisfied
1 2 3 4 5 6 7

14. How likely are you to return to _____ in the future?

Definitely Will Not Return   Definitely Will Return
1 2 3 4 5 6 7

15. How likely are you to recommend _____ to a friend?

Definitely Will Not Recommend   Definitely Will Recommend
1 2 3 4 5 6 7

16. Frequency of Patronage
How often do you eat at _____ ?

1 = Occasionally (Less than once a month)
2 = Frequently (1–3 times a month)
3 = Very Frequently (4 or more times a month)

Section 4: Classification Questions

Please circle the number that classifies you best.

17. Number of Children at Home

1   None
2   1–2
3   More than 2 children at home

Exhibit 11.19   *continued*

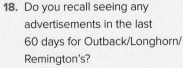

18. Do you recall seeing any advertisements in the last 60 days for Outback/Longhorn/ Remington's?

0	No
1	Yes

19. Your gender

0	Male
1	Female

20. Your age in years

1	18–25
2	26–34
3	35–49
4	50–59
5	60 and Older

21. Your annual gross household income

1	$20,000–$35,000
2	$35,001–$50,000
3	$50,001–$75,000
4	$75,001–$100,000
5	More than $100,000

22. Competitors: Most familiar with _____?

1	Outback
2	Longhorn
3	Remington's

Thank you very much for your help. Click on the submit button to exit the survey.

Exhibit 11.20   Average Importance Ratings for Restaurant Selection Factors

		X1—Large Portions	X2— Competent Employees	X3—Food Quality	X4—Speed of Service	X5— Atmosphere	X6— Reasonable Prices
				Statistics			
N	Valid	200	200	200	200	200	200
	Missing	0	0	0	0	0	0
Mean		4.95	3.12	6.09	5.99	4.74	5.39

Researchers focused their initial analysis of the data on the importance ratings for the restaurant selection factors. The importance ratings are variables X_1–X_6 in the Remington's database. Exhibit 11.20 shows that food quality and speed of service are the two most important factors. To create this exhibit, the click-through sequence is ANALYZE → DESCRIPTIVE STATISTICS → FREQUENCIES. Highlight variables X_1–X_6 and move them to the Variable(s) box. Then go to the Statistics box and check "Mean," and then click Continue, and OK. The least important factor is competent employees (mean = 3.12). This does not mean employees are not important. It simply means they are less important compared to the other factors included in the survey. In sum, respondents wanted good food, fast service, and reasonable prices.

The next task was to examine the perceptions of the three restaurant competitors. Using the restaurant image factors, the consultant conducted an ANOVA to see if there were any differences in the perceptions of the three restaurants (Exhibits 11.21 and 11.22). To create these exhibits, the click-through sequence is ANALYZE → COMPARE MEANS → ONE-WAY ANOVA. Highlight variables X_7–X_{12} and move them to the Dependent List box, and then highlight variable X_{22} and move it to the Factor box. Next go to the Options box, check "Descriptive," and then click Continue, and OK.

We show the results in Exhibits 11.21 and 11.22. We provide an overview of the findings from Exhibits 11.20 to 11.22 in Exhibit 11.23.

The findings of the survey were quite revealing. On the most important factor (food quality), Remington's rated the highest (mean = 6.86; see Exhibit 11.23), but Outback

| **Exhibit 11.21** | One-Way ANOVA for Restaurant Competitors |

Descriptives

		N	Mean
X7 -- Large Portions	Outback	86	3.57
	Longhorn	65	2.77
	Remington's	49	3.39
	Total	200	3.27
X8 -- Competent Employees	Outback	86	5.15
	Longhorn	65	3.25
	Remington's	49	2.49
	Total	200	3.88
X9 -- Food Quality	Outback	86	6.42
	Longhorn	65	5.12
	Remington's	49	6.86
	Total	200	6.11
X10 -- Speed of Service	Outback	86	4.35
	Longhorn	65	3.02
	Remington's	49	2.27
	Total	200	3.41
X11 -- Atmosphere	Outback	86	6.09
	Longhorn	65	4.35
	Remington's	49	6.59
	Total	200	5.65
X12 -- Reasonable Prices	Outback	86	5.50
	Longhorn	65	5.00
	Remington's	49	5.49
	Total	200	5.34

Exhibit 11.22   One-Way ANOVA of Differences in Restaurant Perceptions

ANOVA

		Sum of Squares	df	Mean Square	F	Sig.
X7 — Large Portions	Between Groups	24.702	2	12.351	17.349	.000
	Within Groups	140.253	197	.712		
	Total	164.955	199			
X8 — Competent Employees	Between Groups	259.779	2	129.889	242.908	.000
	Within Groups	105.341	197	.535		
	Total	365.120	199			
X9 — Food Quality	Between Groups	98.849	2	49.425	110.712	.000
	Within Groups	87.946	197	.446		
	Total	186.795	199			
X10 — Speed of Service	Between Groups	150.124	2	75.062	102.639	.000
	Within Groups	144.071	197	.731		
	Total	294.195	199			
X11 — Atmosphere	Between Groups	169.546	2	84.773	136.939	.000
	Within Groups	121.954	197	.619		
	Total	291.500	199			
X12 — Reasonable Prices	Between Groups	10.810	2	5.405	8.892	.000
	Within Groups	119.745	197	.608		
	Total	130.555	199			

Exhibit 11.23   Summary of ANOVA Findings from Exhibits 11.20–11.22

		Competitor Means			
Attributes	**Rankings***	**Outback**	**Longhorn**	**Remington's**	**Sig.**
X7—Large Portions	4	3.57	2.77	3.39	.000
X8—Competent Employees	6	5.15	3.25	2.49	.000
X9—Food Quality	1	6.42	5.12	6.86	.000
X10—Speed of Service	2	4.35	3.02	2.27	.000
X11—Atmosphere	5	6.09	4.35	6.59	.000
X12—Reasonable Prices	3	5.50	5.00	5.49	.000
N = 200 total		86	65	49	.000

*Note: Rankings are based on mean importance ratings of attributes.

was a close second (mean = 6.42). Remington's was also rated the highest on atmosphere (mean = 6.59), but that factor was fifth most important. For speed of service (second most important) and competent employees (least important), Remington's was rated the lowest of the three competitors.

| Exhibit 11.24 | Importance-Performance Chart for Remington's Steak House |

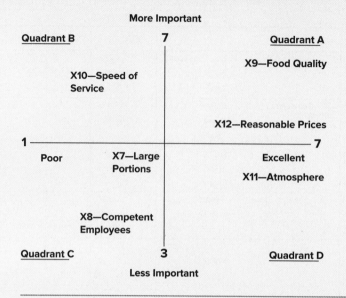

An easy way to convey the results of an image analysis is to prepare an importance performance chart (IPC). To prepare this chart, calculate the mean values for the importance and performance questions for each of the restaurants.Then use these means to plot the position of each restaurant on a perceptual map. The IPC for Remington's Steak House is shown in Exhibit 11.24. The chart shows that in terms of food quality and prices, Remington's is doing well. But there are several areas for improvement, particularly in comparison to the competition. The competitive restaurants can be plotted on a separate perceptual map. An IPC (perceptual map) has quadrants (A–D) that are described as follows:

Quadrant A: Modifications are needed.
Quadrant B: Good job—no need to modify.
Quadrant C: Don't worry—low priority.
Quadrant D: Rethink—a possible overkill.

Hands-On Exercise

1. What are other areas of improvement for Remington's?
2. Run post-hoc ANOVA tests between the competitor groups. What additional problems or challenges did this reveal?
3. What new marketing strategies would you suggest?

Summary

Explain measures of central tendency and dispersion.

The mean is the most commonly used measure of central tendency and describes the arithmetic average of the values in a sample of data. The median represents the middle value of an ordered set of values. The mode is the most frequently occurring value in a distribution of values. All these measures describe the center of the distribution of a set of values. The range defines the spread of the data. It is the distance between the smallest and largest values of the distribution. The standard deviation describes the average distance of the distribution values from the mean. A large standard deviation indicates a distribution in which the individual values are spread out and are relatively farther away from the mean.

Describe how to test hypotheses using univariate and bivariate statistics.

Marketing researchers often form hypotheses regarding population characteristics based on sample data. The process typically begins by calculating frequency distributions and averages, and then moves on to actually test the hypotheses. When the hypothesis testing involves examining one variable at a time, researchers use a univariate statistical test. When the hypothesis testing involves two variables, researchers use a bivariate statistical test. The Chi-square statistic permits us to test for statistically significant differences between the frequency distributions of two or more groups. Categorical data from questions about sex, race, profession, and so forth can be examined and tested for statistical differences. In addition to examining frequencies, marketing researchers often want to compare the means of two groups. There are two possible situations when means are compared. In independent samples the respondents come from different populations, so their answers to the survey questions do not affect each other. In related samples, the same respondent answers several questions, so comparing answers to these questions requires the use of a paired-samples t-test. Questions about mean differences in independent samples can be answered by using a t-test statistic.

Apply and interpret analysis of variance (ANOVA).

Researchers use ANOVA to determine the statistical significance of the difference between two or more means. The ANOVA technique calculates the variance of the values between groups of respondents and compares it with the variance of the responses within the groups. If the between-group variance is significantly greater than the within-group variance as indicated by the F-ratio, the means are significantly different. The statistical significance between means in ANOVA is detected through the use of a follow-up test. The Scheffé test is one type of follow-up test. The test examines the differences between all possible pairs of sample means against a high and low confidence range. If the difference between a pair of means falls outside the confidence interval, then the means can be considered statistically different.

Utilize perceptual mapping to present research findings.

Perceptual mapping is used to develop maps that show perceptions of respondents visually. These maps are graphic representations that can be produced from the results of several multivariate techniques. The maps provide a visual representation of how companies, products, brands, or other objects are perceived relative to each other on key attributes such as quality of service, food taste, and food preparation.

Key Terms and Concepts

Analysis of variance (ANOVA) 297

Chi-square (X^2) analysis 291

Follow-up test 299

F-test 297

Independent samples 294

Interaction effect 301

Mean 274

Median 275

Mode 275

n-way ANOVA 300

Perceptual mapping 304

Range 277

Related samples 294
Standard deviation 278

t-test 294
Variance 278

▆▆ Review Questions

1. Explain the difference between the mean, the median, and the mode.
2. Why and how would you use Chi-square and *t*-tests in hypothesis testing?
3. Why and when would you want to use ANOVA in marketing research?
4. What will ANOVA tests not tell you, and how can you overcome this problem?

▆▆ Discussion Questions

1. The measures of central tendency discussed in this chapter are designed to reveal information about the center of a distribution of values. Measures of dispersion provide information about the spread of all the values in a distribution around the center values. Assume you were conducting an opinion poll on voters' approval ratings of the job performance of the mayor of the city where you live. Do you think the mayor would be more interested in the central tendency or the dispersion measures associated with the responses to your poll? Why?

2. If you were interested in finding out whether or not young adults (21–34 years old) are more likely to buy products online than older adults (35 or more years old), how would you phrase your null hypothesis? What is the implicit alternative hypothesis accompanying your null hypothesis?

3. The level of significance (alpha) associated with testing a null hypothesis is also referred to as the probability of a Type I error. Alpha is the probability of rejecting the null hypothesis on the basis of your sample data when it is, in fact, true for the population of interest. Because alpha concerns the probability of making a mistake in your analysis, should you always try to set this value as small as possible? Why or why not?

4. Analysis of variance (ANOVA) allows you to test for the statistical difference between two or more means. Typically, there are more than two means tested. If the ANOVA results for a set of data reveal that the four means that were compared are significantly different from each other, how would you find out which individual means were statistically different from each other? What statistical techniques would you apply to answer this question?

5. **EXPERIENCE MARKETING RESEARCH**. Nike, Reebok, and Converse are strong competitors in the athletic shoe market. The three use different advertising and marketing strategies to appeal to their target markets. Use one of the search engines on the Internet to identify information on this market. Go to the websites for these three companies (**www.Nike.com**; **www.Reebok.com**; **www.Converse.com**). Gather background information on each, including its target market and market share. Design a questionnaire based on this information and survey a sample of students. Prepare a report on the different perceptions of each of these three companies, their shoes, and related aspects. Present the report in class and defend your findings.

6. **SPSS EXERCISE**. Form a team of three to four students in your class. Select one or two local franchises to conduct a survey on, such as Subway or McDonald's. Design a brief survey (10–12 questions) including questions like ratings on quality of food, speed of service, knowledge of employees, attitudes of employees, and price, as well as several demographic variables such as age, address, how often individuals eat there, and day of week and time of day. Obtain permission from the franchises to interview their customers at a convenient time, usually when they are leaving. Assure the franchiser you will not bother customers and that you will provide the franchise with a valuable report on your findings. Develop frequency charts, pie charts, and similar graphic displays of findings, where appropriate. Use statistics to test hypotheses, such as

"Perceptions of speed of service differ by time of day or day of week." Prepare a report and present it to your class; particularly point out where statistically significant differences exist and why.

7. **SPSS EXERCISE**. Using SPSS and the Santa Fe Grill employee database, provide frequencies, means, modes, and medians for the relevant variables on the questionnaire. The questionnaire is shown in Chapter 10. In addition, develop bar charts and pie charts where appropriate for the data you analyzed. Run an ANOVA using the work environment perceptions variables to identify any differences that may exist between male and female employees, and part-time versus full-time employees. Be prepared to present a report on your findings.

8. **SPSS EXERCISE**. Review the Marketing Research in Action case for this chapter. There were three restaurant competitors—Remington's, Outback, and Longhorn. Results for a one-way ANOVA of the restaurant image variables were provided. Now run post-hoc ANOVA follow-up tests to see where the group differences are. Make recommendations for new marketing strategies for Remington's compared to the competition.

Examining Relationships in Quantitative Research

Learning Objectives   After reading this chapter, you will be able to:

1. Understand and evaluate the types of relationships between variables.
2. Explain the concepts of association and co-variation.
3. Discuss the differences between Pearson correlation and Spearman correlation.
4. Explain the concept of statistical significance versus practical significance.
5. Understand when and how to use regression analysis.
6. Understand the value and application of structural modeling.

Data Mining Helps Rebuild Procter & Gamble as a Global Powerhouse

Procter & Gamble (P&G) is a global player in consumer household products, with 20 world-ranking brands such as Tide, Folgers, Febreze, Mr. Clean, and Pringles. Three billion times a day, P&G products touch the lives of consumers around the world. Yet, several years ago the company saw its status in jeopardy. While many businesses, including P&G, pursue three overall marketing objectives—to get customers, keep customers, and grow customers—P&G realized it had to change its traditional marketing strategies and tactics in order to rebuild its global image and practices. The new approach was based on answering three key questions: (1) Who are the targeted consumers for each brand? (2) What is the company's desired brand equity or positioning? and (3) How should it be achieved?

P&G, a leader in brand management, turned to information technology and customer relationship management to design their new brand building strategy. From internal employee surveys they recognized a need to recommit to a customer-centric approach. Understanding employees' attitudes concerning what P&G was doing "right" and "wrong" helped reestablish five fundamental focal points as operating objectives: (1) respecting the consumer as the "boss" and delivering superior consumer value; (2) making clear strategic choices about where to compete and how to win; (3) being a leader in innovation and branding; (4) leveraging P&G's unique, global operating structure; and (5) executing with excellence as well as more rigorous financial and operating discipline.

P&G mines the information in its data warehouse to retool customer models for its global brand and distributor markets. One objective of the brand models is to acquire new customers worldwide for its brands as well as cross selling the brands to current customers. Another objective is to use product innovation and acquisition to expand the type of products sold worldwide. Statistical models with high predictive capability were modified and validated for each of the brands' market segments. The models considered factors such as household purchasing power, length of residence, family size, age, gender, attitudes toward a brand, media habits, purchase frequencies, and so on. The results suggest P&G has made progress in its rebuilding efforts. Brand equity in 19 of 20 of their major brands is growing—30 million times a day consumers choose P&G brand products. Internally, employee confidence in P&G is growing—56 percent of all P&G employees believe P&G is moving in the right direction compared to only 26 percent a year ago. To learn more about P&G's turnaround, go to **www.pg.com**.

Examining Relationships between Variables

Relationships between variables can be described in several ways, including *presence, direction, strength of association,* and *type*. We will describe each of these concepts in turn.

The first issue is whether two or more variables are related at all. If a systematic relationship exists between two or more variables, then a relationship is *present*. To measure whether a relationship exists, we rely on the concept of statistical significance. If we test for statistical significance and find that it exists, then we say that a relationship is present. Stated another way, we say that knowledge about the behavior of one variable enables us to make a useful prediction about the behavior of another. For example, if we find a statistically significant relationship between perceptions of the quality of Santa Fe Grill food and overall satisfaction, we would say a relationship is present.

If a relationship is present between two variables, it is important to know the *direction*. The direction of a relationship can be either positive or negative. Using the Santa Fe Grill example, a positive relationship exists if respondents who rate the quality of the food high are also highly satisfied. Alternatively, a negative relationship exists between two variables if low levels of one variable are associated with high levels of another. For example, as the number of service problems experienced when dining at the Santa Fe Grill increases, satisfaction is likely to decrease. Thus, number of service problems is negatively related to customer satisfaction.

An understanding of the strength of association also is important. Researchers generally categorize the *strength of association* as no relationship, weak relationship, moderate relationship, or strong relationship. If a consistent and systematic relationship is not present, then there is no relationship. A weak association means the variables may have some variance in common, but not much. A moderate or strong association means there is a consistent and systematic relationship, and the relationship is much more evident when it is strong. The strength of association is determined by the size of the correlation coefficient, with larger coefficients indicating a stronger association.

A fourth important concept is the *type* of relationship. If we say two variables are related, then we pose this question: "What is the nature of the relationship?" How can the link between Y and X best be described? There are a number of different ways in which two variables can share a relationship. Variables Y and X can have a **linear relationship,** which means the strength and nature of the relationship between them remain the same over the range of both variables, and can be best described using a straight line. A second type of relationship between Y and X is a **curvilinear relationship,** which means the strength and/or direction of the relationship changes over the range of both variables. For example, the relationship can be curvilinear if moderate levels of X are strongly related to high levels of Y, whereas both low and high levels of X are only slightly related. For example, if moderate

Linear relationship An association between two variables whereby the strength and nature of the relationship remains the same over the range of both variables.

Curvilinear relationship A relationship between two variables whereby the strength and/or direction of their relationship changes over the range of both variables.

levels of fear appeal in an advertisement are strongly related to positive attitudes toward the ad, whereas both low and high levels of fear appeal are only slightly related, then the relationship between strength of fear appeal and attitude toward the ad would be curvilinear.

A linear relationship is much simpler to work with than a curvilinear relationship. If we know the value of variable X, then we can apply the formula for a straight line ($Y = a + bX$) to determine the value of Y. But when two variables have a curvilinear relationship, the formula that best describes the linkage is more complex. Therefore, most marketing researchers work with relationships they believe are linear.

Marketers are often interested in describing the relationship between variables they think influence purchases of their product(s). There are four questions to ask about a possible relationship between two variables. First, "Is there a relationship between the two variables of interest?" If there is a relationship, "How strong is that relationship?" "What is the direction of the relationship?" and "Is the relationship linear or nonlinear?" Once these questions have been answered, the researcher can interpret results, make conclusions, and recommend managerial actions.

◼◖ Covariation and Variable Relationships

Covariation The amount of change in one variable that is consistently related to the change in another variable of interest.

Since we are interested in finding out whether two variables describing our customers are related, the concept of covariation is a very useful idea. **Covariation** is defined as the amount of change in one variable that is consistently related to a change in another variable. For example, if we know that DVD purchases are related to age, then we want to know the extent to which younger persons purchase more DVDs. Another way of stating the concept of covariation is that it is the degree of association between two variables. If two variables are found to change together on a reliable or consistent basis, then we can use that information to make predictions that will improve decision making about advertising and marketing strategies.

Scatter diagram A graphic plot of the relative position of two variables using a horizontal and a vertical axis to represent the values of the respective variables.

One way of visually describing the covariation between two variables is with the use of a **scatter diagram.** A scatter diagram plots the relative position of two variables using horizontal and vertical axes to represent the variable values. Exhibits 12.1 through 12.4 show some examples of possible relationships between two variables that might show up on a scatter diagram. In Exhibit 12.1, the best way to describe the visual impression left by the dots representing the values of each variable is probably a circle. That is, there is no particular pattern to the collection of dots. Thus, if you take two or three sample values of variable Y from the scatter diagram and look at the values for X, there is no predictable pattern to the values for X. Knowing the values of Y or X would not tell you very much (maybe nothing at all) about the possible values of the other variable. Exhibit 12.1 suggests there is no systematic relationship between Y and X and that there is very little or no covariation shared by the two variables. If we measured the amount of covariation shared by these two variables, which you will learn how to do in the next section, it would be very close to zero.

In Exhibit 12.2, the two variables present a very different picture from that of Exhibit 12.1. There is a distinct pattern to the dots. As the values of Y increase, so do the values of X. This pattern can be described as a straight line or an ellipse (a circle that has been stretched out from both sides). We could also describe this relationship as positive because increases in the value of Y are associated with increases in the value of X. That is, if we know the relationship between Y and X is a linear, positive relationship, we would know the values of Y and X change in the same direction. As the values of Y increase, so do the values of X. Similarly, if the values of Y decrease, the values of X should decrease as well.

Exhibit 12.1 No Relationship between *X* and *Y*

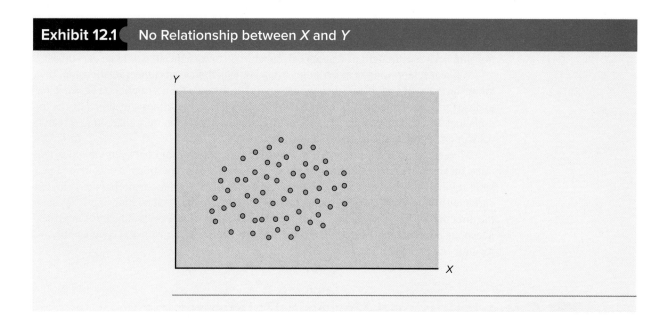

Exhibit 12.2 Positive Relationship between *X* and *Y*

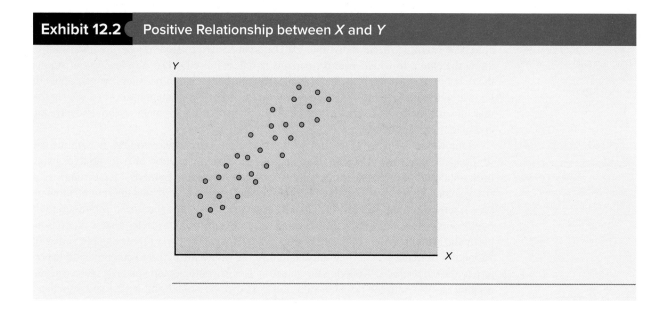

If we try to measure the amount of covariation shown by the values of *Y* and *X*, it would be relatively high. Thus, changes in the value of *Y* are systematically related to changes in the value of *X*.

Exhibit 12.3 shows the same type of pattern between the values of *Y* and *X*, but the direction of the relationship is the opposite of Exhibit 12.2. There is a linear pattern, but now increases in the value of *Y* are associated with decreases in the values of *X*. This type of relationship is known as a *negative relationship*. The amount of covariation shared between the two variables is still high because *Y* and *X* still change together, though in a direction opposite from that shown in Exhibit 12.2. The concept of covariation refers to

Exhibit 12.3	Negative Relationship between *X* and *Y*

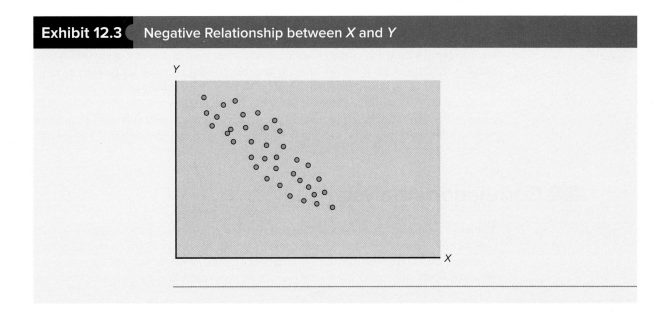

Exhibit 12.4	Curvilinear Relationship between *X* and *Y*

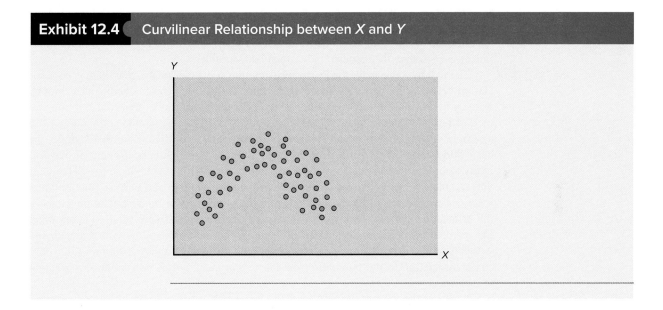

the strength of the relationship between two variables, not the direction of the relationship between two variables.

Finally, Exhibit 12.4 shows a more complicated relationship between the values of *Y* and *X*. This pattern of dots can be described as *curvilinear*. That is, the relationship between the values of *Y* and the values of *X* is different for different values of the variables. Part of the relationship is positive (increases in the small values of *Y* are associated with increases in the small values of *X*), but then the relationship becomes negative (increases in the larger values of *Y* are now associated with decreases in the larger values of *X*).

This pattern of dots cannot be described as a linear relationship. Many of the statistics marketing researchers use to describe association assume the two variables have a linear relationship. These statistics do not perform well when used to describe a curvilinear relationship. In Exhibit 12.4, we can still say the relationship is strong, or that the covariation exhibited by the two variables is strong. But now we cannot talk very easily about the direction (positive or negative) of the relationship, because the direction changes. To make matters more difficult, many statistical methods of describing relationships between variables cannot be applied to situations where you suspect the relationship is curvilinear.

◀◼ Correlation Analysis

Scatter diagrams are a visual way to describe the relationship between two variables and the covariation they share. For example, a scatter diagram can tell us that as income increases, the average consumption of Starbucks coffee increases too. But even though a picture is worth a thousand words, it is often more convenient to use a quantitative measure of the covariation between two items.

Pearson correlation coefficient A statistical measure of the strength of a linear relationship between two metric variables.

The **Pearson correlation coefficient** measures the degree of linear association between two variables. It varies between −1.00 and 1.00, with 0 representing absolutely no association between two variables, and −1.00 or 1.00 representing a perfect link between two variables. The correlation coefficient can be either positive or negative, depending on the direction of the relationship between two variables. But the larger the correlation coefficient, the stronger the association between two variables.

The null hypothesis for the Pearson correlation coefficient states that there is no association between the two variables and the correlation coefficient is zero. For example, we may hypothesize there is no relationship between Starbucks coffee consumption and income levels. If a researcher collects measures of coffee consumption and income from a sample of the population and estimates the correlation coefficient for that sample, the basic question is "What is the probability of getting a correlation coefficient of this size in my sample if the correlation coefficient in the population is actually zero?" That is, if you calculate a large correlation coefficient between the two variables in your sample, and your sample was properly selected from the population of interest, then the chances the population correlation coefficient is really zero are relatively small. Therefore, if the correlation coefficient is statistically significant, the null hypothesis is rejected, and you can conclude with some confidence the two variables you are examining do share some association in the population. In short, Starbucks coffee consumption is related to income.

Earlier in the chapter, we stated that the first question of interest was "Does a relationship between *Y* and *X* exist?" This question is equivalent to asking whether a correlation coefficient is statistically significant. If this is the case, then you can move on to the second and third questions: "If there is a relationship between *Y* and *X*, how strong is the relationship?" and "What is the best way to describe that relationship?"

The size of the correlation coefficient can be used to quantitatively describe the strength of the association between two variables. Some rules of thumb for characterizing the strength of the association between two variables based on the size of the correlation coefficient are suggested in Exhibit 12.5. Correlation coefficients between .81 and 1.00 are considered very strong. That is, covariance is strongly shared between the two variables under study. At the other extreme, if the correlation coefficient is between .00 and .20, there is a good chance the null hypothesis will not be rejected (unless you are using

Exhibit 12.5	Rules of Thumb about the Strength of Correlation Coefficients

Range of Coefficient	Description of Strength
±.81 to ±1.00	Very Strong
±.61 to ±.80	Strong
±.41 to ±.60	Moderate
±.21 to ±.40	Weak
±.00 to ±.20	Weak to no relationship

a large sample). These interpretations of the strength of correlations are suggestions and other ranges and descriptions of relationship strength are possible depending on the situation.

In addition to the size of the correlation coefficient, we also must consider its significance level. How do we do this? Most statistical software, including SPSS, calculates the significance level for a computed correlation coefficient. The SPSS software indicates statistical significance, which is the probability that the null hypothesis will be rejected when in fact it is true. For example, if the calculated correlation coefficient between Starbucks coffee consumption and income is .61 with a statistical significance of .05, this means we would expect to get that result only five times out of 100 solely by chance—if there is not a relationship between the two variables. Thus, we reject the null hypothesis of no association, and conclude that Starbucks coffee consumption and income are related. In the SPSS output, statistical significance is identified as the "Sig." value.

Pearson Correlation Coefficient

In calculating the Pearson correlation coefficient, we are making several assumptions. First, we assume the two variables have been measured using interval- or ratio-scaled measures. If this is not the case, there are other types of correlation coefficients that can be computed which match the type of data on hand. A second assumption is that the relationship we are trying to measure is linear. That is, a straight line describes the relationship between the variables of interest.

Use of the Pearson correlation coefficient also assumes the variables you want to analyze have a normally distributed population. The assumption of normal distributions for the variables under study is a common requirement for many statistical techniques. But determining whether it holds for the sample data you are working with is sometimes difficult, and research analysts too often take the assumption of normality for granted.

SPSS Application—Pearson Correlation

We use the restaurant database to examine the Pearson correlation. The Santa Fe Grill owners anticipate that the relationship between satisfaction with the restaurant and likelihood to recommend the restaurant would be significant and positive. Looking at the database variables you note that information was collected on "Likely to Recommend" (variable X_{24}) and Satisfaction (variable X_{22}). To examine this research question, the owners of the Santa Fe Grill want to look only at their customers. The null hypothesis is no relationship exists between Santa Fe Grill customer satisfaction and likelihood of recommending the restaurant.

To select the Santa Fe Grill survey responses (253) from the total sample of 405 responses, the click-through sequence is DATA → SELECT CASES. First click on the Data pull-down menu and scroll down and highlight and click on Select Cases. You now see the Select Cases dialog box where the default is All cases. Click on the If condition is satisfied option, and then on the If tab. Next highlight the screening variable X_s4 and click on the arrow box to move it into the window. Now click on the equals sign and then 1 to select the Santa Fe customers (coded 1). Next click Continue and then OK and you will be analyzing only the Santa Fe Grill customers. Thus, your output will have the results for only one restaurant. Remember too that all data analysis following this change will analyze only the Santa Fe customers. To analyze the total sample you must follow the same sequence and click again on All cases.

With SPSS it is easy to compute a Pearson correlation between these two variables and test this hypothesis. Once you have selected the Santa Fe customers, the SPSS click-through sequence is ANALYZE → CORRELATE → BIVARIATE, which leads to a dialog box where you select the variables. Transfer variables X_{22} and X_{24} into the Variables box. Note that we will use all three default options: Pearson correlation, two-tailed test of significance, and flag significant correlations. Next go to the Options box, and after it opens click on Means and Standard Deviations and then Continue. Finally, click on OK at the top right of the dialog box SPSS to calculate the Pearson correlation.

Exhibit 12.6 SPSS Pearson Correlation Example for Santa Fe Grill Customers

Descriptive Statistics

	Mean	Std. Deviation	N
X22—Satisfaction	4.54	1.002	253
X24—Likely to Recommend	3.61	.960	253

Correlations

		X22—Satisfaction	X24—Likely to Recommend
X22—Satisfaction	Pearson Correlation	1	.776[*]
	Sig. (2-tailed)		.000
	N	253	253
X24—Likely to Recommend	Pearson Correlation	.776[*]	1
	Sig. (2-tailed)	.000	
	N	253	253

*Correlation is significant at the 0.01 level (2-tailed).

Interpretation of Results The Pearson correlation results are shown in Exhibit 12.6. As you can see in the Correlations table, the correlation between variable X_{24}–Likely to Recommend and X_{22}–Satisfaction is .776, and the statistical significance of this correlation is .000. Thus, we have confirmed our hypothesis that satisfaction is positively related to "likely to recommend." When we examine the means of the two variables, we see that satisfaction (4.54) is somewhat higher than likely to recommend (3.61) but we know the pattern of the responses to these questions is similar. That is, there is covariation between the responses to the two variables: As one goes up, so does the other (and as one goes down, so does the other). In short, more satisfied respondents are more likely to recommend Santa Fe Grill.

It is important for the Santa Fe Grill owners to know the relationship between satisfaction and recommendation likelihood. But equally important is finding out there is considerable room for improvement in both satisfaction and intentions to recommend. These variables are measured on a 7-point scale and both means are near the midpoint of the scale. The owners need to find out why satisfaction is so low as is likelihood of recommending the restaurant. Basically, they need to "drill down" into the other survey data and identify ways to improve the situation. In examples later in this chapter, we show you how to do that.

Substantive Significance of the Correlation Coefficient

When the correlation coefficient is strong and significant, you can be confident that the two variables are associated in a linear fashion. In our Santa Fe Grill example, we can be reasonably confident that likelihood of recommending the restaurant is in fact related to satisfaction. When the correlation coefficient is weak, two possibilities must be considered: (1) there is not a consistent, systematic relationship between the two variables; or (2) the association exists, but it is not linear, and other types of relationships must be investigated further.

Coefficient of determination (r²) A number measuring the proportion of variation in one variable accounted for by another. The r^2 measure can be thought of as a percentage and varies from 0.0 to 1.00.

When you square the correlation coefficient, you arrive at the **coefficient of determination,** or r^2. This number ranges from .00 to 1.0 and shows the proportion of variation explained or accounted for in one variable by another. In our Santa Fe Grill example, the correlation coefficient was .776. Thus, the $r^2 = .602$, meaning that approximately 60.2 percent of the variation in likelihood to recommend is associated with satisfaction. The larger the size of the coefficient of determination, the stronger the linear relationship between the two variables being examined. In our example, we have accounted for 60 percent of the variation in likelihood of recommending Santa Fe Grill by assessing its relationship to satisfaction.

There is a difference between statistical significance and substantive significance. Thus, you need to understand *substantive significance*. In other words, do the numbers you calculate provide useful information for management? Since the statistical significance calculation for correlation coefficients depends partly on sample size, it is possible to find statistically significant correlation coefficients that are too small to be of much practical use to management. This is because large samples result in more confidence that a relationship exists, even if it is weak. For example, if we had correlated satisfaction with the likelihood of recommending the Santa Fe Grill to others, and the correlation coefficient was .20 (significant at the .05 level), the coefficient of determination would be .04. Can we conclude that the results are meaningful? It is highly unlikely the results are meaningful since the amount of shared variance is only 4 percent. Always look at both types of significance (statistical and substantive) before you develop conclusions.

Influence of Measurement Scales on Correlation Analysis

Sometimes research questions can be measured only with ordinal or nominal scales. What options are available when ordinal scales are used to collect data, or when the data simply cannot be measured with an interval scale or better? The **Spearman rank order correlation coefficient** is the recommended statistic to use when two variables have been measured using ordinal scales. If either one of the variables is represented by rank order data, the best approach is to use the Spearman rank order correlation coefficient, rather than the Pearson correlation.

Spearman rank order correlation coefficient A statistical measure of the linear association between two variables where both have been measured using ordinal (rank order) scales.

SPSS Application—Spearman Rank Order Correlation

The Santa Fe Grill customer survey collected data that ranked four restaurant selection factors. These data are represented by variables X_{26} to X_{29}. Management is interested in knowing whether "Food Quality" is a more important selection factor than "Service." Since these variables are ordinal, the Pearson correlation is not appropriate. The Spearman correlation is the appropriate coefficient to calculate. Variables X_{27}–Food Quality and X_{29}–Service are the variables we will use.

The owners want to know in general what factors influence the choice of a restaurant. Therefore, in this analysis the total sample of 405 responses is analyzed. The SPSS click-through sequence is ANALYZE → CORRELATE → BIVARIATE, which leads to a dialog box where you select the variables. Transfer variables X_{27} and X_{29} into the "Variables" box. You will note the Pearson correlation is the default along with the two-tailed test of significance, and flag significant correlations. "Uncheck" the Pearson correlation and click on "Spearman." Then click on "OK" to execute the program.

Interpretation of Results The SPSS results for the Spearman correlation are shown in Exhibit 12.7. As you can see in the Correlations table, the correlation between variable X_{27}–Food Quality and X_{29}–Service is −.130, and the significance value is above .01 (see footnote to Correlations table). Thus, we have confirmed there is a statistically significant relationship between the two restaurant selection factors, although it is very small. The negative correlation indicates that a customer who ranks food quality high in importance tends to rank service significantly lower in importance.

Exhibit 12.7 SPSS Spearman Rank Order Correlation

Correlations

			X27—Food Quality	X29—Service
Spearman's rho	X27—Food Quality	Correlation Coefficient	1.000	-.130[*]
		Sig. (2-tailed)		.009
		N	405	405
	X29—Service	Correlation Coefficient	-.130[*]	1.000
		Sig. (2-tailed)	.009	
		N	405	405

*Correlation is significant at the 0.01 level (2-tailed).

Exhibit 12.8	Median Example for Restaurant Selection Factors

Statistics				
	X26—Price	X27—Food Quality	X28—Atmosphere	X29—Service
N Valid	405	405	405	405
Missing	0	0	0	0
Median	2.00	1.00	3.00	3.00

SPSS Application—Calculating Median Rankings To better understand the Spearman correlation findings, we need to calculate the median rankings of the four selection factors. To do this, the SPSS click-through sequence is ANALYZE → DESCRIPTIVE STATISTICS → FREQUENCIES. Click on variables X_{26}–X_{29} to highlight them and then on the arrow box for the Variables box to use them in your analysis. We use all four selection factors because this will enable us to examine the overall relative rankings of all the restaurant selection factors. Next, open the Statistics box and click on median and then Continue. For the Charts and Format options we will use the defaults, so click on OK to execute the program.

Interpretation of Results The SPSS results for median rankings are shown in the Statistics table in Exhibit 12.8. Recall that medians are descriptive data and can only be used to describe respondents. Based on the coding for this variable, the factor with the lowest median is ranked the highest and is the most important, and the factor with the highest median is the least important, since the four selection factors were ranked from 1 to 4, with 1 = most important, and 4 = least important. Food quality is ranked as the most important factor (median = 1.0) while atmosphere and service are the least important (median = 3.0). The Spearman rank correlation compared food quality (median = 1) with service (median = 3.0), so food quality is significantly more important in restaurant selection than service.

◼◼ What Is Regression Analysis?

Correlation can determine if a relationship exists between two variables. The correlation coefficient also tells you the overall strength of the association and the direction of the relationship between the variables. However, managers sometimes still need to know how to describe the relationship between variables in greater detail. For example, a marketing manager may want to predict future sales or how a price increase will affect the profits or market share of the company. There are a number of ways to make such predictions: (1) extrapolation from past behavior of the variable; (2) simple guesses; or (3) use of a regression equation that includes information about related variables to assist in the prediction. Extrapolation and guesses (educated or otherwise) usually assume that past conditions and behaviors will continue into the future. They do not examine the influences behind the behavior of interest. Consequently, when sales levels, profits, or other variables of interest to a manager differ from those in the past, extrapolation and guessing do not explain why.

Bivariate regression analysis is a statistical technique that uses information about the relationship between an independent or predictor variable and a dependent variable to make predictions. Values of the independent variable are selected, and the behavior of the dependent variable is observed using the formula for a straight line. For example, if you wanted to find the current level of your company's sales volume, you would apply the following straight-line formula:

> Sales volume $(Y) = \$0 + $ (Price per unit $= b$) $\times$ (Number of units sold $= X$)

You would not expect any sales volume if no units are sold. Thus, the constant or x-intercept is $0. Price per unit ($b$) determines the amount that sales volume (Y) increases with each unit sold (X). In this example, the relationship between sales volume and number of units sold is linear.

Once a regression equation has been developed to predict values of Y, we want to find out how good that prediction is. A place to begin is to compare the values predicted by our regression model with the actual values we collected in our sample. By comparing this actual value (Y_i) with our predicted value (Y), we can tell how well our model predicts the actual value of our dependent variable.

A couple of points should be made about the assumptions behind regression analysis. First, as with correlation, regression analysis assumes a linear relationship is a good description of the relationship between two variables. If the scatter diagram showing the positions of the values of both variables looks like the scatter plots in Exhibits 12.2 or 12.3, this assumption is a good one. If the plot looks like Exhibits 12.1 or 12.4, however, then regression analysis is not a good choice. Second, even though the terminology of regression analysis commonly uses the labels *dependent* and *independent* for the variables, these labels do not mean we can say one variable causes the behavior of the other. Regression analysis uses knowledge about the level and type of association between two variables to make predictions. Statements about the ability of one variable to cause changes in another must be based on conceptual logic or preexisting knowledge rather than on statistical calculations alone.

Finally, the use of a simple regression model assumes (1) the variables of interest are measured on interval or ratio scales (except in the case of dummy variables, which are discussed on our website, **www.mhhe.com/hairessentials3e**), (2) the variables come from a normal population, and (3) the error terms associated with making predictions are normally and independently distributed.

Fundamentals of Regression Analysis

A fundamental basis of regression analysis is the assumption of a straight line relationship between the independent and dependent variables. This relationship is illustrated in Exhibit 12.9. The general formula for a straight line is

$$Y = a + bX + e_i$$

Bivariate regression analysis A statistical technique that analyzes the linear relationship between two variables by estimating coefficients for an equation for a straight line. One variable is designated as a dependent variable and the other is called an independent or predictor variable.

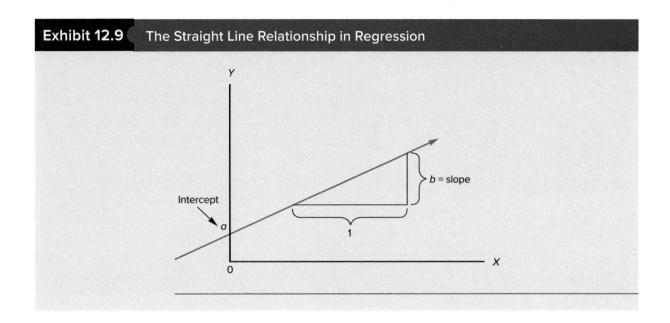

Exhibit 12.9   **The Straight Line Relationship in Regression**

where

Y = the dependent variable

a = the intercept (point where the straight line intersects the Y-axis when $X = 0$)

b = the slope (the change in Y for every 1 unit change in X)

X = the independent variable used to predict Y

e_i = the error for the prediction

In regression analysis, we examine the relationship between the independent variable X and the dependent variable Y. To do so, we use the actual values of X and Y in our data set and the computed values of a and b. The calculations are based on the **least squares procedure.** The least squares procedure determines the best-fitting line by minimizing the vertical distances of all the data points from the line, as shown in Exhibit 12.10. The best fitting line is the regression line. Any point that does not fall on the line is the result of **unexplained variance,** or the variance in Y that is not explained by X. This unexplained variance is called error and is represented by the vertical distance between the estimated straight regression line and the actual data points. The distances of all the points not on the line are squared and added together to determine the *sum of the squared errors,* which is a measure of total error in the regression.

In the case of bivariate regression analysis, we are looking at one independent variable and one dependent variable. However, managers frequently want to look at the combined influence of several independent variables on one dependent variable. For example, are digital recorder/player purchases related only to age, or are they also related to income, ethnicity, gender, geographic location, and education level? Similarly, in the Santa Fe Grill database, we might ask whether customer satisfaction is related only to perceptions of the restaurant's food taste (X_{18}), or is satisfaction also related to perceptions of friendly employees (X_{12}), reasonable prices (X_{16}), and speed of service (X_{21})?

Least squares procedure
A regression approach that determines the best-fitting line by minimizing the vertical distances of all the points from the line.

Unexplained variance The amount of variation in the dependent variable that cannot be accounted for by the combination of independent variables.

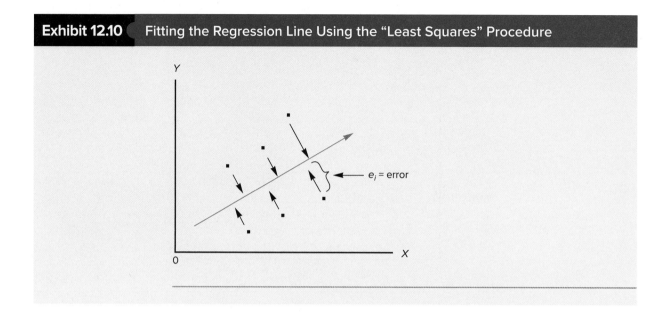

Exhibit 12.10 Fitting the Regression Line Using the "Least Squares" Procedure

Multiple regression is the appropriate technique to measure these multivariate relationships. We discuss bivariate or simple regression analysis before moving on to multiple regression analysis.

Developing and Estimating the Regression Coefficients

Regression uses an estimation procedure called ordinary least squares (OLS) that guarantees the line it estimates will be the best fitting line. We said earlier that the best prediction would be one in which the difference between the actual value of Y and the predicted value of Y was the smallest. **Ordinary least squares** is a statistical procedure that results in equation parameters (a and b) that produce predictions with the lowest sum of squared differences between actual and predicted values. The betas (b) are the **regression coefficients.** If a b is large, the variable is a better predictor of Y.

Error in Regression The differences between actual and predicted values of Y are represented by e_i (the error term of the regression equation). If we square these errors for each observation (the difference between actual values of Y and predicted values of Y) and add them up, the total would represent an aggregate or overall measure of the accuracy of the regression equation.

SPSS Application—Bivariate Regression

Let's illustrate bivariate regression analysis. Suppose the owners of the Santa Fe Grill want to know if more favorable perceptions of their prices are associated with higher customer satisfaction. The obvious answer would be "of course it would." But how much improvement would be expected in customer satisfaction if the owners improved the perceptions of prices? Bivariate regression provides information to answer this question.

Ordinary least squares
A statistical procedure that estimates regression equation coefficients that produce the lowest sum of squared differences between the actual and predicted values of the dependent variable.

Regression coefficient An indicator of the importance of an independent variable in predicting a dependent variable. Large coefficients are good predictors and small coefficients are weak predictors.

In the Santa Fe Grill customer database X_{22} is a measure of customer satisfaction, with 1 = Not Satisfied At All and 7 = Highly Satisfied. Variable X_{16} is a measure of respondents' perceptions of the reasonableness of the restaurant's prices (1 = Strongly Disagree, 7 = Strongly Agree). To examine this research question, the owners of the Santa Fe Grill are most interested in their own customers. The null hypothesis is that there is no relationship between X_{22}–Satisfaction and X_{16}–Reasonable Prices for the Santa Fe Grill customers.

To select the Santa Fe Grill survey responses (253) from the total sample of 405 responses, the click-through sequence is DATA → SELECT CASES. First click on the Data pull-down menu and scroll down and highlight and click on Select Cases. You now see the Select Cases dialog box where the default is All cases. Click on the If condition is satisfied option, and then on the If tab. Next highlight the screening variable X_s4 and click on the arrow box to move it into the window. Now click on the equal sign and then 1 to select the Santa Fe customers (coded 1). Next click Continue and then OK and you will be analyzing only the Santa Fe Grill customers. Thus, your output will have the results for only one restaurant.

To run the bivariate regression, the SPSS click-through sequence is ANALYZE → REGRESSION → LINEAR. Click on X_{22}–Satisfaction and move it to the Dependent Variable window. Click on X_{16}–Reasonable Prices and move it to the Independent Variables window. We use the defaults for the other options so click OK to run the bivariate regression.

Exhibit 12.11 contains the results of the bivariate regression analysis. The table labeled "Model Summary" has three types of R in it. The R on the far left is the correlation coefficient (.479). The R-square is .230—you get this value by squaring the correlation coefficient (.479) for this regression. The R-square shows the percentage of variation in one variable that is accounted for by another variable. In this case, customer perceptions of the Santa Fe Grill's prices accounts for 23.0 percent of the total variation in customer satisfaction with the restaurant.

Interpretation of Results The ANOVA table shows the F-ratio that indicates the statistical significance of the regression model. The variance in X_{22}–Customer Satisfaction that is associated with X_{16}–Reasonable Prices is referred to as explained variance. The remainder of the total variance in X_{22} that is not associated with X_{16} is referred to as unexplained variance. The F-ratio compares the amount of explained variance to the unexplained variance. The larger the F-ratio, the more variance in the dependent variable that is associated with the independent variable. In our example, the F-ratio is 74.939, and the statistical significance is .000—the Sig. value on the SPSS output—so we can reject the null hypothesis that no relationship exists between the two variables. Moreover, we can conclude that the perception of reasonable prices is positively related to overall customer satisfaction.

The Coefficients table shows the regression coefficient for X_{16} (reasonable prices). The column labeled "Unstandardized Coefficients" indicates the unstandardized regression coefficient (b) for X_{16} is .347. The column labeled "Sig." shows the statistical significance of the regression coefficient for X_{16}, as measured by the t-test. The t-test examines the question of whether the regression coefficient is different enough from zero to be statistically significant. The t statistic is calculated by dividing the regression coefficient by its standard error (labeled Std. Error in the Coefficients table). If you divide .347 by .040, you will get a t value of 8.657, which is significant at the .000 level.

The Coefficients table also shows the result for the Constant component in the regression equation. This item is a term in the equation for a straight line we discussed earlier.

Exhibit 12.11 SPSS Results for Bivariate Regression

Model Summary

Model	R	R Square	Adjusted R Square	Std. Error of the Estimate
1	.479*	.230	.227	.881

*Predictors: (Constant), X16—Reasonable Prices

ANOVA†

Model		Sum of Squares	df	Mean Square	F	Sig.
1	Regression	58.127	1	58.127	74.939	.000*
	Residual	194.688	251	.776		
	Total	252.814	252			

*Predictors: (Constant), X16—Reasonable Prices
†Dependent Variable: X22—Satisfaction

Coefficients*

Model		Unstandardized Coefficients		Standardized Coefficients	t	Sig.
		B	Std. Error	Beta		
1	(Constant)	2.991	.188		15.951	.000
	X16—Reasonable Prices	.347	.040	.479	8.657	.000

*Dependent Variable: X22—Satisfaction

It is the X-intercept, or the value of Y when X is 0. If the independent variable takes on a value of 0, the dependent measure (X_{22}) would have a value of 2.991. Combining the results of the Coefficients table into a regression equation, we have

Predicted value of $X_{22} = 2.991 + .347 \times$ (value of X_{16}) + .881 (avg. error in prediction)

The relationship between customer satisfaction and reasonable prices is positive. The regression coefficient for X_{16} is interpreted as "For every unit that X_{16} (the rating of reasonable prices) increases, X_{22} (satisfaction) will increase by .347 units." Recall that the Santa Fe Grill owners asked, "If the prices in our restaurant are perceived as being reasonable, will this be associated with improved customer satisfaction?" The answer is "yes," because the model was significant at the .000 level, and the R-square was .230. Thus, 23 percent of the dependent variable satisfaction was explained by the single independent variable reasonable prices.

Significance

Once the statistical significance of the regression coefficients is determined, we have answered the first question about our relationship: "Is there a relationship between our dependent and independent variable?" In this case, the answer is "yes." But recall our discussion of statistical versus substantive significance. The logic of that discussion also applies when we evaluate whether regression coefficients are meaningful. A second question to ask is "How strong is that relationship?" The output of regression analysis includes the coefficient of determination, or r^2—which describes the amount of variation in the dependent variable associated with the variation in the independent variable. The regression r^2 also tells you what percentage of the total variation in your dependent variable you can explain by using the independent variable. The r^2 measure varies between .00 and 1.00, and is calculated by dividing the amount of variation you have been able to explain with your regression equation by the total variation in the dependent variable. In the previous Santa Fe Grill example that examined the relationship between reasonable prices and satisfaction, the r^2 was .230. That means 23.0 percent of the variation in customer satisfaction is associated with the variation in respondents' perceptions of the reasonableness of prices.

When examining the substantive significance of a regression equation, you should look at the size of the r^2 for the regression equation and the size of the regression coefficient. The regression coefficient may be statistically significant, but still relatively small, meaning that your dependent measure won't change very much for a given unit change in the independent measure. In our Santa Fe Grill example, the unstandardized regression coefficient was .347, which is a relatively weak relationship. When regression coefficients are significant but small, we say a relationship is present in our population, but that it is weak. In this case, Santa Fe Grill owners need to consider additional independent variables that will help them to better understand and predict customer satisfaction.

Multiple Regression Analysis

Multiple regression analysis A statistical technique which analyzes the linear relationship between a dependent variable and multiple independent variables by estimating coefficients for the equation for a straight line.

In most problems faced by managers, there are several independent variables that need to be examined for their influence on a dependent variable. **Multiple regression analysis** is the appropriate technique to use for these situations. The technique is an extension of bivariate regression. Multiple independent variables are entered into the regression equation, and for each variable a separate regression coefficient is calculated that describes its relationship with the dependent variable. The coefficients enable the marketing researcher to examine the relative influence of each independent variable on the dependent variable. For example, Santa Fe Grill owners want to examine not only reasonable prices, but also customer perceptions of employees, atmosphere, and service. This gives them a more accurate picture of what to consider when developing marketing strategies.

The relationship between each independent variable and the dependent measure is still linear. Now, however, with the addition of multiple independent variables, we have to think of multiple independent variables instead of just a single one. The easiest way to analyze the relationships is to examine the regression coefficient for each independent variable, which represents the average amount of change expected in Y given a unit change in the value of the independent variable you are examining.

Beta coefficient An estimated regression coefficient that has been recalculated to have a mean of 0 and a standard deviation of 1. Such a change enables independent variables with different units of measurement to be directly compared on their association with the dependent variable.

With the addition of more than one independent variable, we have some new issues to consider. One is the possibility that each independent variable is measured using a different scale. To solve this problem, we calculate the standardized regression coefficient. It is called a **beta coefficient,** and it shows the change in the dependent variable for each unit change in the independent variable. Standardization removes the effects of using different scales of measurement. For example, years of age and annual income are measured on different scales. Beta coefficients will range from .00 to 1.00, and can be either positive or negative. A positive beta means as the size of an independent variable increases then the size of the dependent variable increases. A negative beta means as the size of the independent variable increases then the size of the dependent variable gets smaller.

Statistical Significance

After the regression coefficients have been estimated, you must examine the statistical significance of each coefficient. This is done in the same manner as with bivariate regression. Each regression coefficient is divided by its standard error to produce a t statistic, which is compared against the critical value to determine whether the null hypothesis can be rejected. The basic question is still the same: "What is the probability we would get a coefficient of this size if the real regression coefficient in the population were zero?" You should examine the t-test statistics for each regression coefficient. Many times not all the independent variables in a regression equation will be statistically significant. If a regression coefficient is not statistically significant, that means the independent variable does not have a relationship with the dependent variable and the slope describing that relationship is relatively flat: the value of the dependent variable does not change at all as the value of the statistically insignificant independent variable changes.

When using multiple regression analysis, it is important to examine the overall statistical significance of the regression model. The amount of variation in the dependent variable you have been able to explain with the independent measures is compared with the total variation in the dependent measure. This comparison results in a statistic called a **model F statistic** which is compared against a critical value to determine whether or not to reject the null hypothesis. If the F statistic is statistically significant, it means the chances of the regression model for your sample producing a large r^2 when the population r^2 is actually 0 are acceptably small.

Model F statistic A statistic that compares the amount of variation in the dependent measure "explained" or associated with the independent variables to the "unexplained" or error variance. A larger F statistic indicates that the regression model has more explained variance than error variance.

Substantive Significance

Once we have estimated the regression equation, we need to assess the strength of the association. The multiple r^2 or multiple coefficient of determination describes the strength of the relationship between all the independent variables in our equation and the dependent variable. The larger the r^2 measure, the more of the behavior of the dependent measure is associated with the independent measures we are using to predict it. For example, if the multiple r^2 in our Canon copier example above were .78, that would mean we can explain 78 percent of the variation in sales revenue by using the variables sales force size, advertising budget, and customer attitudes toward our copier products. Higher values for r^2 mean stronger relationships between the group of independent variables and the dependent measure.

To summarize, the elements of a multiple regression model to examine in determining its significance include the r^2, the model F statistic, the individual regression coefficients for each independent variable, their associated t statistics, and the individual beta coefficients. The appropriate procedure to follow in evaluating the results of a regression analysis is (1) assess the statistical significance of the overall regression model using the F statistic and its associated probability; (2) evaluate the obtained r^2 to see how large it is; (3) examine the individual regression coefficients and their t statistics to see which are statistically significant; and (4) look at the beta coefficients to assess relative influence. Taken together, these elements give you a comprehensive picture of the answers to our three basic questions about the relationships between dependent and independent variables.

Multiple Regression Assumptions

Homoskedasticity The pattern of the covariation is constant (the same) around the regression line, whether the values are small, medium, or large.

Heteroskedasticity The pattern of covariation around the regression line is not constant around the regression line, and varies in some way when the values change from small to medium and large.

Normal curve A curve that indicates the shape of the distribution of a variable is equal both above and below the mean.

The ordinary least squares approach to estimating a regression model requires that several assumptions be met. Among the more important assumptions are (1) linear relationship, (2) **homoskedasticity,** and (3) normal distribution. The linearity assumption was explained earlier and illustrated in Exhibits 12.9 and 12.10. Exhibit 12.12 illustrates **heteroskedasticity.** The pattern of covariation (dots representing the values of X and Y) around the regression line is narrow on the left and very wide on the right (increases in width). In such a situation, the predictive ability of the regression model would change as the values range from small to large. For the regression model to predict accurately the dots must be approximately equal distances from the regression line, whether the values are small, medium, or large—a situation referred to as homoskedasticity. A **normal curve** is shown in Exhibit 12.13. A regression model assumes both the independent and dependent variable distributions are normally distributed. The SPSS regression software has options to check these assumptions. All of these assumptions should be met. The general regression model predicts reasonably well, however, with moderate deviations from linearity, homoskedasticity, and normality.

SPSS Application—Multiple Regression

Regression can be used to examine the relationship between a single metric dependent variable and one or more metric independent variables. If you examine the Santa Fe Grill customer database, you will note that the first 21 variables are metric independent variables. They are lifestyle variables and perceptions of the restaurant, measured using a 7-point rating scale with 7 representing the high end of the scale and 1 the low end. Variables X_{22}, X_{23}, and X_{24} are metric-dependent variables measured on a 7-point rating scale. Variable X_{25}–Frequency of

---

| **Exhibit 12.12** | **Example of Heteroskedasticity** |

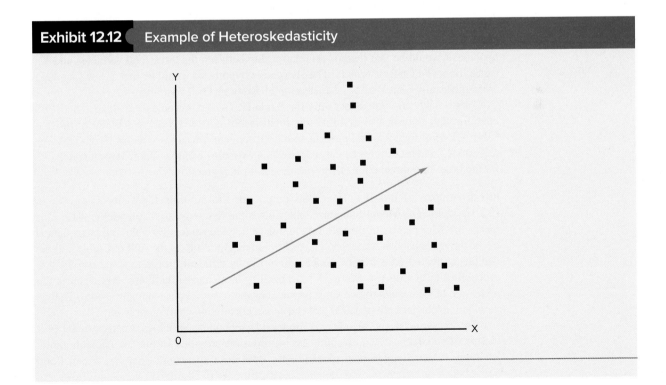

Exhibit 12.13	Example of a Normal Curve

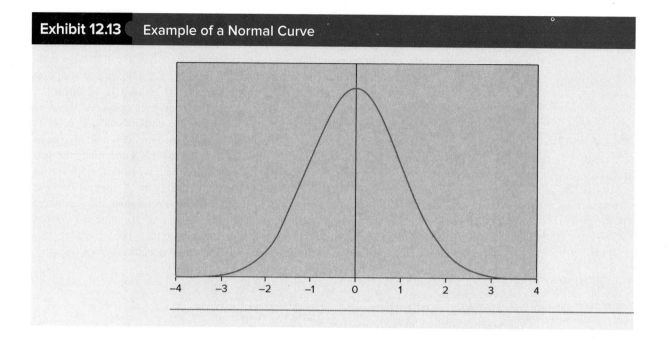

Eating, X_{30}–Distance Driven, X_{31}–Ad Recall, and X_{32}–Gender are nonmetric. Variables X_{26} to X_{29} also are nonmetric variables because they are ranking data, and thus cannot therefore be used in regression.

An example of a problem to examine with multiple regression is the relationship between perceptions of the food in the restaurant and overall customer satisfaction. In this case, the single metric-dependent variable is X_{22}–Satisfaction, and the independent variables would be X_{15}–Fresh Food, X_{18}–Food Taste, and X_{20}–Food Temperature. The null hypothesis would be that there is no relationship between the three food variables and X_{22} for the Santa Fe Grill customers. The alternative hypothesis would be that X_{15}, X_{18}, and X_{20} are significantly related to X_{22}–Satisfaction of Santa Fe Grill customers.

First, make sure you select only the Santa Fe Grill customers to analyze. The SPSS click-through sequence to examine this relationship is ANALYZE → REGRESSION → LINEAR. Highlight X_{22} and move it to the Dependent Variables window. Highlight X_{15}, X_{18}, and X_{20} and move them to the Independent Variables window. We will use the defaults for the other options so click OK to run the multiple regression.

Interpretation of Results The SPSS output for the multiple regression is shown in Exhibit 12.14. The Model Summary table shows the R-square for this model is .417. This means that 41.7 percent of the variation in satisfaction (dependent variable) can be explained by the three independent variables. The regression model results in the ANOVA table indicate that the R-square for the overall model is significantly different from zero (F-ratio = 59.288; probability level (Sig.) < .000). This probability level means there are .000 chances the regression model results come from a population where the R-square actually is zero. That is, there are no chances out of 1,000 that the actual correlation coefficient is zero.

To determine if one or more of the food independent variables are significant predictors of satisfaction, we examine the information provided in the Coefficients table. Looking at the Standardized Coefficients Beta column reveals that X_{15}–Fresh Food has a beta coefficient of .767 that is significant (.000). Similarly, X_{18}–Food Taste and

| Exhibit 12.14 | SPSS Results for Multiple Regression |

Model Summary

Model	R	R Square	Adjusted R Square	Std. Error of the Estimate
1	.646*	.417	.410	.770

*Predictors: (Constant), X20 — Proper Food Temperature, X15—Fresh Food, X18 — Excellent Food Taste

ANOVA†

Model		Sum of Squares	df	Mean Square	F	Sig.
1	Regression	105.342	3	35.114	59.288	.000*
	Residual	147.472	249	.592		
	Total	252.814	252			

*Predictors: (Constant), X20—Proper Food Temperature, X15—Fresh Food, X18—Excellent Food Taste
†Dependent Variable: X22—Satisfaction

Coefficients†

Model		Unstandardized Coefficients		Standardized Coefficients	t	Sig.
		B	Std. Error	Beta		
1	(Constant)	2.144	.269		7.984	.000
	X15—Fresh Food	.660	.068	.767	9.642	.000
	X18—Excellent Food Taste	-.304	.095	-.267	-3.202	.002
	X20—Proper Food Temperature	.090	.069	.096	1.312	.191

*Dependent Variable: X22—Satisfaction

X_{20}–Food Temperature have beta coefficients of -0.267 (Sig. $< .002$) and 0.096 (Sig. $< .191$), respectively. This means we can reject the null hypothesis that none of the food variables are related to X_{22}–Customer Satisfaction. Thus, this regression analysis tells us customer perceptions of food in the Santa Fe Grill, for two of the food variables, are good predictors of the level of satisfaction with the restaurant.

But we need to be cautious in interpreting these regression results. The first question is "Why is X_{20}–Proper Food Temperature not significant?" A second important question is raised by the negative sign of X_{18}–Food Taste (-0.267). The negative sign indicates that less favorable perceptions of food taste are associated with higher levels of satisfaction. This result is clearly not logical and needs to be examined further to understand why this is happening.

First, let's review the meaning of standardized coefficients (beta). Recall that the size of the individual coefficients shows how strongly each independent variable is related to the dependent variable. The signs (negative or positive) also are important. A positive sign indicates a positive relationship (higher independent variable values are associated with higher dependent variable values). A negative sign indicates a negative relationship. When the independent variables are highly correlated with each other, the

Exhibit 12.15	Correlation Matrix of Regression Model Variables

Correlations

		X22— Satisfaction	X15—Fresh Food	X18— Excellent Food Taste	X20—Proper Food Temperature
X22—Satisfaction	Pearson Correlation	1	.627*	.393*	.430*
	Sig. (2-tailed)		.000	.000	.000
	N	253	253	253	253
X15—Fresh Food	Pearson Correlation	.627*	1	.770*	.686*
	Sig. (2-tailed)	.000		.000	.000
	N	253	253	253	253
X18—Excellent Food Taste	Pearson Correlation	.393*	.770*	1	.721*
	Sig. (2-tailed)	.000	.000		.000
	N	253	253	253	253
X20—Proper Food Temperature	Pearson Correlation	.430*	.686*	.721*	1
	Sig. (2-tailed)	.000	.000	.000	
	N	253	253	253	253

*Correlation is significant at the 0.01 level (2-tailed).

Multicollinearity A situation in which several independent variables are highly correlated with each other. This characteristic can result in difficulty in estimating separate or independent regression coefficients for the correlated variables.

signs of the beta coefficients may be reversed in a regression model, and coefficients that are significant may be insignificant. This is what happened in this example. The food variables (independent variables) are highly correlated and therefore can be described as exhibiting **multicollinearity.**

Because multicollinearity can create problems in using regression, analysts must always examine the logic of the signs and significance levels of the regression betas when independent variables are highly correlated. If a hypothesized relationship is the opposite of what is anticipated, one must look at a simple bivariate correlation of the two variables. This can be seen in Exhibit 12.15, which clearly shows the significant positive correlation of .393 between X_{22}–Satisfaction and X_{18}–Food Taste. Note also that there is a significant positive correlation of .430 between X_{22}–Satisfaction and X_{18}–Food Temperature. These bivariate correlations show the problem of using multiple regression when the independent variables are highly correlated.

When are the correlations between independent variables in multiple regression high enough to cause a problem? In the authors' experiences, problems typically arise when the independent variables are correlated at a level of .50 or higher. Note in Exhibit 12.15 that all three independent variables are correlated at a level of .68 or higher. Thus, it is not surprising that this problem arose. To deal with this problem researchers typically follow one of two approaches. One approach is to create summated scales consisting of the independent variables that are highly correlated. The other approach, computing factor scores, is beyond the scope of this book.

Additional discussion of multicollinearity or nonmetric dummy variables in regression is beyond the scope of this book. To help you understand these topics, we have placed material on our website at **connnect.mheducation.com**.

Examination of the SPSS tables reveals that there is a lot of information provided that we did not discuss. Experts in statistics may use this information, but managers typically do not. One of the challenges for you will be to learn which information is most important to analyze and present in a report.

What Is Structural Modeling?

Our analysis of multivariate modeling has focused on multiple regression. The model in Exhibit 12.16 shows how multiple regression could be used to understand what work environment factors might influence commitment among employees of the Santa Fe Grill restaurant. The model has a single dependent variable (Commitment) and four work environment independent variables (pay, teamwork, management/supervision, and work). To run a multiple regression model using the Samouel's Employee data, you would have to select a single question to represent each of the four independent variables in the model, and one question for the dependent variable. For example, question 5 could be used to measure pay, question 4 could measure team, question 3 could measure management, question 1 could measure work, and question 14 could measure the single dependent variable commitment (see Exhibit 10.2 for these specific questions). This regression model has two stages—the four independent variables are one stage and the single dependent variable is the second stage.

In today's complex business environment, we often encounter situations that involve more than two stages in a multivariate model, and in which concepts are more accurately measured with more than a single variable. The model shown in Exhibit 12.17 has three stages—the first stage is the four independent variables (constructs) representing the work environment, each measured with three separate questions; the second stage is the Commitment construct, measured with four separate questions; and the third stage is the ultimate dependent variable Performance, measured with only a single question. Note that the Commitment variable in this path model operates as both a dependent variable of the four work environment variables and as an independent variable predicting performance. The commitment variable in the model is also referred to as an intervening or mediating variable. A three-stage path model like this cannot be analyzed with multiple regression. You must use structural modeling, generally referred to as structural equation modeling (SEM).

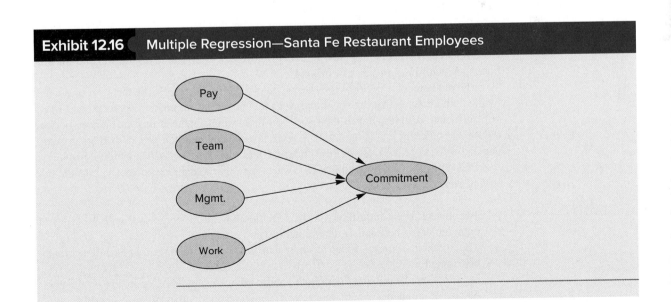

Exhibit 12.16   Multiple Regression—Santa Fe Restaurant Employees

Exhibit 12.17 Structural Equation Model—Santa Fe Restaurant Employees

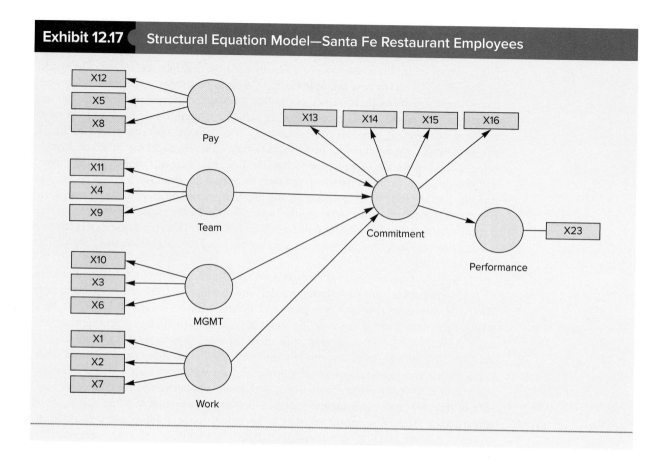

The most appropriate type of SEM for this problem is called partial least squares, or simply PLS-SEM. The calculation of a solution is very similar to ordinary least squares regression, but is extended to obtain a solution for path models with more than two stages and variables measured with more than a single question. The statistical objective of the calculations is to maximize the variance explained in the dependent variables. There also is user-friendly software available to students at no charge—SmartPLS (**www.smartpls.de**). A Powerpoint file explaining how to use this software is available on the website for this book (**www.mhhe.com/hairessentials4**).

The path model is developed based on theory. In Exhibit 12.17, the theory represented by the path model is that the way employees feel about pay, team, management, and work will influence commitment to their job, and that commitment in turn influences performance. Specifically, employees that are more favorable about their pay, coworkers, managers, and work in general, are more committed, and therefore perform at a higher level.

PLS-SEM is becoming popular in business and marketing research because of the following advantages:

1. The measurement requirements are very flexible and it works well with all types of data, including nominal, ordinal, interval, and ratio data.
2. The method is nonparametric so it can be applied to data that is not normally distributed.
3. Solutions can be obtained with both small and large samples. Depending on the complexity of the model, a sample size of 50 or so respondents is often acceptable.

4. Solutions are possible with very complex models based on 100+ questions and many constructs.

5. Many types of analysis are possible, such as group comparisons, mediation, moderation, and importance-performance analysis.

6. The SmartPLS software is very user friendly—just draw a picture of your path model, import your data, and use point-and-click and drag-and-drop motions to run the software. The output includes many assessment tools, including Cronbach's Alpha reliability, validity testing, and explained variance (R^2).

The next section demonstrates the application of the SmartPLS software to help you understand the factors that may be influencing the Santa Fe Grill employees to perform at a higher level.

An Example of Structural Modeling

Management of the Santa Fe Grill wants their employees to be highly motivated to provide excellent service to their customers. As noted earlier, theory suggests that pay, teamwork, management, and work influence commitment to an employer, and ultimately lead to higher performance. These proposed relationships are based not only on theory, but also on practical knowledge, logic, and business experience.

There are five structural paths in the path model shown in Exhibit 12.18. The structural paths are represented by the four single-headed arrows from pay, team, management,

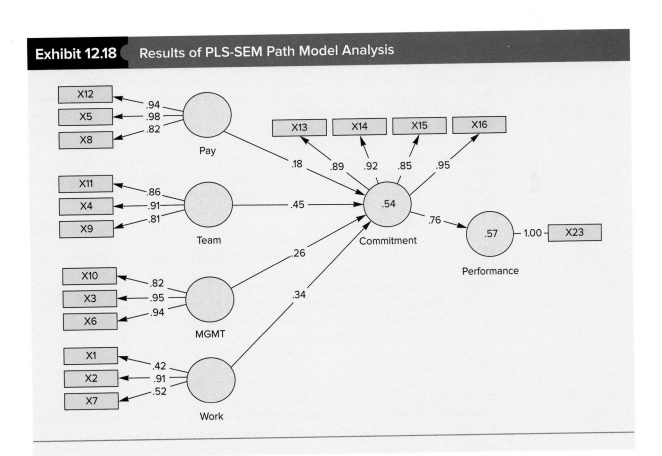

Exhibit 12.18 Results of PLS-SEM Path Model Analysis

and work to commitment, and the one single-headed arrow from commitment to performance. Each of these five structural paths is a hypothesis:

1. The more satisfied employees are with their pay, the more committed they are to the restaurant.
2. The more favorable employees are about how their teams are functioning, the more committed they are to the restaurant.
3. The more favorable employees are about management, the more committed they are to the restaurant.
4. The more favorable employees are about their work at the restaurant, the more committed they are to the restaurant.
5. The more committed employees are to the restaurant, the higher their job performance.

The results from testing the hypotheses using the SmartPLS software are shown on the structural model in Exhibit 12.18. The relationships between the six constructs and the variables (questions) that measure the constructs are referred to as the **outer model.** For example, the pay construct is measured by three variables—X12, X5, and X8. The outer model is thus the six constructs in the path model and the relationships between these six constructs and the variables that measure the constructs. The five structural relationships (single-headed arrows) between the six constructs in the model are referred to as the **inner model.**

PLS-SEM results are examined in a two-step sequence. The first step assesses the outer model, also referred to as the measurement model. The second step assesses the inner model. The numbers on the outer model arrows connecting the constructs with the measured variables are correlations. These correlations are evaluated based on their size and statistical significance. The general guideline is the size of the correlations should be .70 or larger, but smaller correlations are sometimes considered acceptable. Looking at the correlations for the six constructs (see Exhibit 12.19), all are larger than the .70 guideline, except for X1 and X7 on the work construct. In addition, X1 is not statistically significant at the .05 level but X7 is. Since the sample size is N = 77, some researchers would consider the .09 for X1 acceptable, but the size of the correlation still does not meet recommended guidelines. Basically, researcher judgment is involved in deciding these issues. Questions X1 and X7 are definitely weak, and many researchers would likely remove both X1 and X7 from the model and rerun it with fewer measured variables.

The SmartPLS software also provides the Cronbach's Alpha internal consistency reliability measure for all constructs. The reliability is the following: pay = .93; team = .83; MGMT = .87; work = .44; and commitment = .92 (internal consistency reliability is not appropriate for single item constructs, such as performance). The reliability of all constructs is acceptable, except for the work construct.

The second step involves evaluating the results for the inner model. The numbers on the inner model arrows connecting the constructs are structural coefficients (not correlations). These coefficients are similar to regression coefficients (standardized betas), and are also evaluated based on their size and statistical significance. The larger the size of the coefficients, the stronger the path relationship between the two constructs. The sizes of the coefficients on all relationships are meaningful (see Exhibit 12.20). All paths are statistically significant (< 0.05), except the Pay → Commitment relationship. The lack of significance is likely due to the small sample size (N = 77), and under these circumstances, many researchers would consider a .07 significance level acceptable.

Exhibit 12.19	Outer Measurement Model Evaluation

Constructs	Size	Statistical Significance
Pay		
X12	.94	.00
X5	.98	.00
X8	.82	.00
Team		
X11	.86	.00
X4	.91	.00
X9	.81	.00
Management		
X10	.82	.00
X3	.95	.00
X6	.94	.00
Work		
X1	.42	.09
X2	.91	.00
X7	.52	.05
Commitment		
X13	.89	.00
X14	.92	.00
X15	.85	.00
X16	.95	.00
Performance		
X23	1.00	.00

Exhibit 12.20	Inner Path Model Evaluation

Structural Path	Size	Statistical Significance
Pay → Commitment	.18	.07
Team → Commitment	.45	.00
MGMT → Commitment	.26	.00
Work → Commitment	.34	.00
Commitment → Performance	.76	.00

Exhibit 12.21 Results of Revised PLS-SEM Path Model

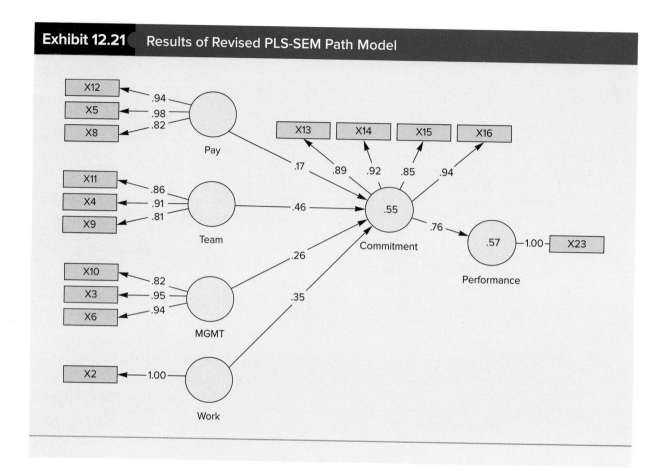

The small size and lack of significance of the outer model correlations of the work construct, in combination with the low reliability of the construct, dictate that corrective measures must be taken to improve this construct. The entire construct could be removed from the model. But before taking that action it is appropriate to delete the poorly performing measured variables. Variables X1 and X7 were removed and the model was run again. The results of the revised model are shown in Exhibit 12.21. Overall, these model results are very similar to the previous one, except that the work construct measured with a single variable (X2) now meets acceptable guidelines, as do all other constructs.

The final concept to evaluate is the predictive ability of the structural model. The four independent variable work environment constructs predict 55 percent of the variance (R^2) in the commitment construct, and the commitment construct predicts 57 percent of the variance (R^2) in the performance construct (see numbers inside constructs in Exhibit 12.21). These are excellent results for this predictive model, and are very useful for the owners of the Santa Fe Grill restaurant in better understanding how to supervise their employees. It should be noted that our analysis has only focused on the basic assessment tools for PLS-SEM analyses. A more comprehensive explanation of the PLS-SEM method can be found in this book (Hair Jr, Joseph F., G. Tomas M. Hult, Christian M. Ringle, and Marko Sarstedt, A primer on partial least squares structural equation modeling (PLS-SEM), 2nd ed. (Thousand Oaks, CA: Sage Publications, in press)).

MARKETING RESEARCH IN ACTION
The Role of Employees in Developing a Customer Satisfaction Program

The plant manager of QualKote Manufacturing is interested in the impact his year-long effort to implement a quality improvement program is having on the satisfaction of his customers. The plant foreman, assembly-line workers, and engineering staff have closely examined their operations to determine which activities have the most impact on product quality and reliability. Together, the managers and employees have worked to better understand how each particular job affects the final delivered quality of the product as the customer perceives it.

To answer his questions about customer satisfaction, the plant manager conducted an internal survey of plant workers and managers using a 7-point scale (endpoints are 1 = Strongly Disagree and 7 = Strongly Agree). His plans are to get opinions from within the company first and then do a customer survey on similar topics. He has collected completed surveys from 57 employees. The following are examples of the topics that were covered in the questionnaire:

- Data from a variety of external sources such as customers, competitors, and suppliers is used in the strategic planning process. Independent variable A10.
- Customers are involved in the product quality planning process. Independent variable A12.
- Customer requirements and expectations of the company's products are used in developing strategic plans and goals. Independent variable A17.
- There is a systematic process to translate customer requirements into new/improved products. Independent variable A23.
- There is a systematic process to accurately determine customers' requirements and expectations. Independent variable A31.
- The company's product quality program has improved the level of customer satisfaction. Dependent variable A36.
- The company's product quality program has improved the likelihood that customers will recommend us. Dependent variable A37.
- Gender of the employee responding: Male = 1; Female = 0. Classification variable A40.

A multiple regression was run using SPSS with responses of the 57 employees as input to the model. The dependent variable was A36 and the independent variables were A10, A12, A17, A23, and A31. The output is shown in Exhibits 12.22 and 12.23. There is a database of QualKote employee responses to these questions available in SPSS format at **connect.mheducation.com**. The database is labeled QualKote MRIA_Essn 3e.sav.

Results indicate a statistically significant relationship between the metric-dependent variable (A36–Satisfaction) and at least some of the five metric independent variables. The R^2 for the relationship is 67.0 and it is statistically significant at the .000 level. This suggests that when employees have more favorable perceptions about some aspects of the implementation of the quality improvement program, they also believe the program has improved customer satisfaction.

Exhibit 12.22 QualKote Descriptive Statistics

Descriptive Statistics

	Mean	Std. Deviation	N
A36—Product Quality Program has Improved Customer Satisfaction	4.81	.953	57
A10—Data from Variety of Sources Used in Planning	5.00	1.414	57
A12—Customers Involved in Product Quality Planning	3.60	1.334	57
A17—Customer Data Used in Planning	2.28	1.176	57
A23—Systematic Process to Translate Customer Requirements into Products	4.53	1.104	57
A31—Systematic Process to Determine Customer Requirements	2.89	.838	57

Hands-On Exercise

1. Will the results of this regression model be useful to the QualKote plant manager? If yes, how?
2. Which independent variables are helpful in predicting A36–Customer Satisfaction?
3. How would the manager interpret the mean values for the variables reported in Exhibit 12.22?
4. What other regression models might be examined with the questions from this survey?

Exhibit 12.23 Multiple Regression of QualKote Satisfaction Variables

Model Summary

Model	R	R Square	Adjusted R Square	Std. Error of the Estimate
1	.819*	.670	.638	.574

*Predictors: (Constant), A31—Systematic Process to Determine Customer Requirements, A10—Data from Variety of Sources Used in Planning, A12—Customers Involved in Product Quality Planning, A17—Customer Data Used in Planning, A23—Systematic Process to Translate Customer Requirements into Products

ANOVA[†]

Model		Sum of Squares	df	Mean Square	F	Sig.
1	Regression	34.095	5	6.819	20.723	.000*
	Residual	16.782	51	.329		
	Total	50.877	56			

*Predictors: (Constant), A31—Systematic Process to Determine Customer Requirements, A10—Data from Variety of Sources Used in Planning, A12—Customers Involved in Product Quality Planning, A17—Customer Data Used in Planning, A23—Systematic Process to Translate Customer Requirements into Products
[†]Dependent Variable: A36—Product Quality Program has Improved Customer Satisfaction

Coefficients*

Model		Unstandardized Coefficients		Standardized Coefficients		
		B	Std. Error	Beta	t	Sig.
1	(Constant)	.309	.496		.624	.535
	A10—Data from Variety of Sources Used in Planning	.314	.068	.466	4.587	.000
	A12—Customers Involved in Product Quality Planning	.294	.066	.411	4.451	.000
	A17—Customer Data Used in Planning	.208	.080	.257	2.614	.012
	A23—Systematic Process to Translate Customer Requirements into Products	.296	.108	.343	2.744	.008
	A31—Systematic Process to Determine Customer Requirements	.020	.136	.017	.145	.885

*Dependent Variable: A36—Product Quality Program has Improved Customer Satisfaction

Summary

Understand and evaluate the types of relationships between variables.

Relationships between variables can be described in several ways, including presence, direction, strength of association, and type. Presence tells us whether a consistent and systematic relationship exists. Direction tells us whether the relationship is positive or negative. Strength of association tells us whether we have a weak or strong relationship, and the type of relationship is usually described as either linear or nonlinear.

Two variables may share a linear relationship, in which changes in one variable are accompanied by some change (not necessarily the same amount of change) in the other variable. As long as the amount of change stays constant over the range of both variables, the relationship is termed linear. Relationships between two variables that change in strength and/or direction as the values of the variables change are referred to as curvilinear.

Explain the concepts of association and covariation.

The terms *covariation* and *association* refer to the attempt to quantify the strength of the relationship between two variables. Covariation is the amount of change in one variable of interest that is consistently related to change in another variable under study. The degree of association is a numerical measure of the strength of the relationship between two variables. Both these terms refer to linear relationships.

Discuss the differences between Pearson correlation and Spearman correlation.

Pearson correlation coefficients are a measure of linear association between two variables of interest. The Pearson correlation coefficient is used when both variables are measured on an interval or ratio scale. When one or more variables of interest are measured on an ordinal scale, the Spearman rank order correlation coefficient should be used.

Explain the concept of statistical significance versus practical significance.

Because some of the procedures involved in determining the statistical significance of a statistical test include consideration of the sample size, it is possible to have a very low degree of association between two variables show up as statistically significant (i.e., the population parameter is not equal to zero). However, by considering the absolute strength of the relationship in addition to its statistical significance, the researcher is better able to draw the appropriate conclusion about the data and the population from which they were selected.

Understand when and how to use regression analysis.

Regression analysis is useful in answering questions about the strength of a linear relationship between a dependent variable and one or more independent variables. The results of a regression analysis indicate the amount of change in the dependent variable that is associated with a one-unit change in the independent variables. In addition, the accuracy of the regression equation can be evaluated by comparing the predicted values of the dependent variable to the actual values of the dependent variable drawn from the sample. When using regression the assumptions should be checked to ensure the results are accurate and not distorted by deviations from the assumptions.

Understand the value and application of structural modeling.

Structural modeling enables researchers to analyze complex multivariate models. The most appropriate structural modeling method for marketing research applications is partial least squares structural equation modeling (PLS-SEM). The PLS-SEM method is an extension of ordinary least squares multiple regression and the statistical objective is to maximize the variance explained in the dependent variable(s). The primary advantages of the method are the ability to examine complex structural models with three or more stages, to include constructs/variables measured with several questions, to analyze data with non-normal distributions, and to obtain solutions with smaller sample sizes.

Key Terms and Concepts

Beta coefficient 333

Bivariate regression analysis 328

Coefficient of determination (r^2) 325

Covariation 319

Curvilinear relationship 318

Homoskedasticity 335

Heteroskedasticity 335

Least squares procedure 329

Linear relationship 318

Model F statistic 334

Multicollinearity 338

Multiple regression analysis 333

Normal curve 335

Ordinary least squares 330

Partial least squares (PLS-SEM) 340

Pearson correlation coefficient 322

Regression coefficient 330

Scatter diagram 319

Spearman rank order correlation coefficient 326

Structural Modeling 339

Unexplained variance 329

Review Questions

1. Explain the difference between testing for significant differences and testing for association.
2. Explain the difference between association and causation.
3. What is covariation? How does it differ from correlation?
4. What are the differences between univariate and bivariate statistical techniques?
5. What is regression analysis? When would you use it?
6. What is the difference between simple regression and multiple regression?

Discussion Questions

1. Regression and correlation analysis both describe the strength of linear relationships between variables. Consider the concepts of education and income. Many people would say these two variables are related in a linear fashion. As education increases, income usually increases (although not necessarily at the same rate). Can you think of two variables that are related in such a way that their relationship changes over their range of possible values (i.e., in a curvilinear fashion)? How would you analyze the relationship between two such variables?

2. Is it possible to conduct a regression analysis on two variables and obtain a significant regression equation (significant F-ratio), but still have a low r^2? What does the r^2 statistic measure? How can you have a low r^2 yet still get a statistically significant F-ratio for the overall regression equation?

3. The ordinary least squares (OLS) procedure commonly used in regression produces a line of "best fit" for the data to which it is applied. How would you define best fit in regression analysis? What is there about the procedure that guarantees a best fit to the data? What assumptions about the use of a regression technique are necessary to produce this result?

4. When multiple independent variables are used to predict a dependent variable in multiple regression, multicollinearity among the independent variables is often a concern. What is the main problem caused by high multicollinearity among the independent variables in a multiple regression equation? Can you still achieve a high r^2 for your regression equation if multicollinearity is present in your data?

5. **EXPERIENCE MARKETING RESEARCH.** Choose a retailer that students are likely to patronize

and that sells in both catalogs and on the Internet (e.g., Victoria's Secret). Prepare a questionnaire that compares the experience of shopping in the catalog with shopping online. Then ask a sample of students to visit the website, look at the catalogs you have brought to class, and then complete the questionnaire. Enter the data into a software package and assess your finding statistically. Prepare a report that compares catalog and online shopping. Be able to defend your conclusions.

6. **SPSS EXERCISE.** Choose one or two other students from your class and form a team. Identify the different retailers from your community where wireless phones, digital recorders/players, TVs, and other electronics products are sold. Team members should divide up and visit all the different stores and describe the products and brands that are sold in each. Also observe the layout in the store, the store personnel, and the type of advertising the store uses. In other words, familiarize yourself with each retailer's marketing mix. Use your knowledge of the marketing mix to design a questionnaire. Interview approximately 100 people who are familiar with all the retailers you selected and collect their responses. Analyze the responses using a statistical software package such as SPSS. Prepare a report of your findings, including whether the perceptions of each of the stores are similar or different, and particularly whether the differences are statistically or substantively different. Present your findings in class and be prepared to defend your conclusions and your use of statistical techniques.

7. **SPSS EXERCISE.** Santa Fe Grill owners believe their employees are happy working for the restaurant and unlikely to search for another job. Use the Santa Fe Grill employee database and run a bivariate regression analysis between X_{11}–Team Cooperates and X_{17}–Likelihood of Searching for another Job to test this hypothesis. Could this hypothesis be better examined with multiple regression? If yes, execute a multiple regression and explain the results.

Communicating Marketing Research Findings

Chapter 13

1. Understand the objectives of a research report.
2. Describe the format of a marketing research report.
3. Discuss several techniques for graphically displaying research results.

4. Clarify problems encountered in preparing reports.
5. Understand the importance of presentations in marketing research.

It Takes More than Numbers to Communicate

Visual display of data is not easy, and even research experts do not always do it well. After all, the kinds of people who are good at statistics are not necessarily the ones who are good at visual presentation. Nevertheless, the ability to present data visually in a way that is illuminating is important in writing research reports.

The person most known for his expertise in presenting visual data is Professor Edward Tufte. The author of several books on the topic, including *The Display of Quantitative Information*, Professor Tufte hails from the field of political science, but his advice applies to any field. Business graphics have the same goals as any other graphics: to convey information, to summarize reasoning, and to solve problems. Tufte explains the importance of visual displays of data: "Good design is clear thinking made visible, and bad design is stupidity made visible. . . . So when you see a display filled with chart junk, there's a deeper corruption: they don't know what they're talking about."[1]

Tufte has implicated poor presentation of statistics and information in the *Challenger* disaster. A NASA PowerPoint slide show buried statistics revealing that rubber O-ring seals in the boosters tended to leak at low temperatures. The failure of an O-ring ultimately resulted in the death of seven astronauts. Of course, poor graphic presentations rarely have such dramatic or tragic consequences. However, business opportunities are missed, time is wasted, and audiences are bored.

The *New York Times* calls Professor Tufte the Leonardo da Vinci of data presentation. Tufte emphasizes that presenting statistics well is not about creating slick graphics. "The task is not to have 'high-impact' presentations, or 'point, click, wow,' or 'power pitches.' The point is to explain something. . . . The right metaphor for presentations is not power or PowerPoint. . . . It's not television or theater. It's teaching."[2]

Value of Communicating Research Findings

No matter how well research projects are designed and implemented, if the results cannot be effectively communicated to the client, the project is not a success. While the chapter introduction focuses on presentations, marketing research reports are communicated in writing as well. An effective marketing research report is one way to ensure the time, effort, and money that went into the research project will be completely realized. The purpose of this chapter is to introduce the style and format of the marketing research report. We identify how the marketing research report is designed and explain the objectives of each section. We then discuss industry best practices regarding effective presentation of research reports.

Marketing Research Reports

A professional marketing research report has four objectives: (1) to effectively communicate the findings of the marketing research project; (2) to provide interpretations of those findings in the form of sound and logical recommendations; (3) to establish the credibility of the research project; and (4) to serve as a future reference document for strategic or tactical decisions.

The first objective of the research report is to effectively communicate the findings of the marketing research project. Since a major purpose of the research project is to obtain information to answer questions about a specific business problem, the report must explain both how the information was obtained and what relevance it has to the research questions. A detailed description of the following topics should be communicated to the client:

1. The research objectives
2. The research questions
3. Literature review and relevant secondary data
4. A description of the research methods
5. Findings displayed in tables, graphs, or charts
6. Interpretation and summary of the findings
7. Conclusions and recommendations

In Chapter 9, we explained how to write a qualitative research report. Quantitative reports include the same general information as do qualitative reports. But some of the issues faced in developing a research report are different. The objectives and questions in qualitative research tend to be broader, more general, and more open-ended than in quantitative research. The literature review and relevant secondary data may be integrated in the analysis of findings in qualitative data analysis, rather than being presented separately from other findings. The description of research methods in both qualitative and quantitative research helps to develop credibility for both kinds of research projects, but different kinds of evidence are offered in developing credibility in quantitative and qualitative analyses. Data display is important in both methods. Qualitative researchers rarely present statistics, but they are the bread and butter of a quantitative presentation. Writing conclusions and recommendations is the final step in both qualitative and quantitative reports.

Too often, quantitative researchers are so concerned about doing statistical analyses they forget to provide a clear, logical interpretation of their results. Researchers must recognize that clients are seldom knowledgeable about sampling methods and statistics. Thus, researchers must present technical or complex information in a manner that is understandable to all parties. Many words used to teach research to students are not necessary in a marketing research report. For example, the word *hypothesis* seldom appears in a marketing research report. When Crosstabs, ANOVAs, *t*-tests, correlation, and regression are used, they are presented with simplicity and clarity. The name of the analysis technique may not even be used in the presentation and reporting of results. Most market researchers do not even include information about statistical significance in their reports, although we recommend that you do so.

In writing a report, researchers must cross the gap from doing and understanding statistics to communicating findings in a way that is completely understandable to nontechnical readers. Most researchers are comfortable with statistics, computer outputs, questionnaires, and other project-related material. In presenting results to the client, researchers should keep the original research objectives in mind. The task is to focus on the objectives and communicate how each part of the project is related to the completion of the objectives.

For example, Exhibit 13.1 is from a research presentation that illustrates a research objective: identifying senior segments with respect to Internet adoption and use. While a

| Exhibit 13.1 | Findings from Senior Internet Adoption Study |

Senior Internet Adoption Segments

	Light Use	Heavy Use
Self Adoption 20%	**Demographics** High income and education, more male	**Demographics** High income and education, younger, more male
	Self-Directed Values Low curiosity and proactive coping	**Self-Directed Values** High curiosity and proactive coping
	Technology Attitudes/Behavior Low technology discomfort	**Technology Attitudes/Behavior** Earliest adoption
	Medium technology optimism, innovativeness **12%**	Low technology discomfort High technology optimism, innovativeness **8%**
Helped Adoption 21%	**Demographics** Medium education and income, more female	**Demographics** Medium income and education, more female
	Self-Directed Values Medium curiosity and proactive coping	**Self-Directed Values** High curiosity and proactive coping
	Technology Attitudes/Behavior Latest adoption	**Technology Attitudes/Behavior** High technology discomfort
	High technology discomfort	High technology optimism, innovativeness **8%**
	Medium technology optimism, innovativeness **13%**	
Non-Adopters 59%	**Demographics** Low income, and education, more female, older	
	Self-Directed Values Low curiosity and high proactive coping	
	Technology Attitudes/Behavior High technology discomfort, low technology optimism, and low innovativeness	

great deal of numerical data was used to prepare the chart, the data have been reduced to a format that is compact and easy to understand. In this chapter, we show you how to use graphics to summarize the statistical analyses covered in our text. These graphics can be used in presentations and in written marketing research reports. Researchers are always looking for ways to summarize information in a meaningful and compact way. They must be careful, however, that results are still easy to interpret and they should provide text to help readers focus on important points. In this chapter, we provide suggestions on how to present various kinds of analysis graphically. Our exhibits show PowerPoint slides, but the same graphics can be used as part of a narrative report. There are always multiple ways to present the same data, and researchers must use their creativity and continually think about if and how their presentation and/or report makes the points they want to make.

In addition to presenting results in an easy-to-understand fashion, the research report or presentation must establish **credibility** for the research methods, findings, and conclusions. This can be accomplished only if the report is accurate, believable, and professionally organized. These three dimensions cannot be treated separately, for they collectively operate to build credibility in the research document. For the report to be accurate, all of the input must be accurate. No degree of carelessness in handling data, reporting of statistics, or incorrect interpretation can be tolerated. Errors in mathematical calculations, grammatical errors, and incorrect terminology diminish the credibility of the entire report.

Clear and logical thinking, precise expression, and accurate presentation create **believability.** When the underlying logic is fuzzy or the presentation imprecise, readers may have difficulty understanding what they read. If readers do not understand what they read, they may not believe what they read. It is important to note that whenever findings are surprising, or are different from what the client expects, research analysts can expect to be questioned. The methodology will be scrutinized to find an explanation that explains away the surprising findings. Sampling method, question wording, and nonresponse error are some of the most common ways of explaining away surprising findings. Researchers must anticipate these questions and have clear explanations for all findings. The accompanying Marketing Research Dashboard covers the role of critical thinking in reporting marketing research.

Finally, the credibility of the research report is affected by the quality and organization of the document itself. The report must be clearly developed and professionally organized. The overall look of the report must not only clearly communicate results, but also convey the professionalism of the research effort. Also, the document must reflect the preferences and technical sophistication of the reader. Reports are written to reflect three levels of readers: (1) readers who will read only the executive summary; (2) readers who will read the executive summary and look at the body of findings more closely; and (3) readers with some technical expertise, who may read the entire report and look to the appendix for more detailed information.

It is helpful to prepare an outline of all major points, with supporting details in their proper position and sequence. The report should have sections that address each of the research objectives. Use short, concise sentences and paragraphs. Always select wording consistent with the background and knowledge of readers. Rewrite the report several times. This will force you to remove clutter and critically evaluate the document for improvements.

The fourth objective of the research report is to be a reference. Most marketing research studies cover a variety of different objectives and seek to answer several research questions. This is accomplished in the report using both statistical and narrative formats. To retain all of this information is virtually impossible for the client. As a result, the research report becomes a reference document that is reviewed over an extended period.

Many marketing research reports become a part of a larger project conducted in various stages over time. It is not uncommon for one marketing research report to serve as a baseline for additional studies. Also, many reports are used for comparison purposes.

Credibility The quality of a report that is related to its accuracy, believability, and professional organization.

Believability The quality of a report that is based on clear and logical thinking, precise expression, and accurate presentation.

Critical thinking is the art of analyzing and evaluating thinking with a view to improving it. While critical thinking is important to almost anything we do, it is especially important in evaluating and reporting research results. Many barriers to effective critical thinking have been identified, and several of these are directly applicable to reporting research.

Confirmation Bias

Confirmation bias exists when researchers interpret the evidence to fit pre-existing beliefs. Researchers must seek to find evidence that disproves their preexisting beliefs in order to avoid falling into this trap. Surprising findings should be evaluated relative to methodological and sampling choices that might have contributed to the findings. However, surprising findings should not be rejected or ignored outright.

Generalizing from Samples

When a sample is small or has not been randomly chosen, researchers must be very careful in making generalizations. Many samples in marketing research are not ideal. Even when researchers seek to draw random samples, they may face challenges in recruiting the sample that result in the sample being biased in subtle ways. Researchers must always seek to think about how the sampling method might have affected their results.

Claiming Causal Relationships between Variables That Aren't Really There

Some facts may be correlated in your data, but the relationship may be merely a statistical coincidence or the correlation may be caused by a third variable. To claim causation, researchers must be sure the appropriate research design was used.

Wrong Construct

In evaluating survey results, you may find that a construct is mislabeled because the items don't actually measure what they claim to measure. Evaluating the reliability and validity of constructs is essential to accurate reporting of scientific research.

Methodological Biases

Methodological choices can bring biases with them. For example, respondents are less forthcoming about some issues on the telephone as compared to an online survey. Long surveys may result in respondent fatigue and inaccurate answers. Word choice, graphics usage, and order of questions can affect responses. Researchers must actively think about how methodological issues may have affected their results.

In reporting results and making presentations, researchers must apply critical thinking skills to ensure their findings are presented objectively and accurately. Being sensitive to the above barriers so they can be overcome, or at least minimized, will help researchers to prepare better presentations.

For example, they are used to compare promotional changes, image building tactics, or even strengths and weaknesses of the firm.

■ Format of the Marketing Research Report

Every marketing research report is unique in that it is based on the needs of the client, the research purpose, and the study objectives. Yet all reports contain some common elements. Although the terminology may differ among industries, the basic format discussed in this section will help researchers plan and prepare reports for various clients. The parts common to all marketing research reports are the following:

1. Title page
2. Table of contents
3. Executive summary
   a. Research objectives
   b. Concise statement of method
   c. Summary of key findings
   d. Conclusion and recommendations

4. Introduction
5. Research method and procedures
6. Data analysis and findings
7. Conclusions and recommendations
8. Limitations
9. Appendixes

Title Page

The title page indicates the subject of the report and the name of the recipient, along with his or her position and organization. Any numbers or phrases to designate a particular department or division also should be included. Most important, the title page must contain the name, position, employing organization, address, telephone number of the person or persons submitting the report, and the date the report is submitted.

Table of Contents

The table of contents lists the topics of the report in sequential order. Usually, the contents page will highlight each topical area, the subdivisions within each area, and corresponding page numbers. It is also common to include tables and figures and the pages where they can be found.

Executive Summary

Executive summary The part of a marketing research report that presents the major points; it must be complete enough to provide a true representation of the document but in summary form.

The **executive summary** is the most important part of the report. Many consider it the soul of the report, insofar as many executives read only the report summary. The executive summary presents the major points of the report. It must be complete enough to provide a true representation of the entire document but in summary form. Make sure your executive summary can stand alone. The rest of your report supports the key findings included in the summary, but the overview provided by the executive summary must nevertheless seem complete. While the executive summary comes near the front of the report, it should actually be written last. Until all the analyses are done, researchers cannot determine which findings are most important.

The executive summary has several purposes: (1) to convey how and why the research was undertaken; (2) to summarize the key findings; and (3) to suggest future actions. In other words, the executive summary must contain the research objectives, a concise statement of method, a summary of the findings, and specific conclusions and recommendations.

Research objectives should be as precise as possible, but not longer than approximately one page. The research purpose along with the questions or hypotheses that guided the project should also be stated in this section. Exhibit 13.2 shows a PowerPoint slide from a presentation that summarizes research objectives for a project in which employees' reactions to their company's consumer ads were measured. After explaining the research purpose and objectives, a brief description of the sampling method, the research design, and any procedural aspects are addressed in one or two paragraphs. Following this is a statement of key findings.

Exhibit 13.3 shows a slide that summarizes a few of the key findings from a research project. The findings presented in the summary must agree with those found in the findings section of the full report. Only key findings that relate to the research objectives should be included.

Finally, the summary contains a brief statement of conclusions and recommendations. The conclusion section of the report summarizes your findings. Conclusions concisely

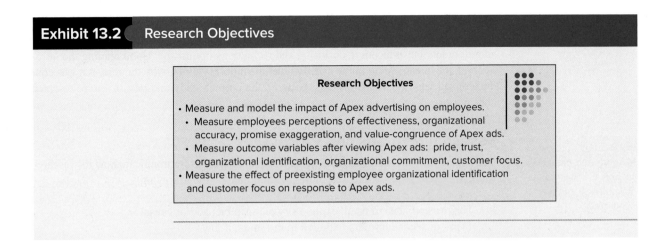

Exhibit 13.2   Research Objectives

Research Objectives

- Measure and model the impact of Apex advertising on employees.
  - Measure employees perceptions of effectiveness, organizational accuracy, promise exaggeration, and value-congruence of Apex ads.
  - Measure outcome variables after viewing Apex ads: pride, trust, organizational identification, organizational commitment, customer focus.
- Measure the effect of preexisting employee organizational identification and customer focus on response to Apex ads.

Exhibit 13.3   Selected Key Findings from a Research Project

Key Findings

- Apex employees identify strongly with Apex, averaging 6.3 on a 7-point scale across all Organizational Identity items.
- Perceived advertising effectiveness with consumers has strong effects on all outcome variables. Employees thus <u>care</u> about the effectiveness of advertising. In particular, effectiveness is very strongly associated with employee pride.
- The perception that ads portray the organization accurately has moderate to strong effects on all outcome variables. Employees thus desire for Apex to be portrayed in ads consistent with how they see their company.

explain research findings and the meaning that can be attached to the findings. Recommendations, in contrast, are for appropriate future actions. Recommendations focus on specific marketing tactics or strategies the client can use to gain a competitive advantage. Conclusions and recommendations typically are stated in one to two paragraphs.

Introduction

Introduction Contains background information necessary for a complete understanding of the report.

The **introduction** contains background information necessary for a complete understanding of the report. Definition of terms, relevant background information, and the study's scope and emphasis are communicated in the introduction. The introduction also lists specific research objectives and questions the study was designed to answer, as well as hypotheses, length of the study, and any research-related problems. Usually hypotheses are not stated formally. They are stated in everyday language. For example, a research team can summarize their hypotheses about the variables they believe will affect senior Internet adoption as follows: "We expected the following factors to be positively related to senior adoption: income, education, curiosity, and technology optimism." Upon reading the introduction, the client should know exactly what the report is about, why the research was conducted, and what relationships exist between the current study and past or future research endeavors.

Research Methods and Procedures

Methods-and-procedures section Communicates how the research was conducted.

The objective of the **methods-and-procedures section** is to communicate how the research was conducted. Issues addressed in this section include the following:

1. The research design used: exploratory, descriptive, and/or causal.
2. Types of secondary data included in the study, if any.
3. If primary data were collected, what procedure was used (observation, questionnaire) and what administration procedures were employed (personal, mail, telephone, Internet)?
4. Sample and sampling processes used. The following issues are usually addressed:
   a. How the sample population was defined and profiled.
   b. Sampling units used (for example, businesses, households, individuals).
   c. The sampling list (if any) used in the study.
   d. How the sample size was determined.
   e. Was a probability or nonprobability sampling plan employed?

Many times when writing the methods-and-procedures section, the writer gets bogged down in presenting too much detail. If on completion of this section, the reader can say what was done, how it was done, and why it was done, the objective of the writer has been fulfilled. A presentation slide summarizing the methodology used in the senior adoption of the Internet study appears in Exhibit 13.4.

Exhibit 13.4	Slide Summarizing Research Methodology

CRITO *Consortium*
University of California, Irvine

Research Methodology

- National telephone survey of seniors 65+
- Questions appended to IDC's technology panel
- 200 Internet users and 245 nonusers (random sample)
- Questions measured:
  — Values
    • Curiosity and self-efficacy (proactive coping)
  — Technology attitudes/behavior
    • Technology optimism, technology discomfort, technology innovativeness
  — Internet use
    • Amount and variety of use; attitudes towards use
  — Demographics
    • Age, education, income, sex

CENTER FOR RESEARCH ON INFORMATION TECHNOLOGY AND ORGANIZATIONS

Data Analysis and Findings

The body of the marketing research report consists of the study's findings. Data analysis requirements differ for each project, so the presentation of findings will be somewhat different for each project. No matter how complicated the statistical analysis, the challenge for researchers is to summarize and present the analysis in a way that makes them easy to understand for nonspecialists. Findings should always include a detailed presentation with supporting tables, figures, and graphs. All results must be logically arranged to correspond with each research objective or research question listed in the report. This portion of the report is not simply an undifferentiated dump of the findings. When reporting results, no writer should claim the results are "obvious," or "self-evident." Rather, report writers both present and interpret their results. Their knowledge of the industry—gleaned through literature review and experience, helps analysts interpret results. The researcher must decide how to group the findings into sections that facilitate understanding. Best practices suggest that tables, figures, and graphs be used when results are presented. Graphs and tables should provide a simple summation of the data in a clear, concise, and nontechnical manner. Text is used to explain the findings in graphs and tables.

When writing the report, the information must be explained in the body of the report in a straightforward fashion without technical output and language. Technical information most readers will have trouble understanding is best suited for the appendix section of the report. Below are several strategies for presenting analyses using graphs and tables. There is probably no one best way to present a particular analysis. Instead there often are several effective ways to portray a particular finding or set of findings. We discuss some specific methods to illustrate frequencies, crosstabs, *t*-tests, ANOVAs, correlations, and regressions. With some patience, you can master the simpler presentation techniques in this chapter. If you become comfortable working with the chart editor in SPSS, you will find there are many more options we have not covered. Once you have mastered the basic techniques, you can teach yourself more by experimenting with the chart editor in SPSS. In addition, you can convert your SPSS data into an Excel spreadsheet and use the graphing functions from Excel to present your findings.

Reporting Frequencies   Frequencies can be reported in tables, bar charts, or pie charts. For example, Exhibit 13.5 contains a table illustrating the results for the research question "How

---

Exhibit 13.5   Findings Illustrating Simple Readable Results of Frequencies

Frequency of Eating at Santa Fe Grill

	Frequency	Percent	Valid Percent	Cumulative Percent
Very infrequently	49	19	19	19
Somewhat infrequently	62	25	25	44
Occasionally	43	17	17	61
Somewhat frequently	59	23	23	84
Very frequently	40	16	16	100.0
Total	253	100.0	100.0	

frequently do you eat at the Santa Fe Grill?" This table illustrates the data output in a simple and concise manner, enabling the reader to easily view how often respondents eat at the Santa Fe Grill. Notice that all digits past the decimal point have been removed. This is common practice in reporting percentages in marketing research. The extra digits create clutter without providing very much information. Moreover, because most research involves sampling error, carrying percentages out past the decimal point is misleading. Researchers usually cannot estimate the results with the degree of precision the extra decimal points imply.

Using Bar Charts to Display Frequencies Exhibit 13.6 shows the simplest type of bar chart that can be made in SPSS. If you are using SPSS version 20 or higher, you will have to choose "LEGACY DIALOGUES" from the "GRAPH" menu before executing each command in this chapter.

To make a bar chart, the SPSS click-through sequence is GRAPH → Legacy Dialogues → BAR. Leave the default on "Simple" and under "Data in chart are," you also use the default of "Summaries for groups of cases." Next click the Define tab to get the screen shown in Exhibit 13.7. On this screen you will usually want to change the default choice from "N of cases" to "% of cases." On the left side of your screen, highlight the name of the variable you want in your bar graph (in this case, the variable is "Major") and move it across to the window that says "Category Axis," and click OK. SPSS will then generate your bar graph.

To make changes to the graph, you double-click the chart in the output, which will take you to a chart editor. There you will find several options for the chart. Double-clicking

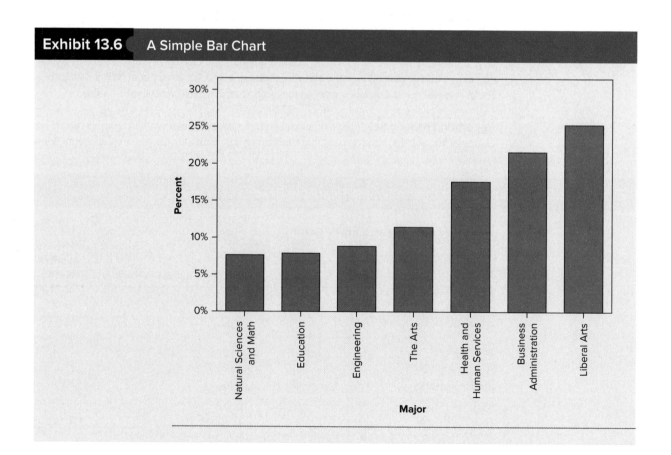

Exhibit 13.6   A Simple Bar Chart

Exhibit 13.7 Making a Simple Bar Graph in SPSS

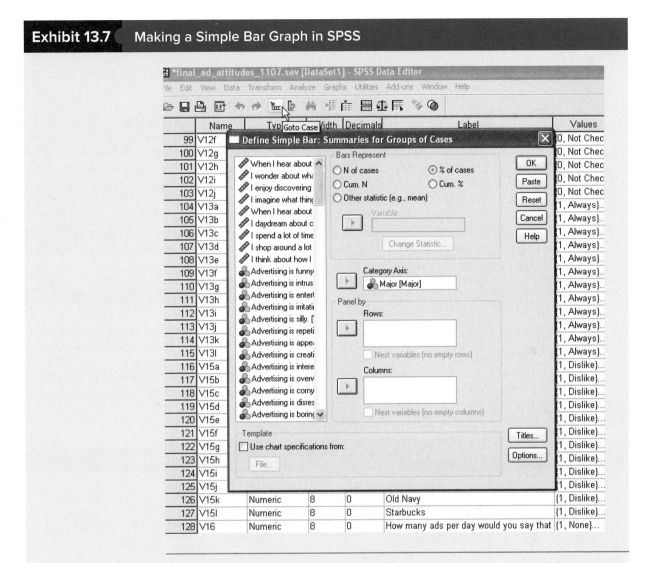

on any of the elements in your chart brings up the relevant menu for customizing that particular element. For example, double-clicking on the bars in the chart will bring up a Properties menu with several tabs. To produce the graph shown in Exhibit 13.6, we chose the Categories tab on the Properties menu. On the Categories menu, we selected the "sort by" option and then "statistic/ascending." This option arranges the graph by lowest percent to highest percent, which makes the graph easier for readers to understand.

By experimenting with various tabs on the Properties menu, students will find they can change the color, font, and font size on the graph. It is often desirable to enlarge the font if the graph will be exported to either Word or PowerPoint. The orientation of the bar labels can be changed as well. If you click on the bar labels while in the chart editor, the Properties menu will appear, and one of the tabs will be "Labels and Ticks." Using this menu, the orientation of labels can be chosen: vertical, horizontal, or staggered. You should experiment with options until everything on your graph is clear and readable. Then, you can right-click on your finished chart, choose the "copy chart" option, and cut and paste the result to a Word or PowerPoint document. The finished result is shown in Exhibit 13.6.

Portraying Frequencies Using Pie Charts Pie charts are particularly good at portraying the relative proportion of response to a question. The process for creating a pie chart is similar to that used for creating the bar chart. From the SPSS menu, choose GRAPH → Legacy Dialogues → PIE. A menu will appear with three radio buttons. The default choice "Summaries for groups of cases" is the correct option for a simple pie chart. Click "Define" and a new menu will appear. On this menu, although "N of cases" is the default option, in most cases you, will be more interested in reporting percentages, so click the button next to "% of cases." Move the variable name from the variable list (in this case V16, which is labeled "How many ads per day do you pay attention to?") into the blank next to "Define Slices by." Then click OK. SPSS will now create your chart in an output file.

As with the bar chart, when you double-click on the pie chart in the output file, you will open the chart editor in SPSS. From the toolbar in the editor, you can choose "Elements → Show Data Labels" and the percentages will be displayed on the pie chart for each slice. However, remove any extra digits after the decimal place from the percentages displayed in your chart. You can double-click on the percentages box, which will give you a Properties menu. Choose the Number Format tab and next to decimal places, enter 0 (see Exhibit 13.8). Note that if you don't click in the right place, the Properties menu may not show the appropriate tab. If you don't see the tab you want on the Properties menu, try double-clicking the relevant part of the chart that you want to change again.

If you spend some time investigating the Options and Properties menus, you will see that you can make fonts bigger, change the font style, and alter the color and appearance

---

Exhibit 13.8 Changing the Properties of a Pie Chart in the SPSS Chart Editor

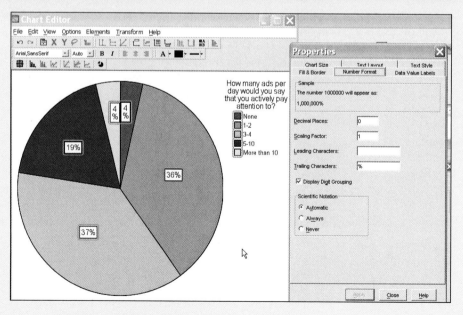

of the slices in the pie. When you are done, you can right-click on the chart and copy and paste it into Word or PowerPoint.

Reporting Means of Thematically Related Variables Researchers may want to report the means of several thematically related variables in the same chart or table. This can be accomplished with either a bar chart or a table. A table may be preferred when a researcher feels that the entire question needs to be portrayed in order to fully understand the findings. Exhibit 13.9 shows a table that was constructed in PowerPoint using the table function. The results of the table are based on SPSS output, using the command sequence Analyze → Descriptive Statistics → Frequencies. A menu will appear, and then you click the Statistics button near the bottom of that menu. Then choose "Mean" and "Standard Deviation." Click OK, and the results will be generated by SPSS.

Note that the items in the table have been ordered from the highest to the lowest average. Sorting responses in this manner often facilitates reader understanding. There are two other important elements of the table to note: (1) the maximum value of 7 is clearly indicated so that readers can easily compare the mean to the maximum possible score and (2) the mean and standard deviations are shown with only one digit past the decimal. While percentages should have no decimals past the decimal point, means should generally display one digit past the decimal point.

It is also possible to portray thematically related means on a bar chart in SPSS. In order to do so, you begin as you did when portraying one variable by choosing Graphs → Bar from the toolbar and leaving the default bar chart type "Simple" selected. However,

---

Exhibit 13.9   **A Table Summarizing Means of Thematically Related Items**

College Students' Attitudes towards Advertising

Item	Number of Responses	Average 7 = Strongly Agree	Standard Deviation
Ads can be a good way to learn about products.	312	5.2	1.5
The purpose of marketing is to attract customers by learning what they want.	308	5.2	1.5
Advertising is an interesting business.	308	5.2	1.5
Advertising sometimes encourages me to seek out more information about products I am interested in.	312	5.0	1.5
I think it would be fun to work for an advertising agency.	306	4.5	1.9
Overall, I am satisfied with advertising.	308	4.3	1.3
Advertising is usually designed to sell things that people don't really need.	310	4.3	1.8
Advertising appeals to the selfishness in human beings.	303	3.6	1.8
If there was less advertising, the world would be a better place.	304	3.4	1.7
I try to avoid advertising whenever possible.	304	3.3	1.7
Advertising is bad for society.	310	2.6	1.5

Exhibit 13.10 Using the Bar Chart Function in SPSS to Summarize Thematically Related Means

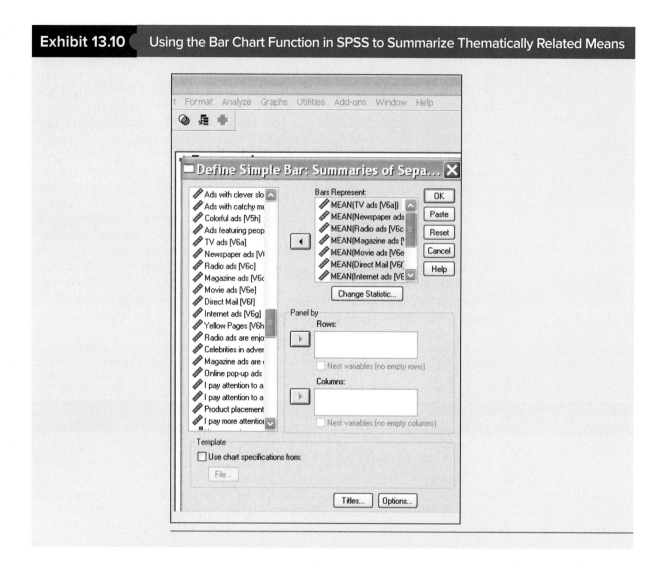

you will change the default at the bottom of the menu from "Summaries of groups of cases" to "Summaries of separate variables." Then click "Define." From there, move the variables you want in the graph from the variable list on the left into the window labeled "Bars Represent" (see Exhibit 13.10). The default is "Mean" so you will not have to change any options. Once you click OK, the bar graph will be created. When you double-click on the bar chart in the output, this will take you to the chart editor. As we explained previously in the chapter, you can double-click elements within the chart and change the properties and the appearance of the bar chart. Exhibit 13.11 shows a finished image that has been cut and pasted to a PowerPoint slide. An interpretation has been added to the slide to facilitate reader comprehension.

Reporting Crosstabs (Bar Charts) The bar chart function in SPSS can be used to display Crosstabs. Once again, you can start with Graphs → Bar → Summaries for groups of cases. From there, choose "Cluster" rather than the default option "Simple" and click "Define." Under "Bars Represent," choose "% of cases." Your independent or predictor

Exhibit 13.11   A Bar Chart Displaying Multiple Thematically Related Means

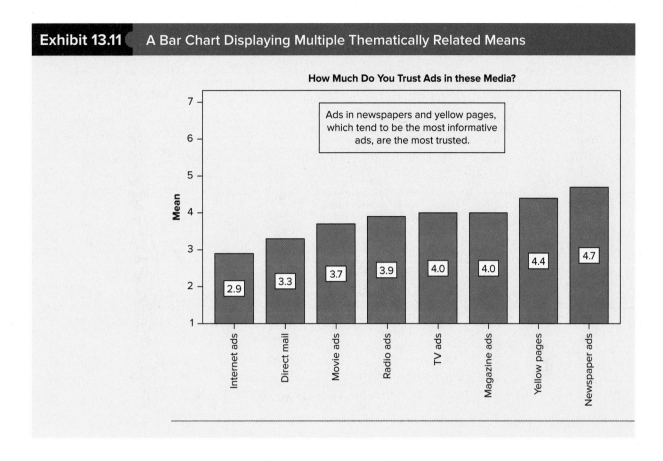

How Much Do You Trust Ads in these Media?

Ads in newspapers and yellow pages, which tend to be the most informative ads, are the most trusted.

variable should be entered in the "Category Axis" blank. In this case, gender is the independent variable. The variable you are explaining, in this case, liking of the Carl's Jr. Paris Hilton ad, is entered into the "Define Clusters" blank (see Exhibit 13.12). Then click OK, and the Crosstab bar chart will be created. As with the other charts, you can double-click on the graph to bring up the chart editor.

Because this particular Crosstab crosses only two categories by two categories, we excluded the bars representing "don't like" from the graph. This is because in a 2 × 2, once you know the values for one category, the other category is completely defined (the two categories must add to 100 percent). Removing a category is straightforward. You can double-click on any of the bars in the graph. This will bring up the Properties menu. One of the tabs will be "Categories." You will see the categories displayed on the menu. If you click on the category you want to exclude (in this case, "Don't Like"), and then click the red **X** button next to the box labeled "Order," the label will be moved to the box below under "Excluded." Click "Apply" and your Crosstab will now display only one category of the outcome variable, in this case the percentage of respondents within each sex who liked the Carl's Jr. Paris Hilton ad. The resulting graph is displayed in Exhibit 13.13.

Reporting *t*-Tests and ANOVAs (Bar Charts) Exhibit 13.14 shows a table created in PowerPoint with information from SPSS output that pictures the results of five different *t*-tests that are thematically related. Each *t*-test compares outcome measures for two groups: men and women. The average for each gender for each variable appears in the cells. Again, significant p-values are indicated.

Exhibit 13.12 Using the SPSS Bar Chart Function to Portray Crosstabs

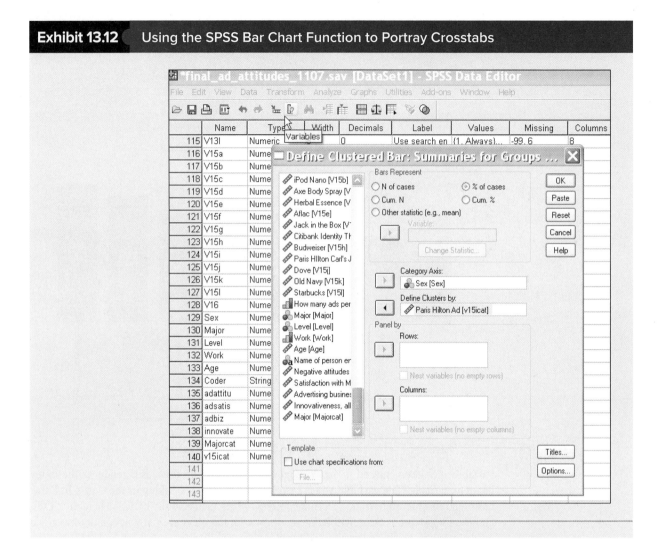

Both *t*-tests and ANOVAs can be displayed on bar charts created in SPSS. Our example will focus on using the bar charts for an ANOVA, but the command sequence within SPSS is the same. Start with Graphs → Bar → Simple. Leave the box chosen next to "Summaries are groups of cases," and click "Define." On the next screen (pictured in Exhibit 13.15), under "Bars Represent," choose "other" and enter the outcome variable (in this case, "Liking for Touching/Emotional" ads) into the blank under "Variable." For "Category Axis," enter the independent variable (in this case "Major"). Then click OK and the graph will be produced. Using "Options" we added a title and a footnote to the graph. Click on the *y*-axis, which shows the scale that we used in the survey, and you get the Properties menu along with a tab labeled "Scale." In that menu, we changed the minimum to 1 and the maximum to 7 (the endpoints in the actual scale). SPSS will often change the scale points represented to maximize the space in the chart, but the resulting default chart may distort your findings. In many cases, you will want to change the axis to show the actual endpoints of your scale. A footnote shows an ANOVA analysis performed to examine the significance of categorical differences. The final graph is displayed in Exhibit 13.16.

Exhibit 13.13	Bar Chart Portraying a Crosstab

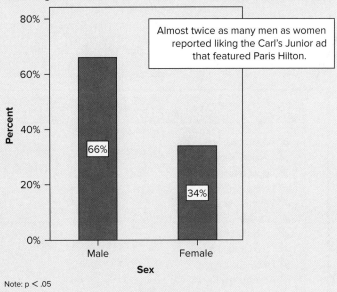

Percentage of Men and Women Who Like Paris Hilton's Carl's Junior Ad

> Almost twice as many men as women reported liking the Carl's Junior ad that featured Paris Hilton.

66%

34%

Percent

Male   Female

Sex

Note: $p < .05$

Exhibit 13.14	A Table Showing *t*-Tests

What Kind of Ads are Effective?

Ad Element	Mean (max=7)	
Informational	Male	4.3*
	Female	4.8
Humorous	Male	5.8
	Female	6.0
Touching/	Male	4.0*
Emotional	Female	4.8
Sex appeal	Male	5.5*
	Female	4.7
Ads with attractive models	Male	5.4*
	Female	4.5
Colorful ads	Male	4.3*
	Female	5.0

Women are more likely than men to say that informational, emotional, and colorful ads are effective. Men are more likely to say that sex appeals and attractive models are effective in advertising. Men and women rate the effectiveness of humor similarly.

*$p<.05$

Exhibit 13.15 Using SPSS to Create Bar Charts to Display ANOVA Results

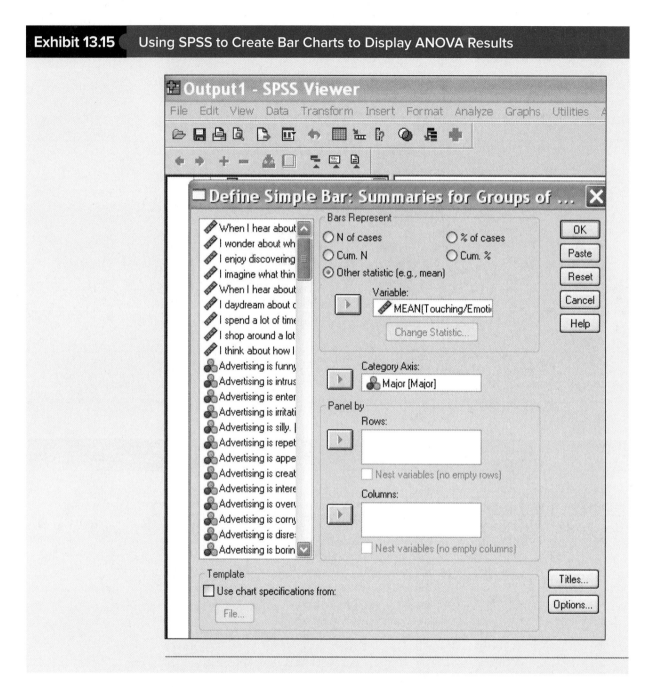

Reporting Correlation and Regression Correlations may be included in a report to illustrate relationships between several variables that are later used in a regression or to show the relationship of several variables to an outcome variable of interest. Exhibit 13.17 is a table showing the correlation of several variables with overall satisfaction for a retailer named Primal Elements. To facilitate comparison of the sizes of the correlations, they are arranged from strongest to mildest. Note that the negative correlation is sorted by its strength because the negative value indicates the direction of the relationship only. The

Exhibit 13.16	Bar Chart Portraying ANOVA Results

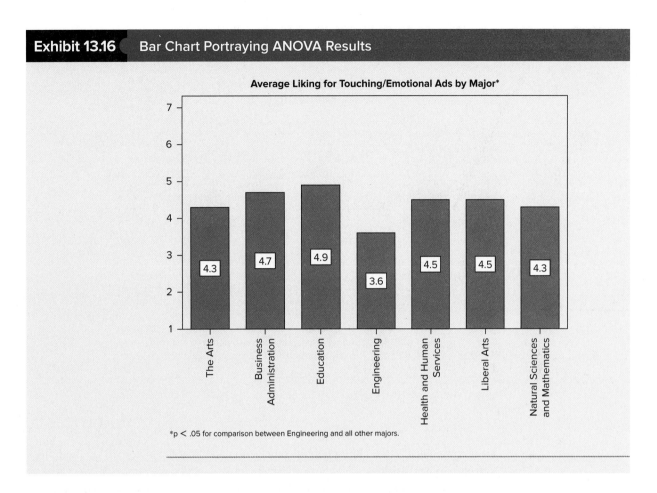

Average Liking for Touching/Emotional Ads by Major*

The Arts: 4.3
Business Administration: 4.7
Education: 4.9
Engineering: 3.6
Health and Human Services: 4.5
Liberal Arts: 4.5
Natural Sciences and Mathematics: 4.3

*$p < .05$ for comparison between Engineering and all other majors.

Exhibit 13.17	Correlations of Item Ratings with Overall Satisfaction with Primal Elements

Item	Correlation
Store atmosphere	.59*
How intimidating the store is	−.30*
Expense of products	−.25*
Interior appearance of store	25*
Quantity of information workers provide about products	.21*
Exterior appearance of store	.16

*$p<.05$, N = 94. Correlations vary in strength from −1 to +1 with 0 meaning "no relationship."

significance levels are once again indicated with a star. The sample size is included on the graph in the footnote if the sample size used in the correlation analysis is different from the overall sample size reported in the methodology section of the report. The interpretation of the table is not included in the exhibit, but accompanying text would explain the strong role

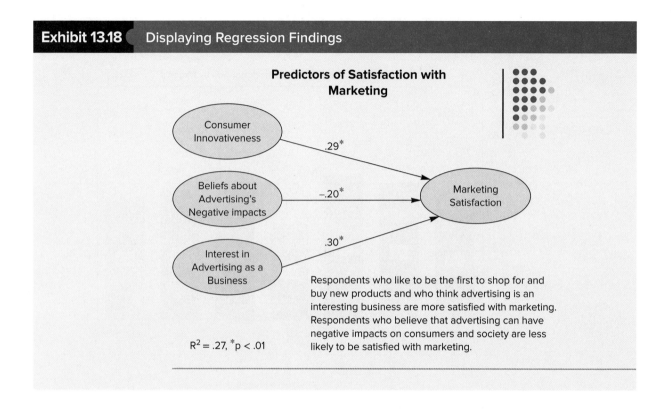

Exhibit 13.18 Displaying Regression Findings

Predictors of Satisfaction with Marketing

Consumer Innovativeness → .29* → Marketing Satisfaction

Beliefs about Advertising's Negative impacts → −.20* → Marketing Satisfaction

Interest in Advertising as a Business → .30* → Marketing Satisfaction

Respondents who like to be the first to shop for and buy new products and who think advertising is an interesting business are more satisfied with marketing. Respondents who believe that advertising can have negative impacts on consumers and society are less likely to be satisfied with marketing.

$R^2 = .27,$ *$p < .01$

of perceptions of store atmosphere in satisfaction and may focus as well on the milder effects of other variables.

Recall that regression is a multivariate technique that estimates the impact of multiple explanatory or independent variables on one dependent variable. One of the simplest ways to present regression findings is to create a diagram in Word or in PowerPoint that pictures the predictor and the outcome variables with arrows showing the relationships between the variables (see Exhibit 13.18). These diagrams were referred to as conceptual models in Chapter 3. The title of the analysis clearly describes the picture ("Predictors of Satisfaction with Marketing"). The standardized betas are portrayed above the appropriate arrow because the beta shows the strength of the relationship between the independent and dependent variables. As in the other pictured analyses, a star may be used to indicate statistical significance. The R^2 (.27) appears in the diagram; the three variables together explain 27 percent of the variance in attitudes toward marketing. The text summarizes the information provided by the regression analysis in the picture.

Conclusions and Recommendations

Conclusions and recommendations are derived specifically from the findings. As illustrated in Exhibit 13.19, conclusions are descriptive statements generalizing the results, not necessarily the numbers generated by statistical analysis. Each conclusion directly references research objectives.

Recommendations are generated by critical thinking. The task is one where the researcher must critically evaluate each conclusion and develop specific areas of applications

Exhibit 13.19   Illustration of Conclusions in a Marketing Research Presentation

Conclusions

- Four primary factors are related to satisfaction with and eating at the Santa Fe Grill—food quality, service, value, and atmosphere.
- Food quality is the most important factor influencing satisfaction with and eating at the Santa Fe Grill.
- Service at the Santa Fe Grill is the second-most important factor influencing satisfaction with and eating at the restaurant.
- Perceptions of the Santa Fe Grill food quality and service are favorable.
- Perceptions of value and atmosphere are relatively less favorable.
- Perceptions of the Santa Fe Grill on all four factors—food, service, value, and atmosphere—are significantly less favorable for the less frequent patrons.
- Perceptions of the Santa Fe Grill on two factors—food and service—are significantly less favorable than they are for Jose's Southwestern Café.
- More frequent patrons of the Santa Fe Grill have lifestyles that characterize them as Innovators and Influencers.
- Employees of Santa Fe Grill do not evaluate their team coworkers very favorably.

for strategic or tactical actions. Recommendations must address how the client can solve the problem at hand through the creation of a competitive advantage.

Exhibit 13.20 outlines the recommendations that correspond to the conclusions displayed in Exhibit 13.19. You will notice each recommendation, unlike the conclusion, is in the form of a clear action statement.

Exhibit 13.20   Illustration of Recommendations in a Marketing Research Presentation

Recommendations

- Advertising messages should emphasize food quality and service since these are the most important factors influencing satisfaction.
- If advertisements include people, they should be characterized as innovative in their lifestyles.
- Focus group research needs to be conducted to learn why perceptions of value and atmosphere are less favorable than perceptions of food quality and service.
- The focus group research also needs to examine why perceptions of less frequent patrons of the Santa Fe Grill are significantly less favorable than those of more frequent patrons.
- The current study collected data from customers of the Santa Fe Grill and Jose's Southwestern Café. In the future, data should be collected from noncustomers.
- Focus group research needs to be conducted to learn why employees are not very favorable about their coworkers.

Limitations

Limitations Weaknesses in research methodology that might affect confidence in research conclusions.

Researchers always strive to develop and implement a flawless study for the client. But all research has limitations. Researchers must note the **limitations** of a project, and speculate intelligently about if and how the limitations may have affected their conclusions. Common limitations associated with marketing research include sampling bias, financial constraints, time pressures, and measurement error.

Every study has limitations, and the researcher has to make the client aware of them. Researchers should not be embarrassed by limitations but rather admit openly that they exist. However, limitations should not be stated in a way that undermines the credibility of the entire project. Researcher reports address limitations, but do so in a way that develops reasonable confidence in the conclusions made in the report. Treatment of limitations in the research report usually involves a discussion of results and accuracy. For example, researchers should tell clients about the generalizability of the results beyond the sample used in the study. Any weaknesses in specific scales should be addressed, along with other potential sources of nonsampling error. If limitations are not stated and are later discovered by the client, mistrust and skepticism toward the entire report may result. When properly reported, limitations rarely diminish the credibility of the report but instead improve client perceptions of the quality of the project.

Appendixes

Appendix A section following the main body of the report; used to house complex, detailed, or technical information.

An **appendix,** many times referred to as a "technical appendix," contains complex, detailed, or technical information not necessary for the formal report. Common items contained in appendixes include the questionnaire or data collection instrument used for the research project, interviewer forms, statistical calculations, and detailed sampling maps. Researchers know the appendix is rarely read in the same context as the report itself. In fact, most appendixes are treated as points of reference in the report. That is, information in the appendix is cited in the report to guide the reader to further technical or statistical detail.

◼ Common Problems in Preparing the Marketing Research Report

Industry's best practices suggest five problem areas that may arise in writing a marketing research report:

1. *Lack of data interpretation.* In some instances, researchers get so involved in constructing results tables that they fail to provide proper interpretation of the data in the tables. The researcher always provides unbiased interpretation of any findings.
2. *Unnecessary use of complex statistics.* To impress clients, many researchers unnecessarily use sophisticated multivariate statistical techniques. In many research reports, the most sophisticated statistical technique required will be a Chi-square test. Avoid using statistical methods unless they are essential to derive meaning from the data.
3. *Emphasis on packaging instead of quality.* Many researchers go out of their way to make reports look classy or flamboyant using sophisticated computer-generated graphics. While professional graphic representation of the results is essential in the report, never lose sight of the primary purpose—to provide valid and credible information to the client.

4. *Lack of relevance.* Reporting data, statistics, and information that are not consistent with the study's objectives can be a major problem when writing the report. Always develop the report with the research objectives clearly in focus. Avoid adding unnecessary information just to make the report longer. Always remain in the realm of practicality. Suggest ideas that are relevant, doable, and consistent with the results of the study.

5. *Placing too much emphasis on a few statistics.* Never base all conclusions or recommendations on one or a few statistically significant questions or results, but on the weight of evidence from your literature review, secondary data, and the pattern of results in your entire report. Always attempt to find substantial supporting evidence for any recommendation or conclusion.

The final research document is the end product of the researcher. Individual credibility can be enhanced or damaged by the report, and credibility is what helps a researcher gain repeat business and referrals from clients. The quality, dedication, and honesty one places into the report have the potential to generate future business, career promotions, and salary raises.

The Critical Nature of Presentations

Presentation of marketing research results can be as important as, if not more important than, the results of the research itself. This is true for several reasons. First, any research, no matter how well done or how important, cannot be properly acted upon if the results are not effectively communicated to those who will use the information in making decisions. Managers need accurate information if they are going to make good decisions, and if they do not understand the marketing research findings, they may well make poor decisions that lead to difficulty not only for the organization but also for individuals in the organization affected by those decisions. Second, the report or presentation is often the only part of the marketing research project that will be seen by those commissioning the report. Senior managers often do not have the time to review all aspects of a research project, so they rely on the researcher to carry out the research properly and then present the findings clearly and concisely. Third, the content and presentation form of the research are closely intertwined. Poorly organized presentations presented in an unclear, lengthy, difficult-to-access format often lead audiences to discount the content.

Guidelines for Preparing Oral Presentations

In almost all situations, the results of marketing research must be presented in a well-documented written report, and summarized in an effective oral presentation to the client. The primary goal of the oral presentation is to condense complex research-oriented information (sampling concepts, statistics, graphs, figures, etc.) into an interesting, informative, and conclusive discussion. Effectively communicating marketing research information is more of an art than a science—an art associated with being a dynamic and credible communicator. A few simple best practices can be very helpful in providing a professional presentation:

1. Don't let the visual component of the presentation detract from the information being communicated. Keep the visual presentation simple and avoid flamboyant graphics and unnecessary audio.

2. Always be friendly, honest, warm, and open in your oral communication. Being too formal, stuffy, or overbearing can lead to a lack of interest in your discussion.

3. Be knowledgeable and confident in your delivery. If necessary, have experts available (research analysts, statisticians, technicians) to complement or facilitate your presentation.
4. Have a well-organized and inspiring dialogue prepared. Practice your presentation with others in your research team, as well as mentally in front of a mirror (or recording device) before you make the presentation to the client.
5. Be an effective active listener. Understand questions and comments arising from the audience. If no questions or comments are being posed within the first five minutes of the presentation, open up the discussion for questions.

Guidelines for Preparing the Visual Presentation

The visual presentation is a separate but equally important component of the marketing research report. The visual presentation has one primary goal: to provide a visual summary of the marketing research report, designed in a manner that will complement and enhance oral communication of the written marketing research report.

In many cases, Microsoft PowerPoint is the preferred method of preparing the visual marketing research presentation. Given the versatility of PowerPoint, the visual presentation may employ graphics as simple as those in this chapter. But these presentations may also employ a full multimedia array of techniques, including sound, animation, color graphics, and video. Regardless of the complexity of the presentation, industry practices suggest the following guidelines:

1. Begin with a slide showing the title of the presentation and the individual(s) doing the presentation. In addition, the client and the marketing research firm should also be identified.
2. A sequence of slides should be developed indicating the objectives of the research and the specific research questions to be addressed, followed by the research methodology employed and a description of the sample surveyed.
3. Additional slides should be developed that highlight the research findings or particular results of the study which the researcher deems important for communication purposes.
4. Finally, the presentation should conclude with recommendations, conclusions, and research implications as they pertain to the study at hand.

MARKETING RESEARCH IN ACTION
Who Are the Early Adopters of Technology?

The latest digital recorder/players do a lot more than just record material. The latest devices include hard drives and programming guides with lots of functionality. Stand-alone digital devices use the same access and storage technology as PCs, but in addition they provide a home theater platform. The devices have menus that let you easily jump to a specific point within a recording and multiple shows over an extended period of time can be recorded.

The recording and storage market is large and rapidly getting much larger. No longer limited to home entertainment playback boxes, it is being combined with increasing numbers of consumer electronics products: computers, wireless phones and other portable devices, appliances, and industrial systems.

DVDs hit the market in the late 1990s and enjoyed very fast growth. Indeed, the DVD market experienced the most rapid rise of any consumer electronics technology ever introduced. The total annual market for all types of digital recorder/player systems (players, recorders, set-tops, PCs) is expected to exceed 700 million units in 2012. But shipments of Blu-ray devices are starting to account for a significant portion of the disc player and recorder market and are expected to outsell DVD players by 2015, when sales of Blu-ray player unit shipments are expected to reach 105 million.

Digital player/recorders have caught the imagination and interest of consumers. Set-top boxes boomed in sales due not only to their functionality, but also to their rapidly falling prices. The average selling price fell from about $500 in 1998 to less than $100 in major retail outlets in 2012, with some units selling for as low as $35.

Two of the biggest challenges of electronics marketers are (1) the successful introduction of new technology-based product innovations into consumer markets and (2) stimulating the diffusion of those innovations to profitable penetration levels. To meet these challenges, researchers must gain clearer insights into the key factors consumers use in deciding whether to adopt technology innovations in consumer electronics.

Researchers recently completed a study to investigate opinions of potential purchasers of digital recorder/player devices. The study compares the innovator and early adopter segments with regard to product usage, digital device purchase likelihood, demographics, and related issues. The primary questions addressed were: "Are there attitudinal and behavioral differences between consumers who are innovators versus those who are early adopters?" and "Can these differences be systematically associated with purchase likelihood of digital recorder/players?"

Using an Internet panel, data were collected from a sample of 200 individuals. The sample frame was consumers with annual household incomes $20,000 or more and ages 18 to 35 years. Data were collected over a two-week period. Participants had to be living in North America because the market study was limited to this geographic area. The questionnaire included questions about innovativeness, lifestyle, product, and brand image. Some of the questions employed interval level measures while others were nominal and ordinal. There is a database for the questions which is available in SPSS format at **www.mhhe.com/hairessentials3e**. The database is labeled Digital Recorder Survey MRIA 3e.sav. A copy of the questionnaire is provided in Exhibit 13.21.

Exhibit 13.21	Questionnaire for Electronics Products Opinion Survey

This is a project being conducted by a marketing research class at the University of Oklahoma. The purpose of this project is to better understand the attitudes and opinions of consumers toward electronics products. The questionnaire will take only a few minutes to complete, and all responses will remain strictly confidential. Thank you for your help on this project.

I. Attitudes

The following questions relate to your attitudes about shopping for electronics products. On a scale of 1 to 7, with 7 being Strongly Agree and 1 being Strongly Disagree, please circle the number that best expresses your degree of agreement with each of the following statements.

	Strongly Disagree						Strongly Agree
1. The Internet is a good place to get lower prices.	1	2	3	4	5	6	7
2. I don't shop for specials.	1	2	3	4	5	6	7
3. People come to me for advice.	1	2	3	4	5	6	7
4. I often try new brands before my friends and neighbors.	1	2	3	4	5	6	7
5. I would like to take a trip around the world.	1	2	3	4	5	6	7
6. My friends and neighbors come to me for advice and consultation.	1	2	3	4	5	6	7
7. Coupons are a good way to save money.	1	2	3	4	5	6	7
8. I seldom look for the lowest price when I shop.	1	2	3	4	5	6	7
9. I like to try new and different things.	1	2	3	4	5	6	7

10. To what extent do you believe you need a DVD player? Please indicate on the scale provided below:

Product I Definitely Do Not Need						Product I Definitely Need
1	2	3	4	5	6	7

11. How likely are you to purchase a digital recorder/player in the next year? Please indicate whether you are moderately likely or highly likely to purchase a digital recorder/player. (*Note:* Respondents who were not likely to purchase a digital recorder/player were screened out of the survey.)

6 = Moderately Likely
7 = Highly Likely

II. Classification Information

Please tell us a little about yourself. We use the data for classification purposes only.

12. What is the highest level of education you have attained? (Check only ONE.)

a. ___ High school graduate
b. ___ College graduate

Exhibit 13.21 *continued*

13. Electronics Products Ownership. Please indicate the level of electronics products ownership that best describes you.

   a. ___ Own few electronics products.

   b. ___ Own a moderate number of electronics products.

   c. ___ Own many electronics products.

14. Please check the category that best indicates your total annual household income before taxes. (Check only ONE.)

   a. ___ $20,000–$35,000

   b. ___ $35,001–$50,000

   c. ___ $50,001–$75,000

   d. ___ $75,001–$100,000

   e. ___ More than $100,000

THANK YOU FOR SHARING YOUR OPINIONS WITH OUR MARKETING RESEARCH CLASS.

To begin the analysis, researchers classified respondents as innovators or early adopters. The Innovativeness scale consisted of five variables: x3, x4, x5, x6, and x9. Cluster analysis was utilized to identify respondents who rated themselves higher (more innovative) on these five scales. The analysis produced 137 Innovators and 63 Early Adopters. This categorical variable (x14) was then used to learn more about the respondents. The initial variables we examine here are x10–Digital recorder/player Product Perceptions, x11–Purchase Likelihood, and x16–Price Consciousness. The results are shown in Exhibit 13.22.

All of the comparisons are significantly different. Looking first at variable x10, the mean value for innovators is larger than for early adopters (5.5 vs. 3.2). This indicates that innovators believe they need a digital recorder/player much more than do early adopters. A similar finding is true for variable x11–Purchase Likelihood (coded 1 = highly likely and 0 = moderately likely). The higher mean value for innovators (.8 vs .1) indicates they are much more likely to purchase a digital recorder/player. Finally, looking at x16–Price

Exhibit 13.22 Comparison of Innovators and Adopters

	Group	N	Mean	Sig.
x10—Digital recorder/Player Perceptions	**0 = Early Adopters**	63	3.2	
	1 = Innovators	137	5.5	
	Total	200	4.7	.00
x11—Purchase Likelihood	**0 = Early Adopters**	63	.1	
	1 = Innovators	137	.8	
	Total	200	.6	.00
x16—Price Conscious	**0 = Early Adopters**	63	.6	
	1 = Innovators	137	.4	
	Total	200	.5	.01

Conscious we see that innovators are less price conscious than are early adopters (.4 vs .6; coded 1 = more price conscious and 0 = less price conscious).

This study suggests that digital recorder/players have left the innovation stage of the diffusion process and are making inroads into the early adopter phase, and beyond. But digital recorder/player manufacturers and retail marketers alike must continue to develop strategies that attract more potential early adopters as well as create awareness and desire among the early majority.

Hands-On Exercise

1. What other issues can be examined with this survey?
2. What problems do you see with the questionnaire?
3. What are the important topics to include in a presentation of the findings?

Summary

Understand the objectives of a research report.

The key objective of a marketing research report is to provide the client with a clear, concise interpretation of the research project. The research report is a culmination of the entire study and therefore must communicate the systematic manner in which the study was designed and implemented. Secondary objectives of the report are to provide accurate, credible, easy-to-understand information to the client. The end result of the report is its ability to act as a reference document to guide future research and serve as an information source.

Describe the format of a marketing research report.

The research report generally includes the following: a title page, a table of contents, and an executive summary, which includes a statement of the research objectives, a detailed statement of the research method and procedures, a brief statement of findings, and conclusions and recommendations. Following the executive summary are the introduction of the report, a description of the methodology employed, and a discussion of data analysis techniques and findings. The final elements are conclusions and recommendations, and a description of limitations. An appendix may include technical explanations or documentation.

Discuss several techniques for graphically displaying research results.

A vast array of graphic techniques is available to display research results. A variety of bar charts can be used to display analyses from simple frequencies to Crosstabs, t-tests and ANOVA. As well, pie charts can be used to display the results of frequencies. Tables are especially helpful for portraying related results, including means, t-tests, and correlations. Conceptual models showing relationships between variables are often used to portray regression results.

Clarify problems encountered in preparing reports.

Problem areas that may arise in the preparation of the research report are (1) lack of data interpretation, (2) unnecessary use of multivariate statistics, (3) emphasis on packaging rather than quality, (4) lack of relevance, and (5) placing too much emphasis on a few statistical outcomes.

Understand the importance of presentations in marketing research.

Presentations are important because research results must be effectively communicated to those seeking to use the information in decision making. The report or presentation may be the only part of the research project that will be seen by those commissioning the report. The content of the research and the presentation form of the research are closely intertwined.

Key Terms and Concepts

Appendix 374

Believability 356

Credibility 356

Executive summary 358

Introduction 359

Limitations 374

Methods-and-procedures section 360

Review Questions

1. What are the seven components of the marketing research report? Briefly discuss each component and why it is important.
2. In the context of the marketing research report, what is the primary goal of the executive summary?
3. What are the primary topics/issues that need to be addressed in the research methods-and-procedures section of a marketing research report?
4. Why are conclusions and recommendations included in a marketing research report?
5. What are the common problems associated with the marketing research report?
6. Why is it important to explain limitations in your marketing research report?

Discussion Questions

1. **EXPERIENCE MARKETING RESEARCH.** Go to the following website: **www.microsoft.com/Education /Tutorials.aspx**. Complete the Tutorials dialog box by typing in "higher education" in the Grade Level box, "technology" in the Learning Area box, and "PowerPoint" in the Product box. After selecting and completing the tutorial, provide written comments on the benefits you received by taking this tutorial.
2. Select the Santa Fe Grill data or one of the other databases provided with this text (see Deli Depot; Remington's; QualKote; or Digital Recorder Survey on the website), analyze the data using the appropriate statistical techniques, prepare a PowerPoint presentation of your findings, and make the presentation to your research class.
   a. Select an appropriate variable from the data set and prepare a simple bar chart of the findings in SPSS.
   b. Select an appropriate variable from the data set and prepare a simple pie chart of the findings in SPSS.
   c. Select a group of thematically related items that are on metric scales. Present the results in a table and also in a bar chart using SPSS.
   d. Find two categorical items that are appropriate for a Crosstab and present your results in a bar chart made with SPSS.
   e. Find a categorical independent variable and interval level dependent variable. Present the results in a bar chart made with SPSS.
   f. Choose an outcome variable that can be explained by two or more independent variables. Run a regression and then develop a diagram (using PowerPoint or Word) that displays your findings.
3. There are several PowerPoint presentations for the Santa Fe Grill Restaurant study on the book's website at **http://connect.mheducation.com**. The presentations demonstrate how findings of a statistical analysis of data from a survey can be reported. Review the presentations and select the one you believe most effectively communicates the findings. Justify your choice.

Glossary

A

Ability to Participate The ability of both the interviewer and the respondent to get together in a question-and-answer interchange.

Alpha Factor The desired or acceptable amount of difference between the expected and the actual population parameter values; also referred to as the *tolerance level of error*.

Alternative Hypothesis A statement that is the opposite of the null hypothesis, where the difference in reality is not simply due to random error.

Analysis of Variance (ANOVA) A statistical technique that determines whether two or more means are statistically different from each other.

Appendix A section at the end of the final research report used to house complex, detailed, or technical information.

Archives Secondary sources of recorded past behaviors and trends.

Area Sampling A form of cluster sampling where clusters are formed by geographic designations such as cities, subdivisions, and blocks. Any geographic unit with boundaries can be used, with one-step or two-step approaches.

Assignment Property The employment of unique descriptors to identify each object in a set.

Availability of Information The degree to which the information has already been collected and assembled in some type of recognizable format.

B

Bad Questions Any question or directive that obscures, prevents, or distorts the fundamental communications between respondent and researcher.

Bar Code A pattern of varied-width electronic-sensitive bars and spaces that represents a unique code of numbers and letters.

Behavior Intention Scale A special type of rating scale designed to capture the likelihood that people will demonstrate some type of predictable behavior toward purchasing an object or service.

Behavioral Targeting Displaying ads at one website based on the user's previous surfing behavior.

Believability The quality achieved by building a final report that is based on clear, logical thinking, precise expression, and accurate presentation.

Benefit and Lifestyle Studies Studies conducted to examine similarities and differences in needs; used to identify two or more segments within a market for the purpose of identifying customers for the product category of interest to a particular company.

Beta Coefficient An estimated regression coefficient that has been recalculated to have a mean of 0 and a standard deviation of 1. This statistic enables the independent variables with different units of measurement to be directly compared on their association with the dependent variable.

Bias A particular tendency or inclination that skews results, thereby preventing accurate consideration of a research question.

Bivariate Regression Analysis A statistical technique that analyzes the linear relationship between two variables by estimating coefficients for an equation for a straight line. One variable is designated as a dependent variable, and the other as an independent (or predictor) variable.

Brand Awareness The percentage of respondents having heard of a designated brand; brand awareness can be either unaided or aided.

Branded Black-Box Methodologies Methodologies offered by research firms that are branded and do not provide information about how the methodology works.

Bulletin Board An online research format in which participants agree to post regularly over a period of 4–5 days.

C

Call Record Sheet A recording document that gathers basic summary information about an interviewer's performance efficiency (e.g., number of contact attempts, number of completed interviews, length of time of interview).

Case Studies An exploratory research technique that intensively investigates one or several existing situations which are similar to the current problem/opportunity situation.

Categorization Placing portions of transcripts into similar groups based on their context.

Causal Hypotheses Theoretical statements about relationships between variables that indicate a cause-and-effect relationship.

Causal Research Research that focuses on collecting data structures and information that will allow the decision maker or researcher to model cause–effect relationships between two or more variables under investigation.

Census A study that includes data about or from every member of a target population.

Central Limit Theorem (CLT) The theoretical backbone of sampling theory. It states that the sampling distribution of the sample mean ($\bar{x}$) or the sample proportion ($\bar{p}$) value derived from a simple random sample drawn from the target population will be approximately normally distributed provided that the associated sample size is sufficiently large (e.g., when n is greater than or equal to 30). In turn, the sample mean value ($\bar{x}$) of that random sample with an estimated sampling error (S_g) (estimated standard error) fluctuates around the true population mean value (m) with a standard error of s/n and has a sampling distribution that is approximately a standardized normal distribution, regardless of the shape of the probability frequency distribution curve of the overall target population.

Chi-square (χ^2) Analysis Assesses how closely the observed frequencies fit the pattern of the expected frequencies and is referred to as a "goodness-of-fit test."

Cluster Sampling A method of probability sampling where the sampling units are selected in groups (or clusters) rather than individually. Once the cluster has been identified, the elements to be sampled are drawn by simple random sampling or all of the units may be included in the sample.

Code of Ethics A set of guidelines that states the standards and operating procedures for ethical decisions and practices by researchers.

Codes Labels or numbers that are used to track categories in a qualitative study.

Code Sheet A sheet of paper that lists the different themes or categories for a particular study.

Coding The activities of grouping and assigning values to various responses.

Coefficient Alpha See *Cronbach's Alpha*.

Coefficient of Determination (r^2) A statistical value (or number) that measures the proportion of variation in one variable accounted for by another variable; the r^2 measure can be thought of as a percentage and varies from .00 to 1.00.

Commercial/Syndicated Data Data that have been compiled and displayed according to some standardized procedure.

Common Methods Variance (CMV) A biased variance that results from the measurement method used in a questionnaire.

Comparative Rating Scale A scale format that requires a judgment comparing one object, person, or concept against another on the scale.

Comparative Scale Scale used when the scaling objective is to have a respondent express an attitude, feeling, or behavior about an object (or person, or phenomenon) or its attributes on the basis of some other object (or person, or phenomenon).

Comparison The process of developing and refining theory and constructs by analyzing the differences and similarities in passages, themes, or types of participants.

Competitive Intelligence Analysis Specific procedures for collecting daily operational information pertaining to the competitive companies and markets they serve.

Completeness The depth and breadth of the data.

Completion Deadline Date Part of the information included in a cover letter that directly communicates to a prospective respondent the date by which his or her completed questionnaire must be returned to the researcher.

Complexity of the Information One of the two fundamental dimensions used to determine the level of information being supplied by the information research process; it relates to the degree to which the information is easily understood and applied to the problem or opportunity under investigation.

Computer-Assisted Telephone Interview (CATI) The computer controls and expedites the interviewing process.

Computer-Assisted Telephone Survey A survey that uses a fully automated system in which the respondent listens to an electronic voice and responds by pushing keys on a touch-tone telephone keypad.

Concept and Product Testing Research information for decisions on product improvements and new product introductions.

Conceptualization Development of a model that shows variables and hypothesized or proposed relationships between variables.

Confidence The certainty that the true value of what we are estimating falls within the precision range we have selected.

Confidence Interval A statistical range of values within which the true value of the target population parameter of interest is expected to fall based on a specified confidence level.

Confidence Levels Theoretical levels of assurance of the probability that a particular confidence interval will accurately include or measure the true population parameter value. In information research, the three most widely used levels are 90 percent, 95 percent, and 99 percent.

Confidentiality to Client The agreement between a researcher and the client that all activities performed in the process of conducting marketing research will remain private and the property of the client, unless otherwise specified by both parties.

Confidentiality to Respondent The expressed assurance to the prospective respondent that his or her name, while known to the researcher, will not be divulged to a third party, especially the sponsoring client.

Confirmation/Invitation Letter A specific follow-up document sent to prospective focus group participants to encourage and reinforce their willingness and commitment to participate in the group session.

Conformance to Standards The researcher's ability to be accurate, timely, mistake free, and void of unanticipated delays.

Conjoint Analysis A multivariate technique that estimates the utility of the levels of various attributes or features of an object, as well as the relative importance of the attributes themselves.

Consent Forms Formal signed statements of agreement by the participants approving the taping or recording of the information provided in group discussions and releasing that data to the moderator, researcher, or sponsoring client.

Constant Sums Rating Scale A scale format that requires the respondents to allocate a given number of points, usually 100, among several attributes or features based on their importance to the individual; this format requires a person to value each separate feature relative to all the other listed features.

Construct A hypothetical variable made up of a set of component responses or behaviors that are thought to be related.

Construct Development An integrative process of activities undertaken by researchers to enhance understanding of what specific data should be collected for solving defined research problems.

Construct Development Error A type of nonsampling (systematic) error that is created when the researcher is not careful in fully identifying the concepts and constructs to be included in the study.

Constructs Hypothetical variables composed of a set of component responses or behaviors that are thought to be related.

Construct Validity The degree to which researchers measure what they intended to measure.

Consumer-Generated Media Blogs, bulletin boards, and social media platforms.

Consumer Panels Large samples of households that provide certain types of data for an extended period of time.

Content Analysis The technique used to study written or taped materials by breaking the data into meaningful aggregate units or categories using a predetermined set of rules.

Content Validity That property of a test which indicates that the entire domain of the subject or construct of interest was properly sampled. That is, the identified factors are truly components of the construct of interest.

Control Group That portion of the sample which is not subjected to the treatment.

Control Variables Extraneous variables that the researcher is able to account for according to their systematic variation (or impact) on the functional relationship between the independent and dependent variables included in the experiment.

Convenience Sampling A method of nonprobability sampling where the samples are drawn on the basis of the convenience of the researcher or interviewer; also referred to as accidental sampling. Convenience sampling is often used in the early stages of research because it allows a large number of respondents to be interviewed in a short period of time.

Convergent Validity The degree to which different measures of the same construct are highly correlated.

Cost Analysis An analysis of alternative logistic system designs that a firm can use for achieving its performance objective at the lowest total cost.

Covariation The amount of change in one variable that is consistently related to the change in another variable of interest.

Cover Letter A separate letter that either accompanies a self–administered questionnaire or is mailed prior to an initial interviewer contact call and whose main purpose is to secure a respondent's willingness to participate in the research project; sometimes referred to as a *letter of introduction*.

Cover Letter Guidelines A specific set of factors that should be included in a cover letter for the purpose of increasing a prospective respondent's willingness to participate in the study.

Credibility The quality that comes about by developing a final report that is accurate, believable, and professionally organized.

Critical Questions Questions used by a moderator to direct the group to the critical issues underlying the topics of interest.

Critical Tolerance Level of Error The observed difference between a sample statistic value and the corresponding true or hypothesized population parameter.

Critical z Value The book z value and the amount of acceptable variability between the observed sample data results and the prescribed hypothesized true population values measured in standardized degrees of standard errors for given confidence levels.

Cronbach's Alpha A widely used measurement of the internal consistency of a multi-item scale in which the average of all possible split-half coefficients is taken.

Cross-Researcher Reliability The degree of similarity in the coding of the same data by different researchers.

Cross-Tabulation The process of simultaneously treating (or counting) two or more variables in the study.

This process categorizes the number of respondents who have responded to two or more questions consecutively.

Curbstoning Cheating or falsification of data during the collection process that occurs when interviewers fill in all or part of a survey themselves.

Curvilinear Relationship An association between two variables whereby the strength and/or direction of their relationship changes over the range of both variables.

Customer-Volunteered Information Data provided by the customer without solicitation.

Customized Research Firms Research firms that provide tailored services for clients.

Cycle Time The time that elapses between taking a product or service from initial consumer contact to final delivery.

D

Data Facts relating to any issue or subject.

Data Analysis Error A "family" of nonsampling errors that are created when the researcher subjects the data to inappropriate analysis procedures.

Database A collection of secondary information indicating what customers are purchasing, how often they purchase, and how much they purchase.

Data Coding Errors The incorrect assignment of codes to responses.

Data Editing Errors Inaccuracies due to careless verifying procedures of data to computer data files.

Data Entry The direct inputting of the coded data into some specified software package that will ultimately allow the research analyst to manipulate and transform the data into usable information.

Data Entry Errors The incorrect assignment of computer codes to their predesignated location on the computer data file.

Data Mining The process of finding hidden patterns and relationships among variables/characteristics contained in data stored in the data warehouse.

Data Reduction The categorization and coding of data that is part of the theory development process in qualitative data analysis.

Data Silo Collection of data by one area of a business that is not shared with other areas.

Data Validation A specific control process that the researcher undertakes to ensure that his or her representatives collected the data as required. The process is normally one of recontacting about 20 percent of the selected respondent group to determine that they did participate in the study.

Data Warehouse A central repository for all significant pieces of information that an organization collects.

De-Anonymizing Data Combining different publicly available information to determine consumers' identities, especially on the Internet.

Debriefing Analysis The technique of comparing notes, thoughts, and feelings about a focus group discussion between the moderator, researcher, and sponsoring client immediately following the group interview.

Decision Opportunity The presence of a situation in which market performance can be significantly improved by undertaking new activities.

Defined Target Population A specified group of people or objects for which questions can be asked or observations made to develop the required information; also referred to as the *working population*. A precise definition of the target population is essential when undertaking a research project.

Deliberate Falsification When the respondent and/or interviewer intentionally gives wrong answers or deliberately cheats on a survey.

Demographic Characteristics Physical and factual attributes of people, organizations, or objects.

Dependence Techniques Multivariate procedures when one or more of the variables can be identified as dependent variables and the remaining as independent variables.

Dependent Variable A singular observable attribute that is the measured outcome derived from manipulating the independent variable(s).

Depth The overall number of key data fields or variables that will make up the data records.

Description The process of discovering patterns, associations, and relationships among key customer characteristics.

Descriptive Research Research that uses a set of scientific methods and procedures to collect data that are used to identify, determine, and describe the existing characteristics of a target population or market structure.

Direct (positive) Directional Hypothesis A statement about the perceived relationship between two questions, dimensions, or subgroups of attributes that suggests that as one factor moves in one direction, the other factor moves in the same direction.

Direct Mail Survey A questionnaire distributed to and returned from respondents via the postal service.

Directness of Observation The degree to which the researcher or trained observer actually observes the behavior/event as it occurs; also termed *direct observation*.

Discriminant Validity The degree to which measures of different constructs are uncorrelated.

Discriminatory Power The scale's ability to significantly differentiate between the categorical scale responses (or points).

Disguised Sponsorship When the true identity of the person or company for which the research is being conducted is not divulged to the prospective respondent.

Disproportionately Stratified Sampling A stratified sampling method in which the size of each stratum is independent of its relative size in the population.

Diversity of Respondents The degree to which the respondents in the study share some similarities.

Domain of Observables The set of observable manifestations of a variable that is not itself directly observable. A domain represents an identifiable set of components that form the construct of interest.

Drop-off Survey A questionnaire that is left with the respondent to be completed at a later time. The questionnaire may be picked up by the researcher or returned via some other mode.

E

Editing The process in which the interviews or survey instruments are checked for mistakes that may have occurred by either the interviewer or the respondent during data collection activities.

Electronic Test Markets Test procedures that integrate the use of selected panels of consumers who use a special identification card in recording their product purchasing data.

Element The name given to the object about which information is sought. Elements must be unique, countable, and, when added together, make up the whole of the target population.

Emic Validity An attribute of qualitative research that affirms that key members within a culture or subculture agree with the findings of a research report.

Empirical Testing The collection of data in the real world using research instruments and then subjecting that data to rigorous analysis to either support or refute a hypothesis.

Ending Questions Questions used by a focus group moderator to bring closure to a particular topic discussion; encourages summary-type comments.

Error The difference between the true score on a research instrument and the observed score.

Estimated Sample Standard Deviation A quantitative index of the dispersion of the distribution of drawn sampling units' actual data around the sample's arithmetic average measure of central tendency; this sample statistical value specifies the degree of variation in the data responses in a way that allows the researcher to translate the variations into normal curve interpretations.

Estimated Sample Variance The square of the estimated sample standard deviation.

Estimated Standard Error of the Sample Statistic A statistical measurement of the sampling error that can be expected to exist between the drawn sample's statistical values and the actual values of all the sampling units' distributions of those concerned statistics. These indexes are referred to as *general precision*.

Estimates Sample data facts that are transformed through interpretation procedures to represent inferences about the larger target population.

Ethnography A form of qualitative data collection that records behavior in natural settings to understand how social and cultural influences affect individuals' behaviors and experiences.

Executive Dashboard An intranet for a select group of managers who are decision makers in the company.

Executive Interview A person-administered interview of a business executive. Frequently, these interviews will take place in the executive's office.

Executive Summary The part of the final research report that illustrates the major points of the report in a manner complete enough to provide a true representation of the entire document.

Expected Completion Rate (ECR) The percentage of prospective respondents who are expected to participate and complete the survey; also referred to as the *anticipated response rate*.

Experiment An empirical investigation that tests for hypothesized relationships between dependent variables and one or more manipulated independent variables.

Experimental Design Reliability The degree to which the research design and its procedures can be replicated and achieve similar conclusions about hypothesized relationships.

Experimental Research An empirical investigation that tests for hypothesized relationships between dependent variables and manipulated independent variables.

Exploratory Research Research designed to collect and interpret either secondary or primary data in an unstructured format.

External Secondary Data Data collected by outside agencies such as the federal, state, or local government; trade associations; or periodicals.

External Validity The extent to which the measured data results of a study based on a sample can be expected to hold in the entire defined target population. In addition, it is the extent that a causal relationship found in a study can be expected to be true for the entire defined target population.

Extraneous Variables All variables other than the independent variables that affect the responses of the test subjects. If left uncontrolled, these variables can have a confounding impact on the dependent variable measures that could weaken or invalidate the results of an experiment.

F

Field Experiments Causal research designs that manipulate the independent variables in order to measure the dependent variable in a natural test setting.

Finite Correction Factor (fcf) An adjustment factor to the sample size that is made in those situations where the drawn sample is expected to equal 5 percent or more of the defined target population. The fcf is equal to the overall square root of $N - n/N - 1$.

Focus Group Facility A professional facility that offers a set of specially designed rooms for conducting focus group interviews; each room contains a large table and comfortable chairs for up to 13 people, with a relaxed atmosphere, built-in audio equipment, and normally a one-way mirror for disguised observing by the sponsoring client or researcher.

Focus Group Incentives Specified investment programs to compensate focus group participants for their expenses associated with demonstrating a willingness to be a group member.

Focus Group Moderator A person who is well trained in interpersonal communications; listening, observation, and interpretive skills; and professional mannerisms and personality. His or her role in a session is to draw from the participants the best and most innovative ideas about an assigned topic or question.

Focus Group Research A formalized qualitative data collection method for which data are collected from a small group of people who interactively and spontaneously discuss one particular topic or concept.

Follow-up Test A statistical test that flags the means that are statistically different from each other; follow-up tests are performed after an ANOVA determines there are differences between means.

Forced-Choice Scale Measurements Symmetrical scale measurement designs that do not have a logical "neutral" scale descriptor to divide the positive and negative domains of response descriptors.

Formal Rating Procedures The use of structured survey instruments or questionnaires to gather information on environmental occurrences.

F-ratio The statistical ratio of between-group mean squared variance to within-group mean squared variance; the F value is used as an indicator of the statistical difference between group means in an ANOVA.

Frequency Distributions A summary of how many times each possible response to a scale question/setup was recorded by the total group of respondents.

F-test The test used to statistically evaluate the difference between the group means in ANOVA.

Functional Relationship An observable and measurable systematic change in one variable as another variable changes.

G

Garbage In, Garbage Out A standard phrase used in marketing research to represent situations where the process of collecting, analyzing, and interpreting data into information contains errors or biases, creating less than accurate information.

Gatekeeper Technology Any device used to help protect one's privacy against intrusive marketing practices such as telemarketing solicitors, unwanted direct marketers, illegal scam artists, and "sugging" (caller ID, voice messengers, answering machines).

Generalizability The extent to which the data are an accurate portrait of the defined target population; the representativeness of information obtained from a small subgroup of members to that of the entire target population from which the subgroup was selected.

General Precision The amount of general sampling error associated with the given sample of data that was generated through some type of data collection.

Graphic Rating Scale Descriptors A scale point format that presents respondents with some type of graphic continuum as the set of possible responses to a given question.

Group Dynamics The degree of spontaneous interaction among group members during a discussion of a topic.

Groupthink A phenomenon in which one or two members of a group state an opinion and other members of the group are unduly influenced.

H

Heteroskedasticity The pattern of covariation around the regression line is not constant around the regression line, and varies in some way when the values change from small to medium and large.

Homoskedasticity The pattern of the covariation is constant (the same) around the regression line, whether the values are small, medium, or large.

Hypothesis A yet-unproven proposition or possible solution to a decision problem that can be empirically tested using data that are collected through the research process; it is developed in order to explain a relationship between two or more constructs or variables.

I

Iceberg Principle The general notion indicating that the dangerous part of many marketing decision problems is neither visible nor well understood by marketing managers.

Importance-Performance Analysis A research and data analysis procedure used to evaluate a firm's and its competitors' strengths and weaknesses, as well as future actions that seek to identify key attributes that drive purchase behavior within a given industry.

Incidence Rate The percentage of the general population that is the subject of a market research study.

Independent Samples Two or more groups of responses that are tested as though they may come from different populations.

Independent Variable An attribute of an object whose measurement values are directly manipulated by the researcher, also referred to as a *predictor* or *treatment variable*. This type of variable is assumed to be a causal factor in a functional relationship with a dependent variable.

In-Depth Interview A structured process of a subject's being asked a set of semi-structured, probing questions by a well-trained interviewer usually in a face-to-face setting.

Information Objectives The clearly stated reasons why data must be collected; they serve as the guidelines for determining the data requirements.

Information Requirements The identified factors, dimensions, and attributes within a stated information objective for which data must be collected.

Information Research Process The 10 systematic task steps involved in the four phases of gathering, analyzing, interpreting, and transforming data and results into information for use by decision makers.

Information Research Questions Specific statements that address the problem areas the research study will attempt to investigate.

In-Home Interview A person-administered interview that takes place in the respondent's home.

Integration The process of moving from the identification of themes and categories to the development of theory.

Interaction Effect Multiple independent variables in an ANOVA can act together to affect dependent variable group means.

Intention to Purchase A person's planned future action to buy a product or service.

Interdependence Techniques Multivariate statistical procedures in which the whole set of interdependent relationships is examined.

Internal Reliability The extent to which the items of a scale represent the same domain of content and are highly correlated both with each other and summated scale scores. It represents the degree to which the components are related to the same overall construct domain.

Internal Secondary Data Facts that have been collected by the individual company for accounting and marketing activity purposes.

Internal Validity The certainty with which a researcher can state that the observed effect was caused by a specific treatment; exists when the research design accurately identifies causal relationships.

Internet Survey The method of using the Internet to ask survey questions and record responses of respondents.

Interpersonal Communication Skills The interviewer's abilities to articulate the questions in a direct and clear manner so that the subject understands what she or he is responding to.

Interpretive Bias Error that occurs when the wrong inference about the real world or defined target population is made by the researcher or decision maker due to some type of extraneous factor.

Interpretive Skills The interviewer's capabilities of accurately understanding and recording the subject's responses to questions.

Interval Scales Any question/scale format that activates not only the assignment and order scaling properties but also the distance property; all scale responses have a recognized absolute difference between each of the other scale points (responses).

Interviewer Error A type of non-sampling error that is created in situations where the interviewer distorts information, in a systematic way, from respondents during or after the interviewer/respondent encounter.

Interviewer Instructions The vehicle for training the interviewer on how to select prospective respondents, screen them for eligibility, and conduct the actual interview.

Introduction Contains background information necessary for a complete understanding of the report.

Introductory Questions Questions used by a focus group moderator to introduce the general topic of discussion and opportunities of reflecting their past experiences.

Introductory Section Gives the respondent an overview of the research.

Inverse (negative or indirect) Directional Hypothesis A statement about the perceived relationship between two questions, dimensions, or subgroupings of attributes which suggests that as one factor moves in one direction, the other factor moves in an opposite fashion.

Iteration Working through the data several times in order to modify early ideas and to be informed by subsequent analyses.

J

Judgment Sampling A nonprobability sampling design that selects participants for a sample based on an experienced individual's belief that the participants will meet the requirements of the research study.

K

Knowledge Information becomes knowledge when someone, either the researcher or the decision maker, interprets the data and attaches meaning.

Knowledge Level Degree to which the selected respondents feel they have knowledge of or experience with the survey's topics.

L

Laboratory Experiments Experiments conducted in an artificial setting.

Leading Question A question that tends to purposely elicit a particular answer.

Least Squares Procedure A regression approach that determines the best-fitting line by minimizing the vertical distances of all the points from the line, also referred to as OLS.

Likert Scale A special rating scale format that asks respondents to indicate the extent to which they agree or disagree with a statements.

Limitations A section of the final research report in which all extraneous events that place certain restrictions on the report are fully communicated.

Linear Relationship An association between two variables whereby the strength and nature of the relationship remains the same over the range of both variables.

Literature Review A comprehensive examination of available information that is related to your research topic.

Lottery Approach A unique incentive system that pools together either individual small cash incentives into a significantly larger dollar amount or a substantial nonmonetary gift and then holds a drawing to determine the winner or small set of winners. The drawing procedure is designed so that all respondents who complete and return their survey have an equal chance of receiving the larger reward.

M

Mail Panel Survey A representative sample of individual respondents who have agreed in advance to participate in a mail survey.

Mail Surveys Surveys sent to respondents using the postal service.

Mall-Intercept Interview An interview technique in which mall patrons are stopped and asked for feedback. The interview may take place in the mall's common areas or in the research firm's offices at the mall.

Marketing The process of planning and executing pricing, promotion, product, and distribution of products, services, and ideas in order to create exchanges that satisfy both the firm and its customers.

Marketing Knowledge A characteristic that complements a researcher's technical competency.

Marketing Research The function that links an organization to its market through the gathering of information. The information allows for the identification and definition of market-driven opportunities and problems. The information allows for the generation, refinement, and evaluation of marketing actions.

Marketing Research Online Communities (MROCs) Purposed communities whose primary purpose is research.

Market Intelligence The use of real-time customer information (customer knowledge) to achieve a competitive advantage.

Market Performance Symptoms Conditions that signal the presence of a decision problem and/or opportunity.

Mean The arithmetic average of all the responses; all values of a distribution of responses are summed and divided by the number of valid responses.

Measurement Rules for assigning numbers to objects so that these numbers represent quantities of attributes.

Measurement/Design Error A "family" of nonsampling errors that result from inappropriate designs in the constructs, scale measurements, or survey measurements used to execute the asking and recording of people's responses to a study's questions.

Measures of Central Tendency The basic sample statistics that could be generated through analyzing the collected data; they are the mode, the median, and the mean.

Measures of Dispersion The sample statistics that describe how all the data are actually dispersed around a given measure of central tendency; they are the frequency distribution, the range, and the estimated sample standard deviation.

Mechanical Devices High-technology instruments that can artificially observe and record either current behavioral actions or physical phenomena as they occur.

Mechanical/Electronic Observation Some type of mechanical or electronic device is used to capture human behavior, events, or marketing phenomena.

Median The sample statistic that splits the data into a hierarchical pattern where half the data are above the median statistic value and half are below.

Media Panels Selected households that are primarily used in measuring media viewing habits as opposed to product/brand consumption patterns.

Member Checking Asking key informants to read the researcher's report to verify that the analysis is accurate.

Memoing Writing down thoughts as soon as possible after each interview, focus group, or site visit.

Method Bias The error source that results from selecting an inappropriate method to investigate the research question.

Methods-and-Procedures Section Communicates how the research was conducted.

Mode The most frequently mentioned (or occurring) raw response in the set of responses to a given question/setup.

Model F Statistic A statistic that compares the amount of variation in the dependent measure "explained" or associated with the independent variables to the "unexplained" or error variance. A larger F statistic value indicates that the regression model has more explained variance than error variance.

Moderator's Guide A detailed document that outlines the topics, questions, and subquestions that serve as the basis for generating the spontaneous interactive dialogue among the focus group participants.

Modified Likert Scale Any version of the agreement/disagreement-based scale measurement that is not the original five-point "strongly agree" to "strongly disagree" scale.

Monetary Compensation An individual cash incentive used by the researcher to increase the likelihood of a prospective respondent's willingness to participate in the survey.

Multicollinearity A situation in which several independent variables are highly correlated with each other. This characteristic can result in difficulty in estimating separate or independent regression coefficients for the correlated variables.

Multiple-Item Scale Designs Method used when the researcher has to measure several items (or attributes) simultaneously in order to measure the complete object or construct of interest.

Multiple Regression Analysis A statistical technique that analyzes the linear relationships between a dependent variable and multiple independent variables by estimating coefficients for the equation for a straight line.

Multivariate Analysis (Techniques) A group of statistical techniques used when there are two or more measurements on each element and the variables are analyzed simultaneously.

Mystery Shopper Studies Studies in which trained, professional shoppers visit stores, financial institutions, or companies and "shop" for various products and assess service quality factors or levels.

N

Negative Case Analysis Deliberately looking for cases and instances that contradict the ideas and theories that researchers have been developing.

Negative Relationship An association between two variables in which one increases while the other decreases.

Netnography A research technique that draws on ethnography but uses "found data" on the Internet that are produced by virtual communities.

Nominal Scales Question/scale structures that ask the respondent to provide only a descriptor as the response; the response does not contain any level of intensity.

Nomological Validity The extent to which one particular construct theoretically networks with other established constructs which are related yet different.

Noncomparative Scale Scale used when the scaling objective is to have a respondent express an attitude, emotion, action, or intention about one specific object (person, phenomenon) or its attributes.

Nondirectional Hypothesis A statement regarding the existing relationship between two questions, dimensions, or subgroupings of attributes as being significantly different but lacking an expression of direction.

Nonmonetary Compensation Any type of individual incentive excluding direct cash (e.g., a free T-shirt) used by the researcher to encourage a prospective respondent's participation.

Nonparticipant Observation An ethnographic research technique that involves extended contact with a natural setting, but without participation by the researcher.

Nonprobability Sampling Sampling designs in which the probability of selection of each sampling unit is not known. The selection of sampling units is based on the judgment or knowledge of the researcher and may or may not be representative of the target population.

Nonresponse Error An error that occurs when the portion of the defined target population not represented or underrepresented in the response pool is systematically and significantly different from those that did respond.

Nonsampling Error A type of bias that occurs in a research study regardless of whether a sample or census is used.

Normal Curve A curve that indicates the shape of the distribution of a variable is equal both above and below the mean.

North American Industry Classification System (NAICS) Codes numerical industrial listings designed to promote uniformity in data reporting procedures for the U.S. government.

Not at Home A specific type of nonresponse bias that occurs when a reasonable attempt to initially reach a prospective respondent fails to produce an interviewer/respondent encounter.

Null Hypothesis A statement of no relationship between two variables.

n-**way ANOVA** This is a type of ANOVA that can analyze several independent variables at the same time.

O

Object Any tangible item in a person's environment that can be clearly and easily identified through the senses.

Objectivity The degree to which a researcher uses scientific procedures to collect, analyze, and create nonbiased information.

Observation Research Systematic observation and recording of behavioral patterns of objects, people, events and other phenomena.

Observing Mechanism How the behaviors or events will be observed; *human observation* is when the observer is either a person hired and trained by the researcher or the researcher himself; *mechanical observation* refers to the use of a technology-based device to do the observing rather than a human observer.

One-Way Tabulation The categorization of single variables existing in the study.

Online Surveys Survey data collected using the Internet.

Opening Questions Questions used by a focus group moderator to break the ice among focus group participants; identify common group member traits; and create a comfort zone for establishing group dynamics and interactive discussions.

Opportunity Assessment The collection of information on product-markets for the purpose of forecasting how they will change in the future. This type of assessment focuses on gathering information relevant to macroenvironments.

Optical Scanner An electronic device that optically reads bar codes; this scanner captures and translates unique bar code numbers into product information.

Ordinal Scales A question/scale format that activates both the assignment and order scaling properties; the respondent is asked to express relative magnitudes between the responses to a question.

Ordinary Least Squares A statistical procedure that estimates regression equation coefficients which produce the lowest sum of squared differences between the actual and predicted values of the dependent variable.

Overall Incidence Rate (OIR) The percentage of the defined target population elements who actually qualify for inclusion in the survey.

Overall Reputation The primary dimension of perceived quality outcomes. Quality of the end product can be gauged in direct proportion to the level of expertise, trust, believability, and contribution the research brings to the client.

P

Parameter The true value of a variable.

Participant Observation An ethnographic research technique that involves extended observation of behavior in natural settings in order to fully experience cultural or subcultural contexts.

Pearson Correlation Coefficient A statistical measure of the strength and direction of a linear relationship between two metric variables.

Peer Review A process in which external qualitative methodology or topic area specialists are asked to review the research analysis.

Perceptual Map A graphic representation of respondents' beliefs about the relationship between objects with respect to two or more dimensions (usually attributes or features of the objects).

Performance Rating Scale Descriptors A scale that uses an evaluative scale point format that allows the respondents to express some type of postdecision evaluative judgment about an object.

Person-Administered Survey A survey in which an individual interviewer asks questions and records responses.

Phantom Respondents A type of data falsification that occurs when the researcher takes an actual respondent's data and duplicates them to represent a second (nonexisting) set of responses.

Physical Audits (or Traces) Tangible evidence (or artifacts) of

some past event or recorded behavior.

Population The identifiable total set of elements of interest being investigated by a researcher.

Population Mean Value The actual calculated arithmetic average parameter value based on interval or ratio data of the defined target population elements (or sampling units).

Population Proportion Value The actual calculated percentage parameter value of the characteristic of concern held by the target population elements (or sampling units).

Population Size The determined total number of elements that represent the target population.

Population Specification Error An incorrect definition of the true target population to the research question.

Population Standard Deviation A quantitative index of the dispersion of the distribution of population elements' actual data around the arithmetic average measure of central tendency.

Population Variance The square of the population standard deviation.

Positioning The desired perception that a company wants to be associated with its target markets relative to its products or brand offerings.

Positive Relationship An association between two variables in which they increase or decrease together.

PowerPoint A software package used to develop slides for electronic presentation of the research results.

Precision The degree of exactness of the data in relation to some other possible response of the target population; the acceptable amount of error in the sample estimate.

Predictions Population estimates that are carried into a future time frame; they are derived from either facts or sample data estimates.

Predictive Validity The extent to which a scale can accurately predict some event external to the scale itself.

Pretesting The conducting of a simulated administering of a designed survey (or questionnaire) to a small, representative group of respondents.

Primary Data Data structures of variables that have been specifically collected and assembled for the current research problem or opportunity situation; they represent "firsthand" structures.

Primary Information Firsthand facts or estimates that are derived through a formalized research process for a specific current problem situation.

Probability Distribution of the Population The relative frequencies of a population's parameter characteristic emulating a normal bell-shaped pattern.

Probability Sampling Sampling designs in which each sampling unit in the sampling frame (operational population) has a known, nonzero probability of being selected for the sample.

Problem Definition A statement that seeks to determine precisely what problem management wishes to solve and the type of information necessary to solve it.

Project Costs The price requirements of doing marketing research.

Projective Techniques A family of qualitative data collection methods where subjects are asked to project themselves into specified buying situations and then asked questions about those situations.

Propensity Scoring Weighting underrepresented respondents more heavily in results.

Proportionately Stratified Sampling A stratified sampling method in which the size of each stratum is proportional to its relative size in the population.

Purchase Intercept Interview An interview similar to a mall intercept except that the respondent is stopped at the point of purchase and asked a set of predetermined questions.

Purposive Sampling Selecting sample members to study because they possess attributes important to understanding the research topic.

Q

Qualitative Research Research methods used in exploratory research designs where the main objective is to gain a variety of preliminary insights to discover and identify decision problems and opportunities.

Quality of the Information One of the two fundamental dimensions that is used to determine the level of information being provided by the research process; it refers to the degree to which the information can be depended on as being accurate and reliable.

Quantitative Research Data collection methods that emphasize using structured questioning practices where the response options have been predetermined by the researcher and administered to significantly large numbers of respondents.

Questionnaire A set of questions and scales designed to generate data to address research objectives.

Questionnaire Development Process A series of logical activities that are undertaken to design a systematic survey instrument for the purpose of collecting primary data from (respondents).

Questionnaire Format/Layout The combination of sets of question/scale measurements into a systematic structured instrument.

Question/Setup Element The question and/or directive that element of a questionnaire; it is one of the three elements that make up any scale measurement.

Quotas A tracking system that collects data from respondents and helps ensure that subgroups are represented in the sample as specified.

Quota Sampling The selection of participants based on specific quotas regarding characteristics such as age, race, gender, income, or specific behaviors. Quotas are usually determined by research objectives.

Quota Sheets A simple tracking form that enhances the interviewer's ability to collect data from the right type of respondents; the form helps ensure that representation standards are met.

R

Random-Digit Dialing A random selection of area code, exchange, and suffix numbers.

Random Error An error that occurs as the result of chance events affecting the observed score.

Randomization The procedure whereby many subjects are assigned to different experimental treatment conditions, resulting in each group's averaging out any systematic effect on the investigated functional relationship between the independent and dependent variables.

Random Sampling Error The statistically measured difference between the actual sampled results and the estimated true population results.

Ranges Statistics that represent the grouping of data responses into mutually exclusive subgroups with each having distinct identifiable lower and upper boundary designation values in a set of responses.

Rank-Order Rating Scale A scale point format that allows respondents to compare their responses to each other by indicating their first preference, then their second preference, then their third preference, etc., until all the desired responses are placed in some type of rank order, either highest to lowest or lowest to highest.

Rating Cards Cards used in personal interviews that represent a reproduction of the set of actual scale points and descriptions used to respond to a specific question/setup in the survey. These cards serve as a tool to help the interviewer and respondent speed up the data collection process.

Ratio Scales Question/scale formats that simultaneously activate all four scaling properties; they are the most sophisticated scale in the sense that absolute differences can be identified not only between each scale point but also between individuals' responses. Ratio scales request that respondents give a specific singular numerical value as their response to the question.

Reachable Rate (RR) The percentage of active addresses on a mailing list or other defined population frame.

Recursive A relationship in which a variable can both cause and be caused by the same variable.

Regression Coefficient An indicator of the importance of an independent variable in predicting a dependent variable. Large standardized coefficients are good predictors and small coefficients are weak predictors.

Refusal A particular type of nonresponse bias that is caused when a prospective respondent declines the role of a respondent.

Related Samples Two or more groups of responses that originated from the sample population.

Relationships Associations between two or more variables.

Reliability The extent to which the measurements taken with a particular instrument are repeatable.

Reliability of the Scale The extent to which the designed scale can reproduce the same measurement results in repeated trials.

Reliability of Service The researcher's ability to be consistent and responsive to the needs of the client.

Reputation of the Firm The culmination of a research firm's ability to meet standards, reliability of service, marketing knowledge, and technical competency for purposes of providing quality outcomes.

Research Instrument A microscope, ruler, questionnaire, scale, or other device designed for a specific measurement purpose.

Research Objectives Statements that the research project will attempt to achieve. They provide the guidelines for establishing a research agenda of activities necessary to implement the research process.

Research Proposal A specific document that serves as a written contract between the decision maker and researcher.

Research Questions Section The second section of the questionnaire that focuses on the research questions.

Respondent Characteristics The attributes that make up the respondents being included in the survey; three important characteristics are diversity, incidence, and participation.

Respondent Error The type of nonsampling errors that can occur when selected prospective respondents cannot be initially reached to participate in the survey process, do not cooperate, or demonstrate an unwillingness to participate in the survey.

Respondent Participation The overall degree to which the selected people have the ability and the willingness to participate as well as the knowledge of the topics being researched.

Response Error The tendency to answer a question in a unique systematic way. Respondents may consciously or unconsciously distort their answers and true thoughts.

Response Order Bias Occurs when the order of the questions, or of the closed-end responses to a particular question, influences the answer given.

Response Rate The percentage of usable responses out of the total number of responses.

Retailing Research Research investigations that focus on topics such as trade area analysis, store image/perception, in-store traffic patterns, and location analysis.

S

Sample A randomly selected group of people or objects from the overall membership pool of a target population.

Sample Design Error A family of nonsampling errors that occur when sampling plans are not appropriately developed and/or the sampling process is improperly executed by the researcher.

Sample Mean Value The actual calculated arithmetic average value based on interval or ratio data of the drawn sampling units.

Sample Percentage Value The actual calculated percentage value of the characteristic of concern held by the drawn sampling units.

Sample Selection Error A type of sample design bias that occurs when an inappropriate sample is drawn from the defined target population because of incomplete or faulty sampling procedures.

Sample Size The determined total number of sampling units needed to be representative of the defined target population.

Sample Statistic The value of a variable that is estimated from a sample.

Sampling The process of selecting a relatively small number of elements from a larger defined group of elements so that the information gathered from the smaller group allows one to make judgments about that larger group of elements.

Sampling Distribution The frequency distribution of a specific sample statistic value that would be found by taking repeated random samples of the same size.

Sampling Error Any type of bias in a survey study that is attributable to mistakes made in either the selection process of prospective sampling units or determining the size of a sample required to ensure its representativeness of the larger defined target population.

Sampling Frame A list of all eligible sampling units for a given study.

Sampling Frame Error An error that occurs when a sample is drawn from an incomplete list of potential or prospective respondents.

Sampling Gap The representation difference between the population elements and sampling units in the sample frame.

Sampling Plan The blueprint or framework used to ensure that the data collected are, in fact, representative of a larger defined target population structure.

Sampling Units Those elements that are available for selection during the sampling process.

Scale Dimensions and Attributes Element The components of the object, construct, or concept that is being measured; it identifies what should be measured and is one of the three elements of a scale measurement.

Scale Measurement The process of assigning a set of descriptors to represent the range of possible responses that an individual gives in answering a question about a particular object, construct, or factor under investigation.

Scale Points The set of assigned descriptors that designate the degrees of intensity to the responses concerning the investigated characteristics of an object, construct, or factor; it is one of the three elements that make up scale measurements.

Scale Reliability The extent to which a scale can produce the same measurement results in repeated trials.

Scanner-Based Panel A group of participating households which have an unique bar-coded card as an identification characteristic for inclusion in the research study.

Scatter Diagram A graphic plot of the relative position of two variables using a horizontal and a vertical axis to represent the values of the respective variables.

Scientific Method The systematic and objective process used to develop reliable and valid first-hand information.

Screening Forms A set of preliminary questions that are used to determine the eligibility of a prospective respondent for inclusion in the survey.

Screening Questions Also referred to as *screeners* or *filter questions;* are used on most questionnaires. Their purpose is to identify qualified prospective respondents and prevent unqualified respondents from being included in the study.

Secondary Data Historical data structures of variables that have been previously collected and assembled for some research problem or opportunity situation other than the current situation.

Secondary Information Information (facts or estimates) that has already been collected, assembled, and interpreted at least once for some other specific situation.

Selection Bias Contamination of internal validity measures created by inappropriate selection and/or assignment processes of test subjects to experimental treatment groups.

Selective Coding Building a story-line around one core category or theme; the other categories will be related to or subsumed to this central overarching category.

Selective Perception Bias A type of error that occurs in situations where the researcher or decision maker uses only a selected portion of the survey results to paint a tainted picture of reality.

Self-Administered Survey A survey in which respondents read the survey questions and record their responses without the assistance of an interviewer.

Semantic Differential Scale A special type of symmetrical rating scale that uses sets of bipolar adjectives and/or adverbs to describe some type of positive and negative poles of an assumed continuum; it is used to capture respondents' cognitive and affective components of specified factors and create perceptual image profiles relating to a given object or behavior.

Semistructured Question A question that directs the respondent toward a specified topic area, but the responses to the question are unbounded; the interviewer is not looking for any preconceived right answer.

Sensitive Questions Questions concerning income, sexual beliefs or behaviors, medical conditions, financial difficulties, alcohol consumption, and so forth that respondents are likely to respond to incorrectly.

Sentence Completion Test A projective technique where subjects are given a set of incomplete sentences and asked to complete them in their own words.

Simple Random Sampling (SRS) A method of probability sampling in which every sampling unit has an equal, nonzero chance of being selected. Results generated by using simple random sampling can be projected to the target

population with a prespecified margin of error.

Single-Item Scale Descriptors A scale used when the data requirements focus on collecting data about only one attribute of the object or construct being investigated.

Situational Characteristics Factors of reality such as budgets, time, and data quality that affect the researcher's ability to collect accurate primary data in a timely fashion.

Situation Analysis An informal process of analyzing the past, present, and future situations facing an organization in order to identify decision problems and opportunities.

Skip Interval A selection tool used to identify the position of the sampling units to be drawn into a systematic random sample design. The interval is determined by dividing the number of potential sampling units in the defined target population by the number of units desired in the sample.

Skip Questions Used if the next question (or set of questions) should be responded to only by respondents who meet a previous condition.

Snowball Sampling A nonprobability sampling method that involves the practice of identifying a set of initial prospective respondents who can, in turn, help in identifying additional people to be included in the study.

Social Desirability A type of response bias that occurs when the respondent assumes what answer is socially acceptable or respectable.

Social Media Monitoring Research based on conversations in social media.

Spearman Rank Order Correlation Coefficient A statistical measure of the linear association between two variables where both have been measured using ordinal (rank-order) scale instruments.

Split-Half Test A technique used to evaluate the internal consistency reliability of scale measurements that have multiple attribute components.

Standard Deviation The measure of the average dispersion of the values in a set of responses about their mean.

Standard Error of the Population Parameter A statistical measure used in probability sampling that gives an indication of how far the sample result lies from the actual population measure we are trying to estimate.

Standard Industrial Classification (SIC) Codes The numerical scheme of industrial listings designed to promote uniformity in data reporting procedures for the U.S. government.

Standardized Research Firms Research firms that provide general results following a standard format so that results of a study conducted for one client can be compared to norms.

Staple Scales Considered a modified version of the semantic differential scale; they symmetrically center the scale point domain within a set of plus (+) and minus (−) descriptors.

Statistical Conclusion Validity The ability of the researcher to make reasonable statements about covariation between constructs of interest and the strength of that covariation.

Store Audits Formal examinations and verifications of how much of a particular product or brand has been sold at the retail level.

Strata The subgroupings that are derived through stratified random sampling procedures.

Stratified Purposive Sampling Selecting sample members so that groups can be compared.

Stratified Random Sampling (STRS) A method of probability sampling in which the population is divided into different subgroups (called strata) and samples are selected from each stratum.

Structured Questions Questions that require the respondent to make a choice among a limited number of prelisted responses or scale points; they require less thought and effort on the part of the respondent; also referred to as *closed-ended questions*.

Subject Debriefing Fully explaining to respondents any deception used during research.

Subjective Information Information that is based on the decision maker's or researcher's past experiences, assumptions, feelings, or interpretations without any systematic assembly of facts or estimates.

Subject's Awareness The degree to which subjects consciously know their behavior is being observed; *disguised observation* is when the subject is completely unaware that he or she is being observed, and *undisguised observation* is when the person is aware that he or she is being observed.

Sugging/Frugging Claiming that a survey is for research purposes and then asking for a sale or donation.

Supervisor Instructions A form that serves as a blueprint for training people on how to execute the interviewing process in a standardized fashion; it outlines the process by which to conduct a study that uses personal and telephone interviewers.

Survey Instrument Design Error A "family" of design or format errors that produce a questionnaire that does not accurately collect the appropriate data; these nonsampling errors severely limit the generalizability, reliability, and validity of the collected data.

Survey Instrument Error A type of error that occurs when the survey instrument induces some type of systematic bias in the response.

Survey Research Methods Research design procedures for collecting large amounts of data using interviews or questionnaires.

Symptoms Conditions that signal the presence of a decision problem or opportunity; they tend to be observable and measurable results of problems or opportunities.

Syndicated (or Commercial) Data Data and information that have been compiled according to some standardized procedure which provides customized data for companies such as market share, ad effectiveness, and sales tracking.

Syndicated Business Services Services provided by standardized research firms that include data made or developed from a common data pool or database.

Systematic Error The type of error that results from poor instrument design and/or instrument construction causing scores or readings on an instrument to be biased in a consistent manner; creates some form of systematic variation in the data that is not a natural occurrence or fluctuation on the part of the surveyed respondents.

Systematic Random-Digit Dialing The technique of randomly dialing telephone numbers, but only numbers that meet specific criteria.

Systematic Random Sampling (SYMRS) A method of probability sampling that is similar to simple random sampling but requires that the defined target population be naturally ordered in some way.

T

Table of Random Numbers A table of numbers that has been randomly generated.

Tabulation The simple procedure of counting the number of observations, or data items, that are classified into certain categories.

Target Market Analysis Information for identifying those people (or companies) that an organization wishes to serve.

Target Population A specified group of people or objects for which questions can be asked or observations made to develop required data structures and information.

Task Characteristics The requirements placed on the respondents in their process of providing answers to questions asked.

Task Difficulty How hard the respondent needs to work to respond, and the level of preparation required to create an environment for the respondent.

Technical Competency The degree to which the researcher possesses the necessary functional requirements to conduct the research project.

Technology-Mediated Observation Data collection using some type of mechanical device to capture human behavior, events, or marketing phenomena.

Telephone Interview A question-and-answer exchange that is conducted via telephone technology.

Test Marketing A controlled field experiment conducted for gaining information on specified market performance indicators or factors.

Theoretical Sampling Selecting sample members based on earlier interviews that suggest that particular types of participants will help researchers better understand the research topic.

Theory A large body of interconnected propositions about how some portion of a certain phenomenon operates.

Thick Description An ethnographic research report that contextualizes behavior within a culture or subculture.

Topic Sensitivity The degree to which a specific question or investigated issue leads the respondent to give a socially acceptable response.

Traditional Test Markets Test markets that use experimental design procedures to test a product and/or a product's marketing mix variables through existing distribution channels; also referred to as *standard test markets*.

Trained Interviewers Highly trained people, with excellent communication and listening skills, who ask research participants specific questions and accurately record their responses.

Trained Observers Highly skilled people who use their various sensory devices to observe and record either a person's current behaviors or physical phenomena as they take place.

Transition Questions Questions used by a moderator to direct a focus group's discussion toward the main topic of interest.

Triangulation Addressing the topic analysis from multiple perspectives, including using multiple methods of data collection and analysis, multiple data sets, multiple researchers, multiple time periods, and different kinds of relevant research informants.

***t*-Test** Also referred to as *t* statistic, a hypothesis test procedure that uses the *t*-distribution; *t*-tests are used when the sample size of subjects is small (generally less than 30) and the standard deviation is unknown.

Type I Error The error made by rejecting the null hypothesis when it is true; represents the probability of alpha error.

Type II Error The error of failing to reject the null hypothesis when the alternative hypothesis is true; represents the probability of beta error.

U

Undisguised Sponsorship When the true identity of the person or company for which the research is being conducted is directly revealed to the prospective respondent.

Unexplained Variance In multivariate methods, it is the amount of variation in the dependent construct that cannot be accounted for by the combination of independent variables.

Unit of Analysis Specifies whether data should be collected about individuals, households, organizations, departments, geographical areas, or some combination.

Unstructured Questions Question/scale formats that require respondents to reply in their own words; this format requires more thinking and effort on the part of respondents in order to express their answers; also called *open-ended questions*.

V

Validity The degree to which a research instrument serves the purpose for which it was constructed; it also relates to the extent to which the conclusions drawn from an experiment are true.

Variability A measure of how data are dispersed; the greater the dissimilarity or "spread" in data, the larger the variability.

Variable Any observable, measurable element (or attribute).

Variance The average squared deviations about a mean of a distribution of values.

Verbatims Quotes from research participants that are used in research reports.

W

Willingness to Participate The respondent's inclination or disposition to share his or her thoughts.

Wireless Phone Survey The method of conducting a marketing survey in which the data are collected on standard wireless phones.

Word Association Test A projective technique in which the subject is presented with a list of words or short phrases, one at a time, and asked to respond with the first thoughts that comes to mind.

Wrong Mailing Address A type of nonresponse bias that can occur when the prospective respondent's mailing address is outdated or no longer active.

Wrong Telephone Number A type of nonresponse bias that can occur when the prospective respondent's telephone number either is no longer in service or is incorrect on the sample list.

Z

Zaltman Metaphor Elicitation Technique (ZMET) A visual research technique used in in-depth interviewing that encourages research participants to share emotional and subconscious reactions to a particular topic.

z-test (also referred to as z statistic) A hypothesis test procedure that uses the z distribution; z-tests are used when the sample size is larger than 30 subjects and the standard deviation is unknown.

Endnotes

CHAPTER 1

1. Allen Vartazarian, "Why Geofencing is the Next Mobile Research Must-Have," *Quirk's Marketing Research Review,* July 2013, p. 56.
2. Allen Vartazarian, "Advances in Geofencing," www. Quirks.com, December 29, 2014, accessed February 7, 2016.
3. Dan Seldin, Gina Pingitore, Lauri Alexander, and Chris Hilaire, "Capturing the Moment: A Feasibility Test of Geofencing and Mobile App Data Collection," www.casro.org, 2014, accessed February 7, 2016.
4. Allen Vartazarian, "7 Ways Geofencing is Transforming Mobile Marketing Research," *Instantly Blog,* blog.instant.ly, September 17, 2014, accessed February 4, 2016.
5. American Marketing Association, *Official Definition of Marketing Research,* 2009, www .marketingpower.com.
6. Dan Ariely, *Predictably Irrational: The Hidden Forces That Shape Our Decisions* (New York: HarperCollins, 2009).
7. "Shopper Insights for Consumer Product Manufacturers and Retailers," www.msri.com /industry-expertise/retail.aspx, accessed March 23, 2012.
8. David Burrows, "How to Use Ethnography for In-depth Consumer Insights," May 9, 2014, *Marketing Week*, accessed February 7, 2016.
9. Kurt Lewin, *Field Theory in Social Science: Select Theoretical Papers by Kurt Lewin* (London: Tavistock, 1952).
10. Sheena S. Iyangar and Mark R. Lepper, "When Choice Is Demotivating: Can One Desire Too Much of a Good Thing?," *Journal of Personality & Social Psychology* 79, no. 6 (December 2000), pp. 995–1006.
11. "Survey of Top Marketing Research Firms," *Advertising Age,* June 27, 1997.
12. "Fostering Professionalism," *Marketing Research,* Spring 1997.
13. Ibid.
14. Bureau of Labor Statistics, www .bls.gov/ooh/Business-and -Financial/Market-research -analysts.htm, *Occupational Outlook Handbook,* "Market Research Analysis," March 29, 2012.
15. Steve Smith, "You've Been De-Anonymized," Behavioral Insider, MediaPost.com, April 3, 2009, www.mediapost.com /publications/?fa=Articles .showArticle&art_aid=103467.
16. ICC/ESOMAR International Code on Social and Market Research, April 3, 2009, http:// www.esomar.org/index.php /codes-guidelines.html. Reprinted by permission of ESOMAR.

CHAPTER 2

1. Robert Kenneth Wade and William David Perreault, "The When/What Research Decision Guide," *Marketing Research: A Magazine and Application* 5, no. 3 (Summer 1993), pp. 24–27; and W. D. Perreault, "The Shifting Paradigm in Marketing Research," *Journal of the Academy of Marketing Science* 20, no. 4 (Fall 1992), p. 369.

CHAPTER 3

1. Mark Walsh, "Pew: 52% Use Mobile While Shopping," *Media-Post News*, January 30, 2012; Aaron Smith, "The Rise of In-Store Mobile Commerce,"*Pew Internet & American Life,* January 30, 2012, http://pewinternet.org /Reports/2012/In-store-mobile-commerce.aspx; Ned Potter, "'Showrooming': People Shopping in Stores, Then Researching by Cell Phone, says Pew Survey," *ABC World News,* January 31, 2012, http://abcnews.go.com /Technology/pew-internet -showrooming-half-cell-phone-use rs-research/story?id=15480115# .Ty2tIlx5GSo.
2. Sally Barr Ebest, Gerald J. Alred, Charles T. Brusaw, and Walter E. Oliu, *Writing from A to Z: An Easy-to-Use Reference Handbook,* 4th ed. (Boston: McGraw-Hill, 2002).
3. Ibid., pp. 44–46 and 54–56.
4. Mintel.com, "About Mintel, About Market Intelligence," www.Mintel.com/about-Mintel, accessed April 8, 2016.
5. GfK Custom Research North American, "GfK Roper Consulting," www.gfkamerica.com/practice _areas/roper_consulting/index .en.html, accessed April 14, 2009.
6. Youthbeat, www.crresearch .com, accessed April 24, 2009.
7. Nielsen Media Research, "Anytime, Anywhere Media Measurement," June 14, 2006, p. 1, a2m2.nielsenmedia.com.
8. David C. Tice, "Accurate Measurement & Media Hype: Placing Consumer Media Technologies in Context,"

www.knowledgenetworks.com
/accuracy/spring2007/tice.html,
accessed April 29, 2009; Jacqui
Cheng, "Report: DVR Adoption to
Surge Past 50 Percent by 2010,"
www.arstechnica.com
/gadgets/news/2007/report-dvr
-adoption-to-surge-past-50
-percent-by-2010.ars-, accessed
April 29, 2009; Dinesh C. Sharma,
"Study: DVR Adoption on the Rise,"
CNET News, http://news.cnet.com
/Study-DVR-adoption-on-the
-rise/2100-1041_3-5182035.html.

CHAPTER 4

1. Merlyn A. Griffiths and Mary
   C. Gilly, "Dibs! Customer Ter-
   ritorial Behaviors," *Journal of
   Services Research* 15, no. 2
   (2012), pp. 131–49; Bryant
   Simon, *Everything but the Cof-
   fee* (Berkeley: University of
   California Press, 2009); Irwin
   Altman, *The Environment and
   Social Behavior: Privacy, Per-
   sonal Space, Territory,
   Crowding* (Monterey, CA:
   Wadsworth, 1975).
2. Yvonne Lincoln and Egon G.
   Guba, "Introduction: Entering
   the Field of Qualitative
   Research," in *Handbook of
   Qualitative Research,* eds. Nor-
   man Denzin and Yvonne Lin-
   coln (Thousand Oaks, CA:
   Sage, 1994), pp. 1–17.
3. Gerald Zaltman, *How Customers
   Think: Essential Insights into the
   Mind of the Market* (Boston:
   Harvard Business School, 2003).
4. Melanie Wallendorf and Eric J.
   Arnould, "We Gather Together:
   The Consumption Rituals of
   Thanksgiving Day," *Journal of
   Consumer Research* 19, no. 1
   (1991), pp. 13–31.
5. Dennis W. Rook, "The Ritual
   Dimension of Consumer Behav-
   ior," *Journal of Consumer
   Research* 12, no. 3 (1985),
   pp. 251–64.
6. Alfred E. Goldman and Susan
   Schwartz McDonald, *The Group
   Depth Interview: Principles and
   Practice* (Englewood Cliffs, NJ:
   Prentice Hall, 1987), p. 161.

7. Mary Modahl, *Now or Never:
   How Companies Must Change
   Today to Win the Battle for
   Internet Consumers* (New York:
   HarperCollins, 2000).
8. Power Decisions Group, "Market Research Tools: Qualitative
   Depth Interviews," 2006,
   www.powerdecisions.com
   /qualitative-depth-interviews.cfm.
9. Harris Interactive, "Online
   Qualitative Research," 2006,
   www.harrisinteractive.com
   /services/qualitative.asp.
10. Mary F. Wolfinbarger, Mary
    C. Gilly and Hope Schau, "Lan-
    guage Usage and Socioemo-
    tional Content in Online vs.
    Offline Focus Groups," Winter
    American Marketing Associa-
    tion Conference, Austin, TX,
    February 17, 2008.
11. Online Focus Groups, "Video-
    Diary Qualitative Research Soft-
    ware," www.qualvu.com/video
    diary, accessed April 17, 2009.
12. Zaltman, *How Customers Think.*
13. Ibid.
14. Robert M. Schindler, "The Real
    Lesson of New Coke: The Value
    of Focus Groups for Predicting
    the Effects of Social Influence,"
    *Marketing Research: A Magazine
    of Management & Applications,*
    December 1992, pp. 22–27.
15. Ray Poynter, "Chatter Matters,"
    Marketing power.com, Fall
    2011, pp. 23–28.
16. Al Urbanski, "'Community'
    Research," Shopper Marketing,
    November 2009, Communispace
    .com, January 7, 2011.
17. Ibid.
18. Poynter, "Chatter Matters."
19. Stephen Baker, "Following the
    Luxury Chocolate Lover,"
    Bloomberg Businessweek, March
    25, 2009.
20. Julie Wi. Schlack, "Taking a Good
    Look at Yourself," November 7,
    2011, Research-live.com.
21. Poynter, "Chatter Matters."
22. Clifford Geertz, *Interpretation
    of Cultures* (New York: Basic
    Books, 2000).
23. Richard L. Celsi, Randall L. Rose,
    and Thomas W. Leigh, "An

Exploration of High-Risk Leisure
Consumption through Skydiving,"
The Journal of Consumer Research
20, no. 1 (1993), pp. 1–23.
24. Jennifer McFarland, "Margaret
    Mead Meets Consumer Fieldwork:
    The Consumer Anthropologist,"
    Harvard Management Update,
    September 24, 2001, http://hbswk
    .hbs.edu/archive/2514.html.
25. Arch G. Woodside and Elizabeth
    J. Wilson, "Case Study Research
    Methods for Theory Building,"
    *Journal of Business and Indus-
    trial Marketing* 18, no. 6/7
    (2003), pp. 493–508.
26. Gerald Zaltman, "Rethinking Mar-
    ket Research: Putting People Back
    In," *Journal of Marketing Research*
    34, no. 4 (1997), pp. 424–37.
27. Emily Eakin, "Penetrating the
    Mind by Metaphor," *The New
    York Times,* February 23, 2002,
    p. B11; also see Zaltman, *How
    Consumers Think.*
28. Eakin, "Penetrating the Mind by
    Metaphor."
29. Sam K. Hui, Eric T. Bradlow,
    and Peter S. Fader, "Testing
    Behavioral Hypotheses Using
    an Integrated Model of Grocery
    Store Shopping Path and Pur-
    chase Behavior," *Journal of
    Consumer Research* 36 (October
    2009), pp. 478–93.
30. Poynter, "Chatter Matters."
31. Poynter, "Chatter Matters."
32. David Murphy and Didier
    Truchot, "Moving Research For-
    ward," *RWConnect,* December 22,
    2011, Esomar.org.
33. Poynter, "Chatter Matters,".
34. Angela Hausman, "Listening
    Posts in Social Media: Discus-
    sion from Ask a Marketing
    Expert," January 16, 2011,
    www.hausmanmarketresearch
    .org.
35. Surinder Siama, "Listening
    Posts for Word-of-Mouth Mar-
    keting," *RWConnect,* January
    16, 2011, Esomar.org.
36. Peter Turney, "Thumbs Up or
    Thumbs Down? Semantic
    Orientation Applied to Unsuper-
    vised Classification of Reviews,"
    Proceedings of the Association for

Computational Linguistics, 2002, pp. 417–24; Bo Pang, Lillian Lee, and Shivakumar Vaithyanathan, "Thumbs Up? Sentiment Classification Using Machine Learning Techniques," Proceedings of the Conference on Empirical Methods in Natural Language Processing, 2002, pp. 79–86; Bo Pang and Lillian Lee, "Seeing Stars: Exploiting Class Relationships for Sentiment Categorization with Respect to Rating Scales," Proceedings of the Association for Computational Linguistics, 2005, pp. 115–24; Benjamin Snyder and Regina Barzilay, "Multiple Aspect Ranking Using the Good Grief Algorithm," Proceedings of the Joint Human Language Technology/North American Chapter of the ACL Conference, 2007, pp. 300–07.

37. Michelle de Haaff, "Sentiment Analysis, Hard But Worth It!" *CustomerThink,* March 11, 2010.

38. Tanzina Vega, "E*Trade's Baby Creates the Most Online Buzz," *The New York Times,* December 28, 2011.

39. "Social Media Monitoring Overview," www.g2crowd.com /categories/social-media -monitoring#before-you-buy, accessed March 6, 2016.

40. Robert V. Kozinets, "The Field behind the Screen: Using Netnography for Marketing Research in Online Communities," *Journal of Marketing Research* 39 (February 2002), p. 69.

41. Ibid., pp. 61–72.

CHAPTER 5

1. Terry L. Childers and Steven J. Skinner, "Toward a Conceptualization of Mail Survey Response Behavior," *Psychology and Marketing* 13 (March 1996), pp. 185–225.

2. Kathy E. Green, "Sociodemographic Factors and Mail Survey Response Rates," *Psychology and Marketing* 13 (March 1996), pp. 171–84.

3. Michael G. Dalecki, Thomas W. Ivento and Dan E. Moore, "The Effect of Multi-Wave Mailings on the External Validity of Mail Surveys," *Journal of Community Development Society* 19 (1988), pp. 51–70.

4. "Mobile Memoir: The Power of the Thumb," April 2004, Mobile Memoir LLC 2004, www.kinesissurvey.com /phonesolutions.html.

5. Leslie Townsend, "The Status of Wireless Survey Solutions: The Emerging Power of the Thumb," *Journal of Interactive Advertising* 6, no. 1 (2005), p. 52. http://jiad.org/vol6/no1 /townsend/index.htm.

6. "Mobile Memoir: The Power of the Thumb."

7. Townsend, "The Status of Wireless Survey Solutions."

8. "Consumers Ditching Landline Phones," *USA Today,* May 14, 2008, p. 1B.

9. Townsend, "The Status of Wireless Survey Solutions."

10. Kevin B. Wright, "Research Internet-Based Populations: Advantages and Disadvantages of Online Survey Research, Online Questionnaire Authoring Software Packages, and Web Survey Services," *Journal of Computer-Mediated Communication* 10, no. 3 (April 2005), http://jcmc.indiana.edu/vol10 /issue3/wright.html.

11. Maryann J. Thompson, "Market Researchers Embrace the Web," *The Industry Standard,* January 26, 1999, www.thestandard .com/article/0,1902,3274,00.html.

CHAPTER 6

1. Ian Paul, "Mobile Web Use Explodes," *PC World,* March 16, 2009.

2. Joseph F. Hair, Jr., Robert P. Bush, and David J. Ortinau, Marketing Research: A Practical Approach for the new Millennium (Burr Ridge, IL: Irwin/McGraw l-Hill 2000) p. 330. Actual prices of lists will vary according to the number and complexity of characteristics needed to define the target population.

3. Nielsen Online, www.nielsen -online.com/resources.jsp? section=pr_netv&nav=1, accessed July 27, 2009.

4. J. Michel Dennis, Larry Osborn, and Karen Semans, "Comparison Study: Early Adopter Attitudes and Online Behavior in Probability and Non-Probability Web Panels," at http://www.knowledgnetworks /accuarcy/spring2009; accessed on April 29, 2009.

CHAPTER 7

1. Kaylene C. Williams and Rosann L. Spiro, "Communication Style in the Salesperson-Customer Dyad," *Journal of Marketing Research* 12 (November 1985), pp. 434–42.

2. Kenneth C. Schneider, "Uniformed response rates in survey research: New evidence," Journal of Business Research 13 (2) (April 1985), pp. 153–62; also Del I. Hawkins and Kenneth A. Coney, "Uninformed Response Error in Survey Research," Journal of Marketing Research 18 (3) (August 1981), pp. 370–74; also at DOI: 10.2307/3150978.

3. Roobina Ohanian, "Construction and Validation of a Scale to Measure Celebrity Endorsers' Perceived Expertise, Trustworthiness, and Attractiveness," *Journal of Advertising* 19, no. 3 (1990), pp. 39–52; and Robert T. W. Wu and Susan M. Petroshius, "The Halo Effect in Store Image Management," *Journal of Academy of Marketing Science* 15 (1987), pp. 44–51.

4. Rajendar K. Garg, "The Influence of Positive and Negative Wording and Issues Involvement on Response to Likert Scales in Marketing Research," *Journal of the Marketing Research Society* 38, no. 3 (July 1996), pp. 235–46.

5. See www.burke.com and Amanda Prus and D. Randall Brandt, "Understanding Your Customers—What You Can Learn from a Customer Loyalty Index," *Marketing Tools* (July/August 1995), pp. 10–14.

CHAPTER 8

1. Barry J. Babin, Mitch Griffin, and Joseph F. Hair, Jr., "Heresies and sacred cows in scholarly marketing publications," *Journal of*

Business Research, 69 (8) (August 2016), pp. 3133–3138; also Christie M. Fuller, Marcia J. Simmering, Guclu Atinc, Yasemin Atinc, and Barry J. Babin, "Common method variance detection in business research," *Journal of Business Research* 69 (8) (August 2016), pp. 3192–3198.

2. Harman, H.H. (1976), *Modern Factor Analysis,* 3rd ed. (Chicago, IL: The University of Chicago Press, 1976).

3. Mario Callegaro, "Web Questionnaires: Tested Approaches from Knowledge Networks for the Online World," Spring 2008, www.knowledge networks.

CHAPTER 9

1. Diane M. Martin, John W. Schouten, and James McAlexander, "Claiming the THrottle: Multiple Femininities in a Hyper-Masculine Subculture," Consumption, Markets and Culture 9, no. 3 (2006), pp. 171–205; Sam Bendall, RidaApart.com, December 23, 2015, "Female Motorcycle Ownership Rise," accessed April 8, 2016.

2. Barney G. Glaser and Anselm Strauss, *The Discovery of Grounded Theory: Strategies for Qualitative Research* (Chicago, IL: Aldine, 1967); also see Anselm Strauss and Juliet M. Corbin, *Basics of Qualitative Research: Grounded Theory Procedures and Techniques* (Newbury Park, CA: Sage, 1990).

3. Alfred E. Goldman and Susan Schwartz McDonald, *The Group Depth Interview: Principles and Practice* (Englewood Cliffs, NJ: Prentice Hall, 1987), p. 161.

4. Matthew B. Miles and A. Michael Huberman, *Qualitative Data Analysis: An Expanded Sourcebook* (Thousand Oaks, CA: Sage, 1994).

5. Susan Spiggle, "Analysis and Interpretation of Qualitative Data in Consumer Research," *Journal of Consumer Research* 21, no. 3 (1994), pp. 491–503.

6. Mary Wolfinbarger and Mary Gilly, "Shopping Online for Freedom, Control and Fun," *California Management Review* 43, no. 2 (Winter 2001), pp. 34–55.

7. Mary C. Gilly and Mary Wolfinbarger, "Advertising's Internal Audience," *Journal of Marketing* 62 (January 1998), pp. 69–88.

8. Wolfinbarger and Gilly, "Shopping Online for Freedom, Control and Fun."

9. Richard L. Celsi, Randall L. Rose, and Thomas W. Leigh, "An Exploration of High-Risk Leisure Consumption through Skydiving," *Journal of Consumer Research* 20, no. 1 (1993), pp. 1–23.

10. Robin A. Coulter, Linda L. Price, and Lawrence Feick, "Rethinking the Origins of Involvement and Brand Commitment: Insights from Post-socialist Central Europe," *Journal of Consumer Research* 31, no. 2 (2003), pp. 151–69.

11. Hope J. Schau and Mary C. Gilly, "We Are What We Post? Self-Presentation in Personal Web Space," *Journal of Consumer Research* 30, no. 3 (2003), pp. 385–404; Albert M. Muniz and Hope J. Schau, "Religiosity in the Abandoned Apple Newton Brand Community," *Journal of Consumer Research* 31, no. 4 (2005), pp. 737–47; Mary Wolfinbarger, Mary Gilly, and Hope Schau, "A Portrait of Venturesomeness in a Later Adopting Segment," working paper 2006; Lisa Penaloza, "Atravesando Fronteras/Border Crossings: A Critical Ethnographic Exploration of the Consumer Acculturation of Mexican Immigrants," *Journal of Consumer Research* 21, no. 1 (1993), pp. 32–54.

12. Anselm Strauss and Juliet Corbin, *Basics of Qualitative Research: Grounded Theory Procedures and Techniques* (Beverly Hills, CA: Sage, 1990).

13. Goldman and McDonald, *The Group Depth Interview;* also see Miles and Huberman, *Qualitative Data Analysis.*

14. Miles and Huberman, *Qualitative Data Analysis.*

15. Alfred E. Goldman and Susan S. McDonald, *The Group Depth Interview* (Englewood Cliffs, NJ: Prentice Hall, 1987), p. 176.

16. Glaser and Strauss, *The Discovery of Grounded Theory;* also see Strauss and Corbin, *Basics of Qualitative Research.*

17. Yvonne S. Lincoln and Egon G. Guba, *Naturalistic Inquiry* (Beverly Hills, CA: Sage, 1985), p. 290.

18. Caroline Stenbecka, "Qualitative Research Requires Quality Concepts of Its Own," *Management Decision* 39, no. 7 (2001), pp. 551–55.

19. Glaser and Strauss, *The Discovery of Grounded Theory;* also see Strauss and Corbin, *Basics of Qualitative Research.*

20. Goldman and McDonald, *The Group Depth Interview.*

21. Ibid., p. 147.

22. Ibid., p. 175.

23. Rebekah Nathan, *My Freshman Year: What a Professor Learned by Becoming a Student* (Ithaca, NY: Cornell University Press, Sage House, 2005).

CHAPTER 10

1. Barry Deville, "The Data Assembly Challenge," *Marketing Research Magazine,* Fall/Winter 1995, p. 4.

CHAPTER 11

1. For a more detailed discussion of analysis of variance (ANOVA), see Gudmund R. Iversen and Helmut Norpoth, *Analysis of Variance* (Newbury Park, CA: Sage, 1987); and John A. Ingram and Joseph G. Monks, *Statistics for Business and Economics* (San Diego, CA: Harcourt Brace Jovanovich, 1989).

CHAPTER 13

1. David Corcoran, "Talking Numbers with Edward R. Tufte; Campaigning for the Charts That Teach," *The New York Times,* February 6, 2000, www.NYTimes.com.

2. Ibid.

Name Index

A

Alexander, Lauri, 400
Alred, Gerald J., 400
Altman, Irwin, 401
Ariely, Dan, 6
Arnould, Eric J., 401
Atinc, G., 403
Atinc, Y., 403

B

Babin, B., 403
Babin, Barry J., 402
Baker, Stephen, 401
Barzilay, Regina, 402
Bradlow, Eric T., 401
Brandt, D. Randall, 402
Brusaw, Charles T., 400
Burrows, David, 400

C

Callegaro, Mario, 403
Cardwell, Annette, 15
Carnahan, Ira, 15
Celsi, Richard L., 401, 403
Cheng, Jacqui, 401
Childers, Terry L., 402
Coney, K. A., 402
Corbin, Juliet M., 403
Corcoran, David, 403
Coulter, Robin A., 403
Craig, C. Samuel, 5

D

Dalecki, M. G., 402
de Haaff, Michelle, 402
Denzin, Norman, 401
Deville, Barry, 403
Dickerson, M., 403
Douglas, Susan P., 4, 5

E

Eakin, Emily, 401
Ebest, Sally Barr, 400
Enos, Lori, 10

F

Fader, Peter S., 401
Fastoso, Fernando, 5
Feick, Lawrence, 403
Fuller, C., 403

G

Garg, Rajendar K., 402
Geertz, Clifford, 401
Gilly, Mary C., 240, 244, 245, 401, 403
Glaser, Barney G., 403
Goldman, Alfred E., 401, 403
Green, Kathy E., 402
Griffin, Mitch, 402
Griffiths, Merlyn A., 401
Guba, Egon G., 401, 403

H

Hair, Joseph F., Jr., 402
Harman, H.H., 403
Harzing, Anne Wil, 5
Hausman, Angela, 401
Hawkins, Del I., 402
Hilaire, Chris, 400
Hoffman, Scott, 37
Huberman, A. Michael, 403
Hui, Sam K., 401

I

Ilvento, T. W., 402
Iversen, Gudmund R., 403
Iyangar, Sheena S., 400

K

Kozinets, Robert V., 99, 402

L

Lee, Lillian, 402
Leigh, Thomas W., 401, 403
Lepper, Mark R., 400
Lewin, Kurt, 9, 400
Lincoln, Yvonne, 401
Lincoln, Yvonne S., 403
Lopez, Ricardo, 100

M

Mandese, Joe, 37
Martin, Diane M., 403
McAlexander, James, 403
McDonald, Susan Schwartz, 401, 403
McFarland, Jennifer, 401
Miles, Matthew B., 403
Modahl, Mary, 401
Moore, D. E., 402
Muniz, Albert M., 403
Murphy, David, 401

N

Nathan, Rebekah, 403
Norpoth, Helmut, 403

O

Ohanian, Roobina, 402
Oliu, Walter E., 400

P

Pang, Bo, 402
Paul, Ian, 402
Penaloza, Lisa, 403
Perreault, W. D., 400
Petroshius, Susan M., 402
Pingitore, Gina, 400
Potter, Ned, 400
Poynter, Ray, 401
Price, Linda L., 403
Prus, Amanda, 402

R

Regan, Keith, 10
Reiche, B. Sebastian, 5
Romero, Donna, 91
Rook, Dennis W., 401
Rose, Randall L., 401, 403

S

Schau, Hope J., 403
Schindler, Robert M., 401
Schlack, Julie Wi, 401
Schneider, K. C., 402

Schouten, John W., 403
Schwab, Charles, 29
Seldin, Dan, 400
Sharma, Dinesh C., 401
Shulby, Bill, 25
Siama, Surinder, 401
Simon, Bryant, 401
Skinner, Steven J., 402
Smith, Steve, 400
Snyder, Benjamin, 402
Spiggle, Susan, 403
Spiro, Rosann L., 402
Stenbecka, Caroline, 403
Strauss, Anselm, 403

T

Thompson, Maryann J., 402
Tice, David C., 400

Townsend, Leslie, 402
Truchot, Didier, 401
Tufte, Edward R., 403
Turney, Peter, 401

U

Urbanski, Al, 401

V

Vaithyanathan, Shivakumar, 402
Vartazarian, Allen, 400
Vega, Tanzina, 402

W

Wade, R. K., 400
Wade, Will, 15
Wallendorf, Melanie, 401
Walsh, Mark, 400

Whitelock, Jeryl, 5
Williams, Kaylene C., 402
Wilson, Elizabeth J., 401
Wind, Yoram, 4, 5
Wolfinbarger, Mary, 240, 244, 245, 401, 403
Wolverton, Troy, 10
Woodside, Arch G., 401
Wright, Kevin B., 402
Wu, Robert T. W., 402

Z

Zaltman, Gerald, 93, 401

Subject Index

A

ABI/Inform, 54, 56
Ability to participate, 121
Abstract constructs, 162
Accuracy, of secondary data, 52
Acme Rent-A-Car, 15
AC Nielsen, 11, 95
Adoption and diffusion theory, 9
Advertising
  online, 37
Advertising Age study, 10
Africa, emerging market in, 4
Agree-Disagree scales, 161
Alternative hypothesis, 283
  defined, 68
Amazon.com, 8, 10
Ambiguous questions, 182
American Airlines, 136
American Bank, Baton Rouge study, 193
American Business Lists, Inc., 138
American Express, 77
American Marketing Association (AMA)
  code of ethics, 16
  marketing research, defined, 5
Analysis of variance (ANOVA),
  297–300
  n-Way. *See* n-Way ANOVA
  one-way, 297, 298
  post-hoc, 300
  reporting, 367–370
  statistical significance in, 297–298
Analytics (application of statistics), 8
ANOVA. *See* Analysis of variance
  (ANOVA)
Appendix, research report, 374
Apple, 77, 135
Arbitron Ratings, 11
Area sampling, 145
Attitude scales, 173–177
  behavioral intention scale, 176–177
  Likert scale, 173–174
  semantic differential scale, 174–176

B

Bad questions, 197–198
Balanced scale, 170
Bank of America, 26

Bar charts, 362–364
  and ANOVA reporting, 367–370
  reporting crosstabs, 366–367
  and *t*-test reporting, 367–370
Behavior
  purchase, scanner data and, 247
  scales used to measure, 173–177
Behavioral intention scale, 176–177
Behavioral targeting, 8
Believability, 356
Benefit and lifestyle studies, 9
Benito Advertising, 42
Beta coefficient, 333–334
  defined, 333
Between-group variance, 297
Bias
  questions and, 198
  response order, 203
  and secondary data evaluation, 52–53
Big data, 4
Bing, 56
Bivariate regression analysis, 328
  defined, 328
  SPSS application, 330–332
Bivariate statistical tests, 287–288
"Black-box" methodologies, 12–13
Blogs, 56
Bookmarking tools, 57
BP (British Petroleum), 90
Brainstorming, 65
Branded "black-box" methodologies, 13
Branding, 7
Brand management, 317–318
Brick-and-mortar stores, 49–50
Budget, survey research method selection
  and, 118
Bulletin board format, 84
Burke, Inc.
  customer loyalty prediction, 159–160
  Secure Customer Index, 184–185
Burke Market Research, 11
Buzz marketing, 56

C

Call records, 211
Careers, in marketing research, 22–23
Carolina Consulting Company, 25

Carter, Dan, 25
Case studies
  defined, 91
  Deli Depot, 267–270
  early adopters of technology, 377–380
  Lee Apparel Company, test marketing,
    128–129
  Santa Fe Grill Mexican Restaurant. *See*
    Santa Fe Grill Mexican Restaurant
    case study
Catalog of Government Publications, 58
Causal hypotheses, 65
Causal research, 122–127. *See also*
  Survey research methods
  defined, 37, 122
  descriptive research *vs.,* 122–123
  experimentation in, 123–124
  objective of, 77
  value of, 108
Cell phones. *See* Mobile phones
Census
  data, 57–58
  defined, 38, 136
Central limit theorem (CLT), 138–139
Charts, preparation of, 281
Children's Wish Foundation, 147
Chi-square analysis, 290–293
  defined, 291
  SPSS application, 292–293
  value calculation, 291–292
ClickZ.com, 56
Client/research buyer
  ethical issues with, 12
  unethical activities of, 15
Closed-ended questions, 195
Cluster sampling
  advantages, 146
  area sampling, 145
  defined, 145
  disadvantages, 146
Coca-Cola, 26, 77, 89, 160
Codes
  defined, 224
Code sheet, 224, 225
Codes of ethics, 16. *See also* Ethics
Coding, 256–259
  defined, 256

example, 226
selective, 227–228
Coefficient alpha, 168
Coefficient of determination, 325
Commercial (syndicated) data. *See*
 Syndicated data
Common methods variance (CMV),
 203–205
Communispace, 100
Comparative rating scale
 constant-sum scales, 178, 179
 defined, 177
 examples of, 179
 rank-order scales, 178
Completion time frame, survey research
 method selection and, 118
Complex questions, 183
Computer-aided telephone interviewing
 (CATI), 5, 113–114
ComScore, 135
Concept testing, 7
Conceptualization, 66
Conceptual Model
 development of, 63–67
 hypotheses and. *See* Hypothesis
Conclusion drawing, in qualitative research,
 231–235
Conclusions, research report, 372–373
Consistency, of secondary data, 52
Constant-sum scales, 178, 179
Construct development, 161–163
Constructs
 abstract, 162
 defined, 63, 161
 development of, 161–163
 in hypotheses, 66
 list of, 34
 marketing maven, 63, 64
Consumer culture/subculture, 4, 6
Consumer panels, 60–61
Consumer privacy, data collection tools and, 4
Consumer Report on Eating Share Trends
 (CREST), 60
Contact records, 211
Content analysis, 89
Content validity, 169
Control variables, 124
Convenience sampling
 advantages, 146
 defined, 146
 disadvantages, 146
Convergent validity, 169
Cookies, computer, 26
Correlation analysis, 322–327
 influence of measurement scales on,
 326–327
 Pearson correlation coefficient, 322–325
Cosmetics, post-socialist European women's
 involvement with, 234–235

Covariation, 319–322
 defined, 319
 scatter diagram, 319
 and variable relationships, 319–322
Cover letter
 defined, 208
 guidelines for developing, 208
 usage, 209
Creative and Response Research
 Services, 61
Credibility
 cross-researcher reliability, 232
 defined, 233, 356
 emic validity, 232
 in qualitative research, 231–235
 of secondary data, 52
 triangulation, 233, 235
Critical thinking, and marketing
 research, 357
Cross-researcher reliability, 232
Cross-tabulation, 261, 288–290
Cultural differences, marketing research
 and, 4
Curbstoning, 13, 249
Curvilinear relationship, 318, 321
Customer loyalty
 Santa Fe Grill Mexican Restaurant,
 159–160
Customer privacy, ethical issues with, 15
Customer satisfaction surveys, 36
Customized research firms, 11

D

Data
 census, 57–58
 completeness of, 118–119
 from data warehouses, 258
 deanonymizing, 15
 "found," 79
 generalizability, 119
 interpretation, and knowledge creation, 40
 missing, 259–261
 organizing, 261
 precision, 119
 preparation. *See* Data preparation
 primary. *See* Primary data
 scanner, and purchase behavior, 247
 secondary. *See* Secondary data
 syndicated, 59–60
 transformation into knowledge, 30–31
 visual display of, 353
Data analysis
 bar charts. *See* Bar charts
 components of, 224
 data reduction. *See* Data reduction
 pie charts, 364–365
 qualitative. *See* Qualitative data analysis
 quantitative. *See* Quantitative data analysis
 reporting frequencies, 361–362

in research design phase, 39
Data coding. *See* Coding
Data collection
 consumer panels, 60–61
 interviewer instructions, 211
 qualitative data. *See* Qualitative data
 collection methods
 questionnaire design, 194
 in research design phase, 39
 screening questions, 211
 supervisor instructions, 210
 tools. *See* Data collection tools
 wireless phone survey, 114–115
Data collection tools
 challenges with digital technology, 4
 consumer privacy and, 4
Data display, 230–231
 types of, 231
Data editing. *See* Editing, data
Data entry, 259–261
 defined, 259
 error detection, 259
 missing data, 259–261
 organizing data, 261
Data mining, 317–318
Data preparation, 248–249
 coding, 256–259
 data entry, 259–261
 editing, 251–255
 validation, 249–251
Data reduction, 223–230
 categorization, 224, 226–227
 comparison, 227
 defined, 224
 integration, 227
 iteration, 228
 negative case analysis, 228
 tabulation, 228–230
Data tabulation. *See* Tabulation, in
 qualitative data analysis; Tabulation, in
 quantitative data analysis
Data validation, 249–251
 completeness, 250
 courtesy, 250
 curbstoning, 249
 defined, 249
 fraud, 250
 procedure, 250
 process of, 250–251
 screening, 250
Data warehouses, data from, 258
Deanonymizing data, 15
Debriefing analysis, 89
Defined target population, 137
Dell Computers, 26
Dependent variables
 defined, 63, 122
Depth interviews. *See* In-depth interviews (IDI)
Descriptive hypotheses, 64

Descriptive research, 36–37. *See also* Survey
    research methods
    causal research *vs.,* 122–123
    defined, 36
    objective of, 77
    and surveys. *See* Surveys
    value of, 108
Descriptive statistics, 264–266. *See also*
    Cross-tabulation; One-way tabulation
Desk research, 50. *See also* Secondary data
Discriminant validity, 169
Discriminatory power, 170
Disproportionately stratified sampling, 143
Distribution
    marketing research applied to, 7–8
Diversity, respondent, 120
Do-it-yourself (DIY) research, 6
Double-barreled questions, 181–182, 197
Doubleclick, 14
Double negative question, 183
Drop-off survey, 116
DVRs, 62

E
EasyJet, 90
Editing, data
    and data preparation, 251–255
    defined, 251
Emic validity, 232
Equivalent form reliability technique, 168
Error detection, 259
Errors
    nonsampling, 110
    sampling, 109–110, 139
ESOMAR, 16
E-tailers/e-tailing, 8
E-tailing, 10
Ethics, 12–16
    branded "black-box" methodologies, 13
    client/research user, unethical activities
        of, 15
    codes of ethics, 16
    curbstoning, 13
    data privacy, 15
    deanonymizing data, 15
    in general business practices, 12–13
    and professional standards, 13–14
    respondent abuse, 14–15
    sources of issues, 12
    unethical activities by respondents, 16
Ethnography, 9
    defined, 91
    nonparticipant observation, 91
    participant observation, 91
Executive summary, 358–359
    defined, 358
    purpose of, 358
Experimental research. *See also* Causal
    research

test marketing. *See* Test marketing
    types of, 126
    validity concerns with, 124–126
    variables, 123, 124
Experiments
    defined, 122
    field, 127
    laboratory, 127
Exploratory research
    defined, 36
    focus group interviews, 82–89
    in-depth interviews, 81–82
    netnography, 99
    objectives, 36
    observation methods. *See* Observation
        methods
    qualitative research methods, 76–93
    sentence completion tests, 93
    word association tests, 92
    Zaltman Metaphor Elicitation
        Technique, 93
External research providers, 10–11
External secondary data, 54–62
    defined, 50
    government sources, 57–58
    popular sources, 54, 56–57
    scholarly sources, 57
    syndicated data, 59–60
External validity, 125, 126
Extraneous variables, 124

F
Facebook, 97
Facebook, impact on data collection, 4
Face validity, 169
Fair Isaac & Co., 273
Federal Express, marketing careers at,
    22–23
Field experiments, 127
Final research report, 41
Focus group interviews, 82–89
    advantages of, 89
    analyzing results, 89
    bulletin board format, 84
    conducting discussions, 87–88
    content analysis, 89
    debriefing analysis, 89
    groupthink, 89
    locations, 86
    number of participants, 84
    participants, 85–86
    phases for conducting, 84–89
    planning phase, 85–86
    purposive sampling, 86
    size of, 86
    stratified purposive sample, 86
    theoretical sampling, 86
Focus group moderator
    defined, 87

guide for, 87
    in main session, 88
Focus group research, 5. *See also* Focus
    group interviews
    defined, 82
Follow-up tests, 299
Forced-choice scale, 171
Ford Motor Company, 211
Format, research report, 357–374
    appendix, 374
    conclusions and recommendations, 372–373
    data analysis and findings, 361–372
    executive summary, 358–359
    introduction, 359–360
    limitations, 374
    methods-and-procedures section, 360
    table of contents, 358
    title page, 358
Frequency distribution, 172
Frugging, 14
F-test, 297

G
Gatekeeper technologies, 26
Generalizable data, 119
Geofencing, 3
Gfk Research, 4
GfK Roper Consulting, 61
Globalization, challenges to marketing
    research, 26
Godiva Chocolates, 90
Google, 8, 56
    Android-based G1, 135
Google Scholar, 57, 69
Government sources, external secondary
    data, 57–58
GPS system, 15
Graphic rating scales, 177–178
Grounded theory, 222
Group depth interview. *See* Focus group
    interviews
Groupthink, 89

H
Harmon One Factor test, 204, 205
Harris Interactive, 5
Heteroskedasticity, 335
Hibernia National Bank, 163
Hispanics, and qualitative research, 100
The Home Depot, 90
Homoskedasticity, 335
Hypothesis
    alternative. *See* Alternative hypothesis
    causal, 65
    constructs in, 66
    defined, 67
    descriptive, 64
    development of, 281–283
    formulating, 64

null. *See* Null hypothesis
projective, 93
testing. *See* Hypothesis testing
Hypothesis testing, 67–68
   parameter, 68
   sample statistic, 68

I

IBM, 10, 26
Iceberg principle, 32, 33
Image assessment surveys, 36
Image positioning, Remington's Steak
   House, 306–312
Incidence rate, 120–121
Independent samples
   defined, 294
   related samples *vs.,* 293–294
   t-test, 295–296
Independent variables
   defined, 63, 122
In-depth interviews (IDI), 75, 76
   advantages of, 82
   characteristic of, 82
   defined, 81
   as qualitative data collection method,
      81–82
   skills required for conducting, 82
   steps in conducting, 82, 83
Information overload theory, 9
Information research process
   defined, 27
   need for, 27–29
   overview, 29–31
   phases of. *See* Phases, of research process
   primary data sources, 26
   sampling as part of, 136–137
   scientific method, 30
   secondary data sources, 26
   transforming data into knowledge, 30–31
   value of measurement in, 160
In-home interview, 111
Inner model, 342
Integration, 227
Interaction effect, 301
Interactive Advertising Bureau (IAB), 51, 57
Internal consistency, scale reliability, 168
Internal research providers, 10
Internal secondary data, 54
   defined, 50
   list of, 55
Internal validity, 125
International marketing research, challenges
   of, 4–5
Internet
   deanonymizing data, 15
   geofencing, 3
   mobile searches, 135–136
   netnography, 99
   online surveys, 116–118

search engine marketing, 135
social media monitoring, 97–98
Internet marketing research, 12
Internet surveys. *See* Online surveys
Interpersonal communication skills, for in-
   depth interview, 82
Interpretive skills, for in-depth
   interview, 82
Interval scales
   defined, 165
   examples of, 166
   overview, 165–166
Interviewer instructions, 211
Interviews
   computer-assisted telephone, 5, 113–114
   curbstoning, 13
   in-depth. *See* In-depth interviews (IDI)
   in-home, 111
   mall-intercept, 112
   subject debriefing, 14
   sugging/frugging, 14
Introduction, research report, 359–360
Introductory section, questionnaires, 203
iPhone, 135
Iteration, 228

J

J. D. Power and Associates, 61, 77, 137
Johnson Properties, Inc., 42
Judgment sampling, 147

K

KISS (Keep It Simple and Short) test, 207
Knowledge
   creation, data interpretation and, 40
   defined, 30
   transforming data into, 30
Knowledge level, respondents, 121–122
Kodak, 10
Kraft Foods, 10, 90

L

Laboratory (lab) experiments, 126–127
Latin America, emerging market in, 4
Leading/loaded questions, 197
Leading question, 182
Least squares procedure, 329
Lee Apparel Company, 128–129
Lexus/Nexus, 54, 56
Likert scale, 117, 173–174
Limitations, research report, 374
Linear relationship
   defined, 318
Listening platform/post, 98
Listening skills, for in-depth interview, 82
Literature reviews, 34–35
   conducting, 51–54
   constructs and, 63–64
   defined, 51

Santa Fe Grill Mexican Restaurant case
   study, 69
secondary data sources, evaluation of,
   51–53
secondary research for, 62–63
value of, 50–51
Loaded question, 182
Loitering time, 3
Lotame Solutions, Inc., 36, 37
Lowe's Home Improvement, Inc., 35

M

Magnum Hotel
   loyalty program, 107–108
   Preferred Guest Card Program, 42–44
Mail panel survey, 116
Mail surveys, 116
Mall-intercept interview, 112
Mapping, perceptual. *See* Perceptual
   mapping
Marketing blogs, 56
Marketing maven construct, 63, 64
Marketing mix variables, marketing research
   and, 6–9
Marketing research
   critical thinking and, 357
   defined, 5
   distribution decisions, 7–8
   ethics in. *See* Ethics
   and four Ps, 6
   growing complexity of, 4–5
   industry. *See* Marketing research industry
   international, 4–5
   and marketing mix variables, 6–9
   pricing decisions, 8
   process. *See* Marketing research process
   promotional decisions, 8
   questionnaires in. *See* Questionnaires
   role and value of, 6–10
   role of secondary data in, 50–51
   sampling in. *See* Sample/sampling
   situations when not needed, 28
Marketing Research Association (MRA), 15
Marketing researchers, management
   decision makers *vs.,* 28
Marketing research ethics. *See* Ethics
Marketing research industry
   careers in, 22–23
   changing skills and, 11
   types of, 10–11
Marketing research process, 5. *See*
   Information research process
   changing view of, 26–27
   phases of. *See* Phases, of research process
   secondary data and, 53–54
Marketing research report. *See* Research report
Marketing Research Society, 16
Marketing research tools, 6
Marketing Resource Group (MRG), 43, 107

Marketing Science Institute (MSI.org), 9
Marketing theory
  examples of, 9
Market segmentation research, 9
Marriott Hotels, 26
Mazda Motor Corporation, 137
McDonald's, 26, 281–282
Mean, 274–275
  analysis of variance. *See* Analysis of
    variance (ANOVA)
  comparing means, 293–297
  defined, 274
  n-Way ANOVA, 303–304
Measurement. *See also* Constructs; Scale
    measurement
  defined, 160
  process, overview of, 160–161
  value in information research, 160
Measures of central tendency, 172, 274–277
  mean. *See* Mean
  median. *See* Median
  mode. *See* Mode
  SPSS applications, 276
Measures of dispersion, 172, 277–280
  range, 277–278
  SPSS applications to calculate, 278–279
  standard deviation, 278–279
  variance, 279
Median
  defined, 275
Media panels, 61
Member checking, 222
Memoing, 228
Mercedes-Benz, 87
Methods-and-procedures section, 360
Middle East, emerging market in, 4
Mintel, 61
Missing data, 259–261
Mobile phones. *See also* Wireless phone
    survey
  used while shopping, 49–50
  with web interactions, 135–136
Mode, 275–276
  defined, 275
Model F statistic, 334
Moderators. *See* Focus group moderator
Moderator's guide, 87
MPC Consulting Group, 191
Multicollinearity, 338
Multiple-item scale, 180
Multiple regression analysis, 333–338
  assumptions, 335
  beta coefficient, 333–334
  defined, 333
  SPSS application, 335–338
  statistical significance, 334
  substantive significance, 334
Multisource sampling, 143
Mystery shopping, 5

N

NAICS (North American Industry
    Classification System) codes, 59
Namestomers, 7, 11
Narrative inquiry, 75
National Eating Trends (NET), 60
National Hardwood Lumber Association, 53
Natural language processing (NLP), 98
Negative case analysis, 228
Negative relationship
  covariation, 320, 321
  defined, 65
Netnography, 99
Neuromarketing, 4
The New York Times, 56
NFO (National Family Opinion), 26
Nominal scales
  defined, 164
  examples of, 164
Noncomparative rating scales
  defined, 177
  graphic rating scales, 177–178
Nonforced-choice scale, 171
Nonparticipant observation, 91
Nonprobability sample size, 150
Nonprobability sampling
  convenience sampling, 146
  defined, 140
  judgment sampling, 147
  quota sampling, 147
  in research design development, 38
  snowball sampling, 147
Nonresponse error, 110
Nonsampling errors, 110, 139–140
  defined, 139
  nonresponse error, 110
  respondent errors, 110
  response error, 110
Normal curve, 335
North American Industry Classification
    System (NAICS) codes, 59
Novartis, 90
NPD Group, 60
Null hypothesis, 283
  for ANOVA, 297
  defined, 68
  for Pearson correlation coefficient, 322
n-Way ANOVA, 300–305
  defined, 300
  interaction effect, 301
  means, 303–304
  perceptual mapping, 304–305
  SPSS application, 301–302

O

Objectives, research. *See* Research objectives
Observation methods, 93–99
  benefits of, 97
  characteristics of, 94, 95

limitations of, 97
  listening platform/post, 98
  selection of, 96–97
  social media monitoring, 97–98
  types of, 94–96
Observation research
  defined, 94
  methods. *See* Observation methods
  overview, 93–94
One-on-one interviews. *See* In-depth
    interviews; In-depth interviews (IDI)
One-way ANOVA, 297, 298
One-way tabulation, 261–264
Online focus groups, 84
  bulletin board format, 84
  disadvantage of, 84
Online research
  retailing research, 8
Online surveys, 116–118
  considerations, 205–207
  defined, 116
  propensity scoring, 118
Open-ended questions
  responses to, 255
  unstructured questions as, 195
Opinion mining, 98
Optimal allocation sampling, 143
Oral presentation, guidelines for preparing,
    375–376
Ordinal scales
  defined, 164
  examples of, 165
  overview, 164–165
Ordinary least squares, 330
Outer model, 342

P

Paired sample, 294
  t-test, 296
Parameter, 68
Participant observation, 91
Participants, in focus group, 85–86
PathTracker, 96
Pearson correlation coefficient, 322–325
Peer review, 235
People for the Ethical Treatment of Animals
    (PETA), 53
Perceptual mapping, 304–305
  applications in marketing research, 305
  defined, 7
Person-administered survey methods
  advantages of, 112
  defined, 111
  disadvantages of, 112
  in-home interview, 111
  mall-intercept interview, 112
Petesting, questionnaires, 39
Pew American and Internet Life, 49
Phases, of research process, 29–41

communicate results, 40–41
research design, selection of. *See*
    Research design
research problem, determination of,
    31–36. *See also* Research problem
    determination
Phone surveys. *See* Telephone-administered
    surveys
Pie charts, 364–365
Pilot studies, 192–193, 207
Place, marketing research applied to, 6, 7–8
PlayStation Underground, 27
Population
    defined, 137
    defined target. *See* Defined target population
    in sampling theory, 137
Population parameter, 283
Population variance, 148
Positioning, 7
Positive relationships, 65
Precision
    data, 119
    defined, 148
Predictably Irrational (Ariely), 6
Presentation, research report, 375–376
    oral, guidelines for preparing, 375–376
    visual, guidelines for preparing, 376
Pretesting questionnaires, 193, 207
Price/pricing
    e-tailing, 10
    marketing research applied to, 6, 8
    unethical, 13
Primary data
    defined, 26
    qualitative research, 76
    research design selection, 37–38
Privacy issues
    ethical challenges, 15
    gatekeeper technologies and, 26
Private communities, 89–90
Probability sample size, 148–150
Probability sampling
    cluster sampling, 145–146
    defined, 140
    in research design development, 38
    simple random sampling, 140–141
    stratified random sampling, 143–145
    systematic random sampling, 141–142
Procter & Gamble (P&G), 10, 90, 317–318
Product, marketing research applied to, 6–7
Product dissatisfaction, 239–240
Product testing, 7
Projective hypothesis, 93
Projective techniques
    defined, 92
    disadvantage of, 92
    sentence completion tests, 93
    word association tests, 92
    Zaltman Metaphor Elicitation Technique, 93

Project Planet, 5
Promotion, marketing research applied to, 6, 8
Propensity scoring, 118
Proportionately stratified sampling, 143
Purposed communities, 89
Purposive sampling, 86

Q
Quaker Oats, 120
Qualitative data analysis
    categorization, 224, 226–227
    code sheet, 224
    conclusion drawing/verification,
        231–235
    data display, 230–231
    grounded theory, 222
    member checking, 222
    nature of, 222
    process of, 223–235
    quantitative analysis *vs.*, 222–223
    research reports. *See* Research report, in
        qualitative research
    triangulation, 233, 235
Qualitative data collection methods
    focus group interviews, 82–89
    in-depth interviews, 81–82
Qualitative research, 4. *See also* Exploratory
        research
    advantages of, 80
    case study. *See* Case studies
    credibility in, 231–235
    defined, 79
    disadvantages of, 80
    ethnography, 91
    Hispanics and, 100
    overview of, 78–80
    private communities, 89–90
    and product dissatisfaction, 239–240
    projective techniques, 92–93
    purposed communities, 89
    quantitative research *vs.*, 78
    samples in, 38
    value of, 76–77
QualKote Manufacturing, 345–347
Qualtrics, 117
QualVu, 84
Quantitative data analysis. *See also*
        Statistical analysis
    coding, 256–259
    data entry, 259–261
    data preparation, 248–249
    data tabulation, 261–266
    Deli Depot examples, 267–270
    editing, 251–255
    grounded theory, 222
    qualitative data analysis *vs.*, 222–223
    validation, 249–251
Quantitative research, 4. *See also*
        Quantitative data analysis

defined, 77
goals of, 78
listening platform/post, 98
opinion mining, 98
overview of, 77–78
qualitative research *vs.*, 78
sentiment analysis, 98
social media monitoring, 97–98
Questionnaire design, 39, 193–207
    American Bank example, 193–207
    bad questions in, 197–198
    call records, 211
    common methods variance, 203–205
    considerations in, 205
    cover letter, 208, 209
    data collection methods, 194
    evaluating, 203–207
    example of banking survey, 199–202
    implementation of survey, 207
    online survey considerations, 205–207
    question/scale format, 197–198, 203
    quotas, 211
    research questions section, 203
    response order bias, 203
    screening questions, 203
    sensitive questions in, 195
    skip questions, 198
    steps in, 193
Questionnaires
    defined, 192
    Deli Depot example, 269–270
    design. *See* Questionnaire design
    electronic products opinion survey,
        378–379
    introductory section, 203
    petesting, 39
    pilot study, 192–193
    pretesting, 193
    samples and, 136–137
    "smart," 204
    wording of, 195, 196–197
Questions
    ambiguous, 182
    bad, 197–198
    and bias, 198
    closed-ended, 195
    complex, 183
    double-barreled, 181–182, 197
    double negative, 183
    leading, 182
    leading/loaded, 197
    loaded, 182
    open-ended. *See* Open-ended questions
    screening, 203, 211
    sensitive, 195
    skip, 198
    structured, 195, 196
    unanswerable, 197
    unstructured, 195

Quotas, 211
Quota sampling, 147

R

Range, 277–278
Rank-order scales, 179
Ratio scales
    defined, 166
    examples of, 167
    overview, 166
Recommendations, research report, 372–373
Recursive relationship, 227
Referral sampling, 147
Regression analysis, 327–338
    beta coefficient, 333–334
    bivariate, 328
    fundamentals of, 328–330
    least squares procedure, 329
    multiple. *See* Multiple regression analysis
    ordinary least squares, 330
    regression coefficients, 330
    straight line relationship, 329
    structural modeling, 339–344
    unexplained variance, 329
Regression coefficients
    beta coefficient, 333–334
    defined, 330
    statistical significance of, 332–333
Related samples
    defined, 294
    independent samples *vs.,* 293–294
Relationships
    and conceptualization, 66
    correlation analysis, 322–327
    curvilinear, 318, 321
    defined, 63
    linear, 318
    negative. *See* Negative relationship
    positive, 65
    regression analysis, 327–338
    strength of association, 318
    between variables, 318–319
Reliability
    cross-researcher, 232
    scale measurement, 167–168
Remington's Steak House, 306–312
Research design
    causal, 37
    data analysis, 39
    data collection/preparation, 39
    data sources, 37–38
    descriptive, 36–37
    execution of, 39–40
    exploratory, 36
    measurement issues and scales, 38–39
    overview of, 77
    sampling design/size, 38
    selection of, 36–39
Research firms, ethical issues with, 13

Research objectives
    causal research, 77
    descriptive research, 77
    questionnaire development, 193–194
Research problem determination, 31–36
    iceberg principle, 32, 33
    identify and separate out symptoms, 32–33
    information needs, identification/clarification, 32–34
    information value, 36
    relevant variables, determination of, 34
    research objectives, specification, 36
    research questions, 34–35
    research request, purpose of, 32
    situation analysis, 32
    unit of analysis, determination of, 34
Research proposal, 10
    defined, 41
    development of, 41
    example, 42–44
    outline of, 40
Research questions, defining, 34–35
Research questions section, 203
Research report
    conclusions, 237
    data/findings, analysis of, 236–237
    format of. *See* Format, research report
    introductory portion of, 236
    objectives, 354–357
    presentation of. *See* Presentation, research report
    problems in preparing, 374–375
    recommendations, 237
    value of, 354
    writing, 235–237
Respondent errors, 110
Respondents
    ability to participate, 121
    abuse of, 14–15
    characteristics, 120–122
    diversity of, 120
    ethical issues with, 12
    incidence rate, 120–121
    knowledge level, 121–122
    participation, 121–122
    unethical activities by, 16
    willingness to participate, 121
Response error, 110
Response order bias, 203
Retail Diagnostics Inc., 11
Retailing research, 8
Rocking-chair interviewing, 13

S

Sample/sampling, 4
    defined, 38, 136
    design, development of, 38
    errors, 109–110

independent *vs.* related, 293–294
    nonprobability sampling. *See* Nonprobability sampling
    paired, 294
    as part of research process, 136–137
    plans. *See* Sampling plans
    probability. *See* Probability sampling
    purposive, 86
    quality assessment tools, 139–140
    and questionnaires design, 136–137
    size. *See* Sample size
    SPSS to select, 151
    stratified purposive, 86
    theoretical, 86
    theory. *See* Sampling theory
    value of, 136–137
Sample size
    determination, 148–151
    nonprobability, 150
    population variance, 148
    probability, 148–150
    sampling from small population, 150
Sample statistic
    defined, 68
Sampling error, 109–110
    defined, 139
Sampling frame
    defined, 138
    sources of, 138
Sampling plans
    defined, 152
    probability, 38
    steps in developing, 152–153
Sampling theory, 137–140
    central limit theorem, 138–139
    factors underlying, 138–139
    population, 137
    sampling frame, 138
    terminology, 137
Sampling units
    defined, 137
Santa Fe Grill Mexican Restaurant case study, 17, 18–19
    customer loyalty, 159–160
    customers surveys, 19, 139
    database, splitting, 276
    employee questionnaire, 252–254
    literature review, 69
    n-Way ANOVA results, 302
    proposed variables, 92
    qualitative research, usage of, 238
    questionnaire design, 212–216
    and research questions/hypotheses development, 67
    sampling plan development, 154
    and secondary data usage, 58
    systematic random sample for, 142
Scale descriptors
    balanced scale, 170

defined, 163
discriminatory power of, 170
forced-choice scale, 171
graphic rating scale, 177–178
nonforced-choice scale, 171
unbalanced scale, 170
Scale development, 169–173
adapting established scales, 172–173
balanced scale, 170
criteria for, 169–172
discriminatory power of scale descriptors, 170
forced-choice *vs.* nonforced scale descriptors, 171–172
measures of central tendency and dispersion, 172
negatively worded statements, 172
questions, understanding of, 169–170
unbalanced scale, 170
Scale measurement, 163–167
clear wording for scales, 180
defined, 163
development of. *See* Scale development
interval scales, 165–166
multiple-item scale, 180
nominal scale, 164
ordinal scale, 164–165
scale descriptors, 163
scale points, 163–164
single-item scale, 180
Scale points, 163–164
defined, 163
Scale reliability, 167–168
coefficient alpha, 168
defined, 167
equivalent form technique, 168
internal consistency, 168
split-half test, 168
test-retest technique, 167–168
Scale validity, 168–169
content validity, 169
convergent validity, 169
discriminant validity, 169
face validity, 169
Scanner-based panels, 95–96
Scanner data, and purchase behavior, 247
Scanner technology, 95–96
scanner-based panels, 95
Scatter diagram
defined, 319
negative relationship, 320, 321
Scheffé procedure, 299
Scholarly sources, 57
Scientific method, 30
Scientific Telephone Samples, 138
Screening questions, 203, 211
Search engine marketing (SEM), 135
Secondary data
additional sources of, 55

defined, 26, 50
external. *See* External secondary data
government reports used as sources, 58
internal. *See* Internal secondary data
and marketing research process, 53–54
research design selection, 37–38
role of, 50–51
search, variables sought in, 53
sources. *See* Secondary data sources
study using, 49–50
Secondary data sources. *See also* Literature review
consumer panels, 60–61
evaluation of, 51–53
media panels, 61
store audits, 62
triangulating, 62
Secure Customer Index (SCI), 184–185
Segmentation studies, 9
Selective coding, 227–228
Self-administered survey, 115–118
advantages of, 115
defined, 115
disadvantages of, 115
drop-off survey, 116
mail panel survey, 116
mail surveys, 116
online survey, 116–118
Semantic differential scale, 174–176
Sensitive questions, 195
Sentence completion tests, 93
Sentiment analysis, 98
Services marketing research, 9
Shopper marketing, 8
Short-term private communities, 90
Simple random sampling
advantages of, 141
defined, 140
disadvantages of, 141
Single-item scale, 180
Situation analysis, 32
Skip questions, 198
"Smart" questionnaires, 204
Snowball sampling, 147
Social media monitoring, 97–98
Sony, 27
Spearman rank order correlation coefficient, 326–327
Split-half test, 168
SPSS (Statistical Product and Service Solution)
ANOVA, 298–300
bivariate regression analysis, 330–332
to calculate measures of central tendency, 276
to calculate measures of dispersion, 278–279
Chi-square analysis, 292–293
independent samples *t*-test, 295–296

n-way ANOVA, 301–302
paired samples *t*-test, 296
Pearson correlation coefficient, 323–325
sample selection, 151
Standard deviation, 278–279
Standardized research firms, 11
Starbucks, 3, 75, 297
Statistical analysis
analysis of variance. *See* Analysis of variance (ANOVA)
bivariate statistical tests, 287–288
charts, 281
chi-square analysis, 290–293
cross-tabulation, 288–290
facilitating smarter decisions, 273
hypotheses. *See* Hypothesis
independent *vs.* related samples, 293–294
measures of central tendency, 274–277
measures of dispersion, 277–280
n-Way ANOVA, 300–305
Remington's Steak House example, 306–312
sample data, analyzing relationships of, 283–300
statistical technique, selection of, 283–285
univariate statistical tests, 286–287
value of, 274–281
Stealth marketing, 56
Store audits, 62
Stratified purposive sample, 86
Stratified random sampling, 143–145
advantages, 144–145
defined, 143
disadvantages, 144–145
disproportionately, 143
multisource, 143
optimal, 143
proportionately, 143
steps in drawing, 143, 144
Structural modeling, 339–344
example of, 341–344
Structured questions, 195, 196
Subject debriefing, 14
Sugging, 14
Supervisor instruction form, 210
Survey Gizmo, 117
surveygizmo.com, 117
Surveymonkey.com, 117
Survey research
central limit theorem, 138
and university residence life plans, 191–192
Survey research methods
advantages of, 109
defined, 109
disadvantages of, 109
errors in, 109–110
person-administered, 111–112

Survey research methods (*Continued*)
 respondent characteristics, 120–122
 selection of, 118–122
 self-administered, 115–118
 situational characteristics, 118–119
 task characteristics, 119–120
 telephone-administered, 112–115
 types of, 110–118
Survey Sampling, Inc., 138
Survey Sampling Inc., 11
Survey Sampling International (SSI), 136
Syndicated business services, 11
Syndicated data, 59–60
 companies, 61
 consumer panels, 60–61
 defined, 60
 media panels, 61
Systematic random sampling
 advantages of, 141
 defined, 141
 disadvantages of, 141
 steps in drawing, 142

T

Table of contents, research report, 358
Tabulation, in qualitative data analysis
 role of, 228–230
Tabulation, in quantitative data analysis,
 261–266
 cross-tabulation, 261
 defined, 261
 descriptive statistics, 264–266
 graphical illustration of data, 264
 one-way, 261–264
Target population
 defined, 38
Task characteristics, and survey research
 methods selection, 119–120
Technology
 and complexity of marketing research, 4
 gatekeeper technologies, 26
 marketing research on early adopters of,
 377–380
Technology-mediated observation, 94–95
Telephone-administered surveys
 computer-assisted telephone interviews,
 113–114

defined, 112
 wireless phone survey, 114–115
Territorial behavior, 75–76
Test marketing
 defined, 127
 Lee Apparel Company example, 128–129
Test-retest reliability technique, 167–168
Theoretical sampling, 86
"Third places," 75–76
Threadless.com, 117
3Com, 5
Thriving on Chaos (Peters), 273
Time Spent methodology, 36, 37
Title page, of research report, 358
Topic sensitivity, 120
Total variance, 297
Triangulation, 233, 235
TSN Global, 60
t-test, 294–296
 defined, 294
 independent samples, 295–296
 paired samples, 296
 reporting, 367–370
Twitter, 4, 97

U

Unanswerable questions, 197
Unbalanced scale, 170
Underground marketing, 56
Unexplained variance, 329
Unit of analysis, 34
Univariate statistical tests, 286–287
 SPSS application, 287
Unstructured questions, 195
UpSNAP, 135
U.S. Census Bureau, 57, 192
U.S. Television Index (NTI) system, 95

V

Validity, 124–126
 defined, 125
 emic, 232
 external, 125, 126
 internal, 125
 scale, 168–169

Variables
 causal research design, 123
 and conceptualization, 66
 control, 124
 defined, 63, 123
 dependent. *See* Dependent variables
 extraneous, 124
 independent. *See* Independent variables
 indicator, 161
 list of, 34
 negative relationships, 65
 positive relationship, 65
 relationships between, 318–319
 relevant, determination of, 34
 in secondary data search, 53
Variance, 279
 unexplained, 329
Verbatims, 237
Verification, qualitative research,
 231–235
Verizon, 90
VideoDiary, 84
Visual presentation, guidelines for
 preparing, 376

W

The Wall Street Journal, 56
Walmart, 26, 90, 247
Web-based bookmarking tools, 57
Willingness to participate, 121
Wireless phone survey, 114–115
Within-group variance, 297
Word association tests, 92
Wording, of questionnaires, 195, 196–197
Worldwide, Inc., 26

Y

Yahoo!, 56
Youthbeat, 61

Z

Zaltman Metaphor Elicitation Technique
 (ZMET), 93
Zoomerang.com, 117